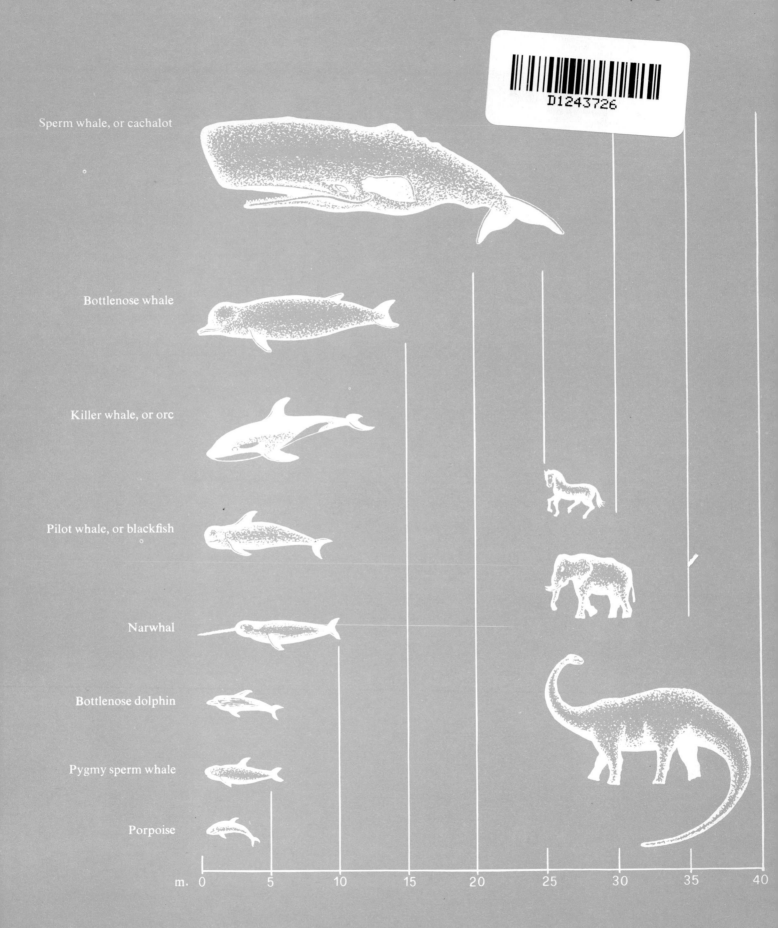

Sperm whale, or cachalot

Bottlenose whale

Killer whale, or orc

Pilot whale, or blackfish

Narwhal

Bottlenose dolphin

Pygmy sperm whale

Porpoise

m. 0   5   10   15   20   25   30   35   40

MAMMALS IN THE SEAS

DATE DUE

Mammals in the seas

Volume IV

Small Cetaceans, Seals, Sirenians and Otters

Selected papers of the
Scientific Consultation on the Conservation and Management
of Marine Mammals and their Environment

FAO ADVISORY COMMITTEE ON
MARINE RESOURCES RESEARCH
WORKING PARTY ON MARINE MAMMALS

with the cooperation of the
UNITED NATIONS ENVIRONMENT PROGRAMME

FOOD AND AGRICULTURE ORGANIZATION OF THE UNITED NATIONS

Rome, 1982

The designations employed and the presentation of material in this publication do not imply the expression of any opinion whatsoever on the part of the Secretariats of the Food and Agriculture Organization of the United Nations and the United Nations Environment Programme concerning the legal status of any country, territory, city or area or of its authorities, or concerning the delimitation of its frontiers or boundaries.

Bibliographic entry:

FAO Advisory Committee on Marine Resources Research.
Working Party on Marine Mammals (1982).
FAO Fish. Ser., (5) Vol. 4: ... p.
Mammals in the seas. Volume 4. Small cetaceans. Seals. Sirenians and otters.
Selected papers of the Scientific Consultation on the conservation and management of marine mammals and their environment. Bergen, 1976.
Marine mammals. Marine ecology. Surveys.
Stock assessment. Population structure. Cetacea.
Pinnipedia. Sirenia. *Enhydra lutris.*

P-43
ISBN 92-5-100514-1

Printed in Italy

PREPARATION OF THIS VOLUME

This volume, the last of the four volumes in the series, contains the corrected versions of those papers selected for final publication, the originals of which were distributed to participants in and contributors to the Scientific Consultation on the Conservation and Management of Marine Mammals and their Environment, held in Bergen, Norway, in 1976.

The papers contained in the present volume were edited by Ms J. Gordon Clark. The abstracts were edited by Mr J. Goodman, and the bibliographic citations by Ms G.A. Soave.

The volumes in this series are being published as follows:

MAMMALS IN THE SEAS

FAO Fisheries Series No. 5

Volume 3

General papers and large cetaceans

Selected papers of the Scientific Consultation on the Conservation and Management of Marine Mammals and their Environment

Volume 4

Small cetaceans, seals, sirenians and otters

Selected papers of the Scientific Consultation on the Conservation and Management of Marine Mammals and their Environment

Contents

VII

SIRENIANS AND OTTERS

EDITOR'S NOTE

Contributors to the Bergen Scientific Consultation on the Conservation and Management of Marine Mammals produced some 140 formal papers (some of which were reprints from existing publications) and a number of working group documents. Of these some 70 have been selected for inclusion in Volumes III and IV and several others have been published elsewhere. A large proportion received preliminary editorial attention from Mr John K. Goodman, who also was responsible for the preparation of the abstracts.

The papers published here have been written by mathematical scientists, field observers, economists, fisheries biologists, conservationists and anthropologists. Their content spans modelling of population dynamics, anatomical details, conservation aspects and considerations of the unseen influence on scientists and managers alike. They are variable in length and in scope. They provide a much needed overview of marine mammal status, management problems and science, and reflect the lack of knowledge in many areas. Cetaceans large and small share pride of space with the pinnipeds, while the sirenians and marine otter occupy regrettably few pages.

In editing this varied assembly, I have tried only to ensure that the language was good and the structure clear, and to correct any inconsistencies that appeared within papers. A fairly obvious order was chosen: general papers first, covering management objectives and modelling techniques, followed by papers on large cetaceans (Volume III); then papers on small cetaceans, seals, sirenians and otters (Volume IV). Within each group, papers are arranged into species status papers, generally in some form of geographical order, and other more general issues including specific population modelling techniques.

One problem will be familiar to many readers. The terms population, stock, breeding population, herd, school and other such varied usage of the English language tend to assume as many meanings as there are authors, and sometimes more. While I do not believe that I have succeeded in standardizing throughout, I have in general used the terms in the following way:

- *discrete breeding population:* that which is thought to be or is an independent genetic unit (see paper by Rørvik and Jonsgård);
- *population:* those animals of the species inhabiting a defined geographical area, but not necessarily discrete breeding populations nor containing complete discrete breeding populations;
- *stock:* any desired grouping of animals, usually for management purposes (thus the Area IV stock of fin whales is a stock for which a quota may be set, but it may or may not represent a discrete breeding population);
- *herd:* a group of small cetaceans, possibly containing several discrete breeding populations; and
- *school:* a group of small cetaceans travelling together.

I would like to thank authors for their painstaking checking of references and of final proofs; the extra work involved for those authors to whom English is not a mother tongue is often not appreciated, and I sincerely hope that the text we have agreed between us reflects in English what they would have wished to say in their own language.

JOANNA GORDON CLARK

SMALL CETACEANS

PRELIMINARY REPORT OF THE BIOLOGY, CATCH AND POPULATIONS OF *PHOCOENOIDES* IN THE WESTERN NORTH PACIFIC

T. KASUYA

Abstract

This study suggests the existence of 3 intraspecific populations of *Phocoenoides* in the western North Pacific and adjacent seas based on geographical differences in the ratio of the colour phases of external pigmentation; it reviews the migration, exploitation and population state of each. Phases of external pigmentation are classified as: (i) black-type, entirely black with no white area on the flank; (ii) *dalli*-type, white area on flank extends laterally to level of dorsal fin; and (iii) *truei*-type, white area on flank reaches laterally to base of flipper, usually with slight to heavy mottling of dark spots on the flank.

A general north and south seasonal migration seems to predominate for all 3 populations of *Phocoenoides*. The Japanese east coast population is composed mostly of animals of the *truei*-type and is distributed mainly in waters off the Pacific coast of northern Japan. This population is the most peculiar of the 3 suggested in its restricted range, its possibly small size and the possibility that it may be exploited the most heavily. In winter and spring, about 6 000 animals are harvested annually in Miyagi and Iwati prefectures from this population and, in summer, an additional unknown number are killed incidentally in the salmon gillnet fishery. Relevant biological parameters indicate a high ratio of immature animals in the catch and a high mortality rate; the decline in catch-per-unit of effort in recent years is significant and should be watched carefully. Improved analysis of this population's current state requires collection of additional biological data and information on the size of the incidental catch in the salmon gillnet fishery. The second population, composed only of *dalli*-type porpoises, is found in the Bering Sea and the offshore waters of the northwestern North Pacific; the limit of its eastern range is unknown. This population is caught incidentally in the salmon gillnet fishery, with estimated annual mortality from 10 000 to more than 20 000 animals – there is no data suggesting a decrease in the size of the population, however. Reliable collection of catch statistics and an independent collection of relevant biological information associated with the incidental fishery is needed. An additional population of *Phocoenoides* of the *dalli*-type is found in the Sea of Japan and the Okhotsk Sea. It is not exploited in Japanese coastal waters at present except probably for an incidental catch in gillnets of small salmon fishing boats; several earlier periods of direct exploitation are known from 1937 to 1966. More study is needed to determine the identity of the population on the west coast of the Kamchatka Peninsula.

Résumé

L'auteur pense qu'on peut distinguer trois populations intraspécifiques de *Phocoenoides* dans le secteur ouest du Pacifique nord et les mers limitrophes en se fondant sur les variations géographiques dans la proportion des couleurs de la pigmentation externe. Il étudie les migrations, l'exploitation et l'état des stocks dans chacune de ces trois sous-populations. Les diverses pigmentations externes sont classifiées comme suit: (i) type noir, entièrement noire sans tache blanche sur les flancs; (ii) type *dalli*, la tache blanche du flanc s'étend latéralement jusqu'au niveau de la nageoire dorsale; (iii) type *truei*, la plage blanche du flanc s'étend latéralement jusqu'à la base de la nageoire, généralement avec des taches noires plus ou moins importantes sur le flanc.

Une migration saisonnière vers le nord et vers le sud semble prédominer dans les trois populations de *Phocoenoides*. La population de la côte est du Japon semble comprendre surtout des animaux du type *truei* et fréquente principalement les eaux au large de la côte Pacifique du nord du Japon. Sur les trois, cette population est celle qui offre le plus de caractéristiques particulières par son domaine restreint, sa taille probablement faible et par la possibilité que son exploitation soit la plus forte. En hiver et au printemps, environ 6 000 animaux sont capturés chaque année dans les préfectures de Miyagi et d'Iwati et en été, un nombre inconnu d'exemplaires est détruit fortuitement dans la pêche du saumon au filet maillant. Les paramètres biologiques indiquent un nombre élevé d'animaux immatures dans les prises et un taux de mortalité également élevé. Le fléchissement de la CPUE au cours des dernières années est notable et devrait être surveillé de près. Pour pouvoir mieux analyser l'état actuel de cette population, il faudrait recueillir des données biologiques supplémentaires et des informations sur le niveau des captures fortuites dans la pêche du saumon au filet maillant. La deuxième population, composée uniquement de marsouins du type *dalli*, fréquente la mer de Béring et les eaux au large du secteur nord-ouest du Pacifique nord. On ignore sa limite orientale. Cette population est affectée accessoirement par la pêche du saumon au filet maillant et la mortalité annuelle serait estimée entre 10 000 et plus de 20 000 animaux. Il n'existe cependant aucune donnée laissant penser à un fléchissement de la population. Il faudrait recueillir des statistiques de captures fiables et réunir de façon indépendante des informations biologiques à l'occasion des prises accessoires. Une autre population de *Phocoenoides* de type *dalli* se trouve dans la mer du Japon et la mer d'Okhotsk. Elle n'est pas exploitée actuellement dans les eaux littorales du Japon sauf, peut-être, dans le cas de quelques prises accidentelles dans les filets maillants des petits bateaux de pêche au saumon. On sait que l'exploitation directe a été pratiquée pendant plusieurs périodes entre 1937 et 1966. Il faudrait effectuer des études supplémentaires pour déterminer l'identité de la population fréquentant la côte ouest de la péninsule du Kamtchatka.

Extracto

Este estudio sugiere que existen tres poblaciones intraespecíficas de *Phocoenoides* en el noroeste del Pacífico y en los mares adyacentes, basándose para ello en las diferencias de la pigmentación externa según la zona geográfica, y examina los movimientos migratorios, la explotación y la situación de cada una de las poblaciones. Según la pigmentación externa, se clasifican en: (i) tipo negro – animales totalmente negros, sin ninguna superficie blanca en el costado; (ii) tipo *dalli* – con una zona blanca en el costado que se extiende lateralmente hasta el nivel de la aleta dorsal; y (iii) tipo *truei* – con una zona blanca en el costado que llega lateralmente hasta la base de la aleta, con frecuencia salpicada de manchas negras de mayor o menor intensidad.

En las tres poblaciones de *Phocoenoides* parece predominar un movimiento migratorio general hacia el norte y hacia el sur, según las estaciones. La población de la costa oriental del Japón está compuesta principalmente por animales de tipo *truei* y se encuentra sobre todo en las aguas situadas frente a la costa del Pacífico del norte del Japón. Esta población es la más peculiar de las tres cuya existencia sugiere, por razón de su área limitada de distribución, el pequeño volumen que probablemente tiene la población y la posibilidad de que sea relativamente la más explotada. Durante el invierno y la primavera se capturan anualmente unos

4

6 000 animales de esta población en las prefecturas de Miyagi e Iwati, y durante el verano un número no determinado de animales resultan muertos accidentalmente en la pesquería de salmón con redes de enmalle. Los parámetros biológicos revelan un elevado porcentaje de animales inmaduros en las capturas y un alto índice de mortalidad; la disminución de la captura por unidad de esfuerzo en los últimos años es importante y ha de vigilarse atentamente. Para poder analizar mejor la situación actual de esta población es necesario recoger más datos biológicos e información sobre las capturas accidentales de esta población en la pesquería de salmón con redes de enmalle. La segunda población, compuesta principalmente por marsopas de tipo *dalli*, tiene su área de distribución en el mar de Bering y en las aguas de media altura del noroeste del Pacífico. No se conoce el límite oriental de su área de distribución. Esta población se captura accidentalmente en la pesquería de salmón con redes de enmalle, con una mortalidad anual que se estima entre 10 000 y más de 20 000 animales, a pesar de lo cual no hay datos que indiquen una disminución de la población. Es necesario recoger estadísticas fidedignas de captura y recopilar independientemente información biológica aprovechando las capturas accidentales. En el mar de Japón y el mar de Ojotsk se encuentra otra población de *Phocoenoides* del tipo *dalli*. Actualmente no se explota en aguas costeras del Japón, si se exceptúa la probabilidad de que se capturen accidentalmente algunos ejemplares en las redes de enmalle de las pequeñas embarcaciones salmoneras; se sabe que entre 1937 y 1966 se explotó directamente en algunas ocasiones. Son necesarios más estudios para determinar la identidad de la población que se encuentra en la costa occidental de la península de Kamchatka.

T. Kasuya
Ocean Research Institute, University of Tokyo, 1-15-1 Minamidai, Nakano-ko Tokyo 164, Japan

Introduction

Kuroda (1954) concluded, based mainly on the distribution and schooling behaviour of the porpoise, that *Phocoenoides dalli* (True, 1885) and *P. truei* (Andrews, 1911) belong to one species, and that the latter constitutes one small population living off the Pacific coast of northern Japan. Furthermore, the facts that some intermediate variations in the pigmentation of the body (Nishiwaki, Kasuya and Houck, 1966) were found and that no biometrical difference was detected between the porpoises representing the two colour types caught off the Pacific coast of Japan, Okhotsk Sea and Aleutian waters (Kasuya, unpublished) strongly support the conclusion of Kuroda (1954).

In this preliminary report the three populations of *Phocoenoides* in the western North Pacific and adjacent seas were tentatively separated based on the geographical difference of the ratio of the colour phases of external pigmentation; the migration, exploitation, and the status of the population are then discussed for each stock of the species.

Further study on the biology of this porpoise in the northwestern Pacific is being conducted.

Materials

The sighting records of small cetaceans in the North Pacific referred to here were mainly collected by myself in the period from 1968 to August 1975 through the various cruises of the research vessels *Tanseimaru*, *Hakuhomaru*, *Hayachinemaru* and *Enoshimamaru*, and of the whaling ship *Ginseimaru* No. 2. The records of the incidental catch of *Phocoenoides* by the research vessels in the salmon gillnet fishery, *Kitagamimaru* and *Iwatemaru*, were provided by Mr. S. Nagahora and Mr. J. Iwagiri for the 1970, 1971, 1972 and 1973 seasons.

Similar information from the research vessel *Hokushinmaru* was provided by Mr. T. Okazaki for the year 1973. These data were very valuable because of the highly reliable identification of *P. dalli* and *P. truei*. Other ancillary records of sporadic catches or of sightings provided by Dr. Y. Naito and Mr. N. Miyazaki are used. Besides the above data, the sighting or sporadic catch records reported by Kuroda (1956), Masaki (1972), Matsui and Uchihashi (1943), Mizue and Yoshida (1965), Mizue, Yoshida and Takemura (1966), Nishiwaki (1967), Nemoto *et al.* (1966), Seno (1940) and Shimazu (1971) are used in this report.

The biological data of 810 porpoises taken in the porpoise hunt in the Sanriku region (Aomori, Iwate and Miyagi prefectures, or northeastern Pacific coast of Japanese main island) were collected by myself from January to April, in 1972 and 1974.

As shown in Table 1 the statistics of the porpoise hunt in the last 12 years were collected from most of the fish markets in the Sanriku region. These statistics give only the monthly weight of the porpoise measured after removal of the viscera, the price of porpoise sold, and the monthly cumulative number of harpoon fishing boats. Though the last can be used as a kind of measure of fishing effort, it is incomplete because it does not include the numbers of boats which came back with no catch. In the case of Kesennuma Fish Market the catch of porpoises by harpoon is not separated from that by other methods. However, it is not important in this study because there are no other fishing boats which can take many porpoises in the winter season and because the amount of porpoises landed at this market is very small. Though the statistics of the Ishinomaki and Shiogama Fish Market were not studied, the landings of porpoises at these markets are negligible.

The number of porpoises and the weight of each animal are recorded only on the copy of the fishermen's receipts and they are usually discarded after a short period. Accordingly, the data on the body weight of each animal was collected from Otsuchi Fish Market (from

Table 1. Source of statistics used in this study

Fish market	1963	1964	1965	1966	1967	1968	1969	1970	1971	1972	1973-75
Miyako (39°39'N, 141°57'E)	P(D)	PD	PD	PD	PD	PD	PD	PD	PD	PD	PD
Yamada (39°28'N, 141°57'E)	X	P	P	PD	PD	PD	PD	PD	PD	PD	PD
Funakoshi (39°27'N, 141°58'E)	X	X	X	X	X	XD	PD	PD	PD	PD	PD
Otsuchi (39°19'N, 141°55'E)	PD	PD	PD	PD	PD	PD	PD	PD	PD	PD	PD
Kamaishi (39°14'N, 141°53'E)	PD	PD	PD	PD	PD	PD	PD	PD	PD	PD	PD
Ofunato (39°04'N, 141°43'E)	P(D)	PD	PD	PD	PD	PD	PD	PD	PD	PD	PD
Hosoura (39°00'N, 141°44'E)	X	X	X	X	X	X	X	X	X	PD	PD
Kesennuma (38°54'N, 141°34'E)	PD	PD	PD	XD	XD	XD	XD	XD	XD	XD	XD
Onagawa (38°26'N, 141°27'E)	PD	PD	PD	PD	PD	PD	PD	PD	PD	PD	PD

X: virtually no harpoon fishing for porpoise; P: porpoise fishing with harpoon operated; D: catch or effort data collected; (D): data from January to March not available.

January 1972 to February 1974) and from Funakoshi Fish Market (from January to March 1974).

Populations of *Phocoenoides* in the western North Pacific

In this study the external pigmentation of *Phocoenoides* is, where necessary, classified into *dalli*-type, *truei*-type and black-type. The last indicates the animal which is entirely black. The *dalli*-type is represented by the animals on which the white area on the flanks extends to the level of the dorsal fin. In animals of this type no spot, or only very slight spottings, on the white area of the flank can be seen. On the *truei*-type the white area reaches to the base of the flipper, and there are usually some spots on the flank varying from very slight to very heavy. In the case of heavy mottling, which is rather rare, the spots are usually restricted to the area between the level of the base of the flipper and the level of the dorsal fin, where the colour should be black on the animals of the *dalli*-type. Even if this part is heavily mottled, the animals are classed as *truei*-type, as the white background is distinguishable. In newborn animals or full-term foetuses of the *dalli*-type, the area on the flank between the base of the flipper and the dorsal fin is of lighter pigment than the corresponding part of the adult (see Plate I of Mizue and Yoshida, 1965). This is comparable with the fact that the corresponding part of the juvenile animal of the *truei*-type is light grey. However, even in juveniles, the two types can be distinguished without difficulty because of the clearness of the anterior margin of the white area and the darker pigmentation of the corresponding part in the *dalli*-type.

Figs. 1-6 and Tables 2 and 3 show the three types of *Phocoenoides* and their geographical distribution. All the animals sighted by me in the southern Okhotsk Sea and two animals caught at the west coast of Kamchatka Peninsula (Seno, 1940) belonged to the *dalli*-type.

7

FIG. 1. – *Truei*-type, a slightly greyish area on the chest region, slightest spotting. 186 cm, male, Sanriku, 10 February 1972.

FIG. 2. – *Truei*-type, heavy spotting, Sanriku, February 1972.

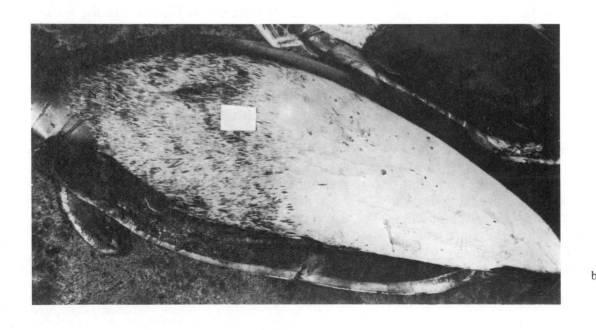

FIG. 3. – *Truei*-type, extremely heavy spotting on the chest region. The irregular dark streaks are of blood. 193 cm, female, Sanriku, 8 February 1974.

FIG. 4. — *Dalli*-type. Chest region is slightly pale, which changes to black on the adult. 100.5 cm, female. 52°13'N, 171°51'E, 21 July 1973.

FIG. 5. — Black-type. White areas on the chest and dorsal fin are reflection of light. 207 cm, male, Sanriku, 13 February 1972.

Table 2. Number of sightings or sporadic catch of *Phocoenoides* and percentage of *truei*-type
Area 1: West of 143°30'E; Area 2: 143°30'E-155°E; Area 3: 155°E-170°E; Area 4: 170°E-170°W

| Month | Sea of Japan | | Okhotsk Sea | | Pacific Ocean | | | | | | | | Bering Sea [1] | |
| | | | | | Area 1 | | Area 2 | | Area 3 | | Area 4 | | | |
	No.	%	No.	%	No.	%	No.	%	No.	%	No.	%	No.	%
Feb.					44	100								
Mar.					25	100								
Apr.	24	0							2	0	4	0		
May	84	0	6	0	26	68.4	4	25.0			5	0		
June	2	0	7	0	188	97.9	4	0	50	6.0	19	0	10	0
July			67	0	30	33.3	65	58.5	30	36.7	15	0		
Aug.							4	100						
Sep.			98	0			11	100						
Oct.							11	90.9						
Nov.					12	0								
Dec.					23	0								
Total	112	0	178	0	348	80.5	99	64.6	82	17.1	43	0	10	0

[1] Bering Sea: West of 170°W.

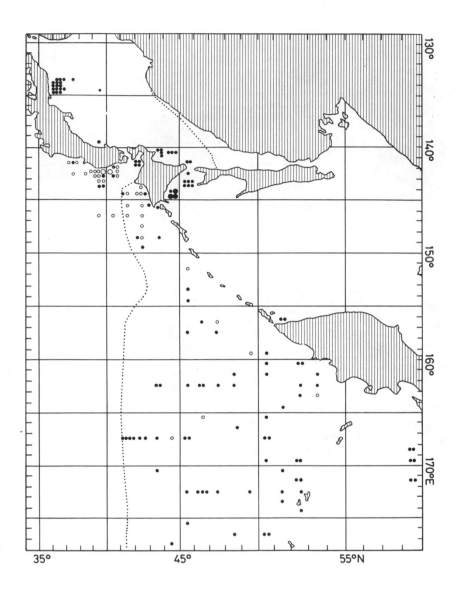

FIG. 6. – Positions of sighting or of sporadic catch of *Phocoenoides*. Open circle: *truei*-type, closed circle: *dalli*-type, half closed: a school with two types, dotted line: 18.3°C (65°F) surface water in August (U.S. Navy Hydrographic Office, 1944). Larger circle indicates 10 schools, and the smaller 1.

Table 3.   Ratio of 3 types of pigmentation in the catch off Sanriku and Tajima coasts

Month	Tajima [1]			Sanriku					Total
	dalli-type		black-type		*dalli*-type		*truei*-type		
	No.	%	No.	%	No.	%	No.	%	
Jan.			1	0.5	6	2.7	215	96.8	222
Feb.	2	100	1	0.3	10	3.4	287	96.3	298
Mar.	302	100	1	0.4	14	5.0	266	94.6	281
Apr.	1 381	100					9	100	9
May	176	100							
Total	1 861	100	3	0.4	30	3.7	777	95.9	810

[1] Noguchi, 1946.

In the Sea of Japan, all the sightings off the west coast of Hokkaido and in the central part of the Sea of Japan were of the *dalli*-type. Matsui and Uchihashi (1943) reported that only *dalli*-type are found off the Tajima coast (southern coast of the Sea of Japan), based on the 33 animals caught by a research vessel and 630 animals landed by the local fishermen. Noguchi (1946) wrote that *P. truei* (*truei*-type) is scarce off the Tajima coast, without giving his reasons. However, as only *P. dalli* (*dalli*-type) are shown in his appendix-Table 1 showing the sex and body lengths of 197 *Phocoenoides* caught off Tajima coast, it is reasonable to conclude that no animals of the *truei*-type are found there. The monthly catch of *dalli*-type in Table 3 is cited from the appendix-Table 2 of Noguchi (1946) showing the catch off the Tajima coast in 1942 and 1943, which data were originally taken from the statistics from Minato village on the Tajima coast.

In the Bering Sea and in the northern North Pacific east of 170°E, only the *dalli*-type is observed. The ratio of *truei*-type increases in the southwest part of the North Pacific, and attains a maximum of 96 % as seen in the catch off Sanriku coast (Table 3). As the fishing area off Sanriku coast is within the range of about 50 nautical miles from the coast, its range coincides approximately with the central part of Area 1 in Table 2. Accordingly, the ratio of *truei*-type in the catch off the Sanriku coast and that of animals sighted in the Pacific Area 1 coincides fairly well except for 12, 23 and 2 animals of the *dalli*-type sighted in November, December and May, respectively, off the southern coast of Hokkaido (entrance of Uchiura Bay) corresponding to Pacific Area 1.

The above suggests that there are possibly three populations in the western North Pacific and adjacent seas. The first is a population off the Pacific coast of Japan, which is composed mostly of the animals of *truei*-type and is distributed mainly in the waters off the Pacific coast of northern Japan. In the winter season they migrate up to Choshi (35°44'N, 140°50'E) as reported by Noguchi (1946). However, only a few members of this population

appear to migrate as far as this, since landings of *Phocoenoides* at Choshi Fish Market could not be confirmed (Miyazaki, pers. comm.). The southernmost record of *Phocoenoides* on the Pacific coast of Japan is thought to be in Suruga Bay (34°45'N, 138°30'E) in March (Kuroda, 1940). Though the position where this animal was caught and the colour type are not certain, it is not impossible to expect it in Suruga Bay because the water temperature can be below 17°C in the area where the migration of *Phocoenoides* is expected (see Table 4). In the summer season most of the animals of this population stay off the east coasts of Hokkaido and of the southern Kurile Islands, which feature is shown in Fig. 6 and Table 2 of this report and Fig. 3 of Ohsumi (1974). However, few individuals seem to migrate up to the east coast of the southern Kamchatka Peninsula. Possibly this is a population living in the coastal waters near to the edge of the Oyashio Current.

Though it is not certain whether the porpoises of the *dalli*-type and of the black-type found off Sanriku coast belong to that population or are migrants from other populations, I am inclined to choose the former hypothesis and consider that the ratio of the three types is at equilibrium in the population. This assumption seems to be correct because the ratio of *truei*-type in Pacific Area 1 is almost stable in the seasons from January to June (Tables 2 and 3).

The second population is that which has its range in the Bering Sea and the offshore waters of the northwestern North Pacific. The southwestern part of the range of this population overlaps the northern and eastern range of the Japanese east-coast population. The animals of this population seem to have a north and south migration in accordance with the season (Ohsumi, 1974). The eastern boundary of this population is not known.

The third population of *Phocoenoides* is found in the Sea of Japan and in the Okhotsk Sea. As all the porpoises of this species in these waters are composed of the *dalli*-type, they are considered not to belong to the Japanese

11

east-coast population. The fact that the *truei*-type migrates in the summer season to the waters east of the Kurile Islands but not to the west of them suggests that the Kurile Islands may be a barrier to the distribution of the porpoise, and that the *dalli*-type observed in the southern part of Okhotsk Sea is separated from the offshore western North Pacific population. According to Noguchi (1946) the catch of *Phocoenoides* off Tajima coast was highest from late March to early May, then the catch was replaced by *Lagenorhynchus*. My own observation shows that *Phocoenoides* is scanty in April, May and June in the central and southern Sea of Japan, but that many *Phocoenoides* are found off the west coast of Hokkaido and are continuously distributed as far as the Okhotsk Sea (Fig. 6 and Table 2), and the porpoises are abundant in the southern Okhotsk Sea in July and September. This strongly indicates that the porpoises spend the winter in the southern Sea of Japan and move to the Okhotsk Sea in the summer. The absence of *Phocoenoides* and the presence of many *Tursiops* and *Pseudorca* in winter at the Tsuchima Strait (34°N, 129°30'E) suggest that *Phocoenoides* does not migrate to the East China Sea.

Ohsumi (1974) showed that many small cetaceans were incidentally captured by the

Table 4. Occurrence of schools of Delphinid species in the western North Pacific in relation to the surface water temperature

Surface water temperature (°C)	Dalli-type	Truei-type	Phocoenoides sp.	Phocoena	Lagenorhynchus	Orcinus	Pseudorca	Globicephala	Grampus	Tursiops	Delphinus	S. coeruleoalba	S. attenuata	Total
3.0- 3.9	4													5
4.0- 4.9	4													4
5.0- 5.9	6	1												7
6.0- 6.9	14	2												16
7.0- 7.9	10	1		1	1									13
8.0- 8.9	14	5	1	1	1									22
9.0- 9.9	2	10	10	1	1	2								26
10.0-10.9	3	5	6		1									15
11.0-11.9	12	2		1	3									18
12.0-12.9	9	1	2		10									22
13.0-13.9	9				5									14
14.0-14.9	12	1			3									16
15.0-15.9	20	10	3		2			1						36
16.0-16.9	3	12	1		3	2		2						23
17.0-17.9		3			9	1	1	2		2				18
18.0-18.9				2	2	2		1	1			1		9
19.0-19.9					6			7	1		1	3	2	16
20.0-20.9					1			6	1	3	1	7		22
21.0-21.9	2	1			1		1	6	2	2	3	1	2	20
22.0-22.9							1	10		11	5	2	1	31
23.0-23.9							3	3	3	12	1	5		26
24.0-24.9							1	3	2	4	1		3	15
25.0-25.9							1	1	5	3	3	3		17
26.0-26.9								2	2	3	5			12
27.0-27.9								1		1	1			3
28.0-28.9								2		2				4
Total	124	54	24	6	49	7	8	47	17	43	21	22	8	430

salmon gill-net fishery off the west coast of the Kamchatka Peninsula. These may be of the *dalli*-type, but their identity is not certain.

The four schools of 37 *Phocoenoides* of the *dalli*-type observed in May, November and December off the southwest coast of Hokkaido (42°20'N, 141°E, entrance of Uchiura Bay) indicate that some animals of the populations in the seas of Japan and Okhotsk or in the offshore western North Pacific might migrate to the southern coast of Hokkaido.

Biology and status of population

JAPANESE EAST-COAST POPULATION

Ohsumi (1972) made a complete review of recent Japanese small cetacean hunting based on the official statistics. His study showed that small cetacean fishing in the north of Chiba prefecture is restricted to Miyagi and Iwate prefectures or to the middle and southern part of the Sanriku region. The method of hunting is described by Pilleri (1971) and Ohsumi (1972).

Phocoenoides hunting in the Sanriku region is done by hand harpoon only in the season when other fishing opportunities are scarce. Almost all the porpoises caught in this region have in recent years been sent to Shizuoka and Yamanashi prefectures, where *Stenella* spp. caught off the coast of Izu Peninsula is also consumed; a very small amount is sent to Yamagata and Akita prefectures. The season usually starts between 21 and 31 January and closes in early April. Almost no boats operate harpoon fishing in May but it increases again in June with the arrival of swordfish. As swordfish are a much more profitable product of harpoon fishing, and as the price of porpoise becomes extremely low after April as a result of the consumers' eating customs, the fishermen do not catch porpoises in the summer season. As a result, the catch of porpoises from January to April is 93.5 % of the total

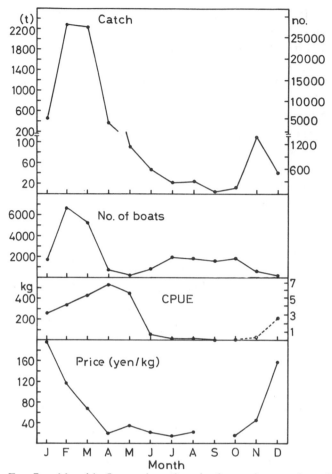

FIG. 7. – Monthly fluctuation of catch of porpoise, number of harpoon fishing boats and CPUE in the years from 1962 to 1973 at Sanriku coast, and price of porpoise at the fish markets of the same region in 1973.

catch. These features are shown in Fig. 7 based on the statistics of the last 12 years from various fish markets in the Sanriku region.

In the porpoise fishing season, when I stayed to study 810 *Phocoenoides* in the Sanriku region, no catch of other species of cetaceans was observed. And even in the records of Funakoshi and Otsuchi Fish Markets for the years from 1972 to 1974 in the months from January to April, only 9 other small cetacean species are found, 0.2 % of the 3 998 animals recorded. This is because *Phocoenoides* is predominant in the season and in the area, and because the price of other species is too low compared with that of *Phocoenoides*. Accord-

13

ingly, it is safe to say that the catch of other species is a negligible fraction of the winter catch. As shown in Fig. 7, the weight of landed porpoise shows a rise in November. This is affected by a big catch (107 tons) in November 1964 recorded at Kesennuma Fish Market. As the catch from various offshore fishing operations is landed at this market, it is reasonable to consider that this big landing of porpoise was made by another type of fishing boat, probably by a purse seiner. The species landed may not be *Phocoenoides*. If this catch is excluded, and the November 1964 catch is assumed to be 7 tons as in the case of the preceding month, the catch per 1 harpoon boat (CPUE) shows a smooth change as shown by an open circle and dotted lines in Fig. 7.

While sightings of *Phocoenoides* occur from September to July off the Sanriku region, the peak of migration is considered from the CPUE to be in April. The catch of *Phocoenoides* in the Sanriku region seems to occur before the peak of the north-bound migration. This suggests that, if the arrival of the porpoises is delayed by the effect of oceanographic conditions, the catch and CPUE of the year can be largely influenced. As *Phocoenoides* is rare in the waters with a surface water temperature above 17°C (Table 4), the migration of these porpoises to the Sanriku region in the summer season must be negligible.

As shown in Fig. 3, *Phocoenoides* smaller than 164 cm in body length are not taken in this fishery. The length 164 cm corresponds to the age of about 1 year (Mizue, Yoshida and Takemura, 1966). This and the fact that the lactating or lactating and simultaneously pregnant females are only 5.1 % and 8.5 % of the mature females, respectively, suggest that the suckling calf and the mother rarely come to the bow of the ship and are not usually taken by a harpoon. The ratio of pregnant or resting females is 84.7 % and 1.7 % respectively.

The ratios of immature animals in the catch of females in January, February and March are 52.6 %, 60.0 % and 70.4 %, respectively. Though the occurrence of maturity in males has not yet been studied the tendency

seems to be the same as with females, because the ratio of smaller animals increases in March (Fig. 8). The sex ratio also changes with the season (Table 5). These facts suggest the occurrence of segregation by growth stage and sex. But this problem must be solved in future based on more samples.

The mean weight of *Phocoenoides* (after removal of all viscera) changes with the season. This is probably related to the segregation of the animals mentioned above. It is, however, safe to say that the mean weight is about 81 kg (Table 6). This figure is used here to calculate the number of animals from the records of catch statistics by weight.

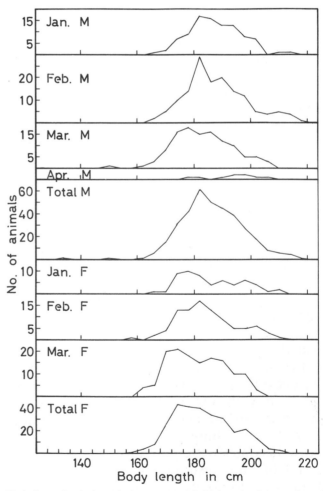

FIG. 8. — Body length frequency of *Phocoenoides* caught at Sanriku coast in 1972 and 1974. M and F indicate males and females respectively.

Table 5. Sex ratio of *Phocoenoides* in the catch off Sanriku coast

Month	Female	Male	Male/Female
Jan.	75	147	1.99
Feb.	111	173	1.56
Mar.	157	122	0.78
Apr.		9	–
Total	343	451	1.31

Fig. 4 shows the annual fluctuation of the catch, number of boats operated (day X No.), and the weight of porpoise caught by a day's work of a boat (CPUE, kg) in the months from January to April. This indicates that the catch per annum of *Phocoenoides* in the Sanriku region fluctuated between 4 500 and 7 500 animals. This value is slightly lower than the total catch of small cetaceans in this region shown by Ohsumi (1972). But it must be noted that the official statistics cited by Ohsumi

Table 6. Mean body weight of *Phocoenoides* in the catch off the Sanriku coast

1: 1 to 10; 2: 11 to 20; 3: 21 to end of month

Month		No. of animals	Total weight (kg)	Mean weight (kg) (without viscera)
	1	99	7 932	80.1
Jan.	2	263	22 736	86.4
	3	584	49 650	85.0
	1	542	43 561	81.1
Feb.	2	926	76 123	82.2
	3	341	26 440	77.5
	1	599	46 126	77.0
Mar.	2	380	29 088	76.5
	3	134	10 319	77.0
	1	24	2 005	83.5
Apr.	2	95	7 597	80.0
	3	2	180	90.0
Total		3 989	322 157	80.8

(1972) include the summer season catch which probably contains other species, and that the number of animals were calculated by an unknown method.

The most important feature of the catch is the rapid decrease of CPUE in recent years. If the number of the harpoon fishing boats which came back to port with no catch are included in the effort, the decline of the CPUE would be even more conspicuous. It must also be noted that the size of the porpoise hunting boats is increasing compared with the past. This must have changed the CPUE.

Fig. 9 indicates that the number of Dall's porpoise caught per day of operation by harpoon fishing boats (CPUE) has declined in recent years. It remains to be considered whether this reflects a decline in the population, taking account of the most recent data.

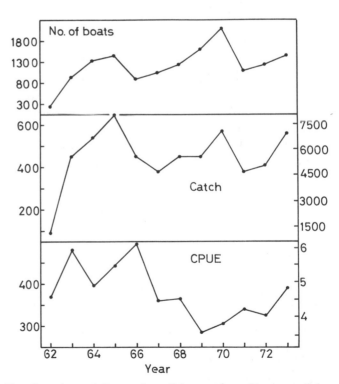

FIG. 9. – Annual fluctuation of the number of harpoon fishing boats, catch of porpoise (left scale weight in tons, right scale number of porpoises calculated from the weight), and CPUE (left scale weight in kg, right scale number of porpoises calculated from the weight) at Sanriku coast in the months from January to April.

15

Table 7 shows the catch of porpoise off the Sanriku coast. The catch is considered to consist mostly of Dall's porpoise caught by harpoon fishing, except for a small number in the summer. *Phocoenoides* are also landed at Ishinomaki Fish Market (38°24'N, 141°18'E), but as the total landing of all delphinids there is only a few tons annually, the statistics are not included in Table 7. The effort data include only the number of harpoon fishing boats which landed a catch; the boats that returned without porpoises are not included.

The declining trend of CPUE did not continue through the 1975 season, for which a high value was recorded, as high as in 1966. Miyazaki, Kasuya and Nishiwaki (1964) showed that the annual fluctuation in the catch of striped dolphin (*Stenella coeruleoalba*) and spotted dolphin (*S. attenuata*) off Sagami Bay, approximately 450 km south of the *Phocoenoides* ground, is correlated with the fluctuation of the Kuroshio Current. The cycle of the fluctuation in the catch is 8 or 9 years (Kasuya, 1976) and there is a 7 to 9 year fluctuation cycle in the velocity, volume of water transported and the meander of the Current (Nitani, 1975). As the striped dolphin off the Pacific coast of Japan seems to be densely distributed near the northern boundary of this current, in the years when the Kuroshio Current, is near the coast the concentration of this species will

also be found there. It is not unreasonable to expect a similar effect of the current on the catch of *Phocoenoides*, because the southeastern boundary of the population is the edge of the Kuroshio Current. Actually, the relationship between the catch (N) of the two species of *Stenella* by drive fishery off Sagami Bay and the CPUE of Dall's porpoise by harpoon fishing is expressed by the following equation:

$$CPUE = 0.000159N + 3.41$$
$$correlation\ coefficient = 0.63$$

This strongly suggests that the catch of Dall's porpoise and that of two kinds of *Stenella* are affected directly or indirectly by a common factor, presumably the annual fluctuation of the Kuroshio Current. Accordingly, the variation of the CPUE shown in Table 7 is probably not a good indicator of changes in abundance of this population.

For better analysis of the status of the population, information on the amount of incidental catch of this population by salmon gill-net fishery off the west coasts of Hokkaido and southern Kurile Islands and information on the relationship between oceanographical conditions and the migration of the porpoise are needed.

The effect of past fur seal poaching on hunting patterns should be checked. The de-

Table 7. Catch statistics of porpoises off the Sanriku coast [1]

	1963	1964	1965	1966	1967	1968	1969	1970	1971	1972	1973	1974	1975
Total catch (tons)	731	763	742	645	416	486	568	651	421	419	584	522	594
Total catch (No.) [2]	9 040	9 440	9 180	7 980	5 150	6 020	7 020	8 060	5 210	5 190	7 230	6 470	7 350
Winter catch (tons) [3]	448	536	650	451	381	448	449	578	375	406	560	455	559
Winter catch (No.) [2][3]	5 540	6 630	8 040	5 590	4 710	5 540	5 550	7 150	4 640	5 020	6 930	5 630	6 920
Boat days (No.) [3]	937	1 364	1 459	914	1 058	1.232	1 586	1 876	1 102	1 243	1 430	1 561	1 064
Catch per boat (No.) [3]	5.9	4.9	5.5	6.1	4.5	4.5	3.5	3.8	4.2	4.0	4.8	3.6	6.5
Striped dolphin (No.) [4]								3 130	5 307	3 315	7 235	6 799	11 715
	8 269	8 535	6 103	15 649	14 351	8 198	4 626						
Spotted dolphin (No.) [4]								435	2 697	0	662	1 162	1 615

[1] Nine fish markets from Miyako to Onagawa (shown in Table 1).
[2] Calculated from the weight assuming 80.8 kg per animal.
[3] From January to April, only the cases where both catch and effort data were available are included.
[4] Catch by drive fishery off Sagami Bay. The season (October to January) is indicated by the year of closure of season.

gree of such poaching is unknown; only some porpoise hunting vessels took seals, and it is unknown what proportion of porpoises and seals they took.

OFFSHORE POPULATION IN THE WESTERN NORTH PACIFIC AND BERING SEA

This population is caught incidentally in a salmon gill-net fishery. This problem has been analysed by Ohsumi (1974). The biology of the cetaceans killed in the salmon fishery was studied by Mizue and Yoshida (1965), Mizue, Yoshida and Takemura (1966) and Koga (1969). These studies showed that the incidental catch by the salmon gill-net fishery is mostly of Dall's porpoise (*dalli*-type). Ohsumi suggested that the catch rate changes with the area, season, and the kind of net. Furthermore, he showed that the catch rate of the porpoise has not shown a tendency to decrease in the past 10 years.

Mizue and Yoshida (1965) say that the reported catch of Dall's porpoise is more than 1 000 animals per fleet, and that if the unreported animals were included, the catch would be more than 2 000 animals. Based on this datum and some other data obtained separately (Mizue, Yoshida and Takemura, 1966) the total number of porpoises killed by Japanese salmon gill-net fishing fleets (11 fleets in 1964) were calculated to be more than 10 000 animals (Mizue and Yoshida, 1965) or certainly more than 20 000 animals (Mizue, Yoshida and Takemura (1966).

Ohsumi (1974) cited Fukuhara's calculation based on the catch rate by U.S. research vessels and total commercial net length. This gives a figure of 11 800 Dall's porpoises (Ohsumi, 1974). However, there is a problem in this calculation, in that the actual length of the net used by the fishing boats is not known and it is generally believed that the salmon gill-net fishing boats use more net than permitted by the officials.

Accordingly, the best estimate of the number of porpoises killed by the salmon

gill-net fishery seems to be that made by Mizue, Yoshida and Takemura (1966).

SEA OF JAPAN-OKHOTSK SEA POPULATION

The commercial exploitation of this population in the southern Okhotsk Sea was started in 1937 (Hirashima and Ono, 1944) and seems to have been continued at least until 1945 (Noguchi, 1946). According to Ohsumi (1972, appendix III) annual catches of small cetaceans fluctuated between 200 and 1 800 off the coast of Hokkaido in the years 1957 to 1966; afterwards the catch was almost negligible. Judging from the information from fishermen at Abashiri on the northern coast of Hokkaido, most of the above catch is considered to have been made off the Okhotsk coast and to have consisted of *Phocoenoides*. The fishing season was from July to September with a peak in July and August (Hirashima and Ono, 1944). It is doubtful whether porpoises which were killed incidentally in the salmon gill-net fishery off the west coast of the Kamchatka Peninsula (Ohsumi, 1974) belong to this population; however, the salmon gill-net fishery in this area was stopped in recent years.

The exploitation of this population in the Sea of Japan was started in 1941 off the coast of the Tajima region (Matsui and Uchihashi, 1943a), and operated until at least 1945 (Noguchi, 1946). However, after 1960 the catch of small cetaceans was almost negligible or zero (see column of Hyogo in the appendix

Table 8. Annual catch of small cetaceans off the Tajima coast

Year	*Phocoenoides*	*Lagenorhynchus*	Unknown
1941	30	64	117
1942	710	59	16
1943	1 484	75	63
1944	507	69	60

III of Ohsumi, 1972). The catch of *Phocoenoides* in Table 8 is cited from Noguchi (1946). Though Noguchi (1946) suggested a possible decrease in the population of *Phocoenoides* off the Tajima coast relative to that of *Lagenorhynchus*, the decrease in *Phocoenoides* can more reasonably be explained by the difficulty of offshore fishing during the war and the relatively higher catch of *Lagenorhynchus*, the coastal species.

Discussion

Among the three populations of *Phocoenoides* suggested here, the population off the Pacific coast of Japan is most peculiar in that it has a restricted range, maybe small and maybe the most heavily exploited. In the winter and spring seasons about 6 000 animals are annually harvested from this population, and in the summer unknown numbers are incidentally killed in the salmon gill-net fishery.

In the mature females caught off the Sanriku coast the frequencies of the animals with 1, 2, 3 and 9 corpora in the ovaries are 10, 4, 1 and 1, respectively. The average number of corpora of mature females is only 1.8. Even if the high ratio of immature animals can be explained by the difference in migration or in behaviour related to the age or reproductive conditions of the animals, such a low corpora number must indicate a high mortality rate in the population. Accordingly, the decline of the CPUE in recent years should be watched carefully and more biological data should be collected to analyse the status of this population.

For the offshore population in the western North Pacific and Bering Sea, there is no data to suggest a decrease in the population and the population is considered to be in better condition. However, it is desirable to establish a system for collecting reliable information on the number of porpoises killed by the commercial salmon gill-net fishing fleet. The ships should have several biologists on board to collect biological information on these porpoises because information prepared by the fishermen or by the inspector is not highly reliable.

The population in the Sea of Japan and Okhotsk Sea is not exploited in Japanese coastal waters except for the probable incidental catch by small salmon fishing boats with gill nets. More study is needed to determine the identity of the population off the west coast of Kamchatka Peninsula.

Acknowledgements

Mr. S. Nagahora and Mr. J. Iwagiri of the Iwate Prefectural Fisheries Research Laboratory, Mr. T. Okazaki of the Far Seas Fisheries Research Laboratory kindly recorded the colour type of the porpoises caught incidentally by the research vessels in salmon gill-net fishery. Dr. Y. Naito of Tokyo University of Fisheries and Dr. N. Miyazaki of the Ocean Research Institute provided the sporadic record of porpoises in Japanese coastal waters. This study is indebted also to the crews of the research vessels *Hayachinemaru*, *Enoshimamaru*, *Hakuhomaru* and *Tanseimaru*, crews of the whaling boat *Ginseimaru No. 2*, and to the staffs of various fish markets in the Sanriku region for their cooperation. I would like to convey my deep appreciation to all who assisted and cooperated in this study.

References

HIRASHIMA, A. and S. ONO, Porpoise fishing off the coast
1944   of the Abashiri region. *Mon. News Hok-* *kaido Prefect. Fish. Res. Lab.*, 1(2): 82-90 (in Japanese).

KASUYA, T., The stock of striped dolphin. *Geiken Tsu-*
1976 *shin (News Whales Res. Inst.),* (295): 19-20, (296):29-38.

KOGA, S., On the Dall's porpoise, *Phocoenoides dalli*
1969 (True), caught by the Japanese salmon fishing gill-net in the northern waters of the Asian side. *J. Shimonoseki Univ. Fish.,* 18(1):53-63 (in Japanese).

KURODA, N., On the cetaceans in Suruga Bay. *Shoku-*
1940 *butsu Oyobi Dobutsu,* 8(5):825-34 (in Japanese).

—, On the relationship between *Phocoenoides dalli* and
1954 *P. truei. Bull. Yamashina Ornithol. Res. Inst.,* 5:44-6 (in Japanese).

—, Observation of marine mammals in the northern
1956 North Pacific. *J. Mammal. Soc. Jap.,* 1(3):36-9 (in Japanese).

MASAKI, Y., Whale cruise in the Bonin Island and Ma-
1972 riana Island area. *Geiken Tsushin (News Whales Res. Inst.),* (249):35-42 (in Japanese).

MATSUI, K. and K. UCHIHASHI, On Dall's porpoise off
1943 the Tajima coast (preliminary report). *Hyogoken chutokyoiku Hakubutsugaku Zasshi,* 8(9):35-9 (in Japanese).

—, On Dall's porpoise off the Tajima coast. *Dobutsu-*
1943a *gaku Zasshi (Zool. Mag., Tokyo),* 55(2):67-8 (in Japanese).

MIYAZAKI, N., T. KASUYA and M. NISHIWAKI, Distribu-
1974 tion and migration of two species of *Stenella* along the Pacific coast of Japan. *Sci. Rep. Whales Res. Inst., Tokyo,* (26):227-43.

MIZUE, K. and K. YOSHIDA, On the porpoises caught by
1965 the salmon fishing gill-net in the Bering Sea and the North Pacific Ocean. *Bull. Fac. Fish. Nagasaki Univ.,* 19:1-36 (in Japanese).

MIZUE, K., K. YOSHIDA and A. TAKEMURA, On the eco-
1966 logy of the Dall's porpoise in the Bering Sea and the North Pacific Ocean. *Bull. Fac. Fish. Nagasaki Univ.,* 21:1-21 (in Japanese).

NEMOTO, K. *et al.,* Observation and tagging of whales by
1966 Tanseimaru in Sanriku and Hokkaido waters. *Geiken Tsushin (News Whales Res. Inst.),* (173):1-10 (in Japanese).

NISHIWAKI, M., Observation and tagging of whales by
1967 Tanseimaru in 1966. *Geiken Tsushin (News Whales Res. Inst.),* (187):1-4 (in Japanese).

NISHIWAKI, M., T. KASUYA and W.J. HOUCK, On the
1966 variation of the white area on the flank of True's and Dall's porpoises. Abstract of the lecture in the autumn meeting of Japanese Association of Scientific Fisheries. 15 (in Japanese).

NITANI, H., Variation of the Kuroshio south of Japan. *J.*
1975 *Oceanogr. Soc. Japan,* 31(4):154-73.

NOGUCHI, E., Dolphin and its utilization. *In* Utilization
1946 of dolphins and scomber fishery, by E. Noguchi and A. Nakamura. Tokyo, Kasumigeseki Shobo, 36 p. (in Japanese).

OHSUMI, S., Catch of marine mammals, mainly of small
1972 cetaceans, by local fisheries along the coast of Japan. *Bull. Far Seas Fish. Res. Lab.,* (7):137-66.

—, Incidental catch of cetaceans with salmon gill-net.
1974 Document prepared for IWC/Small Cetacean Meeting, 9 p.

PILLERI, G., An inhuman method of capturing small
1971 odontocetes in Japan. *In* Investigations on Cetacea, edited by G. Pilleri. Berne, Brain Anatomy Institute, vol. 3, Part 2:347-8.

SENO, J., On two specimens of porpoise captured off the
1940 coast of Ozernaya, Kamchatka. *Bull. Jap. Soc. Sci. Fish.,* 8(6):357-64 (in Japanese).

SHIMAZU, Y., Whale marking cruise off the Sanriku
1971 coast. *Geiken Tsushin (News Whales Res. Inst.),* (233): 1-9 (in Japanese).

US NAVY HYDROGRAPHIC OFFICE, World atlas of sea
1944 surface temperature. Washington, D.C., Govt. Printer, H.O. No. 225, 2nd ed.

THE STOCK OF *STENELLA COERULEOALBA* OFF THE PACIFIC COAST OF JAPAN

T. Kasuya and N. Miyazaki

Abstract

This paper presents a detailed study of the size and sustainable yield of the population of striped dolphins, *Stenella coeruleoalba*, off the Pacific coast of Japan through analysis of biological data and catch statistics gathered since the mid-1990s to the present (biological materials from schools caught in 1967-73), from drive or hand harpoon fisheries or both, in a number of prefectures on the east coast of Japan. The mean annual catch of *S. coeruleoalba* in the late fifties to early sixties can be roughly estimated at 14 000 animals, with the largest catches occurring in the prefectures of Shizuoka (Izu Peninsula), Chiba (Choshi) and Wakayama (Taiji). The estimated mean annual catches in these prefectures were 11 000, 1 500 and 630 animals, respectively. Population assessment includes analysis of the following parameters: sex ratio, attainment of sexual maturity, length of calving interval, accumulation rate of corpora, age composition and total mortality of females and natural mortality rate.

Although the accuracy involved is not completely satisfactory, the study will allow the following conclusions. The population of *S. coeruleoalba* off the Pacific coast of Japan initially included more than 320 000 animals and was decreased in size by exploitation to about 220 000-250 000 animals by the late fifties to early sixties. The present population size is estimated to be 130 000-180 000, which is close to the level producing the maximum sustainable yield of 4 000-6 000 dolphins per year. The population presently being exploited is possibly a small coastal one migrating seasonally along eastern Japan. A drive fishery started for this population in 1973 at Taiji has increased the total catch of *S. coeruleoalba* in recent years. This tendency will continue and if adequate regulations are not introduced will decrease the size of the population rapidly.

Résumé

Les auteurs présentent des données détaillées sur la taille et le rendement soutenu de la population de dauphins rayés, *Stenella coeruleoalba,* au large de la côte Pacifique du Japon. Ils analysent les paramètres biologiques et les statistiques de captures recueillis depuis le milieu du vingtième siècle jusqu'à nos jours (matériaux biologiques provenant des bancs capturés en 1967-73) au cours des pêches par rabattage ou au harpon à main – ou des deux opérations – pratiquées dans plusieurs préfectures de la côte est du Japon. Les captures annuelles moyennes de *S. coeruleoalba* de la fin des années 50 au début des années 60 peuvent être estimées approximativement à 14 000 animaux, les plus fortes captures se situant dans les préfectures de Shizuoka (Péninsule d'Izu), de Chiba (Choshi) et de Wakayama (Taiji). L'estimation des captures annuelles dans ces préfectures était, respectivement, de 11 000, 1 500 et 630 animaux. L'estimation des populations comprend l'analyse des paramètres suivants: rapport des sexes, âge de la maturité sexuelle, longueur de l'intervalle entre deux parturitions, taux d'accumulation des corpora, composition par âge, mortalité totale des femelles et taux de mortalité naturelle.

Bien que l'exactitude ne soit pas entièrement satisfaisante, l'étude permet de tirer les conclusions suivantes. La population de *S. coeruleoalba* au large de la côte Pacifique du Japon était initialement supérieure à 320 000 animaux et a été réduite par l'exploitation à environ 220 000-250 000 à la fin des années 50 et au début des années 60. La taille de la population actuelle est estimée à 130 000-180 000, ce qui est proche du niveau assurant le rendement maximal soutenu de 4 000-6 000 dauphins par an. La population actuellement exploitée est peut-être une petite population côtière accomplissant une migration saisonnière le long du Japon oriental. Une pêche par rabattage, pratiquée à Taiji depuis 1973, a augmenté les captures totales de *S. coeruleoalba* ces dernières années. Cette tendance se poursuivra et elle aura pour effet, faute des règlements appropriés, de réduire rapidement la taille de la population.

Extracto

Se hace un estudio detallado del volumen y el rendimiento sostenible de la población de delfín rayado (*Stenella coeruleoalba*) de la costa del Pacífico del Japón partiendo de los datos biológicos y las estadísticas de captura recogidos desde mediados de siglo hasta la actualidad en las pesquerías de esa especie con arpones mecánicos o de mano de varias prefecturas de la costa oriental del Japón (el material biológico procede de grupos de animales capturados en 1967-73). Las capturas anuales medias de *S. coeruleoalba* a finales de los años cincuenta y principios de los sesenta pueden estimarse aproximadamente en 14 000 animales. Las cifras máximas corresponden a las prefecturas de Shizuoka (península de Izu), Chiba (Choshi) y Wakayama (Taiji), con capturas anuales medias estimadas de 11 000, 1 500 y 630 animales, respectivamente. La evaluación de la población incluye un análisis de los siguientes parámetros: proporción de los sexos, edad de madurez sexual, tiempo que transcurre entre dos partos, índice de acumulación de córpora, composición por edades, mortalidad total de las hembras y mortalidad natural.

Aunque la exactitud de los datos no es plenamente satisfactoria, el estudio permite llegar a las siguientes conclusiones. La población de *S. coeruleoalba* de la costa del Pacífico del Japón contaba inicialmente con más de 320 000 animales y a finales de los años cincuenta y principios de los sesenta había disminuido, a causa de la explotación, a unos 220 000-250 000. La población actual se calcula en 130 000-180 000 delfines, cifra próxima al nivel que permite el rendimiento máximo sostenible (4 000-6 000 al año). Es posible que la población que se explota actualmente sea una pequeña población costera que emigra estacionalmente a lo largo de la costa oriental del Japón. La explotación de esta población con arpones mecánicos, que comenzó en 1973 en Taiji, ha hecho aumentar en los últimos años la captura total de *S. coeruleoalba*. Esta tendencia proseguirá y, si no se introduce una reglamentación adecuada, determinará una rápida disminución de la población.

T. Kasuya
Ocean Research Institute, University of Tokyo, 1-15-1 Minamidai, Makano-ko Tokyo 164, Japan

N. Miyazaki
Department of Marine Sciences, University of the Ryukyus, Shuri, Naha City Okinawa 903, Japan

Introduction

On the Pacific coast of Japan, *Stenella coeruleoalba* have been caught mainly off Taiji (33°36'N, 135°56'E), off the coasts of Izu Peninsula (34°40'N, 140°50'E). The statistics of the catch of this species at Taiji and on the coasts of Izu Peninsula were analysed by Miyazaki, Kasuya and Nishiwaki (1974) and the influence of the Kuroshio current on the fluctuation in the catch of the species off the east coast of Izu Peninsula was demonstrated. Ohsumi (1972) and Miyazaki, Kasuya and Nishiwaki (1974) suggested that the *S. coeruleoalba* caught at the four localities might belong to one population.

The life history and part of the schooling behaviour was studied by Kasuya (1972) based on the animals caught by the driving method off the east coast of Izu Peninsula. Further analysis of the school structure is now being made by Miyazaki. These studies indicated that the schools are not independent population units, but that frequent exchange of members occurs between schools. This means that if the population is exploited the effect of fishing mortality is distributed to other schools of the population and changes their age composition.

This study intends to estimate the size and sustainable yield of the population now exploited off the Pacific coast of Japan based on the total mortality coefficient obtained through the relationship between ovulation and age, on the length of the calving interval estimated from the composition of the catch, and on the natural mortality coefficient assumed from that of *S. attenuata*.

Materials and method

Biological materials were obtained by us from 1, 2, 7, 6, 19 and 2 schools of *S. coeruleoalba* caught in 1967, 1968, 1970, 1971, 1972 and 1973 respectively, off the east coast of Izu Peninsula or off Taiji on the coast of Kii Peninsula. Other ancillary information on the structure of 19 schools provided by Prof. M. Nishiwaki, Dr. S. Ohsumi and Dr. T. Tobayama is used in this study. They were caught off the Izu coast in the years between 1952 and 1970.

The age of the animals was at first determined by examination of the dentinal growth layers using the method of Kasuya, Miyazaki and Dawbin (1974). The number of corpora in the ovaries were counted by the usual method (Kasuya, Miyazaki and Dawbin, 1974). The probable corpora atretica were not included. Then the real age of mature females was calculated using the accumulation rate of the corpora.

The catch of *S. coeruleoalba* was estimated based on the records given by Ohsumi (1972) and Miyazaki, Kasuya and Nishiwaki (1974), and on information collected at Choshi Fish Market.

Population parameters [1]

SEX RATIO

The sex ratio of *S. coeruleoalba* was checked based on data from 9 372 animals. No significant annual fluctuation of the ratio was found. Table 1 shows the sex ratios at different growth stages expressed as the ratio of females to the whole population. The suckling dolphins are animals less than 172 cm in body length, which correspond approximately to 1 ¼ years of age (Kasuya, Miyasaki and Dawbin, 1974). There are fewer females than males at any growth stage (ranging from 45.7 to 48.3 %).

In the present study, the sex ratio 0.476

---

[1] Some of the parameters were re-estimated by Kasuya (1976), but these have little effect on the estimates of the present status of the population obtained in this study.

Table 1. Sex ratio of _S. coeruleoalba_

Stages	No. of animals	Ratio of females
Foetus	661	0.469
Suckling	744	0.483
Others	7 967	0.457

obtained by combining 661 foetuses and 744 suckling calves is used as the sex ratio at birth. This ratio is slightly higher than the corresponding value of _S. attenuata_ 0.450, calculated based on the 238 animals in Kasuya, Mayasaki and Dawbin (1974) and unpublished data of one additional school caught in January 1974.

ATTAINMENT OF SEXUAL MATURITY

Kasuya (1972) showed that females of _S. coeruleoalba_ attain sexual maturity at between 7 and 11 years with a mean age of 8.8 years. A mean age of 9.1 years was recently obtained by Miyazaki (1975) based on more material including Kasuya's data; his age determination of animals between 1 and 12 years was, however, biased by 0.27 years to the higher side of Kasuya's reading, so the difference between the two estimates is not significant. Accordingly, the age of 9 years is used in this study as the age of the female at the attainment of sexual maturity. There seems to be no significant difference between the sexes in the age at sexual maturity (Kasuya, 1972; Miyazaki, 1975).

At present there is no way of checking any change in the age at maturity, which might occur as the population decreases. However, as the age mentioned above is still higher than the corresponding value of unexploited _S. attenuata_ (Kasuya, Miyazaki and Dawbin, 1974), a decrease in age at maturity may not have occurred in _S. coeruleoalba_.

Though the annual fluctuation in body length of females where 50 % of the animals are sexually mature was checked for the data collected between 1952 and 1973, it shows only random fluctuation in the range from 208.7 to 213.2 cm and shows no significant change. The mean body length at the attainment of sexual maturity estimated from the above 2 336 females (from 198 to 237 cm) is 211.5 cm. The corresponding value for males is 218.3 cm (Miyazaki, 1975). In the same study he concluded that the mean weight of testis at the attainment of sexual maturity is 16.5 g (1 testis). As shown in Table 2, the ratio of sexually mature animals in the catch of the drive fishery has increased gradually since 1952. This problem is left for future analysis.

CALVING INTERVAL

The mean length of calving intervals is estimated from the gestation period and the ratio of the number of adult females to that of pregnant animals. Though it is difficult to estimate the gestation period of _S. coeruleoalba_ off the Pacific coast of Japan correctly because of the restricted fishing season and the between-school peculiarity of the foetal length, the figure of 12 months obtained by Kasuya (1972) seems to be the present best estimate. If the gestation period is taken to be 1 year, the ratio mentioned above is the mean length of the calving interval in years.

The mean lengths of the calving interval estimated for each year are shown in Table 3 and Fig. 1. Though all the females with corpus luteum were considered to be pregnant, as the corpus luteum of ovulation seems to persist for only a short period (Kasuya, Miyazaki and Dawbin, 1974) and the frequency of unsuccessful ovulation is low, the error will not be large. In Fig. 1, the data represented by only 1 school are combined with the data of the next year to eliminate the bias of a school. These mean calving intervals show a gradual decrease in recent years. We consider that this is a response of the population to the decrease of the population level. Though this phenomenon must be analysed in relation to the level of

Table 2. Ratio of adult dolphins in the catch of *S. coeruleoalba* in drive fishery

	Suckling [1]		Juvenile		Adult [2]		Total		No. of Schools
	No.	%	No.	%	No.	%	No.	%	
Females									
1952-57	80	8.7	460	50.1	379	41.2	919	100	8
1958-67	108	15.8	224	32.8	351	51.4	683	100	8
1968-73	171	7.1	832	34.7	1 397	58.2	2 400	100	39
Total	359	9.0	1 516	37.9	2 127	53.1	4 002	100	55
Males									
1952-57	74	5.4	748	54.9	541	39.7	1 363	100	8
1958-67	122	19.8	242	39.4	251	40.8	615	100	8
1968-73	189	6.9	1 260	46.1	1 282	47.0	2 731	100	39
Total	385	8.2	2 250	47.8	2 074	44.0	4 709	100	55

[1] Up to 172 cm in body length.
[2] 212 cm or more (females); 219 cm or more (males).

the population, as the population level is not available, the relationship between calving interval and the calendar year was obtained as a first step. However, this problem is dealt with later. When the calendar year is shown by x and the mean length of calving interval by y, the following relationship (r = − 0.61) obtains

$$y = -0.054553x + 109.829 \quad \ldots \quad (1)$$

In the case of unexploited populations of *S. attenuata,* the calving interval was estimated from the scars in the ovaries to be between 2 and 6.5 years, and the mean from the ratio of pregnant females to be 4.19 years (Kasuya, Miyazaki and Dawbin, 1974). These 2 sets of

Table 3. Numbers of females at various reproductive stages and the ratios to pregnant females

Year	No. of schools	Pregnant (P)		P and L		Lactating (L)		Resting		Total	
		No.	ratio	No.	ratio	No.	ratio	No.	ratio	No.	ratio
1952	1	5	0.83	1	0.16	1	0.16	4	0.67	11	1.83
1953	1	4	1.00	0	0.00	17	4.25	0	0.00	21	5.25
1957	3	61	0.94	4	0.06	124	1.91	13	0.20	202	3.11
1958	1	49	0.89	6	0.11	32	0.58	0	0.00	87	1.58
1961	2	8	0.89	1	0.11	19	2.11	4	0.44	32	3.56
1967	1	3	0.60	2	0.40	41	8.20	9	1.80	55	11.00
1968	2	85	0.98	2	0.02	101	1.16	26	0.30	214	2.46
1970	7	63	0.93	5	0.07	72	1.06	52	0.77	192	2.82
1971	3	22	1.00	0	0.00	27	1.23	8	0.36	57	2.59
1972	16	330	0.98	5	0.02	157	0.47	29	0.09	521	1.56
1973	2	81	0.79	22	0.21	69	0.67	8	0.08	180	1.75

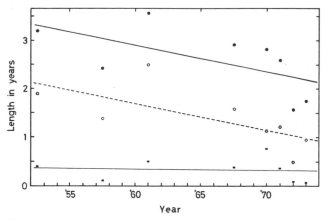

FIG. 1. – Annual fluctuation of the reproductive parameters. Closed circles and thick solid line indicate the length of calving interval, open circles and dotted line length of lactation, and squares and thin solid line the length of resting period.

figures obtained independently show a good coincidence. If the mean calving interval of 4.2 years is expected for *S. coeruleoalba* at the initial population level, 1 936 is obtained from formula (1) as the date when the calving interval began to shorten in the population. This is not unreasonable because heavy exploitation seems to have started in the twenties, with the introduction of motor vessels.

If the annual change in the total lactation period or that of the sum of the lactation period and the period lactating and simultaneously pregnant, is estimated, there is a relationship $y = -0.055343x + 110.174$, $r = -0.69$. This indicates that the mean of the total lactation period in 1973 is 0.98 years or 46 % of that in 1952. On the other hand the length of resting period seems to have been almost unchanged ($y = -0.002773x + 5.787$, $r = -0.09$). Accordingly, it is considered that the shortening of the calving interval is mainly caused by the shortening of the lactation period. Possibly, the resting period (0.37 years in 1952 and 0.32 years in 1973) will not have much plasticity, because it is already close to the interval of the mating seasons, which are recently suspected by Miyazaki (1975) to occur 3 times in a year. The numbers of females lactating and simultaneously pregnant are scarce and are strongly affected by the school structure. For example, in a school with many females near the end of lactation, the ratio of lactating and simultaneously pregnant females is rather high. For these reasons, the detection of annual changes in the frequency of occurrence of such females is difficult at present.

Table 4 shows the relative frequency of reproductive stages expressed as the ratio to the numbers of pregnant females. Though the data were obtained from catches from 1968 to 1973 as more than half of them were taken in the year 1972 when the ratio of pregnant females was extraordinarily high, the calving interval in Table 4 is lower than the value expected in Fig. 1 for the corresponding years. As shown in this Table, the mean calving interval is very short in age classes of 12 growth layers or less. This might easily have been expected because these age classes contain many females in their first pregnancy. However, the length of total lactation and of calving interval even show an increase between age classes of 13-16 tooth layers and age classes of over 17 layers. This indicates that the mean calving

Table 4. **Frequency of reproductive stages shown by the ratio to pregnant females**

Tooth layers	Sample no.	Pregnant (P)	P & L	Lactating (L)	Resting	Total
≤ 12	187	0.984	0.016	0.410	0.123	1.533
13-16	289	0.937	0.063	0.654	0.164	1.818
$-17 \leq$	219	0.895	0.105	0.952	0.133	2.086
Total	695	0.940	0.060	0.658	0.142	1.801

interval and mean lactation period increase with the age of the animal. A similar result was also reported by Kasuya, Miyazaki and Dawbin (1974) on *S. attenuata*. Accordingly, if the relative abundance of old adult females decreases as the result of exploitation, the mean calving interval may decrease. However, it is unreasonable to attribute the decrease in the calving interval accompanied by the decrease of the population entirely to the above phenomenon. Possibly the larger part will be attributed to the decrease in the calving interval in each age class.

ACCUMULATION RATE OF CORPORA

The accumulation rate of dentinal layers is considered to be 1 layer per annum in case of

S. coeruleoalba and *S. attenuata* (Kasuya, 1972; Kasuya, Miyasaki and Dawbin, 1974). Fig. 2 shows the relationship between the number of corpora lutea and albicantia and the age indicated by the number of growth layers in dentine. The fact that the mean number of tooth layers corresponding to each number of corpora does not show much increase in animals with 5 or more corpora indicates that the estimation of age by counting the tooth layers is unreliable after the age of about 16 growth layers and that the age is often underestimated. However, in animals between 10 and 15 years of age, the relationship between age and number of corpora is almost linear. As the ratio of immature females is only 12 and 4 % of total females in age groups of 10.5 and 11.5 years, respectively, indicating the negligible influence of newly

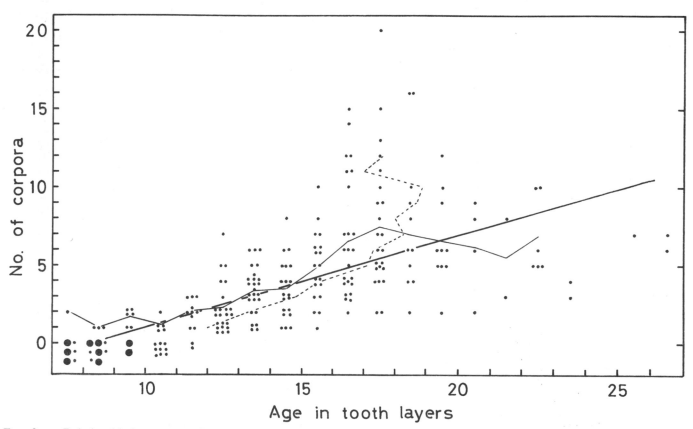

FIG. 2. — Relationship between number of the corpora in ovaries and the number of tooth layers. Small circle indicates one animal, and the larger 10 animals, dotted line means number of tooth layers at each corpora number, thin solid line means number of corpora of mature animals at each number of tooth layers. For thick solid line see text cited from Miyazaki (1975).

mature females, the straight-line part of the relationship will indicate the accumulation rate of the corpora. If the relationship between age (x) and mean number of corpora (y) is calculated by the least squares method for the above age range, the following formula is obtained and shown by a thick solid line in Fig. 2.

$$y = 0.590x - 4.875 \quad \ldots\ldots\ldots\ldots \quad (2)$$

Accordingly, it is considered that the mean accumulation rate of the corpora is 0.590 per annum or that the mean interval between ovulations is 1.70 years.

AGE COMPOSITION AND TOTAL MORTALITY OF MATURE FEMALES

The mean age of mature females corresponding to each number of corpora was calculated based on the mean age at the attainment of sexual maturity, 9 years, and the annual accumulation rate of corpora obtained above. The result of the calculation is shown in Table 5 and Fig. 3. The age thus calculated does not give the mean age of the animals with a certain number of corpora but the mean age on the occurrence of a certain number of ovulations. However, this problem is not important in this study, because it does not change the total mortality rate calculated from it. On the age composition in Fig. 3 the highest frequency is observed at 4 ovulations or at the age of 14.1 years. If the total mortality coefficient (z) is calculated by the least squares method for all the age classes above this point, $Z = 0.1365$ is obtained.

For comparison, if the total mortality coefficient is calculated from the right slope of the age composition based on the tooth layers, the values 0.248 and 0.267 are obtained for males and females respectively (thin straight line in Figs. 4 and 5). These values are extreme-

Table 5. Age composition of mature female of *S. coeruleoalba* calculated from the corpora number

No. of corpora	Age	1968	1970	1971	1972	1973	Total
1	9.0	13	14	6	42	23	98
2	10.7	18	7	7	54	12	98
3	12.4	10	9	5	49	21	94
4	14.1	15	13	3	61	12	104
5	15.8	13	14	1	38	12	78
6	17.5	9	11	5	41	8	74
7	19.2	10	8	2	28	5	53
8	20.9	5	5	1	16	5	32
9	22.6	4	5	1	7	4	21
10	24.3	5	4	1	11	6	27
11	25.9	2	2	2	9	2	17
12	27.6	7	2	–	8	7	24
13	29.3	4	1	1	3	3	12
14	31.0	3	–	–	8	1	12
15	32.7	1	3	–	4	1	9
16	34.4	1	2	1	2	–	6
17	36.1	–	–	2	2	1	5
18	37.8	1	1	–	1	1	4
19	39.5	–	–	–	–	–	–
20	41.2	–	–	–	1	–	1
21	42.9	–	–	–	–	–	–
22	44.6	1	–	–	–	1	2
23	46.3	–	–	–	–	–	–
24	48.0	–	–	–	–	–	–
25	49.7	–	1	–	–	–	1

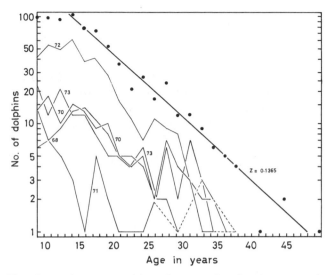

FIG. 3. – Age composition of mature females. Age was calculated from corpora number and accumulation rate of corpora. Numerals indicate the year, and closed circle the total. For solid line see text.

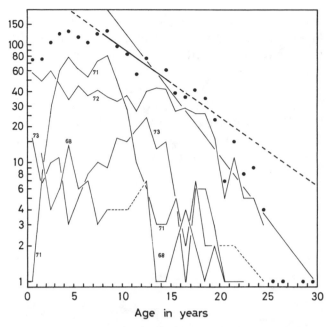

FIG. 4. – Age composition of male dolphins based on the growth layers in dentine (1 layer/year). Numerals indicate the year, closed circle the total, and the thick line the total mortality coefficient z = 0.1365 applied for the age range of solid line. For a thin straight line see text.

ly high and considered to be unreasonable as in the case of *S. attenuata* (Kasuya, Miyazaki and Dawbin, 1974).

NATURAL MORTALITY

There is no direct way of estimating the natural mortality of *S. coeruleoalba*. It is, in this study, derived from the corresponding value of *S. attenuata* at the initial population level.

The mean natural mortality coefficient of sexually mature females of *S. attenuata* is 0.077 (Kasuya, Miyazaki and Dawbin, 1974) or 0.079 (Kasuya, 1976). However, the age of the oldest female of *S. attenuata* estimated from the number of ovulations is about 5 years younger than the corresponding figure of *S. coeruleoalba,* in spite of a lower ovulation rate in *S. attenuata.* So we suspect that the lifetime of *S. coeruleoalba* is about 10 % longer than that of *S. attenuata,* and that the former species has a lower natural mortality rate. Accordingly, if the estimation of the natural mortality coefficient 0.079 is correct for the adult females of *S. attenuata,* the corresponding fig-

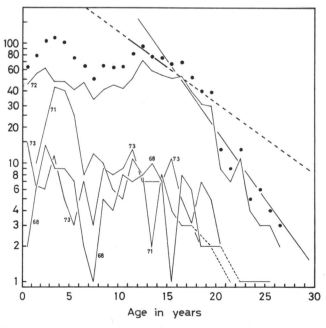

FIG. 5. – Age composition of female dolphins based on the growth layers in dentine. For further explanation see Fig. 4.

T. KASUYA & N. MIYAZAKI

ure of *S. coeruleoalba* seems to be about 0.07. However, the 2 hypothetical natural mortality coefficients of adult females, 0.07 and 0.08, are used in the present study.

As shown in Figs. 4 and 5, large annual fluctuations of the age composition of immature dolphins are observed; furthermore, there are 2 low frequency age classes seen in the total age composition, one at 6 or 7 years of age and

the other at 0 to 2 years. They seem to be caused by the between-school difference of the age composition, segregation of dolphins at premature age class, and by the higher loss rate of juvenile calves during the driving (Kasuya, 1972). These phenomena make it difficult to estimate the mortality rate of immature animals.

In the present study the natural mortal-

FIG. 6. – Some dolphins are separated with a net from a school of striped dolphins kept in Kawana harbour, and are going to be landed. Two high speed scouting boats are seen at the centre beyond the net. November 1973.

FIG. 7. – A dead striped dolphin on the landing platform of Kawana Fishermen's Cooperative Union. November 1973.

ity of the immature animals is estimated as follows.

When A = number of immature females
B = number of mature females
C = mean calving interval in years
L = mean litter size
l_x = number of females at the age of x years
m = age of the female at the attainment of sexual maturity
s = ratio of females at birth
μ_1 = mean natural mortality coefficient of immature female
μ_2 = mean natural mortality coefficient of mature female
f = fishing mortality coefficient

the following relations occur in a population at equilibrium:

$$A = l_0 \int_0^m e^{-(\mu_1+f)x}\, dx = \frac{-l_0}{\mu_1+f}[e^{-(\mu_1+f)m}-1] \quad (3)$$

$$B = l_m \int_m^\infty e^{-(\mu_2+f)(x-m)}\, dx = \frac{l_0 \cdot e^{-(\mu_1+f)m}}{\mu_2+f} \quad (4)$$

$$l_0 = B \cdot \frac{s \cdot L}{C} \quad \dots\dots\dots\dots\dots \quad (5)$$

If C = 4.2, L = 1, m = 9, s = 0.476, $\mu_2 = 0.07$ or 0.08, and f = 0, formulae (4) and (5) give the following estimates for μ_1.

$\mu_1 = 0.05354$, when $\mu_2 = 0.07$
$\mu_1 = 0.03870$, when $\mu_2 = 0.08$

Catch of S. coeruleoalba

As the mortality of animals born before 1959 is dealt with in the present study, it is necessary to use the mean annual catch of the species in the corresponding years. However, as the statistics of pre-1956 catches are not available in most cases, it was estimated from the catch of the recent years.

Considering the catch of dolphins in each prefecture shown in the Appendix III of Ohsumi (1972), it is presumed that the prefectures where significant numbers of S. coeruleoalba might have been caught are Fukushima, Ibaraki, Chiba, Shizuoka and Wakayama.

In Wakayama prefecture the catch was small before 1956 and increased in recent years. The catch of dolphins in this prefecture is almost entirely landed at Taiji and is composed of Steno, Tursiops, S. attenuata and S. coeruleoalba. The catch statistics of Stenella spp. are reported by Miyazaki, Kasuya and Nishiwaki (1974), and it is considered that most of the catch of Stenella is represented by S. coeruleoalba. The mean number of S. coeruleoalba caught in the years when the catch was stable (from 1963 to 1970) is 630 animals per year.

All animals taken in Shizuoka prefecture in Ohsumi (1972) are considered to have been caught on the coast of Izu Peninsula by the driving method. The annual catch of dolphins in Shizuoka prefecture has been reduced since 1967. This coincides with the year when the cooperative operation was started by 2 fishermen's cooperative unions on the east coast of the peninsula. The number of S. coeruleoalba caught on the Izu coast (Miyazaki, Kasuya and Nishiwaki, 1974) and the number of dolphins caught in Shizuoka prefecture (Ohsumi, 1972) show fairly good concidence. Furthermore, as it was confirmed by Tobayama (1969) that the catch of dolphins off the Izu coast is mostly S. coeruleoalba and that other species are negligible (3.3 % from 1963 to 1968), all the catch in Shizuoka prefecture was considered in this study to be S. coeruleoalba. The mean annual catch thus calculated from the statistics in Ohsumi (1972) is about 11 000 for the years from 1957 to 1966.

According to the old annual statistics provided by Dr. S. Ohsumi, the annual catch of dolphins in the 12 years from 1942 to 1953 at Arari and Kawana on the Izu coast has been as follows:

31

	Range	Total	Mean
Arari	277-20 131	88 730	7 394
Kawana	0- 5 311	24 032	2 003

Even if the catch at the other 6 villages that were whaling in that period on the Izu coast is included, the mean annual catch in Shizuoka prefecture would not have exceeded 12 000 animals as their operation was less intensive (Dr. S. Ohsumi, pers. comm.). This indicates that, admitting a large annual fluctuation, the mean annual catch was almost stable in the years from 1942 to 1966.

In Chiba prefecture the catch of dolphins was high in the years from 1957 to 1964 (Ohsumi, 1972) and the mean annual catch was 1 900 dolphins. According to our information obtained at Choshi Fish Market, where most of the dolphins are landed in this prefecture, the dolphins were mainly caught with hand harpoons and *S. coeruleoalba* is the preferred catch of fishermen in the months from October to January, but in February to April smaller numbers of *Lagenorhynchus* and *Lissodelphis* are landed. Though we have not verified this information, it is reasonable to think that most of the dolphin catch is composed of *S. coeruleoalba* because this species is sold at a higher price. In this study it was tentatively guessed that 80 % of the catch in Chiba prefecture, 1 500 dolphins per year, represents *S. coeruleoalba*.

The annual catch of dolphins in the 2 prefectures of Ibaraki and Fukushima in the years from 1957 to 1964 fluctuated between 132 and 1 805 with an average of 880 dolphins, and after 1965 the catch was almost negligible. The ratio of *S. coeruleoalba* in the catch of the former period seems to be low because they were located in the north and some *Phocoenoides* caught in the winter season may have been included. In the present study a total catch of 1 000 was presumed for the catch of *S. coeruleoalba* in Fukushima and Ibaraki prefectures and for the unreported catch in the various parts of the Pacific coast of Japan.

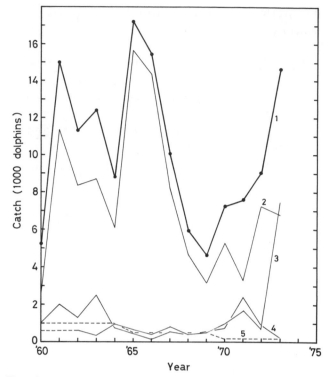

FIG. 8. – Catch of *S. coeruleoalba* off the Pacific coast of Japan. 1 indicates total, 2 Shizuoka (Izu coast), 3 Taiji, 4 Chiba, and 5 other catch. The catch at Taija and that in total Japan in 1973 was recently corrected as 1 000 and 8 200 dolphins respectively (Kasuya 1976), and the catch in 1974 at Taiji and Izu coast was 763 and 11 715 dolphins respectively.

From the above, a rough estimate of the mean annual catch of *S. coeruleoalba* in the late fifties to early sixties off the Pacific coast of Japan is obtained as follows:

Shizuola pref. (Izu Pen.)	11 000
Chiba pref. (Choshi)	1 500
Wakayama pref. (Taiji)	630
Other catches	1 000
Total catch	14 000

The catch statistics for *S. coeruleoalba* after 1960 are estimated as shown in Fig. 6, based on Ohsumi (1972), Miyazaki, Kasuya and Nishiwaki (1974) and our unpublished data.

Population analysis

POPULATION SIZE IN LATE FIFTIES TO EARLY SIXTIES

In drive fishing for dolphin no selection of the animals is expected. In harpoon fishing, there can be a difference in the catchability of dolphins according to growth stage, sex, or the reproductive condition of the female, because only the animals which come to the bow of a boat are usually harpooned, and lactating females accompanied by a suckling calf seem to be less attracted by a boat. However, as the catch has mostly been effected by the driving method, the difference in the catchability of *S. coeruleoalba* is negligible.

If the mean annual catch of *S. coeruleoalba* in the period between the late fifties and early sixties (14 000 animals) is divided by the annual fishing mortality rate, the estimation of the mean population size of *S. coeruleoalba* in the corresponding period is obtained as 218 000 or 255 000 (Table 6).

RECENT STATUS OF THE POPULATION

If the annual recruitment and the catch are added to the above population estimate, the annual fluctuation of the population can be roughly traced.

Table 6. **Estimates of population of *S. coeruleoalba* off the Pacific coast of Japan in the late fifties to early sixties**

Total mortality coefficient	0.1365	0.1365
Natural mortality coefficient, adult female	0.07	0.08
Fishing mortality coefficient	0.0665	0.0565
Fishing mortality rate	0.0643	0.0549
Mean annual catch	14 000	14 000
Population	218 000	255 000

As mentioned in the former section, equations (4) and (5) must obtain in an exploited population at equilibrium. The next relation is obtained from (4) and (5).

$$l_0 = \frac{s \cdot L}{C} \cdot \frac{l_0 \cdot e^{-(\mu_1 + f)m}}{\mu_2 + f} \quad \dots \quad (6)$$

As the parameters s, C, μ_1 and μ_2 were already estimated, and the litter size (L) is considered to be 1.0, the value of f or the sustainable fishing mortality coefficient is obtained for each year. Though it is mathematically incorrect to assume a stationary condition for this population, if the f obtained above is used, the population at the beginning of a year is calculated by the following method, assuming that the catch is made at the end of a year.

$$S_{n+1} = S_n (1 + R_n) - F_n \quad \dots \dots \quad (7)$$

$$R_n = 1 - e^{-f} n \quad \dots \dots \dots \quad (8)$$

S_n indicates the population size of both sexes in the year n, F_n total catch, and R_n sustainable fishing mortality rate or net recruitment rate in

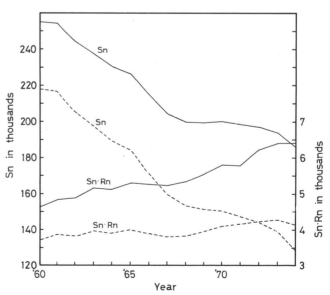

FIG. 9. – Annual fluctuation of the population (S_n) and annual net recruitment ($S_n \cdot R_n$) of *S. coeruleoalba* off the Pacific coast of Japan. Dotted line is based on the assumption of $\mu_2 = 0.07$, and solid line $\mu_2 = 0.08$.

the same year. From this calculation it is suggested that the population decreased rapidly after 1960 except for the years from 1968 to 1972 (Fig. 7). The population level at the beginning of 1974 was about 120 000 ($\mu_2 = 0.07$) or 186 000 ($\mu_2 = 0.08$).

MAXIMUM SUSTAINABLE YIELD

A linear relationship is found, as shown in Fig. 8, between the net recruitment rate (R_n in %) and stock size (S_n) in thousands mentioned above. The relationships are

$$R = -0.01601S + 5.145, \text{ when } \mu_2 = 0.07 \quad (9)$$

or

$$R = -0.02077S + 7.068, \text{ when } \mu_2 = 0.08 \quad (10)$$

Then the sustainable yield is given by $R \cdot S$, as shown in Fig. 8. When the natural mortality coefficient of adult females (μ_2) is assumed to be 0.07, the maximum sustainable yield of 4 100 dolphins is obtained at the population level of 161 000, which is about

32 000 above the level in 1974. The sustainable fishing rate (R) and sustainable yield at 1974 level are 3.09 % and 3 980, respectively. On the other hand, if $\mu_2 = 0.08$ is assumed, the population level producing the maximum yield of 6 000 animals is 170 000, which is about 16 000 below the population level in 1974. The sustainable fishing rate and sustainable yield in 1974 are 3.21 % and 5 960, respectively. Though these figures show minor differences with the annual sustainable yield ($S_n \cdot R_n$) shown in Fig. 7, it is caused by the process of converting the net recruitment-year relationship into net recruitment-population relationship.

The initial population level of the stock is estimated from the relationships (9) or (10), with insufficient accuracy, as the point with no net recruitment. They are 321 000 ($\mu_2 = 0.07$) or 340 000 ($\mu_2 = 0.08$). However, there is no certain reason to expect that the linear relationships of (9) or (10) can be extended to the initial population level. It is also probable that the gradient change is smaller at a higher population level or that there is a time lag between the change in the recruitment rate and the decrease of the population. If such a case occurs, the initial population level calculated above indicates only a minimum estimation, and the population level expressed in Fig. 9 can be larger than the real value.

CALVING INTERVAL – POPULATION LEVEL RELATIONSHIP

The relationship between the mean calving interval and the population level shown by the ratio to the initial population obtained above is shown in Fig. 9. The information on the calving interval in the 1952-53 seasons was not plotted, because the population level was not available. The population level in the 1957-58 seasons was extrapolated from that in 1960, based on the catch statistics reported by Ohsumi (1972) and the method used here. The relationship calculated by the least squares method is

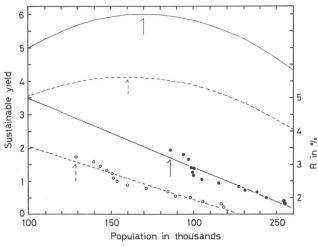

FIG. 10. – Relationship between population size and net recruitment rate (R in %, straight lines), and sustainable yield in thousands (curves). Open circle and dotted line indicate the assumption of $\mu_2 = 0.07$, closed circle and solid line $\mu_2 = 0.08$, arrows the level of population producing the maximum sustainable yield and that in 1974.

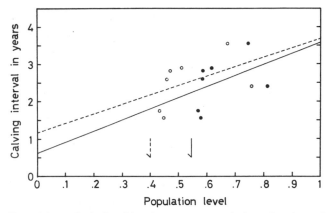

FIG. 11. – Relationship between population level and mean length of calving intervals. Dotted line and open circles indicate the case of $\mu_2 = 0.07$, and solid line and closed circles $\mu_2 = 0.08$. Arrow indicates the level in 1974.

$$C = 2.508P + 1.168, \quad \mu_2 = 0.07 \qquad (11)$$
$$C = 2.945P + 0.620, \quad \mu_2 = 0.08 \qquad (12)$$

when C indicates the calving interval, and P population level.

Though the accuracy of this method is poor because of the inaccuracy of the estimate of the initial population and the scarcity of the data, the calving interval at the population level of 1974 is about 2.2 years as indicated in the former section. And, if the lines are extended, the interval seems to change from above 3.5 years at the initial stage to about 1 year at extremely low population levels. However, it is dubious to expect that the interval could decrease to 1 year, at which point all females must be conceiving just after the parturition.

Discussion

The maximum age of females derived from the present data, admitting the inaccuracy caused by the individual variation of the ovulation rate, is about 50 years. While this may seem too high a figure given our present understanding of small odontocetes, it is not

high when compared with the age reached by *Tursiops* (Kasuya, 1976). In *Tursiops,* which in Japanese coastal waters has larger teeth and thicker layers, it usually becomes difficult to count the dentinal growth layers at ages between 15 and 20 layers. However, on an old animal with exceptionally clear layers, 35 layers were observed in the dentine, as was space in the pulp cavity for the accumulation of 10 or more layers. This observation might suggest that the lifetime of dolphins is longer than that expected from the tooth layers.

Though the 2 sets of natural mortality coefficients are used in the present study, we are inclined to think that the lower natural mortality of adult females $\mu_2 = 0.07$ might be closer to the truth for 2 reasons. One is the comparison of 2 kinds of *Stenella* mentioned above. The other is the speed of the decrease of the population. The catch statistics at Arari and Kawana suggest that the mean annual catch of *S. coeruleoalba* in the period between 1942 and 1953 was at least 10 000 dolphins. This indicates a probable decrease of the population at a rate of more than 6 000 per annum, or more than 108 000 in the 18 years from 1942 to 1959. Even if it is assumed that the population in the 1942 season was close to the initial level, the estimated population based on the higher mortality of the adult female allows the decrease of only 85 000 in the 18 years. On the other hand, the lower mortality gives a more reasonable figure of 103 000. The resolution of this problem must be left for the future because the estimates of the natural mortality coefficient and of the catch statistics are still too uncertain.

Another uncertainty in the present population analysis is related to the estimation of the calving intervals at the initial population level. If the interval is shorter than 4.2 years assumed based on the knowledge of *S. attenuata,* it gives a higher mortality rate at the immature stage and a consequently lower recruitment rate and a more rapid decrease in the population. For example, if the calving interval at initial population level is assumed to be 3.75 years as suggested in Fig. 9, the value

35

of μ_1 is 0.06613 ($\mu_2 = 0.07$) or 0.05129 ($\mu_2 = 0.08$) and the net recruitment rate in 1973 is 2.52 % or 2.69 % respectively. These values are about 82 % of the rate estimated in the former section based on the 4.2-year calving interval at the initial level.

Though Miyazaki, Kasuya and Nishiwaki (1974) analysed the fishing effort and catch of the dolphin off the east coast of Izu Peninsula, no indication was found of a decline in the catch per unit effort. This might be because their analyses were made for the period from 1965 to 1973 seasons, when the population was almost stable or the decrease was slow.

However, if the change in fishing area and the efficiency of fishing vessels are considered, the picture is slightly different. The villages on both sides of Izu Peninsula have been responsible for most of the catch of *S. coeruleoalba* in Japan except for in a few recent seasons. In 1897 this fishing was already common in several villages on the peninsula (see Kasuya, 1972). In those days as they operated the driving for *Lagenorhynchus, Globicephala* and *S. coeruleoalba* with rowing or sailing boats, the operation must have been restricted to the coastal waters and the catch of pelagic *S. coeruleoalba* must have been smaller than the present. According to the information of Mr. Suda, Director of the Kawana Fishermen's Cooperative Union, which is one of 2 dolphin fishing groups operative on the Izu coast in recent years, before the introduction of motor vessels they fished within several nautical miles of the coast, and after the introduction of motor vessels in the twenties, the fishing ground expanded to the entrance of Sagami Bay (about 20 nautical miles from the port). However, they started to use several high-speed scouting boats in 1962, when the last dolphin fishing group on the west coast of Izu Peninsula ceased operations (Miyazaki, Kasuya and Nishiwaki, 1974), and in recent years driving has been done from as far out as about 50 nautical miles. This information suggests that the level of the past catch has only been maintained through the improvement of fish-

ing vessels and the expansion of fishing ground. Several dolphin fishing groups did not adopt such a change, which may have been the reason for their ceasing to operate.

Though the fishermen do not deny the possibility of a decrease in the population, they also think that the decrease in the migration of the dolphin into Sagami Bay is the result of the increase of vessel traffic to and from Tokyo Bay cruising across the entrance of Sagami Bay. Even if this might have some effect on migration, it cannot be a perfect explanation because often there are still some schools of *Grampus, Tursiops, Lagenorhynchus* and *S. coeruleoalba* found in Sagami Bay and the striped dolphin sometimes even rides on the bow wave of a boat. Furthermore, the effects of increased vessel traffic cannot explain the cessation of the fishing on the other side (west coast) of the Izu Peninsula.

Though the accuracy is unsatisfactory, the above considerations may lead to the following conclusions. The population of *S. coeruleoalba* off the Pacific coast of Japan was initially more than 320 000 (Table 7). It was reduced by exploitation to the level of about 220 000-250 000, by the late fifties to early sixties. The present status is estimated to be 130 000-180 000, which is close to the level producing the maximum sustainable yield of

Table 7. **Population analyses of *S. coeruleoalba* off the Pacific coast of Japan**

μ_2	0.07	0.08
Initial population	$\geq$ 321 000	$\geq$ 340 000
Population in 1960	218 000	255 000
Population in 1974	129 000	186 000
R at 1974 level	3.09 %	3.21 %
SY at 1974 level	3 980	5 960
Population, MSY [1] level	161 000	170 000
R at MSY level	2.57 %	3.53 %
MSY	4 130	6 010

[1] MSY: Maximum sustainable yield.

4 000-6 000 dolphins per annum. Possibly this population is a small coastal population migrating seasonally along the Pacific coast of Japan. A drive fishery on this population started in 1973 at Taiji on the coast of Kii Peninsula (Miyazaki, Kasuya and Nishiwaki, 1974) has increased the total catch of this dolphin in recent years (Fig. 6). This tendency will continue and will, if no adequate regulations are introduced, decrease the population rapidly.

Acknowledgements

Greatest thanks are due to Prof. M. Nishiwaki, Dr. S. Ohsumi and Dr. T. Tobayama, who provided us with old biological information on the schools caught by drive method. The fishermen's cooperative unions at Kawana, Futo and Taiji are thanked for the cooperation offered us for collecting the samples. This study is technically assisted by Miss S. Wada.

References

KASUYA, T., Growth and reproduction of *Stenella coe-*
1972   *ruleoalba* based on the age determination by means of dentinal growth layers. *Sci. Rep. Whales Res. Inst., Tokyo*, (24):57-9.

–, Reconsideration of life history parameters of the
1976   spotted and striped dolphins based on cemental layers. *Sci. Rep. Whales Res. Inst., Tokyo*, (28):73-106.

KASUYA, T., N. MIYAZAKI and W.H. DAWBIN, Growth
1974   and reproduction of *Stenella attenuata* on the Pacific coast of Japan. *Sci. Rep. Whales Res. Inst., Tokyo*, (26):157-226.

MIYAZAKI, N., School structure of *Stenella coeruleoalba.*
1975   Thesis for Doctor's Degree, Faculty of Agriculture, University of Tokyo (in Japanese).

MIYAZAKI, N., T. KASUYA and M. NISHIWAKI, Distribu-
1974   tion and migration of two species of *Stenella* on the Pacific coast of Japan. *Sci. Rep. Whales Res. Inst., Tokyo*, (26):227-43.

OHSUMI, S., Catch of marine mammals, mainly of small
1972   cetaceans, by local fisheries along the coast of Japan. *Bull. Far Seas Fish. Res. Lab.*, (7):137-66.

TOBAYAMA, T., School size and its fluctuation in the
1969   catch of *Stenella coeruleoalba* in Sagami Bay. *Geiken Tsuchin (Whales Res. Inst. News)*, (217):109-19 (in Japanese).

ON THE CATCH OF THE STRIPED DOLPHIN, *STENELLA COERULEOALBA*, IN JAPAN

M. NISHIWAKI

Abstract

Several species of smaller cetaceans are caught in drive or hand harpoon fisheries or both in local districts of Japan for human consumption, including the striped dolphin, *Stenella coeruleoalba;* True's porpoise, *Phocoenoides dalli truei;* Dall's porpoise, *P. dalli dalli;* white-spotted dolphin, *S. attenuata;* Gill's bottlenosed dolphin, *Tursiops truncatus gilli;* Risso's dolphin, *Grampus griseus;* false killer whale, *Pseudorca crassidens,* and white-sided dolphin, *Lagenorhynchus obliquidens.* The annual catch of all smaller cetaceans in Japan is from 10 000 to 20 000 animals, this figure decreasing slightly in recent years due to a lessened preference for dolphin meat among the people.

S. Coeruleoalba is the species taken most often (one-half to one-third of the total catch), being captured off the southern coast of the island of Honshu in the Koshinsei or Japan current district and then also the Nanki area as it migrates south from September to February; schools then travel back north up the coast from May to June and return out to sea with the Kuroshio Current to unknown summer areas. Catch statistics are presented for the fishery on the east coast of the Izu Peninsula (Koshinsei district) for a recent 10-year period (highest annual catch, 9 149, 1965/66; lowest annual catch, 3 130, 1969/70; catch for most recent year reported, 6 799, 1973/74). Life history data for *S. coeruleoalba* are given including composition of migrating schools, development of young and information about reproduction. The present population size of *S. coeruleoalba* off the Pacific coast of Japan is very difficult to estimate from the available data; the sizes of the annual catch have been similar for about 30 years, however, indicating that the stock may be stable and able to stand present exploitation levels.

Résumé

Plusieurs petites espèces de cétacés sont capturées pour la consommation humaine, à des fins alimentaires, soit par rabattage, soit au harpon à main — soit par les deux méthodes — dans certaines pêcheries japonaises locales. Il s'agit du dauphin rayé, *Stenella coeruleoalba,* du marsouin de True, *Phocoenoides dalli truei,* du marsouin de Dall, *P. dalli dalĺi,* du dauphin à tâches blanches, *S. attenuata,* du souffleur de Gill, *Tursiops truncatus gilli,* du dauphin de Risso, *Grampus griseus,* du faux épaulard, *Pseudorca crassidens* et du dauphin à flanc blanc, *Lagenorhynchus obliquidens.* Au total, les prises annuelles japonaises se sont situées à 10 000-20 000 exemplaires. Le chiffre a légèrement diminué ces dernières années parce que la chair du dauphin est moins appréciée aujourd'hui.

S. coeruleoalba est l'espèce dominante dans les captures (entre le tiers et la moitié); elle est capturée au large de la côte sud de l'île de Honshu dans le district de Koshinsei, ou du courant japonais, ainsi que dans la région de Nanki, quand elle accomplit une migration vers le sud entre septembre et février. Les bancs remontent ensuite la côte vers le nord entre mai et juin, puis ils gagnent le large en suivant le courant de Kuroshio pour se rendre sur des terrains estivaux inconnus. L'auteur présente une statistique des captures effectuées sur la côte est de la péninsule Izu (district de Koshinsei) au cours d'une période récente de 10 années (capture annuelle la plus forte: 9 149 en 1965/66; capture annuelle la plus faible: 3 130 en 1969/70; capture pour la dernière année indiquée: 6 799 en 1973/74). Il fournit des données sur le cycle biologique de *S. coeruleoalba,* notamment la composition des bancs migrateurs, la croissance des jeunes ainsi que des renseignements sur la reproduction. La taille actuelle de la population de *S. coeruleoalba* dans les eaux de la côte Pacifique du Japon est très difficile à estimer à partir des données disponibles. Toutefois, l'importance des prises annuelles a peu varié depuis environ 30 ans, ce qui indique que le stock est probablement stable et peut supporter les niveaux d'exploitation actuels.

Extracto

En algunos distritos del Japón se capturan para consumo humano varias especies de cetáceos de pequeña talla con arpones mecánicos o de mano, entre ellos: delfín rayado, *Stenella coeruleoalba;* marsopa verdadera, *Phocoenoides dalli truei;* marsopa de puerto Dall, *P. dalli dalli;* delfín moteado, *S. attenuata;* tursión Gill, *Tursiops truncatus gilli;* delfín Risso, *Grampus griseus;* pseudo-orca, *Pseudorca crassidens,* y delfín de costado blanco, *Lagenorhynchus obliquidens.* La captura anual de todos estos pequeños cetáceos en el Japón es de 10 000 a 20 000 ejemplares, y ha disminuido ligeramente en los últimos años debido a la menor preferencia de la población por la carne de delfín.

La especie predominante entre las capturadas (de la mitad a un tercio de la captura total) es *S. coeruleoalba,* que se pesca frente a la costa meridonal de la isla de Honshu, en el distrito de Koshinsei, y también en la zona de Naki, cuando emigra hacia el sur entre septiembre y febrero. Luego los animales se desplazan de nuevo hacia el norte a lo largo de la costa, de mayo a junio, para volver al mar con la corriente del Kurosivo, hacia zonas desconocidas donde transcurren el verano. Se dan estadísticas de captura de la pesquería de la costa este de la península de Izu (distrito de Koshinsei) en un período decenal reciente (captura anual más elevada, 9 149, 1965/66; captura anual más baja, 3 130, 1969/70; captura del último año considerado, 6 799, 1973/74). Se dan datos sobre el ciclo vital de *S. coeruleoalba,* en especial sobre la composición de los grupos que se desplazan, el desarrollo de las formas juveniles, y la reproducción. Es muy difícil estimar, sobre la base de los datos disponibles, el volumen actual de la población de *S. coeruleoalba* de las costas japonesas del Pacífico. Las cifras anuales de captura han sido muy parecidas durante unos 30 años, lo que indica que tal vez la población sea estable y capaz de sostener los niveles actuales de explotación.

M. Nishiwaki
Department of Marine Sciences, University of the Ryukyus, Shuri, Naha City Okinawa 903, Japan

Dolphins and porpoises are still eaten in Japan, though not by all Japanese. Fig. 1 shows the districts in which small cetaceans are consumed. The species eaten varies with the district and depends on the harvest from each of the fishing grounds scattered along the Japan Islands and also on the available transportation route from a fishing ground to markets or consumers. True's porpoise (*Phocoenoides dalli truei*) and Dall's porpoise (*Phocoenoides dalli dalli*) are eaten in the Sanriku district, and the striped dolphin (*Stenella coeruleoalba*) is the main species eaten in the area around Odawara City, Kanagawa Prefecture to Hamanako Lake, Shizuoka Prefecture and the so-called Koshinsei district. In Tokyo Metropolis and the cities on its outskirts, there is no tradition of eating dolphin meat. Fishermen from Izu Fishermen's Union catch the dolphins by the drive method and bring them to the neighbouring Koshinsei district. If there is a large catch of True's porpoise in the Sanriku district, surplus animals with their viscera extracted are transported to the fish market of Numazu City, Shizuoka Prefecture, and transferred to the mountain region of Yamanashi Prefecture where they represent an important protein source for the local people, especially in winter. In Nanki, Wakayama Prefecture, meat is eaten in the areas where whaling has been carried out since ancient times and is still in operation. Striped dolphins (*Stenella coeruleoalba*) form the major part of the catch there, and the catch of white-spotted dolphins (*Stenella attenuata*) has recently been increasing. Other species, the Gill's bottlenosed dolphin (*Tursiops truncatus gilli*) for example, are also hunted and even Risso's dolphins (*Grampus griseus*) are hunted and caught. On the Island of Shikoku, consumption of dolphin meat is rare but on Kyushu Island it has been eaten since ancient times in some districts. It is said, but not certain, that in the islands of Iki and Tsu-shima, off the northern shore of Kyushu, there has been no tradition of eating dolphin meat. But on the northwestern coast of Kyushu and in the Islands of Goto, Gill's bottlenosed dolphins, false killer whales (*Pseudorca crassidens*) and white-sided dolphins (*Lagenorhynchus obliquidens*) are commonly caught by a drive fishery and also by hand harpoons. Along the coast of the Sea of Japan, local people of San-in district have harvested Dall's porpoises in considerable numbers for food; fishing there is mainly by hand harpoons. But this fishery has apparently decreased in recent years (Association of Forest and Agricultural Products, 1970-74).

The annual catch of all these species in Japan is 10 000-20 000. Lately, the number has slightly decreased because of a recent slow decrease in people's preference for dolphin meat and because fishermen come to dislike the hard work of catching dolphins, whether by drive or hand harpoon, with lower profits. The striped dolphin forms the largest part, by number, of the total annual catch, about 1/2 to 1/3.

Stenella are naturally offshore animals and only come near the coast for a part of their life. It seems that they eat plenty of food in the sub-Arctic convergence before migrating south. When the water temperature drops, they come along the Kuroshio Current to the coast of the Japan Islands. They come near to Point Inubo (Choshi City) first, between September and November. Some schools come along the coast of Boso Peninsula, Chiba Prefecture, and enter into Sagami Bay, but some others pass round the top of Boso coming to Izu in December or, at the latest, in the beginning of January. At nearly the same time, the northwest wind becomes dominant and the sea is rough, so that searching and driving-in are very difficult by that time and catch ceases automatically. As the season of dolphin fishing moves to the Nanki area, the catch by harpoon begins in Taiji Town, Wakayama Prefecture, and its neighbouring beach. When catches are high, about 50 animals are brought to the fish market every day in times of prosperity but a common figure is 10 animals a day. The meat is sold in the local area where people prefer it. From March to April the catch is small, probably because the main schools go further

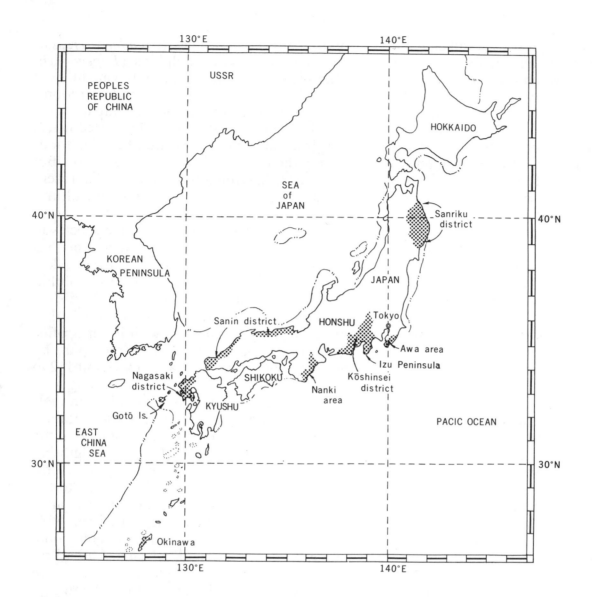

Fig. 1. – Areas of
Japan in which dolphin
meat is eaten.

south. Then from May to June, the schools come back. This time, they go north to the Izu Peninsula. They sometimes come along the west coast of the Izu Peninsula and go into Suruga Bay. About 10 years ago, Arari Fishermen's Union hunted them but they have stopped. Most of the northbound schools do not enter Suruga Bay, but pass Izu and Boso Peninsulas and swim away to the open sea with the Kuroshio Current. Once they have gone, there are no records of them; where they migrate to is utterly unknown (Arari Fishermen's Union, 1964-74) (see Table 1).

Records of the striped dolphin catch have come also from Taiwan, but the number is small, with the largest catch perhaps occurring from February to May. The catch there seems to be done mostly with hand harpoons.

According to Miyazaki (1975) the size of the annual catch on the coast of the Izu Peninsula is closely related to the movement of the Kuroshio Current. If the Kuroshio approaches Iau or Oshima Island, the annual catch is high, but if the Kuroshio stays far out (about 50 miles) from there, the catch is scarce. The Kuroshio Current is recognizable by water temperature; 15°C at 200 m depth is an

Table 1. Catch of southbound *Stenella coeruleoalba* on the east coast of Izu Peninsula in 10 recent years (Arari Fishermen's Union, 1964-74)

	Sep.			Oct.			Nov.			Dec.			Jan.	Feb.	Total
	L	E	M	L	E	M	L	E	M	L	E	M	L	E	
1964-65			50	351	116	173	1 445	467	1 084	1 675	107	533	33	69	6 103
1965-66		29	101	248	1 634	1 229	2 768	135	843	1 967	62	109	24		9 149
1966-67			1 324	191	404	251	1 203	3 253	1 500	50					8 176
1967-68						162	2 325	504	542	131	4 534				8 198
1968-69			169	510	11	1 643	1 345	948							4 626
1969-70				401	145	1 840	355	389							3 130
1970-71	131	1 310	293	603		314	2 197	459							5 307
1971-72		517			25	776			903	1 094					3 315
1972-73		503	1 117	102	631	815	4 067								7 235
1973-74		1 140	512	143	116	3 277	488	975	148						6 799
Total	131	3 499	3 566	2 549	3 082	10 480	16 193	7 130	5 020	4 917	4 703	642	57	69	62 038

E - early; m - middle; L - late part of the month.

indicator. The distance between the current and the positions of the catch may be measured and mapped.

Schools of striped dolphin can be identified as those of mature animals and immature ones. Miyazaki investigated the order of procession in migration as follows. Schools of mature animals are at the centre of the parade and the schools composed of immature animals surround the former. A school of mature animals includes calves shortly after birth and those in the weaning stage.

When the calves reach the age of 2 to 3, they come out of the adult group and join a group of youngsters. At the age of 7 to 9 they reach puberty. Females go back to an adults' group first and males follow them about a year or so later. As for newborn babies, weaning will continue for about a year and a half and while weaning they begin to eat some fish at about 6 months. The cycle of pregnancy may be every 3.39 years and ovulation occurs every 2 years, that is, 0.59 eggs annually. Oestrus may come every 4 months until fertilization.

Usually, there are 300 dolphins on an average in each southbound school, while in a northbound school there are 150-200 dolphins. They apparently divide themselves into more schools. Infrequently, they form a school of more than 1 000 dolphins. Among the many schools of adults and youngsters caught and examined, there were schools in which individuals of both age groups mixed together. The question is whether they were forced to mix by the fishermen driving them or they mixed of their own accord in an emergency.

Based on age determination, it was found that females reach physical maturity at the age of 11.5 and males at 13.5. The oldest among the examined animals was presumed to be a female of 26.5 years and a male of 29.5 years old. The annual catch in the last 10 years on the east coast of Izu Peninsula is shown in Table 1.

Kasuya and Miyazaki (1976) estimated that the size of the population of this species distributed off the Pacific coast of Japan was between 129 000 and 186 000, by dividing the catch by the total mortality coefficient. Though this estimate may deserve consideration, it was based considerably on hypotheses and the data were obtained only from Izu. Considering these particulars, I should emphasize that this number is based only on the data from stocks which have come along the west side of the Kuroshio Current and been caught on the east coast of Izu. Thus, this estimate might not include all the striped dolphins in the offshore waters of Japan which will come to the coast. Moreover, dolphins caught by drive fishery include almost all animals of a school – even recently-born calves are killed and eaten. The fluctuation of stocks at sea is very difficult to estimate from those data. It can, at least, be said that a similar catch figure has been reached every year for about 30 years, and 5 000-10 000 dolphins from the southbound school are still caught. Thus, the stock must be very large. The present size of the annual catch in Japan may not seriously affect the stock, i.e., the stock may sustain the present fishery and remain stable.

References

Arari Fishermen's Union, Catch records of dolphin fi-
1964-74   shery (1964-74) (in Japanese).

Association of Forest and Agricultural Products, Noh-
1970-74   rin Tokei (Statistics of forest and agricultural products) (1970-74) (in Japanese).

KASUYA, T. and N. MIYAZAKI, The stock of *Stenella*
1976   *coeruleoalba* off the Pacific coast of Japan. Paper presented to the Scientific Consultation on the Conservation and Management of Marine Mammals and their Environment, Bergen, Norway, 31 August-9 September 1976. Rome, FAO, ACMRR/MM/SC/25.

MIYAZAKI, N., School structures of *Stenella coeruleoal-
1975   ba*. Thesis for Doctor's Degree, Faculty of Agriculture, University of Tokyo (MS) (in Japanese).

DISTRIBUTION AND DIFFERENTIATION OF STOCK OF *DELPHINUS DELPHIS* LINNAEUS IN THE NORTHEASTERN PACIFIC

W.E. EVANS

Abstract

Delphinus delphis L. occurs in coastal and offshore waters of the northeastern Pacific from the equator to 36°N latitude as well as in the Gulf of California. The range is a band parallelling the west coast of the United States, Mexico and Central America, and extending seaward to 134°W longitude in the northern portion of the range and 115°W longitude in subtropical waters. There are modes in the distribution which indicate increased concentrations of herds at approximately 7°N, 25°N and 32°N latitude. Zones of very low concentrations of herds (hiatuses) are present in the north-south distribution, occurring between 13-20°N and 27-31°N latitude. This decrease in the density of *D. delphis* occurs in the most southerly portion of their range in an area where the mean annual sea surface temperatures are greater than 28°C. The densities of the most common species of delphinid in the tropical eastern Pacific (*Stenella attenuata* and *S. longirostris*) increase in these hiatus areas. The range of the latter two species is a triangle with the base formed by the coastline of Mexico, Central America and Colombia, and the apex extending west to about 10°N latitude, 145°W longitude.

Variations in total body length and certain characteristics of the cranial skeleton are described in quantitative terms. It is concluded that there are at least four distinct populations of *Delphinus* in the northeastern Pacific: (i) a southern California short-snouted population, north of 32°N; (ii) a Baja California short-snouted population between 28° and 30°N; (iii) a southern short-snouted population, south of 15°N, and (iv) a northern neritic long-snouted population, north of 20°N.

Data are presented which indicate that the density of *D. delphis* in the waters off southern California is seasonal and dependent on the mobility of the species, food availability, reproductive state and sea surface temperature. The peak abundances of *Delphinus* within the area of the southern California continental borderland occur in May-June, September-October and in January.

Résumé

On trouve *Delphinus delphis* L. dans les eaux côtières et hauturières du Pacifique nord-oriental entre l'équateur et 36° de latitude nord, ainsi que dans le golfe de Californie. L'aire de distribution s'étend sur une bande parallèle à la côte ouest des Etats-Unis, du Mexique et de l'Amérique centrale, et se prolonge en mer jusqu'à 134° de longitude ouest dans la partie nord et jusqu'à 115° de longitude ouest dans les eaux subtropicales. Des modes de distribution indiquent des concentrations accrues de populations vers les septième, vingt-cinquième et trente-deuxième degrés de latitude nord. Des zones à très faible concentration de populations (hiatus) se trouvent dans la distribution nord-sud, entre 13-20° et 27-31° de latitude nord. Cet abaissement de la densité de *D. delphis* se produit dans la partie la plus méridionale de leur aire de distribution, dans une zone où les températures annuelles moyennes à la surface de la mer dépassent 28°C. Les densités des espèces les plus communes de delphidés dans la zone tropicale du Pacifique oriental (*Stenella attenuata* et *S. longirostris*) s'accroissent dans ces « hiatus ». L'aire de distribution des deux dernières espèces est un triangle dont la base est formée par la côte du Mexique, de l'Amérique centrale et de la Colombie et dont la pointe est située à l'ouest à environ 10° de latitude nord et 145° de longitude ouest.

Les variations de la longueur corporelle totale et certaines caractéristiques du squelette cranien sont décrites en termes quantitatifs. On parvient à la conclusion qu'il existe au moins quatre populations distinctes de *Delphinus* dans le Pacifique nord-oriental: (i) une population à gueule courte dans le sud de la Californie au nord du 32° nord; (ii) une population à gueule courte en basse Californie entre 28° et 30° nord; (iii) une population méridionale à gueule courte au sud du 15° nord; (iv) une population nordique néritique à gueule longue au nord du 20° nord.

Des données sont fournies, indiquant que la densité de *D. delphis* dans les eaux du large au sud de la Californie est saisonnière et dépend de la mobilité des espèces, des disponibilités en aliments, du stade de reproduction et de la température de la surface de la mer. Les sommets de l'abondance pour le *Delphinus* dans l'aire de distribution qui longe le plateau continental au sud de la Californie se situent de mai à juin, de septembre à octobre et en janvier.

Extracto

Delphinus delphis L. vive en las aguas de media altura y costeras del nordeste del Pacífico, desde el Ecuador hasta 36° de latitud norte, así como en el Golfo de California. La zona de distribución es una banda paralela a la costa occidental de los Estados Unidos, México y América Central, que se extiende mar adentro hasta 134° de longitud oeste en la parte septentrional de la zona de distribución y 115° de longitud oeste en aguas subtropicales. Existen formas de distribución que indican mayores concentraciones de manadas a aproximadamente 70°, 25° y 32° de latitud norte. Existen zonas de muy pequeña concentración de manadas (zonas intermedias) en la distribución norte-sur, que viven entre 13-25° y 27-31° de latitud norte. Esta disminución de la densidad de *D. delphis* tiene lugar en la parte más meridional de su zona de distribución, en un área en donde las temperaturas medias anuales en la superficie del mar son superiores a los 28°C. Las densidades de las especies más comunes de delfines en el Pacífico oriental tropical (*Stenella attenuata* y *S. longirostris*) aumentan en estas zonas intermedias. La zona de distribución de las últimas dos especies es un triángulo con la base formada por la línea costera de México, América Central y Colombia, y el vértice extendiéndose en dirección oeste hasta 10° de latitud norte, 145° de longitud oeste.

Las variaciones en toda la longitud del cuerpo y algunas características del cráneo se describen en términos cuantitativos. Se llega a la conclusión de que hay, por lo menos, cuatro poblaciones distintas de *Delphinus* en el nordeste del Pacífico: (i) una población que tiene el hocico corto en California del Sur, al norte de 32°N; (ii) una población que tiene el hocico corto en Baja California entre 28° y 30°N; (iii) una población meridional que tiene el hocico corto, al sur de 15°N y (iv) una población nerítica septentrional de hocico largo, al norte de 20°N.

Los datos presentados indican que la densidad de *D. delphis* en las aguas frente a California del Sur es estacional y depende de la movilidad de las especies, disponibilidad de alimentos, estado reproductivo y temperatura de la superficie del mar. Las máximas abundancias de *Delphinus* dentro del área de las tierras limítrofes continentales de California del Sur tienen lugar en mayo-junio, septiembre-octubre y en enero.

W.E. Evans
Hubbs Sea World Research Institute, 1700 S. Shores Road, Mission Bay, San Diego, California 92109, USA

Introduction

The common dolphin, currently known as *Delphinus delphis,* is distributed worldwide in temperate and sub-tropical waters (Cabrera, 1961), with local variants existing in the Black Sea (Tomilin, 1957), the Mediterranean (Gihr and Pilleri, 1969), along the Atlantic coasts of Europe and Africa (Gihr and Pilleri, 1969; van Bree and Purves, 1972), in the Indian Ocean (van Bree, 1971; Pilleri and Gihr, 1972), the coastal waters of Japan (Nishiwaki, 1965, 1972; Mizue and Yashida, 1960; Ohsumi, 1972), Australia, New Zealand (Gaskin, 1968) and the Pacific coast of South America (Aguayo, 1975). Little has been published about *Delphinus* in the northeastern Pacific. It is considered by some to be the most abundant cetacean in this area (Norris and Prescott, 1961). In 1969, Banks and Brownell discussed the validity of *Delphinus bairdi* and concluded that 2 species of *Delphinus, D. delphis* and *D. bairdi,* were present in the coastal waters of southern California and Baja California, Mexico. The movement patterns of *D. delphis* in the southern California continental borderland have been discussed by Evans (1971, 1974).

The occurrence of *D. delphis* in the temperate and sub-tropical eastern Pacific was noted early by Scammon (1874). However, until the present no comprehensive work has been carried out on these animals. In 1966, I began a study of the biology of *Delphinus* sp.[1] in the northeastern Pacific concentrating on the herds that frequent the coastal and offshore waters of southern California, and, to a lesser extent, stocks that were found in the coastal waters of Baja California, Mexico, and the Gulf of California. After 8 years of observation (1966-74), from surface vessels and aircraft, it is quite evident that this species of delphinid is indeed the most "common" dol-

phin in southern California waters, representing 53 % of all the odontocete cetaceans encountered in 654 observations (Fig. 1). No other species accounted for more than 14 % of the remaining sightings.

When I started work on *Delphinus* sp. in 1966, I intended to define various aspects of the biology of this animal as representative of an unexploited pelagic delphinid. Distribution and movement patterns, feeding behaviour and density in the southern California continental borderland were studied. An attempt was made to relate the distribution to oceanographic parameters in the study area of interest. In 1972 these animals formed an important fraction of the cetaceans killed by the eastern tropical Pacific tuna purse-seine industry (NOAA Tuna Porpoise Review Committee, 1972). The 1973 and 1974 data made available from the porpoise-tuna observer programme of the National Marine Fisheries Service's (NMFS) Southwest Fisheries Center have emphasized the need to summa-

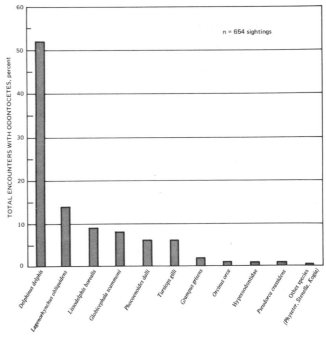

FIG. 1. – Percentage of total encounters during aerial surveys with odontocete cetaceans by species in the southern California Continental Borderland based on 654 sightings. One encounter equals one sighting of an individual or herd of odontocetes, all of the same species.

---

[1] Given the uncertainty that exists over the proper definition of species in this paper, the term *Delphinus* sp. has been used throughout.

rize the data currently available. Data were needed on the numbers and structure of the *Delphinus* stocks in the northeastern Pacific to assess the impact of the fishery on the species.

This study includes (i) a review of the distribution of *Delphinus* sp., (ii) definition of 4 separate stocks of *Delphinus* sp. in the northeastern Pacific, and (iii) a discussion of the monthly changes in the relative abundance of *Delphinus* sp. herds in the southern California continental borderland as a function of seasonal movement pattern.

Distribution of *Delphinus* sp.

The most northerly record of *Delphinus* sp. in the eastern Pacific is a stranded speci-

men from British Columbia, Canada (Giugu-et, 1954). Because it is difficult to determine the initial origin of stranded specimens, they have not been included in the distributional data discussed in this report. Common dolphins have been observed worldwide within the water temperature range 10-28°C, thus including water temperature seasonally found off British Columbia. Observations of herds at sea north of 36°N latitude are based on only 1 reported sighting at 37°18'N latitude (Brownell, 1964).

All verified sightings of *Delphinus* sp. herds collected over a 10-year period from Navy, NOAA and university research ships, commercial tuna fishing vessels and aerial surveys in the northeastern Pacific, indicate that the major distribution is from the equator to 36°N latitude and from 83° to 132°W longitude with some observations of herds to 10°S

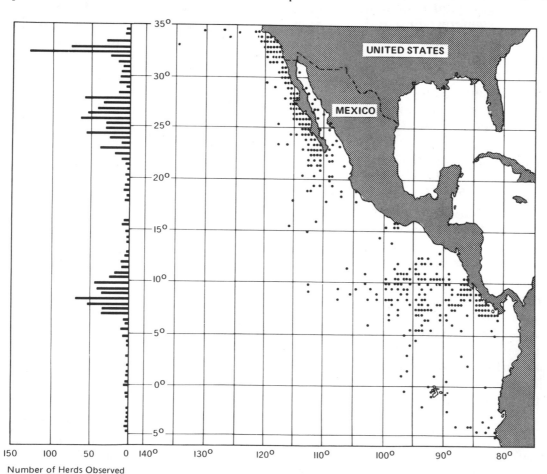

FIG. 2. – Distribution and number of herds sighted in the northeastern Pacific, based on all verified observer sightings available as of October 1974.

Number of Herds Observed

latitude and in the vicinity of the Galapagos Islands (Fig. 2). In this figure, the number of herds sighted as a function of latitude is plotted at the left of the illustration. The dots on the map represent the areas in which herds were observed. From 5° to 32°N, the number of sightings as a function of observer effort has been quite high; and therefore, the modes that occur at approximately 7°N, 25°N and 32°N are probably representative of real increases in the density of *Delphinus* sp. in those areas. The apparent low density of these animals between 13° to 20°N and 27° to 32°N is therefore also indicative of real gaps in the north-south distribution. The decrease in the number of herds sighted south of the equator is the result of a low level of observation effort in that area, with the majority of the sightings reported coming from 1 commercial tuna seiner. Recent survey cruises (1975, 1976) have established the presence of *Delphinus* sp. at 10°S and 125°W, which are not indicated in Fig. 2. Publications which review the distribution data in the aforementioned area (Bruyns, 1971; Marcuzzi and Pilleri, 1971; Aguayo, 1975) indicate that herds of *Delphinus* sp. are present along the west coast of South America at least as far as a latitude of 40°S. The first 2 references indicate a definite gap in the north-south distribution occurring generally south between 5°S and 20°N, which is quite consistent with the data presented in this study.

The distribution of the various races of *Stenella attenuata* and *S. longirostris* reported by Perrin (1974) possibly indicate competitive exclusion. According to Perrin (1972) both *S. attenuata* and *S. longirostris* in the eastern tropical Pacific are distributed from 0° to 25°N latitude and 80° to 146°W longitude. High densities are found between 10° and 20°N latitude and extend westward as far as 146°W longitude, an area apparently not occupied by *Delphinus* sp. Thus, interspecies competition could contribute to the scarcity of *Delphinus* sp. in this area. A comparison by latitude of the areas of distribution and the number of herds sighted for *Delphinus* sp. and the 2 species of *Stenella* is presented in Fig. 3. Most sighting

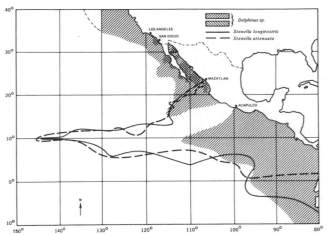

FIG. 3. – The distribution of *D. delphis* in the northeastern Pacific compared with the distribution of *S. longirostris* and *S. attenuata* described by Perrin (1972).

data on *Delphinus* sp. suggest that this species occurs where the sea surface temperatures are below 28°C. Individual sightings of this species have been made in areas where the surface temperature was as high as 30°C; however, in such cases the mixed layer (isothermal water) was shallow, 10-15 m. Furthermore, I have

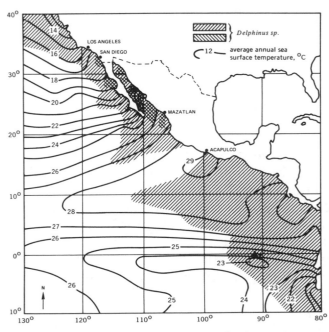

FIG. 4. – The distribution of *D. delphis* in the northeastern Pacific compared to the average annual sea surface temperature (1°C isotherms).

observed surface water temperature in the tropical eastern Pacific that changes as much as 4°C within a distance of 10 nautical miles. If we are to assume sea surface temperature to be a limiting factor in the distribution of *Delphinus* sp. (Fig. 4) it is more meaningful to look at the average annual sea surface temperature. Considering that both the distribution of animals and the sea surface temperature undoubtedly fluctuate seasonally, low *Delphinus* sp. density in the area where the mean annual water temperature is above 28°C could reasonably be interpreted as evidence for a possible thermal barrier. The preference of this species for temperate to sub-tropical waters (Tomilin, 1960) adds support to this interpretation.

Regional stocks

The occurrence of regional variation in various stocks of *Delphinus* sp. has frequently been noted in the literature (Cadanat, 1959; Marcuzzi and Pilleri, 1971; Bruyns, 1971; Nishiwaki, 1967). Unfortunately, these observations have either not been quantified or have been based on conclusions drawn from examination of extremely small samples.

Separation in other areas

According to Barabash-Nikiforov, 1940 (cited by Tomilin, 1957), *D. delphis* L. from the southeastern Black Sea in the vicinity of the city of Batumi are significantly different from those collected from the northwestern Black Sea near Yalta and Novorossiisk. Such morphometric differences as smaller mean total overall length, shorter pectoral flippers, shorter length from the tip of the rostrum to the origin of the dorsal fin were noted. Tomilin, however, questioned the validity of the measurements, stating that true differences of the magnitude observed would be unlikely over

such a short distance (500-700 km). However, Perrin (1972) concluded that, at least in the case of *Stenella,* geographical differences in population can be expected over distances as short as tens of kilometres. The comparison of measurements of 24 specimens of *D. delphis* from the Mediterranean with those of 26 from the Atlantic led Gihr and Pilleri (1969) to conclude that these 2 stocks of *Delphinus* separated by approximately 1 000 km represented 2 races.

NORTHEASTERN PACIFIC

Scammon (1874) suspected that the *D. delphis* in the eastern Pacific might not be the same species as the Atlantic stock. He reportedly sent 2 specimens collected near Point Arguello, California, to the U.S. National Museum. Dall (1873, 1874), noting the elongated and attenuated rostrums, determined that they were a separate species of *Delphinus* which he designated *D. bairdi.* The validity of this species has been questioned several times (Miller, 1936; Hershkovitz, 1966; Rice and Scheffer, 1968).

On the basis of the ratio of rostral length to zygomatic width, Banks and Brownell (1969) concluded that 2 separate species of *Delphinus* occur in the North Pacific, *D. delphis* (ratios 1.53 or less) and *D. bairdi* (ratios 1.55 or higher). However, van Bree and Purves (1972) pointed out that if *D. bairdi* was valid based on this morphometric character, it was not limited to the North Pacific, since they had data on several specimens from the Atlantic and the coastal waters of New Zealand with skull length/width ratios which met the Banks and Brownell criterion for *D. bairdi.* It was further suggested by van Bree and Purves that if the ratio of the rostral length to zygomatic width was indeed a valid character by which to designate a different species of *Delphinus, D. capensis* (Gray, 1828) should be used, since it was also designated based on skull width/length ratios of 1.55 or higher and has chronological precedence.

With the exception of cranial skeletal material obtained from the California Academy of Sciences, San Francisco, and skulls from the Gulf of California provided by Mr. Kenneth Balcomb, which were determined to be mature animals because the premaxillary bones were completely fused, none of the data being discussed has been reported previously. All specimens, except those from the Gulf of California, which were represented by skeletal material only, were sexually mature males (single testes weight of 100 g or more) and females (presence of at least 1 ovarian scar). Where possible, teeth from each individual were sectioned, and animals with less than 4 dentinal layers were excluded from the data base.

Measurements of the zygomatic width and rostrum length were then plotted (Fig. 5) as a scattergram along with similar data from skulls collected in the Gulf of California and the measurements cited by Pilleri and Gihr (1972) for *Delphinus tropicalis* (van Bree, 1971). Data on sexual maturity are available only for those specimens labelled as coastal water, southern California, offshore Baja California (north of 20°N) and tropical eastern Pacific (Costa Rica south of 15°N).

The range of rostral measurements is approximately 5 times greater than that for zygomatic width and appears to be discontinuous. In the group with shorter rostrums (215-274 mm) body length varied from 156 to 226 cm; in the Pacific group with longer rostrums (288-342 mm) body length overall varied from 186 to 243 cm. These measurements for the eastern Pacific specimens were then converted to ratios of rostrum length over zygomatic width (Fig. 6). The 2 separate ranges of ratios similar to those reported by Banks and Brownell (1969) also occur in my specimens. The longer snouted group have ratios with a lower range of 1.52, with the short-snouted group having ratios no greater than 1.49. Moreover, short-snouted forms of *Delphinus* sp. occur not only in the coastal waters of southern California and Baja California, Mexico, but also in the Gulf of California and the tropical eastern Pacific. The present data do not support the supposition by Banks and Brownell (1969) that the short-and long-snouted forms of *Delphinus* sp. in the eastern Pacific are separated geographically, since many of my long-snouted forms were collected at sites only 2-5 nautical miles from some of the collection sites for the short-snouted form. Although the 2 forms are found in the same geographic range, herds of the 2 types do not appear to mix and have never been collected together.

The long-snouted form frequent areas inside the 100-fathom depth contour (Fig. 7). The absence of a long-snouted form in the southern end of the range is probably due more to a lack of data than an actual absence of this variate of *Delphinus* sp. Anecdotal information from commercial tuna purse seine fishermen frequently refers to herds of very

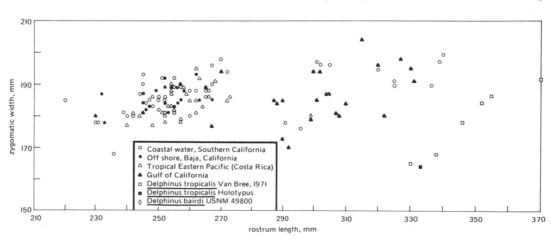

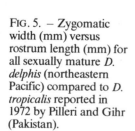

FIG. 5. – Zygomatic width (mm) versus rostrum length (mm) for all sexually mature *D. delphis* (northeastern Pacific) compared to *D. tropicalis* reported in 1972 by Pilleri and Gihr (Pakistan).

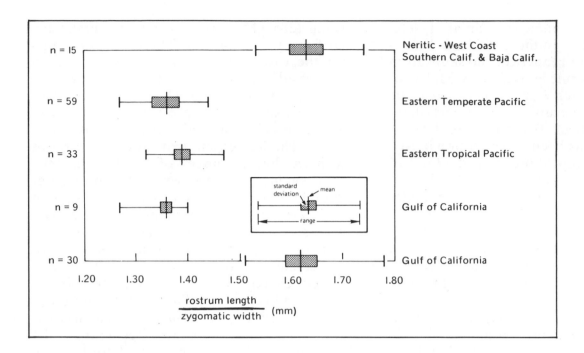

FIG. 6. – Rostrum length/zygomatic width ratios for *Delphinus* from the northeastern Pacific and Gulf of California.

large white-belly porpoise close to shore in the waters off Costa Rica, which they call "untouchables" since they are rarely captured in the seining operation.

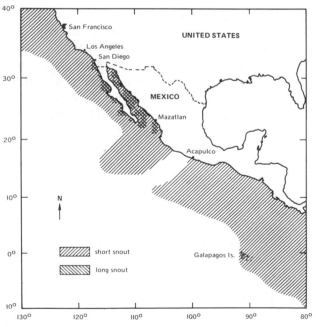

FIG. 7. – Approximate range and distribution of short-snouted and long-snouted *Delphinus* in the northeastern Pacific. Distribution probably fluctuates with season and from year to year depending on water temperatures and food abundance.

Two apparent hiatuses occur in the distribution of *Delphinus* sp. in the northeastern Pacific between latitudes 15°-20°N and latitudes 27°-32°N; they appear to divide the animals into a bimodal northern and a unimodal southern stock. The samples from these regions cannot be separated on the basis of the ratio of rostrum length to zygomatic width. Total overall body length of sexually mature females and males, however, shows a significant difference. The mean total length of 43 females from the southern California and Baja California samples (north of 20°N) is 178.3 cm compared to a mean total length of 196.0 cm for 48 females from the tropical eastern Pacific (south of 15°N) (Fig. 8). A similar difference is found in males from the 2 stocks. Adult male *Delphinus* sp. from the northern stock have a mean total length of 187.5 cm as compared to a mean length of 208 cm for males from the southern stock (Fig. 9).

To further define the differences between the various geographical stocks a stepwise discriminative analysis (Cooley and Lohnes, 1962; Dixon, 1964) was conducted using measurements of skulls from the 4 stocks sampled. These were the short-snouted southern Cal-

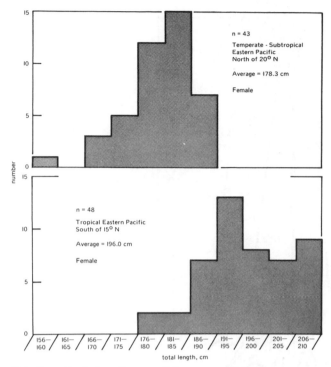

FIG. 8. – Body length overall-frequency histogram, comparing sexually mature female *Delphinus* from the temperate eastern Pacific and the tropical eastern Pacific. Sexual maturity was based on the presence of at least one ovarian scar.

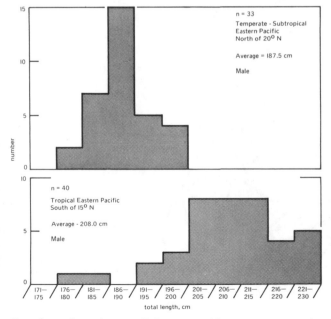

FIG. 9. – Length overall-frequency histogram, comparing sexually mature male *Delphinus* from the temperate and tropical eastern Pacific. Sexual maturity was based on a single testes weight of > 100 grams.

ifornia; short-snouted Baja California; short-snouted, tropical eastern Pacific; and long-snouted, neritic stocks.

Measurements representing those elements of the cranial osteology associated with such functions as hearing, sound production, vision, feeding and respiration were selected (Perrin, 1972). Because of limitations in the state of preparation of the available skeletal material 25 calvarium measurements were used (Table 1, Figs. 10-11). Only specimens

Table 1. Skull morphometrics

Delphinus skull measurements (mm)

1. Condylo-basal length – from tip of rostrum to posteriormost margin of occipital condyles.
2. Length of rostrum – from tip to line across posteriormost limits of antorbital notches.
3. Greatest parietal width, within post-temporal fossae.
4. Greatest preorbital width.
5. Width of rostrum at base – along line across posteriormost limits of antorbital notches.
6. Rostrum width 60 mm from line across posteriormost limits of antorbital notches.
7. Width of rostrum at midlength.
8. Width of rostrum at 3/4 length, measured from posterior end.
9. Length of upper left tooth row – from posteriormost margin of posteriormost alveolus to top of rostrum.
10. Distance from tip of rostrum to internal nares (to mesial end of posterior margin of right pterygoid).
11. Greatest postorbital width.
12. Length of antorbital process of left lacrimal.
13. Greatest length of left post-temporal fossa, measured to crest of raised suture.
14. Greatest width of left post-temporal fossa at right angles to greatest length.
15. Length of left orbit – from apex of preorbital process of frontal to apex of postorbital process.
16. Minor diameter of left temporal fossa proper.
17. Major diameter of left temporal fossa proper.
18. Length of mandibular fossa, measured to mesial rim of internal surface of condyle.
19. Greatest height of left ramus at right angles to greatest length.
20. Length of lower left tooth row – from posteriormost margin of posteriormost alveolus to tip of mandible.
21. Greatest length of left ramus.
22. Width of left premaxilla, measured from nasal septum and perpendicular to main axis of skull.
23. Width of right premaxilla, measured from nasal septum and perpendicular to main axis of skull.
24. Greatest width of external nares.

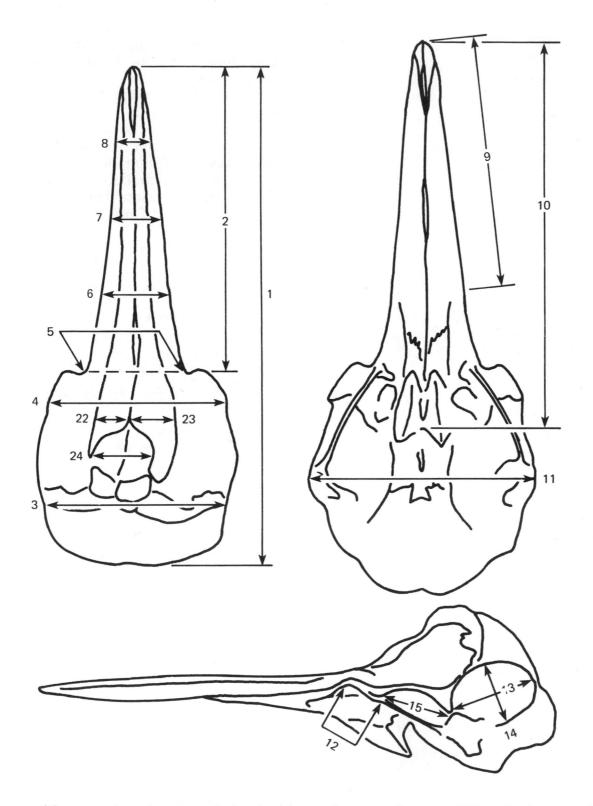

FIG. 10. — Location of skull measurements delineated, elements 1-15 and 21-24.

with more than 4 postnatal dentinal layers in the teeth were used in the variation analyses to avoid biasing the results with ontogenetic changes. This criterion was based on the assumption that the growth of the elements in each of the functional units of the skull would

54

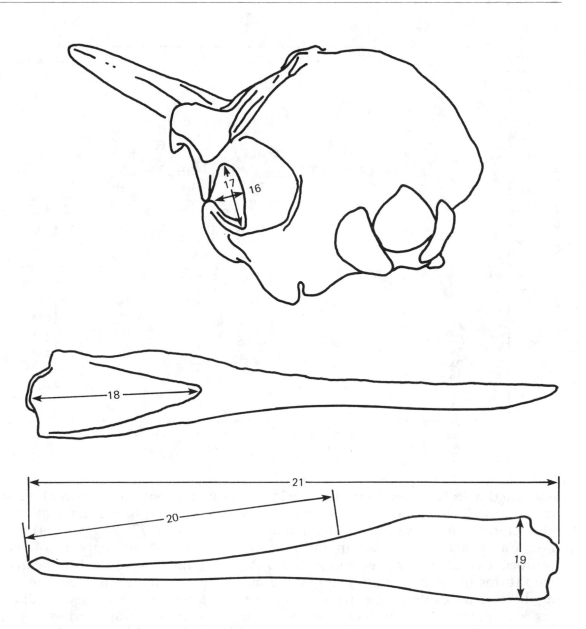

FIG. 11. – Skull measurement delineated as elements 16-21.

be asymptotic by the time 4 or more dentinal layers had been laid down. This was observed in the 2 species of *Stenella* studied by Perrin. Further restrictions were also placed on the selection of specimens to be used in the test sample. The initial analysis was a comparison of the available skull measurements for representatives of all potentially different stocks. The small sample size available for the neritic, long-snouted stock limited the number of variables tested to 16. In order to correct for the wide range in skull length and potential size differences due to sex, all measurements were taken as a percentage of the total skull length (condylo-basal length) for each individual (Fig. 12).

The data on rostral length and zygomatic width (Figs. 5 and 6) indicate a definite separation of the neritic group from the southern California, Baja California, and tropical eastern Pacific stocks. Although less obvious, there is also a significant degree of separation between each of the other 3 groups, especially with regard to the size of the left temporal fossa, which is identified by Perrin (1972) as one of the osteological elements of the skull

55

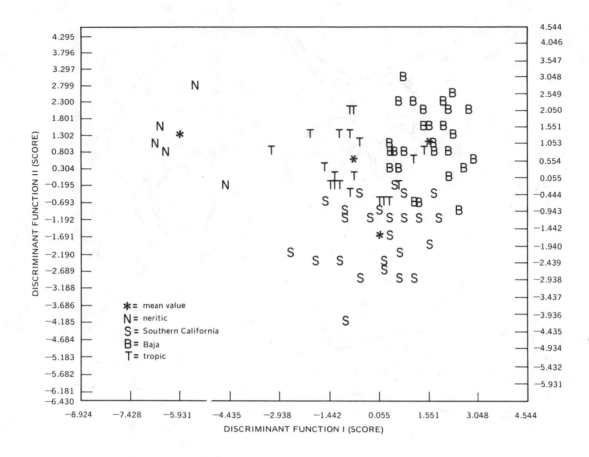

FIG. 12. – Scores of discriminant function I (greatest proportional post-orbital width) versus the scores of discriminant function II (major proportional diameter of the left temporal fossa), for matched samples of *D. delphis* representing the southern short-snouted stock (SoCal), Baja California short-snouted stock (Baja), tropical eastern Pacific short-snouted stock (Tropic) and the northern neritic long-snouted stock (Neritic).

associated with feeding. As in the case of Perrin's coastal form of *S. attenuata,* the post-temporal fossa is larger in the neritic and Baja California forms than in the southern California and southern (eastern tropical Pacific) forms of *Delphinus* sp. Data on the diet for this species of delphinid from Pacific waters are sparse or non-existent except in the case of the southern California stock (Fitch and Brownell, 1968). If, however, one assumes that the types of food organisms consumed by the various geographic stocks of *Delphinus* sp. remain similar at least to family if not to genus and species, it is reasonable to hypothesize that modifications of the feeding apparatus as well as the feeding strategy would occur from northern to southern waters. The water masses and the associated midwater fish fauna of the northeastern Pacific not only change significantly from southern California waters to the waters of the tropical eastern Pacific, but the distribution of suitable food species also var-

ies, becoming discontinuous in the southern portion of the range of *Delphinus* sp. (Robinson, 1972; Briggs, 1974).

Since only 16 of the potential 24 elements were used in the above analysis due to limitations in specimens available from the neritic stock, and additonal discriminative analysis was conducted using 23 of the variables. This time only the southern California (SoCal), the Baja California (Baja), and tropical eastern Pacific (Tropic) samples were considered. To minimize the potential effect of sex and size (from Figs. 8-9 the overall length of the tropical eastern Pacific sample differentiates them from the other 2 groups under consideration), only females were used. These were paired by length class, and all cranial measurements were taken as a percentage of length overall. Although these restrictions placed great limitations on the size of the sample (n for each group reduced to 7) greater confidence can be placed on the validity of the results. The separation of the 3 short-snouted stocks was more obvious (Fig. 13). The 2 most significant discriminating factors were among those excluded in the previous analysis and represent the functional group complexly associated with sound production and respiration: (I) width of the right premaxilla, measured from the nasal septum and perpendicular to the main axis of the skull, and (II) greatest width of the external nares. If the currently popular theories on the mechanisms of sound production are accurate, the differences in the size and relationship of these 2 osteological characters could be associated with variations in vocalization between these 3 stocks (Evans and Prescott, 1962; Evans, Sutherland and Beil, 1964; Norris, 1968, 1969; Norris *et al.*, 1971; Evans, 1973; Evans and Maderson, 1973; Dormer, 1974). Significant differences in the types of sounds or calls produced could result in effective social isolation of the 3 short-snouted stocks (Mayr, 1970; Wynne-Edwards, 1962).

It is clear that the 4 stocks examined so far differ from each other. Now let us examine variation within stocks. Although the number of samples is small, it is possible to compare 2 groups of data on specimens from 2 herds which were assumed to represent different groups, since they were collected at different times of the year and were different in size, composition, behaviour and coloration. Fifteen skull measurements from 5 females collected from 1 herd in June 1971, at 32°50'N, 117°20'W, were compared with those from 5 females collected from 1 herd in September 1971, at 32°40'N, 117°30'W (Fig. 14). Although an exact definition of what constitutes a "herd" in the case of delphinids does not exist, except for the recent essay by Norris and Dohl (1975), the data from the present analysis strongly suggest that at the very least the concept of herd for *Delphinus* sp. certainly includes local discrete breeding populations representing a single limited gene pool within the various stocks being discussed. Further

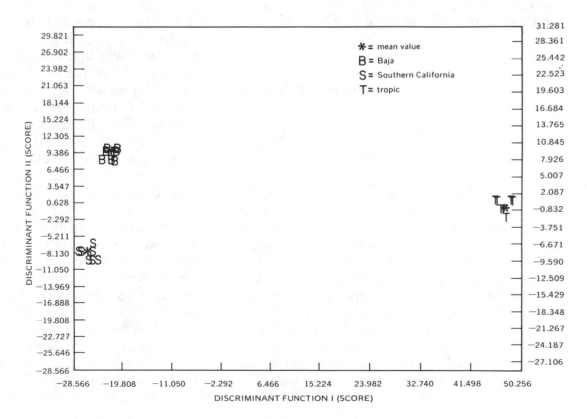

FIG. 13. – Scores of discriminant function I (proportional width of the right premaxilla, measured from the nasal septum and perpendicular to the main axis of the skull) versus scores of discriminant function II (greatest proportional width of the external nares) for matched samples of female *Delphinus* representing the southern California (SoCal), Baja California (Baja) and the tropical eastern Pacific (Tropic) stocks.

analyses based on more extensive data are currently being prepared. If they substantiate these preliminary results, the final outcome will have an important impact not only on our understanding of the term "school" as it applies to delphinids, but, more importantly, to management and conservation approaches.

At present, because of the variability demonstrated within stocks, it would be premature to suggest any change in the current taxonomic nomenclature of *D. delphis* in the northeastern Pacific. More detailed study of the extensive samples of osteological material available from the 4 groups previously mentioned, which is now underway, may change this, especially in the case of the neritic long-snouted stock, which may warrant at least sub-specific status. I feel, however, that we can accept the existence of at least 4 separate stocks of *D. delphis* in the coastal and offshore waters of the northeastern Pacific: (i) a southern California short-snouted stock, north of 32°N; (ii) a Baja California short-snouted stock, 28°-30°N; (iii) a southern short-snouted stock, south of 15°N and (iv) a northern neritic long-snouted stock, north of 20°N.

Delphinus sp. in Southern California waters

RELATIVE ABUNDANCE

In 1962 during research cruises in southern Californian waters, the author started noting the locations, direction of movement and size of herds of *Delphinus* sp. On many occasions additional data including bathythermographs, sound recordings and behavioural observations were also collected. Although the effort was modest in terms of area covered and was not planned as a formal survey or census, certain impressions as to the distribution and numbers of *Delphinus* sp. in the coastal waters of southern California emerged as the data accumulated: herds of

Delphinus sp. were present throughout the year; the size of herds varied from 10-30 to 3 000-4 000 individuals; *Delphinus* sp. were not randomly distributed, but were found consistently in specific areas. These observations led to the start of an aerial survey study in February 1968. One flight per month was made, using commercial fixed- and rotary-wing aircraft. The survey tracks (i.e., a set of predetermined flight patterns) were selected at random but were modified on occasion to avoid areas of naval operation. They are assumed to have sampled the entire study area adequately. Data on time of sighting, location, size of herd, direction of movement, and general behaviour of the herd, sea state and weather, were recorded and photographs were taken. The altitude of the survey flights varied between 150 and 300 m, depending on the type of aircraft used, sea state, and weather conditions. The study area of approximately 20 000 square nautical miles was divided into 100 square nautical mile sectors for the purpose of analysis (Fig. 15). On all the survey flights, areas or sectors in which no sightings were made were recorded as well as records of sightings. The major shortcoming of this survey effort was that consistent estimates of the distance at which a herd was sighted were not made. However, the average sighting distance was ∽ 1.5 nautical miles on either side of the aircraft. Thus, the area censused was assumed to be a corridor 3 nautical miles in width, perpendicular to the direction of the aircraft.

The monthly surveys and the knowledge gained from radio tracking showed that herds of *Delphinus* sp. were extremely mobile, but not randomly distributed (Evans, 1971, 1974). Because of this mobility and non-random distribution, and because numbers of individuals per herd varied from 5 to 3 000, it was decided that line transect theory (Seber, 1973) used by the NMFS Southwest Fisheries Center, La Jolla, California (Perrin, Smith and Sakagawa, 1974; Smith, 1975; Southwest Fisheries Center, 1976) to estimate delphinid population size, could not be applied in this case.

Nevertheless, the surveys have provided

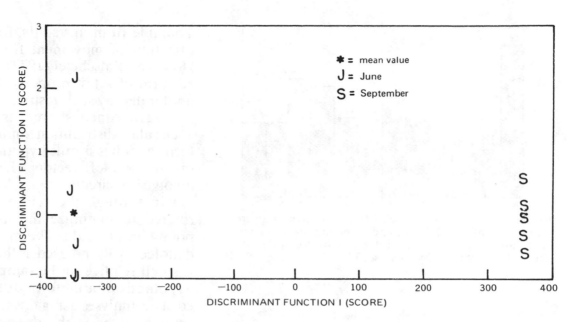

FIG. 14. – Scores of discriminant function I (proportional width of the rostrum at midlength) versus scores of discriminant function II (proportional width of the external nares) for matched samples of female *Delphinus* from two separate herds in southern California waters.

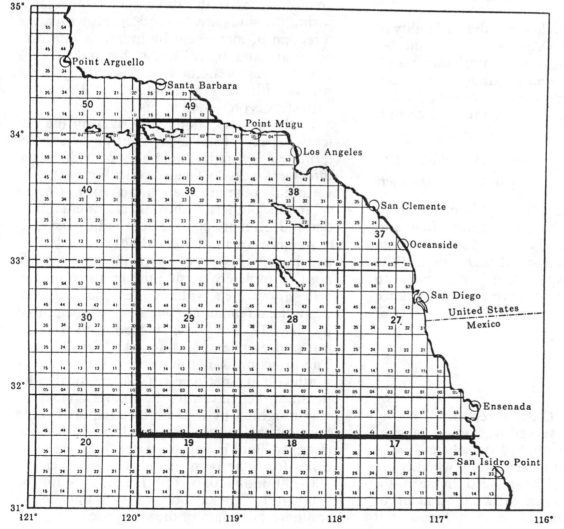

FIG. 15. – Aerial survey area in the southern California Continental Borderland.

59

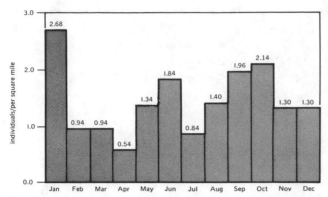

FIG. 16. – Relative abundance of *Delphinus* in the southern California Continental Borderland by month: total area surveyed (distance flown x 3 nautical miles) divided by the estimate of the number of *Delphinus* seen.

some interesting insights into the variability of the movements of *Delphinus* sp. within the southern California continental borderland. By dividing the number of animals seen each month into the area censused (nautical miles flow x 3), a relative monthly index of abundance was obtained:

$$\text{Index of Abundance} = \frac{\text{area censused/month}}{\text{estimated animals seen}}$$

The data indicate that the numbers of *Delphinus* sp. present peaked in January, June and September-October (Fig. 16). Since the area surveyed represents a small percentage of the total range of the species, it is reasonable to assume that the fluctuations in abundance indicate seasonal movements into and out of the study area.

HERD MOVEMENT

On each flight, the direction of movement of all herds observed was noted. Most of the methods, such as that of Batschelet (1965), which could be used to determine whether the movements of *Delphinus* sp. herds in the southern California study area were random or non-random, demand data in a format not available from this study, for example, quantification of movement from a home range. However, Batschelet (1972) suggests a modified form of a test proposed by Ajne, which is not limited by such restrictions.

The Ajne test predicts the uniformity of a circular distribution and in the modified form assumes a null hypothesis of a uniform distribution of vectors. The test procedure involves a circular plot. A straight line *l* is drawn through the centre of the circle and rotated to minimize the number of sample points on one side. The minimum number is denoted by K and used as the test statistic. If K is small relative to the sample size n, the null hypothesis of a uniform distribution is rejected. The analyses using this test indicate that on an annual basis the direction of movement within the study area is random. However, the direction of movement by month is non-random at confidence levels beyond .05. A graphic representation summarizing these results with the year divided into 2 separate semesters is presented in Fig. 17.

These data, along with data on the potential speed of net movement of a herd determined by radio tracking, provide some information as to factors contributing to the variability of monthly abundance of *Delphinus* sp. in the southern California continental borderland. Radiotelemetric data indicate speeds of net movement of 0.77 to 3.20 nautical miles per hour. This mobility could easily move herds completely outside the limits of the aerial survey area within a few days. As an example, a female *Delphinus* sp. was captured by the MV *San Juan*, tagged with a radio transmitter, released, and tracked for 72 hours. The direction of net movement was south by southwest at a net speed of 2.40 nautical miles per hour. Ten days after the animal's release, it was resighted by a commercial sport fishing boat off the coast of Baja California, Mexico (Ranger Bank), approximately 270 nautical miles from the point of release, in a herd of 200-300 individuals still heading south by southwest. This location was well outside the southern boundary of the study area.

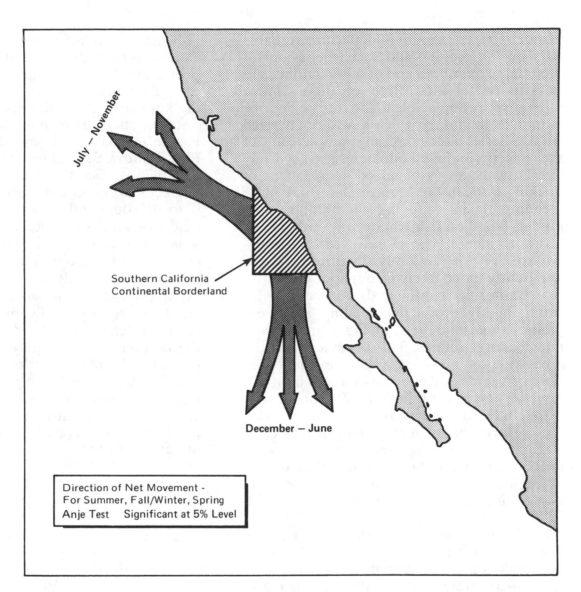

July – November

Southern California
Continental Borderland

December – June

Direction of Net Movement -
For Summer, Fall/Winter, Spring
Anje Test   Significant at 5% Level

FIG. 17. – Direction of movement of *Delphinus* out of the southern California Continental Borderland from July to November (summer/fall semester) and December to June (winter/spring semester).

Discussion

This study has revealed a variety of facets of the life history and behaviour of the common dolphin. Cetaceans, because of their size, mobility and habitat, do not lend themselves to comprehensive life history studies, but through aircraft spotting and survey techniques and through observer data from tuna vessels the outlines of seasonal and daily movement and distribution were learned. In addition, 4 separate stocks of *Delphinus* sp.

distributed from north to south in the northeastern Pacific were identified. Each of these is characterized by features of morphology, and behaviour that appear to be clinal at transition zones. Stocks also occur that may be isolated (neritic long-snouted forms, tropical short-snouted forms).

This study presents data on some aspects of the natural history of the common dolphin considered by Bartholomew (1974) to be important in formulating biologically sound management practices for marine mammals. Recently, research on smaller cetaceans has

61

begun to use as its point of departure available data on the ecology and social behaviour of other large mammals and of other herding and flocking vertebrates. Both of these appear more directly applicable to the study of marine mammals than data which have been derived from fisheries biology. As an example, some of the concepts and methodologies used by Cody (1971) in the study of mixed aggregations of flocking birds in the Mojave Desert are more meaningful in studying delphinids than models based on fish schools. In southern California waters, for instance, herds of *Delphinus* sp. are not randomly distributed. Herds apparently move freely throughout the southern California continental borderland, locating highly productive feeding areas, exploiting them, and then moving on in search of new feeding grounds. This behaviour and the areas of "preference" vary as a function of the time of year. Similar behaviour has been observed by Norris and Dohl (1975) for *S. longirostris* in Hawaiian waters.

The mortality of *Delphinus* sp. incidental to tuna purse-seining operations has always ranked third in numbers to that of the 2 species of *Stenella* involved in the yellow-fin tuna purse-seine fishery (Perrin, 1969, 1972, 1974; Southwest Fisheries Center, 1976).

From observer data in 1971, two sets (2.9 % of the total observed sets) on *Delphinus* sp. resulted in an estimated incidental mortality of 4 200 individuals. In 1972 this increased to 23 sets involving *Delphinus* sp. (8 % of total observed sets) and a projected mortality of 9 000 individuals. The data for 1973 increased concern for the eastern Pacific *Delphinus* sp. stocks. One hundred and five sets (15 % of total observed) included *Delphinus* sp.; 86 % of these sets were south of 15°N and 14 % were north of 20°N. Based on the number of *Delphinus* sp. mortalities observed in this sample, a projected estimated kill of 23 000 individuals was made, to include all boats for the entire year. The incidental mortality statistics for 1974 indicated a significant decrease (4 000) compared to 1973 based on data from 142 sets (14 % of total observed). The 1975, 1976 data

indicate a similar level of effort involving *Delphinus* sp. with projected mortalities of approximately 8 000 animals.

Each year, observer data have expanded the known range of this species. The known distribution of *Delphinus* sp. in the eastern Pacific through 1974 has been illustrated in Figs. 2 and 7. Several research cruises in 1975 and 1976 verified the presence of large herds of *Delphinus* sp. in offshore equatorial waters, 0° to 10° south and as far west as 125°W. The field observations indicate that this stock is separate from the stocks observed in the vicinity of the Galapagos Islands and the Gulf of Panama. Tentatively we are identifying it as the equatorial-oceanic stock. A map delineating the stocks potentially involved in the fishery is presented in Fig. 18. Morphologically, the northern stock is quite distinct from the central and southern stocks (see Figs. 8, 9 and 13). The distinction between the central, southern and equatorial-oceanic stocks at present is only based on distributional data. Whether these range extensions are a result of increased observer effort or a recent shifting of the *Del-*

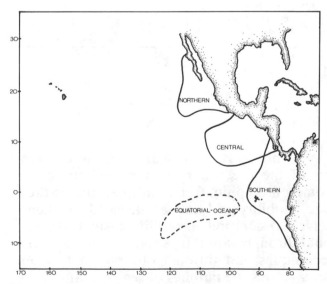

Fig. 18. – Proposed stocks of *Delphinus* Sp. in the tropical eastern Pacific Ocean. The Northern stock is morphologically distinct from the Central/Southern stocks.

phinus sp. population is open for speculation. It is evident that this species is highly mobile and distributed worldwide over a wide range of water temperatures (10°-28°C). It appears to adapt readily to a wide range of ocean habitat types, from the neritic zone of Baja California, Mexico, and essentially enclosed bodies of water such as the Black Sea, to the equatorial offshore waters of the Eastern Pacific. The question arises as to the population response of *Delphinus* sp. as the numbers within the populations of neighbouring species of *Ste-*

nella decrease. Does this provide an opening in the carrying capacity of the tropical eastern Pacific into which *Delphinus* sp. can move? If yellow-fin tuna seek out association with delphinids, is it possible that *Delphinus* sp., which is not normally a preferred animal, may be "recruited" by schools of fish as herds of preferred companions (species of *Stenella*) decrease in numbers? In any of these cases the continued involvement of *Delphinus* sp. in the yellow-fin tuna purse-seine fishery seems assured.

References

AGUAYO, A.L., Progress report on small cetacean research in Chile. *J. Fish. Res. Board Can.*, 1975
32(7):1123-43.

BANKS, R.C. and R.L. BROWNELL, Taxonomy of the common dolphins of the eastern Pacific Ocean. *J. Mammal.*, 50(2):262-71. 1969

BARTHOLOMEW, G.A., The relation of natural history of whales to their management. *In* The whale problem: a status report, edited by W.E. Schevill. Cambridge, Mass., Harvard University Press, pp. 294-303. 1974

BATSCHELET, E., Statistical methods for the analysis of problems in animal orientation and certain biological rhythms. Washington, D.C., American Institute of Biological Science. 1965

—, Recent statistical methods for orientation data. *In* Animal orientation and navigation, edited by S.R. Galler *et al.* Washington, D.C., NASA, Scientific Technical Information Office, pp. 61-91. 1972

BREE, P.J.H. VAN, *Delphinus longirostris* G. Cuvier. *Mammalia, Paris*, 35:345-6. 1971

BREE, P.J.H. VAN and P.E. PURVES, Remarks on the validity of *Delphinus bairdii* (Cetacea, Delphinidae). *J. Mammal.*, 53(2):373-4. 1972

BRIGGS, J.C., Marine zoogeography. New York, McGraw-Hill, 475 p. 1974

BROWN, D.W., D.K. CALDWELL and M.C. CALDWELL. Ob-

servations on the behavior of wild and captive false killer whales, with notes on associated behavior of other genera of captive delphinids. *Contrib. Sci. Los Angeles County Mus.*, (95):1-32. 1966

BROWNELL, R.L., Jr., Observations of odontocetes in central Californian waters. *Norsk Hvalfangsttid.*, 3:60-6. 1964

BRUYNS, W.F.J.M., Field guide of whales and dolphins. Amsterdam. 1971

CABRERA, A., Catálogo de los mamíferos de América del Sur. Orden Cetacea. *Rev. Mus. Argent. Cienc. Nat. 'Bernardino Rivadavia' Inst. Nac. Invest. Cienc. Nat. B. Aires (Zool.)*, 4:603-25. 1961

CADENÂT, J., Rapport sur les petits cétacés ouest-africains. Résultats des recherches entreprises sur ces animaux jusqu'au mois de mars 1959. *Bull. Inst. Fondam. Afri. Noire (A. Sci. Nat.)*, 21(4):1367-409. 1959

CHASE, T.E., Sea floor topography of the central eastern Pacific ocean. *Circ. U.S. Fish. Wildl. Serv.*, (291):33 p. 1968

CODY, M.L., Finch flocks in the Mohave Desert. *Theor. Popul. Biol.*, 2(2):142-58. 1971

COOLEY, W.W. and P.R. LOHNES, Multivariate procedures for the behavioral sciences. New York, John Miley and Sons, Inc., 211 p. 1962

DALL, W.H., Preliminary description of three new spe-

1873   cies of cetacea from the coast of California. *Proc. Calif. Acad. Sci.,* 5:12-3.

DALL, W.H., Catalogue of the cetacea of the North
1874   Pacific Ocean. *In* Marine mammals of the northwest coast of North America, described and illustrated with an account of the American whale-fishery, by C.M. Scammon. San Francisco, John H. Carmany and Co.

DIXON, W.J. (Ed.), BMD BioMedical Computer Pro-
1964   grams. Los Angeles, University of California, Health Sciences Computing Facility, Department of Preventive Medicine and Public Health, School of Medicine, 620 p.

DORMER, K., The mechanism of sound production and
1974   measurement of sound processing in Delphinid Cetaceans. Doctoral Dissertation. University of California, Los Angeles.

EVANS, W.E., Orientation behavior of delphinids: radio-
1971   telemetric studies. *Ann. N.Y. Acad. Sci.,* 188:142-60.

—, Echolocation by marine delphinids and species of
1973   freshwater dolphin. *J. Acoust. Soc. Am.,* 54(1):191-9.

—, Radio-telemetric studies of two species of small
1974   odontocete cetaceans. *In* The whale problem, edited by W.S. Schevill. Cambridge, Mass., Harvard University Press, pp. 385-94.

EVANS, W.E. and P.F.A. MADERSON, Mechanisms of
1973   sound production in delphinid cetaceans: a review and some anatomical considerations. *Am. Zool.,* 13:1205-13.

EVANS, W.E. and J.H. PRESCOTT, Observations of the
1962   sound production capabilities of the bottle-nose porpoise; a study of whistles and clicks. *Zoologica, N.Y.,* 47(3):121-8.

EVANS, W.E., W.W. SUTHERLAND and R.G. BEIL, The
1964   directional characteristics of delphinid sounds. *In* Marine bioacoustics, edited by W.N. Tavolga. Oxford, Pergamon, vol. 1:353-70.

FITCH, J.E. and R.L. BROWNELL, Jr., Fish otoliths in
1968   cetacean stomachs and their importance in interpreting feeding habits. *J. Fish. Res. Board Can.,* 25(12):2561-74.

GASKIN, D.E., Distribution of Delphinidae (Cetacea) in
1968   relation to sea surface temperature off Eastern and Southern New Zealand. *N.Z.J. Mar. Freshwat. Res.,* 2(3):527-34.

GIHR, M. and G. PILLERI, On the anatomy and biometry
1969   of *Stenella styx* Gray and *Delphinus delphis* L. (Cetacea, Delphinidae) of the western Mediterranean. *In* Investigations on Cetacea, edited by G. Pilleri. Berne, Switzerland, Institute of Brain Anatomy, pp. 15-65.

GRAY, J.E., *Delphinus capensis. In* Spicilega zoologica,
1828   Vol. 1. London, Truettel, Wuertz.

GUIGET, C.J., A record of Baird's dolphin (*Delphinus
1954   bairdii* Dall) in British Columbia. *Can. Field Nat.,* 68:136.

HERSHKOVITZ, P., Catalog of living whales. *Bull. U.S.
1966   Natl. Mus.,* (246):259 p.

HUI, C.A., Age and growth correlates of *Delphinus del-
1973   phis.* Masters Thesis, San Diego State University, San Diego, California.

KASUYA, T., Consideration of distribution and migra-
1971   tion of toothed whales off the Pacific coast of Japan based upon aerial sighting records. *Sci. Rep. Whales Res. Inst.,* (23):37-66.

MARCUZZI, G. and G. PILLERI, On the zoogeography of
1971   Cetacea. *In* Investigations on Cetacea, edited by G. Pilleri. Berne, Switzerland, Institute of Brain Anatomy, vol. 3, Pt. 1:101-70.

MAYR, E., Populations, species and evolution. Cam-
1970   bridge, Mass., Belknap Press of Harvard University Press, 453 p.

MILLER, G.S., Jr., The status of *Delphinus bairdii* Dall.
1936   *Proc. Biol. Soc. Wash.,* 49:145-6.

MAIS, K.F., Pelagic fish surveys in the California cur-
1974   rent. *Fish. Bull. Calif. Dep. Fish Game,* (162):79.

MIYAZAKI, N., T. KASUYA and M. NISHIWAKI, Distribu-
1974   tion and migration of two species of *Stenella* on the Pacific coast of Japan. *Sci. Rep. Whales Res. Inst.,* (26):227-43.

MIZUE, K. and K. YOSHIDA, Studies on the little toothed
1960   whales in the west sea of Kyusyu. 1. *Bull. Fac. Fish. Nagasaki Univ.,* (9):33-41.

NISHIWAKI, M., Whales and Pinnipeds. Tokyo Univer-
1965   sity of Tokyo Press, 437 p. (in Japanese).

—, Distribution and migration of marine mammals in
1967 the North Pacific area. *Bull. Ocean Res. Inst.,
Univ. Tokyo,* (1):64 p.

—, General biology. *In* Mammals of the sea: biology
1972 and medicine, edited by S.H. Ridgway.
Springfield, Illinois, C.H. Thomas, pp. 3-204.

NOAA Tuna Porpoise Review Committee, Report.
1972 Washington, D.C., Department of Commerce,
Sept. 8, 63 p.

NORRIS, K.S., Some problems of echolocation in ceta-
1964 ceans. *In* Marine bioacoustics, edited by W.N.
Tavolga. Oxford, Pergamon Press, vol.
1:317-36.

—, Some observations on the migration and orientation
1967 of marine mammals. *In* Animal orientation
and navigation, edited by R.H. Storm.
Corvallis, Oregon, Oregon State University
Press, pp. 101-25.

—, The evolution of acoustic mechanisms in odontocete
1968 cetaceans. *In* Evolution and environment,
edited by E.T. Drake. Yale University Press,
pp. 297-324.

—, The echolocation of marine mammals. *In* The bio-
1969 logy of marine mammals, edited by H.T.
Anderson. New York, Academic Press,
pp. 341-423.

NORRIS, K.S. and T.P. DOHL, The structure and func-
1975 tions of cetacean schools. *In* The behavior of
Cetaceans, edited by L. Herman. New York,
Wiley-Interscience.

NORRIS, K.S. and J.H. PRESCOTT, Observation on Pacific
1969 cetaceans of California and Mexican waters.
Univ. Calif. Publ. Zool., 63(4):291-402.

NORRIS, K.S. *et al.,* The mechanism of sound production
1971 and air recycling in porpoises: a preliminary
report. Proceedings of the Eighth Annual
Conference on Biosonar and Diving Mammals. Stanford Research Institute Stanford,
California.

OHSUMI, S., Catch of marine mammals, mainly small
1972 cetaceans, by local fisheries along the coast of
Japan, *Bull. Far Seas Res. Lab.,* (7):137-66.

OLIPHANT, M.S., California marine fish landings for
1973 1971. *Fish. Bull. Calif. Dep. Fish Game,*
(159):49 p.

PERRIN, W.F., Using porpoise to catch tuna. *World Fish.,*
1969 18(6):41-5.

—, Variation and taxonomy of spotted and spinner
1972 porpoises (genus *Stenella*) of the eastern tropical Pacific and Hawaii. Ph.D. Dissertation,
University of California, Los Angeles, 490 p.

—, Distribution and differentiation of stocks in *Stenella*
1974 in the eastern tropical Pacific. Working Paper
for Meeting of Small Cetaceans Subcommittee of Scientific Committee of IWC, Montreal,
Quebec, Canada, 14 p.

PERRIN, W.F., T.D. SMITH and G.T. SAKAGAWA, Status of
1974 populations of spotted dolphin *Stenella attenuata* and spinner dolphin *Stenella longirostris* in the Eastern Tropical Pacific. *Admin.
Rep. SWFC (Southwest Fish. Cent.) La Jolla,*
(LJ-74-42):21 p.

PILLERI, G. and M. GIHR, Contribution to the knowledge
1972 of Cetaceans of Pakistan with particular reference to the genera *Neomeris, Sousa, Delphinus* and *Tursiops* and description of a new
Chinese porpoise (*Neomeris asiaeorientalis*).
In Investigation on Cetacea, edited by G. Pilleri. Berne, Switzerland, Institute of Brain
Anatomy, vol. 4:107-62.

RICE, D.W. and V.B. SCHEFFER, A list of the marine
1968 mammals of the world. *Spec. Sci. Rep. U.S.
Fish Wildl. Serv. (Fish.),* (579):16 p.

ROBINSON, B.H., Distribution and ecology of midwater
1972 fishes of the eastern North Pacific Ocean. Ph.
D. Dissertation, Biological Sciences, Stanford
University, 175 p.

SCAMMON, C.M., Marine mammals of the northwestern
1874 coast of North America. San Francisco, J.H.
Carmany and Company.

SEBER, G.A.F., The estimation of animal abundance
1973 and related parameters. Riverside, New Jersey, Hafner.

SMITH, T., Estimates of sizes of two populations of por-
1975 poises (*Stenella*) in the eastern tropical Pacific
Ocean. *Admin. Rep. SWFC (Southwest Fish.
Cent.), La Jolla,* (LJ-75-67):106 p.

Southwest Fisheries Center, Progress of research on
1976 porpoise mortality incident to tuna purse-
seine fishing for fiscal year, 1976. *Admin.
Rep. SWFC (Southwest Fish. Cent.) La
Jolla,* (LJ-76-17):134 p.

SQUIRES, J.L., Jr., Measurement of sea surface temper-
1971   ature on the eastern Pacific continental shelf
        using airborne infra-red radiometry, August
        1963-July 1968. *Oceanogr. Rep. U.S. Coast
        Guard,* (47):373-7.

TOMILIN, A.G., Mammals of the U.S.S.R. and adjacent
1957   countries. Vol. 9 Cetacea. Moscow, Akademi
        Nauk S.S.S.R. Issued also by Israel Program
        for Scientific Translation, Jerusalem. IPST
        Catal. No. (1124) (1967).

—, The migrations, geographical races, the thermo-reg-
1960   ulation and the effects of the temperature en-
        vironment on the distribution of cetaceans.
        Migr. Zhivot. (Anim. Popul), (2):3-26.

WYNNE-EDWARDS, V.C., Animal dispersion in relation to
1962   social behaviour. Edinburgh, Oliver and
        Boyd.

STATUS OF POPULATIONS OF SPOTTED DOLPHIN, *STENELLA ATTENUATA*, AND SPINNER DOLPHIN, *S. LONGIROSTRIS*, IN THE EASTERN TROPICAL PACIFIC

W.F. PERRIN, T.D. SMITH and G.T. SAKAGAWA

Abstract

This paper reports progress on assessing the status of three populations of two species of dolphins of the genus *Stenella* involved in the purse-seine fishery for tuna in the eastern tropical Pacific Ocean. The types of data used, the methods used to collect and analyse them and the main assumptions and other sources of uncertainty in the study — as well as the measures taken in some cases to account for these — are summarized.

The size of the population of offshore spotted dolphins (*S. attenuata* sub-species) in 1974 was first estimated to be 2.3-4.9 million, based on an aerial survey. The annual capacity for increase (total births minus natural deaths) was estimated to be 1.4-4.0 %, and the annual rate of observed incidental mortality, based on an estimated kill in 1974 of 79 900-97 300 animals, was estimated to be 1.6-4.2 %. Comparison of these rates indicated that the number of spotted dolphins killed in the fishery in 1974 was at or near the population available after natural mortality. Revised estimates for 1974 give a population size between 3.1-3.5 million dolphins (a preferred, central estimate from a larger range), of which 72 000 were killed in the tuna fishery — this gives an incidental fishing mortality rate of 2.1-2.3 %. This rate was compared with the annual capacity for increase as originally estimated and with an independently figured estimate of the incidental mortality rate the population could tolerate. The population size of a second dolphin involved in the tuna fishery, the eastern spinner dolphin (*S. longirostris* sub-species) was given in revised estimates to be between 1.1-1.2 million (also a preferred, central estimate). The number of animals killed incidentally in 1974 was estimated to be 21 000 animals. The resulting incidental mortality rate, 1.8-1.9 %, was compared with an estimated annual reproductive rate of 8.3 %, the low value of which indicates no apparent response of the population to exploitation. For both the offshore spotted dolphin and the eastern spinner dolphin, the revised estimates indicate that if the sizes of their populations were increasing or decreasing under the levels of fishing mortality in 1974, they were probably doing so at low rates. The impact of the tuna fishery on the whitebelly spinner population (*S. longirostris* sub-species) has not yet been assessed. There is a need for increased acquisition of relevant biological and catch data, expanded surveys of population size and estimation of certain life history parameters.

Résumé

Les auteurs rendent compte des progrès accomplis dans l'évaluation de l'état de trois populations de deux espèces de dauphins du genre *Stenella* touchées par la pêche des thonidés à la senne coulissante dans le secteur est du Pacifique tropical. Un résumé porte sur les types de données utilisées ainsi que leurs méthodes de rassemblement et d'analyse, les principales hypothèses et les autres sources d'incertitude, de même que les mesures prises dans certains cas pour en tenir compte.

La population de dauphins tachetés (sous-espèce de *S. attenuata*) du large a d'abord été estimée en 1974 à 2,3-4,9 millions d'animaux d'après une enquête aérienne. La capacité annuelle d'accroissement (nombre total des naissances moins nombre de morts naturelles) était estimée à 1,4-4 % et le taux annuel de la mortalité accidentelle observée, fondé sur une estimation des morts de 79 900-97 300 animaux en 1974, était évalué à 1,6-4,2 %. La comparaison de ces taux indique que le nombre de dauphins tachetés tués dans les pêches en 1974 était égal ou presque égal à l'excédent de production. La révision des estimations pour 1974 fait apparaître une taille de population de 3,1-3,5 millions de dauphins (estimation centrale préférentielle dans une gamme plus large), dont 72 000 étaient tués dans les opérations de pêche au thon – ce qui donne un taux de mortalité par pêche accessoire de 2,1-2,3 %. Ce taux a été comparé à la capacité annuelle d'accroissement estimée à l'origine et avec une évaluation chiffrée, indépendante, du taux de mortalité accessoire que la population peut supporter. La taille de la population d'un second dauphin touché par la pêche au thon, le dauphin à long bec (sous-espèce de *S. longirostris*), a été indiquée, dans des estimations révisées, comme étant de 1,1-1,2 million d'animaux (ici aussi, une estimation centrale préférentielle). Le nombre de dauphins tués accessoirement en 1974 était estimé à 21 000. Le taux de mortalité accessoire qui en résulte (1,8-1,9 %) a été comparé à l'estimation du taux annuel de reproduction de 8,3 % dont la faible valeur indique que la population ne réagit apparemment pas à l'exploitation. Pour les deux espèces de dauphins, les estimations révisées indiquent que si la taille de leur population augmentait ou diminuait, compte tenu des niveaux de mortalité par capture de 1974, ces taux étaient probablement faibles. On n'a pas encore évalué l'impact de la pêche au thon sur la population de dauphins "white belly" à long bec (sous-espèce de *S. longirostris*). Il est nécessaire de rassembler un plus grand nombre de données sur la biologie et les captures, d'élargir les enquêtes sur la taille des populations et d'effectuer l'estimation de certains paramètres du cycle biologique.

Extracto

Se informa sobre los progresos realizados en la evaluación de la situación de tres poblaciones de dos especies de delfines del género *Stenella* que se capturan accidentalmente en la pesquería de cerco de atún de la parte oriental del Pacífico tropical. Se resumen los datos utilizados, los métodos empleados para recogerlos y analizarlos y las principales hipótesis y otras fuentes de incertidumbre, así como las medidas tomadas en algunos casos para tener estas últimas en cuenta.

La población de delfines moteados de media altura (subespecie de *S. attenuata*) se estimó en 1974, por primera vez, en 2,3-4,9 millones, sobre la base de un reconocimiento aéreo. La capacidad anual de aumento (nacimientos totales menos muertes naturales) se estimó en 1,4-4,0 por ciento, y el índice anual de mortalidad accidental se ha calculado en 1,6-4,2 por ciento, sobre la base de las estimaciones de los animales muertos accidentalmente en 1974 (79 900-97 300). Comparando esos índices se llega a la conclusión de que el número de delfines moteados que se capturaron en la pesquería en 1974 correspondía a la producción excedentaria o se acercaba mucho a ella. Las estimaciones revisadas correspondientes a 1974 arrojan una población de 3,1 a 3,5 millones de delfines (estimación central, preferida, obtenida a partir de una zona de distribución más amplia), de los que 72 000 resultaron muertos en la pesquería de atún, lo que da una mortalidad accidental por pesca de 2,1-2,3 por ciento. Se comparó luego ese índice con la capacidad anual de aumento tal como se había estimado originalmente y con una estimación hecha independientemente de la mortalidad accidental que la población podría tolerar. Por lo que se refiere a la población del otro delfín que se encuentra también en la pesquería de atún, el delfín hilador oriental (subespecie de *S.*

longirostris), las estimaciones revisadas de su población arrojan cifras de 1,1-2,1 millones (se trata también de una estimación central). El número de animales que murieron accidentalmente en 1974 se ha estimado en 21 000. La mortalidad accidental consiguiente (1,8-1,9 por ciento) se comparó con un índice anual estimado de reproducción de 8,3 por ciento, que, al ser tan bajo, indica que no existe respuesta aparente de la población a la explotación. Tanto por lo que se refiere al delfín moteado como al delfín hilador oriental, las estimaciones revisadas indican que, si en 1974 la población estaba aumentando o disminuyendo por debajo de los límites de mortalidad por pesca, probablemente ese aumento o disminución era muy lento. Las repercusiones de la pesquería de atún en la población de delfín hilador de vientre blanco (subespecie de *S. longirostris*) no se han evaluado aún. Es necesario recoger más datos biológicos y de captura, hacer más reconocimientos de la población y hacer estimaciones de algunos parámetros de su ciclo vital.

W.F. Perrin
Southwest Fisheries Center, National Marine Fisheries Service, P.O. Box 271, La Jolla, California 92038, USA

T.D. Smith
Southwest Fisheries Center, National Marine Fisheries Service, P.O. Box 271, La Jolla, California 92038, USA

G.T. Sakagawa
Southwest Fisheries Center, National Marine Fisheries Service, P.O. Box 271, La Jolla, California 92038, USA

Introduction

Tuna fishermen in the eastern tropical Pacific kill dolphins incidentally in the course of their seining operations (Perrin, 1969; NOAA, 1972). About 3 years ago, we set out to assess the impact of this on the dolphin populations.

This report is a very brief summary of portions of a draft report entitled "The porpoise-tuna problem: review of research progress" (draft title), which was written at this laboratory in August-September 1974, and was made available to the public by the National Marine Fisheries Service (NMFS) in October 1974. There have since been adjustments and corrections to the material in that report, mainly because we were working with preliminary 1974 estimates that changed as the year progressed. Details of the data and analyses referred to in this paper are in the draft report. Revised 1976 estimates of 1974 figures have been used in the relevant sections and were derived from NOAA (1975).[1]

Methods

GENERAL APPROACH

Our chief goal in assessing the impact of the fishery was to establish whether or not the populations are declining. We have done this by comparing estimated exploitation rate (number incidentally killed ÷ population size) with capacity for increase (in simplistic terms, birth rate minus natural death rate). The inputs into these 2 basic parameters are laid

out in the flow diagram (Fig. 1). Incidental kill was estimated from the landings of yellowfin tuna from dolphin schools, the number of net sets, and an estimate of average kill per set. Population size was estimated from density estimates extrapolated to known range. Capacity for increase was calculated from estimates of reproductive parameters in the exploited eastern Pacific population and of natural mortality rates in the relatively unexploited western Pacific population.

Two forms of *Stenella attenuata* and 3 of *S. longirostris* exist in the eastern Pacific. The distributions and bases for separation of these forms and their relative importances in the fishery have been described previously (Perrin, 1975). We have concentrated on assessing the status of the most important form, the offshore spotted dolphin (Table 1). We also gave major attention to the eastern spinner dolphin, but have so far only estimated the exploitation rate and not the capacity for increase. For the third major form, the whitebelly spinner, we have thus far estimated only the incidental kill.

MAJOR SOURCES OF DATA

Our major sources of data were the Inter-American Tropical Tuna Commission (I-ATTC), an aerial survey, and the Tunaboat Observer Program.

I-ATTC

The I-ATTC provided data on numbers of purse seine sets on dolphin schools, by vessel class, for the U.S. fleet, and on landings of tuna caught with dolphins by all nations.

Aerial Survey

An aerial survey conducted in January-February 1974 provided data on density of dolphin schools in the eastern tropical Pacific. Approximately 12 000 track miles were flown

---

[1] Since this report was written (1974) and revised (1976) a report of further assessments of status of *Stenella* stocks in the eastern tropical Pacific has been issued: Report of the Workshop on Stock Assessment of Porpoises Involved in the Eastern Pacific Yellowfin Tuna Fishery. Southwest Fisheries Center, Admin. Rep. LJ-76-29, La Jolla, CA, Sept. 1976.

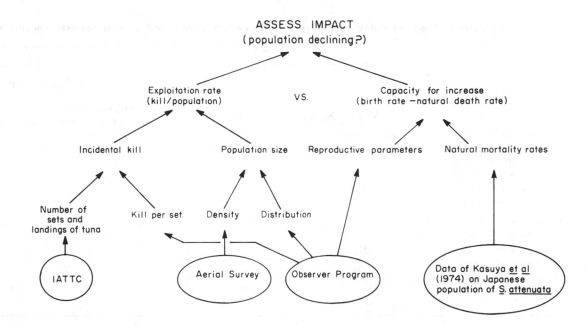

FIG. 1. – Flow diagram for assessing impact of incidental fishing mortality on dolphin populations. Major data sources circled.

in a specially modified Gruman Goose, at an average altitude of about 1 500 ft (Fig. 2). Two observers scanned ahead and to the side. The track lines were selected before the survey, independently of any knowledge of the density of dolphin schools. Range capabilities of the aircraft and locations of suitable airports constrained the choice of track lines.

Observer Program

We have had observers on purse seiners every year since 1971. The observers have collected data on numbers of dolphins killed, on their distribution, and on the sex, age and reproductive condition of a sample of the animals killed. We had observers on 5 cruises in 1971, 12 in 1972, 23 in 1973, and about 40 in 1974. We have also collected data during several cruises chartered to NMFS for gear research.

ESTIMATING INCIDENTAL KILL

Our approach in estimating the incidental kill was to extrapolate from estimates of kill per net set in our observer sample to the entire fishery, based on data from the I-ATTC (Fig. 3). We were faced with several problems in this approach:

— the structure of our sample may or may not be representative of the US fleet;

— we did not sample the non-US fleet;

— the Observer Program was effectively limited to the Commission Yellowfin Regulatory Area (CYRA) (Fig. 4) and did not sample the "outside the line" area to the west where roughly 1/3 of the tuna caught with dolphins is taken.

Adjusting for structure of the observer sample

In looking at our earlier data, we found that dolphin kill per net set is correlated with characteristics of the vessel, mainly size. Beginning in 1974 the tunaboats have been required by law to carry observers when requested, so we have been able since then to design our sample to have about the same

71

Table 1. Populations of spotted and spinner dolphins in the eastern Pacific, and scope of analyses reported in this working paper

Population	Involvement in fishery [1]			Assessment of status [2]				
				Exploitation rate		Capacity for increase		
	Major	Minor?	Negligible	Incidental kill	Population size	Reproductive parameters	Natural mortality	Impact assessed
Coastal spotted dolphin (*S. attenuata* subspecies)		X						
Offshore spotted dolphin (*S. attenuata* subspecies)	X			X	X	X	X	X
Costa Rican spinner dolphin (*S. longirostris* subspecies)			X					
Eastern spinner dolphin (*S. longirostris* subspecies)	X			X	X			X
Whitebelly spinner dolphin (*S. longirostris* subspecies)	X			X				

[1] Major = 1 000 killed incidentally; minor = 100s killed; negligible = 10s or fewer killed.
[2] X = estimates made in present study.

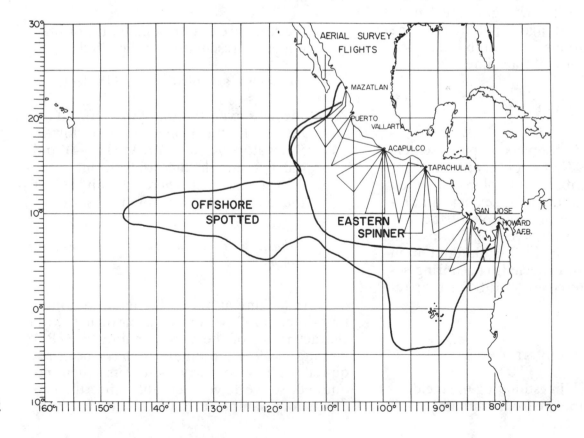

FIG. 2. – Location of track lines on the aerial survey in early 1974. Historical ranges of offshore spotted dolphin and eastern spinner dolphin from Perrin (1974).

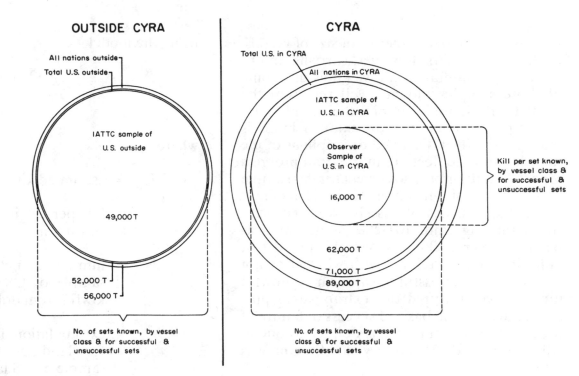

FIG. 3. – Samples used to estimate incidental kill of dolphins in the yellowfin tuna purse seine fishery in the eastern tropical Pacific. Areas of circles are proportional to landings of yellowfin tuna taken in net sets on dolphin schools in 1973. Landings data from I-ATTC.

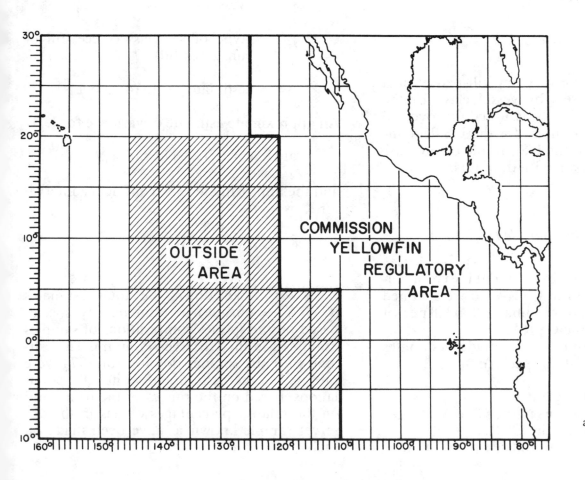

FIG. 4. – The major part of the Inter-American Tropical Tuna Commission regulatory area (CYRA) is shown above. Principal zone of "outside" fishing is also indicated.

structure as the fleet in terms of size of vessels. In the earlier years, however, carrying an observer was voluntary, and we know that some of those samples did not well represent the fleet. In 1971, for example, the sample contained proportionately more small, old vessels than did the fleet. Detailed descriptions of the samples and the fleet are in the draft progress report. We attempted to correct for this sample bias by extrapolating on the basis of kill per set for size-age classes of vessels. We used eight strata ranging from 101-200 (short) tons capacity to over 1 200 tons. We also found that dolphin kill is correlated with whether or not the net set is successful in capturing yellowfin tuna, so we stratified our extrapolating procedure also on the basis of success or failure of the set. A successful set was defined as one in which at least 0.025 ton of yellowfin tuna was taken.

Estimating non-US kill

Since we have very few kill-per-set data and no data on sets by vessel class for the non-US fleet, we simply assumed that over-all kill per set is the same as for the US fleet and extrapolated from the US sample on the basis of tons of tuna taken with dolphins.

Estimating kill outside the CYRA

Virtually no observer data were available from outside the CYRA, so we assumed for the purpose of our estimates that kill per set is the same as in the CYRA.

With this approach, we made 4 estimates of incidental kill (of all species):

(1)   US kill in the CYRA
(2)   kill by all nations in the CYRA
(3)   US kill outside the CYRA
(4)   kill by all nations outside the CYRA,

using the model

$$\hat{K}_g = \hat{C}_g \left(\sum_{i=1}^{8} \sum_{j=1}^{2} N_{ij} \; k_{ij} \right),$$

where

$\hat{K}_g$ = estimated kill

k_{ij} = kill per set in observer sample stratum ij

N_{ij} = number of net sets in I-ATTC sample of US landings of yellowfin from dolphins

$\hat{C}_g$ = extrapolation factor to account for landings not in I-ATTC sample of US landings

i = vessel size class

j = type of set class (successful or unsuccessful)

g = estimate [(1) to (4) above]

An approximate estimate of variance for $\hat{K}_g$ is

$$\text{var} (\hat{K}_g) = C_g^2 [\Sigma\Sigma \; N_{ij}^2 \; \text{var} (k_{ij})]$$

and the approximate 95 % confidence interval for $\hat{K}_g$ is

$$\hat{K}_g \pm 2 \sqrt{\text{var} (\hat{K})}.$$

We broke down the total estimates (CYRA + outside) to estimates by species based on the species compositions of samples examined in the Observer Program. The estimates for the spinner dolphin for 1974 were prorated to the eastern and whitebelly populations, based on the ranges of the forms and on the relative percentages of sets in the observer sample known to have been made on each.

ESTIMATING POPULATION SIZE

We estimated the density of schools of the offshore spotted dolphin and eastern spinner dolphin from data collected in the aerial survey. The basic analytical tool used was line transect theory. When a school was sighted, the perpendicular distance from the track line was estimated. The manner in which the number of sightings declined with distance from the track line was used to determine how much area was effectively searched. Four basic conditions must be met in this approach:

(1)   schools are distributed at random

(2)   transects are placed at random

(3)   probability of sighting a school decreases exponentially with distance from the track line, and

(4)   probability of seeing a school directly on the track line is 1.0.

Making these assumptions, we estimated density as

$$\hat{D} = (n - 1)/2L\bar{Y},$$

where

n   =   number of schools sighted,

L   =   total track miles surveyed, and

$\bar{Y}$ =   average perpendicular sighting distance, in this case about 1 mile.

Variance of the density can be estimated as

$$V(D) = \frac{\hat{D}^2}{n}\left(1 + \frac{n}{n - 2} - \frac{n}{DA}\right)$$

We prorated the overall density estimates into estimates for each stock based on the proportion of the total sightings which were of that stock. We also estimated separately for mixed schools because size of single-stock components in mixed schools is different than size of single-stock schools. We estimated separately for pure spotted schools, pure eastern spinner schools, spotted in mixed schools, and eastern spinner in mixed schools.

We then estimated the total number of schools of each stock and school type by extrapolating the density to the known historical range (Perrin, 1975). This makes the assumption that density of schools in the area sampled is representative of the entire historical range. Variance of the estimate of total schools can be calculated as

$$V(\hat{S}_i) = A_i^2 V(\hat{D}_i),$$

where

$\hat{S}_i$ =   number of schools or schools components of stock-school type i, and

A_i =   area inhabited by schools of stock-school type i

Then, using estimates of average school size (or single-stock component size) from the Observer Program, we estimated the total number of dolphins for each stock-school component type as

$$\hat{N}_i = \hat{C}_i\hat{S}_i,$$

where

$\hat{N}_i$ =   total number of dolphins in stock-school type i, and

$\hat{C}_i$ =   average size of schools of stock-school type i.

Variance can be calculated as

$$V(\hat{N}_i) = V(\hat{C}_i)S_i^2 + V(\hat{S}_i)\hat{C}_i + V(\hat{C}_i)V(\hat{S}_i).$$

75

We then added the single-stock school and mixed-stock school components to obtain an estimate for each of the 2 stocks:

$$\hat{P}_j = \Sigma N_i,$$

where

$$\hat{P}_j = \text{population of stock j.}$$

The variances of N_i are additive. We expressed the population estimates as interval estimates, which were $\pm$ 2 standard deviations from the point estimates. This interval should contain the true value at least 75 % of the time.

We used average school size estimates from the Observer Program, because the sample size from the aerial survey was very small and if used would have greatly increased the variance of the population estimate. This was justified because the aerial estimates did not differ significantly from the Observer Program estimates.

For the 1974 estimates, porpoise-school density estimates from the aerial and ship surveys were made in the aggregate. The ship survey density estimates were also made by stratifying by season and sub-area and computing an average, weighted by the geographical area of each stratum. Additional estimates of density were made which combined the aerial and ship survey. Assuming that the ship survey estimates of density tend to be biased, either due to concentrated fishing for yellowfin tuna associated with dolphins or alternately fishing for yellowfin tuna and other species not associated with dolphins, a correction factor was obtained by the ratio of the aerial survey density to the ship survey density in the period and area of overlap. This ratio was applied to the full range of the ship survey, which is more extensive in areal coverage than the aerial survey. This combined approach additionally assumes that the aerial survey density estimates are accurate and the degree of bias in the ship survey is constant throughout its range.

It is important to note that the estimated population size ranges are ranges of *point* estimates rather than probabilistic confidence intervals. Even though approximate variances were computed for the density and school size estimates and their combination, it is meaningless to try to place a probabilistic confidence interval on the current estimates, because neither the geographical range of each stock is known precisely nor does an estimate of its variance exist. More extensive aerial surveys, ship surveys independent of fishing, or alternate methods will have to be mounted to establish single point estimates with probabilistic confidence bounds.

The major criticisms that can be made of the population estimates are:

— Density of schools may not be the same throughout the ranges. There may be areas of higher or lower density in the unsurveyed offshore parts of the ranges. This could bias the estimates either way.

— The actual range at any time is probably smaller than the historical range. There may be seasonal migrations and year-to-year changes in the range occupied, caused by large-scale environmental fluctuations, e.g. the El Niño condition in 1973. This would bias the estimates upward.

— The assumption that all schools directly on the track line were seen may not be valid. If some schools were missed, this would bias the estimate downward.

ESTIMATING REPRODUCTIVE PARAMETERS

The samples, methods and analyses used in the studies of the life history of S. attenuata are described in detail in Perrin, Coe and Zweifel (1976). The studies were based on about 10 000 specimens collected in the Observer Program. The primary inputs into the status assessment are the estimates of age-specific pregnancy rate. We estimated age by looking at growth layers in the teeth. There are 2 sources of uncertainty in the pregnancy rate estimates. One has to do with the number of growth layers deposited yearly in the teeth, and the other concerns the rate of change of pregnancy rate with age. We could not satisfactorily resolve either of these uncertainties, so the inputs into the assessment model were in terms of alternatives, i.e., 1 layer or 2 tooth layers accumulated yearly in adults, and pregnancy rate being either constant, decreasing "slowly", or decreasing "rapidly" with age (defined below).

ESTIMATING CAPACITY FOR INCREASE

The capacity for increase is basically the difference between the gross annual production and the average annual natural mortality. It changes when the environment or the size of a population changes. It is to be expected that capacity for increase increases when a population is exploited.

The basic approach used to estimate capacity for increase is based on Leslie matrix models. The basic inputs are age-specific pregnancy rates and age-specific natural mortality rates. These rates are combined in a matrix which can be used to project the population forward in time and to determine the capacity for increase implied by the naturality and mortality rates. The model equation of interest here is:

$$\underline{M}\, \vec{N} = \lambda\, \vec{N},$$

where

$\underline{M}$ is the Leslie matrix describing the western Pacific stock,

$\vec{N}$ is the age structure vector, and

λ (lambda) is a scalar constant indicating the annual change in the population size with the life history parameters incorporated in the Leslie matrix $\underline{M}$.

If λ is equal to 1.0, the population neither increases nor decreases in size. If it is less than or greater than 1.0, the population decreases or increases, respectively. The capacity for increase is defined as $(\lambda - 1)/\lambda$.

We do not have estimates of natural mortality rates from the fishery because we cannot separate natural mortality from incidental mortality. Biological data are available for an unexploited spotted dolphin population near Japan (Kasuya, Miyazaki and Dawbin, 1974). These data can be used to derive natural mortality rates to use as first approximations for the rates for the eastern Pacific stock. Kasuya, Miyazaki and Dawbin (1974) did not give estimates of the mortality rates of immature animals more than 1 year old. They did give estimates for the mortality rate of first-year calves. These estimates are very low and are not consonant with an equilibrium population, given the calving intervals, which are more directly calculated and seem reasonable.

Therefore, we estimated new mortality rates for calves and rates for older immature animals indirectly. If the adult mortality rates and the reproductive rates estimated for this stock hold, and if the population is in equilibrium, certain values of mortality rates for calves and older immature spotted porpoise are implied. These implied values are determined as those which satisfy the model equation when $\lambda = 1.0$.

We then determined the capacity for increase for the eastern Pacific stock by combining in one matrix the mortality schedule estimated for the western Pacific stock and the reproductive schedule estimated for the eastern Pacific stock. Analysis of this model yielded the desired estimates of capacity for increase. A basic assumption is that the reproductive rates have increased in the eastern Pacific stock due to a decrease in stock size, while the natural mortality rates have not changed.

These estimates of capacity for increase

can be directly compared to the annual incidental exploitation rate determined as the ratio of the estimate of numbers killed to the estimated population size. If the incidental exploitation rate is less than the capacity for increase, the population should increase; and if it is greater than the capacity for increase, the population should decrease.

It should be noted that this analysis assumed that the incidental mortality occurs equally over all age classes. It also assumes that the population age structure has had time to achieve a stable form. Both of these assumptions, especially the latter, need to be examined further.

Results

OFFSHORE SPOTTED DOLPHIN

Incidental kill

The estimated incidental kill as declined each year since 1972 (Table 2) to about 72 000 in 1974, of which about 75 % is ascribable to the US fleet.

We stress the fact that these estimates must be considered minimal estimates for several reasons, to wit.

— Only animals known to be dead were counted; we have made no attempt to take into account the injured animals, some of which can be presumed to have died after release from the net.

— Kill data were gathered only from US vessels, which probably perform better in preventing incidental mortality than do most non-US seiners. The non-US fleets contain many small, old vessels that were formerly in the US fleet.

— Some observer effect can be presumed. With the stratified approach, the pro-

blem of representation of the fleet in terms of vessel characteristics is solved, but kill rates may be higher on cruises not accompanied by observers than on cruises with observers.

Population size

We saw 54 schools containing offshore spotted dolphins along the 12 000 track miles of the aerial survey. The aerial and ship survey density estimates, along with the geographical ranges and average school sizes resulted in the following total range in estimated population size:

Stock	Estimated total range of population size (millions of animals)
Offshore spotted dolphin	2.8-4.2

The lowest values of the total range result from using the early-season density averages of the combined aerial and ship surveys. The highest values of the total ranges result from using the early-season density averages of the ship survey alone.

The estimated total ranges in population size can be centralized further, because certain of the density estimates are preferred over others. The ship survey is preferred over the aerial survey because of its broader areal coverage. The all-season density averages are preferred over the early-season density averages because of the biases discussed above. The sub-area density averages are preferred over the aggregate density averages because of apparent differences in density among sub-areas. Combining these preferences results in the following centralized ranges in estimated population sizes:

Stock	Estimated centralized range of population size (millions of animals)
Offshore spotted dolphin	3.1-3.5

The lowest values of the ranges result from the combined aerial and ship surveys and the highest result from the ship survey alone. We have no basis to choose between them.

Capacity for increase

The estimate of capacity for increase depends on the choice of alternative assumptions about life history. For tooth layering, the basic options are 1 or 2 layers per year. For reproduction, the basic options are the frequency of reproduction after sexual maturity being constant with age or declining with age. Consideration of all the reasonable alternatives results in a range of estimates of capacity for increase of −2.5 % to +6.6 % per year as shown in Table 3.

None of the alternatives shown in Table 3 can be eliminated with certainty. However, there is some basis for choice. One tooth layer deposited per year has been suggested for the western Pacific population of *S. attenuata* by Kasuya, Miyazaki and Dawbin (1974). One layer per year has also been suggested for other closely related delphinids, including *S. coeruleoalba* (Kasuya, 1972) and *Tursiops truncatus* (Sergeant, Caldwell and Caldwell, 1973). Two tooth layers have been suggested

for *Delphinapterus leucas* (Sergeant, 1973), but this form is less closely related to *Stenella*. Thus, it is reasonable to assume the tooth layering for the spotted dolphin is basically 1 per year.

The estimates of frequency of reproduction with age are based on the relationship between pregnancy rates and numbers of tooth layers. The observed data suggest a decrease in pregnancy rate from 0.6 at 7 layers to 0.4 at 12 layers (Perrin, Coe and Zweifel, 1976). This is termed "decreasing rapidly" in Table 3. The determination of numbers of layers is difficult after the pulp cavity closes at about 12 layers. If the pregnancy rate observed for 12-layer animals is actually the pregnancy rate for all animals age 12 layers or older, then pregnancy rate declines more slowly with age. This is termed "decreasing slowly" in Table 3. Because of the difficulty in reading layers for older animals, it is most reasonable to assume that the reproduction rate either declines slowly with age or is constant with age.

Assuming 1 tooth layer per year and either constant, or slowly decreasing, reproductive rates with age, one obtains a range of estimates of capacity for increase of 1.4-4.0 % (Table 3). Although the other hypotheses cannot be completely ruled out and must be allowed as possibilities, this range represents the most likely values, given present information.

Table 2. Estimated incidental kills of spotted and spinner dolphins in the eastern tropical Pacific, 1971-74, in thousands

Year	Spotted dolphin [1]			Spinner dolphin		
	US	Non-US	Total	US	Non-US	Total
1971	179.7	4.6	184.3	126.4	3.2	129.6
1972	237.6	32.7	270.3	56.7	7.8	64.5
1973	90.6	17.1	107.7	56.9	10.7	67.6
1974			72.0			36.0
						21.0 (eastern)
						15.0 (whitebelly)

[1] Estimates are for 2 populations: (1) coastal spotted and (2) offshore spotted. All of this kill is assigned to the offshore spotted dolphin population, although some coastal spotted dolphin are involved.

Table 3. Possible capacity for increase for *Stenella attenuata* as percent of current population size under alternative assumptions

Reproductive rate with age	Numbers of tooth layers per year	
	One	Two
Constant	2.3 - 4.0	2.9 - 6.6
Decreasing		
Rapidly	− 1.0 - + 0.3	− 2.5 - − 0.8
Slowly	1.4 - 2.6	1.8 - 3.3

Impact of the fishery

The estimate of impact is based on the revised estimates of kill and population size, using 2 approaches to estimating sustainable yield.

Perrin, Coe and Zweifel (1976) estimated that the rate of gross annual production of calves is about 14.4 % of the offshore spotted dolphin population in the eastern Pacific. This estimate is predicted upon their assumption that the samples are representative of the actual population. Perrin, Holts and Miller (1975) estimated the gross annual production rate of calves for spotted dolphin of the western Pacific to be about 8.7 % from data presented by Kasuya, Miyazaki and Dawbin (1974). The western Pacific population is thought to be very lightly exploited and may be in equilibrium; the adult female annual natural mortality rate was estimated to be 7.4 % (Kasuya, Miyazaki and Dawbin, 1974) but juvenile and male mortality rates are probably higher, so the population's average natural mortality rate is probably near the gross annual production rate of calves. Perrin, Coe and Zweifel (1976) suggest that the higher reproductive rate in the eastern Pacific population might be a population response to exploitation, because the individual reproductive parameters differ between the 2 populations in a manner consistent with that hypothesis. If the hypothesis is true, then the reproductive rate of the western Pacific spotted dolphin,

8.7 %, is an estimate of the natural mortality rate, and carrying out the analogy with a simple model indicates that the present eastern Pacific population might sustain an annual incidental fishing mortality rate of 4.4 % or more, if the natural mortality rate were concomitantly depressed. Using this estimate is an alternative to the approach taken in calculating the preliminary estimates, where an age-specific model was used.

The total mortality of offshore spotted dolphins in the eastern Pacific during 1974 is estimated to be 72 000 animals. The central estimates of population size are 3.1-3.5 million animals, with a total range of 2.8-4.2 million animals, giving a central range for the 1974 incidental fishing mortality rate of 2.1-2.3 % and a total range of 1.7-2.6 %. The estimates of the incidental fishing mortality rate are below that indicated as sustainable in the simple model, 4.4 % indicating that the population would increase but at a slow rate of 1.7 % per year or slightly more. The estimates of the incidental fishing mortality rate are within the probably range of that indicated as sustainable in the age-specific model, indicating that if the population were changing it would be doing so at a very low rate (i.e., between decreasing at 1.2 % and increasing at 2.2 % per year). This leads to the tentative conclusion that if the offshore spotted population were changing under the 1974 level of incidental fishing mortality, it was probably doing so at a low rate.

We have done some back extrapolations

on the basis of earlier fishing activity and kill rates to examine the question of whether or not the population is at its original size. The balance of evidence suggests that there has been a decline. We do not know yet how great it has been. These analyses are still being revised and refined.

EASTERN SPINNER DOLPHIN

Incidental kill

The estimated kill of spinner dolphins in 1974 was 36 000, of which 21 000 are estimated to have been eastern spinner dolphins.

Population size

We made 36 sightings of eastern spinner schools on the aerial survey. This extrapolates to a population of 1.0-1.5 million animals, which can be centralized as described for the spotted dolphin, to give a range of 1.1-1.2 million.

Impact of the fishery

Estimates of some life history parameters are available (Perrin, Holts and Miller, 1975). Gross annual reproductive rate was estimated to be 6.4 % for 1973 and 9.8 % for 1974, with a pooled estimate of 8.3 %. This is considerably below the rate estimated for offshore spotted dolphins in the eastern Pacific, suggesting that the stock of the eastern spinner dolphins cannot bear as much *total* mortality as the stock of spotted dolphins. However, depending on the natural mortality rate, it might sustain a higher or lower incidental fishing mortality rate than that of the offshore spotted dolphin. The relatively high rate of reproduction exhibited by the spotted dolphin may be a response to exploitation, as suggested by Perrin, Coe and Zweifel (1976) and Perrin, Holts

and Miller (1975). It is possible that spinner dolphins have been less heavily exploited than spotted dolphins in the past (e.g., prior to 1971); comparisons of several biological parameters with other cetaceans support this contention (Perrin, Holts and Miller, 1975).

In 1974, the estimated central range of population size point estimates of eastern spinner dolphins was 1.1-1.2 million animals, with a total range of 1.0-1.5 million animals. The kill of eastern spinner dolphins in 1974 was estimated to be 21 000 animals. Thus the estimated central range of the annual rate of mortality caused by fishing was 1.8-1.9 %, with a total range of 1.4-2.1 %, which is not appreciably different from that for the offshore spotted dolphin. This, and the apparent absence of populational response to exploitation lead, as for the offshore spotted dolphin, to the tentative conclusion that if the eastern spinner dolphin population was changing in 1974, either increasing or decreasing, it was doing so at a low rate.

WHITEBELLY SPINNER DOLPHIN

For the whitebelly spinner, we know only that an estimated 15 000 were killed. We, as yet, have no estimates of population size or capacity for increase.

Discussion

SHORTCOMINGS OF THE STUDIES

We have established that the aerial survey approach is feasible, but our population estimates are weak because they involve extrapolation to large portions of the ranges that were not surveyed. Also, the estimates based on aerial surveys have high variability due to small sample size. We need an estimate for the whitebelly spinner population. We have not yet surveyed on a large enough scale.

81

The problem of calibration of growth zones in the teeth remains. Until this is settled, the estimates of reproductive parameters are only provisional. We do not, of course, have any estimates yet for the spinner dolphins.

The estimates of measured incidental kill may be inaccurate because of the lack of data for the area outside the CYRA and for the non-US fleet. We also need to estimate the now unmeasured kill.

RECOMMENDATIONS FOR RESEARCH

In order to assess the status of the stocks adequately there is a need to:

— Monitor the sizes of all dolphin stocks involved in the tuna fishery, using expanded surveys that adequately cover the geographical range of each stock. Population estimates should be made over a period of years, so that the existence or absence of trends can be firmly established. Additional sources of potential information, such as I-ATTC data, need to be explored to assist in establishing the history of the status of the stocks.

— Continue to monitor the incidental kill of dolphins in the tuna fishery, through a continued Observer Program or some other scheme. Kill should be estimated stock by stock. An attempt should be made to measure possible effects on dolphins stocks in addition to the presently measured direct incidental mortality.

— Estimate the life history parameters for the several spinner and whitebelly dolphin stocks and resolve the question of toothlayer deposition rate in the spotted dolphin, which is central to estimating parameters.

References

KASUYA, T., Growth and reproduction of *Stenella coe-*
1972   *ruleoalba* based on the age determination by means of dentinal growth layers. *Sci. Rep. Whales Res. Inst., Tokyo*, (24):57-79.

KASUYA, T., N. MIYAZAKI and W. DAWBIN, Growth and
1974   reproduction of *Stenella attenuata* in the Pacific coast of Japan. *Sci. Rep. Whales Res. Inst., Tokyo*, (26):157-226.

National Marine Fisheries Service, The porpoise-tuna
1974   problem: review of research progress (draft title). Washington, D.C., NOAA/NMFS, 164 p.

NOAA Tuna-Porpoise Committee, Report of the
1972   NOAA Tuna-Porpoise Committee. Washington, D.C., NOAA, 63 p.

NOAA, Staff, Porpoise/Tuna Interaction Program
1975   Oceanic Fisheries Division, Southwest Fisheries Center, National Marine Fisheries Service, Progress of research on porpoise mortality incidental to tuna purse seine fishing for fiscal year 1975. *Admin. Rep. Southwest Fish. Cent. (SWFC), La Jolla*, (LF-75-68):98 p.

PERRIN, W.F., Using porpoise to catch tuna. *World Fish.*,
1969   18(6):42-5.

—, Distribution and differentiation of populations of
1975   dolphins of the genus *Stenella* in the eastern tropical Pacific. *J. Fish. Res. Board Can.*, 32 (7):1059-67.

PERRIN, W.F., D.B. HOLTS and R.B. MILLER, Preliminary
1975   estimates of some parameters of growth and reproduction of the eastern spinner porpoise, *Stenella longirostris* subspecies. *Admin. Rep. Southwest Fish. Cent. (SWFC) La Jolla*, (LJ-75-66):33 p.

PERRIN, W.F., J.M. COE and J.R. ZWEIFEL, Growth and
1976   reproduction of the spotted porpoise, *Stenella*

attenuata, in the offshore eastern tropical Pacific. *Fish. Bull. NOAA/NMES*, 74:229-69.

SERGEANT, D.F., Biology of white whales (*Delphinaterus*
1973 *leucas*) in western Hudson Bay. *J.Fish. Res. Board Can.*, 30(8):1065-90.

SERGEANT, D.E., D.K. Caldwell and M.C. Caldwell,
1973 Age, growth and maturity of bottlenosed dolphins (*Tursiops truncatus*) dolphin (*Tursiops truncatus*) from northeast Florida. *J. Fish. Res. Board Can.*, 30(7):1009-11.

STATUS OF THE COCHITO, *PHOCOENA SINUS*, IN THE GULF OF CALIFORNIA

R.L. BROWNELL, Jr.

Abstract

The cochito (*Phocoena sinus*), the smallest member of its genus, is known from 21 confirmed records from the upper Gulf of California and is probably found only in that area. Diagnostic and general morphological characters are given, including the external measurements of two specimens; little to no data are available on other aspects of its biology. Affinities of the axial skeleton and external morphometry suggest that *P. sinus* evolved from a Pleistocene stock of Burmeister's porpoise (*P. spinipinnis*). *P. sinus* has been taken incidentally in the gillnet fishery for totoaba, *Cynoscion macdonaldi*, perhaps since the late forties, and the annual kill during the early seventies may have been in the tens to hundreds. Although the fishery for totoaba was banned in 1975, a small number of cochito will probably continue to be taken in other fisheries and this may have considerable impact on the small population. Research is needed to determine, among other things, the life history of the species and the effects on it of incidental capture in trawl and gillnet fisheries.

Résumé

Le marsouin *Phocoena sinus*, le plus petit des membres de ce genre, est connu sur la base de 21 indications confirmées en provenance de la partie supérieure du golfe de Californie; il est probable qu'on ne le trouve que dans cette zone. L'auteur donne le diagnostic et les caractères morphologiques généraux, y compris les mesures extérieures, de deux spécimens; on ne possède pratiquement aucune donnée sur les autres aspects de sa biologie. Le squelette axial et la morphométrie externe suggèrent que *P. sinus* aurait évolué à partir d'un stock du pléistocène de marsouins de Burmeister (*P. spinipinnis*). *P. sinus* a été capturé accidentellement dans la pêcherie au filet maillant de *Cynoscion macdonaldi*, peut-être depuis la fin des années 40; au cours des premières années 70, la mortalité annuelle pourrait avoir été de l'ordre de dizaines ou de centaines de marsouins. Bien que la pêche de *Cynoscion macdonaldi* ait été interdite en 1975, un petit nombre de *P. sinus* continuera peut-être à se faire prendre dans d'autres pêcheries, ce qui pourrait avoir un retentissement considérable sur cette petite population. Il est nécessaire d'effectuer des recherches pour déterminer, entre autres, le cycle biologique de l'espèce et les effets des captures accessoires dans les pêches au chalut et au filet maillant.

Extracto

El cochito (*Phocoena sinus*), que es el miembro de menor talla de su género, se conoce por 21 avistamientos confirmados en la parte alta del Golfo de California, y probablemente se encuentra sólo en esa zona. Se indican sus características distintivas y sus características

85

morfológicas generales, incluidos los datos obtenidos midiendo dos ejemplares; sobre los demás aspectos de su biología existen muy pocos datos o ninguno. Las afinidades del esqueleto axial y la morfometría externa sugieren que *P. sinus* procede de una población del Pleistoceno de marsopa de burmeister (*P. spinipinnis*). El focénido *P. sinus* se ha capturado accidentalmente en la pesquería con redes de enmalle de totoaba (*Cynoscion macdonaldi*) quizás desde finales de los años cuarenta, y el número de animales muertos anualmente a principios de los años setenta oscila probablemente entre algunas decenas y algunos centenares de animales. Aunque la pesca de totoaba se prohibió en 1975, probablemente seguirán capturándose algunos cochitos en otras pesquerías, lo que podría tener considerables repercusiones en su población, tan reducida. Son necesarias investigaciones para determinar, entre otras cosas, el ciclo vital de la especie y los efectos que tienen en ella las capturas accidentales en las pesquerías de arrastre y de enmalle.

R.L. Brownell Jr.
John Hopkins University, Box 84, Baltimore, Maryland 21205, USA

Introduction

The cochito, *Phocoena sinus*, is the smallest species of *Phocoena*. The range of this species is probably only the upper Gulf of California, Mexico, and it has probably been taken as an incidental catch in the totoaba, *Cynoscion macdonaldi*, fishery for a number of years. This paper reviews what is currently known about the biology and exploitation of *P. sinus*; recommendations are also made for the research needed to determine the status of this species.

Species account

DIAGNOSTIC CHARACTERS

Norris and McFarland (1958) reported that *P. sinus* is distinct from *P. Phocoena* as follows: In *P. sinus* (1) the cranium is smaller in adults, with a relatively much broader and shorter rostrum; (2) the basi-cranial axis is deflected downward at a greater angle, in relation to the horizontal axis of the rostrum; (3) the foramen magnum is relatively larger; (4) the maxillary bone does not enter the orbit but is excluded from it by the lateral margin of frontal bone, instead of completely covering the lateral margin of frontal and entering the orbit; (5) the maxillary leaves a relatively larger exposure of the dorsal aspect of frontal bones, where the latter contact the supraoccipital; (6) the antero-ventral extension of the nasal bones is covered by the mesethmoid; (7) the posterior edge of the palate has a medial U-shaped indentation formed of the medial edges of the rounded, roughly triangular pterygoid bones and the ventral extension of the vomer, which enters the palate just posterior to the palatine bones. In *P. phocoena* the posterior edge of the palate has a W-shaped indentation formed by the pointed, usually acutely triangular pterygoid bones and a central, pointed extension of the palatines, which sometimes cover the ventral extension of the vomer completely, but more often leave it as a small point of bone at their apex; (8) by the lower maxillary and mandibular tooth counts. The teneral external morphology of *P. sinus* is similar to *P. phocoena*, but *P. sinus* differs as follows: (1) total length is less; (2) the flippers are proportionately larger with more concave posterior border; and (3) the dorsal fin is proportionately higher, with a more concave posterior border.

GENERAL CHARACTERS

Additional descriptions of *P. sinus* skulls may be found in Orr (1969) and Noble and Fraser (1971). The only description of the post-cranial elements is that of Noble and Fraser (1971). The only photographs and drawings of skulls are found in Norris and McFarland (1958) and Noble and Fraser (1971).

External measurements are available from 2 specimens (SDMNH 20688 and LACM 28259). These have not been published previously and are given in Table 1. The body proportions of *P. sinus* are closer to those of *P. spinipinnis* than *P. phocoena*.

Little is known of the colour pattern of *P. sinus*, but there is a flipper stripe. It is widest at the anterior insertion of the flipper, and is thinner posteriorly. A narrow component of the flipper stripe extends from the flipper insertion dorsally to the axilla.

The vertebral count is lower than in other species of *Phocoena*: 7 cervical, 12-13 thoracic, 13-15 lumbar, and 29-30 caudal vertebrae with 19-20 chevron bones (Noble and Fraser, 1971; Brownell, unpublished data). The anterior 3 cervicals are fused. The anterior 6 ribs have capitular and tubercular attachments. Six or 7 pairs of sternal ribs are present, with the anterior 3 attached directly to the sternum. The phalangeal formula of SDMNH 20688 is: I-1, II-9, III-8, IV-4 and V-0 (left side). No organ systems have been studied.

DISTRIBUTION

Norris and McFarland (1958) gave the range of *P. sinus* as "certainly occurring in the upper Gulf of California and probably extending south along the Mexican coast", but they questioned the reality of *P. sinus* occurring outside the Gulf of California. Several at-sea sightings of this species have been reported (Norris and McFarland, 1958; Norris and Prescott, 1961). However, all the sightings south of the upper gulf area must be consi-

Table 1. External of measurements of 2 specimens of *Phoca sinus* in mm [1]

	SDMNH 20688	LACM 28259
Total length (tip of upper jaw to fluke notch)	1 390	1 500
Tip of upper jaw		
to gape	80	65
to centre of eye	135	105
to blowhole	140	105
to anterior insertion of flipper	260	265
to tip of dorsal fin	805	840
to centre of anus	960	1 050
Length of right flipper		
anterior insertion to tip	270	280
axilla to tip	190	215
Maximum flipper width	85	100
Dorsal fin		
height, tip to base	115	155
length of base	160	180
Fluke		
width tip to tip	370	370
nearest point of anterior border to fluke notch	100	105
depth of fluke notch	20	20

[1] All measurements of more than 100 mm were rounded off to the nearest 5 mm.

dered as tentative and unconfirmed as they are unsubstantiated by specimens, photographs or descriptions sufficiently detailed to allow positive identification.

A total of 21 confirmed records of *P. sinus* are known (Brownell, unpublished data). Based on these records (Fig. 1), this species appears to be most abundant in the upper part of the gulf. Future studies may show that this is the only place where it is found.

EXPLOITATION

Few details are available on the exploitation of *P. sinus*. The exploitation of totoaba started in the early twenties with hook and line

87

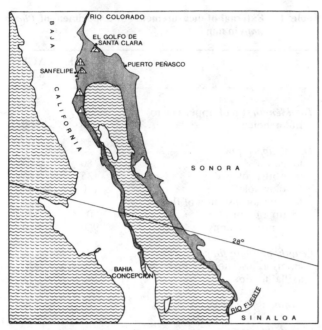

FIG. 1. – The number of confirmed specimens of *Phocoena sinus* in the Gulf of California, Mexico is recorded in the triangles. The totoaba, *Cynoscion macdonaldi*, is known in the stippled area and the main fishing areas are San Felipe, El Golfo de Santa Clara, and Puerto Penasco. The southernmost records of *C. macdonaldi* are Bahia Concepcion and Rio Fuerte. Map modified from Arvizu and Chávez (1972).

fishing and fishermen were using gillnets at least by the late forties. Small cetaceans were taken in this fishery during the late forties, but exact data are lacking on the species and numbers of animals taken (J.E. Fitch, personal communication). The main gillnet fishing areas for totoaba are San Felipe, Baja California; El Golfo de Santa Clara, Sonora; and Puerto Penasco, Sonora. Norris and Prescott (1961) have reported several accounts of *P. sinus* being taken during totoaba gillnet fishing operations around San Felipe, where W.E. Evans (personal communication) reports a catch of 10 porpoises in one day in the early seventies. Available information suggests that the annual incidental kill of *P. sinus* in the 3 main fishing areas of the upper gulf during the early seventies was in the range of tens to hundreds of porpoises.

In 1975 the Mexican Government announced a total closed season on both sport and commercial fishing for totoaba, because the species has declined drastically in recent years (Arvizu and Chávez, 1972; Flanagan and Hendrickson, 1976). If good enforcement capabilities are available, this indefinite ban will decrease the number of porpoises killed in the totoaba fishery. However, gillnet fishing for other sciaenids and sharks will probably continue and these fishing operations probably take some porpoises. Cochitos are also occasionally taken in shrimp trawls (Norris and Prescott, 1961).

REPRODUCTION

Nothing is known about reproduction in this species, but 2 female specimens 1.39 m and 1.50 m in total length were both physically mature.

FOOD HABITS

Fitch and Brownell (1968) reported one *P. sinus* with fish otoliths in its stomach. The fish were identified as grunts (*Orthopristis reddingi*) and Gulf croakers (*Bairdiella icistius*). Both of these fishes are abundant throughout the upper Gulf of California. Remains of squid were also found in the stomach of the same porpoise.

PARASITES

No endoparasites are recorded (Dailey and Brownell, 1972).

PREDATORS

Man is the only known predator of *P. sinus*.

BEHAVIOUR

Only Norris and McFarland (1958) and Norris and Prescott (1961) have reported observations on live *P. sinus*, but these observations were very meagre. Usually 2 porpoises are sighted together (Norris and Prescott, 1961).

REMARKS

Norris and McFarland (1958) have discussed the possible origin of *P. sinus* from *P. phocoena* from the eastern North Pacific or *P. spinipinnis* from the eastern South Pacific. Although *P. sinus* is intermediate in some aspects, they favoured the latter because the cranium of *P. sinus* resembles *P. spinipinnis* more than it does *P. phocoena*. Noble and Fraser (1971) have described an incomplete skeleton of *P. sinus* and compared it with specimens of *P. phocoena* and *P. spinipinnis*. They stated that the axial skeletons of *P. sinus* suggested a closer affinity to *P. spinipinnis* than with *P. phocoena*. The 2 complete axial skeletons that I have collected of *P. sinus* agree with the specimen described by Noble and Fraser (1971). Externally *P. sinus* lacks the peculiarly shaped and tuberculated dorsal fin of *P. spinipinnis*, but the size of the pectorals and other external measurements of *P. sinus* are more similar to *P. spinipinnis* than to *P. phocoena*. Thus, *P. sinus* and *P. spinipinnis* appear to be closely related. *Phocoena sinus* probably evolved as the result of a northward movement of an ancestral *P. spinipinnis* stock into the Gulf of California during one of the Pleistocene glacial ages (Norris and McFarland, 1958).

Recommendations for research

Data are needed on the present catch of *P. sinus* which, although low, may represent a considerable impact on the localized and relatively small population. Additional research needs are to: (i) examine carcasses of stranded or incidentally-taken porpoises to determine the basic life history parameters; (2) review gill-net and trawl fisheries for totoaba, other sciaenids, sharks and shrimps in the upper Gulf of California to determine how long *P. sinus* has been taken incidentally; (3) evaluate the probable impact of future incidental takes of *P. sinus* by fishing operations in the upper Gulf: (4) obtain more information on the total range of *P. sinus*; (5) evaluate the effects on the habitat of the diversion of the Colorado River water for agricultural purposes, and of insecticide contamination in the river; and (6) evaluate the probability of harassment from increasing tourist boat traffic in the upper gulf.

Acknowledgements

I wish to thank W.E. Evans, J.E. Fitch, J.R. Hendrickson, E.D. Mitchell and W.F. Perrin for their assistance during the preparation of this manuscript.

References

ARVIZU, J. and H. CHÁVEZ, Sinopsis sobre la biología de
1972   la totoaba, *Cynoscion macdonaldi* Gilbert, 1890. *FAO Fish. Synops.*, (108): pág. var.

DAILEY, M.D. and R.L. BROWNELL, Jr., A check list of
1972   marine mammal parasites. *In* Mammals of the sea, biology and medicine, edited by S.H. Ridgway. Springfield, Ill., Charles C. Thomas, pp. 528-89.

FITCH, J.E. and R.L. BROWNELL, Jr., Fish otoliths in
1968   cetaceans stomachs and their importance in interpreting feeding habits. *J. Fish. Res. Board Can.*, 25(12):2561-74.

FLANAGAN, C.A. and J.R. HENDRICKSON, Observations
1976   on the commercial fishery and reproductive biology of the totoaba, *Cynoscion macdonaldi*,

in the northern Gulf of California. *Fish. Bull., NOAA/NMFS*, 74(3):531-44.

NOBLE, B.A. and F.C. FRASER, Description of a skeleton
1971   and supplementary notes on the skull of a rare porpoise *Phocoena sinus* Norris and McFarland. *J. Nat. Hist.*, 5:447-64.

NORRIS, K.S. and W.N. MCFARLAND, A new porpoise of

1958   the genus *Phocoena* from the Gulf of California. *J. Mammal.*, 39:22-39.

NORRIS, K.S. and J.H. PRESCOTT, Observations on Pacific cetaceans of California and Mexican waters. *Univ. Calif. Publ. Zool.*, 63:291-402.
1961

ORR, R.T., An additional record of *Phocoena sinus. J. Mammal.*, 50:384.
1969

STATUS OF BURMEISTER'S PORPOISE, *PHOCOENA SPINIPINNIS*, IN SOUTHERN SOUTH AMERICAN WATERS

R.L. Brownell, Jr. and R. Praderi

Abstract

This paper reviews current knowledge of Burmeister's porpoise (*Phocoena spinipinnis*), probably the most abundant coastal small cetacean in southern South American waters and probably existing in two isolated Atlantic and Pacific populations. Although almost nothing is known about the population size or state of either, the Pacific population is the largest of the two, the population in the Atlantic perhaps being limited by competition from four other small cetaceans. Diagnostic and general characters of its morphology are given; very little is known about any other aspect of its biology. Large numbers of this species are taken incidentally in Peru and Chile, though no catch statistics are available. A small number are also taken each year in Argentina and Uruguay. In order to assess the magnitude of this mortality, catch statistics and data relating to its life history should be collected.

Résumé

Les auteurs font le point des connaissances actuelles sur le marsouin de Burmeister (*Phocoena spinipinnis*) qui est sans doute le petit cétacé côtier le plus abondant des eaux australes de l'Amérique du Sud et qui forme probablement deux populations distinctes: celle de l'Atlantique et celle du Pacifique. Encore qu'on ignore presque tout de la taille ou de l'état de l'une et l'autre, la population du Pacifique est la plus importante des deux, la population atlantique étant peut-être limitée par la concurrence de quatre autres petits cétacés. Les auteurs donnent les caractéristiques diagnostiques et générales de la morphologie de ce marsouin; les autres aspects de sa biologie sont très mal connus. Un grand nombre d'animaux est capturé accessoirement au Pérou et au Chili, mais on ne possède pas de statistiques sur les captures. Un petit nombre est aussi capturé chaque année en Argentine et en Uruguay. Il conviendrait de rassembler des statistiques de captures et des données sur le cycle biologique de *P. spinipinnis* pour être à même d'estimer l'ordre de grandeur de la mortalité.

Extracto

Se examinan los conocimientos actuales sobre la marsopa de Burmeister (*Phocoena spinipinnis*), que probablemente es el cetáceo costero de pequeña talla más abundante en las aguas meridionales de Sudamérica y con toda probabilidad está dividido en dos poblaciones aisladas, una en el Atlántico y otra en el Pacífico. Aunque no se sabe casi nada sobre el volumen o la situación de ambas poblaciones, la del Pacífico es la mayor de las dos y es posible que la población del Atlántico se vea limitada a causa de la competencia de otros cuatro pequeños cetáceos. Se indican sus características morfológicas distintivas y generales; se sabe muy poco sobre los demás aspectos de su biología. En Perú y Chile se capturan accidentalmente gran número de animales de esta especie, aunque no se dispone de estadísticas de captura. También en Argentina y Uruguay se captura todos los años un pequeño número de marsopas. Para estimar la importancia de esta causa de mortalidad es necesario recoger estadísticas de captura y datos sobre el ciclo vital de estos animales.

R.L. Brownell, Jr.
Johns Hopkins University, Box 84, Baltimore, Maryland 21205, USA

R. Praderi
Departamento de Zoología, Museo Nacional de Historia Natural, Casilla de Correo 399, Montevideo, Uruguay

Introduction

Burmeister's porpoise (*Marsopa espinosa*) *Phocoena spinipinnis*, is probably the most abundant coastal small cetacean in southern South American waters, and large numbers of these porpoises are taken in Peru and Chile each year incidental to various teleost fisheries. A small number of these porpoises are also taken each year in Argentina and Uruguay. However, very little is known about the state and biology of this species. This paper reports what is currently known about *P. spinipinnis* and recommends research needed to better determine its state.

Species account

DIAGNOSTIC CHARACTERS

The original description of the holotype of *P. spinipinnis* was based on the distinctly shaped dorsal fin (Burmeister, 1865) and in a later report, Burmeister (1869) described skull differences between *P. spinipinnis* and *P. phocoena*. The general external morphology is as in other species of *Phocoena* except for the peculiar shaped dorsal fin and the relatively larger pectorals. The skull in general character is like that of *P. phocoena*, but *spinipinnis* differs as follows: (i) the brain-case is much less compressed from front to back; (ii) in lateral view, the dorsal profile of the supraoccipital bone is in line with the dorsal profile of the rostrum instead of tilted at an angle of slightly over 20°; (iii) the size of the temporal fossa is larger, and (iv) the total tooth count is lower, between 14 and 16 upper teeth on each side (6 specimens) and 17 to 19 lower teeth on each side (6 specimens).

GENERAL CHARACTERS

The only comparative skull description of all four species of *Phocoena* is that of Norris and McFarland (1958). Additional descriptions, photographs and measurements of *P.*

92

spinipinnis skulls may be found in Allen (1925), Praderi (1971), Noble and Fraser (1971) and Pilleri and Gihr (1972). No comparative description has been made of all *Phocoena* species skeletons, but Noble and Fraser (1971) have compared the skeletons of *P. spinipinnis, P. sinus* and *P. phocoena*. Allen (1925) and Pilleri and Gihr (1972) have described and illustrated some post-cranial bones of *P. spinipinnis*. The mean condylobasal length in 10 specimens is 273 mm with a range of 224 to 290 mm.

Burmeister (1865) reported that the total length of the holotype was 1.62 m, but Gallardo (1917) stated that its length remounted was 1.68 m. We have examined specimens from off Punta del Diablo, Uruguay, that were between 1.79 and 1.83+ m in total length.

Little is known about the colour pattern of *P. spinipinnis*, and few external measurements are available (Burmeister, 1869; Allen, 1925).

The vertebral count of one specimen was: 7 cervical, 14 thoracic, 15 lumbar and 32 caudal vertebrae (Allen, 1925). The first 3 cervical vertebrae are fused. The first 8 ribs have capitular and tubercular attachments. Seven pairs of sternal ribs are present, with the anterior 4 attached directly to the sternum. No other organ systems have been studied.

DISTRIBUTION

Along the Atlantic coast of South America this species is known from off Uruguay (Praderi, 1971; Pilleri and Gihr, 1972) and southward to Patagonia, Argentina (Praderi, 1971). On the Pacific side of South America it is known from between Valdivia, Chile (39°50S) northward to Bahia de Paita (05°01S), Peru (Aguayo, 1975; Allen, 1925). The distribution of *P. spinipinnis* along the coasts of southern Argentina and Chile is poorly known, but recently 2 specimens were collected from near Ushuaia, Tierra del Fuego, Argentina (R.N.P. Goodall, pers. comm.).

Sub-species are not recognized but there are probably 2 stocks, one on each side of South America. The distribution of the "Pacific" stock is better known than the Atlantic, and it coincides with the warm-temperate waters (warm-temperate waters as defined by Briggs, 1974) in the eastern South Pacific.

POPULATION DYNAMICS

Nothing is known about the population size and state of either the "Atlantic" or "Pacific" stocks. However, something can be said about these 2 populations based on the habitats in which they exist and the other species of small coastal cetaceans that occur within the range of *P. spinipinnis*. This porpoise is apparently restricted to shallow waters. As the continental shelf is wider on the Atlantic than the Pacific coast, the Atlantic has a larger preferred habitat. This would suggest that the relative population size of *P. spinipinnis* in the Atlantic might be larger than the Pacific population. However, based on our survey of museum specimens, field work, and cath records of this species, the "Pacific" population is by far the larger of the two.

Many small odontocetes restricted to coastal waters have distributions that usually coincide with major zoogeographic regions or coastal provinces within these regions. As noted before, the distribution of *P. spinipinnis* in the eastern South Pacific coincides with the warm-temperate water in this area. In the western South Atlantic, *P. spinipinnis* is known from both warm-temperate and cold-temperate waters, but 4 other species of small cetaceans *Sotalia fluviatilis, Pontoporia blainvillei* (both warm-temperate waters), *Cephalorhynchus commersonii* and *Lagenorhynchus australis* (both cold-temperate waters) are the dominant coastal cetaceans in this area (Brownell, 1974, 1975). This suggests that competetive exclusion may be acting against *P. spinipinnis* in the western South Atlantic, but in the warm-temperate waters of the eastern South

93

Pacific, *P. spinipinnis* is very successful, as no other cetacean competitors exist here.

EXPLOITATION

Some figures recently published on the take of this species in Peru are confusing. Mitchell (1975) stated that Norris reported that 250 000 lb of porpoise meat are sold each year in Peru. Aguayo (1975) and Anon. (1975) reported that the amount was 250 000 lb of porpoise not porpoise meat. The correct figure is "close to 2 000/year". *P. spinipinnis* are taken in Peru (letter of 27/12/74 from K.S. Norris to E. Mitchell). Norris' source for this figure was Jorge Meijia of the Instituto del Mar del Peru. The other reports provide information on the exploitation of *P. spinipinnis* in Peru. Clarke (1962) noted it is commonly offered for sale at the fish market in Chimbote. Grimwood (1969) stated it is frequently taken along the coast by small boat fishermen and at San Andres (13°50′S) they are on sale every day as well as at other fish markets. Actual catch statistics are not available, but information collected on the incidental take of this species in Peru suggests that the 2 000/year figure reported by Norris is a very conservative one (Brownell and J.G. Mead, unpublished data, February 1976).

Aguayo (1975) reported that *P. spinipinnis* is common in northern Chile (Iquique-Antofagasta) and is taken for human consumption. In addition, this species is taken in the provinces of Tarapaca, Antofagasta and Coquimbo in the north; Valparaiso and Concepcion in central Chile; and Valdivia in the south, where fishermen catch small cetaceans accidentally in gillnets (Mitchell, 1975). No catch statistics are available.

A small number of *P. spinipinnis* are also taken each year in Argentina and Uruguay. Castello (1974) reported that these porpoise are occasionally taken in nets by fishermen, and Goodall (Pers. comm.) reported 2 animals taken in nets used for crab fishing, in Argentinian waters. We obtained 4 specimens of this species taken by shark fishermen with gillnets over a 1½ year period off Punta del Diablo, Uruguay (Pilleri and Gihr, 1972).

REPRODUCTION

Almost nothing is known about reproduction in this species, but a near-term foetus (male, 44 cm in total length) was collected on 24 February 1973 from a 1.83+ m carcass (RLB 901) in Uruguayan waters. This suggests that calving can take place during the austral fall. One male (AO 1974-23), 1.80 m in total length, had sexually active testes.

FOOD HABITS

The stomach contents of 1 specimen from off Uruguay was available for study (RP 301). Identifiable remains in this specimen were one *Merluccius hubbsi* and one *Pagrus sedecim*. One unidentified squid was also present.

PARASITES

No endoparasites are recorded (Dailey and Brownell, 1972) but one specimen we examined (RP 301) had nematodes in its stomach.

PREDATORS

Man is an important predator. No natural predators are known, but the killer whale, *Orcinus orca*, is a possibility.

BEHAVIOUR

Nothing is known about the behaviour of this species. Aguayo (1975) observed a group of 8 porpoises at the mouth of the Loa River, Chile (21°25S) in October 1965.

Recommendations for research

The following actions are needed in order to assess the magnitude of the incidental kill of this species properly:

(i) Start a programme to collect statistics on the catch of this and other species of small cetaceans at some of the main localities where they are fished in Peru and Chile.

(ii) Start a programme to collect specimens (teeth, gonads, etc.) from porpoise carcasses so that life history parameters can be estimated.

The above preliminary work must be done before a large-scale research plan (if that is necessary) can be formulated.

Acknowledgements

We thank H.P. Castello, R.N.P. Goodall, J.G. Mead and E.D. Mitchell for their assistance.

References

AGUAYO, A.L., Progress report on small cetacean re-
1975 search in Chile. *J. Fish. Res. Board Can.*, 32(7):1123-43.

ALLEN, G.M., Burmeister's porpoise (*Phocoena spini-*
1925 *pinnis*). *Bull. Mus. Comp. Zool. Harv.*, 67: 251-61.

BRIGGS, J.C., Marine zoogeography. New York,
1974 McGraw Hill, 475 p.

BROWNELL, R.L., Jr., Small odontocetes of the Antarctic.
1974 *Antarct. Map Folio Ser.*, (18):13-9.

BROWNELL, R.L., Jr., Progress report on the biology of
1975 the franciscana, *Pontoporia blainvillei*, in Uruguayan waters. *J. Fish. Res. Board Can.*, 32(7):1073-8.

BURMEISTER, G., Description of a new species of por-
1865 poise in the Museum of Buenos Aires, *Phocoena spinipinnis*, sp. nov. *Proc. Zool. Soc. Lond.*, 1865:228-31.

—, Descripción de cuatro especies de delfínides de la
1869 costa Argentina del Océano Atlántico. *An Mus. Nac. Hist. Nat. B. Aires*, 1(8):367-442.

CASTELLO, H.P., Current cetological investigations in
1974 Argentina. Paper presented to IWC Subcommittee on Small Cetaceans Meeting, Montreal, April 1974. Doc. M. 21 (unpubl.).

CLARKE, R., Whale observations and whale marking off
1962 the coast of Chile in 1958 and from Ecuador towards and beyond the Galapagos Islands in 1959. *Norsk Hvalfangsttid.*, 51:265-87.

DAILEY, M.D. and R.L. BROWNELL, Jr., A check list of
1972 marine mammal parasites. *In* Mammals of the sea, biology and medicine, edited by S.H. Ridgway. Springfield, Ill., Charles C. Thomas, pp. 528-89.

GALLARDO, A., Sobre el tipo de la *Phocoena spinipinnis*
1917 Burmeister. *Physis, B. Aires*, 3(13):83-4.

GRIMWOOD, I.R., Notes on the distribution and status of
1969 some Peruvian mammals 1968. *Spec. Publ. N.Y. Zool. Soc.*, (21):86 p.

MITCHELL, E., Porpoise, dolphin and small whale fish-
1975 eries of the world, status and problem. *IUCN Monogr.*, 3:129 p.

—, (Ed.), Review of biology and fisheries for smaller
1975a cetaceans. *J. Fish. Res. Board Can.*, 32(7): 889-1242.

NOBLE, B. and F.C. FRASER, Description of a skeleton
1971 and supplementary notes on the skull of a rare porpoise *Phocoena sinus* Norris and McFarland. *J. Nat. Hist.*, 5:447-64.

95

NORRIS, K.S. and W.N. MCFARLAND, A new harbour
1958   porpoise of the genus *Phocoena* from the Gulf
        of California. *J. Mamm.*, 39:22-39.

PILLERI, G. and M. GIHR, Burmeister's porpoise *Pho-*
1972   *coena spinipinnis* Burmeister, 1865, off the
        Punta del Diablo, Uruguay. *In* Investigations
on Cetacea, edited by G. Pilleri. Berne, Brain
Anatomy Institute, vol. 4:163-72.

PRADERI, R., Contribucion al conocimiento del genero
1971   *Phocoena* (Cetacea, Phocoenidae) *Rev. Mus.*
        Argent. Cienc. Nat. "Bernardino Rivadavia"
        Inst. Nac. Invest. Cienc. Nat. (Zool.), 7.251-66.

THE PRESENT STATUS OF THE GANGETIC SUSU, *PLATANISTA GANGETICA* (ROXBURGH), WITH COMMENTS ON THE INDUS SUSU, *P. MINOR* OWEN

S. Jones

Abstract

The Gangetic susu, *Platanista gangetica*, is widely distributed in the navigable sectors of the Ganga (Ganges)-Brahmaputra-Meghna river system in India, Bangladesh and Nepal, from the foot of the Himalayas and adjacent eastern hill ranges to the tidal zone, and in part of the Karnaphuli River. The species is non-gregarious, it being very rare that two or more animals are sighted together. A description of the Hooghly River is given as a typical habitat of the susu. Its scientific and common names are also discussed.

The present state of the dolphin's distribution and abundance is reviewed and its population in various sectors is estimated, indicating a total population of approximately 4 000-5 000. From available data, it is believed that there is no depletion in the Gangetic Delta region or in the upper reaches of the Meghna and Brahmaputra Rivers, while in the Ganges proper and its tributaries, the susu is much less numerous than in former days (current estimate, 500-750), primarily due to accidental capture in the nets of fishermen, which also occurs in other areas of its range; no direct fishery for the animal exists. Reliable information of the status of the species is available only for rivers in Bangladesh, where it appears to be increasing in abundance; this may also be the case in the Brahmaputra system in India.

Although the species is in no immediate danger of extermination and has so far been able to withstand heavy pollution in some areas where it is found, its primary habitat (the Ganges river valley and delta region), is the home of approximately 300 million people; dam construction, diversion of water for irrigation and increasing discharge of effluents continue to bring about adverse environment conditions, especially in the Ganges proper. The effects of the Farakka Barrage especially should be monitored. It is recommended that additional research on the Ganges susu, including studies of its general biology, migration, distribution and population size be undertaken with cooperation between the countries concerned. Sanctuaries in selected sections of the river system should be established. Suggestions are given for repopulation of reservoir sections of some tributaries of the Ganges and for transplantation of the species into adjacent river systems.

The Indus susu (*Platanista minor*) was formerly distributed widely in the Indus River and its tributaries. About 400 animals are now thought to survive immediately above the Sukkur Barrage. Hunting of the animal for its oil and the diversion of water for irrigation are the causes of this decline. Complete protection of the species is necessary to prevent its extinction.

Résumé

Le susu du Gange, *Platanista gangetica*, est largement distribué dans les sections navigables du système fluvial Gange-Brahmapoutre-Meghna de l'Inde, du Bangladesh et du

Népal, depuis les contreforts de l'Himalaya et des collines orientales limitrophes jusqu'à la zone d'estuaire et une partie de la rivière Karnaphuli. L'espèce n'est pas grégaire et il est très rare de voir deux animaux ou plus à la fois. L'auteur décrit l'Hooghly, habitat typique du susu. Ses appellations scientifiques et communes sont aussi discutées.

L'auteur indique l'état de la distribution et de l'abondance du dauphin et fournit une estimation de la population des divers secteurs: le total de la population est d'environ 4 000-5 000 animaux. D'après les données disponibles, on pense qu'il n'y a pas de diminution dans la région du delta du Gange ou dans le cours supérieur du Meghna et du Brahmapoutre, alors que dans le Gange même et ses affluents les susus sont bien moins nombreux que par le passé (estimation actuelle: 500-700 animaux), surtout en raison des captures accidentelles dans les filets des pêcheurs, ce qui se produit aussi dans d'autres parties de son domaine. L'animal n'est l'objet d'aucune pêche directe. On ne dispose d'informations fiables sur l'état de l'espèce que pour les cours d'eau du Bangladesh, où il semble son abondance s'accroisse. Ce peut être aussi le cas dans le système du Brahmapoutre, en Inde.

Encore que l'espèce ne soit pas menacée d'extermination immédiate et qu'elle ait pu jusqu'ici résister à la lourde pollution de certaines régions où elle se trouve, son habitat principal (la vallée et le delta du Gange) a une population d'environ 300 millions de personnes; la construction de barrages, le détournement des eaux pour l'irrigation, le déversement croissant des effluents continuent à affecter négativement l'environnement, spécialement dans le Gange proprement dit. Il conviendrait de surveiller spécialement les effets du barrage de Farakka. Il est recommandé que des recherches supplémentaires sur le susu du Gange, y compris l'étude de sa biologie générale, des migrations, de sa distribution et de la taille de la population, soient entreprises en coopération avec les pays intéressés. Il conviendrait de créer des sanctuaires dans des sections sélectionnées du système fluvial. L'auteur fournit des suggestions pour le repeuplement des sections réservoirs de certains affluents du Gange et pour la transplantation de l'espèce dans des systèmes fluviaux voisins.

Le susu de l'Indus (*Platanista minor*) était anciennement largement répandu dans l'Indus et ses affluents. On pense qu'environ 400 animaux survivent aujourd'hui, immédiatement en amont du barrage de Sukkur. Ce déclin a été provoqué par la chasse à l'animal pour en tirer de l'huile et par le détournement des eaux aux fins d'irrigation. Il est nécessaire que l'espèce soit totalement protégée pour éviter son extinction.

Extracto

La platanista del Ganges (*Platanista gangetica*) se encuentra en todos los tramos navegables del sistema fluvial Ganges-Brahmaputra-Meghna (India, Bangladesh y Nepal), desde las estribaciones del Himalaya y las cadenas orientales adyacentes hasta el límite de las mareas, y en algunas zonas del río Karnafuli. Es una especie no gregaria, y es raro ver juntos dos o más animales. Se describe el río Hooghly como hábitat típico de esta platanista y se examinan sus nombres científico y vulgar.

Se estudia la distribución y la abundancia de esta plantanista en la actualidad y se presenta una estimación del volumen de la población en varias zonas, indicando una cifra total del orden de 4 000-5 000 animales. A juzgar por los datos disponibles, no parece que esta especie haya disminuido en número en la región del delta del Ganges o en las cuencas altas del Meghna y del Brahmaputra, mientras en el Ganges propiamente dicho y en sus tributarios es mucho menos numerosa que antiguamente (estimación actual, 500-750), debido principalmente a que algunos animales mueren accidentalmente en las redes de los pescadores, cosa que sucede también en otras zonas del área de distribución de esta especie. No existe explotación directa de estos animales. La única información fidedigna sobre la situación de la especie se refiere a algunos ríos de Bangladesh, donde su número parece ir en aumento. Es posible que suceda lo mismo en el sistema del Brahmaputra, en la India.

Aunque la especie no corre peligro inmediato de extinción y hasta la fecha ha podido resistir a la grave contaminación de algunas de las zonas en que se encuentra, hay que tener presente que en la zona que constituye su hábitat primario (valle del río Ganges y región del delta) viven aproximadamente 300 millones de personas. La construcción de presas, la desviación de aguas para riego y la creciente descarga de aguas residuales siguen haciendo empeorar las condiciones ambientales, especialmente en el Ganges propiamente dicho. Hay que seguir con especial atención los efectos de la construcción de la presa de Farakka. Se recomienda que se inicien nuevas investigaciones sobre la platanista del Ganges, en especial en lo relativo a biología general, movimientos migratorios, distribución y población, con la colaboración de los distintos países interesados. Deberían establecerse santuarios en determinados tramos del sistema fluvial. Se hacen algunas sugerencias para repoblar los embalses de algunos tributarios del Ganges y sobre la posibilidad de trasplantar esta especie a sistemas fluviales adyacentes.

La platanista del Indo (*Platanista minor*) se encontraba antes en todo el río Indo y sus tributarios. Hoy día se cree que sobreviven unos 400 animales, inmediatamente por encima de la presa de Sukkur. Las causas de la disminución de su número son la caza de estos animales, para obtener aceite, y la desviación de aguas para el riego. Es necesario proteger completamente esta especie, para impedir que se extinga.

S. Jones
Department of Zoology, University College, Trivandrum 1, Kerala, India

Introduction

The 2 freshwater dolphins of the subcontinent of India, commonly called susu, distributed in the river systems of the Ganges and the Indus, have been receiving increasing attention in recent years from biologists and conservationists, particularly in view of the threat of extermination faced by the Indus susu. The present status of the Gangetic susu is discussed in this account with some remarks on the Indus susu.

Identification

Anderson (1878) in his exhaustive work considered both to belong to the same species viz., *Platanista gangetica* (Roxburgh, 1801), which is still found in appreciable numbers in the Ganga-Brahmaputra-Meghna River sys-

tem, from the tidal zone to the foot of the mountains. In all the publications of the last few years, including those by the present author, the Latin name of the Indus susu is given as *Platanista indi* Blyth. In a very recent note, van Bree (1976) has pointed out that according to "International Code of Zoological Nomenclature" *indi* Blyth 1859 should be considered a junior synonym of *minor* Owen, 1853. Owen (1853) described *Platanista gangetica* var. *minor* from a skull of the susu from the Indus River.[1] Van Bree (1976) has rightly pointed out that if specific status is given to the Indus susu, it should be known as *Platanista minor* Owen, 1853, on the basis of the recent version of article 23 of the "International Code of Zoological Nomenclature". He also points out that Hershkovitz (1966), in his catalogue of living whales, has listed both names, viz., *minor* Owen and *indi* Blyth in chronological order and that this appears to have escaped the attention of subsequent authors.

---

[1] This skull was destroyed during the second world war.

According to Pilleri and Gihr (1971a), who carried out detailed studies on the skulls of both species, "the nasal crest on the caudo-dorsal edge of the two frontals of the neurocranium constitutes a constant morphological character of a specific nature and is far less prominent in *Platanista indi* than in *P. gangetica*". In the latter it projects above the frontals as a clearly visible ridge to an average height of 10.5 mm in adult specimens while in the Indus susu it is distinctly lower and only projects 1-4 mm. Another character distinguishing the 2 is the difference recorded (Pilleri and Gihr, 1971) in the "caudal height of the maxillary crest that is greater in the dolphins from the Ganges and Brahmaputra (both on the right side and on the left) than in those from the Indus". In addition, the studies by Kasuya (1972) have shown significant difference in the length of the tail portion (anus to tail notch). However, he did not consider the distinguishing characters significant enough to give them specific status and considered them to be 2 sub-species, viz., *Platanista gangetica gangetica* and *Platanista gangetica indi*. In view of the foregoing differences and their separate distribution, I am of the opinion that the Indus susu should be given a specific status with the Latin name of *Platanista minor* Owen, 1853, which has priority over *Platanista indi* Blyth, 1859. Both species are of considerable interest from the point of view both of science and of their survival.

Common names

The common name susu in English is derived from the Hindi names "sus", "susu", "sous", "susa" and "sunsar" which is evidently derived from the breathing sound produced while surfacing. In Bengali-speaking areas, it is known as "susuk", "sishuk", "shushuk" and "sishumachh", the last meaning "sishu-fish", ("machh" = fish). In Assam it is called "hi-ho", "hihoo", "seho", "shuhu" and "sehoo",

and in Sylhet district "hugh" and "huh". In Nepal it is known as "swongsu", and in Sanskrit as "sansar" which means the sea or ocean – presumably meaning an animal of the sea which shows that the ancients knew of its marine origin. The Hindi name "sunsar" would probably have been derived from the above. Many of these local names have been mentioned by Blanford (1888) and Sclatter (1891). The Indus susu is known as "buhlaan" in Sind, Pakistan.

Ganges susu

GENERAL DISTRIBUTION

Platanista gangetica is widely distributed in the broad and deep sections of the Ganges-Brahmaputra-Meghna river system and their major tributaries, from the tidal zone to the foot of the Himalayas, the Garro Hills of Meghalaya and the Cachar Hills of Assam (Fig. 1). The Ganges has its origin in the Himalayas as do its tributaries such as the Jumna,[2] the Gogra, the Gandak and the Kosi, all of which have the susu in their entire course through the plains. Similarly, a number of rivers flow into the Brahmaputra and the Meghna, and the dolphin occurs in all of them except in sections where conditions are unfavourable because of lack of water or the unsuitability of terrain. Anderson (1878) made a comprehensive study of *Platanista* and gave the distribution of the species in the various rivers. According to him "The upward range of this dolphin is apparently only limited by insufficiency of water, and by rocky barriers.

---

[2] The River Jumna originates in the Tehri Garhwal section of the Great Himalayan Range immediately west of the source of the Ganges, and after passing through Delhi and Agra, joins the Ganges at Allahabad as its main tributary. The River Jamuna referred to subsequently in the Brahmaputra system in Bangladesh is not to be confused with the River Jumna in India.

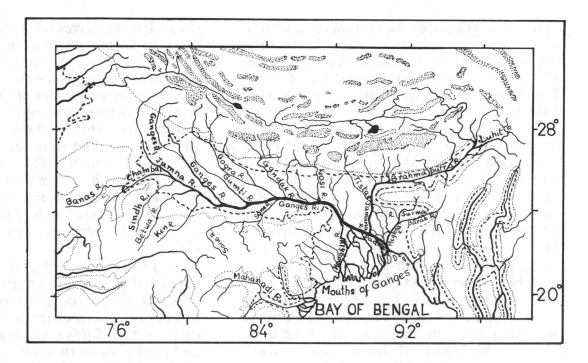

FIG. 1. – The Ganges-Brahmaputra-Meghna River system with the major tributaries. Broken lines (– – –) indicate elevation up to 200 metres and the dotted lines (. . . . .) elevation up to 300 metres above sea level. The stippled areas are mountains over 6 000 metres high. The rise from the plains is abrupt in the north and the east.

As pointed out by Wallick, Hardwick's specimen was obtained 1 000 miles above Calcutta and Cuvier remarks that it ascends the Ganges in great numbers as high as the river is navigable. Even in the month of May, when the Ganges is very low, it extends up to the Jumna as far as Delhi and also enters for a short way all the larger affluents of the main stream. In the Brahmaputra at the same season of the year, it is found throughout the river as far northeast as in such rivers as the Dihing, Dhansiri, Dikku and Disang". He also says that it has never been sighted out at sea. Recently Kasuya and Haque (1972) recorded its occurrence as far up as Dioghat, on the Narayani River of Nepal. This is in the upper section of the Gandak River, which is one of the major tributaries of the Ganges (Fig. 2). At an altitude of 250 m above sea level, Dioghat is about 100 km beyond the farthest limit of the distribution in the river recorded by Anderson. In a personal communication, Dr. Aminul Haque of the Bangladesh Agricultural University, Mymensingh, has informed me that in the Meghna and its tributaries he has seen the susu as far up as Sunamganj in Sylhet district (Fig. 3). According to him, the possibility of its

occurrence further up in the major tributaries of the Meghna cannot be ruled out.

The distribution pattern shows that the animal is essentially passive and non-gregarious, unlike its marine relatives, and though it can move against currents or maintain its position in flooded rivers, it cannot negotiate

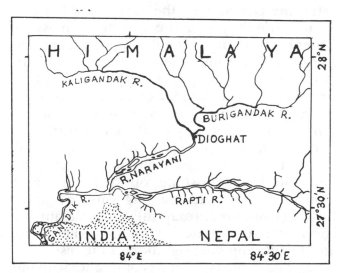

FIG. 2. – The Narayani section of the Gandak River in Nepal just above the Indian border showing Dioghat 250 metres above sea level, the uppermost limit of distribution of the Gangetic susu.

101

rapids and gorges or ascend steep cascades. Its temperature tolerance is evidently of a very wide range from the cold waters of about 10°C, or even less in winter at the foot of the Himalayas, to the warm waters of about 33°C in the tidal areas.

Outside the Ganga-Brahmaputra Meghna river system, the Karnaphuli River at Chittagong was included by Sclatter (1891) in the distributional range of the Gangetic susu, where however it does not now occur. Regarding the presence of a resident population of the susu in the Karnaphuli River at present, Haque (1976) states as follows: "There is a sizeable population of susu in the river Karnaphuli below the Kaptai dam. Above the dam, however, they seem to have disappeared over the short span of 6 or 7 years starting from the tenth year after the construction of the dam. Susu is also reported from another river, Sangu, whose mouth is hardly 10 km from the mouth of the Karnaphuli". This is very interesting and the reason for the disappearance of the animal above the Kaptai dam requires elucidation. Further, the specimens from the river should be compared with those occurring in the Ganga River system.

The Karnaphuli River opens into the Bay of Bengal close to the mouths of the main estuarine complex of the Ganges in Bangladesh through which the combined mass of water of the Ganges, the Brahmaputra and the Meghna flows into the sea (Figs 3 and 8). Owing to the great quantity of fresh water discharged by a number of large rivers, near estuarine conditions prevail in the entire northern section of the Bay of Bengal. During the periods of exceptionally heavy rains and floods, the flood waters from the Gangetic system should be pushing out the salt water along the coast and merging with the water flowing from the Karnaphuli River making it a contiguous freshwater or weakly saline area, and facilitating the migration of the susu.

The Ganges, after its confluence with the last of its major tributaries, the Kosi which has its origin in the Nepal section of the Himalayas, flows into West Bengal and immediately below Farakka gives off its first major distributary or deltaic branch, the Bhagirathi, the lower section of which is known as the Hooghly on which is the city of Calcutta. After the Bhagirathi branches off, the Ganges takes a southeasterly course giving off a number of distributaries which join the mainstream of the Brahmaputra, known as the Jamuna, at Goalundo in Bangladesh, and form the Padma River. This then merges with the Meghna near Chandpur, and flows into the Bay of Bengal through a series of wide estuaries intersected by several islands formed by the deposition of silt.

The Brahmaputra, taking its origin from the Tibetan side of the Himalayan Range, makes its way through a series of gorges and reaches the plains of India in Arunachal Pradesh, north of Saidya, and takes first a westerly and then a southerly course draining some of the heaviest rainfed areas of the world. There is no major diversion of water from this river for irrigation and other purposes and hence there is no significant reduction in flow compared with ancient times. Changes of its course are common in the plains: one major change took place some centuries ago when the main flow between Tistamukhghat and Bahadurabad took a southerly course forming a new river called the Jamuna to meet the Ganges at Goalundoghat. The original Brahmaputra flowing via Jamalpur and Mymensingh to meet the Meghna near Chandpur gradually became a comparatively small river with very much reduced flow of water (Fig. 3).

INCIDENTAL CATCH AND OTHER FACTORS

In the Ganges and its tributaries within India the susu is now seen only in stray numbers. While the rivers are in flood it spreads itself out a little but during summer it falls back to the deep pools which unfortunately are subjected to heavy fishing. No deliberate fishing for the susu is done and as far as possible the fishermen avoid it as it damages the net when it accidentally gets entangled. The nets

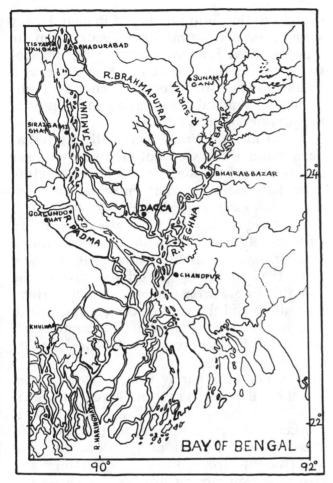

FIG. 3. – The Gangetic delta east of 90"E. For details of the Haringhata River, see Fig. 4.

operated are the large drag nets and seines like the "joha jal"[3] of Bihar or the "mahajal"[4] of Uttar Pradesh (Jones, 1959) and the "ber jal"

and "gai ber jal"[5] of West Bengal (Jones, 1959), which have their modified versions in Bangladesh. Drowning of susu from accidental entanglement in these nets is not uncommon. This brings about a steady depletion in its population, increasing with the advent of synthetic fibres for nets. The passive and defenceless nature of the animal, its low rate of reproduction and public apathy toward its conservation, contribute to the present trend of gradual reduction in its population. Construction of dams on some of the major tributaries of the Ganges and diversion of water for irrigation purposes resulting in a reduced flow, together with the steadily increasing discharge of industrial effluents, have on the whole aggravated the situation by producing adverse environmental conditions. The position would be worse were it not for the fact that the stocks of susu in these areas are steadily replenished by individuals that move up from the extensive deltaic areas of the river system in West Bengal and Bangladesh.

The net operated in the rivers of Bangladesh in which the susu gets accidentally caught is the "jagatberjal" (Jones, 1959).[6] This

---

[3] "*Joha jal*. This is a large hempen round haul net of 5 cm mesh, 90-1 200 m long and 3-4 m broad with a bag about 46 m deep and about 3 m wide at the mouth. It is operated from December to April in the wide and deep stretches of the river with the help of 7 boats, each 7-8 m long, by about 30-40 men" (Jones, 1959).

[4] "*Maha jal*. This is a large dragnet operated with the help of boats in the Ganges. The total length of the net varies from 450 to 650 m and is composed of pieces measuring 14 m × 4.5 to 6 m, the mesh of which will be 2.5 to 6 cm. Empty tins and dried pumpkins are used as floats and baked clay sinkers are attached to the bottom. 30-40 fishermen are required for the operation of the net. The net is employed all the year round except when the river is in flood" (Jones, 1959).

[5] "*Gai ber jal*. This is a very long rectangular seine net measuring 300 or more m with puckerings in the lower portion. The simpler type of seine net without puckerings is known as *ber jal*. The net may be made of either cotton or hemp and the mesh varies from 1 to 5 cm of 5-ply or 5 or 10 counts to 20-ply of 10 counts. The head rope and the foot rope are of the same size, very stout and the depth of the net ranges from 3 to 9 m. Bamboo or wooden floats are attached to the head rope. The net is either shot in the middle of the river by an encircling movement of two boats and then hauled up into the boat after bringing the two ends of the foot rope together or one end is left on shore and the other end is brought round enclosing a very large body of water after which the net is hauled in. When pieces of bamboo are tied across the net to facilitate the hauling operation, it is known as *tana ber jal*. *Ber jal* is generally operated from October-November to May, ..." (Jones, 1959).

[6] "In the large rivers like the Padma and the Meghna very long *ber jals* known as *jagat ber jal*, meaning universe enclosing net, over 1 600 m in length, are used. The operation lasts for several days and a large variety of fish is caught. Though the *jagat ber jal* is not used primarily for hilsa, it also forms one of the catches" (Jones, 1959). The fishing operation is, in principle, in the manner of a fish drive similar to the one described in detail for catching hilsa in the Mahanadi and in the Cauvery (Jones, 1959, 1959a).

103

is only a larger version of the "berjal" used in the rivers of West Bengal, referred to above. This is also known as the "barajal" or "badajal" or "mahajal" meaning big net and "jogatber" and "gogar". The operation of "jagatberjal" involves a large number of men and boats and is carried out only during the dry months when the level of water is low in the rivers. The lower point of the section to be fished is first fenced across by a long net supported on stakes to prevent the escape of any fish and another large net extending from shore to shore and surface to bottom is dragged from a few km upstream gradually reducing the gap between the 2 nets. Any aquatic animal that cannot escape through the 5 cm mesh of the net within the area fished will automatically get caught. The susu is invariably allowed to escape so as to prevent it from damaging the net. In case any dolphin is accidentally drowned it is thrown away to rot on the shore and is fed upon by vultures, mongrels and other carrion eaters. Kasuya and Haque (1972) refer to the capture of 3 specimens of susu from a 5 km stretch of the Brahmaputra near Jamalpur in the course of a "jagatberjal" operation in January 1970.

THE HOOGHLY AS A TYPICAL HABITAT OF THE SUSU

My observations on the Gangetic susu are mainly confined to the Hooghly from Pulta about 30 km to the north of Calcutta, to Diamond Harbour about 60 km to the south. Calcutta is situated about 200 km up from the sea and the tidal influences are felt still beyond as far as Purbastali about 130 km farther to the north. The upper section of the Hooghly above Nabadwip, known as the Bhagirathi, formed the main Ganges or Aadi-Ganga until the 16th century when, due to some natural cause, probably owing to heavy floods, it scoured its way in an easterly direction along one of its spill channels, the Padma, and got linked up with the Jamuna section of the Brahmaputra in Bangladesh and with the Meghna further beyond to flow into the Bay of Bengal. Heavy silting prevents natural flow of water from the Ganges to the Bhagirathi during the dry season from February-March to May-June, as a result of which the Hooghly remains a vast tidal inlet gradually increasing in salinity as the summer months advance.

So far as I know, very little study has been made of any sector of the river system as the habitat of the susu, and I have therefore extracted some relevant information from hydrobiological and fisheries work by my former colleagues, David (1954) and Bose (1956). I was closely associated with their work when I was carrying out fisheries investigations there from 1947 to 1954. The tidal section of the Hooghly from Purbastali immediately north of Nabadwip and the various centres referred to are given in Fig. 4. Table 1 gives some depth and breadth measurements for the Hooghly estuary.

Calcutta is barely 6 m above sea level and the fall of the river from there to the sea is only 1.5-3 cm per km. Tidal influence is marked and there is no well defined tongue of saline water at the bottom. The flood tides into the Hooghly from the sea in summer and post-monsoon months are very much greater in volume and longer in duration than in the monsoon months. The flood tide influx at Calcutta varies from 4 to 6 h in the dry season as against 2.5 to 4 h in the monsoon months. Duration of the ebb tide varies from 6.5 to 8.5 h in the dry months to 7-11.5 h in the monsoon months. The flood tide velocities which vary from 2 to 6 knots during the dry season drop to a little less than 1 knot during the monsoon, while the ebb tide velocities which vary from 2 to 3 knots in summer increase to 4 knots during monsoon. During monsoon months, flood tide influx is 300 m³/sec as against the freshwater discharge of 5 000 m³/sec while during the dry months the spring tide influx is 11 000 m³/sec as against an ebb flow of 2 750 m³/sec. More and more churned-up water is pushed up and retained in the tidal area in summer resulting in the deposition of an increasing quantity of silt in the river. The turbidity which may be as

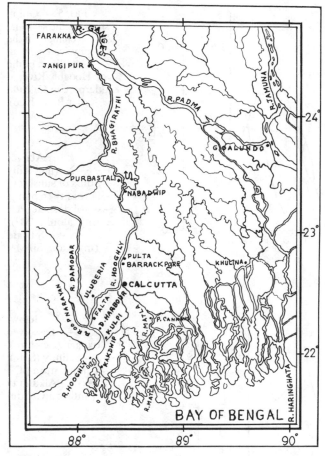

FIG. 4. – The Gangetic delta west of 90"E. The various centres in the Hooghly referred to in the text are indicated.

Table 1. The approximate breadth and depth at some points of the Hooghly estuary

Location	Breadth (km)	Maximum depth at HT during monsoon (m)	Minimum depth at LT during winter (m)
Kulpi	4.6	17.0	10.5
Diamond Harbour	4.65	28.0	21.0
Falta	1.2	21.0	14.0
Uluberia	0.75	22.0	15.0
Calcutta (Kidderpore)	0.75	16.0	9.0
Barrackpore	0.54	18.0	12.0

high as 2 500 ppm during monsoon months comes down to as low as 25 ppm during winter months. A graph showing seasonal variations in a number of physical and chemical parameters in the Hooghly at Calcutta (Kidderpore), as given by Bose (1956), is reproduced in Fig. 5.

The Barrackpore-Pulta area could be considered as the most upstream area coming under saline influence, though incursion of saline waters beyond this point does occasionally occur during the month of April. The water for the city of Calcutta is drawn from here and filtered and purified. The salinity readings here for a year are given below:

	ppm
January-February	8-12
March	10-120
April	10-208
May	26-180
June	18-48
July-December	4-8

In the Calcutta area of the Hooghly the susu is rarely seen during summer while it is common from October to March. From June to October, when freshwater conditions prevail in the lower reaches of the estuary, the susu frequents the areas beyond Diamond Harbour as far as Kakdwip and Sagar Island. The Hooghly is highly polluted, heavily silt-laden and congested with river traffic. Calcutta and the city of Howrah on the opposite bank of the Hooghly have a combined population of about 8 million people and along either side of the river for a distance of over 100 km there are chains of satellite towns radiating in all directions, which together comprise the biggest industrial complex in the country. Despite official restrictions and controls, a large quantity of sewage and over 250 million litres of factory effluents find their way daily into the river, making it one of the most highly polluted waterways in the world. It is interesting that the susu is capable of surviving there, which shows its hardiness. Casualities caused by injury from propellers of steamers and mechanized

105

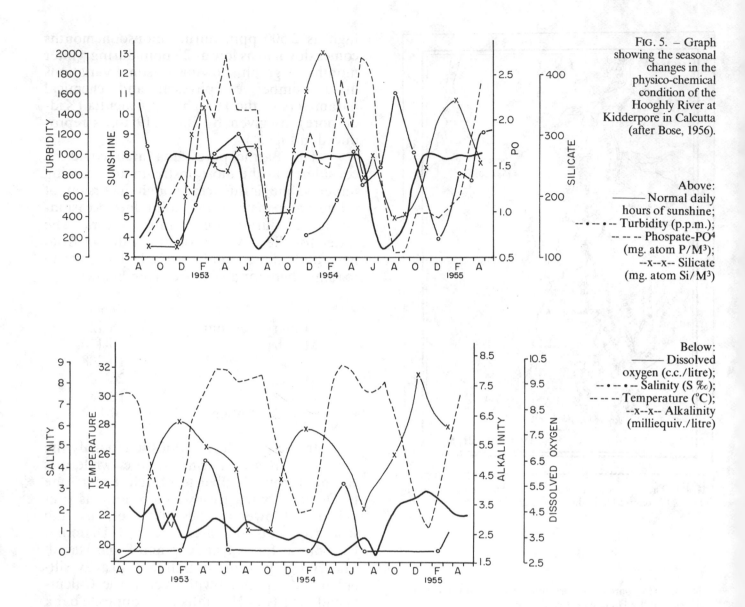

FIG. 5. – Graph showing the seasonal changes in the physico-chemical condition of the Hooghly River at Kidderpore in Calcutta (after Bose, 1956).

Above:
—— Normal daily hours of sunshine;
--•-- Turbidity (p.p.m.);
-- -- Phospate-PO⁴ (mg. atom P/M³);
--x--x-- Silicate (mg. atom Si/M³)

Below:
—— Dissolved oxygen (c.c./litre);
--•-- Salinity (S ‰);
-- -- Temperature (°C);
--x--x-- Alkalinity (milliequiv./litre)

boats are practically unknown and despite its blindness, the dolphin appears to be capable of dodging obstacles and moving objects. In the tidal section of the Gangetic delta in general the behaviour pattern of the susu should be more or less the same. I have seen it in the Matla and beyond Port Canning in Gosaba and in the Sunderbans and as far as the Rai-mangal River toward the east, bordering the Khulna district of Bangladesh, but not in the Kulti section of the Bidhyadhari Spill area where the sewage from the city of Calcutta is discharged.

STATUS AND POPULATION ESTIMATION

In the Ganges below Farakka and in the entire Brahmaputra-Meghna complex of rivers in India and Bangladesh, there are no signs of depletion in susu population, unlike the situation in the Ganges and its tributaries above Farakka. According to Dr. Aminul Haque (personal communication) who made fairly extensive field studies on the distribution and abundance of the dolphin in Bangladesh, it is even believed that the population of the susu is on the increase. The same perhaps could be said of it in the Brahmaputra and its major tributaries within India. The deltaic system of the Ganges is the biggest of its kind in the world, covering an area of about 20 000 km², the greater part of which lies within Bangladesh. It forms a perennial and extensive network of wide and deep rivers and creeks. The entire delta receives from the Ganges and Brahmaputra about 1 200 thousand million m³ of water between the Meghna and Barak and the Surma in the east, and the Damodar and the Roopnarayan in the west. In Bangladesh, as in India and Nepal, there is no deliberate attempt to catch susu, and mortality is confined to the few that are drowned by accidental entanglement in fishing nets. Fortunately, unlike the Indus susu which is deliberately hunted down despite its diminishing numbers and the legal protection it enjoys, no medicinal or aphrodisiac properties are attributed to the meat or oil of the Gangetic susu.

The only reliable information we have on the population of the susu is confined to the observations in the rivers of Bangladesh of Kasuya and Haque (1972), whose table is reproduced below (Table 2). The Ganges-Brahmaputra-Meghna river system in Bangladesh with its deep rivers, extensive network of distributaries and wide tidal inlets is a real haven for the Gangetic susu where it is continuing to hold its own unlike its congener in the Indus.

The total number of individuals sighted from ships and the estimated number per 100 nautical miles (= 186 km) is given in Table 3.

Table 3 shows that the susu population is more dense in the Meghna, in the Padma and in the lower Jamuna, whereas it is comparatively low in the estuary and the upper section of the Jamuna above Sirajganjghat. On the above basis, it is presumed that the population should be comparatively low in the main Brahmaputra above Tistamukhghat flowing through the States of Assam and Arunachal Pradesh in India.

The susu is a non-gregarious animal and it is only very rarely that 2 or more are sighted

Table 2. Seasonal fluctuation of the density of the Ganges dolphin sighted at the station or on the ship (after Kasuya and Haque, 1972)[1]

Month	October		November			December			January	
Decade	2	3	1	2	3	1	2	3	1	2
Brahmaputra										
Khagdahar		xx	x	x	1	0	0	0	0,1	
Govindapur	xx	xx	0	0			0	0	0	
Shambhuganj	xx	xx	xx			0	0	0,1-2	0	
Kewatkhali	xx	0		x	0,1-2	0	0,1	0		
Sutiakhali	xx	x	x	1	0	0,1	0	0	0	
Phulpur	xx			1		0	0	0	0	
Bhabakhali	xx	xx	xx			0	0	0	0	
Kalir Bazar		xx	xx			1-2	0	0		
Meghna										
Bhairab Bazar			xxx	xxx					xxx	
Sandarghat, Dacca		xxx						0		
Chandpur-Dacca										xxx
Jamuna										
Tistamukhghat-Goalundoghat									xxx	xxx

[1] The density was calculated on the basis of counts of the frequency of surfacing individuals and placed under 4 categories: "many", "several", "few" and "none". In cases where the number was known, it was recorded. The observations show that there was a reduction in the population in the Brahmaputra in the Mymensingh area after November, whereas in the Meghna and the Jamuna they were found in appreciable numbers in the rainy season as well as the dry season.

Table 3. Geographical variation of the density of Ganges dolphin based on observations from ships (after Kasuya and Haque, 1972)

Distance from estuary [1]	Locality	Number of sightings	Number of individuals/ 100 miles [1]	Month
0- 30	lower Sundarbans	29	29	January (1970)
30- 60	up to Khulna (upper Sundarbans)	32	67	»
	up to Chandpur (lower Meghna)	34	35	»
60- 90	up to Dacca	95	191	»
90-120	up to Goalundoghat	15	182	»
120-150	up to Sirajganjghat	37	57	»
150-180		37	69	»
180-210	up to Tistamukhghat	4	16	»
130 <	Meghna, upper stream of Bhairab Bazar	540	229	April and May

[1] In nautical miles.

at a time. The observations of Kasuya and Haque in this regard are given in Table 4.

From Table 4 it is seen that 90 % of the sightings and 80.4 % of the total number counted consisted of single individuals. For purposes of record and estimation a single individual or more found in one area was considered to be a school. The frequency distribution of the susu in the rivers as given by them is reproduced in Figs. 6 and 7.

It has been reported by Kasuya and Haque (1972) that the susu frequents narrow sections of rivers, confluences or sections downstream of shallow areas and it is pre-

sumed that this may be due to the availability of food in such places.

To estimate the overall total population of the Gangetic susu in the entire subcontinent we have to divide the complex system of rivers arbitrarily into 4 zones. Of these the first and the most important is what we may call the Gangetic deltaic zone, consisting of the Ganges below Farakka Barrage, the Brahmaputra below Tistamukhghat and the Meghna below Bairab Bazar. This includes the entire Gangetic system in West Bengal (India) and Bangladesh, the Jamuna, the old Brahmaputra and the lower part of the Meghna as far as Bairab

Table 4. School size of the Ganges dolphin (after Kasuya and Haque, 1972)

Locality	Month	No. of individuals in a school									
		1		2		3		4		Total	
		No. of schools	%	No. of schools	%	No. of schools	%	No. of schools	%	No. of schools	%
Tistamukhghat to Goalundoghat	January	73	90.1	5	6.2	2	2.5	1	1.2	81	100.0
Lower Meghna and Sundarbans	January	189	85.9	28	12.7	3	1.4	0	0.0	220	100.0
Upper Meghna	April-May	550	91.5	39	7.0	7	1.3	1	0.2	557	100.0
Total No. of schools	—	772	90.0	72	8.4	12	1.4	2	0.2	858	100.0
Total No. of individuals	—	772	80.4	144	15.0	36	3.8	8	0.8	960	100.0

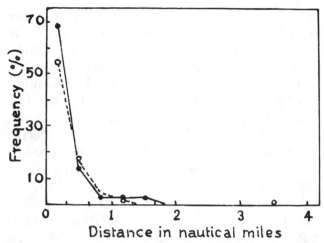

FIG. 6. – Frequency distribution of the length of the course where the Ganges dolphin was sighted at intervals of less than ⅓ nautical mile. Closed circle and continuous line indicate the Jamuna River, and open circle and dotted line, the lower Meghna and Sundarbans (after Kasuya and Haque, 1972).

Bazar in Bangladesh. The Narayanganj-Dacca area will come under this zone. The second zone may be called the Gangetic River zone, comprising the river and its tributaries, almost all of which come within India except some very short stretches that lie in Nepal. The third may be called the Brahmaputra River zone comprising the river and its tributaries above Tistamukhghat, most of which fall within

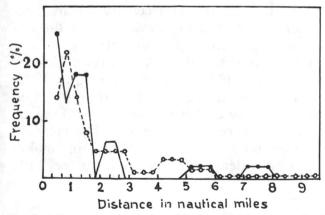

FIG. 7. – Frequency distribution of the length of the course where the Ganges dolphin was not sighted. Where the dolphin was sighted at intervals of less than ⅓ mile, it is dealt as continuous. Closed circle and continuous line indicate the Jamuna River, and open circle and dotted line, the lower Meghna and Sundarbans (after Kasuya and Haque, 1972).

India except a short stretch as far as Dubri, which lies in Bangladesh. The fourth zone may be called the Meghna River zone comprising the upper section of the river above Bairab Bazar. This zone, though a small one, is important from the population point of view of the susu and forms an adjunct to the first zone with which it could even be conveniently included if so desired.

The Gangetic deltaic zone is of vital importance for the survival of the species. It may be said that fortunately the natural features of the habitat, especially its vastness and complexity, combined with the dislike or lack of interest of the people for the meat of susu, have helped to give the animal an advantage. Between the Hooghly in the west and the Sandwip Channel in the east bordering Noakhali, the Ganges and associated rivers open into the Bay of Bengal through several estuaries, each with a separate name. Through these estuaries the combined volume of over 1 200 thousand million m³ of water is discharged annually into the Bay of Bengal. The entire network above the region of saline influence provides several thousand nautical miles of river where the susu lives in comparative safety. On a rough, and conservative, estimate, between 3 000 and 3 500 susu might be found there. In the entire Ganges River zone between 500 and 750 individuals might exist, while in the Brahmaputra River zone the number could be about 500, and in the Meghna River zone above Bairab Bazar about 750. In all, the existing susu population could be estimated at between 4 000 and 5 000, a very satisfactory position when compared to the few hundreds of *Platanista minor* surviving in the Indus River (Mitchell, 1974; Kasuya and Nishiwaki, 1975). It may be said with confidence that under existing conditions it is not in immediate danger of extermination. According to the information furnished by Dr. Aminul Haque of the Bangladesh Agricultural University, the population of susu in Bangladesh is on the increase.

There is, however, no room for complacency. Man's encroachment on nature's domain is multifaceted. The Ganges valley is perhaps the most thickly populated area in the world. The Ganges-Brahmaputra system drains about 1 700 000 km² of land in which live about 300 million people, nearly a tenth of the world's population. There is no need to elaborate on the direct and indirect effect of this vast mass of humanity on the river system. Increasing quantities of water are diverted for irrigation, drinking and even for navigation. The cumulative effect of pollution from factory effluents, other industrial wastes and city sewage is tremendous, though so far the susu has been found to withstand the adverse conditions successfully. Apart from a series of hydroelectric projects in the Himalayan sector, 2 major dams for irrigation purposes have already come up, the Gandhisagar in the Chambal and the Rihand in the Sone, and the main Ganges itself has been bisected by a barrage at Farakka for diversion of water to the Bhagirathi and its tidal section below, known as the Hooghly.

THE FARAKKA BARRAGE AND THE SUSU

In West Bengal the Ganges gives off its first deltaic distributary, the Bhagirathi, which as stated earlier is heavily silted up, as it receives no flow from the Ganges during dry months. The purpose of the barrage, which was commissioned in May 1975, is to circumvent this situation by diverting water from the Farakka Barrage through a 38-km feeder channel with bed width of 151 m and depth of 6.1 m at full supply, linking the Bhagirathi at Jangipur (Fig. 8). The dry weather flow in the Ganges from March to May is 1 250 to 1 500 m³/sec. If 1 000 m³/sec are diverted from this as contemplated, the flow in the Ganges (Padma) until it meets the Jamuna (Brahmaputra) will be reduced to one third to one fifth of its former level. For this reason, a canal from Dubri to Farakka, linking the Brahmaputra with the Ganges, has been suggested but the likelihood of this happening seems to be

rather remote. We have, therefore, to consider the present situation. The population of the susu above Farakka is bound to get isolated from that of the deltaic zone in summer and it remains to be seen if any upward movement will take place even during heavy flood.[7] The stocks of susu in the Hooghly and the adjacent sector of the Gangetic Delta might derive some benefit from the influx of water through the feeder canal during summer months. If any upward or downward movements of individuals occur, they are likely to be uninhibited, with no risk of being caught in fishing nets as would happen in a normal section of the river.

If the conditions created by the Farakka Barrage turn out to be similar to those brought about by the barrages in the Indus, the latter should serve as a lesson to us. It may be argued that since the Farakka Barrage is not for irrigation purposes, it is not as high as those in the Indus and diversion of water will also be confined to the summer months. All the same, it is essential that the population of the susu above the barrage should be carefully watched and studied by the establishment of an observation centre.

GENERAL SUGGESTIONS

Apart from studies of general biology a population estimate is necessary. In this connexion, the pioneering work done by the Cetacean Research Expedition of Tokyo University and Bangladesh Agricultural University (Kasuya, 1972; Kasuya and Haque, 1972) deserves special mention. It is desirable that the entire area of distribution of the Gangetic susu be covered in this manner. The fact that the animal has to surface for breathing makes counting easier. At present we have very little

---

[7] From the information available, it appears that the Farakka Barrage does not constitute a permanent barrier for the movements of the susu in the river.

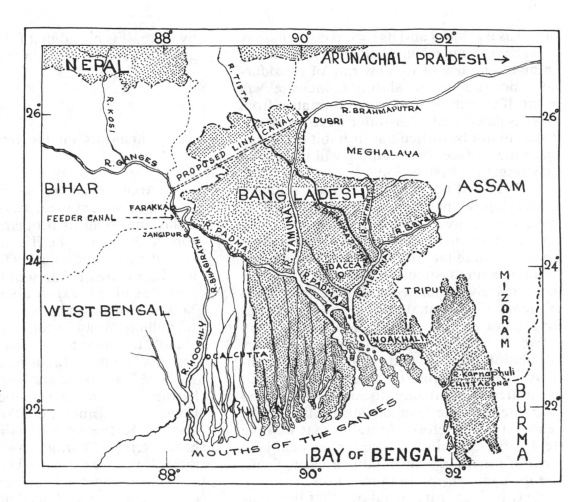

FIG. 8. – The Gangetic delta showing the feeder canal from Farakka on the Ganges to Jangipur on the Bhagirathi and the proposed Ganges-Brahmaputra link canal. Only the major rivers are shown.

idea of its migratory movements. It is known to spread out during certain seasons and retreat to some limited sections of the rivers at other times. The movements of the susu should be studied in a systematic manner. For this, and for population studies, marking experiments should be useful.

Two major dams have been constructed on 2 of the tributaries of the Ganges, the Gandhisagar in the Chambal and Rihand in the Sone, both of which originate in the Vindhya Mountains, facing the southern side of the Gangetic plain. It would be interesting to carry out some transplantation and repopulation experiments with the susu (Jones, 1974). It is not known to be present in these reservoirs, and some specimens from the Jumna and the Ganges could be introduced and their progress

observed. The Chambal held more water in former days when the Aravalli Range and the Malwa Plateau were not denuded of vegetation and the demand for irrigation water was not as high as at present. The repopulation of the susu in the Chambal, based on the Gandhisagar would therefore be of interest. The same could be done with the Sone above the Rihand Dam. At the same time, transplantation of the susu into one or two of the neighbouring river systems having perennial flow of water could also be considered. For this purpose, the Damodar Valley, which is an adjunct of the Gangetic basin, and the Mahanadi in Orissa above the Hirakud Dam could be considered. The introduction of susu should not upset the ecology of these waters. The animal would not destroy the populations of major

111

carps[8] as it is blind and its food consists mainly of catfish, prawns and other bottom-living animals. In view of its slow rate of reproduction, no sudden or alarming increase will occur. If ever its control or extermination from these isolated bodies of water were necessary, it should not be difficult as its habit of coming up to the surface for breathing will make it an easy target for destruction.

We need not wait for a critical situation to develop, as has happened with the Indus susu, before we contemplate action for the conservation and protection of the Ganges susu. Its habitat in the Ganges-Brahmaputra-Meghna system comes within one of the most densely populated and food-poor areas of the world. Fortunately, it is not sought after for food or medicine to any noticeable extent. However, anything can happen under heavy population pressure and the desperate conditions brought about by unexpected natural calamities or manmade disasters. There is no guarantee that the Gangetic susu will be left in peace. It is, therefore, desirable that we take steps sufficiently in advance for the establishment of sanctuaries in suitable areas to facilitate its management and protection.

It is clear from the above that the Gangetic susu deserves more attention than it has received hitherto. After the monumental work of Anderson (1878) about a century ago hardly anything has been done on *Platanista* till interest was revived a few years ago on the initiative of the California Academy of Sciences, San Francisco (Herald, 1969, 1969a), the Brain Anatomy Institute of the University of Berne (Pilleri, 1970) and the Ocean Research Institute of the University of Tokyo (Kasuya, 1972). It is a matter of great satisfaction that interest in research and conservation of the susu is being shown at international level. Given its distribution, the necessary investigations are an international problem. The countries most concerned are India and Bangladesh and cooperative investigations are called for

by them. It is hoped that FAO and IUCN will give the necessary lead in this matter.

Comments on the Indus susu

About a century ago the Indus dolphin, *Platanista minor* Owen, was distributed in the Indus and in all its tributaries from the tidal zone to the foot of the Himalayas. In the main river it was found in a 1 500 km stretch from the deltaic area in the south to Attock in the north, at about 600 m above sea level. The 3 000 km long river has a total drainage area of 1.2 million km² and a combined annual flow of about 210 thousand million m³ of water (see Fig. 9). The main Indus is intersected by the Tarbella Dam in the north above Attock and 6 barrages in the plains, the Kalabagh, the Chasma, the Taunsa, the Guddu, the Sukkur and the Kotri. All the main tributaries also have a series of barrages and dams to harness their water resources. The extensive and ever-increasing diversion of water for irrigation – the biggest of its kind in the world – along a network of canals and distributaries flowing through the desert and semi-arid tracts, and the virtual absence of seasonal rains for replenishment, has reduced the flow to such an extent as to exterminate the susu from all the tributaries, leaving only a small population in a short section of the main river. A few hundred individuals, estimated around 400, survive immediately above the Sukkur Barrage. If things go on as at present, it is only a question of time before these are also exterminated and another name added to the list of extinct species. Kasuya and Nishiwaki (1975) recorded the presence of a few stragglers immediately below the Sukkur Barrage and above the Guddu Barrage but by now they will probably have fallen easy targets to poachers. The present critical state of this dolphin has been pointed out by several workers in recent years (Herald, 1969; Pilleri, 1970; Holloway,

[8] "Major carps" refers to certain species of Indian carp.

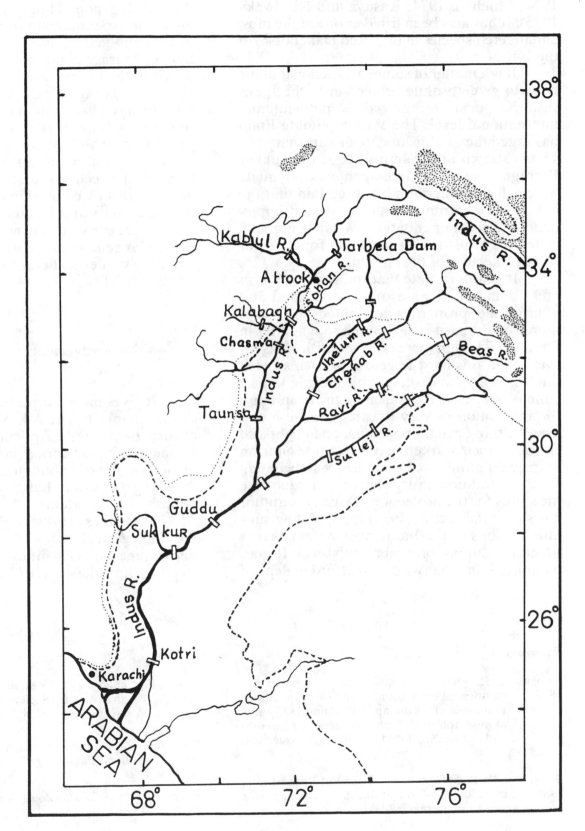

FIG. 9. – The Indus River and its tributaries. Broken lines (– – –) indicate elevation up to 200 metres and dotted lines (. . .) elevation up to 300 metres above sea level. The stippled areas are mountains over 6 000 metres high.

1974; Mitchell, 1974; Kasuya and Nishiwaki, 1975). It has also been listed as one of the most endangered species in the "Red Data Book" of the IUCN.

It is a matter of some satisfaction that the need to give absolute protection to the Indus susu has been recognized at national and international level. The World Wildlife Fund has urged the establishment of a sanctuary in a 75 km stretch of the Indus above the Sukkur Barrage where the river contains adequate water all the year round. It is certain that the Pakistan Government will accept and implement the recommendation. What is urgently called for are stringent measures for the complete protection of the animal.

It is unfortunate that Indus susu oil is in great demand because of the medicinal and aphrodisiac properties attributed to it and therefore the susu is very much sought after in Pakistan. Though there is no scientific basis for this belief, it is hard to get rid of such an idea once it takes hold of gullible people. Apart from propaganda for educating the people and the imposition of very drastic punitive measures for those caught poaching, one might also consider open marketing of substitute oil from marine dolphins to cater to the local demand.

In addition to legislative and educative measures for the protection of susu, the author has suggested (Jones, 1974) repopulating suitable sections of the Indus river system having perennial supply of water, with susu. It goes without saying that we can ill afford to deplete the existing population by removing specimens for experimental purposes. Perhaps the individuals that manage to escape from the Sukkur Barrage could be retrieved and transferred to the reservoir immediately above the Kalabagh Barrage instead of being left to their fate. Susu is a hardy animal and it is known to stand transport well. It is hoped that the above suggestions will receive due consideration from the concerned authorities, and that stringent protective measures will be implemented. In this connexion, the results of experiments on transplantation or introduction of the Gangetic susu in new or depleted sectors in the Gangetic area, if carried out as suggested in the earlier section of this paper, should prove helpful.

Acknowledgements

It gives me great pleasure to express my sincere thanks to Dr. A.K.M. Aminul Haque of the Bangladesh Agricultural University, Mymensingh, for furnishing me with information on the distribution and abundance of the Gangetic susu in Bangladesh from his unpublished observation.

My thanks are due to Dr. P.K. Talwar of the Zoological Survey of India, Calcutta, for sending me the relevant extracts from the account by J. Anderson (1878).

References

ANDERSON, J., Anatomical and zoological researches
1878   comprising an account of the two expeditions to the western Yunnan in 1868 and 1875 and a monograph of the cetacean genera *Platanista* and *Orcaella*. London, Bernard Quaritch, 550 p.

BLANFORD, W.T., Mammalia. *In* Fauna of British India,
1888   including Ceylon and Burma. London, Taylor and Francis, pp. 589-90.

BLYTH, E., Catalogue of the Mammalia in the Museum
1863   of the Asiatic Society, Calcutta. Calcutta, Asiatic Society, vol. 8:200.

BOSE, B.B., Observations on the hydrology of Hooghly
1956   Estuary. *Indian J. Fish.*, 3(1):101-8.

BREE, P.J.J. VAN, *Bull. Zool. Mus. Amsterd.*, 5(17):
1976   139-40.

DAVID, A., A preliminary survey of the fish and fisheries
1954   of a five mile stretch of the Hooghly River
         near Barrackpore. *Indian J. Fish.*, 1(1/2):
         231-55.

HAQUE, A.K.M. AMINUL, Comments on the abundance
1976   and distribution of the Ganges susu, *Platanista gangetica*, and the effects of the Farakka
         Barrage on its population. Paper presented to
         the Scientific Consultation on the Conservation and Management of Marine Mammals
         and their Environment, Bergen, Norway, 31
         August-9 September 1976. Rome, FAO,
         ACMRR/MM/SC/32:2 p.

HERALD, E.S., Field and aquarium study of the blind
1969   river dolphin, *Platanista gangetica*. California
         Academy of Sciences Steinhart Aquarium, 59
         p. (mimeo).

–, Blind river dolphin: first side-swimming cetacean.
1969a   *Science, Wash.*, 166:1408-10.

HERSHKOVITZ, Ph., Catalogue of living whales. *Bull. U.S.*
1966   *Natl. Mus.*, (246):259 p.

HOLLOWAY, C.W., A note on the current status of the
1974   Indus dolphin *Platanista indi* Blyth 1859, in
         Sind Province. Morges, Switzerland, IUCN, 9
         p. (MS).

IUCN, Indus dolphin or susu *Platanista indi* Blyth 1859.
1973   *IUCN Red Data Book*, 1: Mammalia.

JONES, S., Hilsa fishing methods in the Indian region.
1959   Part 1. *J. Bombay Nat. Hist. Soc.*, 56(2):
         250-75.

–, Hilsa fishing methods in the Indian region. Part 2. *J.*
1959a   *Bombay Nat. Hist. Soc.*, 56(3):423-48.

–, A suggestion for the introduction of the Indus
1974   susu and the Gangetic susu into new sectors
         and river systems in the Indian sub-continent
         and establishment of sanctuaries for them.
         Presented to the Scientific Consultation on the
         Conservation and Management of Marine
         Mammals and their Environment, Bergen,

Norway, 31 August-9 September 1976. Rome,
FAO, ACMRR/SC/16:3 p.

KASUYA, T., Some information on the growth of the
1972   Ganges dolphin with a comment on the Indus
         dolphin. *Sci. Rep. Whales Res. Inst., Tokyo*,
         (24):87-108.

KASUYA, T. and A.K.M. AMINUL HAQUE, Some information on the distribution and seasonal
1972   movements of the Ganges dolphin. *Sci.*
         Rep. Whales Res. Inst., Tokyo, (24):109-15.

KASUYA, T. and M. NISHIWAKI, Recent status of the
1975   population of the Indus dolphin. *Sci. Rep.*
         Whales Res. Inst., Tokyo, (27):81-94.

MITCHELL, E., Porpoise, dolphin and small whale fisheries of the world: definition of the problem.
1974   *IUCN Monogr.*, (3).

OWEN, R., Descriptive catalogue of the osteological series contained in the Museum of the Royal
1853   College of Surgeons of England. 2. Mammalia
         placentalia. London, pp. 351-914.

PILLERI, G., Observations on the behaviour of *Platanista*
1970   *gangetica* in the Indus and Brahmaputra Rivers. *In* Investigations on Cetacea, edited by
         G. Pilleri. Berne, Brain Anatomy Institute,
         vol. 2:26-60.

PILLERI, G. and M. GIHR, Zur systematik der gattung
1971   *Platanista* (Cetacea). *Rev. Suisse Zool.*,
         78(3):746-59.

–, Difference observed in the skull of *Platanista gangetica* (Roxburgh 1801) and *Platanista indi*
1971a   (Blyth 1859). *In* Investigations on Cetacea,
         edited by G. Pilleri. Berne, Brain Anatomy
         Institute, vol. 3, Pt. 1: 13-21.

SCLATTER, W.L., Catalogue of Mammalia in the Indian
1891   Museum, Calcutta. Calcutta, Indian Museum,
         Part 2:315-6.

ROXBURGH, W., An account of a new species of *Dolphinus*, an inhabitant of the Ganges. *Asiat. Res.*,
1801   7:170-4.

OBSERVATIONS ON THE ATTITUDE OF PEOPLE IN BANGLADESH TOWARDS SMALL CETACEANS

A.K.M. AMINUL HAQUE

Abstract

In Bangladesh, the smaller cetaceans comprise several species living in estuaries and the sea, including the Irrawaddy dolphin, *Orcaella brevirostris*, common dolphin, *Delphinus delphis* and finless porpoise, *Neophocaena phocaenoides*, and the Ganges susu, *Platanista gangetica*, living in fresh water. All are known by the name "Shushuk" or some variant of it, and there is no organized fishery for any of them, this being accounted for by the favourable attitude of the people towards them. Animals are sometimes accidentally entangled in fishing nets. The salt-water species yield oil, bone and other products, all used as medicine; around February 1976, about 200 animals, including the 3 species above, were caught off Cox's Bazar, but only 19 were collected and processed. If caught accidentally, *P. gangetica* is released alive or, if the animal dies, its oil may be used as an aphrodisiac, medicine or an ingredient in soap; its meat is generally not eaten nor used as livestock feed. At least one family of fishermen kills 50-150 susus each year by harpoon.

Résumé

Au Bangladesh, les petits cétacés comprennent plusieurs espèces vivant dans les estuaires et en mer, le dauphin de l'Iraouaddhi, *Orcaella brevirostris*, le dauphin commun, *Delphinus delphis*, le marsouin, *Neophocaena phocaenoides* et le susu du Gange, *Platanista gangetica*, vivant en eau douce. Tous sont connus sous le nom de "Shushuk" — ou une variante de ce terme — et il n'existe aucune pêche organisée, ce qui s'explique par l'attitude favorable du public à leur égard. Les animaux sont parfois accidentellement emmêlés dans les filets de pêche. Les espèces d'eau salée fournissent de l'huile, des os et d'autres produits, tous employés comme médicaments. Vers février 1976, environ 200 animaux, comprenant les trois espèces ci-dessus, ont été capturés au large de Cox's Bazaar mais 19 seulement ont été ramenés et dépecés. S'il est capturé par accident, *P. gangetica* est relâché vivant ou, si l'animal meurt, son huile peut être employée comme aphrodisiaque, comme médicament ou comme ingrédient du savon; sa chair n'est généralement pas consommée et ne sert pas non plus à l'alimentation animale. Une famille au moins de pêcheurs tue de 50 à 100 susus au harpon chaque année.

Extracto

Entre los cetáceos menores presentes en Bangladesh figuran varias especies que viven en estuarios y en el mar, como el delfín de Irrawady (*Orcaella brevirostris*), el delfín común (*Delphinus delphis*) y la marsopa sin aletas (*Neophocaena phocaenoides*), o en aguas dulces, como la platanista del Ganges (*Platanista gangetica*). Todos ellos se designan con el nombre

117

"shushuk", o una variante de él, y no existe una pesquería organizada de ninguna de esas especies, debido a la actitud favorable de la gente hacia esos animales. Algunos quedan apresados a veces accidentalmente en las redes de pesca. De las especies de agua salada se obtiene aceite, huesos y otros productos, que se utilizan como medicamentos; hacia febrero de 1976 se capturaron frente a Cox Bazaar unos 200 animales de las tres especies de aguas marinas arriba indicadas, pero sólo 19 se recogieron y aprovecharon. Cuando se capturan accidentalmente platanistas del Ganges, se las deja vivas o, si mueren, se utiliza su aceite como afrodisíaco, como medicamento o como ingrediente para jabones; la carne no se come, en general, y se utiliza para piensos. Al menos una familia de pescadores mata anualmente con arpón entre 50 y 150 platanistas.

A.K.M. Aminul Haque
Faculty of Fisheries, Bangladesh Agricultural University, Mymensingh, Bangladesh

Introduction

Several species of small cetaceans occur in Bangladesh waters, of which one is freshwater and the rest are all estuarine and/or marine. While three of the latter forms have been identified as *Orcaella brevirostris*, the Irrawaddy dolphin, *Delphinus delphis*, the common dolphin, and *Neophocaena phocaenoides*, the finless porpoise, all the small cetaceans go by the same popular name, "Shushuk" with local variants, *viz.*, "Shishu", "Shishumachh", "Suchchum", "Huchchum" or "Houm". People in coastal areas, particularly those engaged in fishing, seem to know of at least three marine species that occasionally get entangled in their fishing nets. They differentiate the three species by the presence or absence of a snout, and by body-colours. In February 1960, the author collected one specimen each of *N. Phocaenoides* and *O. brevirostris* that were respectively stranded and washed ashore at Cox's Bazar on two separate occasions. People who live away from the coastal belt are not aware of the marine cetaceans and know only of one species, *Platanista gangetica*, the Ganges susu or "Shushuk".

Status of the fishery

There is no organised fishery for any of the cetaceans in Bangladesh. However, the author has located at least one family of "shikaris" – a type of Hindu fishermen – who harpoon aquatic reptiles and mammals. This is a traditional activity. Some 50 to 150 Ganges susu are killed this way every year.

Attitude towards cetaceans

The lack of an organised fishery for the cetaceans can be explained by the attitude of the people here in general, and the fisherfolk in particular, towards these animals.

MARINE AND ESTUARINE DOLPHINS AND PORPOISES

These marine and estuarine forms yield products believed to have much therapeutic value. For example, (a) the body-oil, collected by keeping the dead animal hanging upside down in the sun, or under a tin-roof, is claimed to be effective against puerperal fever, asthma, and, of course, impotence; (b) oil extracted by boiling the liver, brain, kidney, and blubber, is believed to be a sure cure for piles, asthma, general debility and other similar ailments; (c) bile, collected from the gall-bladder, is used in the treatment of various kinds of ulcerations including those of the stomach; and finally, (d) the skull-bones are made into powder by rubbing on a stone, and used for the treatment of cataracts.

Around February 1976 some 200 specimens of these marine and estuarine forms, representing all three species listed above, were caught in fishing nets in the Bay of Bengal off Cox's Bazar, but only 19 were collected and processed for oil and other products by the sole processor (the "doctor"). The rest were thrown back into the sea.

The marine and estuarine dolphins and porpoises are regarded by the people in coastal areas of Bangladesh with some veneration. This is understood to be due to two reasons. One is that these small cetaceans are believed by them to be "direct descendants" of Adam, the first man, and thus these "sacred" animals must be shown due respect. The other reason is that one of the three commoner species (the white suchchum of the fishermen), apparently *D. delphis*, is credited with a very welcome quality in that if a man is accidentally thrown overboard, they are said to support him from below, and surround and guard him against possible attack from sharks.

GANGES SUSU

The Ganges susu is quite a strong, stout animal that seems to be able to sense the presence of nets in the vicinity (Aminul Haque *et al.*, 1977) despite the fact that it has only vestigial eyes. It does however get caught accidentally in fishing nets, and the fishermen try to untangle the animal before it does their nets much damage. If alive, the susu is usually thrown back into the water. If, on the other hand, the animal dies, it may be taken ashore, where some enterprising individual may collect the carcass for extraction of oil, which has well-known value as an aphrodisiac. It is also claimed to be of much therapeutic value for rheumatism and many other maladies, and has a limited local use in soapmaking and tanning industries. The meat, which the author understands to be quite delicious, is not eaten by any of the local people, although a small section of the Buddhist community may not have any objection to doing so. The bulk of the population is made up of Muslims who, for religious reasons, do not eat susu meat. The meat is not used as livestock feed either.

People in Bangladesh appear to have accepted the Ganges susu as a harmless, water-dwelling neighbour. Even if a fishing net has just been damaged, they never complain about them — an attitude that appears at times to border on indulgence.

References

AMINUL HAQUE, A.K.M. *et al.*, Observations on the be-
1977   haviour and other related aspects of the biol-
        ogy of the Ganges susu, *Platanista gangeti-*
        ca. Sci. Rep. Whales Res. Inst., Tokyo, (29): 87-94.

CURRENT UNDERSTANDING OF THE STATUS OF SMALL CETACEAN POPULATIONS IN THE BLACK SEA

T.D. SMITH

Abstract

A fishery using guns and nets for the common dolphin, *Delphinus delphis*, Azov dolphin, *Phocoena phocoena*, and bottlenose dolphin, *Tursiops truncatus*, in the Black and Azov Seas has been pursued since about 1870 from the USSR, Turkey, Bulgaria and Romania. Steadily declining annual Soviet harvests since the maximum Soviet catch of 135 000-140 000 animals in 1938, despite an increased catching effort, led to seasonal management restrictions by the USSR in 1962, and a complete closure of the fishery in the USSR, Romania and Bulgaria in 1967. The final annual Soviet catches of 5 600-7 400 animals reported for 1964-66 represent a major collapse of the fishery and were accompanied by apparent marked changes in the age and sex composition of the harvest and a change in the species composition from the historically predominant *D. delphis* to predominantly *P. phocoena*. The fishery continues in Turkey with recent reported annual catches approaching the 1938 Soviet maximum; the loss rate is estimated to be high because of the use of guns as the harvesting method.

Limited catch statistics are available since 1927, except for Romania, and are generally reported only for all species combined in total metric weight. Analysis indicates that the exploitation rate was probably excessive at the height of the fishery in 1936 (12.5-20.0 %) and may remain so today for the Turkish fishery (7.9-100.8 %).

Annual Soviet aerial surveys initiated since the 1967 moratorium provide questionable estimates of total population size of Black Sea porpoises. Problems with these estimates and probably also with kill estimates preclude definite understanding of the present state of the population and indicate the need to refine both these statistics. Present observations are confined to recognition that the numbers of porpoise in the Black Sea have declined substantially to marginal levels due to the direct fishery; the present Turkish fishery is important, particularly as it continues now when stocks are probably reduced.

Résumé

Le dauphin commun, *Delphinus delphis*, le "dauphin" de la mer d'Azov, *Phocoena phocoena*, et le souffleur, *Tursiops truncatus*, sont pêchés aux armes à feu et au filet depuis 1870 environ dans la mer Noire et la mer d'Azov par l'URSS, la Turquie, la Bulgarie et la Roumanie. La diminution régulière des captures de l'URSS depuis le maximum soviétique de 135 000-140 000 animaux en 1938, malgré un effort de capture accru, a amené ce pays à adopter des restrictions saisonnières en 1962. La pêche a été entièrement arrêtée par l'URSS, la Roumanie et la Bulgarie en 1967. Le chiffre annuel des dernières captures soviétiques en 1964-66, 5 600-7 400 animaux, représente un effondrement majeur de la pêche, qui s'est accompagné de changements nettement marqués de la composition des captures par âge et par sexe. La composition par espèce était également modifiée, *D. delphis*, qui avait toujours été l'espèce dominante, cédant la place à *P. phocoena*. La pêche se poursuit en Turquie; les captures annuelles récentes signalées avoisineraient le record soviétique de 1938. On estime que le taux de perte est élevé par suite de l'emploi des armes à feu comme méthode d'exploitation.

On possède des statistiques de capture limitées depuis 1927, sauf pour la Roumanie. Elles donnent en général le poids total pour l'ensemble des espèces. L'analyse indique que le taux d'exploitation a été probablement excessif lors de l'apogée de la pêche en 1936 (12,5-20 %) et qu'il peut l'être encore dans la pêcherie turque (7,9-100,8 %).

Les enquêtes aériennes annuelles entreprises par les Soviétiques depuis le moratoire de 1967 fournissent des estimations d'une fiabilité contestable sur la taille totale des populations de marsouins de la mer Noire. L'incertitude de ces estimations et probablement aussi des estimations de la mortalité par pêche ne permet pas de connaître exactement l'état actuel de la population et prouve qu'il est nécessaire d'améliorer ces deux types de statistiques. A l'heure actuelle, on doit se borner à reconnaître que les effectifs des marsouins de la mer Noire ont subi un fléchissement substantiel et sont tombés à un niveau marginal du fait de la pêche directe. La pêche turque actuelle est d'autant plus importante qu'elle se poursuit à un moment où les stocks sont probablement réduits.

Extracto

Desde 1870, aproximadamente, la URSS, Turquía, Bulgaria y Rumania se dedican a la pesca de delfín común, *Delphinus delphis*, marsopa de Azov, *Phocoena phocoena*, y tursión, *Tursiops truncatus*, con redes y armas de fuego, en el mar Negro y el mar de Azov. La continua disminución de las capturas anuales de la Unión Soviética (a pesar del aumento del esfuerzo de captura) respecto a la cifra máxima de 135 000-140 000 animales conseguida en 1938 movió a ese país a introducir en 1962 restricciones, regulando la temporada de caza. En 1967, la URSS, Rumania y Bulgaria vedaron totalmente la captura de esos animales. Las últimas capturas anuales de la Unión Soviética (5 600-7 400 animales), correspondientes a 1964-66, reflejan el gran colapso de esa actividad y revelan notables cambios en la composición por edad y sexo de los animales capturados y en la composición por especies de las capturas, con un predominio de *P. phocoena* frente al predominio tradicional de *D. delphis*. En Turquía prosigue la explotación de esos delfínidos, con capturas que, en los últimos años, según los datos comunicados, se acercan a las cifras máximas de la Unión Soviética de 1938. Se calcula que el índice de pérdidas es elevado debido al empleo de armas de fuego.

Se dispone de estadísticas limitadas de captura desde 1927 (con exclusión de Rumania), que en general se refieren sólo al conjunto de todas las especies, indicando el peso total en unidades métricas. Los análisis realizados indican que probablemente el índice de explotación en el momento culminante de la pesquería (1936) era excesivo (12,5-20 por ciento) y tal vez siga siéndolo hoy día en Turquía (7,9-100,8 por ciento).

Los reconocimientos aéreos realizados anualmente por la Unión Soviética desde la veda de 1967 permiten hacer estimaciones, de valor cuestionable, sobre el volumen total de la población de delfines y marsopas del mar Negro; los problemas inherentes a esas estimaciones y, probablemente también, a las estimaciones de las capturas impiden conocer claramente la situación actual de las poblaciones y ponen de relieve la necesidad de mejorar ambas estadísticas. En la actualidad, lo único que se puede hacer es reconocer que el número de delfines y marsopas del mar Negro ha disminuido sustancialmente, como consecuencia de la explotación, reduciéndose a cifras marginales. Las actuales actividades pesqueras de Turquía son importantes, sobre todo porque probablemente las poblaciones han disminuido.

T.D. Smith
Southwest Fisheries Center, National Marine Fisheries Service, P.O. Box 271, La Jolla, California 92038, USA

Introduction

In 1962, the USSR adopted unilateral management restrictions on whaling in the international multispecies small cetacean fishery in the Black and Azov Seas, which took the form of a restriction on killing during the breeding season. In 1967, whaling by the USSR, Romania and Bulgaria was completely stopped. In Turkey whaling continues. The adoption of management restrictions by the other nations was prompted by steadily declining catches since 1939, and the catastrophic decline in catch in 1964-66.

The information available to me on this fishery comes from: Danilevsky and Tuyutyunnikov, 1968; Zemsky and Yablokov, 1974; Mitchell, in press – draft version; personal communication with Zemsky and Yablokov, December 1964, in La Jolla, California.

There are several other papers referred to in the above papers which would be valuable and copies are being sought. All of the references of which I am aware which may be directly relevant to the status of the Black Sea porpoise populations are listed in the bibliography.

History of the fishery

The catching of small cetaceans in the Black Sea apparently began circa 1870 (Zemsky and Yablokov, 1974). The earliest record I have been able to obtain is from 1927, when a catch of 9 300 animals by Soviet fishermen was reported (Zemsky and Yablokov, 1974).

The available statistics suggest a maximum Soviet catch of 135 to 140 000 animals in 1938. Subsequently, the catch apparently declined, until the whaling stopped in all countries except Turkey in 1966. Available catch statistics for the USSR, Bulgaria and Turkey are given in Table 1; the numbered notes indicate the variety of sources from which they were drawn. No information is available on the magnitude of the Romanian catch, but Jelescu (1960, quoted in Mitchell, 1974) describes the fishing techniques.

There are 3 species of small cetaceans involved in varying degrees in this fishery. These are *Delphinus delphis*, the common dolphin, *Phocoena phocoena*, the harbour porpoise, and *Tursiops truncatus*, the bottlenose dolphin. The catch statistics are generally available only for all species combined, as shown in the notes. It is known, however, that the common dolphin, *D. delphis*, has historically been predominant in the catch. Note that the catch records from the fishery have historically been reported in centners – hundred of kilogrammes. The formal English name for this quantity is quintal, and it corresponds approximately to 220 lb. The 9 300 animals figure reported for 1927 is apparently based on a conversion of one animal to approximately 54 kg (Zemsky and Yablokov, 1974). Thus the 1927 catch was probably first reported as 5 022 centners or 502.2 metric tonnes. The origin of the figure of 54 kg as the average weight of each animal in the catch statistics is unknown to me. Its accuracy depends on both the species composition and the age and sex composition of the catch. As no other conversion factors are available this has been used throughout this report.

Two methods of harvesting are used, guns and nets. The gun method apparently has a very high loss rate of wounded animals. The loss rate with the net fishery is considered small (Zemsky and Yablokov, 1974). Turkey, the only remaining country pursuing this fishery, uses the gun method (Zemsky and Yablokov, 1974).

With these points in mind, it appears that the Soviet fishery reached a peak in 1938 and then declined steadily. Thus, the average pre-war catch is listed as roughly twice that of the average post-war catch. This decline in the catch occurred despite greatly increased effort, both in quantity and quality. For instance, after the war, aerial spotting planes were

123

Table 1. Estimated numbers of small cetaceans killed in the Black Sea, by nation and for all nations, for all species, in thousands. Figures in parentheses indicate average catch over the time period covered by the arrows

Year	USSR	Bulgaria	Turkey	All Nations
1927	9.3[1]			
1928				
1929				
1930				
1931				
1932	(66.)[1]			
1933				
1934				
1935				(250-300)[3]
1936				
1937				
1938	134.-140.[2]			
1939				
1940				
1941*	≈0[18]		>0[19]	
1942*	≈0	1.7[11]	>0	
1943*	≈0		>0	
1944*	≈0		>0	
1945*	≈0		>0	
1946				
1947				
1948				
1949				
1950				
1951				
1952				
1953				
1954			(157-185.2)[7]	
1955	(≈33.0)[4]	31.0[6]		
1956				
1957				
1958				
1959				
1960			30.0-40.0[8]	
1961	46.5[5]			
1962	** [15]			
1963	**			
1964	**			
1965	** (5.6-7.4)[17]			
1966	*** [14] 0.0[16]			3.7[13]
1967	*** 0.0	*** [17] 0.0[17]	3.9[9]	1.0[13]
1968	*** 0.0	*** 0.0	37.4[9]	
1969	*** 0.0	*** 0.0		
1970	*** 0.0	*** 0.0		

Table 1. Estimated numbers of small cetaceans killed in the Black Sea, by nation and for all nations, for all species, in thousands. Figures in parentheses indicate average catch over the time period covered by the arrows (*concluded*)

Year		USSR		Bulgaria	Turkey	All Nations
1971	***	0.0	***	0.0		
1972	***	0.0	***	0.0	35.2[9]	
1973	***	0.0	***	0.0	129.5[9]	
1974	***	0.0	***	0.0		

    * Indicates war years;
  ** Indicates summer season fishery restriction;
*** Indicates complete fishery restriction.

[1] (Zemsky and Yablokov, 1974).
[2] (Zemsky and Yablokov, 1974) maximum catch reported.
[3] (Zemsky and Yablokov, 1974) "Summary catch of all Black Sea countries" to compare with abundance estimate for the thirties from Arseniev, Zemsky and Studenetsskaya, 1973.
[4] (Zemsky and Yablokov, 1974) "(The catch) in 1946-66 ... hardly reached half of this number" referring to 1927-38 average of 66 000 dolphins.
[5] (Zemsky and Yablokov, 1974) apparently maximum catch by USSR since war years.
[6] (Zemsky and Yablokov, 1974) maximum catch by Bulgaria.
[7] (Danilevsky and Tyutyunnikov, 1968).
[8] Mitchell (1975) quoted in Zemsky and Yablokov, 1974.
[9] (Zemsky and Yablokov, 1974).
[11] (Zemsky and Yablokov, 1974).
[12] (Danilevsky and Tyutyunnikov, 1968).
[13] (Danilevsky and Tyutyunnikov, 1968).
[14] (Danilevsky and Tyutyunnikov, 1968).
[15] (Zemsky and Yablokov, 1974) summer fishery restriction as of 1 May 1966.
[16] (Zemsky and Yablokov, 1974) catch effectively zero, amounting to "several dozens a year only".
[17] (Zemsky and Yablokov, 1974).
[18] (Zemsky and Yablokov, 1974).
[19] (Danilevsky and Tyutyunnikov, 1968).

introduced, which increased gear effectiveness (Zemsky and Yablokov, 1974). It does not appear, further, that any respite which may have occurred during the war benefited the porpoise populations appreciably. The catch of 5 600-7 400 animals per year reported for 1964 to 1966 represents a major collapse of the fishery (Danilevsky and Tuyutyunnikov, 1968). Accompanying this there has apparently been a marked change in the composition of the catch, by age, sex and species. It seems that earlier the catch was roughly equally divided between the sexes. In the 1963 and 1964 seasons the catch was composed of 70-75 % young, and pregnant or nursing females. This may have been associated with an extension of the fishing grounds (Danilevsky and Tuyutyunnikov, 1968). Similarly, the predominant species in the catch changed from *D. delphis* (80-90 %) to *P. phocoena* (Danilevsky and Tuyutyunnikov, 1968).

Note that *P. phocoena* is a small animal, with a maximum length of 167 cm for males and 180 cm for females (Tomilin, 1967). The maximum weight appears to be around 56 kg (Danilevsky and Tuyutyunnikov, 1968). This compares with maximum lengths of the order of 2 and 3 m for *D. delphis* and *T. truncatus*, respectively.

Referring again to Table 1, the Turkish fishery as reported is obviously important, and especially now when stocks are probably reduced. Despite the upheaval during the second world war, and the cessation of the Soviet fishery, the Turkish fishery continued (Danilevsky and Tuyutyunnikov, 1968). In addition, the use of guns means that the loss rate is high. In the period 1951-56 the average annual catch exceeded the maximum Soviet annual catch in 1938. Similarly, the reported catch in the last 2 years has approached that 1938 maximum. These data together with the high loss rate, suggest either an extremely intense fishery on a locally greater abundance of porpoise, or

Table 2. Population size estimates in thousands, their natural logarithm, and percent change between years, after Zemsky and Yablokov, 1974.

Year	Tursiops			Delphinus			Phocoena			Total		
	Pop. ('000)	Nat. log.	% Change	Pop. ('000)	Nat. log.	% Change	Pop. ('000)	Nat. log.	% Change	Pop. ('000)	Nat. log.	% Change
1967	65.7	4.19	+ 9.1	145.6	4.98	− 80.6	23.3	3.15	+ 25.3	234.6	5.46	− 44.9
1968	71.7	4.27	+ 91.1	28.3	3.34	− 7.1	29.2	3.37	− 58.2	129.2	4.86	+ 35.8
1969	137.0	4.92	− 73.0	26.3	3.27	+457.0	12.6	2.50	+ 100.8	175.5	5.17	+ 18.5
1970	37.0	3.61	+280.5	146.5	4.99	+ 94.3	24.5	3.20	− 25.3	208.0	5.34	+113.4
1971	140.8	4.95	− 19.4	284.7	5.65	− 11.8	18.3	2.91	− 19.7	443.8	6.10	− 14.6
1972	113.5	4.73	− 72.7	251.0	5.53	− 16.0	14.7	2.67	+ 126.5	379.2	5.94	− 27.4
1973	31.0	3.43		211.0	5.35		33.3	3.51		275.3	5.61	− 15.1
1974	—			—			—			(233.7)		
Mean	85.24		91.0	155.77		111.1	22.21		59.3	263.66		45.0
SDEV	45.46			102.24			7.64			112.35		
SD ERROR	17.18			38.64			2.89			42.46		
MEAN (LN)	4.30			4.73			3.05			5.50		
SDEV (LN)	0.61			1.00			0.36			0.43		
SER (LN)	0.23			0.38			0.14			0.16		

gross inaccuracies in the catch statistics. If the former, it does seem likely that a fishery of this magnitude could cause a reduction in the porpoise populations. This will be discussed in conjunction with the estimates of stock sizes.

With shifting species and age and sex composition it is unlikely that the numbers of dolphin per metric tonne of reported catch has remained constant. With the shift toward *P. phocoena* in the latter part of the fishery the average weight probably declined and hence the estimates of numbers killed are probably too low. In order to evaluate truly the impact of the fishery it is important to be able to determine the numbers of animals rather accurately.

Population sizes

The aggregate population size of all species of porpoise in the Black and Azov Seas was estimated for the thirties at 1.5 to 2.0 million animals (Arseniév, Zemsky and Studenetsskaya, 1973; quoted by Zemsky and Yablokov, 1974).

In conjunction with the Soviet moratorium on harvesting porpoise, aerial surveys have been conducted twice a year since 1967. These have been designed to obtain estimates of the population sizes of the various species, and were apparently the basis of population estimates quoted in *Nature* (Anon., 1974). Since that article [1] additional information on these estimates of population size have become available in Zemsky and Yablokov, 1974. These authors provide estimates by species, as shown in Table 2. It can be seen that these estimates vary considerably from year to year and that no obvious trends are identifiable. In Fig. 1 the natural logarithm of the population

---

[1] Note that in 1973 the population estimate is here given as 800 000, "three times the 1965 figure". I have no figure for 1965 and the 1973 estimate given in Zemsky and Yablokov, 1974, is 275 300 animals.

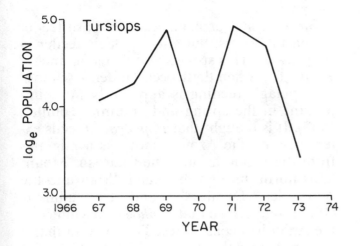

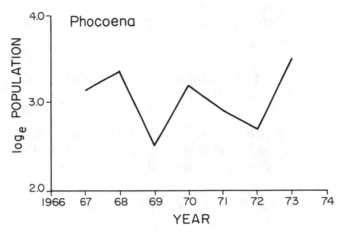

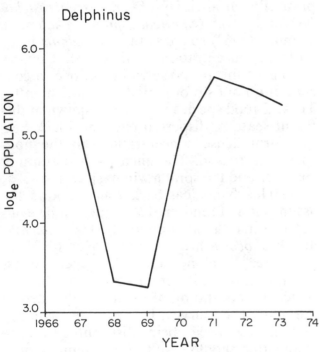

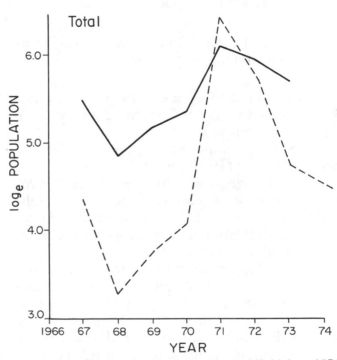

FIG. 1. – Logarithms of population size versus year for estimates of porpoise population size given in Zemsky and Yablokov, 1974, by species and total.

size estimates is plotted against time. It does not seem likely that cetacean populations, with their low reproductive rates and long lifespan, could experience fluctuations of this magnitude.

Some of the assumptions made in deriving these estimates are given. These include: (i) random distribution of porpoise; (ii) search of a path 3.0 km wide, and (iii) counting of one half of the animals in this path.

From personal coversations, I understand that:

— some large schools were seen and counted outside this path;

— the aircraft left the track line if the sighted school was large for a close fly by, and then returned to the track;

— the flight speed was 4 km/min;

— the area of the Black Sea inhabited by porpoise is 413 000 km²;

— there are no small cetaceans in the Azov Sea (because of pollution), and

— the same route-march or trackline was followed on each of the surveys.

The location of this track is not given. It is not known how the results from the 2 surveys were combined each year.

Several comments are given in Zemsky and Yablokov (1974) about these estimates of population size. The estimates of the *Delphinus* population size are considered more reliable than those for *Phocoena* and *Tursiops*, because *Delphinus* is a more pelagic animal and the other 2 more inshore.

The high variability of these estimates, even for the more pelagic *Delphinus* population, appears most likely due to a failure to meet the assumption of randomness of the spatial distribution of the populations. Some information on the biology of these 3 species is of interest here. As mentioned in Zemsky and Yablokov (1974), *Phocoena* and *Tursiops* are generally found nearer shore than *Delphinus*. Sokolov (1971) referring to Kleinenberg (1956) describes *Tursiops truncatus* as feeding generally on benthic organisms, fairly near shore. It is restricted in distribution to the northern and eastern shores of the Black Sea (Tomilin, 1967). Sokolov also describes *Pho-*

coena phocoena as being a benthic fish feeder in coastal waters, but also a pelagic feeder in deep water. This species also feeds on anchovy-like fish when these occur in dense schools. This pelagic feeding is apparently most important in the spring and autumn (Tomilin, 1967). It is thought that *P. phocoena* feeds extensively on the Azov anchovy as it migrates from the region around the Caucasus Mountains north through the Kerch Strait into the Azov Sea. Danilevsky and Tyutyunnikov (1968) suggest also that *P. phocoena* winters on the Anatolian coast (West Turkey) and that it does not enter the Azov Sea. This latter point was also suggested by Yablokov (pers. comm.), citing pollution levels.

In distinction to these other 2 species, *Delphinus delphis* is a pelagic animal, feeding primarily on anchovy (*Engraulis encrasicholus*) and sprat (*Spratella spratus phaleriza*). Tomilin (1967) suggests that *D. delphis* feeds on local concentrations of these fish. Congregations of this porpoise will form over a concentration of fish for periods of 1 to 2 months. These 2 food species apparently spawn at different seasons, dispersed over the Black Sea, but form dense concentrations in the non-spawning season. The anchovy is a summer spawner and the sprat a winter spawner.

This biological background allows the assumption of random distribution to be evaluated. First, the assumption that *T. truncatus* and *P. phocoena* are distributed over the whole Black Sea, let alone randomly, appears questionable. It would seem necessary to obtain a better understanding of the area inhabited at the time of the survey. However, the assumption of these species being distributed over the whole area should result in a systematic bias, not in high variability. Second, the large concentrations of *D. delphis* feeding on the anchovy during the summer (the time of the surveys) will tend to increase the variability of the resulting estimates. As the track lines were not randomly placed this could also result in a possible bias in the estimates. This aspect could be evaluated further by examining the variability between the surveys within a year.

The accurate determination of the area inhabited is important to avoid a consistent bias in the resulting population estimates. Similarly, the accurate determination of the path effectively searched is important. The assumption of seeing one half of the animals within a 3 km path implies an effective path width of 1.5 km, or 0.75 km on a side. One interpretation of this is that the number of sightings made is the same as would have been made if a path 0.75 km on a side had been inspected completely.

Using this figure, one obtains the proportion of the area effectively searched as (8 000 × 1.5/413 000) = 0.029. Thus the number of animals sighted would be divided by this fraction to obtain the total population estimate.

This assumed path width can be checked against 2 other examples. Tomilin (1967) reports on observations made from an aeroplane in the late thirties, referring to Tsalkin (1936-38) and Golenchenko (1939). The sources of these references are not available. Flying at a speed of 130-180 km/h and at 200-500 m altitude, Tomilin suggests it is possible to see dolphin schools up to a maximum distance of about 7 km. He also reports that "most convenient" observation can only be made if the aircraft flies directly over or within approximately 1.5 km of the school. Tomilin notes that visibility deteriorates markedly if the sea state exceeds Beaufort 2. The assumption made about visibility is not inconsistent with these values, although perhaps soewhat conservative.

The second comparison is with figures given in Smith (1975). In an aerial survey in the eastern tropical Pacific in early 1974, the distance of sighting of each school was recorded. An average distance at which schools were sighted of 1.4 km was reported. Following Seber (1973) this average sighting distance can be interpreted as the effective path search on 1 side of the aeroplane.

This can be compared with the value of 0.75 km computed above, suggesting that the visibility in the Black Sea surveys is much less than that in the eastern tropical Pacific survey, or that one or more of the assumptions listed above are false.

Status of the stocks

A simple statistic which can be used to evaluate the impact of harvesting on a population is the crude exploitation rate, the ratio between the total number harvested and the total population size. In the Black Sea porpoise harvesting, the kill is not generally available by species, so it is necessary to compute this ratio for all stocks taken together.

In the thirties the total size of all stocks was estimated at 1.5-2.0 million. Comparing this to the estimated kill in 1936 of 0.25-0.36 million, one obtains a crude exploitation rate in the range of 12.5-20.0 %.

It is difficult to choose a most probable population size from the estimates given in Zemsky and Yablokov. However, if the general range of the estimates of 129 200-444 000 animals is reasonable, the current exploitation rates due to the Turkish kill can be computed. The estimates of the Turkish kill in this decade vary from 35 200-130 000 animals per year. These estimates suggest crude exploitation rates of 7.9-100.8 %. The observation that the Turkish harvesting has continued at high levels in 1973 and 1974 suggests that the population estimates are probably in the high end of the range.

Beyond these crude analyses there is little that can be said about the status of the stocks. The problems with the available estimates of population size, and probably also with the kill estimates, preclude a consistent understanding. It would appear necessary to refine both of those statistics, but especially the population size estimates. As discussed above, this latter would be possible by better determining both the area inhabited at the time of the survey and the effective path width searched.

Summary

I have assembled and reviewed what is available to me on the status of the Black Sea small cetacean populations. It is apparent that a fishery directly on these animals has reduced their abundance to marginal levels. By 1966 this reduction was sufficient to cause management action to be taken in some countries. The kill was probably excessive at the height of the fishery (12.5-20.0 %), and may still be so today (7.0-100.8 %).

However, the information on numbers killed and on numbers in the population is not sufficiently precise to allow for definite statements. Perhaps the most telling observation is that the numbers of small cetaceans in the Black Sea has declined substantially.

References

ARSENIEV, V.A., V.A. ZEMSKY and I.S. STUDENETSSKAYA, 1973 Morskie mlekopitayushchie (Marine mammals). Moskva, Pischevaja Promishlennost'.

DANILEVSKY, N.N. and V.P. TUYUTYUNNIKOV, Present 1968 state of Black Sea dolphins described. *Rybn. Khoz. Mosk.*, 11:25-7.

GOLENCHENKO, Unknown reference in Tomilin (1956) 1939 gives information on early aerial observations of dolphin in Black Sea.

JELESCU, N., The industrial fishery for dolphins in the 1960 Black Sea-Rumanian coast. *Bul. Inst. Cercet. Piscic.*, 19(2):64-70.

KLEINENBERG, S.E., Marine mammals of the Black and 1956 Azov Seas. Moscow, Akademia Nauka.

MITCHELL, E., Porpoise, dolphin and small whale fishe- 1975 ries of the world: status and problems. *IUCN Monogr.*, (3):129 p.

SEBER G.A.F., The estimation of animal abundance and 1973 related parameters. Beckenham, Kent, Griffin.

SMITH, T.D., Estimates of sizes of two populations of 1975 porpoise (*Stenella*) in the eastern tropical Pacific Ocean. *Admin. Rep. Southwest Fish. Cent. (SWFC) La Jolla*, (LJ-75-67).

SOKOLOV, V., Cetacean research in the USSR. *In* In- 1971 vestigations on Cetacea, edited by G. Pilleri. Berne, Switzerland, Brain Anatomy Institute, vol. 3. Pt. 2:317:46.

TOMILIN, A.G., Mammals of the USSR and adjacent 1967 countries. Vol. 9. Cetacea. Jerusalem, Israel Program for Sci. Transl., IPST (1124):742 p. Translation of Zveri SSSR i prilezhashchikh stran: Kitoobraznye (1957).

TSALKIN, V.I., Unknown reference in Tomilin (1967) 1936-38 gives information on early aerial observations of dolphin in Black Sea.

ZEMSKY, V. and A.V. YABLOKOV, Catch statistics, short 1974 history of exploitation and present status of *Delphinus delphis, Tursiops truncatus* and *Phocoena phocoena* in the Black Sea. Working paper presented to the Meeting of the ACMRR/FAO, La Jolla, California.

ANON., Anthill and tiger counting in the Soviet Union. 1974 *Nature, Lond.*, 250:12-3.

CHANGE IN OCCURRENCE OF THE HARBOUR PORPOISE, *PHOCOENA PHOCOENA*, IN DANISH WATERS AS ILLUSTRATED BY CATCH STATISTICS FROM 1834 TO 1970

S.H. Andersen

Abstract

During 24 seasons (November, December and January) from 1834 to 1892, 27 992 harbour porpoises, *Phocoena phocoena*, were taken in the Strait of Lille Baelt, Denmark, with a mean annual harvest of 1 122. Catches during the 2 world wars were between 230 and about 700 animals. From this data and the author's own field observations in 1969/70, when about 20 animals were seen, it can be concluded that the present migration of harbour porpoises through Danish waters is less than before.

Résumé

Au cours des 24 campagnes (novembre, décembre et janvier) qui se sont déroulées de 1834 à 1892, 27 992 marsouins communs, *Phocoena phocoena*, ont été capturés dans le détroit de Lille Baelt, au Danemark, soit une capture annuelle moyenne de 1 122 animaux. Pendant la période s'étendant entre les deux guerres, les captures ont été de 230 à environ 700 animaux. Sur la base de ces données et des propres observations de l'auteur sur le terrain en 1969/70, quand on a aperçu quelque 20 animaux, on peut conclure que les migrations actuelles des dauphins communs à travers les eaux danoises sont inférieures à ce qu'elles étaient.

Extracto

Entre 1834 y 1892, en el curso de 24 campañas (noviembre, diciembre y enero), se capturaron en el Lille Baelt, Dinamarca, 27 992 marsopas comunes, *Phocoena phocoena*, con una captura anual media de 1 122 animales. Durante las dos guerras mundiales las capturas variaron entre 230 y 700 animales. A partir de esos datos, y de las observaciones hechas directamente por el autor en 1969/70, en que avistó 20 animales, se puede concluir que los movimientos migratorios de la marsopa común en aguas danesas son hoy menores que antes.

S.H. Andersen
Fysiologisk Institut, Odense Universit, Niels Bohrs Allé, 5000 Odense, Denmark

131

In many sites of its world wide distribution the harbour porpoise is known to migrate and this held true until about 1950 for the harbour porpoise in Danish and Baltic waters. In early spring the animals were seen migrating through Danish waters to the Baltic Sea. Some stayed in Danish waters, where harbour porpoises are still common most of the year. In November, December and part of January a migration out of the Baltic took place. At this time the animals were schooling, in contrast to the more scattered inward migration in spring.

Today, migration to and from the Baltic Sea has almost completely ceased. This statement is based upon a comparison of the catch of porpoises from 1834 to 1892 with the much lower catch during world wars I and II, and on the author's own observations.

The porpoise hunt in the narrow strait separating the Danish peninsula Jutland from the island of Funen has already been described in English (van Heel, 1962) but the catch statistics from the porpoise hunting guild have not been published before.

The hunting guild dates back to 1593, but written information on hunting yield is only available for the periods 1834-45, 1873-74, and 1880-91. The main product obtained from porpoise catch was oil for lighting. The guild was cancelled in 1898, possibly due to the decreased catch but also due to the competition from cheaper mineral oil products.

The following table gives the catch records available from the porpoise guild's account books.

Catching took place only in November, December, sometimes extending until the middle of January, and the yearly yields seem astonishingly high to Danes of today. The total catch during these three periods totalling 24 years, was 27 992, with a seasonal mean of 1 122 porpoises.

The hunt was resumed in the same waters during the two world wars, and the catches obtained are shown in Table 2.

In 1969-1970 the author was engaged full-time in hunting for live porpoises to be

Table 1. Recorded catches (nos.) of harbour porpoise, *Phocoena phocoena*, by the porpoise hunting guild

Season	No. of catches	Season	No. of catches
1834-35:	1 684	1880-81:	1 831
1835-36:	1 215	1881-82:	1 814
1836-37:	1 416	1882-83:	1 545
1837-38:	653	1883-84:	1 505
1838-39:	886	1884-85:	1 552
1839-40:	657	1885-86:	1 318
1840-41:	683	1886-87:	1 349
1841-42:	793	1887-88:	1 009
1842-43:	1 395	1888-89:	1 589
1843-44:	1 079	1889-90:	992
1844-45:	330	1890-91:	301
1873-74:	1 801	1891-92:	521

kept in captivity. Between April and January, and in the same waters in which the hunters worked in the old days, we observed only about 20 animals, many of which seemed to be the same individuals.

It is concluded from the material presented here that the migration of the harbour porpoise through Danish waters to and from the Baltic Sea is now only a shadow of what it was.

For a discussion on the causes of this alteration see Andersen, 1972.

Table 2. Catches of *Phocoena phocoena* in world wars I and II

Season	No. of catches	
1916-17:	approx.	300
1917-18:	–	600
1918-19:	–	700
1941-42:		230
1042-43:		329
1943-44:		421

References

ANDERSEN, S.H., On the state of stock of common por-
1972   poise in Danish waters. ICES, C.M. Mar.
        Mamm. Comm., 1972/N:6 (mimeo).

VAN HEEL, W.D., Sound and Cetacea. *Neth. J. Sea Res.*,
1962   1(4).

DDT RESIDUES IN BLUBBER OF HARBOUR PORPOISE, *PHOCOENA PHOCOENA* (L.), FROM EASTERN CANADIAN WATERS DURING THE FIVE-YEAR PERIOD 1969-1973

D.E. Gaskin, M. Holdrinet **and** R. Frank

Abstract

Samples of blubber from 60 male and 55 female harbour porpoises (*Phocoena phocoena*) collected from 1969 to 1973, all but 11 from the east and west coast approaches to the Bay of Fundy, were analysed for DDT residues; the results were then compared according to sex, age class and year of collection. Factors complicating the study included variation of the levels of residue in individuals of the same age, perhaps due in part to differences in diet, and the relatively small size of samples. DDT residue levels showed a positive correlation with age in male harbour porpoises and a negative though less pronounced correlation in females, indicating that a significant portion of the accumulated DDT may be passed by females to the foetus or to the calf during lactation. It appears that DDT levels in porpoises of both sexes collected at the end of the study were very markedly lower than those of animals collected at the beginning. No close correlation of residue levels with body size was apparent nor was it possible to detect whether there is any significant annual fluctuation in residue levels. Differences between residue levels in some of the animals collected in North American waters outside the Bay of Fundy and the average levels of the Bay of Fundy group, may be due to differences in reproductive history, in diet, in oceanic conditions and in the amount of DDT that has entered the different habitats.

Résumé

Des échantillons de graisse provenant de 60 mâles et 55 femelles de marsouin commun (*Phocoena phocoena*), prélevés de 1969 à 1973 et provenant tous, sauf onze, des approches côtières est et ouest de la Baie de Fundy, ont été analysés pour détecter la présence de résidus de DDT. Les résultats ont ensuite été comparés selon le sexe, la classe d'âge et l'année de prélèvement. Les facteurs compliquant l'étude comprenaient des variations du niveau des résidus chez des sujets du même âge, dues peut-être à des différences de régime alimentaire et à la taille relativement réduite des échantillons. Les niveaux de résidus de DDT montraient une corrélation positive avec l'âge chez les marsouins mâles et une corrélation négative, bien que moins prononcée, chez les femelles, ce qui indiquait qu'une fraction significative du DDT accumulé peut passer des femelles au fœtus ou au veau pendant l'allaitement. Il apparaît que les niveaux de DDT chez les marsouins des deux sexes recueillis à la fin de l'étude étaient très nettement inférieurs à ceux des animaux pris au début. Aucune étroite corrélation entre le niveau des résidus et la taille du corps n'est apparue et il n'a pas non plus été possible de savoir s'il existe une fluctuation annuelle significative des niveaux de résidus. Les différences de niveaux de résidus chez certains des animaux capturés dans les eaux nord-américaines, hors de la baie de Fundy, et les niveaux moyens du groupe de la baie de

Fundy peuvent être dues à des différences du cycle de reproduction, du régime alimentaire, des conditions océaniques et des quantités de DDT qui ont pénétré dans les différents habitats.

Extracto

Para determinar la presencia de residuos de DDT se analizaron muestras de grasa de 60 machos y 55 hembras de marsopa común (*Phocoena phocoena*) recogidas todas ellas entre 1969 y 1973 y procedentes (exceptuadas 11) de animales capturados en los extremos oriental y occidental de la bahía de Fundy, comparando luego los resultados según el sexo, la clase de edad y el año en que se había recogido la muestra. Entre los factores que complican el estudio pueden citarse la variación en la presencia de residuos entre individuos de la misma edad, debida quizás en parte a diferencias en su dieta alimentaria, y el volumen relativamente pequeño de las muestras. Los residuos de DDT mostraron una correlación positiva con la edad en las marsopas machos y una correlación negativa, aunque menos pronunciada, en las hembras, lo que indica que las hembras pueden pasar una porción importante del DDT acumulado al feto o a la cría durante la lactación. Los niveles de DDT encontrados en marsopas de ambos sexos recogidos a finales del estudio resultaron notablemente inferiores a los presentes en animales recogidos al principio. No se encontró ninguna relación estrecha entre el nivel de los residuos y la talla corporal, ni fue posible detectar la presencia de fluctuaciones anuales importantes en el nivel de los residuos. Las diferencias entre los niveles de residuos de algunos de los animales recogidos en aguas estadounidenses, fuera de la bahía de Fundy, y los niveles medios del grupo de la bahía de Fundy puede deberse a diferencias en el ciclo reproductivo, en la dieta, en las condiciones oceánicas y en la cantidad de DDT que penetra en los distintos hábitats.

D.E. Gaskin
Department of Zoology, University of Guelph, Guelph, Ontario N1G 2W1, Canada

M. Holdrinet
Pesticide Residue Testing Laboratory, Ontario Department of Agriculture, Guelph, Ontario, Canada

R. Frank
Pesticide Residue Testing Laboratory, Ontario Department of Agriculture, Guelph, Ontario, Canada

Introduction

Preliminary findings concerning DDT and dieldrin levels in harbour porpoises, *Phocoena phocoena* (L.), from the Bay of Fundy region during 1969 and 1970 were presented by Gaskin, Holdrinet and Frank (1971). In view of some high levels recorded (averages of 307.00 ppm in extractable fat of weaned and adult males and 214.00 ppm in immature and resting females), sampling was continued in subsequent years to study possible trends in the levels. Since DDT was not being used in large quantities in the watershed regions of the major rivers feeding the Bay of Fundy after 1967, it was hoped that a rather rapid reduction in tissue levels would be observed. In the present paper, some of the results obtained for the 5-year period 1969-73 are discussed. Residues of PCBs and other organochlorine compounds are still under study, and results will be given elsewhere.

Materials and methods

Samples of blubber and other tissues were collected from 115 harbour porpoises (60 males and 55 females) taken during the period June 1969 to September 1973 by shooting at sea or from fish traps, in eastern North American waters. Specimens obtained were aged from examination of thin ground sections of mandibular teeth following the methods and interpretations of Gaskin and Blair (1977). A piece of blubber, 2 × 2 cm in area, free of underlying epaxial muscle and visible connective tissue, was taken from the right-hand side of each specimen 10 cm behind and above the base of the pectoral flipper. Tissues were chilled to seawater temperature (about 10 °C) and frozen to − 20 °C as soon as field conditions permitted (2-7 hours). For chlorinated hydrocarbon analysis, macerated representative samples were subjected to exhaustive soxhlet fat extraction with hexane and 1 g of extracted fat of each was cleared using a 5 % deactivated Florisil r column, following the method of Langlois, Stemp and Liska (1964); Gaskin, Holdrinet and Frank (1971); and Gaskin *et al.* (1973). Chlorinated hydrocarbons were eluted using dichloromethane in hexane. A preliminary gas chromatographic run was used to assess levels of DDTs and PCBs. If significant, a suitable aliquot was dissolved in acetone and run through a column of activated coconut charcoal to separate the DDT group from PCBs, this method being a modification of that described by Berg, Diosady and Rees (1972). 25 % acetone in ether was used to elute the DDT group first; PCBs were removed from the column with benzene. Both fractions were passed through a mixed phase column, and gas chromatography was used for residue qualification and quantification.

Results are presented as obtained, uncorrected for recovery percentages, the latter being checked periodically by fortification directly into the oil obtained from hexane extraction. Average recoveries were: p,p'DDE-98 %; p,p'-TDE-95 %; o,p'-DDT-91 %; p,p'-DDT-90 %, in total. Further studies of the PCB residues are in progress and results will be reported elsewhere, as will data on DDT group residues samples.

Results and discussion

The sex and age class distribution of specimens in this study are shown in Table 1. Unless indicated in the footnote to this table, all specimens were taken in waters around Deer, Campobello and Grand Manan Islands and from the Digby Gut and the Annapolis Basin. Table 2 shows the DDT levels obtained.

The magnitude of organochlorine hydrocarbon residues can be influenced by a number of factors. The most significant of these variables appear to include: (i) the age of

137

Table 1. Age distribution of harbour porpoises from Bay of Fundy approaches collected during 1969-73, with supplementary data on specimens taken outside this immediate area. [1] Numbers of males, females given separately

Years	Year classes																		Totals	
	0		1		2		3		4		5		6		7		8 + [2]			
	M	F	M	F	M	F	M	F	M	F	M	F	M	F	M	F	M	F	M	F
1969	1	0	1	3	0	4	0	0	0	1	1	4	2	0	2	0	1	0	8	12
1970	2	2	3	2	0	0	1	0	0	2	0	0	0	0	1	0	1	1	9	7
1971	2	1	4	3	1	1	0	2	1	0	2	3	0	0	2	0	1	1	14	10
1972	2	0	2	4	3	1	1	0	1	1	2	1	3	0	0	0	1	0	15	7
1973	2	1	3	1	1	2	0	1	0	1	2	2	2	1	0	1	2	1	12	11
Totals	9	4	13	13	5	8	2	3	2	5	7	10	7	1	5	1	6	3	57	47

[1] The other 11 specimens from outside the Bay of Fundy approaches included: 1 from St. Mary's Bay head in 1972 (F, 8); 2 from Narragansett Bay, R.I., in 1971 (F, 1), and 1972 (F, 0); 1 from Boothbay Harbor, Me., in 1971 (F, 1); 1 from southeastern Newfoundland in 1973 (F, 0); 1 from Souris, P.E.I. in 1972 (M, 5); and 5 from the southeastern Atlantic coast of Nova Scotia in 1970 (F, 4); 1971 (F, 6) and 1972 (F, 1; M, 5; F, 7). Sex and ages of these specimens given in parentheses.

[2] Includes five 8-year-olds (M, 3; F, 2); one 9-year-old female; and three males aged 10, 11 and 13 years, respectively.

the specimen; (ii) the regional level of contaminants and the corresponding influx-efflux relationship; (iii) the reproductive state and history of the individual, especially in the case of females, and (iv) the particular diet and feeding regime of the animals concerned. Direct uptake from water is possible, but the quantity of organochlorines obtained by a marine mammal by this route is likely to be very small in comparison to the amount obtained from food. Variation in body size at any given age is not insignificant in this species, but since one might expect larger specimens to have a correspondingly slightly higher proportional food intake, any influence on residue levels probably lies well within the observed individual variation. The latter is large and may be attributed to different exposure to contaminants through dietary preference or food item availability, both of which may vary from one local region to another with time, or to unknown differences in individual physiological condition. In the present study, interpretation is further complicated by the relatively small sample sizes of subcategories, despite the fact that 115 specimens is a respectable total by large mammal standards. Year-class data have been pooled in a number of cases when this seemed appropriate and not misleading.

The majority of animals examined in this study were captured between the end of May and the middle of September during the 5-year study period. The species is strongly migratory in the coastal waters of the Maritime Provinces of Canada (Gaskin, Arnold and Blair, 1974) and the numbers of animals in the Bay of Fundy drop very markedly at the onset of the autumn (Neave and Wright, 1968). It was not possible to ascertain whether there is any significant annual fluctuation in residue levels, but such evidence as is available suggests that this too would be masked by the large degree of individual variation even it if did occur. For example, two 2-year old females, both sexually immature, were taken on 2 and 3 September 1969. Both were between 132 and 133 cm in total body length, and in all other appearances were nearly identical healthy young females. Study of tooth sections suggested that one might have been a month or so older than the other, but probably not more. Yet the fractionally smaller specimen contained 132 ppm of total DDT in extractable fat and the other only 56 ppm. This comparison also seems to militate against close corre-

Table 2. Minimum, maximum and mean (in parentheses) levels of Σ DDT residues in blubber of harbour porpoises (*Phocoena phocoena* (L.)) from the Bay of Fundy approaches, Canada, 1969-73. All results in ppm in extractable fat, from thawed tissue puree

Year classes	0	1	2	3	4	5	6	7	8+
Males									
1969	288.7	150.8	–	–	–	305.4	225.6-226.0	371.0-520.0	447.9
1970	75.1-186.7	163.1-416.0 (267.5)	–	337.0	–	–	–	291.0	326.0
1971	30.3-45.1	46.4-86.5 (65.7)	57.0	–	183.8	169.8-377.8	–	186.2-203.1	556.3
1972	62.7-265.8	50.1-95.6	40.4-81.9 (55.4)	87.3	194.4	74.9-86.5	60.1-107.3 (84.3)	–	411.8
1973	25.4-132.9	16.2-28.1 (23.4)	16.1	–	–	45.1-292.0	89.2-131.9	–	205.7-221.6
Females									
1969	–	183.5-269.5 (212.9)	56.2-352.0 (165.0)	–	290.0	108.9-122.0 (115.6)	–	–	–
1970	154.8-197.3	131.0-436.0	–	–	54.8-142.2	–	–	–	93.7
1971	197.6	76.7-227.9 (160.1)	102.5	87.0-114.1	–	34.1-114.4 (52.5)	–	–	26.4
1972	–	16.3-102.0 (52.7)	92.5	–	17.2	19.0	–	–	–
1973	126.0	32.1	29.9-45.1	42.0	87.2	57.8-64.9	55.5	110.1	15.8

lation of residue levels in blubber with body size.

Data summarized in Fig. 1 show conclusively that in the male harbour porpoises in these waters since 1969, total DDT shows a positive correlation with age, so it can be presumed that whatever the seasonal variation in rates of uptake, presumably mostly from the major food items, which are herring, *Clupea harengus* Linn., and mackerel, *Scomber scombrus* Linn., in this region (Smith and Gaskin, 1974), there continues to be a net uptake over an extended period of time.

The opposite situation occurs in the females, although the correlations are less striking (Fig. 2). There is a clear indication that a biologically significant negative correlation is present between total DDT residue levels and age in these females in each year of the 5-year period. The simplest explanation of this effect is that a significant fraction of the DDT titre in the depot fat is transferred to the foetus or to the calf during lactation. The erratic nature of residue levels in the older females probably relates to reproductive history. Some females may calve almost every year, since we have a

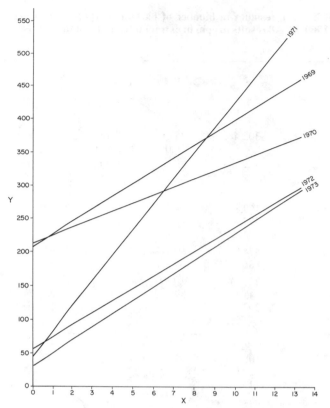

FIG. 1. – Correlation of magnitude of DDT residues in parts per million of extractable fat (Y) with age (x) in male harbour porpoises from the Bay of Fundy approaches during 1969-1973, inclusive. To avoid multiplications involving zero during the statistical analysis, all age classes were treated as x + 1 during computation, thus removing year class 0 one step from the y axis. Fitted equations obtained from the data were as follows:

1969 : y = 187.51 + 19.53x (0.05-P-0.02)
1970 : y = 202.04 + 12.56x (0.10-P-0.05)
1971 : y =   8.82 + 38.33x (0.01-P-0.001)
1972 : y = 37.64 + 18.60x (0.01-P-0.001)
1973 : y =   7.84 + 20.65x (0.01-P-0.001).

ings do not seem to agree with those of Fisher and Harrison (1970), although more work is needed.

In Figs. 3 and 4, the magnitude of residues present in harbour porpoise blubber are shown, segregated by year classes, for the 5-year period. In both sexes, it would seem very clear that total DDT levels are down very markedly by the end of the period from the 1969 levels. Once again, the situation is more clear-cut in the males than in the females. In the case of females age 6-years and older, no relationship could be found; this may result from sample heterogeneity with respect to re-

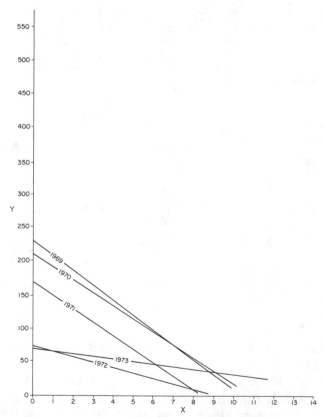

FIG. 2. – Correlation of magnitude of DDT residue in parts per million of extractable fat (Y) with age (x) in female harbour porpoises from the Bay of Fundy approaches during 1969-1973, inclusive. Data treated as indicated in Fig. 1. Fitted equations obtained from the data were as follows:

1969 : y = 249.01 – 21.53x (0.15-P-0.10)
1970 : y = 230.40 – 18.90x (0.20-P-0.15)
    but 1969 + 1970 : y = 238.00 – 19.76x (0.10-P-0.05)
1971 : y = 189.25 – 19.00x (0.01-P-0.001)
1972 : y = 74.16 – 7.83x (0.15-P-0.10)
1973 : y = 69.52 – 1.76x (0.20-P-0.15).

high incidence of simultaneously pregnant and lactating specimens in our samples, yet other females manifestly do not. Such variation in reproduction success would make a great difference in the uptake-efflux ratio over a 5-year period. In the majority of cases, there seems to be unmistakably a net loss of DDT with time. Studies on the female reproductive cycle are continuing; it is presently difficult to distinguish between corpora in the ovaries representing ovulation alone and those representing pregnancy, and our preliminary find-

productive history. There are, of course, other possible explanations, but the above seems most probable. Marginal statistical significance in a number of cases is not regarded as important. Sample sizes are quite small in absolute terms, and the statistical method used is, of course, very sensitive to sample size and to the wide range of individual variation. In some cases, the low level of statistical significance results from inclusion of one specimen with anomalously high levels in the sample.

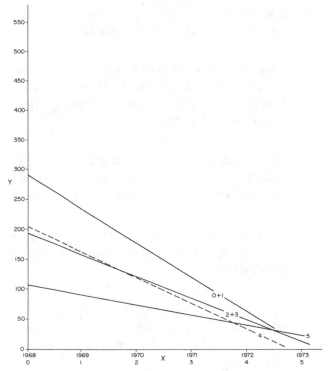

FIG. 4. – Correlation of magnitude of DDT residues in parts per million of extractable fat (y) with the years 1969-1973, inclusive (data collection centred on August) (x), in female harbour porpoises from the Bay of Fundy approaches, segregated by year classes as in Fig. 3. Data for year classes 0 + 1 and 2 + 3 pooled because of small sample sizes. Fitted equations obtained from the data for the respective year class sets were as follows:

$$0 + 1 : y = 291.69 - 49.07x \quad (0.01\text{-}P\text{-}0.001)$$
$$2 + 3 : y = 195.96 - 30.69x \quad (0.05\text{-}P\text{-}0.02)$$
$$4 : y = 205.30 - 37.05x \quad (0.20\text{-}P\text{-}0.15)$$
$$5 : y = 110.99 - 12.84x \quad (0.10\text{-}P\text{-}0.05)$$

6 + : no relationship found.

We were interested to see if animals taken outside the Bay of Fundy approaches differed in residue magnitude from the average levels found within the main collecting region. For what they are worth, considering that only single specimens were obtained in most cases,[1] the results are as follows:

— Prince Edward Island specimen — much higher than the Bay of Fundy average for its sex, age and year.

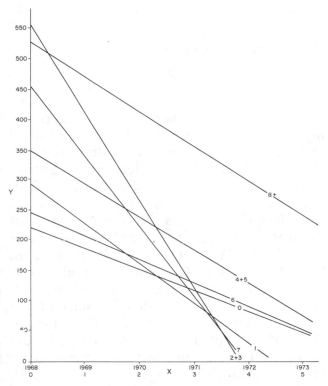

FIG. 3. – Correlation of magnitude of DDT residues in parts per million of extractable fat (y) with the years 1969-1973, inclusive (data collection centred on August) (x), in male harbour porpoises from the Bay of Fundy approaches; statistical calculations of the relationship segregated by year classes 0 to 8 +. Data for age classes 2 and 3, and 4 and 5 have been pooled because of limited sample sizes. Sexual maturity is attained at age 4 in this population. Fitted equations obtained from the data for the respective year class sets were as follows:

$$0 : y = 224.58 - 29.24x \quad (0.15\text{-}P\text{-}0.10)$$
$$1 : y = 290.96 - 54.95x \quad (0.01\text{-}P\text{-}0.001)$$
$$2 + 3 : y = 454.24 - 96.77x \quad (0.01\text{-}P\text{-}0.001)$$
$$4 + 5 : y = 350.00 - 46.20x \quad (P = 0.10)$$
$$6 : y = 249.27 - 34.13x \quad (0.01\text{-}P\text{-}0.001)$$
$$7 : y = 565.10 - 125.43x \quad (0.01\text{-}P\text{-}0.001)$$
$$8 + : y = 531.15 - 48.90x \quad (0.05\text{-}P\text{-}0.02).$$

---

[1] Basic data for these specimens are given in the footnote to Table 1.

141

— Boothbay Harbor specimen — comparable with Bay of Fundy levels.

— Atlantic coast of Nova Scotia specimens – all comparable with Bay of Fundy levels or slightly below average for their sex, age and years.

— Narragansett Bay specimens – significantly lower than average levels for comparable Bay of Fundy specimens.

— Southeastern Newfoundland specimen – much lower than a comparable Bay of Fundy specimen.

— St. Mary's Bay, Nova Scotia, specimen — very low levels compared with equivalent sex and age class specimens in Bay of Fundy.

The latter result was perhaps initially the most surprising, since St. Mary's Bay is so closely adjacent to the Bay of Fundy approaches. The functional ovary, however, was quite heavily scarred indicating an extensive breeding history; furthermore, it would appear that the major item of diet of the few harbour porpoises occurring in the shallow sandy bay is not herring but eel pout, *Macrozoarces americanus* (Bloch & Schneider), (Smith and Gaskin, 1974), so a dietary difference may also be involved.

Relatively high levels in the Bay of Fundy compared with Newfoundland and the coast of Rhode Island may reflect a number of factors. The mixing, tidal flow and upwelling in the mouth of the Bay of Fundy probably contributed to a significant mixing back into the water body of residues which might in other regions stay in the bottom sediments. The nature of the Gulf of Maine and Bay of Fundy currents and their limited relationship with the main North Atlantic drift waters may retard passage of the DDT residues into the open Atlantic to some extent. Relatively cold water temperatures in the region compared with those further offshore may result in slower bacterial action to break down residues. Finally, since the forests of New Brunswick have been more heavily treated with DDT than most other parts of eastern North America, and the major rivers of that province empty into either the Bay of Fundy or the waters adjacent to Prince Edward Island, it is no surprise that the highest residues were found in the specimens from these areas.

Acknowledgements

This study was supported by an operating grant from the National Research Council of Canada (A5863) and by funding from the Donations Committee of Shell Canada Ltd., to whom we express our thanks. Additional field assistance was provided by the Protection Branch of the Fisheries and Marine Service of Environment Canada, particularly by officers based at St. Andrews, N.B., Brand Manan, N.B., Digby, N.S., Chester, N.S., and Souris, P.E.I. Material from the Newfoundland specimen was kindly provided by staff of the Royal Ontario Museum and Dr. Howard Winn of the University of Rhode Island kindly arranged for Narragansett specimens to be sent to us in 1971 and 1972. Messrs. C.W. Walton and M. Smith of the Department of Sea and Shore Fisheries of the State of Maine gave invaluable assistance in obtaining the 1971 specimen from Boothbay Harbor. Our thanks are also extended to the numerous personnel of the Department of Zoology, University of Guelph, who have been involved in this programme over the years and who hopefully have all been previously acknowledged by name in earlier publications. Some difficult logistic problems were solved and boat charter provided by Marine Research Associates of Deer Island, N.B.

References

Berg, O.W., P.L. Diosady and G.A.V. Rees, Column
1972   chromatographic separation of polychlorinated biphenyls from chlorinated hydrocarbon pesticides, and their subsequent gas chromatographic quantification in terms of derivatives. *Bull. Environ. Contam. Toxicol.*, 7:338-47.

Fisher, H.D. and R.J. Harrison, Reproduction in the
1970   common porpoise (*Phocoena phocoena*) of the North Atlantic. *J. Zool., Lond.*, 161:471-86.

Gaskin, D.E. and B.A. Blair, Age determination of
1977   harbour porpoise, *Phocoena phocoena* (L.) in the western North Atlantic. *Can. J. Zool.*, 55(1):18-30.

Gaskin, D.E., P.W. Arnold and B.A. Blair, *Phocoena
1974   phocoena. Mammal. Species*, 42:1-8.

Gaskin, D.E., M. Holdrinet and R. Frank, Organo-
1971   chlorine pesticide residues in harbour porpoises from the Bay of Fundy. *Nature, Lond.*, 233:499-500.

Gaskin, D.E. *et al.*, Mercury, DDT and PCB in harbour
1973   seals (*Phoca vitulina*) from the Bay of Fundy and Gulf of Maine. *J. Fish. Res. Board Can.*, 30:471-5.

Langlois, B.E., A.R. Stemp and B.J. Liska, Analysis of
1964   animal food products for chlorinated insecticides. *J. Milk Food Technol.*, 27:202-4.

Neave, D.J. and B.S. Wright, Seasonal migrations of
1968   the harbour porpoise (*Phocoena phocoena*) and other Cetacea in the Bay of Fundy. *J. Mammal.*, 49:259-64.

Smith, G.J.D. and D.E. Gaskin, The diet of harbour
1974   porpoises (*Phocoena phocoena* (L.)) in coastal waters of eastern Canada, with special reference to the Bay of Fundy. *Can. J. Zool.*, 52(6):777-82.

RADIO TRACKING DUSKY PORPOISES IN THE SOUTH ATLANTIC

B. Würsig

Abstract

In Golfo San José in southern Argentina, dusky porpoises (*Lagenorhynchus obscurus*) were found to live in groups of 6-15 animals. Larger groups form to feed and, afterwards, to copulate and "play". Between December 1973 and May 1975, radio tags were placed on 10 porpoises and they were tracked from a boat and from land. The location of the tagged animals was estimated from the strength of the signal, by triangulation using 2 receivers and by homing and resighting; the latter 2 methods were the most accurate. Three animals were never resighted. Four were resighted with one or more of the same animals present when they had been captured for tagging, showing that there is group cohesion for at least several days. Four animals left Golfo San José after being tagged. Porpoises tracked within 20 km of its mouth travelled with the tidal current while those more than 20 km away from it did not seem to be affected by the direction of the tide. The "minimum mean speed" of 2 porpoises was 2.28 km/h and 3.18 km/h, and both moved faster near the mouth of the bay than away from it. The minimum mean distance travelled daily for all porpoises was 19.2 km, though it was much smaller, 0.7 km, for the one animal studied in wintertime. The movements of this animal were slow and near the shore. Animals studied in the summer moved faster, further from shore and over a larger area. Dives in the summer, despite differences between porpoises, usually lasted longer during the day than at night. Long dives were generally most frequent at dusk. The animal studied in the winter usually had briefer dives during the day than at night.

Résumé

On a observé que les dauphins *Lagenorhynchus obscurus* du golfe de San José, dans le sud de l'Argentine, vivaient en groupes de 6 à 15 animaux. Des groupes plus importants se formaient pour s'alimenter et, ensuite, pour s'accoupler et "jouer". De décembre 1973 à mai 1975, des plaquettes radio ont été placées sur 10 dauphins et suivies depuis un bateau et depuis la terre. L'emplacement des animaux bagués était estimé d'après la force du signal, par triangulation avec deux récepteurs, et par radio-guidage et nouveau repérage visuel; ces deux dernières méthodes se sont révélées les plus précises. Trois animaux n'ont jamais été observés de nouveau. Quatre ont été repérés de nouveau avec un (ou plusieurs) des animaux qui se trouvaient présents lors de la capture aux fins de baguage, ce qui montre qu'il existe une cohésion du groupe durant au moins plusieurs jours. Quatre animaux ont quitté le golfe de San José après avoir été bagués. Les dauphins suivis et repérés jusqu'à 20 km de son ouverture se déplaçaient avec la marée, alors que ceux qui étaient éloignés de plus de 20 km ne semblaient pas être affectés par la direction de la marée. La "vitesse moyenne minimum" de 2 dauphins était de 2,28 km/h et 3,18 km/h et tous deux se déplaçaient plus vite près de l'ouverture de la baie que loin de celle-ci. La distance moyenne minimum parcourue chaque jour par tous les dauphins était de 19,2 km, bien qu'elle ait été très inférieure – 0,7 km – dans le cas du seul animal étudié

145

en hiver. Les mouvements de cet animal étaient lents et il se tenait près du rivage. Les animaux étudiés en été bougeaient plus vite, se trouvaient plus loin du rivage et occupaient une plus grande surface. Les plongées, malgré les différences entre les animaux, duraient généralement plus longtemps le jour que la nuit, en été. Les longues plongées étaient généralement plus fréquentes au crépuscule. Les animaux étudiés en hiver plongeaient habituellement moins longtemps le jour que la nuit.

Extracto

En el golfo de San José, en la costa meridional de Argentina, se han encontrado delfines oscuros (*Lagenorhynchus obscurus*) en grupos de 6 a 15 animales, que se reúnen a veces en grupos mayores para alimentarse y, más tarde, para copular y "jugar". Entre diciembre de 1973 y mayo de 1975 se colocaron marcas radioeléctricas en 10 delfines, siguiendo luego su rastro desde una embarcación o desde tierra. El lugar donde se encontraban los animales marcados se estimó a partir de la potencia de la señal, mediante triangulación con dos receptores, y por el sistema de retorno y reavistamiento. Los dos últimos métodos resultaron los más precisos. Tres de los animales no se reavistaron nunca. Cuatro se avistaron de nuevo en compañía de uno o más de los animales que los acompañaban cuando habían sido capturados y marcados, lo que muestra que existe cierta cohesión entre los grupos, al menos durante varios días. Cuatro animales abandonaron el golfo de San José después de haber sido marcados. Los delfines a los que fue posible seguir dentro de un radio de 20 km de la boca del golfo se desplazaban con las corrientes de la marea, mientras los que se siguieron hasta más allá de 20 km de la boca del golfo no parecían estar afectados por la dirección de la marea. La "velocidad mínima media" de dos delfines resultó de 2,28 km/hora y 3,18 km/hora, y ambos se desplazaban con mayor rapidez en las proximidades de la boca de la bahía que fuera de ella. La distancia media mínima recorrida diariamente por todos los delfines fue de 19,2 km, aunque en el caso del único animal que se estudió durante el invierno resultó mucho menor: 0,7 km. Los movimientos de este animal eran lentos y se desplazaba cerca de tierra. Los animales estudiados durante el verano se desplazaban con mayor rapidez, más alejados de la costa y dentro de una superficie más vasta. En el verano, las inmersiones, a pesar de las diferencias de un animal a otro, resultaron de ordinario más largas durante el día que durante la noche. Las inmersiones largas fueron en general más frecuentes al oscurecer. El animal estudiado durante el invierno realizó de ordinario inmersiones más breves durante el día que durante la noche.

B. Würsig
Division of Natural Sciences, Applied Sciences Building, University of California, Santa Cruz, California, 95064, USA

Introduction

Our knowledge of porpoise social behaviour in wild populations is very limited. In large part, this is because it is hard to mark and recognize individual animals and thus learn much about the behaviour of known individuals under natural conditions. As a result, movement data on most species of porpoises has, in the past, relied mainly on visual sightings of only a few marked individuals. Because it is difficult to recognize and follow such marked animals, the amount of information gained from these studies has been small. Recently, however, experimental use of radio beacons has yielded promising results. Evans (1971, 1974) was able to track *Delphinus delphis* off Southern California and has related the animals' movements to the presence of deep water escarpments and sea mounts. He also found a diurnal variation in their dive patterns. Gaskin, Smith and Watson (1975) successfully tracked 3 *Phocoena* in the Bay of Fundy, and B. Irvine (personal communication) is utilizing radio transmitters to study herd movement and social organization of *Tursiops* in and around the Florida Intracoastal Waterway.

This use of radio tags should, for the first time, make it possible to radio tag an individual animal and follow it for extended periods. In addition, by tagging or recording natural markings of the radioed animal's companions, it would be possible to learn something of the composition and stability of porpoise groups – an obvious first step in understanding their social behaviour. My wife and I undertook to do this with a group of porpoises in a protected South Atlantic bay.

Using existing radio beacons and receiving systems (Martin, Evans and Bowers, 1971), we began a study of dusky porpoises (*Lagenorhynchus obscurus*) in Golfo San José, southern Argentina (42°40′S Lat.), in late 1973. Most important in selecting a study site was the absence of shipping, pleasure boating and other man-made disturbances which haunt the student of natural behaviour in the more populous North. Dusky porpoises, as we found from earlier studies, are present in the bay throughout the year and it is probably true for part at least of their population, that they do not migrate. The porpoises usually travel in small groups of 6-15 individuals. These groups band together into as many as 300 animals during feeding and its attendant after-feeding copulation and "play" behaviour (seen as a profusion of in-air acrobatics).

The main diet of *Lagenorhynchus obscurus* appears to consist of the anchovy *Engraulis anchoita* (Würsig and Würsig, submitted for publication), abundant in the area during most of the year (Boschi and Fenucci, 1972). The porpoises herd schools of these fish into a tight mass against the surface of the water and then feed on them from below while gulls, terns, albatross, petrels and cormorants take advantage of the situation from above. After the porpoises have fed they are not afraid of boats or divers and will readily ride the bow and stern wave of a motorboat. This behaviour allowed the capture and tagging of particular individuals at that time.

Materials and methods

Radio transmitters consisted of a 35 cm long aluminium tube and a 60 cm whip antenna covered with insulation except at the tip. When salt water connected the antenna tip and beacon tube the radio would not transmit, and thus was operating only when the porpoises were at the surface. The transmitter was connected to a fibreglass saddle, brightly painted for easy identification, which was padded inside with open-cell foam and designed to fit over the dorsal fin (unit manufactured by Ocean Applied Research Corp., San Diego, California, Model PT-219). Transmitters emitted a 20 m/sec pulse every 0.6 to

147

1.25 sec on crystal-controlled channels ranging from 27.265 to 27.355 MHz, with a power output of 0.5 watt. Three lithium batteries (Power Conversion, Inc., Westchester, N.Y.) provided enough power for approximately 3 days of continuous operation, up to 15 days mounted on a porpoise. Two quarter-wave adcock antennas were used for reception from home base and mobile land tracking, and a 1/16 wave closed loop antenna with built-in preamplifier was used for tracking from the boat. Two receivers (Model ADFS-210, receivers and antennas by Ocean Applied Research) displayed the bearing of the porpoise on a cathode ray tube (CRT). The approximate distance of the transmitter could be estimated from the amplitude of the auditory signal and from the display on the CRT. At close range (15 km or less) the signal strength meter on the receiver was useful. Triangulation, using 2 receivers, or actual resighting of the porpoise by homing in on the transmitter gave more accurate positions than gauging distance from the receiver by the use of signal strength. The home base antenna was 17 m above Mean Low Water Level, the mobile land antenna was 1.5 m above land, and the boat antenna was 3 m above water surface. The useful range of the system was approximately 50 km. The open loop adcock antenna had an error of ± 5°.

Between 24 December 1973 and 15 May 1975, 10 dusky porpoises were captured while they were riding the bow pressure wave of a 3.5 m (Avon) or 4.5 m (Zodiak) rubber boat (Table 1). The animals were grasped in front of the tail with a device known as a tail grab, home-made from a design by Roger Payne. It was powered by a motorcycle spring and amply padded with neoprene rubber. When the grab fired, the 1 m long handle fell away and the animal was pulled in on the end of a 15 m long rubber cord. Once in the boat, the porpoise was sized and sexed and when possible photographed. The bottom of the boat was outfitted with a 10 cm thick foam mattress, and the animal was kept cool by continuous sprinkling with sea water. A 0.4 cm diameter

hole was bored through the dorsal fin with a cork corer, and the hole was heat-cauterized with a specialtipped soldering gun (Model Quick-Shot, Kemode Co., Westbury, N.Y.). The radio saddle was mounted on the dorsal fin and connected with a bolt designed to corrode in approximately 9 months. Porpoises were out of the water an average of 10 minutes (6-16 minutes).

After release, the radio signal from the porpoise was tape-recorded continuously for the first 24-48 h (Sony TC800B reel-to-reel recorder at 2.4 cm/sec). After that initial period, the signal was sampled by recording a half-hour period every 4 h. These sample recordings were made at 00.15-00.45, 04.15-04.45, 08.15-08.45, 12.15-12.45, 16.15-16.45, and 20.15-20.45 Argentine Local Time (add 3 h for GMT or Coordinated Universal Time). Boat trips to approach the tagged porpoise were made whenever weather permitted, using a different motor than when the animal was captured to try to minimize any possible flight reaction. When the weather was bad, attempts were made to triangulate the porpoise's position by using 2 receivers on land.

During boat trips to the tagged porpoise we tried to identify other animals nearby. To aid in identification we marked some of them with spaghetti tags when possible. The spaghetti tags consisted of 40 cm long brightly coloured plastic streamers coded in 3 colours per tag. They were thin (0.5 cm diam.) and flexible and their 3 cm stainless steel tip was lanced into the thick blubber beside the dorsal fin while the animals rode the pressure wave. Unfortunately, it was found that such tags are usually rejected by the tissue after only a matter of months, leaving a round, white scar under the dorsal fin (Irvine, personal communication and personal observation). During the 2 year stay in Golfo San José we found many such scarred individuals which had apparently been tagged several months previously. Because the tags appeared to hold for the relatively brief periods of radio tracking, however, they proved useful for short-term study.

Results

CAPTURE

None of the porpoises appeared greatly traumatized by the catching and tagging procedure, breathing only slightly faster in the boat (mean breath 1 per 18 sec) than while in the water (mean breath 1 per 23 $\pm$ 2 sec, from stopwatch timing of free-swimming individuals). Except for an occasional tail lash or backward body arch, they did not move. When the dorsal fin was pierced and cauterized, a slight jerk of the body was observed in approximately half of the animals; the others did not react. Although 7 animals bled when their dorsal fin was pierced, cauterizing stopped bleeding in all but 1 instance. In that case (porpoise G), insertion of the tightfitting saddle bolt into the dorsal fin stopped bleeding. Only once (porpoise B) during capture did other animals appear to be alarmed. Groups that had approached the boat before capture generally milled near the boat for approximately 5 minutes after the motor was stopped and the captured animal pulled aboard. This behaviour was indistinguishable from that observed during the many times we stopped the motor without having caught a porpoise. On the other hand, groups which we had to approach and which did not ride the bow wave very well (i.e., which rode about 1 m below the surface instead of higher up) disappeared almost immediately when the motor stopped, whether or not we had captured a porpoise from the group. Porpoise B and its group represented an exception to the above general behaviour, and will be discussed later.

TRACKS AND GROUP COHESION

Table 1 summarizes the length of radio contact with all porpoises captured. Porpoises A, E and C were never resighted after release. They were tracked from shore at Punta Tehuelche and home base. Their movements are shown in Figs. 1 and 2. Porpoises A and E were tagged on the same day in groups separated from each other by only 2 km. They travelled widely different routes within the bay and left it on the same day 3 days after capture. Porpoise C stayed close to shore and near its tagging location for the 6.5 days of radio contact.

The 7 remaining porpoises were all resighted after tagging. Porpoises I and J left the

Table 1. *Lagenorhynchus obscurus* radio-tagged between December 1973 and May 1975

Name	Sex	Length (cm)	Dates of Radio Contact	Number of Days of Radio Contact	Mean Dive Time (sec)	Reason for Loss of Contact
A	M	170 ± 3	Dec. 25 - Dec. 27 1973	2.5	—	leaves the bay
E	F	165 ± 3	Dec. 24 - Dec. 27 1973	2.5	22.0	leaves the bay
C	M	171	Jul. 31 - Aug. 6 1974	6.5	16.9	transmitter failure?
I	M	175	Nov. 30 - Dec. 14 1974	15.0	17.4	batteries used up
G	F	161	Jan. 3 - Jan. 16 1975	13.5	13.8	batteries used up
B	M	165	Jan. 19 - Jan. 20 1975	1.0	34.4	leaves the bay
H	F	173	Jan. 26 - Jan. 28 1975	2.5	28.2	leaves the bay
F	M	160	Apr. 15 - Apr. 17 1975	2.5	20.5	transmitter failure?
J	F	173	Apr. 19 - May 4 1975	15.0	19.2	batteries used up
A'	F	157	May 10 - May 15 1975	5.0	12.4	transmitter failure?
			Total	66.0	Mean 21.0	

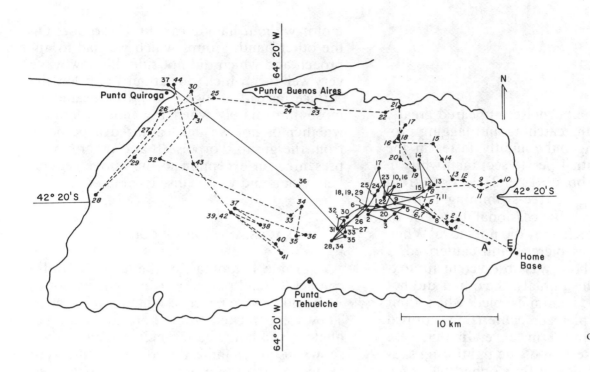

FIG. 1. – Radiotracks
of two dusky porpoises,
1973.

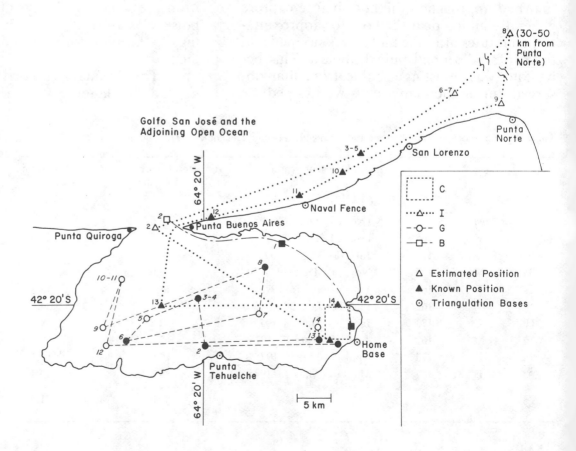

FIG. 2. – Radiotracks
of four dusky porpoises,
1974-1975.

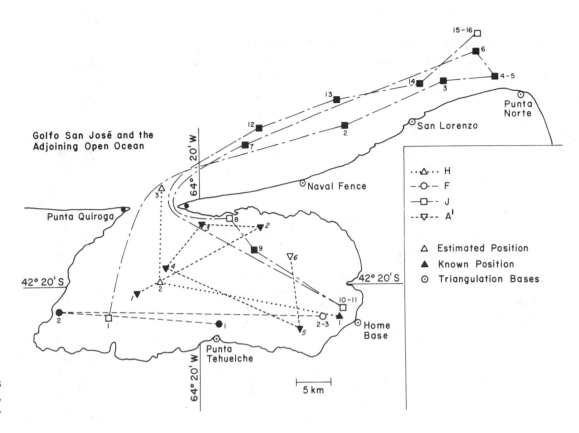

FIG. 3. – Radiotracks of four dusky porpoises, 1975.

bay and were tracked east of Golfo San José to as far as Punta Norte (Figs. 2 and 3). Both came back into the bay after 1 week (I) and 11 days (J). Porpoise J stayed in the bay for 3 more days and then left once again, once more to head east in the ocean.

Porpoises G, B, J and A' were each re-sighted at least once with other identifiable individuals (Table 2). G and A' moved normally while in their groups but their transmitters became fouled with kelp after several days and both were slowed down appreciably.

Porpoise B was captured in a group of only 5 others (3 of which were identified by natural marks). The group swam rapidly away from the boat and toward the middle of the bay as B was being hauled aboard. A large group of about 30 porpoises milled 300 m shoreward of the boat and did not appear to alter its behaviour during and after capture. When porpoise B was released, it swam rapidly in the direction in which its 5 companions had gone, not toward the much closer group near the boat. We approached B that same afternoon and discovered it with its original group, 18 km from the capture site. The entire group remained close together (within approximately 12 m). The group avoided the boat by dodging to the left or right of it as we approached, and headed rapidly toward the mouth of the bay. This behaviour represented th only time that capture had clearly frightened the rest of the group.

MOVEMENT ANALYSIS

The speed with which porpoises A and E moved was calculated from successive positions triangulated at 1-3 h intervals. These successive positions were only a minimum measure of the distance swum, so the mean of these speeds I have called the "minimum mean speed". For porpoise A this speed was 2.28 km/h (35 observations). The minimum speed of porpoise E, tabulated as above,

Table 2. *Lagenorhynchus obscurus* radio-tracking summary

Porpoise	Date Captured Group Size	Dates Resighted Group Size	Other Animals Recognized	Comments
A	Dec. 24, 1973 8-12	–	–	Triangulation and dive time observations only. Moves in eastern part of bay for 2.5 days, then leaves bay.
E	Dec. 24, 1973 8-12	–	–	Triangulation and dive time observations only. Moves throughout bay for 2.5 days, then leaves bay.
C	Jul. 31, 1974 6-8			Stays within 10 km of shore, near capture sight, for 6.5 days.
		Aug. 1 and 2, 1974. Near a group of 250. Boat gets very close but no resighting.	–	–
I	Nov. 30, 1974 10			Travels out of bay and back into it. Only 6 km from capture sight when signal lost.
		Dec. 13, 1974. Alone and 1 km from nearest group of 10.		Moving slowly.
G	Jan. 3, 1975 40 feeding 8-10 staying with boat during part of capture.		–	Moves throughout Golfo San José during the 15 days of radio contact.
		Jan. 3, 1975 (4 hrs. after capture) 8-10 Jan. 4, 1975 alone but 8-10 0.5 to 1.0 km distant. Jan. 8, 1975 8-10.	2 spaghetti tags placed in this group of 8-10. In 8-10 group near G at least one, possibly both, tags of Jan. 3. 2 spaghetti tags of Jan. 3.	Moving well with others and feeding. Apparent copulation by G and a larger adult seen 2X in one hour. Moving slowly. Bothered by radio. Group of 8-10 nearby not feeding. Moving well with others while feeding but slightly slow and lagging behind when not feeding. 30 cm of kelp fouled on the radio.
		Jan. 10, 1975 near, and after one hour with, 100. Jan. 15, 1975 alone, 100 1 to 2 km distant.	At least one tag of Jan. 3, possibly both. –	Kelp and the radio apparently slowing G down. Kelp slowing G down until we are able to free porpoise of it, then moving more normally but still a bit slowly.
B	Jan. 19, 1975 6		One calf, one light sub-adult, one with fin nick.	
		Jan. 19, 1975 (8 hrs. after capture) 6	One calf, one light sub-adult, one with fin nick.	Moving normally with its group. Leaves bay night of Jan. 19-20.

Table 2. *Lagenorhynchus obscurus* **radio-tracking summary** *(concluded)*

Porpoise	Date Captured Group Size	Dates Resighted Group Size	Other Animals Recognized	Comments
H	Jan. 26, 1975 30-40	Jan. 26, 1975 (4 hrs. after capture) alone, but with at least 3 groups of 6-15 0.5 to 2 km distant.	–	Moving slowly, apparently hampered by radio. Leaves bay Jan. 28.
F	Apr. 15, 1975 12-15	Apr. 16, 1975 12-15	–	Moving normally. Appears unbothered by radio. Group has been feeding.
J	Apr. 19, 1975 175-200 feeding	For 3 hrs. immediately after release, within a group of 175-200.	One partial albino	Moving normally with others. Feeding.
		Apr. 27, 1975 alone, near 15 groups of 6-15 each, 0.5 to 5 km distant.	One partial albino in one of the groups.	Moving well. Not feeding.
A'	May 10, 1975 15		One with white spot on dorsal fin, one adult with calf.	
		May 11, 1975 15	One with white spot on dorsal fin, one adult with calf.	Moving normally. Feeding.
		May 12, 1975 15	One with white spot on dorsal fin, one adult with calf.	Moving normally. Feeding.
		May 13, 1975 alone, other groups nearby. May 14, 1975 alone, other groups nearby.	–	Moving slowly. Kelp fouled on radio.

showed an overall mean of 3.18 km/h (40 observations). Travel time of both porpoises was significantly faster near the mouth of Golfo San José than it was over 20 km from the mouth (see Table 3). Because the other 8 porpoises were not triangulated as frequently, speed data for them would be even less accurate and was not calculated. However, the data make it obvious that strong tidal currents near the mouth influenced the movements of all porpoises studied.

To examine how the movements of porpoises relate to tidal currents, I looked at each occasion when a porpoise moved 5 km or more in any 4 h period. Each such movement was put into 1 of 2 groups depending on whether it was closer to or further away than 20 km from the mouth of the bay. Comparison of the direction of movement with the direction of tidal currents gave the results shown in Table 4. Movements not obviously going toward or against the direction of tidal flow and movements bridging tide changes were excluded. The results show that porpoises near the mouth travelled with the current at almost all times, 1 animal (J) swimming against the currents only

153

Table 3. **Minimum mean speed travelled by porpoises A and E**

Porpoise	> 20 km from Mouth		< 20 km from Mouth		Overall
A	# 1	1.85 km/hr (S.D. = 1.128 km/hr) n = 34	# 2	16.85 km/hr (one sample)	2.28 km/hr n = 35
E	# 3	2.04 km/hr (S.D. = 1.366 km/hr) n = 20	# 4	4.32 km/hr (S.D. = 1.236 km/hr) n = 20	3.18 km/hr n = 40

Significance between # 1 and # 2, $p < 0.001$, Student's t-test
Significance between # 3 and # 4, $p < 0.001$, Student's t-test

once. Travel direction of porpoises further than 20 km from the mouth did not appear to be affected by tidal currents (Table 4; tidal currents of Golfo San José are in Figure 4).

The daily mean of minimum travel for all porpoises (as calculated from straight line distances between known points) was 19.2 km (S.D. = 1.79 km). Porpoise C, the only animal studied in winter, deviated sharply from this figure, with a mean of only 0.7 km/day. The difference between amount of movement of C and that of the 9 other porpoises is significant (t-test, $p > 0.01$).

DIVE TIME ANALYSIS

Porpoises differed widely in duration of dives (see Table 1 for means). Nevertheless, despite the great individual variation, a clear day-night pattern emerged that was consistent for animals radiotracked in summer and fall

Table 4. **Number of times porpoises moved 5 km or more with or against tide in a 4-hour period**

Porpoise	< 20 km from Mouth		> 20 km from Mouth	
	With Current	Against Current	With Current	Against Current
E	7 times	0	4 times	1 time
I	2	0	2	0
G	9	0	2	3
B	1	0	0	0
H	1	0	0	0
J	2	1[1]	0	3
Total	22	1	8	7

Difference in movements with or against currents significant ($p < 0.001$, testing equality of percentages).　　No difference in movement with or against currents.

[1] Went through the mouth with the tide, after having approached it against the tide.

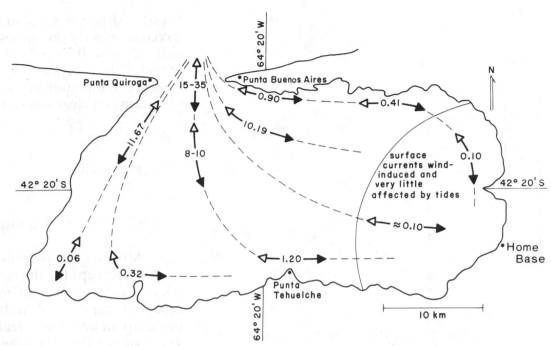

FIG. 4. — Surface currents of Golfo San José
← falling tide ← rising tide
Readings are in km/hr.

(adequate data for breakdown into sessions of day were not available for porpoises A, E, B, and H, however). Nighttime (2015-2045, 0015-0045, 0415-0445) was characterized by short dives, and daytime by long dives. Porpoise C, the only animal to be tracked in winter, showed a strikingly different pattern, usually with briefer dives during the day than at night (Figures 5 and 6). Furthermore, dives lasting 90 seconds or more were more frequent during daytime in summer and fall, with peaks during the 1215-1245 and 1615-1645 samples in different porpoises. In winter (porpoise C), the reverse was once again true (Figure 7).

Dive duration near sunset or dusk exhibited still another pattern. Mean dive duration at dusk increased compared with mean duration of dives preceding or following sunset by 1 hour. A closer look at the data showed that this increase was mainly because of an increase in the number of long dives (≥ 90 sec), which were generally more frequent during dusk than at other times of day or night. This difference, tested for porpoise E, the only animal for which adequate data exist, shows that at least in that porpoise the difference is significant (x^2-test, $p < 0.005$).

Do variations in the weather correspond to a subsequent variation in dive length or amount of time spent at the surface? During stormy days, with wind greater than 40 km/hr, porpoise I spent a significantly greater amount of time at the surface than on "calm" days with wind less than 10 km/hr (n = 12, $p < 0.005$,

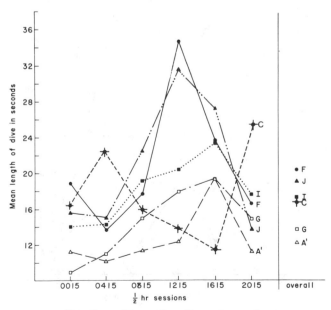

FIG. 5. — Mean dive times for sessions.

155

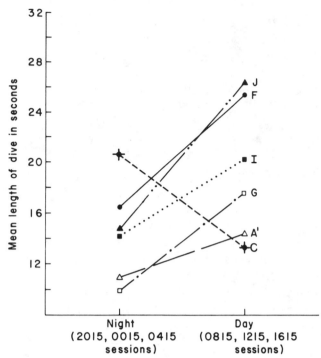

FIG. 6. – Mean dive times night and day.

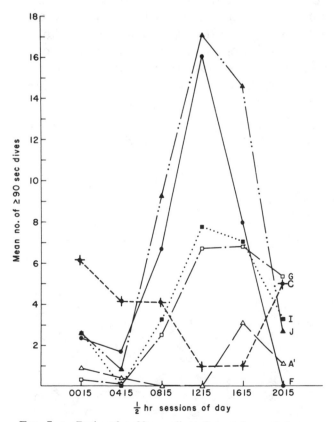

FIG. 7. – Ratio of ≥90 sec dives for sessions of day.

t-test). Porpoises G, J and A′, however, behaved in exactly the opposite way (n = 16, 19 and 12; p < 0.005, 0.005, and 0.05, respectively). Other porpoises could not be tested because of inadequate data (i.e., not enough observations on clear-cut stormy and calm days).

Discussion

CAPTURE AND COHESION

Most tagged porpoises showed no flight reaction (except for the small group with porpoise B). This does not mean, however, that repeated capture of individuals might not build up an avoidance reaction of the capture vessel or possibly any other boat. Porpoises C, I, F, and A′ stayed close to or returned to the vicinity of the capture site during the relatively short life of the radio signal. Therefore, no general avoidance of the area where the animal has been caught appears to exist.

Porpoises G, B, F, and A′ were resighted several times in groups with identified individuals. They demonstrated that small-group cohesion (6-15 animals) is present. On January 8, for example, we repeatedly saw porpoise G lagging behind its group, as its movement apparently was slowed by the radio tag. We encountered it again within its group ½ to 1 hour later. At the same time there were 10 or more other small and large groups in the vicinity, but porpoise G was clearly orienting toward that group which included two spaghetti-tagged individuals that had been near the animal during capture 5 days earlier. The most dramatic example of group cohesion was that of porpoise B of whose group of 5 we identified 3 individuals. Despite having another group of porpoises closer to porpoise B upon its release, we spotted it again later that day moving with its original group. I do not know how the animal oriented to its own group. Random search from group to group is a possibility. It is perhaps more probable that there existed acoustic communication between the group and the recently tagged member, possibly in the form of "signature" sounds as has been described for *Tursiops* (Caldwell and Caldwell, 1965) and for a more closely related animal, *Lagenorhynchus obliquidens* (Caldwell and Caldwell, 1971). In future it may prove fruitful to record underwater sound during tagging and subsequent release for a better understanding of this example of orientation under apparently stressful conditions.

Porpoises I, H, and J, when encountered again, were in the vicinity of another group or groups but were basically alone. Various possibilities exist: 1) these porpoises were lone animals – they had joined a group to feed, were captured after feeding, and then on being released became solitary again: 2) these porpoises were completely abandoned because other animals reacted to the transmitter or because the transmitter slowed them down; 3) these apparently lone animals never found their group after release, and 4) these porpoises were with a group when the boat was not present but left the group when the boat approached.

The first possibility appears unlikely; in 2 years of field studies we only once encountered an apparently solitary dusky porpoise. That the porpoises had been abandoned also appears unlikely because all porpoises resighted were at least near other porpoises, if not immediately adjacent to them. It is possible that they may never have found their group and may not have been accepted into any other group. It is more likely, however, that the porpoises were with a group almost all of the time, but that the approach of the boat frightened off the tagged porpoise while the rest of the group went about its normal activity. Since we were converging on to the tagged individual, we would have missed the rest of its group. This idea appears especially plausible when looking at the behaviour of porpoise G, whom we encountered on January 4, 1975, just minutes after we had met the small groups with which it had travelled a day earlier (2 spaghetti tags in the group). Given the fact that porpoise

G was with "its group", as evidenced by the later sightings of it feeding with the 2 spaghetti-tagged animals, it may be assumed that it moved away from its group to avoid us on January 4, and that we accidentally spotted its nearby group. Furthermore, in looking at resightings of porpoises with "their groups", we, in all but one case (B), found the porpoises feeding or engaged in behaviour (such as heading towards the boat from a distance, breaching near the boat, riding the bow wave well) which from other studies suggested that they had recently been feeding. Many times during this pattern of after-feeding behaviour the animals did not avoid the boat in any way, and this was also so with the tagged animals resighted with groups. Why did porpoise B, whose group did not show feeding or after-feeding behaviour, not leave the group when the boat approached? The answer may be that when we reapproached the group, all animals for some reason were avoiding us. Porpoise B, seemingly as afraid as other nonfeeding tagged porpoises, also tried to avoid the approaching boat but, because the rest of the group used the same avoidance tactics, stayed with the group. This small group was the only one that moved (fled?) immediately to "beyond our sight" when B was tagged. Either an alarm signal was issued or catching of the animal was alarm enough. In the evening, the group still avoided the boat and remained together.

A major problem in this study was the possibility that capturing porpoises and equipping them with radios bothered some of these highly social animals so much that they do not remain with their conspecifics, even though this may only be briefly while the boat is present. A good, comprehensive study of the natural behaviour of porpoises is not likely with equipment that at least at times seems to bother and slow them down. Two animals (G and A) were slowed down badly by kelp strands which became fouled on the radio transmitters. At least 2 others (I and H) were noticeably slowed down apparently by the radio transmitters only. These problems might be solved with a smaller radio and saddle, better streamlined for less

157

drag and to avoid kelp fouling. The antenna should be thinner and more flexible and probably located on the dorsal midline aft of the fin. Perhaps it also could be streamlined to reduce drag (airfoil-shaped instead of round), as has been shown to be of utmost importance in airplane antenna design. Some of these improvements have already been made, with better designed, more streamlined radios on *Tursiops* in Florida waters (B. Irvine, personal communication).

MOVEMENT

Irvine and Wells (1972) suggested that *Tursiops* moved in and out of the Intracoastal Waterway south of Tampa Bay, Florida, with ingoing and outgoing tidal currents. A similar correlation of movement with tidal currents was found in the present study. Not only did radio-tagged animals move through the mouth of Golfo San José with tidal flow, but evidence for movement with the tide was found as far as 20 km from the mouth. Considering the swift currents generated by the large amount of water which must enter and leave this bay during a 6-hour cycle (difference between low and high tide is 6-8 m), this discovery is not very surprising.

The only porpoise to have been studied during the winter was C. It covered significantly less territory than all of the others. This observation appears to fit in well with theodolite data of porpoise movements during the wintertime; slow, nearshore movement which changes direction often and thus keeps the animal in a restricted area (Würsig, in press). On the other hand, radio- (and theodolite-) tracked porpoises during the summertime moved faster, further from shore, and covered a larger area than their wintertime counterparts. This difference may be a reflection of the food supply. Unfortunately little is known of the foodfish *Engraulis anchoita* which appears to be the main diet of the dusky porpoise in Argentine waters (Würsig and Würsig,

submitted). During a research cruise carried out mid-February (summer) of 1970 (Boschi and Fenucci, 1972) anchovy was found throughout the bay. This observation correlated with porpoises found throughout the bay at and around this time. In winter, anchovy are mainly found in more northern latitudes, several hundred kilometers north of the study site (Brandhorst, *et al.*, 1971). It thus appears likely that dusky porpoises are not feeding on anchovy in this area in winter. I do not know what they are feeding on during the slow, near-shore winter movements.

DIVE-TIME PATTERNS

There was a large individual variation in dive times, and it did not appear to be related to animal size or sex. Future analysis may find a relationship between the duration of the dives and environmental factors, but whatever correlation exists is surely complex. Despite differences from porpoise to porpoise, all the animals exhibited a clear day-night variation in length of dives, with nighttime characterized in summer by short dives, daytime (primarily about 1000-1700 hrs) by longer dives. However, in winter night dives became long. Behavioural notes on *Tursiops* species in captivity have shown that nighttime is marked by reduced vocalization (Powell, 1966) and by reduced social interactions (Saayman, Tayler and Bower, 1973, on *Tursiops aduncus*). These data appear to point to nighttime periods of resting or sleeping, but whether or not the short night dives of dusky porpoises during summer represent a similar behaviour is not known. In the winter, porpoises dove only for brief periods during the day. At the same time, they moved slowly and near shore at almost all times, and their activity level appeared low. They therefore appeared to be "resting", and this apparent rest correlates with brief dives (Würsig and Würsig, submitted).

Delphinus delphis studied by Evans (1971, 1974) made long dives during nocturnal hours.

He correlated this with the nightly upward migration of organisms associated with the deep scattering layer. It is not clear from his data whether or not there was a difference in diving pattern between seasons. Long, mainly afternoon, dives which dusky porpoises made in summer occurred during the daily peak of feeding activity (Würsig and Würsig, submitted). It thus appears likely that porpoises were diving deeper at this time, possibly to hunt for fish and herd them toward the surface. Long dives, greater than 90 seconds, were observed during daytime as well as at dusk. Evans (1971) found that *Delphinus delphis* stopped to "mill" and possibly feed around sunset, sunrise, and noon. A similar feeding behaviour may be evident with dusky porpoises but why this should be is not known.

High wind had a definite effect on the amount of time porpoises spent at the surface. However, it varied greatly from porpoise to porpoise. Porpoises J, G, and A' surfaced less in rough weather, while porpoise I exhibited exactly the opposite trend. Various possibilities present themselves: 1) since 3 porpoises studied stayed under the surface significantly more in storm conditions and only 1 did not, porpoises may usually show this behaviour and I could have shown aberrant behaviour, possibly because the radio and its saddle interfered; 2) it could be that the effect does not represent natural behaviour and the tagged porpoises, bothered by the radios, were merely adjusting to surfacing and breathing in different ways; and 3) the effect is real but different for different animals and, most likely, their groups.

Possibility No. 1, less time spent at the surface during high winds, may have highest appeal. Porpoises, like scuba divers, may prefer not to be buffeted by rough seas and therefore stay below the influence of wave action as much as possible. Dive times did not change under these weather conditions, only the amount of time spent at the surface. This therefore does not appear to reflect a change in feeding behaviour. The change appears directly related to sea or wind state.

Summary

Dusky porpoises live in small groups of 6-15 individuals. These small groups come together to form larger aggregations to feed, and then separate again. This behaviour suggests a complex social system.

Three porpoises showed that small groups appear stable over a period of at least several days. Recently tagged porpoises were not bothered by the radio transmitters, but usually after 2 or more days movement was slower than normal and tagged porpoises were more often found alone. Kelp fouling of the radio beacon was a serious problem for at least 2 animals.

Porpoises in Golfo San José are to a large degree affected by tidal currents. They travel within and outside of the bay, but whether they have a territory or have a range and how big it might be is unclear. In summer, dusky porpoises make longer dives during the day than they do at night. This difference is related to feeding in daylight, with periods of relative rest at night. In winter this cycle appears to be reversed.

Acknowledgements

I express may sincere thanks to Dr. Charles Walcott of the State University of New York at Stony Brook. He spent a great deal of effort and time in preparation for this study, and he is in large part responsible for its successful conclusion. I also thank Dr. Roger Payne of the New York Zoological Society for providing equipment and advice throughout the study. I thank Dr. Douglas Smith, Peter Tyack, Jen and Des Bartlett, Hugo Callejas, Jan Wolitzky, Russ Charif, and Chris Clark for providing help and moral support. A special debt of gratitude goes to my wife Melany for assisting in all aspects of the study.

This research was supported by contributions from the New York Zoological Society, the Committee for Research and Exploration of the National Geographic Society, and the State University of New York at Stony Brook.

References

BOSCHI, E.E. and J.L. FENUCCI, Contribución al conoci-
1972   miento de la fauna marina del Golfo San José.
        Physis, B. Aires, 31(82):155-67.

BRANDHORST, W. *et al.*, Evalucación de los recursos de
1971   anchoita (*Engraulis anchoita*) frente a La Ar-
        gentina y Uruguay. 3. *Ser. Inf. Tec. Proy. De-
        sarr. Mar del Plata*, (34):1-39.

CALDWELL, M.C. and D.K. CALDWELL, Individualized
1965   whistle contours in bottlenosed dolphins (*Tur-
        siops truncatus*). *Nature, Lond.*, 207:434-5.

–, Statistical evidence for individual signature whistles in
1971   Pacific white sided dolphins, *Lagenorhynchus
        obliquidens. Cetology*, 3:1-9.

EVANS, W.E., Orientation behaviour of delphinids: radio
1971   telemetric studies. *Ann. N.Y. Acad. Sci.*,
        188:142-60.

–, Radio-telemetric studies of two species of small
1974   odontocete cetaceans. *In* The whale problem: a
        status report, edited by W. Schevill. Boston,
        Mass., Harvard University Press, pp. 386-94.

GASKIN, D.E., G.J.D. SMITH and A.P. WATSON, Prelimi-
1975   nary study of movements of harbour porpoise
        (*Phocoena phocoena*) in the Bay of Fundy using
        radiotelemetry. *Can. J. Zool.*, 53:1466-71.

IRVINE, B. and R.S. WELLS, Results of attempts to tag
1972   Atlantic bottlenosed dolphins *Tursiops trunca-
        tus*). *Cetology*, 13:1-5.

MARTIN, H., W.E. EVANS and C.A. BOWERS, Methods for
1971   radio tracking marine mammals in the open
        sea. *In* Transactions of the IEEE Conference on
        Engineering in the Ocean Environment, Sep-
        tember 1971, San Diego, CA, pp. 44-9.

POWELL, W.A., Periodicity of vocal activity of captive
1966   Atlantic bottlenose dolphins: *Tursiops trunca-
        tus. Bull. South. Calif. Acad. Sci.*, (65):237-44.

SAAYMAN, G.S., C.K. TAYLER and D. BOWER, Diurnal
1973   activity cycles in captive and free-ranging
        Indian Ocean bottlenose dolphins (*Tursiops
        truncatus* Ehrenberg). *Behaviour*, 44:212-33.

WÜRSIG, B., Aspects of the natural history of bottlenose
        and dusky porpoises. National Geographic So-
        ciety Research Reports, 1971 Projects.
        Washington, D.C., National Geographic
        Society (in press).

WÜRSIG, B. and M. WÜRSIG, The behaviour and ecology
        of dusky porpoises, *Lagenorhynchuys obscurus*,
        in the south Atlantic. Submitted for
        publication in *Behaviour*.

SEALS

A DISCRETE POPULATION MODEL FOR THE SOUTH AFRICAN FUR SEAL, *ARCTOCEPHALUS PUSILLUS PUSILLUS*

P.D. SHAUGHNESSY and P.B. BEST

Abstract

A simple model for South African fur seals, *Arctocephalus pusillus pusillus*, was constructed to determine the annual yield of yearlings and abundance of mature females when the population reaches stability and the time taken to reach stability, under various constant sealing rates, and the sensitivity of these to changes in the values of the parameters used. The model assumes a stable initial population and is concerned only with females. Ages at sexual maturity and at first parturition were taken to be 3 and 4 years, respectively; the proportion of newborn pups who were female was set at 40 %. Annual survival rates of animals in their second and third years, in their fourth year and of mature females, were set at 0.7141 each, 0.95 and 0.087, respectively. These parameters were treated as independent of population size. The other rates are density-dependent: the pregnancy rate is described by a linear relationship, and the survival rate of young pups by a geometric one. Pregnancy and survival rates are based on data from northern fur seals, *Callorhinus ursinus*, on the Pribilof Islands.

The model predicts the maximum sustainable sealing rate to be 33 % of female yearlings, when the mature female population stabilizes at about 51 % of its initial size, a condition reached after 180 years and providing an annual harvest of 449 yearlings to every 5 100 mature females. The maximum sealing rate tolerable for a sizeable sustained yield would be about 50 %, so a harvest of 33 % may be dangerous if the model is seriously biased. The model was shown not to be sensitive to changes in the density-independent parameters, but changes in the pregnancy rate and especially in the survival rate of pups, do produce considerable variation in the predicted values (notably a decrease in the maximum sustainable sealing rate) particularly if these rates are assumed to be density-dependent. Thus, it is important that data on these 2 parameters be obtained and that pup production is properly monitored in the meantime.

Résumé

Un modèle simple, destiné à l'otarie à fourrure sud-africaine, *Arctocephalus pusillus pusillus*, a été construit pour déterminer la production annuelle de jeunes et l'abondance de femelles arrivées à maturité quand la population atteint le point de stabilité et le temps mis pour y parvenir, avec divers taux constants de chasse, et leur sensibilité aux changements des valeurs des paramètres employés. Le modèle suppose une population initiale stable et ne porte que sur les femelles. On a considéré que l'âge de maturité sexuelle et à la première parturition était, respectivement, de 3 et 4 ans. La proportion de veaux nouveau-nés femelles a été fixée à 40 %. Les taux annuels de survie des animaux durant leur seconde, troisième et quatrième années et ceux des femelles ont été fixés, respectivement à 0,7141 chaque, 0,95 et 0,087. Ces paramètres ont été traités comme indépendants de la taille de la population. Les autres taux dépendent de la densité: le taux de gestation est décrit par une relation linéaire et le taux de survie des jeunes veaux est décrit par une relation géométrique. Les taux de gestation et de

163

survie se fondent sur des données concernant les otaries à fourrure, *Callorhinus ursinus*, des Pribilov.

Le modèle prévoit que le taux maximum soutenu de chasse est de 33 % pour les veaux femelles quand la population femelle mature se stabilise à environ 51 % de sa taille initiale, condition atteinte après 180 ans et assurant une récolte annuelle de 449 jeunes de l'année par 5 100 femelles matures. Le taux maximum de chasse tolérable pour un rendement soutenu appréciable serait d'environ 50 %, donc une chasse de 33 % pourrait être dangereuse si le modèle est affecté d'une distorsion sérieuse. On a montré que le modèle n'était pas sensible aux changements des paramètres dépendant de la densité, mais les changements du taux de gestation, et spécialement du taux de survie des veaux, produisent des variations considérables dans les valeurs prévues (notamment une diminution du taux maximum soutenu de chasse), particulièrement si l'on suppose que ces taux dépendent de la densité. Il est donc important que les données sur ces deux paramètres soient obtenues et que la production de veaux soit convenablement surveillée entre temps.

Extracto

Se preparó un modelo sencillo para el lobo marino de dos pelos de Sudáfrica, *Arctocephalus pusillus pusillus*, en orden a determinar: el rendimiento anual de animales de un año y la abundancia de hembras maduras cuando la población alcanza la estabilidad; el tiempo necesario para alcanzar la estabilidad, con diversos índices constantes de explotación; y la sensibilidad de éstos a las variaciones en los valores de los parámetros utilizados. El modelo supone una población inicial estable, y se ocupa sólo de las hembras. Se partió de la hipótesis de que las edades de madurez sexual y de primer parto son, respectivamente, 3 y 4 años, y la proporción de cachorros hembras recién nacidos se fijó en 40 por ciento. El índice anual de supervivencia de los animales en el segundo y tercer año se fijó en 0,7141, en el cuarto año, en 0,95, y el índice de supervivencia de hembras adultas, en 0,087. Estos parámetros se trataron como independientes del volumen de la población. Los demás índices dependen de la densidad: el índice de preñez se describe mediante una relación lineal, y el índice de supervivencia de los cachorros mediante una relación geométrica. Los índices de preñez y supervivencia se basan en datos procedentes del oso marino (*Callorhinus ursinus*) de las islas Pribilof.

El modelo prevé que el rendimiento máximo sostenible equivaldrá al 33 por ciento de las hembras de un año, cuando la población de hembras maduras se estabiliza en torno a un 55 por ciento de su número inicial, estado que se alcanza al cabo de 180 años si se permite obtener un rendimiento anual de 449 animales de un año por cada 5 100 hembras maduras. El índice máximo de explotación tolerable para obtener un rendimiento sostenido importante sería del orden del 50 por ciento, por lo que explotar la población al 33 por ciento podría ser peligroso si el modelo estuviera viciado por un grave error sistemático. Se ha mostrado que el modelo no es sensible a variaciones en los parámetros independientes de la densidad, pero los cambios en los índices de preñez y, especialmente, en el índice de supervivencia de los cachorros determinan variaciones considerables en los valores previstos (sobre todo, una disminución de la captura máxima sostenible), especialmente si se supone que esos índices dependen de la densidad. Así pues, es importante obtener datos sobre esos dos parámetros y seguir de cerca, entretanto, la producción de cachorros.

P.D. Shaughnessy
Director, Sea Fisheries Institute, Private Bag, Sea Point 8060, South Africa

P.B. Best
Sea Fisheries Branch, Marine Mammal Laboratory, P.O. Box 251, Cape Town 8000, South Africa

Introduction

The population of South African fur seals has generally been successfully managed since 1891, with some signs of an increase in population size under controlled exploitation (Shaughnessy, 1976). This has been achieved mainly through the direct involvement of the State in sealing, and by adhering strictly to the traditional practices of harvesting seals in their first year of life and, formerly, of harvesting adult bulls. During the last ten years, however, the gradual transfer of sealing from the State to private enterprise, the intensification of the conflict between the pelagic fishing industry and seals (which are viewed either as competitors or as a pest), and the increasing public concern over sealing have meant that future management must be placed on a firmer scientific basis.

As a first step to this end an attempt has been made in this paper to construct a simple mathematical model to determine the effects of certain sealing regimes on population size and to determine the maximum sustainable yield (MSY). Because many of the aspects of fur seal behaviour and biology relevant to this model are unknown for *A.p. pusillus*, frequent reference has been made to the northern fur seal, *Callorhinus ursinus*, of the Pribilof Islands for which a larger body of pertinent data has been published.

The model

The South African sealing industry is directed at both male and female yearlings. Since *A.p. pusillus* is polygynous and management of females is likely to be more critical, the model considers only the effect of exploitation of this sex. The model assumes a stable, unharvested initial population of 10 000 mature females together with the concomitant number of immature females as indicated by the parameters for such a population (1 795, 1 282 and 915 seals aged 1, 2, and 3 years respectively, at the end of each year). In the initial population, the number of mature females dying annually is balanced by the number of juvenile females reaching sexual maturity annually, so that

$$N_0 \, p \, 0.4 \, s_1 \, (1 - F) \, s_2 = N_0 \, (1 - e^{-M_2}) \quad (1)$$

where

N_0 = initial population size of mature females

p = pregnancy rate of mature females

s_1 = survival rate of females from birth to 7 months of age

F = fishing mortality or sealing rate (percentage of female yearlings, surviving initial mortality, that are harvested)

s_2 = survival rate of immature seals after sealing season (from 10 months to 4 years of age)

and

M_2 = instantaneous natural mortality rate of adult females.

The factor 0.4 represents the proportion of female pups at birth in *A.p. pusillus* (Best and Rand, 1975). The term pup is used here to describe seals in their first 3 or 4 months of life until they shed their black, natal coat. From then until 12 months of age they are referred to as yearlings.

The population has been simulated in a real time series. For each simulation the sealing rate is kept constant, but certain parameters are made to vary in response to exploitation. At each iteration of the simulation the numbers of mature females, and of yearling females harvested are recorded. Iteration is continued until a stable population is reached, that is, until the number of females in each age class in successive iterations differs by less than 1.0.

The following symbols refer to the number of female seals in each age class at the end of year t, where year t ends at the beginning of the subsequent pupping season

$P_{1,t}$ = Number of one-year-olds
$P_{2,t}$ = number of two-year olds
$P_{3,t}$ = number of three-year-olds

and

N_t = number of mature females (four years and older).

Further,

$P_{0,t}$ = number of pups born in year t
p_t = pregnancy rate of mature females in year t

and

C_t = catch of female yearlings in year t.

Thus

$$P_{0,t+1} = N_t \cdot p_t \cdot 0.4 \qquad \dots \dots \dots \dots \quad (2)$$
$$P_{1,t+1} = P_{0,t+1} \cdot s_1 (1 - F) \qquad \dots \dots \dots \quad (3)$$
$$P_{2,t+1} = P_{1,t} \cdot s_{2,1} \qquad \dots \dots \dots \dots \quad (4)$$
$$P_{3,t+1} = P_{2,t} \cdot s_{2,2} \qquad \dots \dots \dots \dots \dots \quad (5)$$
$$N_{t+1} = N_t - N_t (1 - e^{-M}2) + P_{3,t} \cdot s_{2,3} \quad (6)$$
$$C_{t+1} = P_{0,t+1} \cdot s_1 \cdot F \qquad \dots \dots \dots \dots \quad (7)$$

where $s_{2,1}$, $s_{2,2}$ and $s_{2,3}$ are the survival rates of seals from age 1 to 2, 2 to 3 and 3 to 4 years, respectively.

The parameters

On the basis of skull suture examination, the age at sexual maturity in female *A.p. pusillus* was taken as 2 years by Rand (1955), with the first pup born at age 3. However, in August and September 1975, 7 female South African fur seals killed in their third year of life in the harvest at Kleinzee were found not to be pregnant. Since these females were tagged as pups in January 1973, we can be sure of their age. Thus we have concluded that females are not mature until at least 3 years of age, and their first parturition occurs at age 4 or later.

Although this parameter has been found to be density—dependent in some pinniped species (Sergeant, 1973), and there are suggestions of a difference in the age of females at sexual maturity between Asian and American herds of *C. ursinus* (Nagasaki, 1961), it has been considered safer here (in the absence of positive evidence of density—dependence) to assume that the age at sexual maturity in *A.p. pusillus* remains constant, irrespective of population size.

The pregnancy rate of *A.p. pusillus* has been given as 70 % by Rand (1952). It can also be calculated from data given in Tables 3 and 7 of Rand (1959) as 63/84 or 75 %. This is a very similar proportion to that described for *C. ursinus*. In the latter species at the Pribilof Islands, this parameter seems to be significantly affected by population density. Pregnancy rates varied from 57.8 % to 62.9 % in the years 1952, 1958-1962; for this period, Chapman (1964) considered 60 % to be the most reasonable estimate. For the period 1916-1922, he considered a figure of 80 % to be a reasonable upper limit to the pregnancy rate. The population level of the Pribilof Islands herd underwent considerable alteration during this time period. From 1925 to 1947 the population increased and exceeded the level estimated to give MSY (Johnson, 1972). The pup population was believed to have levelled off near 600 000 by the early 1950's (Johnson, 1975), and Nagasaki (1961) considered that, for the purposes of yield calculations, the pup production for the Pribilof Islands herd from 1953 to 1956 was equivalent to its maximum.

On the assumption that the density of northern fur seals reached its maximum in the early 1950's (when 600 000 pups were born), then the population level in 1916-1922 (154 000 pups, based on the average of 1916-1922 pup counts (Johnson, 1975)) was about 25 % of that in the early 1950's. Thus a linear relationship between relative adult female population size, N_t/N_0, and the proportion pregnant in year t (p_t) can be calculated as

$$p_t = 0.85 - 0.25\, N_t/N_0.$$

There are no data yet on the natural mortality rate of South African fur seals, either for juveniles or for adults. Given the similarity in reproductive rate and breeding behaviour of *A.p. pusillus* and *C. ursinus*, however, there is no reason to believe that a similar pattern of mortality does not exist in both species. In *C. ursinus* initial pup mortality (on land) is virtually complete by age 6 weeks (Kenyon, Scheffer and Chapman, 1954), and appears to be strongly density—dependent (Chapman, 1961; Nagasaki, 1961). The relationship between mortality of *C. ursinus* pups on land and the number born has been recalculated from the available data (Table 1 and Figure 1). Mortality for the period 1914 to 1922 and in 1924 has been calculated from counts of live and

dead pups (Kenyon, Scheffer and Chapman, 1954), while mortality from 1961 to 1966 has been calculated from counts of dead pups only (Marine Mammal Biological Laboratory, 1969) and the mean of pup population estimates based on tagging and on shearing and sampling (Johnson, 1972). Assuming that the maximum pup population for the Pribilofs was 600 000, the observed mortalities (M_1 %) have been plotted on a logarithmic scale against estimates or counts of the pup population expressed as a proportion of the initial pup population size (x). This gives a least squares estimates of

$$\log_{10} M_1 = 0.0475 + 1.3542\, x.$$

Assuming that pup mortality is similar for both sexes, the initial survival rate of female pups can be expressed as

$$s_1 = 1-0.01\,(10^{0.0475 + 1.3542x})$$

where

$$x = N_t p_t / N_0 p_0.$$

This equation has been inserted into the model to produce estimates of pup survival (s_1) at different levels of pup population size relative to the initial.

Because mortality of pups on land is essentially complete by 6 weeks of age in *C. ursinus*, it is assumed that in *A.p. pusillus* mortality of young pups represents the only natural mortality previous to sealing (which in this species has normally occurred at an age of 6.5 to 10.5 months). Natural mortality after sealing and before recruitment to the mature population is not considered to be density-dependent, despite opinions to the contrary for *C. ursinus* (NPFSC Scientific Committee, 1962). This conclusion is reached after comparing the survival rate of *C. ursinus* females from birth to age 3 for the period 1916-22 ($0.40 \times 1.25 = 0.50$) with that for 1947-52 (0.37 in Chapman, 1964). When the different survival rates for pups on land during these two

Table 1. Relationship between land mortality in northern fur seal pups and number of pups born

Year	No. pups born [1,2] (thousands)	No. pups born/ 600 000 (x)	No. dead pups [1,3] counted	Mortality rate (M_1 %)
1914	93	0.155	1 743	1.9
1915	104	0.173	1 811	1.7
1916	117	0.195	2 482	2.1
1917	128	0.213	3 850	3.0
1918	143	0.238	4 302	3.0
1919	157	0.262	4 834	3.1
1920	168	0.280	4 219	2.5
1921	177	0.295	4 397	2.5
1922	186	0.310	3 223	1.7
1924	208	0.347	5 109	2.5
1961	491	0.818	71 001	14.5
1962	420	0.700	53 748	12.8
1963	393	0.655	39 239	10.0
1964	396	0.660	25 042	6.3
1965	367	0.612	46 308	12.6
1966	413	0.688	27 392	6.6

[1] 1914-1924: from Kenyon, Scheffer and Chapman (1954).
[2] 1961-1966: data are mean of tagging estimates and shearing and sampling estimates, from Johnson (1972).
[3] 1961-1966: including the 5 % oversight factor, from Marine Mammal Biological Laboratory (1969).

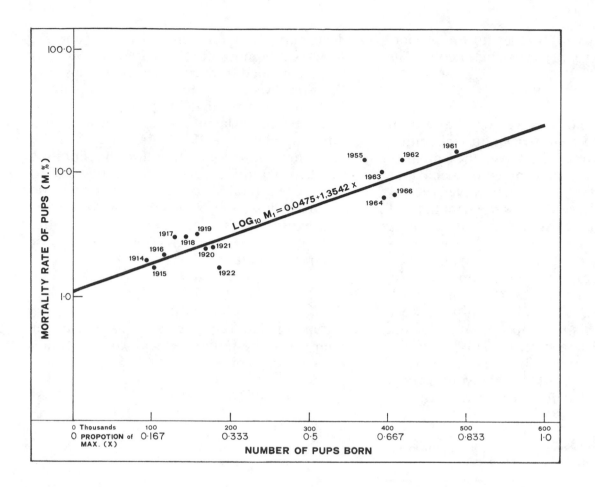

FIG. 1. – Density dependent mortality rate of *Callorhinus ursinus* pups at the Pribilof Islands.

periods are taken into consideration, the subsequent survival rates of juveniles at sea are almost identical (around 0.51), despite great differences in the total population size. In the model therefore annual survival rates for second and third year animals ($s_{2,1}$ and $s_{2,2}$) are taken to be constant, at 0.7141 each, with $s_{2,1}$ including any mortality that might take place after sealing and previous to age one.

No estimates are available for 2 other survival rates of *A.p. pusillus*, namely that for females in their third year and that for mature females. According to Chapman (1964), the survival rate of third and fourth year *C. ursinus* females is high, around 0.94 to 0.95. Therefore a figure of 0.95 has been adopted for $s_{2,3}$.

If the present model is then run for a balanced initial population with the parameters set at the above values, the annual mortality rate of mature *A.p. pusillus* females can

be calculated as 0.087. This figure is considered to be close enough to Chapman's (1964) calculation for *C. ursinus* of 0.11 to be used in the model. No density–dependent changes in these two rates are expected.

Results

(1) *Maximum sustainable harvest of yearlings*

The annual harvest of yearling females, the number of mature females when the population reaches stability and the number of years taken to reach stability under various constant sealing rates are shown in Table 2. The model predicts that the maximum sus-

Table 2. Yield and population size of *A.p. pusillus* females at various sealing rates, with time taken for the population to reach stability

Sealing rate (F)	Annual harvest of yearlings (C_t)	Population size of mature females ($N/_t/N_0$)	Years to stability (t)
0.10	178	0.893	61
0.20	341	0.759	92
0.30	444	0.578	150
0.31	447	0.556	159
0.32	449	0.532	169
0.33	449	0.508	180
0.34	446	0.483	192
0.35	440	0.457	206
0.40	362	0.303	311
0.50	36	0.021	485
0.60	12	0.006	250
0.70	8	0.003	167
0.80	6	0.002	124
0.90	5	0.001	97

tainable sealing rate for yearlings is 33 % of the number of female pups surviving to the beginning of the sealing season, when the mature female population stabilizes at about 51 % of its initial level (Figure 2). That stability is reached after 180 years.

It is interesting to note that the yield curve falls off very rapidly when the sealing rate is increased beyond that giving maximum harvest. The maximum sealing rate tolerable for an appreciable sustained yield appears to be about 50 %. This suggests that even harvesting at the maximum sustainable yield level might be potentially dangerous if there should be a serious bias in the model. Thus the population should be harvested at below the maximum sustainable rate.

(2) Sensitivity analyses

The parameters used in this model have been subjected to sensitivity analyses. In each of these analyses the number of mature females dying annually has been adjusted to balance the number of juvenile females reaching sexual maturity so that the number of mature

females in the initial population remains constant. For the survival rates that are thought to be independent of population density (namely, those for seals in their second, third and fourth years), alteration of the parameters by 3 or 4 percentage points has little effect on the predicted maximum sustainable sealing rate or on the concomitant yield (Table 3). Further, the number of mature females in the resulting stable population either remains unchanged or increases slightly.

Other presumed density-independent parameters that seem to have little effect on the predicted maximum sustainable sealing rate are the sex ratio of newborn pups and the age at sexual maturity in females (Table 4). As the percentage of females among newborn pups is increased from 35 % to 50 %, the model predicts that the maximum sustainable sealing rate is virtually unaltered, the harvest increases, and the number of adult females in the stable population changes only slightly.

Changing the age of first parturition of cows from 4 years to either 3 years or 5 years also has little effect on the maximum sustainable sealing rate and on the predicted harvest of yearlings, but slightly increases the number of adult females in the stable population (Table 4). As would be expected, the number of years taken to reach stability increases as the age of first parturition increases. Unfortunately it was not possible to treat the age of first parturition as a density-dependent parameter. From these analyses it can be concluded that the model is not sensitive to changes in these density-independent parameters.

In using equation (2) to predict the number of pups born, N_t has been used for the number of adult females in the population. Although this is correct for the beginning of the pupping season of year $t + 1$, the number of adult females decreases during the pupping season due to mortality. Since the pupping season lasts for a couple of months rather than a whole year, N_t is considered to be a better estimate of the number of adult females than N_{t+1}. However, if N_t is replaced by N_{t+1}, in equation (2), there is little change to the pre-

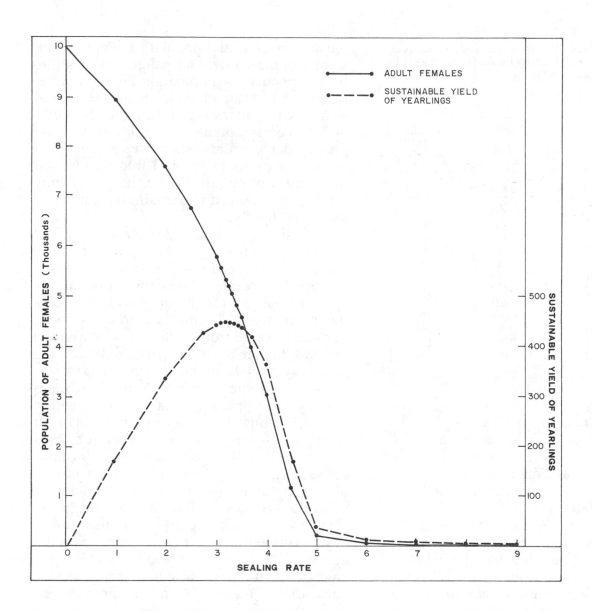

FIG. 2. – Population size and sustainable yield of female South African fur seals at various sealing rates.

dicted maximum sustainable sealing rate, harvest and the number of adult females at stability (Table 4).

The model is sensitive to changes in the pregnancy rate (p_t). This parameter is considered to be density-dependent in *C. ursinus*. The model has also been run with pregnancy rate assumed to be density-independent at the highest and at the lowest values estimated for *C. ursinus* (0.8 and 0.6, respectively). Under these circumstances the predicted maximum sustainable sealing rate and the harvest are considerably reduced (Table 4). The model is less sensitive to changes in the pregnancy rate when this parameter is considered to be density-dependent. If the pregnancy rate relationship is changed so that the pregnancy rate of 0.6 occurs when the number of mature females is 90 % of its initial value rather than at its initial value (i.e., if the number of pups born at the pregnancy rate of 0.6 was 540 000 rather than 600 000) giving $p_t = 0.85 - 0.28\, N_t/N_0$, then the maximum sustainable rate increases slightly to 34.5 % and the harvest also increases (Table 4). On the other hand, if the pregnancy rate relationship is changed so that the pregnancy rate of 0.8 occurs when the number of mature females is 10 % of its initial value rath-

Table 3. Results of sensitivity analysis of density-independent survival rates used in the population model of *A.p. pusillus*

Survival rate	Values of the parameter	Maximum sustainable sealing rate	Maximum sustainable harvest of yearlings	Population size of adult females relative to initial (N_t/N_0)	No. years to stability (t)
$s_{2,1}$	0.670	0.32	450	0.534	175
	0.714 [1]	0.33	449	0.508	180
	0.760	0.33	450	0.510	172
$s_{2,2}$	0.670	0.32	450	0.534	175
	0.714 [1]	0.33	449	0.508	180
	0.760	0.33	450	0.510	172
$s_{2,3}$	0.920	0.32	450	0.534	172
	0.950 [1]	0.33	449	0.508	180
	0.980	0.33	449	0.509	176

[1] All parameters unaltered.

er than 19.25 % (i.e., if the number of pups born at the pregnancy rate of 0.8 was 80 000 rather than 154 000), then the maximum sustainable sealing rate decreases slightly to 31.5 % and the harvest also decreases.

The model is very sensitive to changes in the survival rate of pups (s_1). When this parameter is held constant at its estimated highest and lowest value in *C. ursinus* (0.9826 and 0.8554, respectively), the model predicts that the maximum sustainable sealing rate and harvest are both considerably reduced (Table 4). We have also considered the effect of describing the variation of up survival rate with pup population size by a linear rather than an exponential relationship. For the linear function we used the pup survival rates predicted by the exponential relationship when the number of pups is 1 % and 100 % of its initial value. This leads to be function

$$s_1 = 0.9909 - 0.2431 \times$$

which has the effect of reducing the maximum sustainable rate to 29 %.

These conclusions lead us to stress the importance of obtaining data on pup mortality prior to sealing and on the pregnancy rate of mature females. Projects to monitor these parameters in *A.p. pusillus* are either in cross or being planned.

(3) *Other harvesting regimes.*

Although most *A.p. pusillus* taken are yearlings, recoveries of tagged seals of known age in harvests indicate that a small proportion of older immature seals is also taken. An inspection of the teeth of dead seals showed that the proportion of seals killed that were more than 1 year old at 5 colonies varied between 0.8 % and 11.3 % (Shaughnessy, 1976). In addition, there is a harvest of seals incidental to commercial fishing operations that presumably includes all age-classes. Thus it is instructive to use the population model to predict the maximum sustainable sealing rate, yield and the size of the resulting stable adult female population for a variety of harvesting regimes other than the harvest of yearling seals. Three approaches have been adopted. Firstly, the whole harvest is applied to animals of one of the year-classes. Secondly the harvest

Table 4. Results of sensitivity analysis of some parameters used in the population model of *A.p. pusillus*

Parameter	Maximum sustainable sealing rate	Maximum sustainable harvest of yearlings	No. mature females relative to no. in initial population (N_t/N_0)	No. years to stability
Proportion of female newborn pups:				
0.35	0.325	394	0.522	189
0.40 [1]	0.33	449	0.508	180
0.45	0.32	506	0.533	156
0.50	0.33	561	0.508	157
Age of cow at first parturition:				
3 years	0.32	450	0.533	157
4 years [1]	0.33	449	0.508	180
5 years	0.32	450	0.534	180
Number of mature females in equation (2):				
N_{t+1}	0.325	449	0.520	164
$N_{tl/}$ [1]	0.33	449	0.508	180
Pregnancy rate:				
$p_t = 0.8$, constant	0.19	351	0.626	226
$p_t = 0.6$, constant	0.185	263	0.646	243
$p_t = 0.85 - 0.28\ N_t/N_0$	0.345	460	0.513	169
$p_t = 0.85 - 0.25\ N_t/N_0$ [1]	0.33	449	0.508	180
$p_t = 0.82 - 0.22\ N_t/N_0$	0.315	426	0.517	187
Survival rate of pups:				
$s_1 = 0.9826$, constant	0.175	248	0.496	252
$s_1 = 0.8554$, constant	0.17	216	0.514	263
$s_1 = 0.9909 - 2431x$	0.29	331	0.453	200
$s_1 = 1 - 0.01\ (10^{0.0475 + 1.3542x})$ [1]	0.33	449	0.508	180

[1] All parameters unaltered.

is limited to seals in the 1st and 2nd year-classes, and varying proportions of them are harvested. Finally, these two approaches are combined for a harvest of varying proportions of several age-classes. In each case, the maximum sustainable sealing rate is expressed as the maximum sustainable harvest divided by the number of pups surviving to the beginning of the sealing season. This sealing rate is then comparable to F in the case when only yearlings are harvested.

(i) *Harvest restricted to a single year-class*

For this manipulation of the model, two alterations were made to the equations: firstly, the factor $(1 - F)$ in equation (3) was moved to equation (4), (5) or (6) as required, while equation (3) became

$$P_{1,t+1} = P_{0,1} \cdot s_1;$$

Secondly, equation (7) (defining the catch) was altered accordingly. For example, if the catch is composed of seals in their third year, equation (5) becomes

$$P_{3,t+1} = P_{2,t} \cdot s_{2,2} \cdot (1 - F),$$

and the catch in year t + 1 becomes

$$C_{t+1} = P_{2,t+1} \cdot s_{2,2} \cdot F.$$

The results of these manipulations (Table 5) indicate that both the maximum sustainable harvest and the maximum sustainable sealing rate decrease as the harvest is shifted to older age-classes.

For the mature female class, the maximum sustainable sealing rate is reached when a very small proportion of the mature females is harvested annually (0.4). Further, the model indicates that harvesting 10 % of the adult females each year results in their number being reduced by half in 10 years. Only four years are required if 20 % of the adult females are removed annually.

(ii) *Harvest of 1st and 2nd year animals*

The effect of including various proportions of second year animals in the harvest of yearlings has been analysed by modifying equation (4) to

$$P_{2,t+1} = P_{1,t} \cdot s_{2,1} - h \cdot C_{t+1}$$

and expressing the total catch in year t + 1 as

$$T_{t+1} = C_{t+1} + h \cdot C_{t+1}$$
$$= (1 h) P_{0,t+1} \cdot s_1 \cdot F,$$

where the number of animals harvested in their second year is h times that harvested in their first year. The results of these manipulations (Table 6) indicate that as the proportion of second year animals in the harvest increases, the maximum sustainable harvest and the maximum sustainable sealing rate decrease.

When 5 % of the catch are seals in their second year, the maximum sustainable sealing rate is reduced to 32 % from 33 % when only yearlings are harvested. When 9 % of the catch are second years, the maximum sustainable sealing rate is further reduced to 31 %.

(iii) *Harvest of more than two age-classes*

Table 7 illustrates two examples.

Firstly when the winter harvest consists of 93 % yearlings, 5 % 2nd years and 2 % 3rd years, the maximum sustainable harvest decreases slightly from 449 (when only yearlings are taken) to 433, while the maximum sustainable sealing rate decreases from 33 % to 31 %.

Secondly, when a small proportion of the mature animals (0.005) is taken each year additional to the above harvest of immatures, the maximum sustainable harvest decreases to 407 (382 immatures and 47 matures) and the maximum sustainable sealing rate is 31 %.

Discussion

The harvest of *A.p. pusillus* is directed at young immatures (predominantly yearlings)

Table 5. The effect of harvesting different age-classes on the maximum sustainable yield and population size of *A.p. pusillus* females

Age-class harvested	Value of F for MSY	Maximum sustainable yield	Maximum sustainable sealing rate	No. mature females relative to initial population (N_t/N_0)	No. years to stability (t)
0 +	0.33	449	0.330	0.508	180
1 +	0.325	321	0.232	0.521	173
2 +	0.33	229	0.169	0.508	178
3 +	0.32	218	0.155	0.532	166
Mature	0.04	218	0.157	0.522	137

Table 6. The effect of harvesting various proportions of first and second year animals on the maximum sustainable yield and population size of *A.p. pusillus* females

Proportion of second years in harvest $h/(1+h)$	Value of h	Value of F for MSY	Maximum sustainable yield			Maximum sustainable sealing rate	No. mature females relative to initial population (N_t/N_0)	No. years to stability (t)
			1st year	2nd year	Total			
0 [1]	0	.33	449	0	449	.330	.508	180
0.050	0.053	.305	418	22	440	.321	.514	177
0.091	0.1	.285	384	39	443	.313	.521	168
0.167	.2	.255	351	70	421	.306	.517	169
0.231	.3	.23	316	95	411	.299	.517	176
0.333	.5	.19	264	132	396	.285	.525	173
0.412	.7	.162	227	159	386	.276	.531	170
0.5	1.0	.135	187	187	374	.270	.523	174
0.6	1.5	.105	145	217	362	.263	.519	176
0.667	2.	.085	118	236	355	.255	.525	173
0.8	4.	.05	68	272	340	.250	.508	181
0.85	5.667	.035	50	284	334	.233	.549	163
1 [1]		.325	0	321	321	.232	.521	173

[1] From Table 2.

because this is one of the most common age-classes in the colonies and it produces the most valuable pelts. Changing the emphasis of the harvest to older immatures would not be possible due to their scarcity in the colonies, with the exception of the Cape Cross colony where many of them haul-out regularly on the beach south of the main breeding area. Because pup production of colonies is compara-tively simple to monitor through aerial photography and the tag-recapture technique (Best and Rand, 1975; Shaughnessy, 1976), any errors that occur in the management of the yearling harvest can be rectified relatively promptly. The long time-lags in the response of the population to manipulation make such monitoring essential.

Manipulations of the population model

Table 7. The effect of harvesting various proportions of different age-classes on the maximum sustainable yield and population size of *A.p. pusillus* females

Proportion of immature catch in each age-class			Proportion of mature population harvested	Maximum sustainable yield		Maximum sustainable sealing rate	No. mature females relative to initial population (N_t/N_0)	No. years to stability
0+	1+	2+		Immature	Mature			
1.0 [1]	0	0	0	449	0	.330	.508	180
.95 [2]	.05	0	0	440	0	.321	.514	177
.91 [2]	.09	0	0	443	0	.313	.521	168
.93	.05	.02	0	433	0	.310	.528	171
.92	.05	.02	.005	382	25	.308	.489	183

[1] From Table 2, for comparison.
[2] From Table 6, for comparison.

indicate that the maximum sealing rate for a sustained harvest of young immatures is slightly over 30 % of the number of pups surviving to the beginning of the sealing season. The pup production estimates made by the tag-recapture method (including estimates from the recovery of tags in the harvest) refer to the population size at tagging in mid-January when pups average 6 weeks of age. Since most of the natural mortality in the first year of life occurs in the first few weeks, these pup population estimates will not differ much from the number of pups surviving to the beginning of the sealing season (when they average 8 months of age). Thus the maximum sustainable sealing rate can be applied to these pup production estimates to obtain quotas for the harvest.

Although the harvest is directed at yearlings, more information should be obtained on the mortality rate of adult females incidental to the fishing industry, as the population model indicates that such mortality can strongly affect the maximum sustainable harvest and sealing rate.

In the event of the collapse of the sealing industry for *A.p. pusillus* pelts, the managers of the herds might consider controlling the population level by harvesting adult females, another age-class which is present at the colonies in large numbers at predictable times of the year. However, such a harvest could jeopardize the population since this age-class is very sensitive to even small amounts of harvesting. Thus it is not surprising that the early sealers of *A.p. pusillus* in the 17th and 18th century, who were harvesting indiscriminately and usually during the breeding season, had such a drastic effect on the population level. Furthermore, monitoring the size of the adult female population would be difficult. This could be done indirectly by monitoring the size of the pup population (as is done currently), but would require a knowledge of the pregnancy rate at different population levels.

Acknowledgements

We thank Dr. T.D. Smith of the University of Hawaii for advice on the model, and Mr. B. Kriedemann of the Sea Fisheries Branch for performing the computations.

References

BEST, P.B. and R.W. RAND, Results of a pup-tagging
1975   experiment on the *Arctocephalus pusillus* rookery at Seal Island, False Bay, South Africa. *Rapp. P.-V. Réun. CIEM*, 169:267-73.

CHAPMAN, D.G., Population dynamics of the Alaska fur
1961   seal herd. *Trans. N. Am. Wildl. Nat. Resour. Conf.*, 26:356-69.

–, A critical study of Pribilof fur seal population esti-
1964   mates. *Fish. Bull. USFWS*, 63(3):657-69.

JOHNSON, A., Affidavit. *In* Ocean mammal protection:
1972   hearing before the Sub-Committee on Oceans and Atmosphere of the Committee on Commerce, United States Senate 92nd Congress, 2nd Session, Part I, U.S. Government Printing Office, pp. 783-7.

JOHNSON, A.M., The status of northern fur seal popula-
1975   tions. *Rapp. P.-V. Réun. CIEM*, 169:263-6.

KENYON, K.W., V.B. SCHEFFER and D.G. CHAPMAN, A
1954   population study of the Alaska fur-seal herd. *Spec. Sci. Rep. U.S. Fish. Wildl. Serv. (Wildl.)*, (12):1-77.

NAGASAKI, F., Population study on the fur-seal herd.
1961   *Spec. Publ. Tokai Reg. Fish. Rec. Lab.*, 7:1-60.

Marine Mammal Biological Laboratory, Fur seal inves-
1969   tigations, 1966. *Spec. Sci. Rep. U.S. Fish. Wildl. Serv. (Fish.)*, (584):1-123.

NPFSC Scientific Committee, Report on investigations
1962   from 1958 to 1961. Paper presented to the North Pacific Fur Seal Commission by the

standing Scientific Committee on 26 November 1962, 183 p.

RAND, R.W., Fur seals. Research and management.
1952   *Commer. Ind.*, 11(1):35-40.

—, Reproduction in the female Cape fur seal, *Arctoce-*
1955   *phalus pusillus* (Schreber). *Proc. Zool. Soc.*
        Lond., 124(4):717-40.

—, The Cape fur seal (*Arctocephalus pusillus*). Distri-
1959   bution, abundance and feeding habits off the
        south western coast of the Cape Province.

Invest. Rep. Div. Sea Fish. S. Afr., 34:1-75.

SERGEANT, D.E., Environment and reproduction in
1973   seals. *J. Reprod. Fert.*, Suppl. 19:555-61.

SHAUGHNESSY, P.D., The status of seals in South Africa
1976   and South West Africa. Paper presented to the
        Scientific Consultation on the Conservation
        and Management of Marine Mammals and
        their Environment, Bergen, Norway, 31 Au-
        gust-9 September 1976. Rome, FAO,
        ACMRR/MM/SC/52:30 p.

MODELLING SEAL POPULATIONS FOR HERD MANAGEMENT

C.K. Capstick and K. Ronald

Abstract

A brief description of Allen's life-table model of the population of harp seals, *Pagophilus groenlandicus*, in the western North Atlantic is given, with flow charts of its computer programme. The model operates on the number of seals in each year-class, applying in each year the following sequence: births, deaths by hunting, natural mortality and ageing by one year. The first 3 parameters can be different for each year-class or uniform for the population; the initial size of the population can be taken to be the sum of all year-classes or calculated from a population of pups only.

The model is modified to include a birth rate which is density dependent; this is derived from a density-dependent female maturity rate based on a cumulative normal frequency distribution and on a function describing the recorded drop in age at sexual maturity from about 5½ to 4¾ years between the early fifties and the early sixties. A maximum birth rate and minimum age at first birth are also included, here set at 90 % and age 4, respectively. Within certain limits, the modified model shows a slower rate of decline in the size of declining exploited populations than does the model in which the birth rate is not related to population size: using the model without density dependence, a herd of harp seals constructed from a population of 250 000 pups began to decline toward extinction under 2 different rates of harvesting after 15 and 28 years, respectively; using the other model, the herd began this decline after 19 years in the first case and was still sustainable after 50 years in the second. To help determine whether it is the harvest, natural mortality rates of certain age classes or both, which are causing the decline, the model can be used to simulate the history of the population; with regard to harp seals in the western North Atlantic, if the estimated average natural mortality rate of 11 % per year is near the true mortality rate, examples in this paper indicate that hunting of these seals must be reduced. There is a need to develop stochastic models which can accommodate the chance variations in the values of important parameters of this population.

Résumé

Les auteurs décrivent brièvement le modèle d'Allen basé sur des tableaux de longévité de la population de phoques du Groenland, *Pagophilus groenlandicus*, de l'Atlantique nord-ouest, ainsi que les schémas de son programme d'ordinateur. Le modèle porte sur les effectifs de chaque classe d'âge annuelle en appliquant, pour chaque année, la séquence suivante: naissances, mortalité résultant de la chasse, mortalité naturelle et vieillissement d'un an. Les trois premiers paramètres peuvent être différents pour chaque classe annuelle, ou uniformes pour la population; la taille initiale de la population peut être considérée comme étant la somme de toutes les classes annuelles ou peut être calculée seulement à partir d'une population de nouveau-nés.

Le modèle est modifié pour inclure un taux de natalité dépendant de la densité; il est obtenu à partir d'un taux de maturité des femelles dépendant de la densité, basé sur une distribution de fréquence normale cumulative et sur une fonction décrivant l'abaissement enregistré de l'âge de la maturité sexuelle de 5½ à 4¾ ans entre le début des années 50 et le début des années 60. Un taux maximum de natalité et un âge minimum à la première naissance sont aussi inclus; ils sont fixés ici, respectivement, à 90 % et 4 ans. Dans certaines limites, le modèle modifié fait ressortir un taux plus lent de diminution de la taille des populations exploitées en fléchissement que ne le fait le modèle où le taux de natalité n'est pas lié à la taille de la population: en utilisant le modèle sans dépendance à l'égard de la densité, un troupeau de phoques du Groenland construit sur une population de 250 000 jeunes a commencé à fléchir en direction de l'extinction, avec deux différents taux d'exploitation après 15 ans et 28 ans, respectivement; en utilisant l'autre modèle, le troupeau a manifesté ce déclin après 19 ans dans le premier cas et était toujours exploitable après 50 ans dans le second. Afin de déterminer plus facilement si c'est l'exploitation, le taux de mortalité de certaines classes d'âge, ou une combinaison des deux, qui provoque le déclin, le modèle peut être employé pour simuler l'évolution historique de la population, dans le cas des phoques du Groenland de l'Atlantique nord-ouest, si le taux estimé de la mortalité naturelle moyenne de 11 % par an est proche du véritable taux de mortalité. Les exemples fournis dans le présent rapport indiquent que la chasse de ces phoques doit être réduite. Il est nécessaire d'élaborer des modèles stochastiques qui peuvent tenir compte des variations dues au hasard de la valeur des paramètres importants de cette population.

Extracto

Se presenta una breve descripción del modelo de tablas vitales de Allen para la población de foca de Groenlandia (*Pagophilus groenlandicus*) del noroeste del Atlántico y una descripción de las diversas etapas de la ejecución del correspondiente programa para calculadora. El modelo trabaja sobre la base del número de focas de cada clase anual, aplicando en cada año la siguiente secuencia: nacimientos, muertes por captura, mortalidad natural y determinación de la edad. Los tres primeros parámetros pueden ser diversos según la clase de edad o uniformes para toda la población; para determinar la población inicial puede utilizarse la suma de todas las clases anuales o hacer un cálculo a partir de una población de cachorros solamente.

Se modifica el modelo para incluir un índice de nacimientos dependiente de la densidad, que se obtiene a partir de un índice de madurez de las hembras (dependiente también de la densidad) basado en una distribución cumulativa normal de frecuencias y en una función que describe la disminución que se ha registrado en la edad en el momento de la madurez sexual, que ha bajado de 5½ a 4¾ años entre principios de los años cincuenta y principios de los años sesenta. Se incluye también un índice máximo de nacimientos y una edad mínima en el primer parto, fijados, respectivamente, en 90 por ciento y cuatro años de edad. Dentro de ciertos límites, el modelo modificado muestra un índice más lento de disminución del volumen de las poblaciones explotadas que el modelo en el que el índice de nacimientos no se pone en relación con el volumen de la población: usando el modelo en el que no se tiene en cuenta la densidad de la población, un rebaño de focas de Groenlandia con una población de 250 000 cachorros empieza a disminuir acercándose a la extinción al cabo de 15 y 28 años, con dos índices distintos de explotación; con el otro modelo, el rebaño inicia esa disminución al cabo de 19 años, en la primera hipótesis y sigue dando un rendimiento sostenible al cabo de 50 años en la segunda. Para determinar si es la explotación, la mortalidad natural de determinadas clases de edad, o ambas, lo que determina la disminución, el modelo puede utilizarse para simular la historia de la población. Por lo que se refiere a las focas de Groenlandia del noroeste del Atlántico, si la mortalidad natural media estimada del 11 por ciento al año se acerca a la mortalidad real, los ejemplos citados en este documento indican que es necesario reducir la explotación de esas focas. Es necesario preparar modelos estocásticos que permitan tener en cuenta las variaciones aleatorias de los valores de algunos parámetros importantes de esta población.

C.K. Capstick
Department of Computing and Information Science, University of Guelph, Guelph, Ontario, N1G 2W1 Canada

K. Ronald
College of Biological Science, University of Guelph, Guelph, Ontario, N1G 2W1 Canada

Introduction

During the last twenty years, biologists have become increasingly involved in the modelling and simulation of complex ecological systems, made feasible by the computational speed of electronic computers. The use of such models by fisheries biologists and terrestrial wildlife managers is now common-place in the study of population dynamics and in the evaluation of alternative management strategies for exploited species. Although many pinniped populations are presently exploited by man, the use of simulation models as a scientific and management tool in this process has been limited (Chapman, 1961; Allen, 1975).

Starting from Allen's (1975) life table model of the northwestern Atlantic harp seal (*Pagophilus groenlandicus*) continuous attempts have been made to increase the correspondence between the behaviour of the model and this exploited population. A simultaneous development of input and output facilities for the models is needed, to make them more readily understood, and used, by those responsible for herd management decisions.

This paper sets out to give an expanded account, not previously published, of the basic sequence of operations used to compute Allen's (1975) model of the northwestern Atlantic harp seal. It also describes, as part of the process of model development, one density-dependent pupping relationship, together with other modifications intended to make this particular model more readily available to those concerned with the management of this herd.

The life table model

The basic life table model for harp seals in the Northwest Atlantic is described by Allen (1975). It uses the life table modelling techniques described by Leslie (1945, 1948), making specific adaptations for the Northwest Atlantic harp seal herd. The model operates on the numbers of seals in each of 30 year classes, applying in each year the following major sequence: births, deaths by hunting in the whelping and moulting patches, natural mortality and ageing by one year. The numbers remaining in each year class then form the basic life table data for the next annual cycle of calculations, and so on, over whatever period is being modelled. Birth rates, catch statistics and natural mortalities can be specific to individual year classes or uniform for the population. The initial population can either be specified as the numbers in each year class, or calculated from

179

an initial population of pups only. In the latter case the population constructed corresponds to a stable, unexploited herd.

Overview flowcharts, not previously published, describing the computer programme used to implement this model are shown in Figure 1 (data input) and Figure 2 (annual calculations). The principal modifications made to the original programme concern:

1) Changing the model to operate in interactive mode under IBM's Time Sharing Operating (T.S.O.) system on most standard computer terminals.

2) Alterations to the programme to reduce input errors made on the terminal keyboard.

3) The addition of facilities to implement density-dependent birth rates by age class, as described below.

The possibility of adding density-dependent natural mortality rates for individual age classes is currently being explored.

A model of density-dependent birth rates

Data

Sergeant (1966) gives the basic data on harp seal maturity rates. He states that the herd is divided geographically into 2 distinct breeding populations, one in the Gulf of St. Lawrence (Gulf) and the other off-shore from Newfoundland and Labrador (Front). Consequently the data are presented on a geographical basis. The data show differences between the maturity rates of female seals taken from the 2 geographical stocks, and between samples (from both stocks) taken in the early 1950's and the early 1960's. The mean age at

sexual maturity declined over the decade from 5½ to 4 years in the Front sample, and from 5½ to 5 years in the Gulf sample (Sergeant, 1966).

For the purpose of deriving density-dependent female maturity rates for the herd as a whole, no distinction is made here between Gulf and Front stocks. The geographical distinction in the data has been ignored and the Gulf and Front samples are combined. Instead, they have been divided into two time periods, one for 1951/54 and the other for 1961/65 (Table 1). When time is taken as the distinctive parameter, it will be seen that the age at which 50 % of female seals mature declined from between ages 5 and 6 in 1951/54 to between ages 4 and 5 in 1961/65. These changes in female reproductive maturity correspond to a decline in herd size from approximately 3 million in the early 1950's. (Fisher, 1955), to perhaps 2 million in the early 1960's, as implied by various estimates of pup production in the literature (Sergeant, 1966).

Development of a model

The 1953 maturity data has a mean of 5.49 years ·and a standard deviation of 1.07 years, while the 1964 data has a mean of 4.77 years and a standard deviation of 1.16 years (Figure 3). As the difference between the variances of these 2 samples was not found to be significant at the 0.1 % level, a common standard deviation of 1.118 years was calculated from the pooled variances. This figure was used as the standard deviation of all subsequent maturity ogives. This basic data shows a good fit to a cumulative normal (Gaussian) frequency distribution.

The formula for the cumulative normal frequency distribution is given by:

$$F(X) = \int_{-\infty}^{x} \frac{1}{\sqrt{2\Pi\sigma}} \, e^{-(t-\mu)^2/2\sigma^2} dt \quad \ldots \quad (1)$$

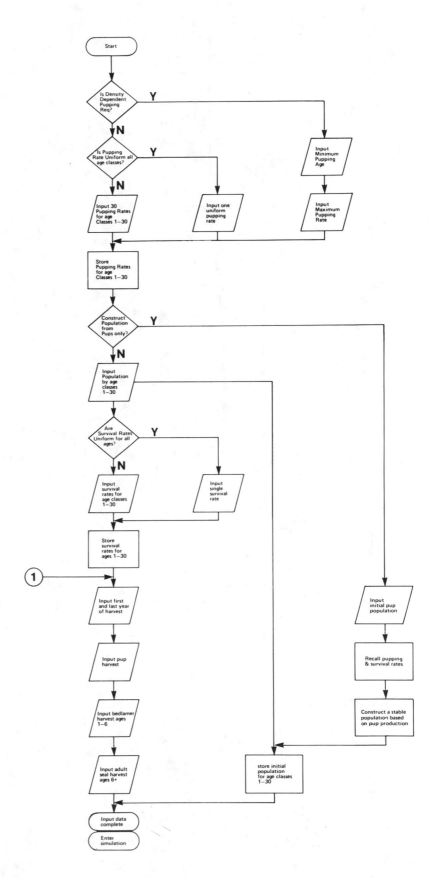

FIG. 1. — Overview flowchart of the data input
section of the model.

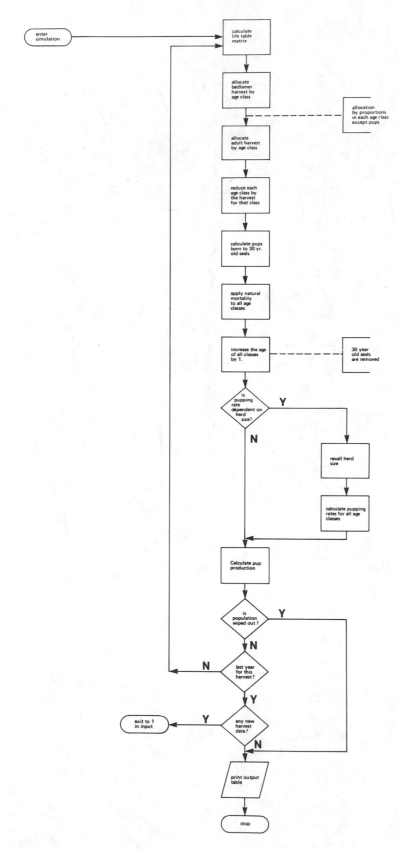

Fig. 2. – Overview flowchart of the annual calculation section of the model.

Table 1. Reproductive states of female harp *Pagophilus groenlandicus* seals for the periods 1951-1954 and 1961-1965. Gulf and Front populations combined. Age at maturity defined as age at first ovulation. From Sergeant (1966)

Age (years)	1951-1954			1961-1965		
	Total	Mature	% Mature	Total	Mature	% Mature
1	6	0	00	28	0	00
2	6	0	00	45	0	00
3	23	0	00	44	3	6.8
4	20	1	5.0	57	13	22.8
5	27	9	33.3	45	28	62.2
6	18	14	77.7	47	39	83.0
7	27	23	85.2	48	47	97.9
8	12	12	100.0	18	18	100.0
9	17	17	100.0	9	9	100.0
10	14	14	100.0	5	5	100.0
11	12	12	100.0	16	16	100.0
12	8	8	100.0	9	9	100.0
13	3	3	100.0	8	8	100.0
14	3	3	100.0	8	8	100.0
15	5	5	100.0	5	5	100.0
16	2	2	100.0	6	6	100.0
17	–	–	–	–	–	–
18	3	3	100.0	8	8	100.0
19	1	1	–	1	1	100.0
20	3	3	100.0	–	–	–
21	1	1	100.0	1	1	100.0
22	–	–	–	1	1	100.0
23	–	–	–	–	–	–
24	1	1	100.0	–	–	–
25	1	1	100.0	–	–	–

where

μ = average age at maturity
σ = standard deviation of age at maturity

Using the cumulative normal frequency distribution as the basis for a density-dependent function has one principal advantage: the normal distribution is completely specified by the mean and standard deviation. If it is reasonable to assume that the standard deviation of these maturity ogives can be regarded as constant, then, to describe a family of reproductive ogives for different herd sizes, the mean is the only parameter which need vary. In terms of harp seal maturities, the mean is defined as the average age at maturity which, for the normal distribution, corresponds to the age group in which 50 % of the females are mature. Maturity is, in turn, defined by Sergeant (1966) for these data as "age at first ovulation".

A density-dependent function relating age at 50 % maturity to herd size is postulated which has the following characteristics:

a) The general relationship is described by the function

$$\mu = F(H) \quad \dots \dots \dots \dots \dots \quad (2)$$

where

μ = average age at maturity and
H = herd size in millions

b) The function should fit the two known points:

183

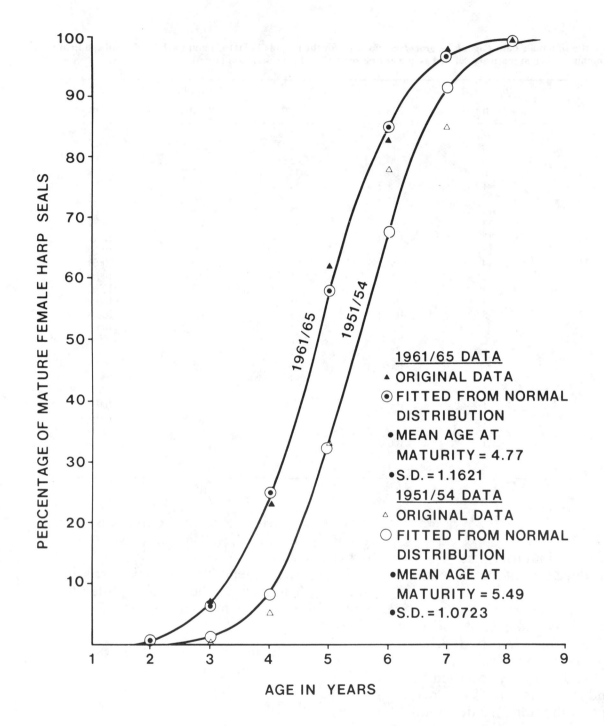

FIG. 3. – Relationship between maturity of female harp seals and age. From Sergeant (1966).

Herd size (Millions)	Average age at maturity
3.0 (1950's)	5.49
2.0 (1960's)	4.77

c) The function should become asymp-

totic at ages 6-7 for large herd sizes, say greater than 5 million.

d) The function should exhibit the greatest rate of change between herd sizes of 3 million and just less than 1 million.

184

Using these characteristics, b) was extrapolated according to c) and d) and a series of possible functions were postulated and fitted using a least squares fitting technique. Exponential and natural logarithmic functions were explored on a trial basic. The best fit was given by a function of the general type:

$$\mu = a + b \log_e H \quad \ldots \ldots \ldots \ldots \quad (3)$$

where μ = average age at maturity
$\quad$ H = herd size in millions
a and b = parameters

The function:

$$\mu = 3.711 + 1.5976 \log_e H \quad \ldots \ldots \quad (4)$$

is proposed as an initial hypothesis describing the relationship between herd size and mean age at maturity (Figure 4). This relationship satisfied all of the characteristics described above.

Using equations 1 and 4, and substituting for μ in the formula for the cumulative normal frequency distribution, the complete model becomes:

$$F(X) =$$

$$\int_{-\infty}^{x} \frac{1}{\sqrt{\Pi}\sigma} e^{-[t-(3.711+1.5976\log_e H)]^2/2\sigma^2} dt \quad (5)$$

where

F(X) $\,$ = proportion of mature female seals at age X
$\quad$ H = herd size in millions
$\quad \sigma$ = standard deviation of age at maturity

When plotted for different herd sizes this model produces a family of maturity ogives as shown in Figure 5.

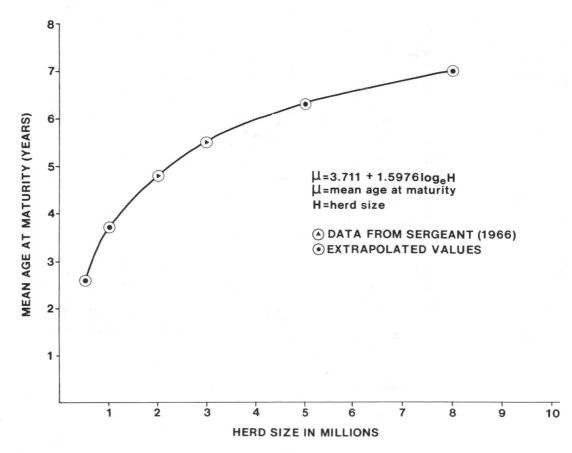

μ=3.711 + 1.5976$\log_e$H
μ=mean age at maturity
H=herd size

Ⓐ DATA FROM SERGEANT (1966)
⊙ EXTRAPOLATED VALUES

FIG. 4. – Proposed relationship between mean age at maturity and herd size for female harp seals.

185

In order to use this theoretical model of female harp seal maturity in a life table model of the harp seal population as a whole, certain constraints are necessary. First, the density-dependent relationship between herd size and female maturity must be converted to a relationship between herd size and birth or pupping rates. As conception takes place in March, previous to the birth of pups in late February/early March of the following year, this simply means moving the ogives for all herd sizes one year to the right (Sergeant, 1966, 1973).

The model used to calculate the proportion of female seals pupping (as distinct from those reaching maturity) is therefore:

$$F(X_p) = \int_{-\infty}^{x_p} \frac{1}{\sqrt{2\Pi\sigma}}\, e^{-[t-(4.711+1.5976\,\log_e H)]^2/2\sigma^2}\, dt \qquad (6)$$

where

$F(X_p)$ = proportion of female seals pupping at age X_p

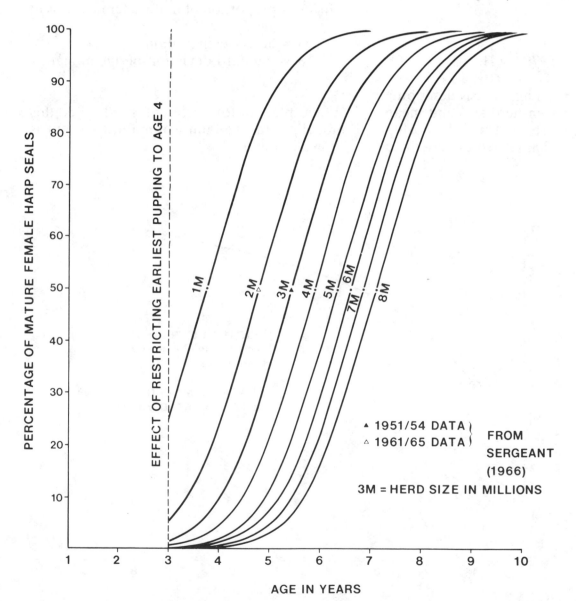

FIG. 5. – Model of relationship between percentage of mature female harp seals and age. For different herd sizes.

H = herd size in millions

σ = standard deviation of age at pupping

Second, allowance must be made for mature females that do not become pregnant, or that become pregnant but do not produce a pup which survives to birth. It is proposed that this be implemented by imposing a maximum on the percentage of seals that produce a pup that survives to birth. There is evidence (Sergeant, 1971; Øritsland, 1971), that this is about 90 %, but in case new evidence might change this in the future, the computer programme implementing the density-dependent birth rate model accepts this percentage as input data.

Similarly, there is, as yet, no evidence that harp seals give birth at any age below 4. Until conflicting evidence is forthcoming, the minimum age at which a female harp seal can give birth is also accepted as input data, and set at age 4. The minimum pupping age can be changed by supplying different values for this parameter as input data. Birth rates for ages less than the minimum pupping age are set equal to zero. The transformed birth rate ogives are shown in Figure 6, with sample restrictions on maximum pupping percentage and minimum pupping age super-imposed.

The effect of density-dependent pupping rates

The effect of density-dependent pupping rates can best be demonstrated on a declining population. The particular simulation runs used in this example are based on a stable, unhunted herd constructed by the

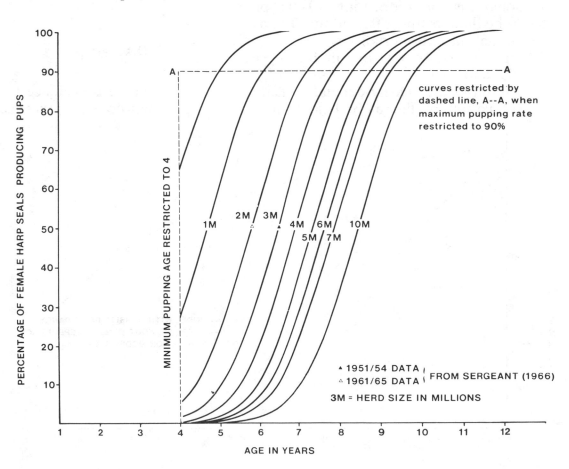

FIG. 6. – Model of relationship between percentage of female harp seals producing pups and age of seals. For different herd sizes.

model from a population of 250 000. The group age class structure of this particular herd is:

Age Group (Years)	Number of Seals (Thousands)
0-1 (pups)	250
1-2 to 5-7	472
6-7 to 29-30	559
Total	1 281

Two hunts were chosen to produce different rates of population decline when density-dependent pupping rates were not in effect. The actual catch in 1976 of about 164 000 seals was apportioned into 134 000 (82 %) adults. The proportions are those estimated from available hunt data for 1973, 1974 and 1975. Using the same proportions, the less severe hunt of 127 000 seals (the 1976 quota plus allocations) was apportioned into 104 000 pups, 15 000 bedlamers and 8 000 adults. The average annual natural mortality was set at 11 %, and the simulation was to run for 50 years from 1976 to 2026.

Without the density-dependent features the simulation of the more heavily hunted

herd stops in 1991 (Figure 7); the more lightly hunted herd simulation stops in 2004 (the simulation model stops when the hunt takes all of the annual pup production, and the first 3 or 4 age classes are empty).

The effect of density dependent pupping rates is different on the two declining populations. In the heavily hunted herd the cessation of the simulation run is delayed from 1991 to 1995, while the simulation of the more lightly hunted herd is still running in 2026 instead of stopping in 2004. Clearly, the efficacy of the proposed density-dependent pupping relationship — as a negative feedback which tends to stabilize the population as a system — is affected by the rate of decline of the population.

Thus, if a population is declining beyond a certain rate (which is as yet undetermined), then no reasonable density-dependent relationship is going to save it.

Discussion

There is evidence to indicate that pupping may occur at earlier ages as the herd size of

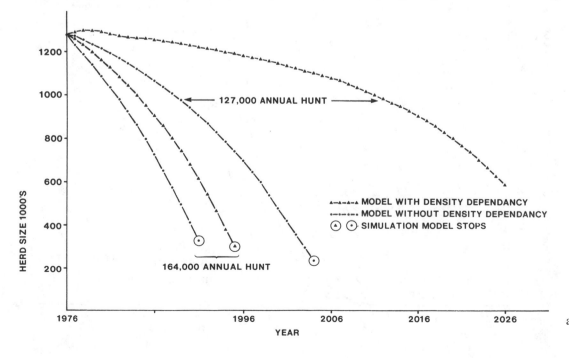

FIG. 7. — The effects of density-dependent pupping rates on a declining population under constant annual hunts of 127 000 and 164 000 seals. Average annual natural mortality 11 %.

the Northwest Atlantic harp seal declines (Sergeant, 1966, 1973). At present the biological data only apply to herd sizes varying between about 2 and 3 million animals, but it is reasonable to assume that such a relationship is not limited to these herd sizes; the only question at issue is its specification.

The relationship proposed here is only one of a number of possible hypotheses, but it does have certain properties which would be expected of any reasonable density-dependent pupping rate mechanism. First, it is unreasonable to assume a linear change of the mean age at maturity with herd size, as this would imply such biological absurdities as minimum breeding ages of 1 or 2 years in very small herds, or very high minimum breeding ages in large herds. The proposed relationship is therefore non-linear, and limited with respect to the range of variables (both age and herd size), over which it holds.

As used in this model, the relationship is limited at small herd sizes by restricting the minimum pupping age. This is specified as an input variable (Figure 1) and constrains the family of ogives in such a way that the pupping rates in the vector below this minimum pupping age are set equal to zero (Figure 6).

The assumption that the relationship becomes asymptotic with respect to the average maturity age at large herd sizes is not likely to be a serious problem in modelling a herd which has declined from an annual pup production of probably more than 600 000 in the early 1950's (Fisher, 1955), to perhaps less than 200 000 in 1975 (Lavigne *et al.*, 1976). The relationship is intended to be included in future forecasts produced by the model, until such time as a "better" proposal is developed.

With the Northwest Atlantic harp seal herd now estimated at a size somewhere less than 1 million to 1.5 million animals, there are some significant implications for herd management. At this size of herd, female seals should be pupping earlier than previously recorded. The hypothesis proposed here suggests that 7 % of females should be pupping at age 3 when the herd size is 1 million, and about 3 %

pupping at age 3 when the herd size is 1.5 million. In herds of this size food is unlikely to be a limiting factor. Since it is also probable that pupping is occurring earlier, all factors favour an increase in herd size. Therefore any further decrease in herd size is likely to be the result of excessive hunting pressure, some other kind of human intervention, or the herd having fallen below some critical size for sustainability.

Forecasts made with the density-dependent feature added to the model are more optimistic than when this feature is omitted, within limits which depend on assumptions about the rate of decline of herd size. In the example given above, either the hunting pressure is too great to allow the pups born earlier to contribute sufficient recruitment into the breeding stock to halt the decline, or the average annual natural mortalities are too high. One approach to estimating natural mortalities is to use the model to simulate the history of the herd. Using known hunt statistics and starting sufficiently far back in time to eliminate the initial conditions from the model, it is possible to derive by experiment the minimum natural mortality rates which generate estimates of pup production and total population which mimic the published historical estimates of these parameters. The estimates from such an approach can then be compared to the estimates of natural mortality derived by Allen (1975), from total annual mortality estimates made by Ricker (1971), and Ulltang (1971). At present, the implications from the examples presented here are, that if an estimated average annual mortality of 11 % is anywhere near the true figure, hunting pressure on the herd must be reduced.

The main advantage of simulation models for herd management is that they allow the effects of alternative management strategies to be evaluated, without affecting the real world which contains the seal herd. Provided the models themselves have been properly tested and evaluated against known biological data, there is no reason why simulation techniques should not be as successful in this field

189

as they have been in industry. Already, as has happened in industrial applications, this model has indicated areas where the data are deficient, and where more research is required to improve our knowledge of herd population dynamics.

This model is essentially deterministic and numerical, and there is a real need to develop stochastic models which can adequately reflect the chance variations in key parameters that are encountered by the harp seal herd. This approach should eventually be expanded to develop an integrated series of ecosystem models using the whole range of known simulation techniques. For instance, energy flows in the ecosystem are much better modelled by continuous simulation techniques, while discontinuous numerical systems are more effectively modelled by using discrete, stochastic simulations. Integration may well involve hybrid simulation techniques and

computers, as well as very large amounts of data. Because of the expense of acquiring such data, marine mammal biologists should cooperate to develop and maintain some central data bank facilities.

Acknowledgements

This research was made possible by a grant from the Donner Canadian Foundation and the continued support of the Special Advisory Committee on Seals and Sealing to the Minister of State (Fisheries), Government of Canada. We thank Dr. D.M. Lavigne for his helpful comments on the original manuscripts, and Dr. N.T. Ison and Mrs. C. Farrell for assistance with the statistics and programming.

References

ALLEN, R.L., A life table for harp seals in the Northwest
1975   Atlantic. *Rapp. P.-V. Réun. CIEM*, 169: 303-11.

CHAPMAN, D.G., Population dynamics of the Alaska fur
1961   seal herd. *Trans. N. Am. Wildl. Conf.*, 26:356-69.

FISHER, H.D., Utilization of Atlantic harp seal popula-
1955   tions. *Trans. N. Am. Wildl. Conf.*, 20:507-18.

LAVIGNE, D.M. *et al.*, An aerial census of western At-
1976   lantic harp seals (*Pagophilus groenlandicus*) using ultraviolet photography. Paper presented to the Scientific Consultation on the Conservation and Management of Marine Mammals and their Environment, Bergen, Norway, 31 August-9 September, 1976. Rome, FAO, ACMRR/MM/SC/33:9 p.

LESLIE, P.H., On the use of matrices in certain popula-
1945   tion mathematics. *Biometrica*, 33:183-212.

–, Some further notes on use of matrices in population
1948   mathematics. *Biometrica*, 35:213-45.

ØRITSLAND, T., The status of Norwegian studies of harp
1971   seals at Newfoundland. *Redbook ICNAF*, 1971(3):185-209.

RICKER, W.E., Comments on the West Atlantic harp seal
1971   herd and proposals for the 1972 harvest. *Res. Doc. ICNAF*, 75/12/143. Appendix.

SERGEANT, D.E., Reproductive rates of harp seals, *Pa-
1966   gophilus groenlandicus* (Erxleben). *J. Fish. Res. Board Can.*, 23(5):757-66.

–, Calculation of production of harp seals in the
1971   Northwest Atlantic. *Redbook ICNAF*, 1971(3):157-84.

–, Environment and reproduction in seals. *J. Reprod.
1973   Fert.*, Suppl. 19:555-61.

ULLTANG, O., Estimates of mortality and production of
1971   harp seals at Newfoundland, 13 p. (MS).

PINNIPED BIOENERGETICS

D.M. Lavigne, W. Barchard, S. Innes and N.A. Øritsland

Abstract

The authors summarize present knowledge of pinniped bioenergetics, concentrating on principles, rather than details for individual species. They emphasize the types of data which are needed to improve understanding of the role of pinnipeds in the marine ecosystem, and consider the utilization of energy by pinnipeds at the organismic and population levels. Pinnipeds are also considered as a component of a complex marine ecosystem, with comments on community energetics in relation to management. Lastly the authors consider the systems approach to management, a strategy which requires increased inputs of manpower and money, but one which will lead to a greater understanding of the complexity of ecological interactions in natural systems. This understanding should lead to more enlightened utilization and conservation of natural resources. Much of the work done on pinniped energetics relates to the harp seal, *Pagophilus groenlandicus*, and this is reflected in the paper. An extensive bibliography is provided.

Résumé

Les auteurs font le point sur les connaissances actuelles en bioénergétique des pinnipèdes, insistant surtout sur les principes, plutôt que sur les détails relatifs aux différentes espèces. Ils soulignent les types de données qui sont nécessaires pour mieux connaître le rôle joué par les pinnipèdes dans l'écosystème marin et examinent l'utilisation de l'énergie par les pinnipèdes, au niveau des organismes individuels et de la population. La note étudie également les pinnipèdes en tant qu'éléments d'un écosystème marin complexe, et présente certains commentaires sur l'énergétique collective, en rapport avec l'aménagement. Enfin, les auteurs traitent de l'approche des systèmes en matière d'aménagement; c'est une stratégie qui exige un apport accru de main-d'œuvre et de moyens financiers, mais elle peut aboutir à faire mieux comprendre la complexité des actions réciproques qui s'exercent dans les systèmes naturels. Cette compréhension devrait conduire à utiliser et à conserver d'une manière plus intelligente les ressources naturelles. La majeure partie des travaux existants consacrés à l'énergétique des pinnipèdes concernent le phoque du Groenland (*Pagophilus groenlandicus*), comme il ressort du document. Une bibliographie détaillée complète l'ouvrage.

Extracto

Los autores resumen los conocimientos actuales sobre la bioenergética de los pinnípedos, centrando la atención en los principios más que en los detalles de cada especie. En especial, los autores señalan los tipos de datos que se necesitan para poder comprender mejor el papel de los pinnípedos en el ecosistema marino y estudiar la utilización de la energía por los pinnípedos a nivel de organismo y de población. Asimismo, se estudian los pinnípedos como parte del complejo ecosistema marino y se formulan observaciones sobre energética de las manadas en relación con la ordenación. Por último, los autores analizan la manera de abordar sistemáticamente la ordenación, estrategia que requiere cada vez más insumos de mano de obra y dinero, pero que puede llevar a una mejor comprensión de la complejidad de las interacciones ecológicas en los sistemas naturales. Esta comprensión permitirá utilizar y conservar más racionalmente los recursos naturales. Los trabajos sobre energética de los pinnípedos se refieren sobre todo a la foca de Groenlandia, *Pagophilus groenlandicus*, como queda bien patente en esta publicación. El trabajo contiene una extensa bibliografía.

D.M. Lavigne
College of Biological Science, Department of Zoology, University of Guelph, Guelph, Ontario N1G 2W1, Canada

W. Barchard
College of Biological Science, Department of Zoology, University of Guelph, Guelph, Ontario N1G 2W1, Canada

S. Innes
Department of Zoology, University of Kansas, Lawrence, Kansas 66044, USA

N.A. Øritsland
Institute of Zoophysiology, University of Oslo, Postboks 1051, Blindern, Oslo 3, Norway

"Let me give one example of a problem in the ecology of seals ... We may be pushing near the limits of the fish resource and, if so, we have an apparent reason for killing all seals that feed on fish. But first it will have to be shown that, with fewer seals, there would be more fish, and I don't believe that anyone has demonstrated this outside the simplest aquatic model. When we take seals from the ocean, what sort of holes are left?"
Scheffer (1975)

Introduction

As man continues to exploit and deplete the natural resources of the sea, it becomes essential that new and improved management strategies be developed in order to conserve these resources. Future management policies must allow for prolonged and efficient utilization of marine resources and their mainten-ance at some optimal and stable level, minimizing the input of energy involved in exploitation, as well as maximizing output.

In order to realize these objectives, it will be necessary to develop a "system" approach to management (Watt, 1966). Single species models must be replaced by multispecies system simulations based on a knowledge of the various biotic and abiotic components within the ecosystem.

Since Lindeman's (1942) classic paper, it has become commonplace to study ecosystems in terms of energy flow, and it is now generally accepted that a knowledge of energy flow provides the most reliable basis for evaluating the role of a particular population within its community (Odum, 1971). In order to optimize management strategies for exploited populations, including those of many pinnipeds, productivity or rate of biomass (i.e., energy), production must be understood.

To date, management of pinniped species has been based primarily on "trial and error", or in a few instances on various types of single species population models (Chapman, 1961; Allen, 1975; Benjaminsen and Lett, 1976; Capstick, Lavigne and Ronald, 1976). Such management has been, and is, inadequate. It is now necessary to study pinnipeds as component members of a complex community.

The emphasis has been on estimating numbers of pinnipeds in particular populations with occasional estimates of population biomass (Laws, 1960). The importance in an ecosystem of large organisms tends to be under-emphasised by the use of numbers, and over-emphasised by the use of weights and biomass; the reverse tends to be true for small organisms (Clarke, 1946; Odum, 1971). Such data may however be used to calculate rates of change and energy flow within populations. The bioenergetic approach not only provides a more reliable estimate of the importance of a population within its community, but is equally applicable to all populations in all environments, regardless of differences, in terms of numbers and size, of organisms, species, and populations. Energy is the common currency of ecosystems (Odum, 1971).

It thus becomes necessary to identify the various factors which determine the efficiency of energy use at each step, or trophic level, within the ecosystem. Loss of energy at each trophic level is significantly large, such that few food pyramids have more than 5 levels (Watt, 1968). Respiration losses increase from producers to consumers. Increased mobility, for instance, to search for food, or to migrate, requires increased energy. It has been suggested that efficiency is greatest in larger animals near the top of the food pyramids, i.e. the high energy expenditure and increased respiration of predators is a function of increased activity, which in turn increases the probability of finding prey species (Watt, 1968), but even this generalization requires further clarification.

The present view of pinnipeds seems to be that they are relatively inefficient predators,

with an ecological efficiency of less than 10 %. Estimates of ecological efficiency for pinnipeds are, however, limited. An estimate of 6 % was obtained for western Atlantic harbour seals *Phoca vitulina* (Boulva, 1973), and 0.5 % for harp seals *Pagophilus groenlandicus* (Sergeant, 1973). The disparity between these estimates probably reflects how little we know about pinniped bioenergetics, rather than how much we know about their ecological efficiency and their role in the ecosystem. Only research will provide the answer which is important for present and future management decisions.

In several parts of the world, pinnipeds are one component of a multispecies fishery. Gulland (1970) noted that the exploitation of several species at different trophic levels in a given area can result in difficult management problems. Not only do fishermen complain about the activities of other fishermen in the same area, but also about the predators feeding on prey which are themselves exploited by man (Gulland, 1970). Pinnipeds do not escape these management controversies. In the western Atlantic fishermen support an increased annual hunt, so as to further reduce populations of harp (*Pagophilus groenlandicus*) and hooded (*Cystophora cristata*) seals, which reportedly damage fishing gear and compete with man for common food resources such as herring *Clupea harengus*, cod *Gadus morhua*, and capelin *Mallotus villosus* (Fisheries Council of Canada, 1974, 1975). In the eastern Pacific, a similar controversy surrounds competition between man and northern fur seal *Callorhinus ursinus* for pollack *Theragra chalcogramma* (Sergeant, 1976). Such management problems can only be resolved through a knowledge of the quantitative relationships between predator and prey, including the weight of prey consumed to produce a unit weight of predator (Gulland, 1970).

Despite man's past and current philosophy of harvesting the oceans (Christy, 1973), it is now frequently stated that man can make the best use of incident solar radiation (energy) by cropping the trophic pyramid as close to the plant layer as possible, if not at the plant layer itself (Watt, 1968). Such considerations may lead to the suggestion that we should not be overly concerned about exterminating pinniped populations, especially given their apparently low efficiency. In fact, in energetic terms we might do well to extirpate our competitors (e.g. the pinnipeds) and base our future fisheries at lower trophic levels. It is probably true that such a policy would maximize short-term productivity by minimizing the wastage of energy at each succeeding trophic level (Watt, 1968). It could however impair long-term productivity by reducing diversity, thus creating instability within the system (Watt, 1968; Margalef, 1968). Even this warning is open to discussion; Goodman (1975), in a recent and extensive review, concluded that there is no such simple relationship between diversity and stability in ecosystems. At present there is no easy solution to the problem of developing appropriate management policies.

Nevertheless, a knowledge of bioenergetics would appear to be a necessary prerequisite for enlightened ecosystem management. This has been recognized in the area of fisheries management (Beamish, Niimi and Lett, 1975) and major steps in this direction have been taken in the area of terrestrial wild life management (Moen, 1973). No such synthetic review of the present knowledge of pinniped bioenergetics has been made. Many papers relevant to this discussion have been produced over the years, but few (e.g., Boulva, 1973) have attempted to construct an energy budget for even a single population of pinnipeds.

The purpose of this paper is to summarize what is known of pinniped bioenergetics as it relates to ecosystem management. No attempt will be made, however, to review all that is presently known about pinniped bioenergetics. Many of the examples used will refer to the harp seal, with reference to other species being made where possible, or when necessary to demonstrate a concept. This is partly because relatively more is known about harp seal energetics than about most other pinnipeds,

and it is the species with which we are most familiar. In fact, the details of bioenergetics for a particular species are less important for the purposes of this paper than the concepts which may be extended to any species, with emphasis on the sorts of data which are needed to improve our understanding of the role of pinnipeds in the marine ecosystem. It is hoped that areas requiring further research will be recognised and incorporated into future research programmes, so that future management of marine mammals may be more effective.

Initially we consider the utilization of energy by pinnipeds at the organismic level of organization (in reality most of the data are collected by examining individual members of a population). Then we look at population energetics with respect to such important features as birth rates, mortality rates, etc. Finally, we briefly consider pinnipeds as component members of a complex marine ecosystem, and make some preliminary comments about community energetics in relation to management.

Energy utilization by pinnipeds

GENERALIZED BIOENERGETIC SCHEME

The generalized bioenergetic scheme or pattern of energy flow through higher vertebrates is illustrated in Fig. 1 (Harris, 1966; Moen, 1973; Church and Pond, 1974; Beamish, Niimi and Lett, 1975; Kleiber, 1975). Although this scheme may be tentatively applied at the population level, assuming no synergisms, measurements are in fact made at the organismic or individual level of organization. Since the flow of energy through an individual, a population, and an ecosystem is unidirectional, and in accordance with the laws of thermodynamics (Gallucci, 1973), the generalized scheme represents an energy budget which must be balanced. Although variations on this conventional scheme have

FIG. 1. – Conventional schematic of energy utilization by animals [1]

GROSS ENERGY (GE) of food (heat of combustion)

Faecal Energy (FE)

1. undigested food
2. enteric microbes and their products
3. secretions into the gastro-intestinal tract
4. cellular debris from gastro-intestinal tract

APPARENT DIGESTIBLE ENERGY (DE)

Urinary Energy (UE)
1. food origin
2. endogenous origin
Gaseous products of digestion (primarily methane)

METABOLIZABLE ENERGY (ME) [2]

Heat Increment [3] (HI)
(wasted heat unless animal is below lower critical temperature)
1. heat of nutrient metabolism
2. heat of fermentation

NET ENERGY (NE)

MAINTENANCE ENERGY (NE_m)
1. Basal metabolism [3]
2. Voluntary activity [3]
3. Energy to keep body warm if below thermal neutral environment, and when need for heat energy is above that supplied by heat increment
4. energy to keep body cool when above the thermal neutral environment

PRODUCTION ENERGY (NE_p)
1. energy storage foetus, semen, growth, fat, milk, hair, etc.
2. work (part of this is lost as heat)

---

[1] Adapted from Harris, 1966; Moen, 1973; Church and Pond, 1974; Beamish, Niimi and Lett, 1975; Kleiber, 1975.
[2] When ME is corrected to nitrogen equilibrium, it is known as N-corrected metabolizable energy (ME_n).
[3] These items are expended as heat.

been proposed (Harris, 1966; Beamish, Niimi and Lett, 1975) which are more correct representations of the physiological processes operating within the animal, it is only practical at present to quantify the various components of the simplified scheme. Most bioenergetic studies of wildlife populations have followed this plan.

Some of the components of the scheme have been examined and studied in pinnipeds, but little attempt has been made to quantify all the components for any particular species. The problems of conducting experimental work with pinnipeds are well known, but these should not deter attempts to quantify the bioenergetic scheme. If certain components cannot be measured directly, a first approximation may be gained from available data on other mammals. This can be modified later as the results of experiments with pinnipeds become available. It should always be borne in mind that the parameters being measured may be somewhat altered by the conditions of captivity. Some data can also be collected directly from animals in the field, though there are considerable problems in obtaining a representative sample of a wild population of pinnipeds, or, for that matter, of any wild mammalian population (Caughley, 1966).

However, variations and fluctuations in components are usually much greater than those which occur in entire systems (Odum, 1971). Thus, while the problems noted above should not be overlooked, they should not deter examination of pinnipeds from a more holistic point of view than has been done in the past.

We now consider each of the components in the bioenergetic scheme, noting areas which have been studied, and identify areas which require further consideration and experimentation.

GROSS ENERGY OF FOOD

A major component in any bioenergetics study is food consumption. What is consumed, and how does the species utilize the nutritional components, one of which is energy? Food energy is the gross energy (GE) of the food entering the animal, or population, per unit weight of food (kcal g^{-1}). This initial figure may be estimated in a number of ways. Therefore, it is important to have a detailed understanding of the food habits of the particular pinniped under consideration. Gross energy intake may then be estimated indirectly from the proximate composition of food items consumed, using the energetic equivalents for carbohydrate, protein, and lipid (Table 1). An alternative method for estimating food energy is to determine the heat of combustion of food items using bomb calorimetry (Górecki, 1975). In either case it is particularly important to take into account seasonal changes in feeding habits and in the proximate composition of food items when estimating food energy intake on an annual basis. In general, interchanging food items only affects the gross energy value of the food if the percentage of fat changes, since fat has approximately twice the energy value of carbohydrate or protein (Table 1).

It would be pointless to review what is

Table 1. Caloric equivalents (kcal g^{-1} dry weight) for a typical fat, a typical carbohydrate, and a typical protein at the gross energy (GE), apparent digestible energy (DE), and metabolizable energy (ME) stages of the generalized bioenergetic scheme (Fig. 1) [1]

Substance	GE	DE	ME
Fat	9.4	9.0	9.0
Carbohydrate	4.15	4.0	4.0
Protein	5.65	5.20	4.0

[1] From Pike and Brown (1975). Other caloric equivalents are commonly found in the literature. In general their deviance from these typical values will be small. For example, Church and Pond (1974) give values of 9.45, 4.10, and 5.65 for the GE of fat, carbohydrate and protein, respectively.

known about food habits of pinnipeds in general. What follows is a description of the food habits of one species, the harp seal, throughout the year. This is used to illustrate the present problems associated with obtaining estimates of gross energy intake for pinnipeds, and to formulate a tentative energy budget for this species.

Harp seal pups are nursed with an extremely fat-rich milk, characteristic of phocid seals, and marine mammals in general. Since milk is part of the production energy of female seals (Fig. 1), a detailed discussion of pinniped milk will be deferred.

During the short 2- to 3- week nursing period, rapid changes occur in the young harp seal. It increases its weight quickly from about 7 kg at birth to perhaps 35 kg (Fig. 2), largely as a result of acquiring a 5 cm layer of insulating subcutaneous blubber. In this period the pup becomes truly homeothermic. It is weaned at about 2½ to 3 weeks of age, and left on the whelping ice by the mother who enters the water to mate. The pup is now in the midst of its first moult, losing the neonatal white coat and replacing it with the spotted immature, or beater, pelt. The young seal may not enter the water for some time, and probably experiences a post-nursing drop in body weight (Fig. 2).

While food habits of immature and adult harp seals are not well defined in quan-

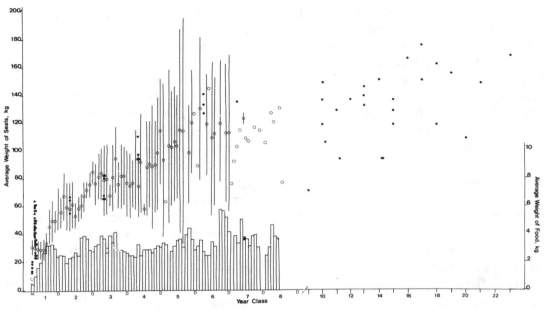

FIG. 2. – Growth data for the harp seal, *Pagaphilus groenlandicus.* Solid circles represent field data collected in March-April 1976 off the east coast of Canada. Open circles (± S.D.) represent data obtained from captive seals over the last 8 years (Ronald, pers. comm.). The histogram indicates average weight of food, *Clupea harengus,* consumed by these captive animals (Ronald, pers. comm.).

titative terms, changes in diet with season and with age have been recognized (Sergeant, 1973).

On entering the water, the beaters begin to feed on small pelagic crustaceans such as amphipods and euphausids, e.g. *Thysanoessa* (Sergeant, 1973). At 2-3 months these juvenile seals begin their first northward migration (Sergeant, 1965), by which time they are feeding on fish, primarily capelin (Sergeant, 1973).

Immature and adult harp seals reach the northern end of their spring migration in late May and June (Sergeant, 1965, 1973). In west Greenland waters they feed on spawning runs of capelin as well as euphausids (Sergeant, 1973). Some harp seals, mainly adults, which migrate to northwest Greenland and into the eastern Canadian Arctic, feed on arctic cod *Boreogadus saida,* and various crustaceans including euphausids, mysids, and amphipods (Sergeant, 1973).

Kapel (1973) summarized the feeding habits of harp seals in west Greenland waters during the summer. He reported large regional variations, with capelin, polar cod, and Greenland halibut *Reinhardtius hippoglossoides* being the main fish species consumed, and shrimp *Pandalus* sp. being the dominant invertebrate prey. Regional variations in diet were such that in some areas invertebrates (crustaceans) comprised 70 % to 100 % of stomach contents, while in other areas capelin was the main prey species and the crustacean content dropped below 4 %.

In late fall, harp seals begin their southward migrations ahead of the Arctic pack ice (Sergeant, 1965). Arriving in the Gulf of St. Lawrence and off the east coast of Newfoundland, they feed on capelin, euphusids, and herring (Sergeant, 1973).

Their exact location and feeding habits during much of January and February remain largely unknown. It has been suggested that they feed off the Grand Banks of Newfoundland (Andrews, 1951) but there seems to be little recent evidence to support this suggestion.

In late February and in early March,   197

adult females reappear on the ice in the Gulf of St. Lawrence and on the Front, off Newfoundland, to give birth. It has been suggested that during and immediately following parturition and lactation, females feed intermittently or very little, mainly on decapod crustaceans such as *Pandalus* sp. (Sergeant, 1973, 1976, 1976a). Sivertsen (1941) also concluded that female harp seals consume an insignificant amount of food at this time and noted a concomitant reduction in the thickness of the blubber layer.

Prior to and after parturition, nursing, weaning and mating, harp seals wintering in the Gulf of St. Lawrence from January to April feed mainly on capelin, but occasionally on other pelagic fish, euphausids, decapods and cephalopod molluscs (Sergeant, 1973).

On the Front, in the same period, immature (non-breeding animals aged about 1-5 years) and adult seals feed on decapod crustaceans (of which 80 % may be *Pandalus* sp.) more frequently than on fish (Sergeant, 1973).

Moulting adults, during April and May, feed mainly on capelin in the Gulf, as well as on such rough fish species as sea raven *Hemitripterus americanus* and shorthorn sculpin *Myoxocephalus scorpius*. On the Front, moulting seals may feed on capelin, Atlantic cod, flatfish, and some of the spinier species such as redfish *Sebastes marinus* (Sergeant, 1973). Intermittently, feeding en masse seems to take place from the large ice floes used as moulting patches.

From this complex annual feeding cycle the harp seal emerges as a eurytrophic organism, often feeding simultaneously at a variety of trophic levels, perhaps, like harbour seals (Boulva, 1973), concentrating somewhat on fish species. It would appear that harp seals, like many other pinnipeds (Geraci, 1975), are opportunistic in their feeding habits, at any given time eating those species which are present in the greatest numbers and easiest to catch.

Stomach content data for harp seals, as summarized above, and similar data for many other pinniped species, are of very limited use in bioenergetic studies. The results of the harp seal analyses, for example, have been expressed either in terms of frequency (Sergeant, 1973), volume (Fisher and MacKenzie, 1955), or percentage of stomachs containing various prey items (Myers, 1959). No single criterion, whether it be numbers, frequency of occurrence, volume, or weight, is usually adequate to provide meaningful results from a series of stomach content analyses (Korschgen, 1971). In particular, measurements of frequency as employed by Sergeant (1973) only indicate that an item was consumed, but provide little information on its relative importance in the diet. Frequency measurements become meaningful when used with volume or weight, expressed as a percentage of the total sample (Korschgen, 1971).

Some of the problems associated with stomach content analyses are difficult to overcome. For example, the high proportion of empty stomachs found in some samples (Sergeant, 1973) present certain difficulties of interpretation. The absence of data for certain times of the year, as in the harp seal during the summer (Sergeant, 1973), can be remedied by research.

For a bioenergetic study we need an estimate of the quantity of food ingested per meal, the frequency of feeding, measurement of the weight, or volume, of the various prey items consumed, and the proximate composition of those prey items. The caloric intake of the animal may then be estimated. Some estimates of these factors have been made for both harp seals (Sergeant, 1973) and harbour seals (Boulva, 1973), using data on captive animals to provide first approximations where sufficient field data were lacking. Field data have been used to estimate food consumption and feeding frequency for the New Zealand fur seal, *Arctocephalus forsteri* (Street, 1964). Additional information may be obtained from the literature. For example, the proximate composition and gross energy of some harp seal prey species are given in Tables 2 and 3 respectively. Again it is important to realize that the caloric content of food species may

Table 2. Proximate composition of some common prey species of the harp seal, *Pagophilus groenlandicus*

Species	Sample [1]	% Moisture	% Protein	% Fat	% Carbohydrates	% Ash	Reference
Clupea harengus [2]	F	61.8-69.0	15.4-19.7	7.5-19.4	—	1.06-2.1	Geraci, 1975
Atlantic herring	?	69.0	17.3	11.3	—	2.1	Altman and Dittmer, 1968
Mallotus villosus [2]	W	77.1-84.1	12.9-15.3	1.8-8.1	—	1.8 -2.2	McCallum *et al.*, 1969 [3]
Capelin	W	77.1-82.3	12.9-15.0	1.8-8.1	—	—	Geraci, 1975
Gadus morhua	F	81.2	14.6-17.6	0.2-0.6	—	1.2	Geraci, 1975
Atlantic cod	?	81.2	17.6	0.3	—	1.2	Altman and Dittmer, 1968
Euphausia superba Euphausid (krill)	M	80.0	17.8	1.3	—	1.4	Geraci, 1975

[1] M = Meat, W = Whole Fish, F = Fillet.
[2] Marked seasonal variations in proximate composition occur in many fish species. In herring, percentage fat may vary from 2 % to 4 % in early spring to 15 % (Stoddard, 1968) or more in early winter. In capelin, percentage fat may be as high as 23.4 in the fall, with the moisture content dropping to 65 % (Devold, 1970, as cited in Jangaard, 1974). For a detailed review of seasonal variation in proximate composition of capelin see Jangaard (1974).
[3] Prespawning and spawning capelin.

Table 3. Gross energy content of some common prey species of harp seal, *Pagophilus groenlandicus*

Species	kcal/gm ash free dry wt.	kcal/gm dry wt.	kcal/gm wet wt.	References
Clupea harengus Atlantic herring	6.4	—	1.9	Cummins and Wuycheck, 1971
	—	—	1.8	Altman and Dittmer, 1968
	—	—	2.0	Geraci, 1975
	—	—	1.6-2.9	Calculated [1]
Mallotus villosus Capelin	—	—	0.9-1.6 [2]	Calculated [1]
Gadus morhua Atlantic cod	—	—	0.8	Altman and Dittmer, 1968
			0.8-1.1	Calculated [1]
Euphausia superba Euphausid (krill)	—	—	1.1	Calculated [1]
Mysis stenolepis Decapoda	—	4.7	1.0	Tyler, 1973
	5.3	—	1.1	Cummins and Wuycheck, 1971
Pandalus montagui	5.6-5.9	—	1.3	Cummins and Wuycheck, 1971
	—	4.6	1.3	Tyler, 1973
Amphipoda	4.9	—	0.9	Cummins and Wuycheck, 1971

[1] Calculated from proximate composition values (see Table 2) obtained from Geraci (1975).
[2] This value must be considered a minimum estimate, based on capelin with a low fat content. At other times of the year, fat levels increase to more than 20 % (Jangaard, 1974) resulting in a dramatic increase in energy content.

vary temporally and spatially, depending primarily on the fat content[1].

Gross energy, however, does not predict the biological value of a particular food item to the consumer, since indigestible portions have approximately the same relative energy content as the digestible portions. A more accurate predictor of the biological value of food is the amount of energy assimilated, or the digestible energy.

DIGESTIBLE ENERGY

Since the efficiency of assimilation of a pinniped, or in fact any animal, is not 100 %, not all of the food consumed (GE) is available to the animal. Some food passes directly through the digestive tract and is lost as faecal energy. The subtraction of faecal energy from the gross energy of the food gives the apparent digestible energy (DE), sometimes termed assimilated or absorbed energy, i.e. the energy which passes through the intestine wall and enters the blood stream of the animal. Digestible energy is often expressed in terms of digestive or absorption efficiency:

$$\text{absorption efficiency} = DE/GE \times 100$$

Absorption efficiencies vary with the composition of the diet (Brody, 1945; Beamish, Niimi and Lett, 1975).

"Digestibility" may more correctly be qualified as "apparent digestibility", since errors are introduced by the indirect method of calculating the energy absorbed. The digestive enzymes secreted into the gastrointestinal tract and the sloughed intestinal lining both give the energy measured for faecal loss too high a value, resulting in an underestimate of the true digestible energy (Harris, 1966).

Although difficult to quantify in the field, estimates of faecal energy loss may be made in captivity. Animals may be fed known amounts of food, which may readily be expressed in calories. Faeces are then collected and the energy content determined using a bomb calorimeter. Fresh faeces should be collected and freeze dried, or even dried below 40 °C (Mahslid, MacDonald and Stock, 1975). It should be noted that the energy content of fish faeces left in water for varying lengths of time changes, (Beamish, Niimi and Lett, 1975) and this will also be the case with seal faeces.

Since it is unlikely that collection of all seal faeces for a known intake of food will be possible, the use of an inert chemical indicator may be necessary to estimate DE even in captive experiments. The most widely used indicator has been chromium sesquioxide (Cr_2O_3) (Czarnocki, Sibbald and Evans, 1961; Arthur, 1970). Alternatively, Petrides (1968) has suggested that radioactive 51-chromium is somewhat easier to use and provides a more accurate method of quantitative analysis.

The magnitude of faecal energy loss is dependent on the digestibility of the food. In general, animal tissue and seed portions of plants show high digestibility, while non-seed portions of plants have low digestibility for monogastrics, due to their high cellulose content. Animals which utilize other animals and seeds for food usually have faecal losses in the range of 5 % to 15 %. Animals consuming cellulose plant materials have evolved adaptations which allow them to utilize the products of microbial digestion.

Faecal energy loss is relatively constant for a variety of mammals (Table 4). Carnivores such as fox *Vulpes fulva* and bobcat *Lynx rufus* have faecal losses of 9 % of the gross energy (Vogtsberger and Barrett, 1973; Golley *et al.*, 1965; Morris, Feyimoto and Berry, 1974) while the insectivorous bat *Lasiurus cinereus* shows a loss of 8.8 % (Brisbin, 1966). Ruminants, because much of their food is undigestible, tend to lose larger amounts of GE through faeces (Table 4).

In the only digestibility study of a pinniped, the DE of ringed seals (*Pusa hispida*) eating herring or capelin was found to be 97 %

---

[1] This is the case with herring which are 2 % to 4 % oil in early spring and 15 % oil in early winter (Stoddard, 1968).

Table 4. Apparent digestible protein, fat, and energy

Species	Protein (%)	Fat (%)	Energy (%)	Reference
Phoca hispida ringed seal	97.3 ± 0.9 (SD)	99.3 ± 0.2	97.0 ± 0.8	Parsons, 1977
Ursus maritimus polar bear	84.2 ± 1.7 (SD) 87.0 ± 4.1	97.7 ± 0.6 94.2 ± 4.5	91.6 ± 1.4 –	Best, 1976 Patton, 1975 (as cited in Best, 1976)
Vulpes fulva red fox	–	–	91 ± 2	Vogtsburger & Barrett, 1973
Alopex lagopus arctic fox	–	–	95	Underwood, 1971
Lynx rufus bobcat	–	–	91	Golley *et al.*, 1965 Morris, Feyimoto & Berry, 1974
Mustela nivalis least weasel	–	–	89.9	Golley, 1960
Canis familiaris dog	70-98 80	87-97 90-95	82-93 –	Orr, 1965 NRC, 1974
Felis catus cat	89	–	–	Greaves & Scott, 1960
Panthera tigris tiger	88.8	–	–	Morris, Feyimoto & Berry, 1974
Panthera leo lion	88.8	–	–	»
Panthera pardus leopard	88.9	–	–	»
Panthera onca jaguar	89.7	–	–	»
Felis concolor puma	92.1	–	–	»
Felis pardalis ocelot	89.1	–	–	»
Felis caracal caracal	87.5	–	–	»
Lynx lynx lynx	90.4	–	–	»
Felis viverrina fishing cat	89.5	–	–	»
Felis tenminckii golden cat	87.7	–	–	»
Felis bengalensis leopard cat	88.4	–	–	»
Felis serval serval	91.9	–	–	»
Taxidea taxus badger	88.1	–	–	»
Peromyscus maniculatus deer mouse	–	–	77.0 ± 2.1	Johnson & Groepper, 1970
Microtus pennsylvanicus meadow vole	–	–	81.1 ± 0.7	»
Clethrionomys gapperi red-backed vole	–	–	78.9 ± 1.6	»
Zapus hudsonius meadow jumping mouse	–	–	71.5 ± 0.5	»

Table 4. Apparent digestible protein, fat, and energy *(concluded)*

Species	Protein (%)	Fat (%)	Energy (%)	Reference
Mus musculus house mouse	–	–	79.5 ± 1.5	»
Dipodomys ordi ord kangarco rat	–	–	95.1 ± 0.4 (oat diet) 97.7 ± 0.2 (barley diet)	» »
Citellus richardsoni Richardson's ground squirrel	–	–	82.2 ± 0.2	»
Citellus tridecemlineatus thirteen-lined ground squirrel	–	–	81.0 ± 1.3	»
Sciurus niger and *S. carolinensis* fox and grey squirrel	–	–	77.0 ± 1.3 95.0 ± 0.7	Smith & Follmer, 1972 »
Oryzomys palustris rice rat	–	–	88-95	Sharp, 1967
Ochotona princeps pika	–	–	68	Johnson & Maxwell, 1966
Lasiurus cinereus hoary bat	–	–	91.0 ± 4.7	Brisbin, 1966
Cryptotia parva least shrew	–	–	90.1	Barrett, 1969
Ovis aries sheep	–	–	66.9-69.7	Ekern & Sundstøl, 1974
wildebeest			62-70	Rogerson, 1968
eland			59-70.2	»

(Parson, 1977). Given the generally varied diet of pinnipeds, a faecal energy loss equivalent to about 9 % to 10 % GE is not unreasonable for our purposes (Table 4). This would suggest that at least 90 % to 91 % of the gross energy (GE) in food is available to the pinniped as apparent digestible energy (DE).

Studies must eventually consider the digestibility of the various food items consumed by specific pinnipeds, as well as seasonal variations in the proximate composition, and thus the energy content, of their diet throughout the year.

METABOLIZABLE ENERGY

Not all of the energy assimilated (DE) is available for use or storage. Some is lost through the production and excretion of urine, which contains the nitrogenous end products of protein katabolism, such as urea, creatine, etc. The amount of energy thus lost depends on the dietary protein balance and the physiological status of the animal (Brody, 1945).

Again, no measurements of urinary loss in pinnipeds are available in the published literature although Parsons (1977) has recently provided estimates for captive ringed seals (Table 5). Such estimates can be made in captivity through the use of a modified "metabolic cage" apparatus such as is commonly used for small mammals (Drodz, 1975).

Estimates of urinary loss for some mammals are given in Table 5. It is important to note that these energy losses should be expressed in terms of % DE or in kcal, but not in % GE, since the urine loss depends on the nitrogen containing substances actually absorbed or mobilized by the animal. From Table 5, and a basic knowledge of the proximate composition of some major food items consumed by pinnipeds (e.g. Table 2), an estimate of urinary energy loss between 7 % and 8 % DE is probably not unrealistic for our purposes.

An estimate of the metabolizable energy (ME) is obtained by subtracting energy loss in the urine and, especially in the case of herbivores, the gaseous products of digestion (Fig. 1). According to our estimates thus far, ME for a harp seal is 82.7 %-84.7 % GE, calculated by:

$$ME = GE - FE - UE \quad \dots\dots\dots \quad (1)$$

where FE and UE are faecal energy and urinary energy losses respectively. This is similar to the 84.6 % figure used by Boulva (1973) for harbour seals. More recent estimates for ringed seals (Parsons, 1977) averaged 88.6 ± 2.6 (1 SD).

In the conventional energetic scheme, metabolizable energy represents the energy which is available to the animal for use or storage. The value of ME is affected by the level of intake of nutrients and must, for comparative purposes, be corrected for growth. Nitrogen-corrected ME or ME_n is calculated according to the equation:

$$ME_n = ME \pm (NB \cdot 7.45 \text{ kcal}) \quad \dots \quad (2)$$

where ME is defined by equation (1) and

$$NB = NI - FN - UN \quad \dots\dots\dots \quad (3)$$

where NB is nitrogen balance or nitrogen retention, i.e. the nitrogen consumed in food (NI) minus both the nitrogen in faeces (FN) and the nigrogen in urine (UN) (Harris, 1966).

If nitrogen is lost from the body (negative nitrogen balance), 7.45 kcal are added to the metabolizable energy (ME) for each gram of nitrogen lost. If nitrogen is retained by the body (positive nitrogen balance), then 7.45 kcal are subtracted from the metabolizable energy (Harris, 1966). The conversion factor (7.45 kcal) was determined for dogs and further research is required to justify its general acceptance (Harris, 1966).

Because of the need to collect urine, ME is extremely difficult to estimate in the field. Therefore, in practice, ME is generally not measured in wild animals.

It is misleading to assume that all of the energy termed ME in many bioenergetic schemes (Table 1) is available to the animal (Beamish, Niimi and Lett, 1975; Harris, 1966). When an animal ingests a meal, the rate of metabolism expressed in units of heat production, or oxygen consumption, increases. This increase has been variously termed spe-

Table 5. Urinary energy loss in some species of mammals expressed as a percentage of gross energy (GE) and digestible energy (DE)

Species	% GE[1]	% DE	Reference
Lynx rufus bobcat	8.0	8.8	Golley *et al.*, 1965
Ovis aries sheep	4.2-5.2	–	Ekern and Sundstøl, 1974
wildebeest	3.8-4.7	6.9-7.8	Rogerson, 1968
eland	3.8-4.8	6.5-8.2	»
cattle	4.0	5.7	Brody, 1945
rabbit	6.7	11.2	»

[1] Low assimilation efficiencies of herbivores are reflected in the urinary energy loss expressed as a percentage of GE.

cific dynamic action (SDA) (Kleiber, 1975; Beamish, Niimi and Lett, 1975), calorigenic effect (Kleiber, 1975), heat increment of feeding (Harris, 1966), and heat of nutrient metabolism (Moen, 1973). Although the biochemistry of the heat increment is not completely understood, the liberated heat energy is generally assumed to result primarily from the deamination of amino acids in the liver (Buttery and Annison, 1973). If protein, lipid and carbohydrate are fed separately, the heat increment amounts to approximately 30 %, 13 %, and 15 % respectively, of the ingested energy (Harper, 1975). A composite diet of protein, lipid, and carbohydrate, however, results in a lower value for heat increment than predicted from the composition of the food (Forbes and Swift, 1944).

This heat energy is lost, and is only of use to a homeotherm such as a pinniped for maintaining a constant deep body temperature in hypothermic environments (Kleiber, 1975; Moen, 1973; Harris, 1966). Although many pinniped species such as the harp seal, hooded seal (*Cystophora cristata*), ringed seal (*Phoca hispida*), Weddell seal (*Leptonychotes weddelli*), etc., spend much, if not all of their lives in cold polar and subpolar waters in close proximity to ice, it is doubtful whether, for these animals, such environments can normally be considered "hypothermic" (Irving and Hart, 1957; Gallivan, 1977). When ambient conditions do drop below the thermal neutral environment, the heat increment may become useful, since it reduces the energy needed for maintenance of homeothermy. The opposite will be true when ambient environmental conditions exceed the thermal neutral zone, since the additional heat must be dissipated. This latter problem may be of minor significance for pinnipeds in the wild with constant access to water, except perhaps when actively swimming and hunting for food. It could be of some significance to animals held in captivity without access to cold water.

Additional energy requirements for absorption, digestion, transportation, and deposition of food materials are presumed to be small and are difficult to separate experimentally from the heat increment of feeding (Beamish, Niimi and Lett, 1975). The term apparent heat increment of feeding may thus be more appropriate to describe the value which is really measured by most experiments.

No estimates of the heat increment of feeding have been made relative to the energy content of food (GE) for pinnipeds. Parsons (1977), however, did report an increase in metabolic rate (27 % and 35 %) in two ringed seals which persisted for 12 to 13 h after feeding. This area of experimentation deserves to be explored further since loss of energy via the heat increment will represent an ecologically significant proportion of the food consumed. Experiments must obviously consider the changes in heat increment that will occur with diets of varying proximate composition (Brody, 1945) such as would occur in the wild on a seasonal basis.

The subtraction of heat increment from the metabolizable energy defined above gives a more realistic estimate of the energy available to the animal for further use or storage (Beamish, Niimi and Lett, 1975). This is termed net energy (Fig. 1) in most generalized bioenergetic schemes.

NET ENERGY

Net energy (NE) is energy which is available to the animal for maintenance of body functions, the production of new tissue, and for doing work. It is generally subdivided into maintenance energy (NE_m) and production energy (NE_p) (Fig. 1).

Maintenance Energy

Maintenance energy is used for basal metabolism, voluntary activity, and in homeotherms, for thermoregulation.

Metabolism

It is generally accepted that the resting metabolic rates (M) of marine mammals, and phocid seals in particular are higher than those of terrestrial mammals (Irving, 1972). Of the few measurements of oxygen consumption which are available for pinnipeds, most have been obtained from restrained seals, and usually from immature animals weighing less than 50 kg. In such cases M has been found to be as much as twice (Irving and Hart, 1957; Luecke, Natarajan and South, 1975) that predicted by Kleiber's (1975) equation for mammals (Fig. 3):

$$M = 70 \, W^{0.75} \qquad (4)$$

where M is measured in kcal/24h and W is body size in kg; $W^{0.75}$ is often termed the metabolic weight (Kleiber, 1975; Harris, 1966).

As Irving (1972) noted, the fact that restrained, immature and presumably growing animals were used to obtain metabolic data for seals, might explain why the results were higher than expected. It is therefore worth stressing that the only experiment which utilized a free-swimming (but extremely quiet) adult seal of known weight in the post-absorptive condition produced an estimate close to Kleiber's equation (Fig. 3) for mammals (Øritsland and Ronald, 1975). More recently Gallivan

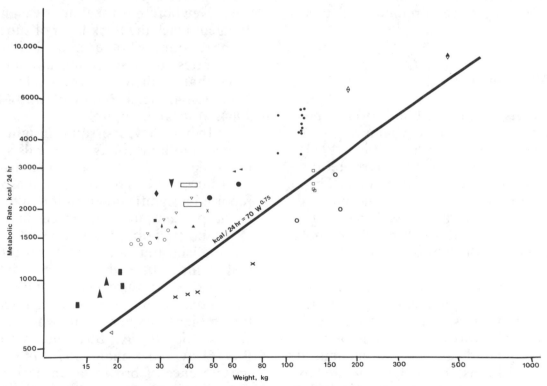

FIG. 3. – Metabolic rates of seals in relation to body size (after Øritsland and Ronald, 1975). ■ *P. vitulina* (see Irving *et al.*, 1953); ▽ *P. vitulina* (see Irving and Hart, 1957); ▲ *P. vitulina* (see Hart and Irving, 1959); ○ *P. groenlandicus* (see Irving and Hart, 1957); wide rectangle, lower: *P. groenlandicus*, not swimming; wide rectangle, upper: *P. groenlandicus*, not swimming; wide rectangle, upper: *P. groenlandicus*, free swimming in 2 m diameter circular tank (Wekstein and Krog, 1971; as cited in Øritsland and Ronald, 1975); ● *P. groenlandicus*, active and, □ resting (Øritsland and Ronald, 1975); ◯ *P. groenlandicus* (see Gallivan, 1977); x *H. grypus* (see Scholander, 1940); ▼ *C. cristata* (see Scholander, 1940); ✕ *P. hispida* (see Parsons, 1977); *L. weddelli* ◈ mean and ♦ minimum determinations (Kooyman, 1975); ▲ *P. groenlandicus* pup, ● *Histriophoca fasciata*, ■ *Eumetopias jubatus* pup, ◀ *O. rosmarus* pup, ◁ *P. vitulina* pup, and ▼ *C. ursinus* (see Iversem and Krog, 1973); and ▲ *Z. californianus* (see Luecke *et al.*, 1975). Determinations for two cetaceans ◈ *Tursiops truncatus*, and ♦ *Phocoena phocoena* are shown for comparison (Kooyman, 1975).

(1977) and Parson (1977) have also found that basal metabolism in confined harp seals and ringed seals respectively falls near, in fact below, Kleiber's equation for mammals (Fig. 3). Øritsland and Ronald (1975) have also noted that the metabolic rate of the harp seal appears to decrease with age (increasing size) and may approach a value of M consistent with Kleiber's (1975) equation.

About 40 % of the body weight of many seals, including the harp seal (Sivertsen, 1941), is blubber, characterized by low metabolic activity. Thus, even a metabolic rate conforming to the expected would still indicate a body core with a high metabolic rate (Øritsland and Ronald, 1975).

Further studies of basal metabolism in pinnipeds are obviously needed to clarify the maintenance energy requirements of these animals.

Thermoregulation

Mammals regulate their deep body temperature at a set point by balancing their heat production with heat loss (Bligh, 1973). Adaptive mechanisms keep the energy required for thermoregulation to a minimum. Thus, under most thermal conditions encountered by a mammal in its normal environment, sufficient heat is evolved through basal metabolism to maintain a constant deep body temperature.

For most mammals at rest, heat production in the post-absorptive state will be at a basal level (equation 4) over a range of environmental temperatures. This range of temperature, designated as the thermoneutral zone (Bligh and Johnston, 1973) is bounded by an upper critical (T_{uc}) and lower critical (T_{lc}) temperature. When ambient air temperatures (T_a) rise above T_{uc}, additional energy is required to activate evaporative heat dissipating mechanisms, such as sweating or panting (Bligh and Johnston, 1973). When temperatures (T_a) drop to T_{lc}, the thermal insulation of a homeotherm is at a maximum (Scholander *et al.*, 1950). As T_a falls below T_{lc}, extra heat energy is required to compensate for the additional heat loss from the animal.

The relationship between heat production and low environmental temperatures ($T_a < T_{lc}$) is approximated by:

$$M = C (T_b - T_a)$$

where M is metabolism expressed in terms of energy flow, T_b is the deep body temperature, T_a is ambient air temperature, and C is the thermal conductance (the inverse value of the insulation) of the animal. Below the lower critical temperature, additional heat production will be relatively small for a well-insulated animal and high for a poorly insulated animal (Scholander *et al.*, 1950, Fig. 10).

Newborn harp seal pups weigh less than 10 kg and lack the thick layer of subcutaneous blubber found in older animals. Basal metabolic rates in these young animals may be twice that predicted by the Kleiber equation (equation 4, Fig. 3) (Davydov and Makarova, 1964; Øritsland, unpubl.).

In recent years, some insight has been gained into how young harp seals survive the initial days of lie in the harsh environment of their nursery. Davydov and Makarova (1965) reported a significant elevation in metabolism in harp seal pups immersed in ice water. Øritsland (unpubl.) found no such increase in metabolism, but rather a depression in deep body temperature when the cold stress was in the form of exposure to wind and rain or sleet conditions, which are often characteristic of the ambient weather on the whelping ice. Recent studies (Grav, Blix and Pasche, 1974; Blix, Grav and Ronald, 1975) have observed the presence of brown fat in harp seal pups. This discovery, the first such observation in any marine mammal (Grav, Blix and Pasche, 1974), suggests that young harp seals may also utilize non-shivering thermogenesis to produce sufficient body heat for survival under adverse conditions, prior to developing an insulating layer of blubber.

Under more favourable weather conditions, when the sun is shining, the young harp seal like many pinnipeds (e.g. Fay and Ray, 1968; Ray and Fay, 1968) may utilize solar radiation as an external source of heat (Øritsland, 1970). The white foetal hair or lanugo transmits and reflects solar radiation down through the pelt where it is absorbed at or near the surface of the skin (Øritsland, 1971). Subsequently thermal infrared radiation (heat) emitted from the skin surface becomes trapped within the pelt. This "greenhouse" effect contributes to a further reduction in heat loss to the environment (Øritsland, 1971). As a result of these adaptations, skin temperatures as high as 41 °C, i.e. higher than the deep body temperature (37° to 38 °C) have been reported in basking harp seal pups (Øritsland and Ronald, 1973).

In the absence of solar radiation, on cloudy days and at night, the young pups appear to seek the shelter of overhanging ice hummocks to escape from winds, and often freezing rain, thereby avoiding weather conditions which would promote further heat loss (Øritsland and Ronald, 1973).

A lower critical temperature of about 8 °C has been reported for harp seals at about three weeks of age after their first moult (Iversen and Krog, 1973). Frisch and Øritsland (1968) had predicted that metabolism should double for a 20 °C depression (8° to −12 °C) in ambient air temperature in seals of this age.

It thus appears that survival under adversely cold weather conditions is achieved by a combination of adaptations, including tolerance to hypothermia, utilization of solar radiation, changes in behaviour, and an ability to increase heat production by oxidation of brown fat deposits.

Research is needed to describe the energy requirements for thermoregulation in harp seal pups adequately. For the present it is reasonable to state that the heat loss of young seals is of the order of twice basal metabolism as predicted by Kleiber's equation (4). This is in fact characteristic of immature animals in general (Denckla, 1970; Nordan, Cowan and Wood, 1970).

There is also a paucity of quantitative data on the thermoregulatory interactions between heat production and heat loss under various ambient conditions in adult pinnipeds (Irving, 1969).

For the purpose of the present discussion the demonstration of the assumed high efficiency of adaptive thermal mechanisms in pinnipeds in general, and the harp seal in particular, will have to rely on a comparative approach. As noted above, well-insulated mammals have a lower T_{lc} and a lower (per degree C) increase (slope) in metabolic rate as T_a drops below T_{lc}, than less well insulated mammals (Scholander et al., 1950). In addition, pinnipeds are relatively large mammals with a small surface-area-to-volume ratio, traits which favour reduced heat loss to the environment (Mayr, 1956). A lower critical temperature has not been reached in immature harp seals in water temperatures down to 0 °C (Irving and Hart, 1957). In harbour seals, however, seasonal changes in T_{lc} have been reported (Hart and Irving, 1959). Øritsland and Ronald (1975) observed that a fat adult harp seal in water of 9 °C had a normal mammalian metabolic rate (as predicted by the Kleiber equation, Fig. 3). Under similar ambient conditions a leaner seal always had a higher metabolic rate. Subsequently, Gallivan (1977) found no evidence in three adult harp seals, of basal metabolic rates higher than that of terrestrial mammals. Temperatures between 1.8° and 28.2 °C were within the zone of thermoneutrality. In addition, Øritsland and Ronald (unpubl. data) and Parsons (1977) have demonstrated normal mammalian metabolic rates (Kleiber, 1975) for ringed seals Phoca hispida.

Thus, it would appear that a fat, and therefore well-insulated, harp seal will have a lower critical temperature below 0 °C in water. Furthermore, the cooling effect of water would be such that a significant increase (< 0.5 M) in metabolic rate in response to further cooling would only occur if the ambient water temperature was depressed to between − 5° and − 10 °C, a condition which is hardly possible.

In air, however, ambient weather conditions might well fall below the seal's critical thermal environment (Moen, 1968). For example, it is possible that pagophilic seals may be trapped on the surface of the ice if leads or breathing holes freeze up (Stirling and McEwan, 1975). Under such conditions metabolic rate would have to increase to maintain deep body temperature. If these conditions persisted and the seal had no access to food, the effects could be lethal (Stirling and McEwan, 1975).

From a bioenergetic point of view, the highly developed thermoregulatory mechanisms found in pinnipeds ensure that little or no significant energy consumption beyond basal levels is necessary for the maintenance of homeothermy. It should be noted, however, that some species may exhibit a significant shift in temperature sensitivity throughout the year and that lean seals in water may have to increase metabolism to meet thermoregulatory demands.

Activity

An active animal requires more energy than a resting animal (Tucker, 1970; Schmidt-Nielsen, 1972; Gold, 1973; Calder and Gold, 1974). Generally, walkers expend more energy per gram to cover a given distance than do flyers (Schmidt-Nielsen, 1972a). Swimmers appear to be more efficient than both walkers and flyers, although most of the evidence has been derived from fish (Tucker, 1970; Schmidt-Nielsen, 1972, 1972a). Gold (1973) has estimated the specific energy cost of locomotion for walking, flying, and swimming to be in the ratio of 15:5:2.

The pinniped body shape is obviously adapted for an aquatic existence (Harrison and King, 1965). The body is streamlined and fusiform, the head is relatively small and rounded with no obvious external pinnae. An indistinct neck merges with a smoothly contoured trunk, and the limbs are highly modified for swimming (Harrison and King,

1965). While direct estimates of the energy cost of locomotion in marine mammals are not readily available in the literature, qualitative observations suggest that pinnipeds are relatively effortless swimmers.

The energy cost of locomotion may, however, be estimated on the basis of hydrodynamic analysis, or more directly by indirect calorimetry, i.e. by determination of oxygen consumption at various swimming speeds.

In the context of hydrodynamics, it is recognized that the movement of water relative to a marine mammal results in a force known as drag or resistance (Hoerner, 1956) operating against the direction of swimming. Since there are inconsistencies and a lack of information in the literature covering the hydrodynamics of marine mammals, a presentation of relevant equations and symbols seems appropriate.

Drag is described by the equation:

$$D = 0.5 \, C \, \rho V^2 A \quad \ldots \ldots \ldots \ldots \quad (5)$$

where

D is drag (force) [mass · length · time^{-2}],
C a non-dimensional drag coefficient
V is swimming speed [length · time^{-1}]
ρ is the density of water [mass · length^{-3}]
A is wetted surface area and is not necessarily equal to the surface area of the animal. It may be referred to as a drag area [length^2].

The drag coefficient (C) is a complex function of the Reynolds number. Reynolds law considers the inertial and viscous forces acting on a submerged body. These forces are expressed as a dimensionless number, the Reynolds number (R_e) with:

$$R_e = lV\rho/\mu = l \cdot V/v \quad \ldots \ldots \ldots \quad (6)$$

where l is the length of the body in the velocity direction [length], and μ is the viscosity of the water [force · time · length^{-2}]. The ratio $v = \mu/\rho$ is called the kinematic viscosity [mass · time^2 · length^{-4}]. For a detailed discussion of the above concepts, the reader is referred to Hoerner (1965), Webb (1975), and Vennard and Street (1975).

Having outlined the forces resisting movement in water, the power needed to overcome the drag is calculated. Power (P), by definition, is the energy required per unit time and may be calculated by:

$$P = D \cdot V \text{ [force} \cdot \text{length} \cdot \text{time}^{-1}]. \qquad (7)$$

Kurbatov and Mordvinov (1974) performed detailed hydrodynamic analyses of harp seals. They defined a functional relationship between R_e and C. Consider a 120 kg harp seal 1.65 m in length (harp seal data bank, University of Guelph). Swimming at 1.95 m s^{-1} this animal would have an R_e of 2.156×10^6 and a corresponding C of 0.015 (Kurbatov and Mordvinov, 1974).

Using the formula:

$$A = 0.08 \, W^{0.67} \text{ [length}^2] \quad \ldots \ldots \ldots \quad (8)$$

for the surface area of a seal (Irving *et al.*, 1935) and $\rho = 1020 \text{ kg m}^{-3}$, the necessary power would be P = 112.3 watts or 96.7 kcal h^{-1}. If an overall swimming efficiency of 0.25 is assumed (Luecke, Natarjan and South, 1975), i.e. 25 % of the net swimming metabolism is converted into thrust, the net cost of locomotion is about 449 watts or 387 kcal h^{-1}, which is about 4 times the basal metabolic rate calculated from Kleiber's equation (Fig. 3). The energetic cost of moving one gram of animal a distance of one kilometer is thus 0.46 cal g^{-1} km^{-1}.

In comparison with the above calculations based on hydrodynamic principles, measurements of oxygen consumption in captive harp seals (Øritsland and Ronald, 1975) swimming at about 2 km h^{-1} produced an estimate of 0.34 cal g^{-1} km^{-1} (Øritsland and Ronald, unpubl.), or 0.12 cal g^{-1} km^{-1} less than that obtained by the first method.

In order to compare these two estimates with available data for other animals (Schmidt-Nielsen, 1972a), a caloric equivalent of 4.7 cal ml^{-1} oxygen consumed (Harper, 1975) was used, corresponding to a non-protein respiratory quotient (RQ) determined for harp seals of between 0.70 to 0.75 (Øritsland and Ronald, 1975). This gave estimates of the net cost of locomotion of 0.1 and 0.07 ml O$_2$ g^{-1} km^{-1} based on hydrodynamic analysis and indirect calorimetry, respectively (Fig. 4).

The experimental determination of oxygen consumption in a swimming seal suggests that the net energy cost of locomotion is similar to that found in fish (Fig. 4). The estimate based on hydrodynamic analysis was slightly higher, very close to the regression line for walking and running animals (Fig. 4).

Luecke, Natarjan and South (1975) provided similar data for an otariid, the California sea lion, *Zalophus californianus*. They reported a net cost of locomotion of 100 kcal h^{-1} (in addition to basal metabolism) to maintain a swimming speed of 240 m min^{-1} (14.4 km h^{-1}). Assuming an average body weight of 31.55 kg (Luecke, Natarjan and South, 1975), this gives an estimate of oxygen consumption of about 0.047 mg O$_2$ g^{-1} km^{-1}. This estimate also falls on the "fish line" and is considerably less than the energetic cost of locomotion for a walking or running animal of the same size (Fig. 4).

A variation of 0.12 cal g^{-1} km^{-1}, may initially seem insignificant. However, its bioenergetic implications become important when the appropriate multiplications with body size, swimming distance, and population size are performed.

Thus, for the harp seal population in the western Atlantic, 0.12 cal g^{-1} km^{-1} must be multiplied by 100 000 g (minimal estimate of average body size), by 10^6 animals, each of which may swim in excess of 6 000 km per year during migration (Sergeant, 1965) and while foraging for food. The difference in the two estimates, when considered in terms of the whole population over one year, is roughly equivalent to 7.2×10^{10} kcal or 7.6×10^6 kg of fat, i.e., 7 600 tonnes of fat, or between 45 000 and 80 000 tonnes (wet weight) of capelin.

Obviously, the energetic cost of swimming constitutes a significant item in the energy budget of the harp seal in particular, and of

209

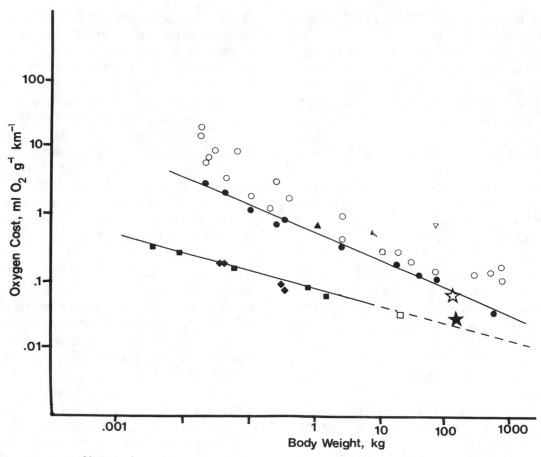

FIG. 4. — The energy cost of locomotion, expressed as the amount of oxygen required to transport 1 g of animal a distance of 1 km (redrawn from Schmidt-Nielsen, 1972b). Small circles — walking and running. Solid circles refer to the net cost of locomotion. Open circles refer to the total oxygen consumption of animals while moving and therefore include the resting O_2 consumption; thus, these points fall above the regression line for net cost. ■ swimming animals (fish). ▲ duck swimming at the surface; man swimming at the surface; ★ energy cost of locomotion for a harp seal, *Pagophilus groenlandicus*, estimated from oxygen consumption experiments (Øritsland and Ronald, 1975) and ☆ from hydrodynamic analysis; and □ an estimate of the net cost of locomotion for a California sea lion, *Zalophus californianus* (from Luecke *et al.*, 1975).

pinnipeds in general. However, the actual quantities involved must be determined by experiments and through field observations, which have yet to be performed.

Respiratory and hydrodynamic factors can both be measured in the laboratory by using water flumes or channels; information thus obtained will be relevant to the problems of drag, critical Reynolds numbers, and swimming efficiencies. Field observations will provide more detailed information on daily and seasonal activity patterns, swimming speeds, and distances travelled. All these data will be needed in order to evaluate properly the energetic cost of locomotion for pinnipeds.

Production Energy

Production energy (NE_p) is utilized for growth and reproduction, and in mammals for the production of hair and milk. Since growth is usually determined from a series of measurements obtained either in the field or from captive animals, a discussion of morphometrics is appropriate at this time. Production energy will then be discussed under the sections foetal growth, post-partum growth during nursing, and subsequent growth as the animal becomes nutritionally self-sufficient and matures into an adult member of the breeding population.

Morphometrics

Measurements of individual animals in a population are often routinely collected by mammalogists in conjunction with other studies. With reference to seals, a list of standard measurements has been proposed (American Society of Mammalogists, 1967). Some of these measurements are particularly important to the study of bioenergetics, including standard length, axillary girth, weight, and blubber thickness. Since weight and blubber thickness may vary seasonally, the date of measurement is important. The age, often obtainable from tooth sections (Laws, 1953; Fisher and Mackenzie, 1954), sex, and reproductive condition of the animal should be noted where possible.

The importance of such fundamental data in relation to bioenergetics cannot be over-emphasized. While they are presently available for a number of pinniped species, there are significant deficiencies, some of which may be difficult to overcome.

For an adequate survey of wild species as many animals as possible should be obtained during each month of the year (Asdell, 1965). This is not always possible for many pinnipeds, but efforts should be made to spread sampling periods over different parts of the year, instead of collecting all the samples for one year at one time. Furthermore, the difficulty of obtaining a random sample of a population (Caughley, 1966) must not be overlooked, and attempts should be made to identify biases.

Reproductive condition should be related to body size noting that body length is often a better measure of body size than weight (Asdell, 1965). In many pinnipeds, length is

less dependent upon incidental factors than body weight and varies less seasonally, in addition it is subject to less variation at puberty (Asdell, 1965).

Much of this information is collected annually by seal biologists. The recommendation that measurements be standardized (American Society of Mammalogists, 1967) bears repeating. Additionally measurements might be recorded on computerized data sheets, suitable for keypunching, which could be stored in a central computer facility and made available to the scientific community on request. Valuable data would thus be preserved for future analyses, and comparative research on various pinnipeds might be stimulated.

The data would also be available to a far greater number of scientists than at present, since most of it is now stored in the filing cabinets of individual scientists, and in restricted reports to various national and international committees. This latter practice has hindered the free exchange of information in marine mammal biology. Valuable information should be published in the primary scientific literature, where (hopefully) it will be subjected initially to critical review before becoming readily available to all interested parties.

Foetal Growth

The gestation period of most pinnipeds can be divided into three parts. Initially, the fertilized ovum undergoes rapid growth to the blastocyst stage of development. This is followed by a period of arrested development, commonly called delayed implantation (Fisher, 1954, 1954a). Later the blastocyst becomes attached to the uterine wall and development continues to parturition as in most other mammals.

A limited amount of relevant information is available on foetal growth in pinnipeds. Foetal length appears to be highly correlated with weight. For grey seals, *Halichoerus gry-*

211

pus, this relationship may be derived from data in the literature (Hewer and Backhouse, 1968):

$$W = 5.75 \cdot 10^{-5} l^{2.75} \quad (r = 0.995) \quad (9)$$

where W is weight in kg and l is length in cm.

A similar equation:

$$W = 6.15 \cdot 10^{-5} l^{2.73} \quad (r = 0.997) \quad (10)$$

may be derived from Scheffer's (1962) data for the northern fur seal *Callorhinus ursinus*.

The striking similarity between the length/weight relationship for a foetal phocid and a foetal otariid suggests that if data are not available for a particular species, the equation

$$W = 6 \cdot 10^{-5} l^{2.74} \quad \dots\dots\dots\dots \quad (11)$$

would be a reasonable first approximation. This is consistent with the generalization that weight is a function of length to the third power (Ricker, 1975).

Data on foetal growth are also available for various other pinnipeds including the harbour seals *P. vitulina richardi* (Bigg, 1969) and *P. vitulina concolor* (Boulva, 1973), and ringed seals (Smith, 1973).

Little is known about the energetic requirements for foetal growth and development in pinnipeds. Moen (1973) has estimated the energy requirements of gestation for white-tailed deer *Odocoileus virginianus* using data from domestic cattle. The total energy requirement for gestation includes the expense of maintaining the pregnant uterus, the energy required for foetal growth, the increase in maternal work and the endocrine influences on the metabolism of the pregnant female (Brody, 1945).

Moen (1973) used cattle data to estimate the daily metabolizable energy cost during gestation. This equation:

$$Q_{ep} = e^{(2.8935 + 0.017t_d)} \quad \dots\dots\dots\dots \quad (12)$$

(where Q_{ep} is the energy requirement [kcal], and t_d is gestation time, i.e. 280 days) was then generalized to a number of ungulate species (Moen, 1973). Further generalization to harp

seals is perhaps questionable due to the large differences in mass and thus metabolic rate (per unit weight) between a 7 kg seal pup and a 45 kg calf. Nevertheless, the cost of pregnancy for cattle, about twice Kleiber's (1975) weight specific basal metabolic rate of the foetus, may be a useful approximation for seals, given the present state of the artscience. This would give an energy requirement of 602.49 kcal/day^{-1} (or 86.07 kcal kg^{-1}/day^{-1}) for the full term harp seal. Use of an exponential growth function similar to Moen's (equation 12) but adjusted for the final metabolic rate of the foetus, results in an average estimate of 19.22 kcal/kg^{-1} (foetal weight)/day^{-1} or approximately 29 000 kcal (ME) per foetus over a gestation period of 215 days assuming a birth weight of 7 kg.

The relatively large size of pinniped foetuses at full term has been noted by Laws (1959). This may be advantageous in cold environments, reducing the surface area to volume ratio, and thus heat loss (Mayr, 1956). It may also be related to the advantages of precocity and/or the reduced limitations to growth afforded by the aquatic environment (Laws, 1959). Whatever the reason for the production of a relatively larger foetus may be, it requires relatively more energy than for most other mammals.

From equation (12) it can be seen that the length of the gestation period influences the energy cost. Having a period of suspended development may ensure that parturition takes place at a particular time of year without much additional energy drain on the female. For example, in the harp seal, birth takes place in the western Atlantic, coincident with the presence of suitable ice for whelping, and suitable food in the form of large concentrations of crustaceans (Sergeant, 1965, 1973a) for the newly-weaned pups.

Milk Production

Milk is the sole source of nourishment for a seal pup during the early stages of its life.

Although the nursing period varies among the pinnipeds (Harrison, 1969), production of milk obviously represents a significant demand on the energy resources of the lactating female.

The gross composition of pinniped (and cetacean) milk differs significantly from that of most mammalian species (Table 6). It contains extremely high concentrations of fat relative to most mammals, and only trace amounts of lactose. This fat-rich milk provides a source of energy for normal metabolic functions and in many species allows the young pinniped, as it matures, to deposit quickly the thick layer of subcutaneous blubber which is so necessary for maintaining homeothermy (Irving, 1969), and thus for survival. This blubber layer is also important in streamlining; it gives the animal buoyancy in water (Kooyman and Drabek, 1968), and enables it to build up sufficient energy reserves to survive the period between weaning and the establishment of nutritional self-sufficiency (Sivertsen, 1941; Laws, 1959; Bryden, 1968; Harrison, 1969).

It is difficult to generalize about the milk composition of pinnipeds. The values reported in Table 6 should not be regarded as absolutes, since it has been established that fat content in milk in some pinnipeds changes during the nursing period. Fat content decreases with time in the harp seal (van Horn and Baker, 1971), increases in the Weddell seal (Kooyman and Drabek, 1968; Stull, Brown and Kooyman, 1967), and reaches a peak somewhere in the middle of the lactation period in the elephant seal *Mirounga leonina* (Bryden, 1968).

Milk output may also change with time (Bryden, 1968). Therefore it is important to record the time relative to the time of parturition at which the sample is obtained for analysis. Standardization of techniques for collection and analysis should also be encouraged since many variables have been shown to affect the results (Silvertsen, 1941), such as whether the samples were obtained from live or dead animals, the presence or absence of blood in the sample, freeze-drying, and the amount of agitation during handling. Despite these problems, the correlations between fat concentration, growth rates, and the length of the nursing period appears to be generally accepted (Laws, 1959).

Fatty acid composition of pinniped milk seems to remain fairly constant over the lactation period (van Horn and Baker, 1971), although it is important to realize that any number of factors, such as diet, temperature, physiological state and genetic constitution, could affect the results (Glass, Troolin and Jenness, 1967). Fatty acid composition of milk and stored fats does not appear to differ significantly in terms of the proportions of the major components. Long-chain unsaturated fatty acids are characteristic of milk fat of seals (Meara, 1952; Ackman and Jangaard, 1965; Ashworth, Ramaiah and Keyes, 1966; Jangaard and Ke, 1968), as well as of whales and polar bears (*Ursus maritimus*) (Glass, Troolin and Jenness, 1967; Jenness, Erickson and Craighead, 1972). It seems that these are derived primarily from plankton and fish (and seals, in the case of the polar bear) which these animals eat (Glass, Troolin and Jenness, 1967). Since the major fatty acid components are virtually in the same proportions in both blubber and milk fat, it would appear that the mobilization of fats from the blubber of the lactating females is accomplished with a minimum of biosynthesis from precursors.

Several authors have suggested that milk composition has evolved in response to the nutrient requirements of the young animal as the major selection pressure (Blaxter, 1961; Ashworth, Ramaiah and Keyes, 1966; Jenness, 1974). However several other factors must be taken into account. The nutritive value of the milk is dependent not only upon its gross composition, but also upon the quantity ingested by the pup (Jenness, 1974). Very little is known about the milk intake of nursing pinnipeds. Bryden (1968) has attempted to give quantitative estimates for the amount of milk produced by the southern elephant seal as well as that consumed by the pup during lactation. Such estimates are only of value in

213

Table 6. Gross composition of pinniped milk. Values for other mammals are given for comparison [1]

Species	% Lipid	% Protein	% Lactose	% Water	Energy kcal/gm [2]	References
PINNIPEDIA						
Phocidae						
Pagophilus groenlandicus	41.5	7.6	0.12	–	–	van Horn & Baker, 1971
harp seal	50.2	6.8	0.69	42.0	5.2	Cook & Baker, 1969
	42.8	12.0	0.0	43.8	–	Sivertsen, 1941
	42.7	10.5	0.0	45.3	–	Sivertsen, 1941
Phoca vitulina	45.0	9.0	–	–	–	Harrison, 1960 [4]
harbour seal						
Halichoerus grypus	53.2	11.2	2.6	–	5.75	Amoroso *et al.*, 1951
grey seal						
Cystophora cristata	40.4	6.7	0.0	49.9	4.21	Sivertsen, 1941
hooded seal						
Leptonychotes weddelli	42.1	15.8	1.0	43.6	4.89	Stull *et al.*, 1967 [3]
Weddell seal	42.2	–	–	–	–	Kooyman & Drabek, 1968
Mirounga angustirostris	29.4	11.7	0.7	–	3.45	as cited in Jenness, 1974
northern elephant seal						
Mirounga leonina	29.3	8.9	–	65.1	–	Bryden, 1968 [3] (in gm/ml)
southern elephant seal						
Otariidae						
Zalophus californianus	34.9	13.6	0.0	–	4.20	Pilson & Kelly, 1962
California sea lion						
Callorhinus ursinus	46.0	–	–	–	–	Wilke, 1959 [4]
northern fur seal	53.3	9.6	0.11	–	5.4	Ashworth *et al.*, 1966
Arctocephalus pusillus	19.0	10.0	–	–	–	Rand, 1956 [4]
South African fur seal						
CETACEA						
Odontoceti						
Delphinapterus leucas	26.9	10.6	0.74	59.0	3.2	Lauer & Baker, 1969
beluga whale						
Tursiops truncatus	16.7	9.6	0.77	–	–	Eichelberger *et al.*, 1940 [5]
bottlenose dolphin						
Stenella graffmani	25.3	8.3	1.9	–	–	Pilson & Waller, 1970
spotted porpoise						
Phocoena sp.	45.8	11.2	1.3	41.1	4.99	Purdie, 1884 [5]
porpoise						
Prodelphinus plagiodon	18.0	9.4	0.63	–	2.25	Eichelberger *et al.*, 1940 [5]
spotted dolphin						
Mysticeti						
Balaenoptera musculus	38.1	12.8	–	47.2	–	Sivertsen, 1941
blue whale	42.3	10.9	1.3	–	4.61	Gregory *et al.*, 1955 [3]
Balaenoptera borealis	22.2	12.0	1.8	–	–	Takata, 1921 [5]
sei whale						
Balaenoptera physalus	30.6	13.1	–	54.1	–	Sivertsen, 1941
fin whale	28.6	11.4	2.6	57.9	3.52	Lauer & Baker, 1969
	51.0	13.0	4.5	–	–	White, 1953 [4]
	32.4	12.8	0.3	–	3.8	Ohta *et al.*, 1953 [3]
Megaptera novaeangliae	38.5	–	–	46.7	–	Pedersen, 1952 [5]
humpback whale	33.0	12.5	1.1	–	3.86	Chittleborough, 1958 [3]

Table 6. Gross composition of pinniped milk. Values for other mammals are given for comparison [1] *(concluded)*

Species	% Lipid	% Protein	% Lactose	% Water	Energy kcal/gm [2]	References
OTHER MAMMALS						
Ursus maritimus	31.4	11.0	0.74	55.1	3.6	Cook *et al.*, 1970
polar bear	33.1	11.8	0.3	–	–	Jenness *et al.*, 1972
Mustela vison	3.6	7.4	8.2	–	1.1	Conant, 1962 [5]
mink	3.3	7.7	10.3	–	–	Conant, 1962 [5]
Alopex lagopus Arctic fox	11.8	12.0	5.4	–	2.01	Dubrovskaya, 1965 [3]
Bos taurus domestic cow	3.7	3.3	4.8	87.0	0.74	Spector, 1956 [5]
Rangifer tarandus caribou - wild	19.1	11.8	2.4	–	2.56	McEwan & Whitehead, 1971
Dipodomys morriami kangaroo rat	23.5	–	–	50.4	–	Kooyman, 1963
Homo sapiens man	4.0	1.3	6.5	87.0	0.72	Schumacher, 1934 [5]

[1] For more complete summary, see Ben Shaul (1962).
[2] Calculated from gross composition using caloric equivalents for lipid, protein, and carbohydrate (Table 1).
[3] As cited in Jenness (1974).
[4] As cited in Harrison (1969).
[5] As cited in Ben Shaul (1962).

indicating the relative amounts involved (Bryden, 1972). Prepartum diet of the female is one of the many factors that may affect milk yield (Church and Pond, 1974).

Linzell (1972) provided a comprehensive review of milk yields and energy cost in different mammalian species. No marine species were discussed in detail, although a tentative estimate of the energy cost of lactation for the blue whale *Balaenoptera musculus* was given. A similar estimate for the sperm whale *Physeter catodon* has been calculated by Lockyer (1976). In most species, the lactating female must increase food intake in order to maintain an energy balance during nursing (Brody, 1945; Linzell, 1972; Moen, 1973; Lockyer, 1976). Many female seals, however, apparently fast or eat very little during the lactation period (Laws, 1959; Sergeant, 1973). This is confirmed by the observation of a marked weight loss in female seals when nursing (Amoroso and Matthews, 1952; Laws, 1959; Sergeant, 1973), which implies that very little

food is taken at this time, or else that little of the assimilated energy is channelled into maintenance.

There are few or no data on stomach capacities of young seals, rates of assimilation, frequency of suckling and the duration of suckling periods, and the quantity of milk ingested during each session. Nor are there values for the volume of milk readily available to the pup at any given time, although Bryden (1968) has obtained some data for the southern elephant seal and Harrison (1969) gives an estimate for the northern fur seal. Adequate estimates of these parameters would be extremely difficult to obtain, however, since a wide variety of extraneous factors may be operative at any given time. Suitable conditions for observation cannot easily be predicted or obtained – for instance it is not known to what extent seal pups suckle at night (Bryden, 1968). The cautious behaviour of female seals, combined with the stresses imposed by capture and restraint, the variety of methods used to obtain samples, the difficulties of obtaining adequate sample sizes, and the general neglect of relevant physiological data for each pup (including exact age, sex, body length and weight, etc.) makes evaluation of present data difficult, and certainly imposes restrictions upon future investigations.

Milk production necessary to meet the energetic requirements of the pup can nevertheless be estimated, and has been calculated in the past (Moen, 1973). An equation for daily milk production (MP in kcal) described below may thus be used as a first approximation:

$$MP = \frac{A + GI + 2(70\,W^{0.75})}{E} \quad (13)$$

where A is an estimate of the net cost of locomotion which in many sedentary young pinnipeds may be negligible [kcal day^{-1}], GI is the daily growth increment which has been estimated for a number of pinnipeds (Lindsey, 1937; Amoroso and Matthews, 1952; Laws, 1953; Templeman, 1966) expressed in energy units [kcal day^{-1}]. The factor 2 accounts for the higher basal metabolic rates (equation 4) reported in young animals and discussed previously, and E is the net energy coefficient for milk, which represents the proportion of milk (energy) consumed which is available to the pup as net energy (NE). Moen (1973) used a value of E = 0.80 in his calculations. To express daily milk production in grams of milk, equation 13 must be divided by the energy equivalent for milk (Moen, 1973) which in harp seals is about 4.8 kcal g^{-1} (Table 6).

The equation describing the total milk production (MP$_T$) during the nursing period would then be:

$$MP_T = \sum_{i=1}^{n} \frac{A + GI + 2(70\,W_i^{0.75})}{E} \quad (14)$$

where n is the length of the nursing period [days] and W$_i$ is the weight of the pup on the ith day where W$_1$ = weight at birth, W$_2$ = W$_1$ + GI, W$_3$ = W$_2$ + GI etc. MP$_T$, however, does not represent the total energy cost to the female to produce milk. The actual cost of milk production will be somewhat higher and for dairy cattle has been estimated to be over 1.6 times the energy contained in milk (Crampton and Harris, 1969). Thus, for seals, the total energy cost of milk production for the lactating female will be higher than MP$_T$. Lacking data to the contrary, an estimate of 1.6 MP$_T$. will be assumed.

Using equation 14, above, we have calculated MP$_T$ for harp seals as approximately 240 000 kcal, using a GI of 1.6 kg day^{-1} (Templeman, 1966), converted to kcal using the caloric equivalent for whole ringed seal pups of 5.215 kcal g^{-1} (Stirling and McEwan, 1975). Activity (A) of very young harp seal pups is negligible and no estimates of the cost of locomotion for older pups are available. Thus A was assumed to be zero, with any minor activity taken care of by assuming that the pups' basal metabolism is twice the theoretical M = 70 W$^{0.75}$. This MP$_T$ may thus correspond to an energy cost to the lactating female of about 384 000 kcal, equivalent to 42.7 kg of body fat. For a fasting 150 kg female harp seal, this represents a 28 % weight loss during the lactation period. This is remarkably similar to the 26 % weight loss reported for a nursing grey seal (Amoroso and Matthews, 1952). If the female seal eats during the nursing period, this theoretical weight loss may not be realized.

Postnatal Growth

Postnatal growth in pinnipeds is characterized by a rapid initial increase in body size during the first year (Laws, 1959), followed by a more gradual increase until about the time the animal reaches sexual maturity.

A large amount of information has been collected on growth rates of pinnipeds. Laws (1959) provided a detailed review of growth for eleven species of phocids, two otariids, and one odobenid. Subsequently, additional growth data have been provided for various pinnipeds including harbour seals (Bigg, 1969;

Boulva, 1973), ringed seals (Smith, 1973), harp seals (Sergeant, 1973) and southern elephant seals (Bryden, 1969).

Growth rates in pinnipeds vary. In general, smaller-sized species grow more slowly than larger ones (Laws, 1959), and there also appears to be an inverse relationship between longevity and rate of growth, or final size (Laws, 1959).

Body length is a less variable measure of body size than body weight, particularly in the case of pinnipeds exhibiting seasonal (and individual) variations in body weight. The relationship between body length and weight may again (see earlier section – *Foetal Growth*) be described by the general equation (Laws, 1959):

$$W = ql^3 \quad \ldots\ldots\ldots\ldots\ldots\ldots \quad (15)$$

The value of q reported in the literature for postnatal growth is about 0.02 (W and l measured in metric units) for the northern fur seal, and between 0.03 and 0.04 in the southern elephant seal (Laws, 1959). Laws (1959) suggested that the values for q for the elephant seal are probably consistent with those of most other phocids, but that for the leopard seal *Hydrurga leptonyx*, q must have a lower value. Sufficient weight and length data are still not available to test this suggestion for many species.

For the purposes of the present discussion, growth of individual animals is of importance because it represents a significant portion of the production energy during the first few years of life. To provide baseline information for our extrapolations on individual energy budgets and ecological efficiency we will restrict detailed discussion to what is presently known about postnatal growth in harp seals. Brief reference to other species will be made where possible.

The harp seal pup at birth is approximately 0.65-0.90 m long and weighs (on the basis of a small sample) between 7 and 14 kg. As noted by Laws (1959), this is large in relation to the size of the female. For example,

recent data obtained for 4 female harp seals and their pups indicate a mean ratio of pup weight to maternal weight shortly after parturition of 1:8.6. This suggests a ratio at birth in the order of 1:10 for the harp seal, compared with 1:6 for the harbour seal and 1:15 for the southern elephant seal (Laws, 1959). The mean ratio of pup length to maternal length for our small sample was 1:9.

At birth, only a very small proportion of the body weight of a harp seal pup is comprised of blubber (Grav, Blix and Pasche, 1974). This is also true for many neonatal phocids (Irving, 1972), including the grey seal (Widdowson, 1950).

In most mammals, female milk yields are probably insufficient to allow maximum growth of the young (Blaxter, 1961; Jenness, 1974), and it is therefore thus assumed that growth of the young animal tends towards an optimum rather than the maximum. However, the pattern of growth in pinnipeds appears to be different from that of terrestrial mammals, where generally the sequence of development is from nervous tissue to bone, muscle and fat (Abrams, 1968; Bryden, 1969). In pinnipeds, initial postnatal development involves the deposition of fat into a subcutaneous layer of blubber, which provides the bulk of the initial weight gain during the nursing period (Bryden, 1968). Recent unpublished data collected for harps seals, demonstrates that this fat deposition may account for early "growth". Towards the end of the nursing period, when sculp weight (weight of skin, with hair and blubber attached) reaches about 50 % of body weight, there is no further increase in the proportion of body fat. Subsequent growth involves increases in organ size, muscle biomass, and body size (length) in general.

Weight gains of young pinnipeds are well documented. Pups of *M. Leonina* have an average weight gain of about 6.8 kg day^{-1} (Laws, 1953). Similar values are available for *L. weddelli* (3.2 kg day^{-1}) (Lindsey, 1937), and *H. grypus* (1.4 kg day^{-1}) (Amoroso and Matthews, 1952). The young harp seal may gain about 1.6 kg day^{-1} (Templeman, 1966). Otariids and odobenids have much slower growth rates. Pups of *Arctocephalus forsteri* gain an average of 0.024 kg day^{-1} over a period of 240 days (Crawley, 1975) and a captive walrus, *Odobenus rosmarus*, was reported to gain between 0.23 and 0.5 kg day^{-1} amounting to a total of 145.5 kg in the first year of life (Harrison, 1969).

Growth curves have been constructed for various pinniped species (Laws, 1959). This requires some measure of the age, e.g. from tooth sections (Laws, 1953; Fisher and Mac Kenzie, 1954), and of body size (length or weight).

Data from wild and captive harp seals (Ronald, pers. comm.) have been used to construct a preliminary growth curve for harp seals (Fig. 2). There is considerable variability in these data, as might be expected since weight and not length was used to measure body size (Laws, 1959; Asdell, 1965). It is interesting to note that there is no significant statistical difference ($p < 0.05$) between the captive and the wild data. The captive data are thus useful in that the amount of food consumed and therefore the caloric intake of these animals is known.

Available morphometric data on harp seals are at present incomplete. Additional data which are required include blubber thickness of a seasonal basis, body length and axillary girth as a function of weight and age, etc. There is also a paucity of morphometric data available for harp seals during the summer, although such information is presently being collected. Further detailed morphometric samples are required at other times of the year as well.

An equation may be derived from the available data to give a general description of the growth of harp seals during the first 10 to 15 years of life such that:

$$W = 39.9 + 15.6x - 0.52x^2 \quad (r = 0.95) \quad (16)$$

where W is body weight [kg] and x is age in years. This equation must be considered very preliminary since it is based on both captive and wild data. Further wild data, including length/weight data collected throughout the year will provide a better basis for describing the harp seal growth curve, but until such data are forthcoming, our calculations will include the above estimates of harp seal growth.

ENERGY REQUIREMENTS OF INDIVIDUAL ANIMALS

Since the energy requirements of an individual animal depend primarily upon its basal metabolic requirements, its activity, and its production in the form of growth, milk production, etc., the preceding sections may therefore be summarized by constructing a very preliminary energy budget for a harp seal.

Data from captive animals (Fig. 2) may be used to estimate food consumption for harp seals, and from there the daily energy available to an adult harp seal (Table 7). It would appear that between 46.9 and 51.8 kcal kg^{-1} day^{-1} are available as net energy.

When expressed as a percentage of Gross Energy (67.7 to 74.6 – Table 7), this value is seen to be similar to the value of 75.2 %

Table 7. Estimate of net energy available to adult harp seals *Pagophilus groenlandicus*, based on consumption of herring, *Clupea harengus*, by captive harp seals[1] aged older than 6 years (Fig. 2)

Stage of Utilization[2]	% GE	Partitioning of daily food intake	
		kcal day^{-1}	kcal kg^{-1} day^{-1}
GE	100	7322	69.3
DE	90 -91	6590 -6663	62.4-63.1
FE	9 -10	659 - 732	6.2- 6.9
ME	82.7-84.7	6055.5-6202	57.3-58.7
UE	6.3-7.3	461 - 534	4.4- 5.1
HI	10 -15[3]	732 -1098	6.9-10.4
NE	67.7-74.7	4957 -5469.5	46.9-51.8

[1] The mean of these animals (106 kg) will be used for calculations.
[2] In Table 8, since these are the only animals for which food comsumption data are available.
[3] See Fig. 1 for an explanation of terms used from Forbes and Swift (1944).

determined for rats fed a mixed diet of beef protein and lard (Forbes and Swift, 1944).

Energy requirements for adult harp seals may also be estimated (Table 8), and most of the calculations have already been made. Estimates of the energetic cost of swimming and pursuit of food are pure speculation. These areas require considerable attention in the near future, although the former will be easier to measure directly than the latter. We have assumed that an adult harp seal may spend 50 % of its time sleeping or resting, 25 % swimming, and 25 % swimming actively in "pursuit of food". Oxygen consumption values observed for captive harp seals (Øritsland and Ronald, 1975) have been used to provide an estimate of the energetic costs of these activities (Table 8).

This approach to energy budgets is similar to that described by Moen (1973). Although our estimates for the harp seal (Table 9) are hypothetical, the order of magnitude appears to be correct (Parsons, 1977). Daily energy requirements for adult harp seals are about twice the basal metabolic rate (M),

which appears reasonable when compared to the few species of ungulates for which similar data exist. This assumes that basal metabolism in pinnipeds, like other mammals, is close to the theoretical value predicted by Kleiber's (1975) equation, but there is no general agreement on this point. The validity of these results may therefore warrant further discussion.

The daily energy requirement including the energy cost of activity of the lactating harp seal at about 9 times M is very high. It appears to be near the upper limit of the energy requirement for the lactating Friesian cow and blue whale, both of which may exceed 8 times M (Table 9) without including the energy cost of activity. This requirement, however, lasts only for the duration of lactation which probably does not exceed 18 days (Templeman, 1966) and may be as short as 10 to 12 days (Sivertsen, 1941). Lactating harp seals are no doubt in negative energy balance and like many lactating pinnipeds lose weight; they have been reported to lose 18.1 kg of blubber (a 31 % reduction in blubber weight). This evidence suggests that our estimates are not unreasonable.

Finally, it is of interest to compare the estimated energy available to a harp seal (Table 7) with the energy requirements of the same animal (Tables 8 and 9). We estimated that the net energy (NE) available to the captive harp seals was 46.9 to 51.8 kcal kg^{-1} day^{-1} (Table 7). An adult harp seal requires, according to our estimates, a minimum of 45 kcal kg^{-1} day^{-1} (21.84 + 9.9 + 13.1 kcal kg^{-1} day^{-1}, Table 8). There is, therefore, some evidence that our crude energy budget is a satisfactory approximation, until actual estimates of many of the parameters are forthcoming. Supporting this conclusion, Parson (1977) found that the minimum energy requirements for ringed seals were between 35 and 55 kcal kg^{-1} day^{-1}.

Table 8. Energy requirements of an adult harp seal, *Pagophilus groenlandicus*, based on a hypothetical activity regime (energy requirements of pregnancy and lactation are also noted)

Activity	% of day	Energy requirement (NE) kcal kg^{-1} day^{-1}
Basal Metabolism	100	21.8 [1]
Swimming	25	9.9 [2]
Pursuit of food	25	13.1 [1]
Resting	50	Basal
Growth	assumed to be	0.0
Reproduction		
pregnancy		1.1 [3]
lactation		199.91 [4]

[1] Based on hypothetical 106 kg seal referred to in Table 7.
[2] Øritsland and Ronald's (1975) estimates of oxygen consumption for swimming harp seals were used to derive these estimates, since suitable data were not available. The energy cost of swimming corresponds to the average oxygen consumption during 1 h experiments. The energy cost involved in "pursuit of food" corresponds to the maximum oxygen consumption value reported in their paper.
[3] Energetic cost of pregnancy over 215 days of the year (see p. 212), 29 000 kcal (ME), adjusted to NE by removing HI equivalent to 15 % GE (Table 7).
[4] Energetic cost of milk production, 384 000 kcal over a lactation period of 18 days (see page 216).

Population energetics

The preceding description of energy flow through individual animals may also be

Table 9. Comparison of daily energy requirements of various mammals expressed in terms of multiples of basal metabolism (equation 4)

Species	Daily Energy Requirements	References
Pagophilus groenlandicus (harp seal)		
male	2.05	this paper
pregnant female	2.06	this paper
lactating female	9.15	this paper
Odocoileus virginianus (white-tailed deer)		
adults	1.23-1.98	Moen, 1973
lactating female	2.3	Moen, 1973
Cervus canadensis (elk or wapiti)		
spikebull	1.44-1.82	Moen, 1973
maturebull	1.74	Moen, 1973
Antilocapra americana (pronghorn)		
adult	1.40-1.45	Moen, 1973
Bos taurus (Friesian cow)		
Lactating female	4-9 [1]	Linzell, 1972
Mus musculus (mouse)		
lactating female	2-3 [1]	Linzell, 1972
Alopex lagopus (Arctic fox)		
lactating female	5 [1]	Linzell, 1972
Sus scrofa (pig)		
lactating female	3-5 [1]	Linzell, 1972
Homo sapiens (man)		
lactating female	0.4-2 [1]	Linzell, 1972
Balaenoptera musculus (blue whale)		
lactating female	1-8 [1]	Linzell, 1972
Physeter catodon (sperm whale)		
lactating female	.88 [1]	Lockyer, 1976

[1] Values consider only lactation and ignore cost of other activities. Milk energy values extrapolated from a graph, and BMR calculated from Kleiber (1975).

used to calculate the rate of energy flow in a population. Energy flow, or the rate of assimilation in a population, provides the most reliable basis for evaluating the observed fluctuations in population density, and for determining the role of a population within its community (Odum, 1971).

At present, population assessments of pinnipeds are usually based on estimates of numbers which are obtained in a variety of ways, including different census techniques (e.g. Lavigne and Ronald, 1975), mark-recapture experiments (Sergeant, 1975), etc. Occasionally, more detailed studies of the dynamics of specific pinniped populations have been carried out. These analyses incorporate information on the age structure of the population usually into some form of life table model, with estimates of birth rate, death rate, the sex ratio, age at maturity, etc. For example, such analyses exist for the harp seal (Allen, 1975), harbour seal (Bigg, 1969; Boulva, 1973), ringed seal (Smith, 1973), grey seal (Hewer, 1964), Weddell seal (Stirling, 1971), southern elephant seal (Laws, 1960), and northern fur seal (Chapman, 1961). From an ecological point of view, however, numbers alone tend to underestimate the importance of large animals such as pinnipeds within an ecosystem (Odum, 1971).

Attempts to estimate population biomass have rarely been made for pinnipeds (Laws, 1960; Boulva, 1973; Sergeant, 1973). This can easily be accomplished if estimates of the age distribution, age-specific growth rates, and population size are available. Population biomass is more commonly estimated by multiplying an average body weight for an animal within the population by the total number of animals in the population (Sergeant, 1973). Such estimates must at best be considered very approximate. Density-dependent changes in growth rates (Scheffer, 1955; Laws, 1973) are known in certain pinnipeds, with the suggestion that concomitant changes in reproductive rates may also take place (Sergeant, 1966, 1973a). Such changes may occur "naturally" or as a result of human exploitation of the population resulting in a reduction in population density (Sergeant, 1966, 1973a; Laws, 1973). These changes are probably related to the availability of food (Sergeant, 1966, 1973a;

Laws, 1973). In high density populations gregarious and hierarchical social behaviour exhibited by many pinnipeds (McLaren, 1958) may also mediate density-dependent changes which result in reduced recruitment. In any case, estimates of population biomass at any one time may be misleading if used to measure the importance of a species within a particular system. In contrast to numerical estimates such biomass estimates tend to overestimate the importance of large organisms within a system (Odum, 1971).

The most realistic approach to studying populations within ecosystems is thus to integrate numerical data and biomass estimates, taking into account respiration, which accounts for much of the energy flow in most situations (Odum, 1971). Only two attempts have been made, to our knowledge, to describe energy flow within a pinniped population (Boulva, 1973; Parsons, 1977). Boulva's analysis, based on a hypothetical harbour seal population, indicated that of the gross energy (GE) consumed, about 15 % was lost as "rejecta" (faeces and urine), 79 % was lost as "respiration" (heat losses including basal metabolism, and the various heat increments, etc.) while 6 % was realized as production (including growth, reproduction, and animals removed from the population by harvesting, and natural mortality).

Calculations made in this paper produce rather similar population estimates of energy flow in a harp seal population. Briefly, of the gross energy consumed by western Atlantic harp seals, it would appear on the average that 17 % is lost as "rejecta", 80 % is lost as "respiration", while production represents about 3 % of gross energy. These findings are discussed in more detail under ecological efficiency.

In summary, while little has been done to date to estimate the rates of energy flow through pinniped populations, it is important to stress that this approach will provide a more realistic basis on which to manage pinniped stocks in the future. The limitations of using only numerical or biomass data to assess pinniped populations, especially those currently exploited by man, must be recognized.

Community energetics

The ultimate aim of this paper was to discuss pinniped bioenergetics in relation to ecosystem management. It has been suggested that the systems approach will eventually provide the best information for managing pinniped populations. This is particularly true in those instances where pinnipeds represent only one component in a multispecies fishery, or when exploitation of previously unhunted populations is contemplated.

The information required for such an approach includes a knowledge of the flow of energy and material through the ecosystem and some quantitative description of the specific pathways involved. This requires a detailed knowledge of trophic or feeding relationships, and other interactions between the various components within the system. Individual species are no longer the important consideration at this level of discussion (Kerr, 1974).

TROPHIC RELATIONSHIPS

In general, pinnipeds occupy a relatively high position in marine trophic webs. Many species are, however, eurytrophic, feeding on a variety of invertebrate and vertebrate prey species which themselves occupy a variety of trophic levels.

A trophic web for a particular pinniped may be constructed from a detailed knowledge of its prey species. For most species the components of the trophic web may change with age, and with season, and such variations in feeding habits are important to note.

A simplified trophic web for the harp seal in the western Atlantic is shown in Fig. 5.

221

Unfortunately, quantitative data on the rates of energy transfer within this trophic web are not available at the present time. Nevertheless, the complexity of possible trophic interactions emphasizes the naivety of managing exploited pinniped populations on the basis of single species population models. Of the species shown in Fig. 5, man exploits not only harp seals, but also flatfish, Atlantic cod, silver hake, cephalopod molluscs, sand lances (*Ammodytes*) and pelagic decapods (e.g. *Pandalus* sp.) (Sergeant, 1973, 1976a), capelin, redfish, and herring (Templeman, 1966; Pinhorn, 1976). It is self-evident that changes in one trophic level will have effects on other levels within the system. This is an especially important consideration at the present time when there is some controversy about the status of

western Atlantic harp seal stocks and their future management (Benjaminsen and Lett, 1976; Capstick, Lavigne and Ronald, 1976; Mercer, 1977; IUCN, 1977; Lavigne, 1976, 1977). In addition, stocks of herring, flatfish, cod, and redfish are also over-exploited and depleted in the western Atlantic (Pinhorn, 1976; Winters, 1975). Furthermore, it is not unreasonable to predict that increased harvests of capelin may be anticipated in the next few years, while fin whales *Balaenoptera physalus* and minke whales *Balaenoptera acutorostrata*, which both feed on capelin, have not been hunted by Canadian whalers in the western Atlantic since 1972 (Pinhorn, 1976).

This is then an example of an exploited pinniped population representing only one component of a multi-species fishery. Signifi-

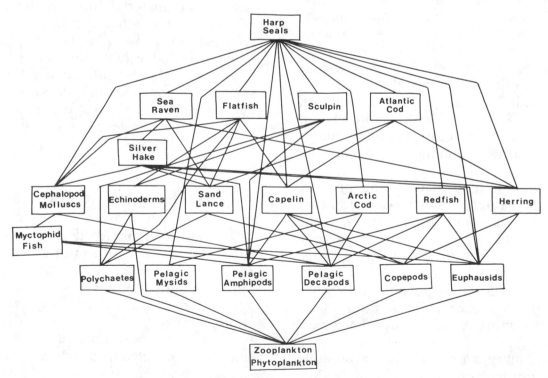

FIG. 5. — A simplified trophic web for the harp seal *Pagophilus groenlandicus*. This diagram summarizes the trophic relationships of harp seals on an annual basis without regard for changes in food habits associated with differences in season or age of seals, nor does it differentiate between important prey species and those which are consumed occasionally. The trophic relationships become more complicated and of significance to management when it is noted that many of the fish species consumed by harp seals are also commercially exploited by man, as is the harp seal itself. In addition, whale species, formerly exploited in the western Atlantic, are also involved in this trophic web, as both fin whales *Balaenoptera physalus* and minke whales *Balaenoptera acutorostrate* compete with seals and man for capelin *Mallotus villosus*. (Compiled from various sources.)

cant trophic interactions between the exploited populations (Fig. 5) no doubt occur, but these are complex and poorly understood.

All of these exploited species are being "managed" at the present time. However, from an ecosystem point of view, there are problems in determining the appropriate levels of catch for each species simultaneously. Conventionally, calculations of maximum sustainable yield (MSY), in terms of numbers or biomass, have provided a basis for managing individual populations (Christy, 1973). However, when ecologically interrelated species are being harvested, yield from each species cannot be maximized simultaneously. To take a maximum yield from one population will result in less than maximum yield of the other, either through over- or under-utilization (Christy, 1973). The above comments stress the need for additional quantitative information on predator-prey interactions (Gulland, 1970), intra- and inter-specific competition, and ultimately on energy flow through the trophic web. They also emphasize the problems of basing management decisions solely on results of numerical, single species models.

It is therefore not yet possible to provide an adequate, quantitative description of the flow of energy through the trophic web given in Fig. 5. We can however make some preliminary estimates of energy flow through the harp seal component as noted under "Population Energetics". Some estimates of ecological efficiency for this species are provided below.

ECOLOGICAL EFFICIENCY

Although many different "ecological efficiencies" have been reported in the literature, no commonly accepted and standardized definition of the term exists. The concept is virtually meaningless, unless a complex array of ambiguous and confusing terms is clarified. To reduce the confusion, we have adopted Kozlovsky's (1968) scheme and refer the reader to his thorough discussion of this subject.

An ecological efficiency may be defined as a ratio of any of the various parameters of energy flow in or between trophic levels of a natural community, in or between populations of organisms, or in or between individual organisms (Odum, 1971). The primary concern in this paper is the impact of pinniped populations on other components within the ecosystem, especially where man and pinnipeds compete for the same food resources. For this reason we will limit discussion to Kozlovsky's (1968) ecological efficiency denoted as EE 5-0. This particular ecological efficiency has been described by a variety of terms including:

1. Efficiency of transfer to the next level in terms of ingested energy (Patten, 1959).

2. Ecological efficiency (Slobodkin, 1960, 1962; MacFayden, 1963).

3. Gross efficiency of yield to ingestion (Wiegert, 1964).

4. Ecological growth efficiency (Odum, 1971).

5. Gross production efficiency (Ricklefs, 1973).

Regardless of the name, EE 5-0 may be defined as follows (Kozlovsky, 1968):

$$EE\ 5\text{-}0 = \frac{\text{Energy passed to trophic level } n+1}{\text{Ingestion at trophic level } n}$$

In other words, EE 5-0 is the ratio of energy available to trophic level $n + 1$ to the energy ingested or removed from trophic level $n - 1$ by trophic level n, or simply a measure of the efficiency with which materials and energy are transferred between levels (Turner, 1970).

Table 10 summarizes a number of EE 5-0 values (expressed as a percentage) for animals from several trophic levels. Values for pinnipeds at least must be qualified since they really refer to populations and not to an entire trophic level within the ecosystem. In analysing the trends of EE 5-0, Kozlovsky (1968) has shown that ecological efficiency "decreases at levels above trophic level 2, so that values below 10 % should not be considered anomalous". In fact, Turner (1970) argued that "on the basis of available data, the ecological efficiency of populations of homeothermic animals cannot exceed 2-3 %" while Steele (1974) suggested that ecological efficiencies for mammals range between 2 to 5 %.

Some of the confusion about ecological efficiency EE 5-0 arises because of the so-called "ten per cent law" (Sutton and Harmon, 1973). Slobodkin (1961) pointed out that the ratio of food assimilated at n − 1 to that assimilated at n "will tend to converge on some relatively narrow range of values around 10 %". The relatively constant values of Lindemann's (1942) efficiency (or progressive efficiency, as this ratio is commonly known) have been confused by some with those of EE 5-0, but as Table 10 shows, few if any animals approach a value of 10 % for EE 5-0.

Misuse and misinterpretation of Slobodkin's (1960) definition of ecological efficiency has further compounded the confusion in the literature (Sergeant, 1973). This was:

$$\text{ecological efficiency} = \frac{\text{Yield at n}}{\text{Ingestion at n}}$$

which pertains only to a steady state population where yield for any given time period is the same as production for that time period.

Very few real estimates of EE 5-0 have been made for whole populations because of the information required i.e., population structure, whether the population is stable, increasing or decreasing (Turner, 1970), growth, ingestion and productivity, prey species, seasonal variation in the type and quantity of prey taken, and variations in their caloric content. Data of this sort for any single pinniped species are not readily available. However, using approximations from other mam-

mals where necessary, we have incorporated information on population structure (Allen, 1975; Benjaminsen and Lett, 1976; Capstick, Lavigne and Ronald, 1976) age specific growth and food consumption (Fig. 2), the caloric content of food (Table 3), and of seals (Stirling and McEwan, 1975), energy required for gestation and lactation, and estimates of mortality from hunting and natural causes to provide a rough estimate of EE 5-0 for harp seals (Table 10).

The mean estimate of EE 5-0 for harp seals in the western Atlantic was 3.9 % (range 1.92-4.94) for 7 calculations made on different age distributions generated by two harp seal population models (Benjaminsen and Lett, 1976; Capstick, Lavigne and Ronald, 1976). One such calculation is shown in Table 11.

Sergeant (1973) has provided the only other estimate of ecological efficiency for the harp seal (0.5 %). Admittedly (Sergeant, 1973), this was only a first approximation and even less specific values for growth and ingestion were used than in this paper. He also considered pup production as his only factor of yield, which is not a true estimate. Yield is the energy transferred to the next trophic level via natural mortality (e.g. predation, decomposition) and in the case of exploited species, via hunting mortality as well. Sergeant also used biomass estimates, which tend to over-estimate the impact of large organisms on the ecosystem (Odum, 1971), rather than the rate of energy transfer. To demonstrate this, Parsons (1977) repeated Sergeant's (1973) calculations using energy values rather than biomass and this increased the estimate of ecological efficiency to 1.76 %.

Our value of about 3.9 % for EE 5-0 is in line with expected results for homeotherms (Turner, 1970) and mammals (Steele, 1974) and does not support Sergeant's (1973) generalization that "Harp seals (as perhaps other sea mammals) are therefore inefficient converters of fish flesh."

Only two other estimates of ecological efficiency for pinnipeds are presently available. Boulva (1973) estimated 6 % for harbour

Table 10. Comparative values of EE 5-0 (%) for animals from various trophic levels

Species	Ingestion	Production	$\dfrac{\text{Production}}{\text{Ingestion}} \times 100$	Reference
Littorina inornata marine gastropod	645 kcal/m^2/yr	40.6 kcal/m^2/yr	6.29	Odum & Smalley, 1959[1]
grasshoppers (3 species)	71 »	4.0 »	5.63	Odum, Connel & Davenport, 1962[1]
Alburnus alburnus bleak	–	–	6.6	Mann, 1965
Rutilus rutilus roach	–	–	5.5	Mann, 1965
Marsh wren	125 kcal/m^2/yr	0.5 kcal/m^2/yr	0.4	Kale, 1965[1]
Sylvilagus audubonii desert cottontail rabbit	1.08 »	0.03 »	2.8	Chew & Chew, 1970
Lepus californicus jack rabbit	4.6 »	0.12 »	2.6	Chew & Chew, 1970
Microtus pennsylvanicus meadow vole	25 »	0.52 »	2.1	Golley, 1960
Dipodomys merriami kangaroo rat	7.2 »	0.05 »	0.69	Chew & Chew, 1970
Adenota kob thomasi Uganda kob	74.1 »	0.81 »	1.1	Buechner & Golley, 1967
Odocoileus virginianus white-tailed deer	52.6 »	0.64 »	1.2	Davis & Golley, 1963
Loxodonta africanus African elephant	71.6 »	0.34 »	0.47	Petrides, Golley & Brisbin, 1965
Bos taurus domestic cow	14.3 »	0.86 »	6.0	Petrides, Golley & Brisbin, 1965
Mustela rixosa least weasel	.582 »	.013 »	2.2	Golley, 1960
Phoca vitulina harbour seal	704 224 × 10^3 kcal/yr	41 695 × 10^3 kcal/yr	5.9[3]	Boulva, 1973
Pagophilus groenlandicus harp seal	–	–	0.525	Sergeant, 1973
Pagophilus groenlandicus harp seal	–	–	3.9[3]	This paper
Phoca hispida ringed seal	–	–	3.8[3]	Parsons, 1977
Physeter catodon sperm whale	–	–	<1-14.3[2]	Lockyer, 1976

[1] As cited in Ricklefs (1973).
[2] Ranges for first year suckling calf to physically mature adults.
[3] Population structure taken into account.

seals, which may be somewhat high. A critical value in his analysis seems to be the caloric content of food, and when our estimate of caloric content of food (harp and harbour seals consume reasonably similar food items), is substituted in Boulva's calculations, his estimate becomes 3.5 %. Parsons (1977) using a congruent analysis to Boulva (1973) calculated an ecological efficiency for ringed seals of 3.8 %. Both of these calculations incorporated

225

Table 11. Calculation of EE 5-0 for harp seals, *Pagophilus groenlandicus*, in the western Atlantic

$$EE\ 5\text{-}0 = \frac{\text{Population Production}}{\text{Population Ingestion}} \times 100$$

where production equals:

Natural mortality	$5\ 648 \times 10^{10}$ kcal y^{-1}
Hunting mortality	$4\ 057^1 \times 10^{10}$ kcal y^{-1}
	$9\ 707 \times 10^{10}$ kcal y^{-1}

and ingestion equals:

Gross Energy of Food[7] $2\ 612 \times 10^{12}$ kcal y^{-1}

$$EE\ 5\text{-}0 = \frac{9\ 705 \times 10^{10}}{2\ 612 \times 10^{12}} \times 100 = 3.72\ \%\ ^1$$

[1] Seven different age distributions were used in calculations of EE 5-0 for harp seals. The estimates ranged from 1.92-4.94 with a mean of 3.9 %. For an unexploited population and stable age distribution the EE 5-0 was 2.34 %. This last value is most comparable to the estimates of Boulva (1973) and Parsons (1977) for harbour seals and ringed seals respectively.

The following parameters were used in the above calculation:

Age class	n[2] (in thousands)	caloric content (kcal gm^{-1})	ingestion rate (kcal/day^{-1}/animal^{-1})	average weight (g)[5]	natural mortality[6]
		5.215[3]			
0	376	3.15[3]	3 980.6[4]	38 399	0.20
1	209	4.24	5 654.0	64 416	.16
2	154	4.24	6 596.6	79 788	.13
3	152	4.24	5 617.8	85 982	.11
4	93	4.24	6 741.2	100 492	.10
5	96	4.24	7 576.8	112 358	.095
6	87	4.24	7 322.2	105 620	.095
7	85	4.24	7 322.2	105 620	.095
8	55	4.24	7 322.2	105 620	.095
9	34	4.24	7 322.2	105 620	.095
10	32	4.24	7 322.2	106 620	.095
11	31	4.24	7 322.2	105 620	.095
12	28	4.24	7 322.2	105 620	.095
13	30	4.24	7 322.2	105 620	.095
14	25	4.24	7 322.2	105 620	.095
15	16	4.24	7 322.2	105 620	.095
16	16	4.24	7 322.2	105 620	.095
17	11	4.24	7 322.2	105 620	.095
18	15	4.24	7 322.2	105 620	.095
19	7	4.24	7 322.2	105 620	.095
20	6	4.24	7 322.2	105 620	.095
21	4	4.24	7 322.2	105 620	.10
22	5	4.24	7 322.2	105 620	.12
23	3	4.24	7 322.2	105 620	.15
24	4	4.24	7 322.2	105 620	.19
25	4	4.24	7 322.2	105 620	.24

[2] Age distribution was taken from Benjaminsen and Lett (1976).
[3] Upper value is for pups at or just after weaning, the lower for pups from weaning to 1 year of age (Stirling and McEwan, 1975).
[4] Values for pups from weaning to 1 year.
[5] All members assumed to feed 300 days during year (Sergeant, 1973), average daily consumption being calculated from data used in Fig. 2.
[6] Hypothetical values from Capstick, Lavigne and Ronald (1976).
[7] Ingestion was computed from [5] for all animals in an age class [2]. Also included was an estimate for gross energy of producing a pup to the weaning stage multiplied by the number in age class 0.

a stable age distribution and considered only natural mortality as yield.

Clearly, more work is required before realistic ecological efficiencies for pinnipeds can be calculated and adequate assessments of the impact of pinnipeds on the ecosystem can be made. All values of EE 5-0 for pinnipeds available to date (Boulva, 1973; Sergeant, 1973; this MS; Parsons, 1977) must be considered to be very preliminary and totally insufficient criteria on which to base management decisions.

The systems approach to management

A "systems" approach has yet to be recognized as a feasible alternative to present management practices. Before it can be contemplated, much additional information on pinniped bioenergetics will be required, as well as on other areas which affect the functioning and productivity of ecosystems. These include the availability of nutrients within the system, meteorological influences and the presence of man-made pollutants. In systems where various components are harvested by man, the economics of exploitation must also be considered when making decisions about future management (Christy, 1973).

Leopold (1949), in his now classic book, recognized the land as a unit system, comprised of interdependent biotic and abiotic components. More recently, others (Watt, 1966; Gulland, 1970; Odum, 1971) have emphasized the need and value of this approach to modern ecology.

The important point is that a system can only be studied by viewing it as a whole (Watt, 1966), and cannot be grasped by studying only its components (Watt, 1966; May, 1974). Even though this has been recognized, few attempts at large scale work have been made. Patten (1972) summarized the work presently completed on the International Biological Programme North American Grassland Biome

Study while Botkin and Miller (1974) discussed attempts to model the Brookhaven Forest and several authors (Smith, 1970; Milner, 1972; Vandyne, 1972; Goodall, 1972) have outlined the requirements and difficulties of such an approach, but it seems that there has been little action. While the difficulties of such action are clear, the consequences of present day management practices may be less easily recognized; nevertheless, numerous examples of inadequate conservation of natural resources have become obvious in recent years.

The effects of introducing species into novel environments are well known and documented. Less numerous are accounts of the effects on the functioning of ecosystems of removing species. Paine (1966) demonstrated the effects of removing a single species from an intertidal invertebrate system. In less than two years, a fifteen species community collapsed to one of 8 species. Laws (pers. comm.) has noted the effects of reduced numbers of baleen whales in the Southern Ocean. Here, there is evidence that removal of one member of an ecosystem allows other species, such as crab-eater seals (*Lobodon carcinophagus*), the fur seal *Arctocephalus gazella* and krill-eating penguins, to expand their populations into the niche now unfilled by whales.

The variable effects of introducing or removing species raise the question of ecosystem stability. The relationship between diversity and stability in ecosystems has recently been reviewed (Goodman, 1975). It was found that there is no simple relationship between the two, but this does not mean that there is no relationship at all. Dunbar (1973) raised the possibility of the need for large spaces and large time factors to produce stability in the Arctic ecosystem. Another recent review (Chew, 1974) suggested that although consumers may not remove a significant portion of production, they may be necessary for regulation of ecosystems.

Thus, the systems approach to management is necessary, but research in this field requires large commitments of manpower and money (i.e. energy). The advantages will, how-

227

ever, certainly outweigh the costs. By approaching the management of pinniped stocks, and indeed, all natural renewable resources in this manner, we will gain some understanding of the complexity of ecological interactions in natural systems. Such understanding will undoubtedly contribute to more enlightened utilization (and hopefully conservation) of natural resources in the future.

Acknowledgements

This compilation of available information on the ecological energetics of pinnipeds was initiated at the request of Dr. Ole Mathiesen, as a result of the UN/FAO/ACMRR *ad hoc* Group III meeting in Seattle, Washington in September 1975. A draft MS was submitted to the Scientific Consultation on Marine Mammals, Bergen, Norway, 31 August to 9 September 1976 as ACMRR/MM/SC112. Subsequently, the MS was edited, and many of the calculations were reworked to incorporate new information and to correct errors in the original MS. No attempt was made to include or synthesize all information published since August 1976. A few additions were made, in particular new data from two recent theses by J. Gallivan and J. Parsons.

Preparation of this paper was aided by the support of several individuals. We especially thank Professor K. Ronald, Dean, College of Biological Science, University of Guelph, for permission to use unpublished data on the growth of harp seals in captivity, and for the use of his Pinniped Bibliography. Professor C. Capstick, Department of Computing and Information Science, University of Guelph, provided access to a harp seal population model which was used to generate age distributions for our calculations. K. Kalpakis and P. Reynolds assisted with the compilation of data and constructed the figures, R. Stewart with the analysis of unpublished field data, and G. Nancekivell with the laborious task of checking and proofreading the final MS.

We thank J. Gulland, P.F. Lett, J. Parsons, and G.C. Ray for volunteering comments on the original MS.

This work was made possible through the financial support of the Donner Canadian Foundation; the Special Advisory Committee on Seals and Sealing to the Minister of State for Fisheries, Government of Canada; and the National Research Council of Canada. In addition, W.W. Barchard received support from an O'Brien Foundation Fellowship while S. Innes was a recipient of a Canadian National Sportsman's Show Scholarship and a University of Guelph Graduate Research Scholarship. Attendance of the senior author at the Bergen Consultation was made possible by funds from the Canadian Friends of the International Ocean Institute. We particularly thank S. Holt and M. Bruce for their encouragement and support.

References

ABRAMS, J.T., Nutrition of the captive wild herbivore.
1968   *Symp. Zool. Soc. Lond.*, 21:41-62.

ACKMAN, R.G. and P.M. JANGAARD, The grey (Atlantic)
1965   seal, fatty acid composition of blubber from a lactating female. *Can. J. Biochem.*, 43:251-5.

ALLEN, R.L., A life table for harp seals in the Northwest
1975   Atlantic. *Rapp. P.-V. Réun. CIEM*, 169:303-11.

ALTMAN, P.L. and D.S. DITTMER, Metabolism: biologi-
1968   cal handbook. Bethesda, Maryland, Federation of American Societies for Experimental Biology.

American Society of Mammalogists, Committee on
1967   Marine Mammals, Standard measurements of seals. *J. Mammal.*, 48:459-62.

AMOROSO, E.C. and L.H. MATTHEWS, Reproduction and
1952 lactation in the seal. *Rep. Int. Congr. Physiol. Pathol. Anim. Reprod. Artif. Insem.*, 2: 192-203.

AMOROSO, E.C. *et al.*, Lactation in the grey seal. *J. Physiol.*, 113:4-5.
1951

ANDREWS, C.W., The hazardous industry of North At-
1951 lantic sealing. *Anim. Kingd.*, 54:66-94.

ARTHUR, D., The determination of chromium in animal
1970 feed and excreta by atomic absorption spectrophotometry. *Can. Spectrosc.*, 15:134-6.

ASDELL, S.A., Reproduction and development. *In* Phy-
1965 siological mammalogy, edited by W.V. Mayer and R.G. van Gelder. London, Academic Press.

ASHWORTH, V.S., G.D. RAMAIAH and M.C. KEYES, Spe-
1966 cies difference in the composition of milk with special reference to the northern fur seal. *J. Dairy Sci.*, 49:1206-11.

BARRETT, G.W., Bioenergetics of a captive least shrew,
1969 *Cryptotis parva. J. Mammal.*, 50:629-30.

BEAMISH, F.W.H., A.J. NIIMI and P.F.K.P. LETT,
1975 Bioenergetics of teleost fishes: environmental influences. *In* Comparative physiology-functional aspects of structural materials, edited by L. Bolis, H.P. Maddrell and K. Schmidt-Nielsen. Amsterdam, North-Holland Publishing Co.

BENJAMINSEN, T. and P.F. LETT, A stochastic model for
1976 the management of the northern Atlantic harp seal *Pagophilus groenlandicus* population. *ICNAF Res. Doc.*, 76/X/130.

BEN SHAUL, D.M., The composition of the milk of wild
1962 animals. *In* International zoo yearbook, edited by C. Jarvis and D. Morris. London, Zoological Society of London.

BEST, R.C., Ecological energetics of the polar bear
1976 (*Ursus maritimus* Phipps 1774). M.Sc. Thesis. University of Guelph, Guelph, Ontario, Canada.

BIGG, M.A., The harbour seal in British Columbia. *Bull.*
1969 *Fish. Res. Board Can.*, (172):33 p.

BLAXTER, K.L., Lactation and the growth of the young.
1961 *In* Milk: the mammary gland and its secretion, edited by S.K. Kon and A.T. Cowie. New York, Academic Press, vol. 2.

BLIGH, J., Temperature regulation in mammals and
1973 other vertebrates. Amsterdam, North-Holland Publishing Co.

BLIGH, J. and K.G. JOHNSTON, Glossary of terms for
1973 thermal physiology. *J. Appl. Physiol.*, 35:941-61.

BLIX, A.S., H.J. GRAV and K. RONALD, Brown adipose
1975 tissue and the significance of the venous plexuses in pinnipeds. *Acta Physiol. Scand.*, 94:133-5.

BOTKIN, D. and R. MILLER, Complex ecosystem models
1974 and predictions. *Am. Sci.*, 62:448-53.

BOULVA, J., The harbour seal, *Phoca vitulina concolor*, in
1973 eastern Canada. Ph.D. Thesis. Dalhousie University, Halifax, Nova Scotia, Canada.

BRISBIN, I.L., Energy utilization in a captive hoary bat.
1966 *J. Mammal.*, 47:719-20.

BRODY, S., Bioenergetics and growth, with special refer-
1945 ence to the efficiency complex in domestic animals. New York, Hafner Publishing Co., Inc.

BRYDEN, M.M., Lactation and suckling in relation to
1968 early growth of the southern elephant seal, *Mirounga leonina* (L.). *Aust. J. Zool.*, 16:739-48.

–, Relative growth of the major body components of
1969 the southern elephant seal, *Mirounga leonina* (L.). *Aust. J. Zool.*, 17:153-77.

–, Growth and development of marine mammals. *In*
1972 Functional anatomy of marine mammals, edited by R.J. Harrison. New York, Academic Press, vol. 1:1-79.

BUECHNER, H.K. and F.B. GOLLEY, Preliminary esti-
1967 mates of energy flow in Uganda kob (*Adenota kob thomasi* Newmann). *In* Secondary productivity of terrestrial ecosystems. (Principles and methods), edited by K. Petrusewicz. Poland, Pánstwowe Wydawnictwo Nankowe.

BUTTERY, P.S. and E.F. ANNISON, Considerations of the
1973 efficiency of amino acid and protein metabolism in animals. *In* The biological efficiency of protein production, edited by J.G.W. Jones. Cambridge, Cambridge Univesity Press.

CALDER, W.A. and A. GOLD, Energy cost of animal loco-
1974   motion. *Science, Wash.*, 184:1098.

CAPSTICK, C.K., D.M. LAVIGNE and K. RONALD, Popula-
1976   tion forecasts for Northwest Atlantic harp seals,
        Pagophilus groenlandicus. *ICNAF Res. Doc.*,
        76/X/132.

CAUGHLEY, G., Mortality patterns in mammals. *Ecology*,
1966   47:906-18.

CHAPMAN, D.G., Population dynamics of the Alaskan fur
1961   seal herd. *Trans. North Am. Wildl. Nat. Resour.
        Conf.*, 26:356-69.

CHEW, R.M., Consumers as regulators of ecosystems: an
1974   alternative to energetics. *Ohio. J. Sci.*,
        74:359-70.

CHEW, R.M. and A.E. CHEW, Energy relationships of the
1970   mammals of a desert shrub (*Larrea tridenata*)
        community. *Ecol. Monogr.*, 40:1-21.

CHRISTY, F.T., Jr., Alternative arrangements for marine
1973   fisheries: an overview. Washington, D.C., Re-
        sources for the Future, Inc.

CHURCH, D.C. and W.C. POND, Basic animal nutrition
1974   and feeding. Oregon, O and B Books.

CLARKE, G.L., Dynamics of production in a marine area.
1946   *Ecol. Monogr.*, 16:321-35.

COOK, H.W. and B.E. BAKER, Seal milk. 1. Harp seal
1969   (*Pagophilus groenlandicus*) milk: composition
        and pesticide residue content. *Can. J. Zool.*,
        47:1129-32.

COOK, H.W. *et al.*, Polar bear milk. 4. Gross composition,
1970   fatty acids and mineral constitution. *Can. J.
        Zool.*, 48:217-9.

CRAMPTON, E.W. and L.E. HARRIS, Applied animal nu-
1969   trition. San Francisco, W.H. Freeman and Co.

CRAWLEY, M.C., Growth of New Zealand fur seal pups.
1975   *N.Z.J. Mar. Freshwat. Res.*, 9(4):539-45.

CUMMINS, K.W. and J.C. WUYCHECK, Caloric equivalents
1971   for investigations in ecological energetics.
        Commun. Inst. Assoc. Theor. Appl. Limnol.,
        (18).

CZARNOCKI, J., I.R. SIBBALD and E.V. EVANS, The deter-
1961   mination of chromic oxide in samples of feed
        and excreta by acid digestion and spectropho-
        tometry. *Can. J. Anim. Sci.*, 41:167-79.

DAVIS, D.E. and F.B. GOLLEY, Principles in mammalogy.
1963   New York, Reinhold Publishing Corp.

DAVYDOV, A.F. and A.R. MAKAROVA, Changes in heat
1964   regulation in newborn seals on transition to
        aquatic forms of life. *Fed. Proc. Fed. Am. Soc.
        Exp. Biol. (Trans. Suppl.)*, 24(II):T562-6.

DAVYDOV, A.F. and A.R. MAKAROVA, Changes in the
1965   temperature of the skin of the harp seal during
        ontogenesis, as related to the degree of cooling.
        Transl. Ser. Fish. Res. Board Can., (816).

DENCKLA, W.D., Minimal oxygen consumption in the
1970   female rat, some new definitions and meas-
        urements. *J. Appl. Physiol.*, 29:263-74.

DRODZ, A., Metabolic cages for small rodents. *In* Me-
1975   thods for ecological bioenergetics, edited by W.
        Grodzinski, R.Z. Klebowski and A. Duncan.
        IBP Handb., (24).

DUNBAR, M.S., Stability and fragility in Arctic ecosys-
1973   tems. *Arctic*, 56:179-85.

EKERN, A. and F. SUNDSTØL, Energy utilization of hay and
1974   silage by sheep. *In* Energy metabolism of farm
        animals, edited by K.H. Menke, H.I. Lontzsch
        and I.R. Reichl. *Publ. Eur. Assoc. Anim. Prod.*,
        (14):221-4.

FAY, F.H. and G.C. RAY, Influence of climate on the
1968   distribution of walruses, *Odobenus rosmarus*
        (Linnaeus). 1. Evidence from thermoregulatory
        behaviour. *Zoologica, N.Y.*, 53:1-14.

FISHER, H.D., Studies on reproduction in the harp seal
1954   *Phoca groenlandica* Erxleben in the Northwest
        Atlantic. Ph.D. Thesis. McGill University,
        Montreal, Quebec, Canada.

—, Delayed implantation in the harbour seal, *Phoca
1954a   vitulina* (L.). *Nature, Lond.*, 173:879.

FISHER, H.D. and B.A. MACKENZIE, Rapid preparation of
1954   tooth sections for age determinations. *J. Wildl.
        Manage.*, 18:535-7.

—, Food habits of seals in the maritimes. *Progr. Rep. Atl.
1955   Coast Stn.*, (61):5-9.

Fisheries Council of Canada, Resolutions passed at an-
1974   nual meeting in Ottawa. *Bull. Fish. Counc.
        Can.*, May issue: 3-4.

—, Resolution passed at annual meeting in Halifax. Seals.
1975   *Bull. Fish. Counc. Can.*, May issue: 3.

FORBES, E.B. and R.W. SWIFT, Associative dynamic effect
1944   of protein, carbohydrate and fat. *J. Nutr.*, 27:453-68.

FRISCH, J. and N.A. ØRITSLAND, Insulative changes in the
1968   harp seal during moulting. *Acta Physiol. Scand.*, 74:637-8.

GALLIVAN, G.J., Temperature regulation and respiration
1977   in the freely diving harp seal (*Phoca groenlandica*). M.Sc. Thesis. University of Guelph, Guelph, Ontario, Canada.

GALLUCCI, V.F., On the principles of thermodynamics in
1973   ecology. *Annu. Rev. Ecol. System.*, 4:329-57.

GERACI, J.R., Pinniped nutrition. *Rapp. P.-V. Réun.*
1975   *CIEM*, 169:312-23.

GLASS, R.L., H.A. TROOLIN and R. JENNESS, Compara-
1967   tive biochemical studies of milk. 4. Constituent fatty acids of milk fats. *Comp. Biochem. Physiol.*, 22:415-25.

GOLD, A., Energy expenditure in animal locomotion.
1973   *Science, Wash.*, 181:175-276.

GOLLEY, F.B., Energy dynamics of a food chain of an
1960   old-field community. *Ecol. Monogr.*, 30: 187-206.

GOLLEY, F.B. *et al.*, Food intake and assimilation by
1965   bobcats under laboratory conditions. *J. Mammal.*, 29:442-7.

GOODALL, D.W., Building and testing ecosystem models.
1972   *In* Mathematical models in ecology, edited by J.N.R. Jeffers. *Symp. Br. Ecol. Soc.*, 12.

GOODMAN, D., The theory of diversity-stability relation-
1975   ships in ecology. *Q. Rev. Biol.*, 50:237-83.

GÓRECKI, A., The adiabatic bomb calorimeter. *In*
1975   Methods of ecological bioenergetics, edited by W. Grodzinski, R.Z. Klebowski and A. Duncan. *IBP Handb.*, (24).

GRAV, H.J., A.S. BLIX and A. PASCHE, How do seal pups
1974   survive birth in Arctic winter? *Acta Physiol. Scand.*, 92:427-9.

GREAVES, J.P. and P.P. SCOTT, Nutrition of the cat. *Br.*
1960   *J.Nutr.*, 14:361-9.

GULLAND, J.A., Food chain studies and some problems in
1970   world fisheries. *In* Marine food chains, edited by J.H. Steele. Edinburgh, Oliver and Boyd, pp. 296-315.

HARPER, H.A., Review of physiological chemistry. Los
1975   Altos, California, Lange Medical Publications, 15th ed.

HARRIS, L.E., Biological energy interrelationships and
1966   glossary of energy terms. *Publ. Natl. Acad. Sci. Nat. Res. Counc. U.S.*, (1411):1-35.

HARRISON, R.J., Reproduction and reproductive organs.
1969   *In* The biology of marine mammals, edited by H.T. Andersen. New York, Academic Press, pp. 253-348.

HARRISON, R.J. and J.E. KING, Marine mammals. Lon-
1965   don, Hutchinson and Co.

HART, J.S. and L. IRVING, The energetics of harbour seals
1959   in air and water with special consideration of seasonal changes. *Can. J. Zool.*, 37:447-57.

HEWER, H.R., The determination of age, sexual matu-
1964   rity, longevity, and a lifetable in the grey seal (*Halichoerus grypus*). *Proc. Zool. Soc. Lond.*, 142:593-624.

HEWER, H.R. and K.M. BACKHOUSE, Embryology and
1968   foetal growth of the grey seal, *Halichoerus grypus. J. Zool., Lond.*, 155:507-33.

HOERNER, S.F., Fluid-dynamic drag. New Jersey, Hoer-
1965   ner Fluid Dynamics.

IUCN (International Union for Conservation of Nature
1977   and Natural Resources), The harp seal - cause for unease. *IUCN Bull.*, (8):17,20,22.

IRVING, L., Temperature regulation in marine mammals.
1969   *In* The biology of marine mammals, edited by H.T. Andersen. London, Academic Press, pp. 147-74.

—, Arctic life of birds and mammals including man.
1972   Berlin, Springer-Verlag.

IRVING, L. and J.B. HART, The metabolism and insulation
1957   of seals as bare skinned mammals in cold water. *Can. J. Zool.*, 35:497-511.

IRVING, L. *et al.*, The respiratory metabolism of the seal
1935   and its adjustment to diving. *J. Cell. Comp. Physiol.*, 7:137-51.

IVERSEN, J.A. and J. KROG, Heat production and body
1973   surface in seals and sea otters. *Norw. J. Zool.*, 21:51-4.

JANGAARD, P.M., The Capelin (*Mallotus villosus*): biol-

231

1974   ogy, distribution, exploitation, utilization, and composition. *Bull. Fish. Res. Board Can.*, (186):70 p.

JANGAARD, P.M. and P.J. KE, Principal fatty acids of
1968   depot fat and milk lipids from harp seal (*Pagophilus groenlandicus*) and hooded seal *Cystophora cristata*. *J. Fish. Res. Board Can.*, 25:2419-26.

JENNESS, R., The composition of milk. *In* Lactation: a
1974   comprehensive treatise, edited by B.L. Lawson and V.R. Smith. London, Academic Press, vol. 3.

JENNESS, R., A.W. ERICKSON and J.J. CRAIGHEAD, Some
1972   comparative aspects of milk from four species of bears. *J. Mammal.*, 53:34-57.

JOHNSON, D.R. and K.L. GROEPPER, Bioenergetics of north
1970   plains rodents. *Am. Midl. Nat.*, 84:537-48.

JOHNSON, D.R. and M.H. MAXWELL, Energy dynamics of
1966   Colorado pikas. *Ecology*, 47:1059-61.

KAPEL, F.O., Some second-hand reports on the food of
1973   harp seals in West Greenland waters. ICES C.M. 1973/N:8.

KERR, S.R., Theory of size distribution in ecological
1974   communities. *J. Fish. Res. Board Can.*, 31:1859-62.

KLEIBER, M., The fire of life. New York, John Wiley and
1975   Sons, 2nd ed. rev.

KOOYMAN, G.L., Milk analysis of the kangaroo rat,
1963   *Dipodomys merriami*. *Science, Wash.*, 142:1467-8.

−, Respiratory adaptations in marine mammals. *Am.*
1973   *Zool.*, 13:457-68.

−, Physiology of freely diving Weddell seals. *Rapp. P.-V.*
1975   *Réun. CIEM*, 169:441-4.

KOOYMAN, G.L. and C.M. DRABEK, Observations on the
1968   milk, blood and urine constituents of the Weddell seal. *Physiol. Zool.*, 41: 187-94.

KORSCHGEN, L.J., Procedures for food habit analysis. *In*
1971   Wildlife management techniques, edited by R.H. Giles. Washington, D.C., The Wildlife Society.

KOZLOVSKY, D.G., A critical evaluation of the trophic
1968   level concept. 1. Ecological efficiencies. *Ecology*, 49:48-60.

KURBATOV, B.V. and I.E. MORDVINOV, Hydrodynamic re-
1974   sistance of semiaquatic mammals. *Zool. Zh.*, 53:104-10. Issued also as *Transl. U.S.Jt. Publ. Res. Serv.*, (62536).

LAUER, B.H. and B.E. BAKER, Whale milk composition. 1.
1969   Fin whale (*Balaenoptera physalus*) and beluga whale (*Delphinapterus leucas*) milk: gross composition and fatty acid constituents. *Can. J. Zool.*, 47:95-7.

LAVIGNE, D.M., The present status of western Atlantic
1976   harp seals: a management consideration. *ICNAF Res. Doc.*, 76/X/133.

−, Stock assessment and management of western Atlan-
1977   tic harp seals. Paper presented to the 2nd Symposium of Endangered North American Wildlife and Habitat, St. Louis, Mo., 1-5 June, 1977.

LAVIGNE, D.M. and K. RONALD, Improved remote sensing
1975   techniques for evaluating seal populations. ICES C.M. 1975/N:12.

LAWS, R.M., A new method of age determination in
1953   mammals with special reference to the elephant seal (*Mirounga leonina* Linn.). *Sci. Rep. Falkland Isl. Depend. Surv.*, (2).

−, Accelerated growth in seals, with special reference
1959   to the Phocidae. *Norsk Hvalfangsttid.*, (9):425-52.

−, The southern elephant seal (*Mirounga leonina* Linn.)
1960   at South Georgia. *Norsk Hvalfangsttid.*, (10/11:466-76, 520-42.

−, Effects of human activities on reproduction in the
1973   wild. *J. Reprod. Fert.*, Suppl. 19:523-32.

LEOPOLD, A., A Sand County almanac. New York, Bal-
1949   lantine Books, Inc.

LINDEMAN, R., The trophic-dynamic aspect of ecology.
1942   *Ecology*, 23:399-418.

LINDSEY, A.A., The Weddell seal in the Bay of Whales,
1937   Antarctica. *J. Mammal.*, 18:127-44.

LINZELL, J.L., Milk yield, energy loss in milk, and mam-
1972   mary gland weight in different species. *Dairy Sci. Abstr.*, 34:351-60.

LOCKYER, C., Estimates of growth and energy budget for
1976   the sperm whale, *Physeter catodon*. Paper presented to the Scientific Consultation on the

Conservation and Management of Marine Mammals and their Environment, Bergen, Norway, 31 August-9 September 1976, Rome, FAO, ACMRR/MM/SC/38:33 p.

LUECKE, R.H., V. NATARJAN and F.E. SOUTH, A mathematical biothermal model of the California sea lion. *J. Thermal Biol.*, 1:35-45.
1975

MACCALLUM, W.A. *et al.*, Newfoundland capelin: proximate composition. *J. Fish. Res. Board Can.*, 26(8):2027-35.
1969

MACFAYDEN, A., Animal ecology, aims and methods. Bath, Pitman Publishing.
1963

MAHSLID, L., I.A. MACDONALD, and M.J. STOCK, Loss of energy associated with ovendrying. *Proc. Nutr. Soc.*, 34:58A.
1975

MANN, K.H., Energy transformations by a population of fish in the River Thames. *J. Anim. Ecol.*, 34:253-75.
1965

MARGALEF, R., Perspectives in ecological theory. Chicago, University Chicago Press.
1968

MAY, R.M., Stability and complexity in model ecosystems. *Princeton Univ. Press Monogr. Popul. Biol.*, (6).
1974

MAYR, E., Geographic character gradients and climatic adaptation. *Evolution*, 10:105-8.
1956

MCEWAN, E.H. and P.E. WHITEHEAD, Measurement of the milk intake of reinder and caribou calves using tritiated water. *Can. J. Zool.*, 49:443-9.
1971

MCLAREN, I.A., Some aspects of growth and reproduction of the bearded seal, *Erignathus barbatus* (Erxleben, 1777). *J. Fish. Res. Board Can.*, 15(2):219-27.
1958

MEARA, M.L., The component acids of the milk fat of a grey Atlantic seal. *Biochem. J.*, 51:590-3.
1952

MERCER, M.C., The seal hunt. Ottawa, Department of fisheries and the Environment, Information Branch, Fisheries and Marine Service.
1977

MILNER, C., The use of computer simulation in conservation management. *In* Mathematical models in ecology, edited by J.N.R. Jeffers. *Symp. Br. Ecol. Soc.*, 12.
1972

MOEN, A.N., The critical thermal environment: a new look at an old concept. *Bioscience*, 18:1041-3.
1968

—, Wildlife ecology: an analytic approach. San Francisco, W.H. Freeman and Co.
1973

MORRIS, J.C., J. FEYIMOTO and S.C. BERRY, The comparative digestibility of a zoo diet fed to 13 species of felid and a badger. *Int. Zoo Yearb.*, 14:169-71.
1974

MYERS, B.J., The stomach contents of harp seals (*Phoca groenlandica* Erxleben) from the Magdalen Islands, Quebec. *Can. J. Zool.*, 37:378.
1959

National Research Council (NRC), Nutrient requirements of dogs. Washington, D.C., National Academy of Science.
1974

NORDAN, H.C., I.McT. COWAN and A.J. WOOD, The feed intake and heat production of the young black-tailed deer (*Odocoileus hemionus columbianus*). *Can. J. Zool.*, 48:275-82.
1970

ODUM, E.P., Fundamentals of ecology. Philadelphia, W.B. Saunders Co.
1971

ODUM, E.P. and A.E. SMALLEY, Comparison of population energy flow of a herbivorous and a deposit-feeding invertebrate in a salt marsh ecosystem. *Proc. Natl. Acad. Sci.*, 45:617-22.
1959

ODUM, E.P., C.E. CONNELL and L.B. DAVENPORT, Population energy flow of three primary consumer components of oldfield ecosystems. *Ecology*, 43:88-96.
1962

ØRITSLAND, N.A., Energetic significance of absorption of solar radiation in polar homeotherms. *In* Antarctic ecology, edited by M.W. Holdgate. London, Academic Press, vol. 1:464-70.
1970

—, Wavelength-dependent solar heating of harp seals (*Pagophilus groenlandicus*). *Comp. Biochem. Physiol.*, 40A:359-61.
1971

ØRITSLAND, N.A. and K. RONALD, Effect of solar radiation and wind chill on skin temperature of the harp seal, *Pagophilus groenlandicus* (Erxleben, 1777). *Comp. Biochem. Physiol.*, 44A:519-25.
1973

—, Energetics of the free diving harp seals (*Pagophilus groenlandicus*). *Rapp. P.-V. Réun. CIEM*, 169:451-4.
1975

ORR, N.W.M., The food requirements of Antarctic sledge dogs. *In* Canine and feline nutritional requirements, edited by O. Graham-Jones. London, Pergamon Press.
1965

PAINE, R.T., Food web diversity and species diversity.
1966   Am. Nat., 100:65-75.

PARSONS, J.L., Metabolic studies on ringed seals (Phoca
1977   hispida). M.Sc. Thesis. University of Guelph,
Guelph, Ontario, Canada.

PATTEN, B.C., An introduction to the cybernetics of the
1959   ecosystem: the trophicdynamic aspect. Ecology,
40:221-31.

—, A simulation of the shortgrass prairie ecosystem. Si-
1972   mulation, Dec. issue: 177-86.

PETRIDES, G.A., The use of 51-chromium in the determi-
1968   nation of energy-flow and other digestive characteristics in animals. Proc. Symp. Recent Adv.
Trop. Ecol., 1968:25-31.

PETRIDES, G.A., F.B. GOLLEY and I.L. BRISBIN, Energy
1965   flow and secondary productivity. In A practical
guide to the study of the productivity of large
herbivores, edited by F.B. Golley and H.K.
Buechner. IBP Handb., (7).

PIKE, R.L. and M.L. BROWN, Nutrition: an integrated
1975   approach. Toronto, John Wiley and Sons Inc.

PILSON, M.E.Q. and A.L. KELLY, Composition of the milk
1962   from Zalophus californianus, The California sea
lion. Science, Wash., 135:104-5.

PILSON, M.E.Q. and D.W. WALLER, Composition of milk
1970   from spotted and spinner porpoises. J. Mammal., 51:74-9.

PINHORN, A.T. (ed.), Living marine resources of New-
1976   foundland-Labrador: status and potential.
Bull. Fish. Res. Board Can., (191):64 p.

RAY, G.C. and F.H. FAY, Influence of climate on the
1968   distribution of walruses, Odobenus rosmarus
(Linnaeus) 2. Evidence from physiological
characteristics. Zoologica, N.Y., 53:19-32.

RICKER, W.E., Computation and interpretation of biolo-
1975   gical statistics of fish populations. Bull. Fish.
Res. Board Can., (194):382 p.

RICKLEFS, R.E., Ecology. Newton, Mass., Chiron Press.
1973

ROGERSON, A., Energy utilization by the eland and wil-
1968   debeest. Symp. Zool. Soc. Lond., 21:153-61.

SCHEFFER, V.B., Body size with relation to population
1955   density in mammals. J. Mammal., 36:493-515.

—, Pelage and surface topography of the northern fur
1962   seal. North Am. Fauna Fish Wildl. Serv.,
(64):1-206.

—, Seals and people. Rapp. P.-V. Réun. CIEM, 169:9-11.
1975

SCHMIDT-NIELSEN, K., Locomotion: energy cost of
1972   swimming, flying, running. Science, Wash.,
177:222-8.

—, How animals work. Cambridge. Cambridge Univers-
1972a   ity Press.

SCHOLANDER, P.F., Experimental investigations on the
1940   respiratory functions in diving mammals and
birds. Hvalrad. Skr., 22:1-131.

SCHOLANDER, P.F. et al., Heat regulation in some arctic
1950   and tropical mammals and birds. Biol. Bull.
Mar. Biol. Lab. Woods Hole, 99:237-58.

SERGEANT, D.E., Migrations of harp seals Pagophilus
1965   groenlandicus (Erxleben) in the Northwest Atlantic. J. Fish. Res. Board Can., 22(2):433-64.

—, Reproductive rates of harp seals, Pagophilus groen-
1966   landicus (Erxleben). J. Fish. Res. Board Can.,
23(5):757-66.

—, Feeding, growth, and productivity of Northwest At-
1973   lantic harp seals (Pagophilus groenlandicus).
J.Fish. Res. Board Can., 30(1):17-29.

—, Environment and reproduction in seals. J. Reprod.
1973a   Fert., Suppl. 19:555-61.

—, Estimating numbers of harp seals. Rapp. P.-V. Réun.
1975   CIEM, 169-274-80.

—, History and present status of harp and hooded seals.
1976   Biol. Conserv., 10:95-117.

—, The relationship between harp seals and fish popula-
1976a   tions. ICNAF Res. Doc., 76/X/125.

SHARP, H.F., Food ecology of the rice rat Oryzomys pa-
1967   lustris (Harlan) in a Georgia salt marsh. J.
Mammal., 48:557-63.

SIVERTSEN, E., On the biology of the harp seal, Phoca
1941   groenlandica Erxleben. Hvairad. Skr., 26:
1-164.

SLOBODKIN, L.B., Ecological energy relationships at the
1960   population level. Am. Nat., 94:213-36.

–, Growth and regulation of animal populations. To-
1961   ronto, Holt, Reinhart, and Winston.

–, Energy in animal ecology. *In* Advances in ecological
1962   research, edited by J.B. Cragg. London, Academic Press, vol. 1:69-101.

SMITH, C.C. and D. FOLLMER, Food preferences of squir-
1972   rels. *Ecology*, 53:82-91.

SMITH, F.E., Analysis of ecosystems. *In* Analysis of tem-
1970   perate forest ecosystems, edited by D.E.
Reichle. New York, Springer-Verlag Inc.

SMITH, T.G., Population dynamics of the ringed seal in
1973   the Canadian eastern Arctic. *Bull. Fish. Res.
Board Can.*, (181):55 p.

STEELE, J.H., The structure of marine ecosystems. Oxford,
1974   Blackwell Scientific Publications, 128 p.

STEIN, Y. and O. STEIN, Selective labelling of adipose
1965   tissue *in vivo*. *In* Handbook of physiology,
edited by A.E. Renold and G.F. Cahill, Jr.
Washington, D.C., American Physiological Society.

STIRLING, I., Population dynamics of the Weddell seal
1971   (*Leptonychotes weddelli*) in McMurdo Sound,
Antarctica, 1966-1968. *In* Antarctic Pinnipedia,
edited by W.H. Burt. *Antarct. Res. Ser.*,
18:141-61.

STIRLING, I. and E.H. McEWAN, The caloric value of
1975   ringed seals (*Phoca hispida*) in relation to polar
bear (*Ursus maritimus*) ecology and hunting
behaviour. *Can. J. Zool.*, 53:1021-7.

STODDARD, J.H., Fat contents of Canadian Atlantic herr-
1968   ing. *Tech. Rep. Fish. Res. Board Can.*, (79):23 p.

STREET, R.J., Feeding habits of the New Zealand fur seal
1964   (*Arctocephalus forsteri*). *Fish. Tech. Rep. Minist.
Agric. Fish. N.Z.*, (9):20 p.

STULL, J.W., W.H. BROWN and G.L. KOOYMAN, Lipids of
1967   the Weddell seal, *Leptonychotes weddelli*. *J.
Mammal.*, 48:642-5.

SUTTON, D.B. and N.P. HARMON, Ecology: selected topics.
1973   New York, John Wiley and Sons Inc.

TEMPLEMAN, W., Marine resources of Newfoundland.
1966   *Bull. Fish. Res. Board Can.*, (154):170 p.

TUCKER, V.A., Energetic cost of locomotion in animals.

1970   *Comp. Biochem. Physiol.*, 34:841-6.

TURNER, F.B., The ecological efficiency of consumer po-
1970   pulations. *Ecology*, 51:741-2.

TYLER, A.V., Caloric values of some North Atlantic
1973   invertebrates. *Mar. Biol.*, 19:258-61.

UNDERWOOD, L.S., The bioenergetics of the Arctic fox
1971   (*Alopex lagopus*). Ph.D. Thesis, Pittsburgh,
Penn., Pennsylvania State University.

VANDYNE, G.M., Organization and management of an
1972   integrated ecological research program with
special emphasis on systems analysis, universi-
ties, and scientific cooperation. *In* Mathematical models in ecology, edited by J.N.R. Jeffers.
Symp. Br. Ecol. Soc., 12.

VAN HORN, D.R. and B.E. BAKER, Seal milk. 2. Harp seal
1971   (*Pagophilus groenlandicus*) milk: effects of
stage of lactation on the composition of the
milk. *Can. J. Zool.*, 49:1085-8.

VENNARD, J.K. and R.L. SREET, Elementary fluid mecha-
1975   nics. Toronto, John Wiley and Sons, Inc.

VOGTSBERGER, L.M. and G.W. BARRETT, Bioenergetics of
1973   captive red foxes. *J. Wildl. Manage.*,
37:495-500.

WATT, K.E.F., The nature of systems analysis. *In* Sys-
1966   tems analysis in ecology, edited by K.E.F. Watt.
New York, Academic Press.

–, Ecology and resource management: a quantitative
1968   approach. Toronto, McGraw-Hill Book Co.

WEBB, P.W., Hydrodynamics and energetics of fish pro-
1975   pulsion. *Bull. Fish. Res. Board Can.*, (190):158
p.

WIDDOWSON, E.M., Chemical composition of newly born
1950   mammal. *Nature, Lond.*, 166:626-8.

WIEGERT, R.G., Population energetics of meadow spit-
1964   tlebugs (*Philaenus spumarius* L.) as affected by
migration and habitat. *Ecol. Monogr.*,
34:217-41.

WILKE, F., Fat content of fur seal milk. *Murrelet*, 39:40.
1958

WINTERS, G.H., Review of capelin ecology and estimation
1975   of surplus yield from predator dynamics.
ICNAF Res. Doc., 75/2.

MONK SEALS ON THE SOUTHWEST COAST OF TURKEY

F. Berkes

Abstract

Interviews with fishermen on the southwest coast of Turkey in the spring and summer of 1976 indicate that 50-100 Mediterranean monk seals (*Monachus monachus*) are present in this area, and that the population is declining in size. Sightings by fishermen were almost all of single animals and included nine sightings, within the last two years, of seals on land near caves perhaps suitable as dens, and of young seals. Monk seals were being seen less often than in the past by fishermen in 11 of 13 communities visited, though this may not necessarily be due to a real reduction in numbers; location where seals were present but have not been seen for two years are given, including 11 possible breeding sites. The scattered distribution pattern of the present population is inconsistent with the assumption of earlier work that monk seals live in colonies, though a group of as many as 5 animals has been reported off Cape Gelidonya and 3 colonies of more than 20 animals each were reported to have disappeared in the last 2-40 years − selection may now be against the formation of permanent colonies and for temporary residence of single animals, especially in rocky areas with caves. Fishermen seem to view monk seals both as a pest they would like to see disappear (because of the damage done by them to nets) and as an intelligent animal they admire. Dircct killing of seals by fishermen is slight but still significant − fishermen in only 5 communities reported deliberate or accidental (drowning in nets) deaths in the past 2 years; large numbers may once have been killed but the difficulty in finding and killing seals and the belief, especially in the Aegean and among older fishermen, that killing them brings bad luck, in part prevent this today. Perhaps more important is the indirect effect on seals of increasing fishing effort and over-fishing. Pollution from Antalya and perhaps also oil of pelagic origin between Datça and Bozburun, may be partly responsible for the decline of the monk seal populations in those areas.

Résumé

Des entretiens avec les pêcheurs de la côte sud-ouest de la Turquie qui ont eu lieu au printemps et en été 1976, indiquent que 50 à 100 phoques-moines de la Méditerranée (*Monachus monachus*) se trouvent dans cette région et que la taille de la population diminue. Les repérages visuels faits par les pêcheurs portaient presque tous sur des animaux isolés; pour neuf d'entre eux, datant des deux dernières années, il s'agissait de phoques se trouvant à terre, à proximité de grottes leur servant peut-être de refuge, et de jeunes phoques. Les pêcheurs de onze des treize communautés visitées aperçoivent les phoques-moines moins souvent que par le passé, encore que ceci ne soit pas nécessairement dû à une réduction réelle des effectifs; les endroits où se trouvaient des phoques mais où l'on n'en a pas vu depuis deux ans sont indiqués, y compris onze sites possibles de reproduction. L'éparpillement de la distribution de la population actuelle ne cadre pas avec l'hypothèse de travaux antérieurs selon laquelle les phoques-moines vivent en colonies, bien qu'un groupe de cinq animaux ait été signalé au large du cap Gelidonya et l'on a rapporté que trois colonies comprenant chacune plus de vingt animaux ont disparu au cours des deux à quarante dernières années. Il est possible que l'évolution soit maintenant contraire à la formation de colonies permanentes et favorable à la résidence temporaire d'animaux isolés, spécialement dans les zones rocheuses comprenant des grottes. Les pêcheurs semblent considérer les phoques-moines à la fois comme une nuisance qu'ils voudraient voir disparaître (en raison des dégâts qu'ils provoquent dans les filets) et comme un animal intelligent qu'ils admirent. Le nombre de phoques tués directement par les pêcheurs est faible mais encore significatif — dans cinq communautés seulement, les pêcheurs ont signalé des morts délibérées ou accidentelles (noyade dans les filets) au cours des deux dernières années; il est possible qu'un grand nombre d'animaux ait été tué autrefois mais la difficulté de les repérer et de les tuer et le fait qu'on croie — spécialement en mer Egée et parmi les vieux pêcheurs — que leur abattage porte malheur évitent en partie que cela se poursuive aujourd'hui. L'élément peut-être le plus important est l'effet indirect sur les phoques d'un effort de pêche croissant et de la surexploitation. La pollution d'Antalya et peut-être aussi le pétrole d'origine pélagique, entre Datça et Bozburun, pourraient être partiellement responsables du déclin des populations de phoques-moines dans ces régions.

Extracto

Algunas entrevistas con pescadores de la costa sudoccidental de Turquía durante la primavera y el verano de 1976 indican que en esa zona se encuentran entre 50 y 100 focas monje del Mediterráneo (*Monachus monachus*) y que el volumen de la población va en disminución. Los avistamientos de los pescadores se refieren casi en su totalidad a animales solos e incluyen nueve avistamientos, hechos en los dos últimos años, de focas en tierra en la proximidad de grutas, que quizá utilicen como madrigueras, y de animales jóvenes. En 11 de las 13 comunidades visitadas, los avistamientos de focas monje eran menos frecuentes que en el pasado, aunque la razón no ha de buscarse necesariamente en una reducción real de su número. Se indica una serie de lugares donde estas focas estaban presentes pero no han sido vistas durante dos años, incluidas 12 posibles zonas de reproducción. La dispersión de la población actualmente existente no está de acuerdo con las hipótesis hechas en trabajos anteriores de que la foca monje vive en colonias, aunque hay noticias de un grupo de cinco animales frente al Cabo Gelidonya y se ha señalado que tres colonias de más de 20 animales han desaparecido entre los últimos 2 y 40 años. Es posible que hoy día la selección se oponga a la formación de colonias permanentes y favorezca la residencia temporal de animales solos, especialmente en zonas rocosas con grutas. Los pescadores consideran a la foca monje como una plaga, que quisieran ver desaparecer (por los daños que causa a las redes), pero la admiran por su inteligencia. Los animales que los pescadores matan directamente son pocos, pero no por eso dejan de tener importancia. Sólo en cinco comunidades los pescadores comunicaron muertes deliberadas o accidentales (por estrangulamiento en las redes) durante los dos últimos años. Es posible que antaño se mataran en gran número, pero la dificultad de localizar y matar a estos animales, y la creencia, especialmente en el Egeo y entre los pescadores más viejos, de que matarlos trae mala suerte, representa hoy día una defensa parcial para esa especie. Tal vez sea más importante el efecto indirecto que tiene en las focas el aumento del esfuerzo de pesca y la sobrepesca. La contaminación procedente de Antalya y quizás también los yacimientos submarinos de petróleo que se encuentra entre Datça y Bozburun pueden haber influido en la disminución de las poblaciones de foca monje de esas zonas.

F. Berkes
Brock University, Department of Biological Sciences, Glenridge Campus, St. Catharines, Ontario L253A1, Canada

The Mediterranean monk seal (*Monachus monachus*) has been known to occur along the coast of Turkey but detailed surveys of this endangered species have been lacking (Mursaloglu, 1964; Ronald and Healey, 1974). This report is based on a brief survey of fishing communities in spring/summer 1976 in southwestern Turkey.

In most cases, between one-third and one-quarter of the fishermen in each community were interviewed and the interviews were open-ended. The information requested included dates of sighting, numbers of seals (young and adult) observed at each sighting and whether they were seen on land or at sea; the local place names within each area were also recorded. Data were also collected on (a) the habitat and biology of the seals, (b) direct and indirect mortality caused by fishermen, fishing activities and other factors, and (c) practices and patterns of marine resource use in the area. Within villages, the results of individual interviews were compared with one another and with the results of group interviews, for consistency. Since fishermen on these coasts tend to use a variety of fishing grounds, it was possible to compare information from different villages about the same area, to verify seal distribution. Information for parts of Gökova Bay and part of the coast between Fethiye and Kaş was not as detailed as for other areas due to an absence of fishermen with recent first-hand knowledge.

The distribution maps, with the exception of the two poorly investigated areas already mentioned, are verifiable and reproduceable. For example, the head of Bodrum Fishermen's Cooperative, an old and experienced fisherman, independently produced a seal distribution map identical, point by point, to the one derived from interviews in the three fishing communities in the area. Fishermen, especially on the Aegean, recognize individual seals in some areas by location, colour, size and habits.

Distribution

Distribution records for *Monachus* for 1976 are indicated in Figure 1. Where many sightings were reported from one locality, one representative mark only was entered[1]. There are nine sites at which, within two years of the study, there have been sightings of seals on land near caves that might be suitable as dens, and also of young seals. All records are sightings of *single* animals with the exceptions of Marmaris Bay where two seals have been seen together, one large and one small (May, 1976),

---

[1] *Editor's note.* The author considers multiple sightings from one locality to be of the same seal or seals.

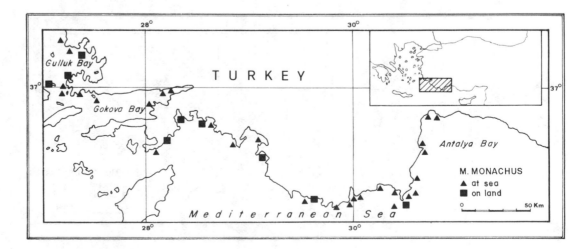

FIG. 1. – Distribution records of *Monachus monachus* on the southwest coast of Turkey, 1976.

and Beşadalar off Cape Gelidonya where as many as five animals have been seen together: three small, one black adult and one very large white/grey (mid-May, 1976). The latter report was confirmed by frequent sightings of seals near Cape Gelidonya by not less than five independent fishing groups from February to early June.

Figure 2 shows those locations at which seals used to be seen but have not been seen within the last two years. Eleven of these sites represent locations at which seals were seen on land near caves and where young seals used to be present. Almost all of these eleven sites occur near towns and villages.

The results indicate that on the southwest coast of Turkey seals do occur, and unpublished data suggest that their occurrence is regular. As documented in Figure 2, however, a number of possible reproductive sites have been lost and seals have disappeared from parts of their former range.

A trend of decreasing seal sightings was confirmed in all but two of thirteen communities. Informants reported seals to be "less frequently seen now as compared to a few years ago". In several communities, however, fishermen attributed this *not* to a real reduction in numbers, but to increasing human interference. This hypothesis is supported by the fishermen's statements that they seldom kill seals who have no other enemy.

Fishermen in only five of thirteen communities reported killing seals (deliberately, or accidentally by drowning in nets) in the past two years. In four of these, only one seal per village was known to have died over the 2-year period, but Fethiye reported several deaths. According to informants, larger numbers were once killed. It would appear, therefore, that any reduction in seal numbers since the 1950's may not readily be attributed to direct killing by fishemen, and that mortality due to this factor is rather low despite the large amount of damage allegedly done by the seals.

The impact of fishermen on *monachus*

Fishermen rank *Monachus* high among "pests" in the study area, others being the dolphin (especially in the Aegean), the spiny dogfish (especially in the Mediterranean) and the marine turtles. Fishermen claim to be able to identify the type of damage from each of these; seal damage looks "as if nets were torn by hand". While dolphins and dogfish usually leave single holes or carry away parts of the net, seals "reduce nets into rags", often leaving a characteristic three-hole pattern similar to that described by Greek fishermen in Ronald and Healey (1974).

There are two main reasons for relatively low seal mortality at the hands of fishermen.

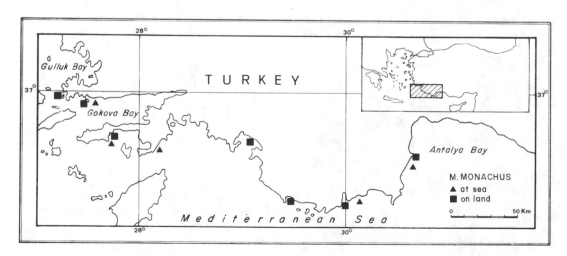

FIG. 2. – Locations where *Monachus monachus* was formerly seen, but has not been sighted within two years of the present study.

First, *Monachus* is difficult to find and to kill. It is a fast swimmer, unpredictable, intelligent, and "seems to sense it whenever we take guns along". Most fishermen say they would be happy to have seals disappear entirely from their area, but at the same time they tell seal stories (especially of epic battles between seals and octopuses), chuckle fondly at photographs of *Monachus* ("yes, that rascal!"), and appear to have great respect for the craftiness and abilities of what they consider to be the most intelligent creature of the sea.

Secondly, many fishermen, especially those on the Aegean, think that killing seals brings bad luck. This belief is strongly held among the older, more traditional fishermen some of whom genuinely feel that "the seal has a right to eat, too". But the belief is losing its hold among the younger, more profit-oriented fishermen, especially those who have a great deal of money invested in efficient, modern fishing gear. Since the 1950's, handmade nets have been replaced by multifilament nylon nets and the length of net set by each fisherman has greatly increased, perhaps by a factor of five since the 1950's.

Persecution by fishermen may be an important cause for the observed scatter in the distribution of *Monachus*. With the exception of Beşadalar, the distribution pattern is inconsistent with the assumption of much of earlier work (Wijngaarden, 1962) that *Monachus* lives in colonies. It may be reasonable to hypothesize that there is strong natural selection against establishing large colonies (over 20 individuals) with a permanent location. According to informants, three such colonies, each with at least five young, at Fethiye, Kalkan west of Kaş, and Ağva south of Kemer were killed off or dispersed between 10 and 40 years ago. It appears that there could be strong selective pressure for mobility, temporary residence and hunting alone, especially in rocky areas offering a choice of caves. In the study area, the coast is rocky almost without interruption west of Finike. East of Finike, however, the only rocky stretch is between Cape Gelidonya and Kemer. Beşadalar off

Cape Gelidonya appears, therefore, to be the best refuge for a population of seals with a range from Finike to Antalya, which is a tourist and commercial centre. This may explain the concentration observed at Beşadalar and nowhere else in the study area.

As is well known, the biological production of the Mediterranean and the Aegean is unusually low and these areas are very susceptible to over-fishing. Surveys carried out simultaneously with the seal study indicated a great increase over the years in the number of fishermen (although many are now entering the tourist industry), increasing size, capability and travelling range (but not numbers) of fishing vessels, and greater fishing effort per fishermen. A possible 5 to 10-fold increase in the total fishing effort since the 1950's without any great increase in the fish catch in the study area suggests over-fishing.

Conclusion

The number of distribution points suggests around 50-100 seals. This is a small population and rather vulnerable to extinction assuming that *Monachus*, a top carnivore, has a low reproductive rate and matures late. Furthermore, there is rather strong evidence that the population is declining. Increasing human disturbance no doubt has a depressing effect on seal populations. Pollution from Antalya may be partly responsible for the contraction of the range and a reduction in the carrying capacity of the area for *Monachus*. A second area in which pollution may be of importance is the Datça-Bozburun coast which is heavily tarred with oil of pelagic origin (there is no known local source of oil). However, cause and effect relationships would be very difficult to establish even if it can be shown that there is more oil pollution here than elsewhere.

If seal mortality due to direct conflict with fishermen seems relatively slight, it is still

241

significant. Perhaps more significant, however, may be the *indirect* effect of increasing fisheries exploitation. The effect of over-fishing on the carrying capacity of an ecosystem for seals, and its population consequences, should not be underestimated.

The study was supported by the International Fund for Animal Welfare (IFAW). I thank Mr. B. Davies of IFAW, and Dr. D.E. Sergeant of Environment Canada and IUCN, to whom I am indebted for suggestions, valuable comments and criticism.

References

MURSALOGLU, B., Occurrence of the monk seal on the
1964   Turkish coasts. *J. Mammal.*, 45:316-7.

RONALD, K. and P. HEALEY, Present status of the Medi-
1974   terranean monk seal (*Monachus monachus*). *Migrat. Ser. UFAW-IUCN, Lond.*, (100).

WIJNGAARDEN, A. VAN, The Mediterranean monk seal.
1962   *Oryx*, 6:270-3.

THE MONK SEAL (*MONACHUS MONACHUS*)

K. Ronald and P.J. Healey

Abstract

The authors present a review of the biology, ecology and exploitation of the Mediterranean monk seal. They briefly review the taxonomy, morphology, and the distribution of the species, which is far less extensive than in earlier times. The world population is about 500-800, made up of small groups widely scattered around the Mediterranean, Black Sea and Atlantic coast of Africa. Population dynamics of the species are considered; whelping is believed to be asynchronous, and may take place all year round. Incidental kills are thought seriously to affect the population. Populations are thought to have declined particularly over the last 100 years, from a possible level of 5 000 animals in the 15th century. Food of the seal is varied, including green algae, various fish and shellfish, and even grapevines. Little is known of the ecology of the species, but it may be that the Mediterranean is unfavourable, and that its true habitat will become the Atlantic. Studies on parasitofauna are briefly reviewed. The limited populations have little effect on human activities and, unless effective conservation measures are adopted immediately, extinction could result within 25 years. Public display is a potential use. Management measures proposed are a thorough survey of habitats, especially in Algeria, an effective biological research programme, education of the public, and restriction of knowledge of the species' distribution in order to avoid pressure from tourists.

Résumé

Les auteurs présentent un compte rendu de la biologie, de l'écologie et de l'exploitation du phoque-moine de Méditerranée. Ils traitent succinctement de la taxonomie, de la morphologie et de la distribution géographique de l'espèce, qui est loin d'être aussi répandue qu'autrefois. La population mondiale atteint environ 500 à 800 individus, qui se répartissent en petits groupes largement dispersés à travers la Méditerranée, la mer Noire et sur la côte atlantique de l'Afrique. La dynamique de la population concernant cette espèce est également mentionnée. La reproduction est, croit-on, asynchrone et la fécondation peut se produire en toute saison de l'année. Les destructions par prises non intentionnelles semblent présenter un sérieux danger pour l'espèce. On pense que les populations de ce phoque ont diminué, particulièrement au cours des 100 dernières années; on estime qu'au quinzième siècle l'espèce comprenait peut-être 5 000 individus. L'alimentation du phoque-moine est variée: elle se compose d'algues vertes, de divers poissons et coquillages et même de raisins. L'écologie de l'espèce est encore mal connue, mais il se pourrait que la Méditerranée soit un milieu défavorable, et que le véritable habitat de ces phoques se déplace vers l'Atlantique. L'ouvrage relate brièvement les études réalisées sur la faune parasitaire. Les populations de cet animal, peu nombreuses, n'exercent qu'un effet limité sur les activités de l'homme et, à moins qu'une protection efficace ne leur soit immédiatement accordée, l'espèce pourrait venir à extinction dans moins de 25 ans. L'exhibition publique pourrait être une solution. Les mesures de gestion

243

proposées sont les suivantes: une étude approfondie des habitats de l'espèce, spécialement en Algérie; un programme efficace de recherche biologique; l'éducation du public; et la limitation des informations divulguées sur la répartition géographique des espèces, cela afin de ne pas éveiller la curiosité des touristes.

Extracto

Los autores presentan un examen de la biología, la ecología y la explotación de la foca fraile del Mediterráneo. Estudian brevemente la taxonomía, la morfología y la distribución de la especie, que es mucho menos amplia que antes. La población mundial de unas 500-800 focas se compone de pequeños grupos extensamente distribuidos en el Mediterráneo, el Mar Negro y la Costa Atlántica de Africa. Se examina la dinámica de población de la especie; se piensa que la cría es asíncrona y que puede tener lugar a lo largo de todo el año. Se cree que las matanzas incidentales afectan gravemente a la población. Se estima que las poblaciones de esta especie, que quizá eran del orden de 5 000 animales en el siglo XV, han disminuido de manera particular en los últimos 100 años. La alimentación de esta foca es variada y se compone de algas verdes, diversos peces y moluscos e incluso de vides. La ecología de la especie es poco conocida, pero es posible que el Mediterráneo no le sea favorable, y que el Atlántico sea su hábitat más apropiado. Se examinan brevemente los estudios sobre parasitofauna. Las escasas poblaciones tienen poco efecto en las actividades del hombre y, si no se adoptan inmediatamente medidas eficaces de conservación, pueden extinguirse en un plazo de 25 años. La exhibición pública de algunos animales constituye un posible aprovechamiento. Se proponen como medidas de ordenación un estudio minucioso de los hábitats, en especial en Argelia, un programa eficaz de investigaciones biológicas, la educación popular y la limitación de las informaciones sobre la distribución de la especie a fin de no atraer a turistas.

K. Ronald
P.J. Healey
College of Biological Science, University of Guelph, Guelph, Ontario N1G 2W1, Canada

Description

TAXONOMY

The published descriptions of the Mediterranean monk seal vary greatly. The original scientific description was made from a specimen stored in Strasbourg by Hermann (1779) who named it *Phoca monachus*. In 1782, Buffon, unaware of Hermann's work, described the same animal and in 1785, Boddaert, using Buffon's description, renamed the seal *Phoca albiventer* (Boddaert, 1785). In 1822, Flemming was the first to suggest the generic name *Monachus*. Other names that have been given to this species of seal are *Phoca bicolor, Phoca leucogaster, Phoca hermanni, Phoca crinita, Monachus mediterraneus, Leptonys monachus, Leptorhynchus monachus, Pelagios monachus, Pelagius* sp., *Pelagus* sp., *Pelagias* sp. and *Rigorn* sp. (King, 1956).

MORPHOLOGY

Monk seal pups, at birth, are approximately 1 m in length and weigh 20 kg. Their coats vary in colour from dark brown to black. The soft, woolly hair, 1.0-1.5 cm in length, does not lie close to the animal's body (Gavard, 1927; King, 1964; Mursaloglu, 1964).

Adult females resemble the pups more than the males in colouring, their fur being dark brown with yellow tips and with no light ventral patch (IUCN, 1966). The mature females weigh from 62.5 to 302 kg and measure approximately 2.8 m in length (King, 1956), although there is one reference to an animal 3.8 m long (Schnapp, Hellwing and Chizelea, 1962). The adult male varies in colour from dark brown to black with slight yellowish patches along the centre of the back and belly. The bristly hair of adult seals is 0.5 cm in length and lies close to the animal's body (Mursaloglu, 1964; Maxwell, 1967). The animal's vibrissae are light yellow to brown in colour, smooth and oval in cross section (Mursaloglu, 1964; Maxwell, 1967; Schnapp, Hellwing and Chizelea, 1962).

Monk seals from the Black Sea are described as being grey, showing a brownish hue dorsally, and a yellowish-white one ventrally. There is a dark dorsal strip which reaches a maximum width of 30 cm in the region of the sternum and a minimum width of 18 cm in the caudal region (Schnapp, Hellwing and Chizelea, 1962). Their recorded lengths and weights have shown considerable variation caused not only by individual differences but also by the age of the animal concerned. The tail is darker than the rest of the body, with yellowish edges, and on the ventral part in the anal region there is a small area of dark brown fur. The front limbs of these Black Sea seals are darkish brown on the inside and light brown on the outer surfaces (Schnapp, Hellwing and Chizelea, 1962).

The dental formula of *M. monachus* is (2/2), c (1/1), m (5/5) in the adult (Allen, 1887) while the milk dentition is (2/2) (1/1) (3/3) (King, 1956).

DISTRIBUTION

Today the Mediterranean monk seal has a far less extensive distribution than in earlier times. The world population of about 500-800 (Ronald and Healey, 1974; IUCN, 1972; Ronald, 1973) is made up of small groups widely scattered around the Mediterranean, Black Sea and Atlantic coast of Africa. As there have been no positive recent sightings it is probable that the monk seal has disappeared altogether from the coasts of Portugal, France (LeGrand, 1977 in a personal communication, suggests that the monk seal still exists on Isle Levant) and Spain (Boulva, unpubl.). A captive female in Lisbon (Ronald and Healey, 1974) has recently died. Reports indicate the existence of monk seals in the Madeiras and the Desertas Islands (Boulva, unpubl.; Møhl, pers. comm.; Vasconcelos, pers. comm.). Other Atlantic ridge islands, where sightings have been made recently are the Canary Islands, Islands of Selvagens, Lanzarote, Fuerteventura, de Lobos, Santa Maria, Cape Verde and Flores (Ronald and Healey, 1974).

The southern limit of the monk seal along the West African coast is 20°49'30"N (Monod, 1923) – approximately the latitude of Cap Blanc, Spanish Sahara – and its limit of distribution is influenced by the temperature of the sea and corresponds to a 20 °C winter isotherm (Budker, 1945). There are few sightings of seals as far north as Morocco on the Atlantic coast (Boulva, unpubl.), the population being concentrated near the Spanish Sahara, particularly in the Cap Blanc region (Duguy, pers. comm.). Two monk seals are being held in captivity at Zoo de Cansado, Nouadhibou, Mauritania (Nicod, pers. comm.).

Along the Mediterranean coast, monk seals are still seen in Morocco, particularly between Al Hoceima and the Algerian border, and also on the Chafarinos Islands, 4 km north of the Moroccan mainland (Boulva, unpubl.; Ronald and Healey, 1974). These seals are scattered all along the coast of Algeria and are thought to be quite numerous here (Boulva, unpubl.; Ronald and Healey, 1974). The only monk seals found near Tunisia are the few which exist on the island of La Galite off the northern coast, at Cap Bon and on the islands of Zembra and Zembretta in the Gulf of Tunis (Boulva, unpubl.; Lachaux, pers. comm.; Massa, 1972; King, 1956). Seals are scattered along the coast of Libya with one confirmed colony in the Gulf of Bomba near Tolmeitha (Norris, 1972). It is almost certain that monk seals do not now occur along the coasts of the United Arab Republic, Egypt, Suez or Israel (Ronald and Healey, 1974), although a dozen or so still live in coastal Lebanon (Le Cavalier, pers. comm.). Monk seals can be found scattered along most of the southern coast of Turkey with occasional rare sightings along the Aegean coast and in the Sea of Marmara (Ronald and Healey, 1974). The most recent reports (May, 1977) concerning the status of the

monk seal in the Black Sea indicate colonies near Butter Cape and Cape Kaliakra on the Bulgarian coast, where it is estimated that several pairs of animals are living under the strict protection of law. A very small colony of 2 or 3 animals inhabits Cape Maslen Nos and there may be a southern breeding colony in the bay of Sveta Parashkeva. During the seventies, reports of monk seal sightings have been received from along the coast to the south of the town of Sozopol (Zakhariev, pers. comm.). There have also been sightings in the Bosphorus as late as the sixties but not since, which may indicate that Black Sea and Mediterranean populations are isolated from each other (Berkes, pers. comm.).

The presence of the monk seal is still reported on many Greek islands in the Aegean Sea although it is rarely found in mainland Greece (Ronald and Healey, 1974; Ronald, 1973; IUCN, 1972). Although it was not thought to live any more along the coasts of Yugoslavia and mainland Italy (Roland and Healey, 1974), in 1975 (Keckes, pers. comm.) a few individuals were reported to be surviving along the Yugoslav coast of the Adriatic Sea between Split and Montegorgano, under full protection. Bruno (1976) cites 15-16 individuals along the Dalmatian Coast. Recent sightings have been made in Sardinia (7 animals), Sicily and the smaller islands of Montecristo, Egadi (Boulva, 1974), Tavolara and Marettimo (Ronald and Healey, 1974). This seal has also been seen recently on the Cerbicales Islands, southeast of Corsica, an area now being considered for a reserve (Boulva, 1977).

To summarize, the Mediterranean monk seal can, at present, be found in the Madeiras, Desertas Islands, Canary Islands, other small Atlantic ridge islands, the "Sahara", the Mediterranean coasts of Morocco, Algeria, Libya, Lebanon and Turkey, a part of the Yugoslav coast, islands off the Tunisian coast, the Greek islands of the Aegean Sea, in the Black Sea along the Bulgarian coast, on Sardinia, Sicily, other small Italian islands and possibly near Corsica.

Population dynamics

PRESENT NUMBERS

As of today, the world population of Mediterranean monk seals would appear to consist of a maximum of 800 animals (Ronald and Healey, 1974). The most recent information on the population status of this seal was obtained by personal communication with persons living or working in the areas where it is found. No formal government censusing or tagging has been carried out. It would appear that at present there are 2 or 3 monk seals near each of the Madeiras, Salvagens and Desertas Islands as of 1973, a few around the Canary Islands and Isla de Lobos and also a few on the islands of Santa Maria, Cape Verde and Flores in 1973. There were at least 50 monk seals on the coast of the Sahara in June 1974, and 2 are presently in captivity in Mauritania. Up until 1973 there were a few seals in Morocco and reports in 1974 indicate a maximum of 100 in Algeria. There were a few seals on the islands off Tunisia in 1972 and there are perhaps 20 to 30 presently in Libya. It is doubtful whether any monk seals are living in Egypt or Israel but perhaps 12 still exist in Lebanon. In 1974 50-60 seals were thought to be living along the Turkish coast but all animals previously reported to be in captivity are now dead. It is interesting to note that most animals occurring along Turkish coasts are older animals which have probably been driven to unsuitable reproductive habitats by human disturbance (Berkes, pers. comm.). Several pairs still exist in the Black Sea on the Bulgarian coast but none are now seen in the Bosphorus. A few survive along a part of the Yugoslav coast. An estimated maximum of 150 monk seals are living in the Greek islands in the Aegean Sea and it is possible that small populations can be found in or near Sardinia, Sicily and Corsica (Ronald and Healey, 1974).

BREEDING

Because newborn pups have been found at different times in the year, it is believed that whelping is asynchronous in this species and may take place all year round. Newborn pups were found on 21 May 1959, 7 July 1973 (Boulva, unpubl.; Duguy, pers. comm.) and 4 July 1974 (Duguy, pers. comm.) at the Sahara colony. A pup was born in the grotto on Kastelorrizo in June 1977; in October a young seal measuring 1.25 m was seen just outside the same cave (Ronald, unpubl.). Little else is known of the breeding habits of the monk seal although it is thought to have a gestation period of 11 months (Troitzky, 1953). The pups are born on land and do not enter the water until they are weaned from their mother at 6-7 weeks. They remain with their mother for 3 years, breeding at 4 years of age (IUCN, 1966; Maxwell, 1967). Because the complete breeding cycle takes 13 months, breeding probably occurs every second year (King, 1956; IUCN, 1966).

INCIDENTAL KILL

The population of Mediterranean monk seals is steadily diminishing. One of the reasons for this is the incidental kill that occurs when, for example, the seals drown in fishing nets or when fishermen attempt to eliminate them by shooting.

HISTORICAL ABUNDANCE

The population of Mediterranean monk seals was probably large once as this animal seems to have been well known by previous generations and even ancient Greeks and Romans like Plutarch, Pliny, Homer and Aristotle wrote of them (Scott, 1971; King, 1964; Maxwell, 1967). A history of sealing along the northwest coast of Africa indicates that at one time there was an abundance of seals in that region. The Portuguese caught seals in the 15th century, which were used for their skins and oil and there may have been as many as 5 000 seals at one time (Monod, 1932). There are 2 islands in this area named Isla de Lobos, indicating an earlier population of monk seals (Monod, 1923; Vasconcelos, pers. comm.). At the time of Admiral W.H. Smith's travels in the early 19th century the monk seal was apparently abundant all along the coasts of Libya and the Arab Republic of Egypt, between Alexandria and Benghazi (Norris, 1972) and formerly it occurred in large numbers along the coast to the west of Alexandria. There are reports of several being killed during the first world war (Flower, 1932). Up to 30 years ago one could see monk seals quite regularly in the Black Sea and even in the Bosphorus (Kosswig, pers. comm.) although even around the end of the 19th and the beginning of the 20th centuries these seals were appearing less often, possibly because of human disturbance of their breeding grounds near the Anatolian and Balkan coasts (Bychkov, pers. comm.). At one time the monk seal was also fairly numerous in Sicily (Riggio, pers. comm.) as it probably was in all areas of its present day distribution. It is particularly during the last century that its population has decreased rapidly everywhere.

Food

The nutritional sources of the Mediterranean monk seal are varied and include green algae (Schnapp, Hellwing and Chizelea, 1962), eels, carp, whiting, sardines, bonito, octopus (Ronald, 1973), lobsters (Bertram, 1943; Gavard, 1927), herring (Bacescu, 1948), *Dentex, Labra* (Boettger, 1951; King, 1956), whitefish, *Mullus surmuletus, Boops boops, Mugil cephalus* (Ronald and Healey, 1974), other flat fish (Maxwell, 1967) and other fish species. These seals are often a nuisance to fishermen as they take fish from their nets and cause damage. They seem to take fewer fish when the nets are set at a depth of 30m (Ronald and Healey, 1974). Feeding mainly in the water, monk seals have been observed to play with their food,

tossing it into the air a number of times before eating it (Ronald and Healey, 1974) and there are also records of seals eviscerating fish and eating the head first (Gavard, 1927). Coastal grapevine owners in Algeria claim that the seal will climb to the grapevines at night to eat the grapes, where grapevines are often grown close to the seashore (Boulva, unpubl.).

Ecosystem

Little is known about this seal's place in the ecosystem. It is possible that, because of high salinities and environmental temperatures, the seal cannot survive in the Mediterranean. Its true habitat may become the Atlantic rather than the Mediterranean.

The parasitology of the Mediterranean monk seal has had limited study. It is known, however, that the helminth fauna of the gastrointestinal tract is fairly diverse, with records of large infections by the nematode *Contracaecum* sp. (Schnapp, Hellwing and Chizelea, 1962). *C. osculatum* (Joyeux and Baer, 1936; Baylis, 1937; Markowski, 1952) and *Terranova* (synonym of *Porrocaecum* and *Phocanema*) *decipiens* occur in lesser numbers (Schnapps, Hellwing and Chizelea, 1962) and *Anisakis pegroffi* (King, 1956) are also found. The Cestoda are represented by *Diphyllobothrium* sp. (Schnapp, Hellwing and Chizelea, 1962), specifically *coniceps, elegans, lanceolatum, hians, latum* and *Diplogenophorus tetrapteus, Bothriocephalus* sp., and an immature form under the name *Cysticerus cellulosae* (King, 1956).

Aesthetic value

As for all marine mammals the particular grace of this group in water is outstanding. Seals are innately curious animals and return man's curiosity with an apparently intelligent regard for man himself.

Effects on human activities of changes in population size

As the number of monk seals is so small there can be little effect on humans. If an increase occurs in their numbers there would be an inconsequential increase in damage to nets and a limited increase in competition with man for food species. A decrease in their population size would not noticeably affect human activities other than causing a loss in an aesthetic species as well as a loss of a biological indicator of the condition of the Mediterranean and parts of the Atlantic.

Vulnerability to extinction

The population of the Mediterranean monk seal is decreasing very rapidly and extinction could result within the next quarter century if effective conservation measures are not adopted immediately. The main reasons for this decrease are human disturbance in various forms and marine pollution, the cause varying with the different areas of distribution. The Libyan population of monk seals, for example, is diminishing possibly due to the increased pollution of the Mediterranean Sea as a result of the oil industry in Libya (Essghaier, pers. comm.) Growing numbers of boats, skin divers, fishermen, etc., in Lebanon are causing a decrease in the monk seal population as is pollution; in earlier years the populations were affected by the introduction of foreign flora and fauna from the Suez Canal, the drop in productivity since 1965 due to the Aswan Dam, killings (very rare) and accidents (Le Cavalier, pers. comm.). Human disturbance of Black Sea monk seals on the breeding grounds near the Anatolian and Balkan coasts caused the eventual disappearance of this animal (Bychkov, pers. comm.). The excess of tourists in Sardinia and Sicily (Casale, 1970; Scott, 1971) as well as on the island of Corsica

(Boulva, unpubl.) has driven the seals from most of these areas. The Mediterranean monk seal is then indeed in danger of extinction and the reasons for this are human disturbance (mainly in the form of tourism and increased settlement of coastline areas) and pollution, although accidental deaths (such as drowning in fishermen's nets) and killings (shootings by fishermen of seals that have become a nuisance to their livelihood) are also causes. The animal's inability to achieve the thermoregulatory and ionic regulatory needs imposed by high salinities and temperatures must also be considered as possible contributors to its decline.

Use of live animals

One of the uses of live monk seals would be for display to the public in zoos. They have been successfully kept in captivity on many occasions in zoos such as the ones in Paris (IUCN, 1966; Jarvis, C., editor, 1965), Ankara (Lucas, J., editor, 1970), Rhodes (Tsimenidis, pers. comm.), Istanbul (Duplaix, N., editor, 1973) and Izmir (Mursaloglu, 1964) but now only 3 are being held, 2 in the Zoo de Cansado, Nouadhibou, Mauritania (Nicod, pers. comm.). Live monk seals could also be used in scientific research, none of which is presently in progress, although there are some plans for the future (Ronald, 1973). Reintroductions from such captive stocks could be made.

Need for conservation and management

Because of the vulnerability of the Mediterranean monk seal, the need for its management and conservation is great. The only countries taking any serious measures are France, Italy, Yugoslavia, Greece, Bulgaria,

Rio de Oro (IUCN, 1972) and Tunisia (Ronald and Healey, 1974). Greece has recently decided to initiate a major plan for the conservation of the species. Other reserves have been suggested for Corsica, Canary Islands, Filfla (south of Malta), Kapidaz (Turkey).

Greece has established 1 reserve in the Sporades Islands of the Aegean and is implementing a series of critical reserves in the Dodecanese Islands, where the largest concentration of monk seals exists. Turkey has established the first game preserve on the Kapidaz Peninsula in the Sea of Marmara. Further reserves or protected areas have been suggested in the Canary Islands, around the Island of Filfla (south of Malta), and a "Parc Naturel" has been suggested for Corsica. The French have established the Association for the Protection of Marine Mammals, with emphasis on the monk seal's survival, and the World Wildlife Fund Will give high priority to projects to restore the monk seal as part of its Marine Programme for 1976-78.

The following measures are recommended for the future protection of the Mediterranean monk seal. A final survey of the listed population centres should be undertaken, particularly in areas like the Algerian coast where fairly large numbers are thought to exist. Governments should be approached and encouraged to undertake conservation measures. At the same time, a research programme should be initiated which includes studies of functional anatomy and physiology, behaviour in the wild and in captivity, sensory physiology, reproductive physiology and behaviour, reproductive potential in the wild and in captivity, the determination of necessary conditions for the successful reintroduction of any captive seals and identification methods for known seals populations (Ronald and Healey, 1974). It is important that people become educated to the seal's essential place in nature and that its presence is brought to the attention of concerned nations. Finally, it is essential that exact details of this animal's present distribution be available only to a small group working on its conservation, to prevent its exploitation by the tourist industry as this would surely lead to its extinction (Ronald and Healey, 1974).

There may be only one opportunity to ensure the survival of the Mediterranean monk seal. That opportunity is NOW.

References

ALLEN, J.A., The West Indian seal (*Monachus tropicalis* Gray). *Bull. Am. Mus. Nat. Hist.*, 2:1-39.
1887

BACESCU, M., Foca un animal pe cale de disperitie in Marea Neogra. *Rev. Stiint. V. Adamachi*, 34(1).
1948

BAYLIS, H.A., On the ascarids parasitic in seals, with special reference to the genus *Contracaecum*. *Parasitology*, 29:121-30.
1937

BERKES, F., Personal communication. Marine Science Centre, McGill University, Montreal, Canada.

BERTRAM, G.C.L., Notes on the present status of the monk seal in Palestine. *J. Soc. Preserv. Fauna Emp.*, 47:20-1.
1943

BODDAERT, P., Elenchus animatium. 1. Quadrupedia. Rotterdam.
1785

BOETTGER, C.R., Notizen zur Verbreitung und ueber die Verwandtschaftsbeziehungen der Moenschsrobbe (*Monachus albiventer* Boddaert). *Zool. Anz.*, 147:303-10.
1951

BOULVA, J., Survey of the Mediterranean monk seal in the western Mediterranean and eastern Atlantic. (Unpubl. MS.)
1974

BRUNO, S., Considerazioni sulla foca monaca mediterranea, storia, distribuzione e stato di *Monachus monachus* (Hermann 1779) nel Mare Adriatico (Mammalia, Pinnipedia, Phocidae). *Ric. Biol. Selvaggina*, Suppl. 8:91-110.
1976

BUDKER, P., Pinnipèdes et siréniens d'Afrique. *Notes*
1945 *Afr.*, 27:4-6.

BYCHKOV, V.A., Personal communication. Central Laboratory for Nature Conservation, Krpvchenko Street, 12 Moscow V-331-USSR.

CASALE, A., Visione d'insieme del complesso ecologico e
1970 faunistico della grotta del Bue Marino. Rome, Associazione Italiana World Wildlife Fund.

DUGUY, R., Personal communication. Centre d'étude des mammifères marins, 28 rue Albert ler, 17000 La Rochelle, France.

DUPLAIX, N. (ed.), International Zoo Yearbook. Hall,
1973 Sussex, Ditchling Press Ltd., vol. 13.

ESSGHAIER, M., Personal communication. Graduate student in 1972 of D.R. Johnson, Univesity of Idaho, Moscow, Idaho, 83843, U.S.A.

FLOWER, S.S., Notes on the recent mammals of Egypt,
1932 with a list of species recorded from the kingdom. *J. Zool., Lond.*, (1932):369-450.

GAVARD, Observations sur le phoque-moine *Monachus*
1927 *albiventer* Bodd faites au Laboratoire de Castiglione. *Bull. Stn. Agric. Pêche Castiglione*, (2):175-211.

HERMANN, J., Beschreibung der Muenchs-Robbe. *Bes-*
1779 *chaef. Ges. Naturforsch. Freunde Berlin*, 48:456-509.

IUCN, Red Data Book. Vol. 1. Mammalia. Morges,
1966 Switzerland, IUCN.

–, Red Data Book. Vol. 1. Mammalia. Morges, Swit-
1972 zerland, IUCN.

JARVIS, C. (ed.), International Zoo Yearbook. London,
1965 Balding and Mansell, Vol. 5.

JOYEUX, C. and J.G. BAER, Cestodes. *Faune Fr.*, 30.
1936

KECKES, S., Personal communication. United Nations Environment Programme, Palais des Nations, Geneva, Switzerland.

KING, J.E., The monk seal (genus *Monachus*). *Bull. Br.*
1956 *Mus. Nat. Hist. (Zool.)*, 3:201-56.

–, Seals of the world. London, British Museum (Natu-
1964 ral History).

KOSSWIG, C., Personal communication. Insirah Sokak 32, Bebek, Istanbul, Turkey.

LACHAUX, M., Personal communication. 7 rue des Etats-Unis d'Amérique, Tunis, Tunisia.

LE CAVALIER, J.-C., Personal communication. Villa Halim Moukheiber, Beit-Mery, Lebanon.

LUCAS, J. (ed.), International Zoo Yearbook. Scotland,
1970 Aberdeen University Press, Vol. 10.

MARKOWSKI, S., The cestodes of pinnipeds in the Arctic
1952 and other regions. *J. Helminthol.*, 26:171-214.

MASSA, B., La foca monaca (*Monachus monachus*
1972 Herm.) esiste ancora in Sicilia. *Atti Soc. Ital., Sci. Nat. Mus. Civ. Stor. Nat. Milan*, 113(4):385-90.

MAXWELL, G., Seals of the world. London, Constable
1967 and Co., Ltd., 151 p.

MONOD, T., Note sur la présence du *Monachus albiven-*
1923 *ter* Bodd sur la côte saharienne. *Bull. Mus. Natl Hist. Nat., Paris*, 29:555-7.

–, Phoques sahariens. *Terre Vie*, 12:257-61.
1932

MURSALOGLU, B., Occurrence of the monk seal on the
1964 Turkish coasts. *J. Mammal.*, 45:316-7.

NEDEV, D., Personal communication. Director General, DSO, Ribno-Stopanstvo, Burgas, Romania.

NICOD, B., Personal communication. Directeur, Zoo de Cansado, Nouadhibou, Mauritania.

NORRIS, W.J.T., Monk seals in Libya. *Oryx*, 11:328-30.
1972

RIGGIO, S., Personal communication. Istituto di Zoologia, Università di Palermo, Via Archrafi 18, 90123 Palermo, Italy.

RONALD, K., The Mediterranean monk seal *Monachus*
1973 *monachus. IUCN Publ. (New Ser.) Suppl. Pap.*, (30):30-41.

RONALD, K. and P. HEALEY, Present status of the Medi-
1974 terranean monk seal. *Migration Ser. UFAW-IUCN Lond.*, (100).

SCHNAPP, B., S. HELLWING and G. CHIZELEA, Contribu-
1962 tions to the knowledge of the Black Sea seal

(*Monachus monachus*) Herm. *Trav. Bucharest Muz. Natl. Int. Nat. "G. Antipa"*, 3:383-400.

SCOTT, W.N., Monk seals in Sardinia. *Rep. Acc. Univ.*
1971   *Fed. Anim. Welf.*, (1970-1971):31-4.

TROITZKY, A., Contributions à l'étude des pinnipèdes à
1953   propos de deux phoques de la Méditerranée
         ramenés de croisière par S.A.S. le prince Rai-
         nier III de Monaco. *Bull. Inst. Océanogr.,*
         Monaco, (1032):1-46.

TSIMENIDIS, N., Personal communication. Institute of
Oceanographic and Fisheries Research, Hydrobiological Station of Rhodes, Greece.

VASCONCELOS, M. de S., Personal communication. Mi-
nisterio de Marinha, Aquario Vasco da Gama,
Lisbon, Portugal.

THE STATUS OF SEALS IN THE UNITED KINGDOM

W.N. BONNER

Abstract

Eight species of pinnipeds have been recorded from the United Kingdom in recent times, but only the grey seal, *Halichoerus grypus*, and the common seal, *Phoca vitulina*, are resident breeding species. Due at least partly to lessened human pressure, the grey seal has increased from a relatively rare species during the late 1800s to a present population of about 69 000 in Great Britain, comprising 60 % of the total world population; in 1966, about 2 000 seals were estimated to live around Ireland, found mainly in the southwest but also on the northern coast, Lombay Island and in the Saltee Islands. Most British grey seals occur in Scotland, with substantial breeding populations in the Outer Hebrides (27 000), North Rona (9 000) and Orkney (14 500) and smaller numbers on the mainland, Fair Isle and in Shetland. The largest English population occurs in the Farne Islands (6 700) with smaller numbers off Norfolk, the Scilly Isles, Cornwall, Wales and the Isle of Man. The common seal may have decreased in numbers, and has a smaller geographical range in the United Kingdom than the grey seal: of the estimated British population of 15 000 or more animals, about 5 450-7 601 (the largest concentration in Europe) are found in the Wash, with smaller groups from the Thames estuary to the River Humber and occasionally in other parts of England and Wales; common seals are found in the larger firths and estuaries of the east coast of Scotland, in Shetland, Orkney and the Outer Hebrides and generally in modest numbers on the Scottish west coast. At least 1 250 common seals were estimated to inhabit waters of Ireland in 1966, mainly on the east and northeast coasts. The species favours relatively sheltered waters, congregating in large groups on sand banks and mud flats, and is relatively sedentary. Grey seals are found on exposed rocky coasts and in strongly tidal waters and show no definite migratory movements, except those made by breeding aggregation during auumn and sub-sequent random dispersal of the young. Identifying physical characters are given for both species. Female grey seals reach sexual maturity at age 4-5, and have a longevity of 35 years and perhaps 46 years. Males rarely breed before age 10 and live to about age 25. An adequate life table for the common seal in the United Kingdom is lacking, mainly due to the lack of specimens.

Competition by seals for the heavily exploited fish stocks around the British Isles has an effect on fisheries, though it is difficult to calculate. Although not certainly known, estimates of average daily food intake of common and grey seals include 5-8.5 kg and 7.5-12.5 kg, respectively; in general gadoids are the most common food item and salmonids, clupeoids and pleuronectids are also prominent. Large aggregations of seals cause considerable direct damage to fisheries, but this has not been quantified; the taking of salmon, usually by grey seals, at fixed salmon nets is the most frequent complaint. The population increase of this species has aggravated the situation in Scotland and northeastern England. The role of seals as the definitive hosts of Anisakine nematodes also has detrimental economic effects on fisheries. Except for these examples, seals play a negligible part in the U.K. economy. Somewhat

253

regular hunting, mostly for pups and related to fisheries protection, takes place in Orkney, the Hebrides, Shetland, on the east and west mainland coasts of Scotland and (as a commercial venture) in The Wash. There is no sport hunting and the recreational use of seals is confined to boat-tripping to offshore concentrations; public opinion is strongly opposed to skin hunting for its own sake.

The Conservation of Seals Act 1970 affects seals in England, Wales and Scotland; licences can be granted for scientific research, commercial exploitation on a sustained yield basis and for management actions to protect fisheries and the environment. The British Government maintains a considerable effort in the field of seal biology; further information is especially needed on the feeding ranges of both species and on their state in certain areas. Seals are protected under the Wildlife Act 1970 in the Irish Republic but are not protected in Northern Ireland.

Résumé

Huit espèces de pinnipèdes ont été signalées au Royaume-Uni dans les temps modernes, mais seuls le phoque gris, *Halichoerus grypus*, et le phoque commun, *Phoca vitulina*, y résident en permanence et s'y reproduisent. Par suite — du moins en partie — d'un fléchissement de la pression humaine, la population de phoques gris, relativement rare à la fin du 19ème siècle a atteint le chiffre actuel d'environ 69 000 animaux en Grande-Bretagne et représente 60 pour cent du total de la population mondiale. On estimait en 1966 qu'environ 2 000 phoques vivaient dans les eaux irlandaises, surtout au sud-ouest, mais aussi, sur la côte nord, l'île de Lombay et les îles Saltee. La plupart des phoques gris britanniques se trouvent en Ecosse, avec de substantielles populations de reproducteurs dans les Hébrides extérieures (27 000), North Rona (9 000) et les Orcades (14 500), ainsi qu'un petit nombre sur la grande terre, à Fair Isle et dans les Shetland. La plus importante population anglaise se trouve sur les îles Farne (6 700), avec de petits groupes au large de Norfolk, des Sorlingues, de la Cornouaille, du Pays de Galles, et de l'île de Man. Le nombre de phoques communs pourrait avoir diminué et son aire géographique est moins étendue au Royaume-Uni que celle du phoque gris. Sur la population britannique évaluée à 15 000 animaux au moins, environ 5 450-7 601 (la plus grande concentration d'Europe) se trouvent dans le Wash, avec des groupes plus restreints allant de l'estuaire de la Tamise jusqu'à la Humber et, occasionnellement, dans d'autres parties de l'Angleterre et du Pays de Galles. Les phoques communs se rencontrent dans les grands bras de mer et estuaires de la côte est de l'Ecosse, aux Shetland, aux Orcades et dans les Hébrides extérieures; on en trouve généralement en petit nombre sur la côte écossaise orientale. On a estimé qu'au moins 1 250 phoques communs vivaient en 1966 dans les eaux irlandaises, surtout sur la côte est et nord-est. L'espèce préfère les eaux relativement abritées, se rassemble en grands groupes sur les bancs de sable et de vase et est relativement sédentaire. Les phoques gris vivent sur les côtes rocheuses exposées et dans les eaux à fortes marées; ils n'ont aucun déplacement migratoire défini, à l'exception des mouvements des reproducteurs en automne et de la dispersion désordonnée subséquente des jeunes. Les caractères physiques distinctifs sont donnés pour les deux espèces. Les femelles de phoque gris atteignent l'âge de maturité sexuelle vers 4-5 ans. Les mâles sont rarement aptes à la reproduction avant 10 ans et vivent jusqu'à 25 ans environ. Il n'existe pas de tableau de longévité approprié au Royaume-Uni pour le phoque commun, surtout par suite du manque de spécimens.

La concurrence des phoques pour les stocks de poissons lourdement exploités des eaux britanniques a des retentissements sur les pêches qu'il est difficile de chiffrer. Bien qu'on manque de certitude, on estime que la ration alimentaire quotidienne du phoque commun et du phoque gris est, respectivement, de 5-8,5 kg et 7,5-12,5 kg. En général, les gadidés constituent l'aliment le plus commun mais les salmonidés, les clupéidés et les pleuronectidés jouent aussi un rôle important. Les vastes concentrations de phoques provoquent des dommages directs considérables dans les pêches mais il a été difficile de les quantifier. Les plaintes les plus fréquentes portent sur le fait que les saumons sont dévorés dans les installations fixes, habituellement par les phoques gris. L'accroissement de la population de cette espèce a aggravé la situation en Ecosse et dans l'Angleterre du nord-est. Le fait que les phoques soient les hôtes définitifs des nématodes Anisakine a aussi un effet économique négatif sur les pêches. Exception faite de ces exemples, les phoques jouent un rôle négligeable dans l'économie du Royaume-Uni. Quelques activités de pêche régulière, touchant surtout les phoques nouveau-nés et liées à la protection des pêches ont lieu aux Orcades, aux Hébrides, aux Shetland, sur les côtes orientales et occidentales de l'Ecosse et (comme entreprise commerciale) dans le Wash. Il n'existe pas de chasse sportive et la valeur récréative des phoques se limite à des excursions en bateau vers les concentrations du large; l'opinion publique est fermement opposée à la chasse du phoque comme fin en soi.

La loi sur la conservation des phoques de 1970 intéresse les phoques d'Angleterre, du Pays de Galles et d'Ecosse. Des permis peuvent être accordés pour la recherche scientifique, l'exploitation commerciale sur la base du rendement eumétrique et l'exploitation rationnelle visant à protéger les pêches et l'environnement. Le gouvernement britannique consacre des ressources considérables aux recherches biologiques sur les phoques. Il est nécessaire d'obtenir des informations complémentaires sur la gamme alimentaire des deux espèces et sur leur état dans certaines zones. Les phoques sont protégés en République d'Irlande par la Loi sur la protection de la nature de 1970; aucune protection n'existe en Irlande du Nord.

Extracto

En el Reino Unido se ha registrado recientemente la presencia de ocho especies de pinnípedos, pero sólo la foca gris (*Halichoerus grypus*) y la foca común (*Phoca vitulina*) se reproducen en sus aguas. Gracias en parte a la disminución de su explotación por parte del hombre, la foca gris ha pasado de ser una especie relativamente rara a finales del siglo pasado a una población actual de unos 69 000 animales en Gran Bretaña, que representan el 60 por ciento de la población mundial total. En 1966, se estimó que vivían alrededor de Irlanda unas 2 000 focas, principalmente en el sudoeste, pero también en la costa septentrional, en la isla Lombay y en las islas Saltee. La mayor parte de las focas grises de Gran Bretaña se encuentran en Escocia, con poblaciones importantes de reproductores en las Hébridas Exteriores (27 000), en North Rona (9 000) y en las Orcadas (14 500), y en menor número en la tierra firme, en la isla Fair y en las Shetland. La población principal de Inglaterra se encuentra en las islas Farne (6 700), y en números menores frente a Norfolk, las islas Scilly, Cornualles, Gales y la isla de Man. El número de focas *P. vitulina* parece haber disminuido, y su zona de distribución en el Reino Unido es menor que la de la foca gris: de los 15 000 o más animales en que se estima la población de Gran Bretaña unos 5 450-7 601 (la mayor concentración de Europa) se encuentran en el Wash, con grupos menores entre el estuario del Támesis y el río Humber y en ocasiones en otras partes de Inglaterra y Gales; se encuentran también focas comunes en los grandes esteros y estuarios de la costa este de Inglaterra, en las Shetland, las Orcadas y las Hébridas Exteriores y en general, en número reducido, en la costa occidental de Escocia. Se calcula que en las aguas de Irlanda había en 1966 como mínimo 1 250 focas comunes, sobre todo en las costas este y nordeste. Estos animales prefieren aguas relativamente protegidas y se congregan en grandes grupos en bancos de arena y llanuras de fango; la especie es relativamente sedentaria. La foca gris se encuentra en costas rocosas expuestas al mar y en aguas con gran movimiento de mareas y no muestra claros movimientos migratorios, si se exceptúan las concentraciones para la reproducción durante el otoño y la posterior dispersión aleatoria de los animales jóvenes. Se indican las características físicas peculiares de ambas especies. Las hembras de foca gris alcanzan la madurez sexual a los cuatro-cinco años de edad y su longevidad es de 35 años y tal vez lleguen a 46. Los machos raramente se reproducen antes de los diez años y alcanzan unos 25 años de edad. No existen buenas estadísticas vitales de la foca

255

común en el Reino Unido, debido principalmente a la falta de ejemplares suficientes para estudio.

La actividad de las focas sobre las poblaciones de peces intensamente explotadas de las Islas Británicas repercute ciertamente en las pesquerías, pero es difícil hacer un cálculo exacto. Aunque no se conoce con certeza, se estima que la ingesta diaria media de alimentos de la foca común y la foca gris es respectivamente de 5-8,5 kg y 7,5-12,5 kg en general, el alimento más común son los gádidos, y también los salmónidos, clupeidos y pleuronéctidos son importantes. Las grandes concentraciones de focas causan daños directos apreciables a las pesquerías, pero no se 'han cuantificado; las quejas más frecuentes se refieren a la depredación de salmones, de ordinario por *H. grypus*, en las redes salmoneras fijas. El aumento de la población de esta especie ha agravado la situación en Escocia y en el nordeste de Inglaterra. También la función de estas focas como hospedante definitivo de los nematodos Anisakine tiene efectos económicos perjudiciales en las pesquerías. Salvo cuanto se ha dicho, las focas desempeñan una función insignificante en la economía del Reino Unido. La caza de focas, sobre todo cachorros y animales que molestan en las pesquerías, se practica con cierta regularidad en las Orcadas, las Hébridas, las Shetland, la costa este y oeste de Escocia y (como empresa comercial) en el Wash. No existe caza deportiva de estos animales, y el valor recreativo de las focas se limita a algunos viajes en embarcaciones para visitar las concentraciones que se encuetran a lo largo de la costa; la opinión pública se opone enérgicamente a la captura de estos animales para aprovechar sus pieles.

La Ley de Conservación de las Focas de 1970 afecta a las focas de Inglaterra, Gales y Escocia; pueden concederse licencias de caza para investigación científica, para explotación comercial sobre la base de un rendimiento sostenido y para proteger las pesquerías y el medio ambiente. El Gobierno Británico realiza considerables esfuerzos en el campo de la biología de las focas; se necesita más información, especialmente sobre las zonas en que se alimentan ambas especies y la situación actual de las poblaciones en algunos lugares. Las focas están protegidas en la República de Irlanda por la Ley de la Fauna de 1970, mientras no están protegidas en Irlanda del Norte.

W.N. Bonner
Life Sciences Division, British Antarctic Survey, Madingley Road, Cambridge CB3 OET, UK

Introduction

The United Kingdom Government maintains a considerable effort in the field of seal biology. The Seals Research Division of the Institute for Marine Environmental Research (a component body of the Natural Environment Research Council) comprises eight scientists and support staff whose sole task it is to study British seals.

Eight species of pinnipeds have been recorded from United Kingdom waters in recent times, but of these only two, the common seal, *Phoca vitulina* L. and the grey seal, *Halichoerus grypus* (Fab.) are resident breeding species. The walrus, *Odobenus rosmarus*; the ringed seal, *Pusa hispida*; the harp seal, *Pagophilus groenlandicus*; the bearded seal, *Erignathus barbatus*; and the hooded seal, *Cystophora cristata*, have been sighted as occasional vagrants. The walrus may have been more abundant in early times, as walrus remains are not infrequent in Bronze and Iron Age deposits. It is possible that the ringed seal, which resembles the common seal and is difficult to distinguish from it in the water, is a regular visitor to Shetland. There is a single record of a California sea lion, *Zalophus californianus*, but this was without doubt an animal that had escaped from captivity (Coulson and Hickling, 1960).

The remainder of this paper is confined to the common seal, of which about 40 per cent of the European stock is to be found in Great Britain, and the grey seal whose British population comprises about 60 per cent of the total world stock.

Identification

Common seal

Adult males: nose to tail
length: 130-160 cm (26 specimens)
exceptionally to 170 cm,
Weight 55-105 kg (22 specimens);

Adult females: nose to tail
length: 120-155 cm (26 specimens)
Weight 45-87.5 kg (19 specimens).
Length at birth 70-97 cm, weight 9-11 kg.

The coat colour and pattern are very variable, usually a mottle of dark spots on a lighter ground, but on the back spots coalesce to produce a pale reticulation on a dark ground. Males are generally darker than females. The coat fades to a brownish tinge prior to moult at the end of summer. Pups are born in first adult pelage, rarely in silver or fawn lanugo. Pup skins from the Wash are paler than those from Scotland and may entirely lack spotting on belly; a similar difference was noted in *P. vitulina* pups from Arctic and maritime Canada (Dunbar, 1949).

Claws on the fore-limbs are short, not much overhanging the tips of the digits; the head is small in relation to body, the top of the head is rounded and the snout is short. Nostrils are at an angle, thus: \/, and almost touching below (Wynne-Edwards, 1954). Teeth: i 3/2 c 1/1 pc 5/5. Check teeth (except 1st) are much longer than broad, set obliquely in the jaw clearly tricuspid with posterior cusps often sub-divided. The inter-orbital region of the skull is slender, the palate anteriorly flat, the posterior palatal foramen enters the palate on maxilla, the posterior border of palate is $\wedge$ shaped; nasals extend beyond the posterior margin of maxilla.

Grey seal

Adult males: nose to tail 195-230 cm ($\bar{x}$ = 207.3, SD = 9.5, N = 25)
Weight 170-310 kg ($\bar{x}$ = 233.0, SD = 37.6, n = 25).
Adult females: nose to tail 165-195 cm ($\bar{x}$ = 179.6, SD = 7.4, n = 25)
Weight 105-186 kg ($\bar{x}$ = 154.6, SD = 24.1, n = 25).
Length at birth 90-105 cm, weight 14.5 kg.

There is marked sexual dimorphism in the coat pattern. Apart from the generally darker tone of the back which shades into the lighter belly there are two tones, a lighter and a darker. In males the darker tone is more extensive forming a continuous dark background with light patches; in females the lighter tone is continuous with dark spots (Hewer and Backhouse, 1959) but the spots are always larger than those of the common seal. The colour varies from almost black in some bulls to silver grey on cream in light females. Yearlings near moult are nearly uniform fawn. Pups born in white lanugo moulted after 2-3 weeks.

Adult males are conspicuously larger than females, with heavy neck and shoulders. The bull's profile is convex, the muzzle wide and heavy; the cow's profile is almost flat, the muzzle more slender. Claws on the fore-limb are long and slender, and overhang the ends of the digits by 2-3 cm. The nostrils are almost parallel and separated below (Wynne-Edwards, 1954). Dentition: i 3/2 c 1/1 pc 5/5 (often 6/5). The cheek teeth are large and strong, nearly circular in cross-section, each with single conical cusp; secondary cusps are insignificant, usually only on 5th upper and 4th of 5th lower pc. The posterior margin on the palate is evenly rounded, the anterior part of the palate strongly arched; the posterior margin of nasals is approximately level with the maxillae; the inter-orbital region wide; the very wide nasal openings and elevated fronto-nasal region are characteristic of this species, but may be confused with *Cystophora cristata* from which it is distinguished by incisors 2/2 in latter.

Distribution and movements

The largest concentrations of seals are to be found in remote areas; this may be a consequence of disturbance by man. Bonner has discussed habitats (1972) and distribution (1976).

Common seals

Common seals are most often to be found in relatively sheltered waters, particularly estuaries, sea-lochs or around island archipelagos. They are the characteristic seals of sand-banks and mud-flats, such as those in the Wash, where they may occur in groups of up to 300, sometimes 500. Around rocky shores as in Shetland or on the west coast of Scotland, they are usually found in small groups, rarely larger than 20-40.

The largest concentration in Europe is in the Wash in eastern England, where the stock is estimated to be between 5 450 and 7 601 (Summers and Mountford, 1975). Much smaller groups occur on sand-banks from the Thames estuary to the Humber. Elsewhere in England and Wales common seals occur only occasionally.

They are also found in the larger firths and estuaries of the east coast of Scotland, though it is doubtful if the species breeds in the Firth of Forth. Populations are associated with the principal offshore island groups – Shetland, Orkney and the Outer Hebrides – though they are absent from the distant islands of North Rona, Sula Sgeir and St. Kilda. The species is generally distributed, though not in large numbers, on the west coast of Scotland and the adjacent islands. It is absent from the Isle of Man and the Channel Islands.

Lockley (1966) estimated that there were at least 1 250 in Ireland, the largest concentrations occurring in the shallow waters of the east and northeast coasts.

They are relatively sedentary animals, and individuals can be seen on the same rock day after day (Venables and Venables, 1955). There is some interchange over small distances and some more extensive movement of young animals. Seals marked as pups in the Wash have been recovered from between North Berwick (Firth of Forth) and the coast of Holland (Bonner and Witthames, 1974). No definite migratory movements are known.

Grey seals

By contrast, grey seals are more often to be found on exposed rock coasts and in strongly tidal waters such as the Pentland Firth. They have a wider geographical range than the common seal in the United Kingdom, occurring from the Scilly Isles to Shetland. In Scotland, where the great majority occur, substantial populations breed in the Outer Hebrides, at North Rona and at Orkney. Smaller groups occur in Shetland and the Inner Hebrides and very small numbers breed on mainland Scottish coasts.

The largest population in England is that of the Farne Islands, off the Northumberland coast. A few occur in the Wash, on one of the outer sands, and a group of about 100-200, which produces 6-15 young each year, is found on a tidal bank at Scroby Sands, off the east Norfolk coast. This habitat, as a breeding station, is unique in Europe, though grey seals breed in large numbers on the sands of Sable Island, Canada. Grey seals are found as a breeding species in small numbers in the Scilly Isles, sparsely on the Cornish coast, on the coasts and off-lying islands of Pembrokeshire and Cardiganshire and in very small numbers on the Lleyn Peninsula and Anglesey in North Wales. Small numbers breed on the Isle of Man.

Lockley (1966) estimated that 2 000 grey seals occurred in Ireland. They are to be found mainly in the south-west, though there are some on the northern coast and others at the Saltee Islands and Lambay Island on the east coast.

Grey seals are widely distributed in coastal waters during the spring and summer but concentrate in comparatively few breeding places in the early autumn, dispersing again after breeding has ended. Boyd (1962) has described their movements in north-west Britain and Bonner (1972) has summarised dispersal of the young. This is a random movement, the young seals radiating out in all seaward directions from their breeding sites. As in the common seal, there are no definite migratory movements but the aggregation in the breeding season impose a more mobile pattern on grey seals.

Status of stocks

This has been reviewed by Bonner (1976) and Summers, Bonner and van Haaften (1978). The most striking change in the British seal population has been the very rapid increase of grey seals since the beginning of this century.

Tables 1 and 2 summarise the population estimates, status and management regimes for grey and common seals respectively.

It was not until 1932 that Gunn noted that grey seals were beginning to frequent the inner islands of the Orkney group (Gunn, 1932): prior to that the seals had been confined to Seal Skerry off North Ronaldsay and perhaps on the skerries of the Pentland Firth. A stock of about 8 750 grey seals of which over 90 % breed on the inner isles is now centred on Orkney. In the Hebrides even more striking increases have taken place. As recently as 1966 only 15 pups were counted at the Monach Isles; in 1976 production was estimated at about 2 572 pups and in the same period production for the whole group reached 6 850. In the Farne Islands accurate counts of the number of pups born have been made since 1956. These increased from 751 in that year to 1 956 in 1970 (Bonner and Hickling, 1971). Numbers have since fallen as a result of extensive culling of adult seals, and in 1976 only 1 420 pups were born (Hickling, Hawkey and Harwood, 1977).

Although early reports were not founded on such extensive observations as are available today, there is little doubt that the grey seal was relatively rare in the late nineteenth century; Ritchie and Calderwood (in Rae, 1960) estimated that there were about 4 000-5 000 grey seals around the United Kingdom in

259

Table 1. **Status of grey seal stocks in Great Britain (from Bonner, 1976, updated with information from the Seals Research Division (SRD), Institute of Marine Environmental Research, NERC)**

Stock	Date of last Survey	Estimated pup Production	Equivalent total Population	Reliability of Estimates	Status	Management
S.W. Britain	1974	800-900 [1]	2 800-3 150	Fair	Unknown	Close season Sep-Dec
Inner Hebrides	1976	1 200	5 000	Fair	Increasing	Close season Sep-Dec
Outer Hebrides	1976	6 850	27 000	Good	Increasing	Part hunted (1 000 pups/year) Monachs totally protected
North Rona	1976	2 500	9 000	Good	Increasing	Totally protected
Shetland	1973	1 000	3 500	Poor	Unknown	Sporadic hunting
Orkney	1976	4 000	14 500	Good	Increasing	Part hunted (1 000 pups/year) otherwise close season Sep-Dec
Farne Islands	1976	1 343 + 82	6 700	Very Good	Increasing	Management objective is stock of 1 000 breeding females, otherwise totally protected
APPROX TOTAL			69 000			

[1] Corwall and Scilly last surveyed in 1973 (Summers, 1974), Wales in 1974 (SRD unpublished data).
[2] 1976 figures not yet available. Projected estimates given here.

1928; these had increased to about 46 000 in 1972. In earlier times grey seal numbers were probably kept in check by human predation during their vulnerable breeding season. During the last 100 years the depopulation of outlying islands and the decline in the crofting-fishing way of life, in which seals were regarded as a valuable resource, have both lessened the pressure on the seals, and provided them with previously unavailable breeding sites.

Common seals do not seem to have undergone similar changes in the same period, and indeed their numbers may have declined, though very few data exist. Their breeding habits may perhaps have made them less vulnerable in earlier days to predation by man, and less able to benefit today from the availability of new breeding sites. Scheffer (1958) raised the question as to whether common seals might be unable to compete successfully with grey seals.

Vital parameters

Bonner (1972) has reviewed the breeding biology of grey and common seals in Europe. A valuable paper by Hewer (1964) has provided a population analysis based on a sample of 295 grey seals of known age. Hewer found that about half the cows were mature (i.e. had ovulated) at age 4 and the rest at age 5. Hewer calculated the longevity of the female to be 35 years but Bonner (1971) recorded a cow shot in the wild aged 46. Males rarely take part in breeding before age 10 and live to about 25 years.

From his data Hewer derived survival rates for a hypothetical stable grey seal population and used these to prepare an analysis of a population producing 1 000 pups by the end of the breeding season. This may be used to calculate the total population where the number of pups born is known. This "pup

Table 2. Status of common seal stocks in Great Britain (from Bonner, 1976, updated with information from the Seals Research Division (SRD), Institute of Marine Environmental Research, NERC)

Stock	Date of last Survey	Estimated total Population	Reliability of Estimate	Status	Management
Inner Hebrides/ West coast Scotland	1975	3 500 + [1]	Moderate	Unknown	Hunted: quota 250 pups/year
Outer Hebrides	1974	1 300 + [2]	Moderate	Unknown	Few pups taken as part of Inner Heb/W. coast quota in some years
Shetland	1973	2 000 [3]	Moderate	Decreasing until 1973	Totally protected since 1973
Orkney	1972	2 000-3 000 [4]	Moderate	Probably static	Hunted: quota 200 pups/year
East coast Scotland	1975	850-1 050 [4]	Poor	Unknown	Sporadic killing of pups and adults to protect salmon netting stations
Wash	1973	5 500-7 651 [5]	Good	Probably static	Hunted: quota 400 pups/year (no hunting in 1974)
APPROX TOTAL		15 000 +			

[1] SRD unpublished data.
[2] SRD unpublished data.
[3] Anderson *et al.* (1974).
[4] Summers, Bonner and van Haaften (1978).
[5] Summers and Mountford (1975).

factor" varies from 3.1 at the beginning of the season to 3.9 at the end. A factor of 3.5 has been used to convert pup counts to total populations in this and many other papers on British grey seals. This factor will apply only to a stable population and special multipliers are required for populations which are changing in size.

No large samples of British common seals have so far been analysed. Harrison (1960) suggested sexual maturity in the Wash seals was reached later than age 3 and was more likely to be age 5 or 6, at least in bulls. Bigg (1969) in his study of *Phoca vitulina richardi* in British Columbia found, in a sample of 138 females, that 20 % matured at age 2, 38 % at age 4 and 8 % at age 5. Males matured between ages 3 and 6, mostly at 5. It is likely that the British seals are similar. Further work is urgently needed on this subject but the collection of material presents difficulties.

Food habits and relations to fisheries

Rae (1960, 1968 and 1973) has studied the feeding habits of Scottish seals extensively. Sergeant (1951) has made observations on the feeding of common seals in the Wash and Anderson *et al.* (1974) have presented some data for grey seals in the Welsh Dee.

In general, seals eat fish and since most fish stocks around the British Isles are heavily exploited it follows that the large amount eaten by seals has an effect on fisheries. Although in many cases the samples studied have been biased towards seals collected at the site of fishing operations it appears that both grey and common seals eat gadoids more commonly than other fish. Salmonids (particularly *Salmo salar*, the salmon), clupeoids (particularly *Clupea harengus*, the herring) and pleuronectids (most often found in the diet of

261

common seals) are also prominent.

The amount of food consumed in the wild is not certainly known. Steven (1934) calculated that grey seals ate 15 lbs (6.8 kg) of fish a day. Rae (1970) supported this and in a later paper (1973) recorded a single meal of 9.98 kg (22 lbs) of salmon taken from the stomach of a male grey seal. Using Keys' (1968) estimate of a food intake of 6-10 % of body weight per day, Bonner (1972) suggested that reasonable estimates of average daily intake were 5-8.5 kg for common seals and 7.5-12.5 kg for grey seals.

Where seals occur in large numbers they cause appreciable damage to fisheries. In Scotland and north-east England the situation has been exacerbated by the rapid increase in grey seal numbers.

The damage most complained of in the United Kingdom but so far unquantified is the taking of salmon from fixed salmon nets, usually by grey seals (Rae and Shearer, 1965). Net damage has declined since synthetic fibres have been substituted for cotton. Fixed gill nets set for cod on the east coast of Scotland are also liable to atack by grey seals, as are ground nets in the Minch and drift nets in various places. Long-lines are affected by seals stripping the bait or taking the fish from the hooks (Rae, 1960).

It is difficult to estimate the effect of seals on wild stocks of fish. Lockie's (1962) attempt to do so for salmon and the Farne Islands stock of grey seals failed to reach firm conclusions because of insufficient data. Since that time, this stock of seals has nearly doubled in size.

The role of seals as the definitive hosts of Anisakine nematodes is also of significance to fisheries. The increase in the incidence of larvae of Terranova decipiens ("cod worm") in the flesh of cod around the British Isles can be correlated with increasing grey seal numbers. Although Terranova is destroyed by all ordinary means of cooking cod, wormy cod is less attractive to the consumer and badly affected cod is unsaleable. The cost of filleting, candling and removing the worms by hand adds greatly to production costs. Grey seals are of greater importance in the transmission of Terranova than common seals (Young, 1972). Adults of another nematode, Anisakis sp. ("herring-worm") are occasionally found in grey seals but more often in porpoises and other Cetacea. The larvae infest herring. Young concluded that grey seals were not hosts of significance to species of Anisakis.

Economic value

Seals play a negligible part in the economy of the United Kingdom, except as pests of commercial fisheries. More or less regular seal hunting, mostly for pups, takes place in Orkney, the Hebrides, Shetland, the east and west mainland coasts of Scotland and in the Wash. Bonner (1969) discussed seal hunting in the United Kingdom and suggested that the aggregate proceeds from sealing did not exceed £ 12 000 a year and that cropping at maximum sustainable yield levels might increase this to £ 50 000 or £ 60 000. Since then both the stocks of seals and the price of skins have increased, but it is unlikely that the total resource would ever exceed a gross value of £ 80 000 a year at present prices. Most seal hunting in the United Kingdom (though not in the Wash) is related to fisheries protection; public opinion is strongly opposed to skin-hunting for its own sake. There is no sport hunting of seals in the United Kingdom. Recreational use of seals (which is locally considerable) is mainly confined to boat-tripping to seal islands – as in the Farne Islands – or seal rocks – as in Cornwall. The value of this use cannot be quantified; it is not directly related to the abundance of seals.

Conservation legislation

The Conservation of Seals Act 1970, which covers England, Wales and Scotland, prohibits for both species, the killing, injuring or taking of seals (or any attempts to do so) during close seasons which cover the breeding seasons (grey seals, 1 September-31 December; common seals, 1 June-31 August). When it appears necessary on conservation grounds a Parliamentary Order can also be made prohibiting absolutely the killing of seals in specified areas. Currently (August 1977) such an order is in force in respect of common seals in Shetland. Neither of these prohibitions applies to seals killed in the immediate vicinity of fishing nets. Licences can be granted to kill or take seals during the close season (most of the hunted pups are taken under such licences) or at any time in a prohibited area, for a variety of reasons. These include scientific purposes, prevention of damage to fisheries, reduction of a population surplus for management purposes, and the use of a population surplus of seals as a resource. Before granting licences, the appropriate Minister will receive advice from a group on which seal biologists, conservation and fishery interests are represented.

The Act also regulates killing methods. The use of poison for killing seals is forbidden except under licence, which may not be granted for the use of strychnine. Firearms must be rifles firing ammunition having a muzzle energy of not less than 600 foot-pounds (83 kg m) and a bullet weighing not less than 45 grains (2.9 g). Licences can be granted to use other weapons to kill seals in special cases and the use of 0.22 rifles for killing pups is generally permitted under licence.

The Act provides the necessary legal foundation to protect seals while at the same time allowing their numbers to be controlled should they locally endanger fisheries, or increase to such a point that harm is caused to the environment. Should the stock of seals be large enough to warrant it licences can be granted to hunters to make use of traditional resources on a sustainable yield basis without harming stocks.

In northern Ireland grey seals were protected by the Grey Seals (Protection) Act, 1914, which expired in 1918. It appears, therefore, that neither species of seal is protected in northern Ireland. There is no legislation affecting seals in the Isle of Man, or the Channel Islands. In the Irish Republic seals of all species are comprehensively protected under the Wildlife Act 1976 though licences may be issued to permit the capturing or killing of seals for educational, scientific or other specified purposes. It is possible under the Act to allow steps to be taken to stop seal damage to fisheries. The Act further restricts the sale of seals or seal-skins to licensed wildlife dealers, a valuable provision which is absent from the UK Act.

Conclusions

Basic population estimates of the main seal assemblies have been made and changes are monitored. Grey seals in the UK have increased and common seals may be declining. Further information is required on the status of grey seals in Shetland, and of common seals on the west coast of Scotland. An adequate life-table for common seals is lacking, but it is difficult to obtain a sufficiently large series of specimens. Further work on the feeding range of seals is needed.

It is hoped that organised research on the status of seals in Northern Ireland and the Irish Republic will begin shortly.

References

ANDERSON, S.S. et al., Grey seals, *Halichoerus grypus*, of
1974   the Dee Estuary and observations on a characteristic skin lesion in British seals. *J. Zool., Lond.*, 174:429-40.

BIGG, M.A., The harbour seal in British Columbia. *Bull.* 1969 *Fish. Res. Board Can.*, (172):33 p.

BONNER, W.N., British seals — a pest, resource or 1969 amenity? *Salmon Net*, 5:32-7.

—, An aged grey seal (*Halichoerus grypus*). *J. Zool.,* 1971 *Lond.*, 164:261-2.

—, The grey seal and common seal in European waters. 1972 *Oceanogr. Mar. Biol.*, 10:461-507.

—, The stocks of grey seals (*Halichoerus grypus*) and 1976 common seals (*Phoca vitulina*) in Great Britain. *Publ. Natl. Environ. Counc. (C)*, (16).

BONNER, W.N. and G. HICKLING, The grey seals of the 1971 Farne Islands 1969 to 1971. *Trans. Nat. Hist. Soc. Northumb.*, 17:141-62.

BONNER, W.N. and S.R. WITTHAMES, Dispersal of com- 1974 mon seals (*Phoca vitulina*) tagged in the Wash, East Anglia. *J. Zool., Lond.*, 174:528-31.

BOYD, J.M., Seasonal occurrence and movement of seals 1962 in north-west Britain. *Proc. Zool. Soc. Lond.*, 138:385-404.

COULSON, J.C. and G. HICKLING, The grey seals of the 1960 Farne Islands 1958 to 1959. *Trans. Nat. Hist. Soc. Northumb.*, 13:151-78.

DUNBAR, M.J., The Pinnipedia of the Arctic and Sub- 1949 arctic. *Bull. Fish. Res. Board Can.*, (85):22 p.

GUNN, J., Orkney the magnetic North. Edinburgh, 1932 Thomas Nelson and Sons.

HARRISON, R.J., Reproduction and reproductive organs 1960 in common seals (*Phoca vitulina*) in the Wash, East Anglia. *Mammalia, Paris*, 24(30):372-85.

HEWER, H.R., The determination of age, sexual matu- 1964 rity, longevity and a life table in the grey seal (*Halichoerus grypus*). *Proc. Zool. Soc. Lond.*, 142:593-624.

HEWER, H.R. and K.M. BACKHOUSE, Field identification 1959 of bulls and cows of the grey seal, *Halichoerus grypus* Fab. *Proc. Zool. Soc. Lond.*, 132:641-5.

HICKLING, G., P. HAWKEY and L.H. HARWOOD, The grey 1977 seals of the Farne Islands: the 1976 breeding season. *Trans. Nat. Hist. Soc. Northumb.*, 42(6):119-25.

KEYS, M.C., A survey of feeding practices for pinnipeds 1968 in zoos and aquariums. Seattle, Washington, Bureau of Commercial Fisheries, Marine Mammal Biological Laboratory, 20 p. (mimeo).

LOCKIE, J.D., Grey seals as competitors with man for 1962 salmon. *In* The exploitation of natural animal populations, edited by E.D. LeCren and M.W. Holdgate. *Symp. Br. Ecol. Soc.*, (2):316-22.

LOCKLEY, R.M., The distribution of grey and common 1966 seals on the coasts of Ireland. *Ir. Nat. J.*, 15:136-43.

RAE, B.B., Seals and Scottish fisheries. *Mar. Res.*, 1960 1960(2):39 p.

—, The food of seals in Scottish waters. *Mar. Res.*, 1968 1968(2):23 p.

—, How much do seals eat daily? *Salmon Net*, 6:20. 1970

—, Further observations on the food of seals. *J. Zool.,* 1973 *Lond.*, 169:287-97.

RAE, B.B. and W.M. SHEARER, Seal damage to salmon 1965 fisheries. *Mar. Res.*, 1965(2):35 p.

SCHEFFER, V.B., Seals, sea lions and walruses: a review 1958 of the Pinnipedia. Stanford, California, Stanford University Press, 154 p.

SERGEANT, D.E., The status of the common seal (*Phoca* 1951 *vitulina*) on the East Anglian coast. *J. Mar. Biol. Assoc. U.K.*, 29(3):707-17.

STEVEN, G.A., A short investigation into the habits, 1934 abundance and species of seals on the North Cornish coast. *J. Mar. Biol. Assoc. U.K.*, 19:489-501.

SUMMERS, C.F., The grey seal (*Halichoerus grypus*) in 1974 Cornwall and the Isles of Scilly. *Biol. Conserv.*, 6(4):285-91.

SUMMERS, C.F. and M.D. MOUNTFORD, Counting the 1975 common seal. *Nature, Lond.*, 253:670-1.

SUMMERS, C.F., W.N. BONNER and J. VAN HAAFTEN, 1978 Changes in the seal population of the North Sea. *Rapp. P.-V. Réun. CIEM*, 172:278-85.

VENABLES, U.M. and L.S.V. VENABLES, Observations on 1955 a breeding colony of the seal *Phoca vitulina* in Shetland. *Proc. Zool. Soc. Lond.*, 125:521-32.

WYNNE-EDWARDS, V.C., Field identification of the
1954   common and grey seals. *Scott. Nat.*, 66:192.

YOUNG, P.C., The relationship between the presence of
1972   larval anisakine nematodes in cod and marine mammals in British home waters. *J. Appl. Ecol.*, 9:459-85.

THE HARP SEAL, *PAGOPHILUS GROENLANDICUS*

K. RONALD, P.J. HEALEY **and** H.D. FISHER

Abstract

The harp seal (*Pagophilus groenlandicus*) is distributed across the northern Atlantic and Arctic Seas from Severnaya Zemlya to the eastern Canadian Archipelago in 3 mainly distinct populations; each undertakes a migration in the late spring to northern areas to feed, and a migration southward in the winter to a distinct breeding and moulting ground on the sea ice. Seals reproducing in the White Sea spend the summer near the ice edge in the Barents and Kara Seas; the Greenland Sea population breeds in waters around Jan Mayen and migrates north to feeding grounds between Spitsbergen and Greenland; and the northwest Atlantic population breeds in the Gulf of St. Lawrence and off the southeast coast of Labrador, and spends the summer from western Greenland to Hudson Bay. The populations are estimated to number 600 000, 100 000 and less than 1 000 000, respectively. External characteristics and coloration are summarized and some distinguishing skull and dentition characters are given. Adult male and female harp seals reach average lengths and weights of 183 cm and 135 kg, and 179 cm and 119.7 kg, respectively; newborns average 103 cm and 11.8 kg. Age at sexual maturity for females varies in each population with a mean perhaps near age 5; males are reported to be sexually mature at age 8. Seals may live for over 30 years. Whelping occurs at different times in each population, and in the 2 breeding groups in the northwest Atlantic, but generally is from late February to early March. Mating takes place about 2 weeks after this, followed by the formation of moulting groups during April. Gestation proper lasts about 7.5 months following an 11-week period of delayed implantation.

The visceral anatomy is described and some organ weights and dimensions are given for both young and adult specimens. Only general anatomic descriptions of the central nervous system of phocid seals are available and there is even less information for harp seals, in particular. Complex morphological and physiological adaptations, especially manifest in the circulatory system, allow this species to make prolonged dives to great depths in search of food. Blood values are discussed. Vision is the harp seal's primary source of sensory information; adaptations in the eye characteristic of those needed for nocturnal as well as daylight vision allow excellent visual sensitivity in both air and water. The anatomy of the harp seal ear is similar in some ways to that of cetaceans as well as terrestrial mammals; although it seems adapted to hearing underwater, it is probably of little use in echolocation. A total of 15 underwater sounds have been recorded and analysed.

Adult harp seals have a varied diet consisting mainly of pelagic fish and pelagic and benthic crustaceans. Annual consumption of food by the northwest Atlantic population has been estimated at 2 000 000 t; comparison of this figure with the annual increment of the population indicates a low ecological efficiency. General maintenance, diet requirements and physiological problems and treatment in captivity, are summarized. *Contracaecum gadi* is the most common of the harp seal's parasites; the species is also the host of preference for the cod worm (*Terranova decipiens*) and is the most important pinniped vector of this nematode in the Gulf of St. Lawrence.

Résumé

Le phoque du Groenland, *Pagophilus groenlandicus*, fréquente l'Atlantique nord et les mers arctiques de Severnaya Zemlya à l'archipel oriental du Canada. On compte trois populations à peu près complètement séparées, qui se déplacent à la fin du printemps vers des latitudes septentrionales pour se nourrir et, en hiver, vers des zones plus au sud pour atteindre un terrain séparé où elles se reproduisent et muent sur les glaces marines. Les phoques qui se reproduisent en mer Blanche passent l'été à la limite des glaces de la mer de Barents et de la mer de Kara. La population de la mer du Groenland se reproduit dans les eaux de l'île de Jan Mayen et gagne, par une migration vers le nord, des terrains d'alimentation entre le Spitzberg et le Groenland. La population de l'Atlantique nord-ouest se reproduit dans le golfe du Saint-Laurent et au large de la côte sud-est du Labrador; elle passe l'été entre le Groenland occidental et la baie d'Hudson. On estime la taille de ces populations, respectivement, à 600 000, 100 000 et moins d'un million. Les auteurs donnent des indications sur les caractéristiques et la coloration externes ainsi que des détails sur le crâne et la dentition. Chez l'adulte, la longueur et le poids moyens sont de 183 cm et 135 kg pour le mâle et de 179 cm et 119,7 kg pour la femelle. Pour les veaux nouveau-nés, les chiffres moyens sont de 103 cm et 11,8 kg. Chez la femelle, l'âge de la maturité sexuelle varie dans chaque population, la moyenne étant peut-être d'environ 5 ans. Chez le mâle, la maturité sexuelle surviendrait à 8 ans. La longévité peut dépasser 30 ans. Les dates de parturition diffèrent dans chaque population et dans les deux groupes de reproducteurs de l'Atlantique nord-ouest mais elles se situent généralement en fin février-début mars. L'accouplement survient environ deux semaines plus tard et il est suivi par la formation de groupes qui muent en avril. La gestation proprement dite dure environ sept mois et demi, après une période de nidation différée de onze semaines.

Les auteurs décrivent l'anatomie interne et indiquent le poids et la dimension de certains organes chez les jeunes et les adultes. On ne possède que des données anatomiques générales sur le système nerveux central des phocidés et on sait moins de choses encore sur le phoque du Groenland en particulier. Des adaptations morphologiques et physiologiques complexes, spécialement apparentes dans le système circulatoire, permettent à ces animaux de plonger longuement à de grandes profondeurs à la recherche de leur nourriture. Certains caractères hématologiques sont examinés. La vision est la source primordiale des informations sensorielles chez le phoque du Groenland. L'œil est adapté à la vision nocturne aussi bien qu'à la grande lumière, de sorte que l'acuité visuelle est excellente dans l'air comme dans l'eau. L'anatomie de l'oreille rappelle à certains égards celle des cétacés et celle des mammifères terrestres. Bien qu'elle semble adaptée à l'audition dans l'eau, elle est probablement de peu d'utilité pour le repérage par écho. On a enregistré et analysé un total de 15 phonations émises sous l'eau.

Le régime alimentaire de l'adulte est varié; il se compose surtout de poissons pélagiques et de crustacés pélagiques et benthiques. La consommation annuelle de nourriture de la population de l'Atlantique nord-ouest a été estimée à 2 millions de tonnes. La comparaison entre ce chiffre et l'accroissement pondéral annuel de la population indique une faible efficacité écologique. Les auteurs donnent quelques indications sur les soins à donner aux animaux en captivité, les besoins alimentaires, les problèmes physiologiques et les traitements à appliquer. Le *Contracaecum gadi* est le parasite le plus commun chez les phoques du Groenland; ce dernier est aussi l'hôte de prédilection du vers de la morue (*Terranova decipiens*) comme il est le plus important vecteur pinnipède de ce nématode dans le golfe du Saint-Laurent.

Extracto

La foca de Groenlandia, *Pagophilus groenlandicus*, se encuentra en el norte del Atlántico y el Mar Artico, desde Severnaya Zemlya hasta el este del archipiélago canadiense, dividida en tres poblaciones principales, que se desplazan a finales de primavera hacia el norte, donde se alimentan y crecen, y en invierno hacia el sur, a una zona bien precisa de cría y muda en los hielos marinos: las focas que se reproducen en el Mar Blanco transcurren el verano cerca del borde de los hielos en los Mares de Barents y Kara, la población del Mar de Groenlandia se reproduce en las aguas que rodean a Jan Mayen y emigra hacia el norte para alimentarse entre Spitzbergen y Groenlandia, y la población del noroeste del Pacífico se reproduce en el Golfo de San Lorenzo y frente a la costa sudoriental del Labrador y transcurre el verano entre el oeste de Groenlandia y la Bahía de Hudson. Sus poblaciones se estiman, respectivamente, en 600 000, 100 000 y menos de un millón de animales. Se presentan brevemente sus características externas y el color de su pelaje y se indican algunos aspectos característicos de su cráneo y dentición. La talla y peso medio de los machos y hembras adultos de estas focas son respectivamente 183 cm y 135 kg y 179 cm y unos 119,7 kg; los recién nacidos tienen por término medio 103 cm y pesan 11,8 kg. La edad de madurez sexual de las hembras varía según la población, con una media que quizás se encuentre próxima a los cinco años de edad; las noticias existentes dicen que los machos alcanzan la madurez sexual a los ocho años. La longevidad máxima supera los 30 años. Las fechas de alumbramiento difieren según las poblaciones, incluidos los dos grupos de reproductores del noroeste del Atlántico, pero en general los partos se producen entre finales de febrero y principios de marzo. La cópula tiene lugar unas dos semanas después del parto, tras lo cual se forman grupos de animales en muda durante el mes de abril; la gestación propiamente dicha dura unos 7,5 meses, tras un período de retraso de implantación de 11 semanas.

Se describe la anatomía visceral y se indican los pesos y dimensiones de algunos órganos de ejemplares jóvenes y adultos; sólo se dispone de descripciones anatómicas generales del sistema nervioso central de los fócidos, y la información disponible sobre *P. groenlandicus*, en concreto, es aún menor. Su compleja capacidad de adaptación morfológica y fisiológica, que se manifiesta especialmente en el sistema circulatorio, permite a esta especie hacer inmersiones prolongadas a grandes profundidades en busca de alimentos. Se examinan los índices sanguíneos. La visión es la fuente principal de información sensorial de la foca de Groenlandia: la adaptación del ojo tanto para la visión nocturna como para la visión con luz clara permite una excelente sensibilidad visual tanto en el aire como en el agua. La anatomía del oído de la foca de Groenlandia es análoga en algunos aspectos a la de los cetáceos y a la de los mamíferos terrestres; aunque parece estar adaptado a la audición bajo el agua, probablemente es poco útil para la orientación por ecos. Se han registrado y analizado en total 15 emisiones de sonidos debajo del agua.

La alimentación de las focas de Groenlandia adultas es muy variada y consiste principalmente en peces pelágicos y crustáceos pelágicos y bentónicos. El consumo anual de especies aptas para alimentación de la población del noroeste del Atlántico se ha calculado en dos millones de toneladas; comparando esta cifra con el aumento anual de la población resulta que su eficiencia ecológica es baja. Se dan datos resumidos sobre su manutención general, necesidades alimenticias, problemas fisiológicos y tratamiento en cautividad. El parásito más común de la foca de Groenlandia es *Contracaecum gadi*; la especie es también uno de los principales hospedantes del parásito del bacalao *Terranova decipiens* y es, entre los pinnípedos, el vector más importante de este nematodo en el Golfo de San Lorenzo.

K. Ronald
Mr P.J. Healey
College of Biological Science, University of Guelph, Guelph, Ontario N1G 2W1, Canada

H.D. Fisher
Department of Zoology, University of British Columbia, Vancouver 8, B.C., Canada

Genus and species

The harp seal was first named *Phoca groenlandica* by Fabricius in 1776. In 1777, however, Erxleben described this animal and is therefore usually credited with the name. *Pagophilus*, which means ice lover (from the Greek words "pagos" meaning ice and "philos" meaning loving), was introduced by Gray in 1850 (Scheffer, 1958). Other scientific names that have been given to this seal include *P. oceanica*, Lepechin; *Callocephalus oceanicus*, Lesson; *Phoca similunaris*, Boddaert; *P. dorsata*, Pallas; *P. mulleri*, Lesson; *Callocephalus groenlandicus*, F. Cuvier; *Phoca albicauda*, Desmarest; *P. desmarestii*, Lesson; *P. pilayi*, Lesson (Brown, 1868). Recently *Pagophilus* was reassigned to subgeneric rank within the inclusive genus "*Phoca*" based on the decision that it, along with *Pusa, Histriophoca* and *Phoca* (sensu stricto), lacked any unique cranial characters that allow generic recognition (Burns and Fay, 1970).

The harp seal has also been given many common names by various nationalities. Sealers refer to the newborn pups as "whitecoats", partly moulted pups as "ragged jackets", the fully moulted pups as "bedlamers" and the adults as Greenland seals, harp, saddle or saddlebacks. French Canadian names include "phoque du Groenland", "loup marin de glace", "loup marin coeur" and "brasseur" (Mansfield, 1967). The Eskimos generally call the seal "kairulik" (Mansfield, 1967) or in Pont Inlet "neitke" (Brown, 1868). Other names are saddleback (English), "svartsida" (Norwegian), "daelja", "daevok" and "aine" (Lapp), "svartsiden" (Danish), "blaudruselur" (Icelandic) and "atak" (Greenland) (Brown, 1868).

There are 3 major populations of harp seals, each with its own distinct breeding ground, one in the White Sea, one in the Greenland Sea north of Jan Mayen and a third utilizing the Gulf of St. Lawrence and the ice off the east coast of Newfoundland. Although there are no obvious morphological diffe-

rences between them, it is believed that the 3 populations rarely mix (Sergeant, 1973).

External characteristics and morphology

The smoothly tapering body of the harp seal is thick and round in the thoracic region. The tail is short, slightly dorso-ventrally flattened and tapers gradually until near the distal extremity. Distally, the limb becomes distinct only from the tarsus. The flippers are composed of five digits united by an interdigital web (Tarasoff *et al.*, 1972). Adult males have 46.8 ± 0.29 labial vibrissae and 3.0 ± 0.88 eye vibrissae (Shustov and Iablokov, 1967).

Coloration and integument

As the harp seal grows it moults (Ronald *et al.*, 1970) as well as changing its coat colour many times, and there is even variation in the coats of full grown adults (King, 1964). The variable aspects are the darkness of the general background, the darkness of the dorsal as compared to the ventral surface, the quantity of spots, their dimensions and hue and the presence of the harp shape (Smirnov, 1924).

The harp seal pups are born with a soft, curly yellowish coat, stained by the amniotic fluids. This turns white during the first 3 days probably as a result of the crystallization of the amniotic fluids. When they are 2 to 4 weeks old the white coat is shed to reveal a short-haired coat of grey, darker dorsally, lighter on the ventral surface and marked with darker grey and black spots (King, 1964). The term ragged jackets is used for pups with loose white hair. There is a great variation in the shade of the ground colour and the degree of spotting but all immatures show the same general pattern (King, 1964). The dorsal areas and upper sides of the yearling seals begin to lighten while the ventral surface darkens causing the spots to be less obvious. The general background of the 2 year coat is light ash grey and the spots are much paler than before. The 3 year old seals are a uniform light ash grey with markings becoming even less distinct. The 4 year olds or young adults may begin to show the mature adult pattern on their coats although this does not become fully developed, especially in the females, for some years after sexual maturity (Smirnov, 1924). Some males as they approach maturity show a very dark coloration. This "sooty" phase is usually lost at the next moult. The adult male harp seal is usually light whitish grey with a horse-shoe shaped black band running along the flanks and across the back. Its head, to just behind the eyes, is black. The face and "harp" of the adult female are paler and may be broken into spots (King, 1964).

The harp seal hair is made up of primary guard and secondary hairs (Tarasoff *et al.*, 1972) and is of some insulative value although the blubber plays an important part in this function (Frisch, Øritsland and Krog, 1974). When in the water the inner part of the woolly underfur retains a stagnant layer of water, 2 mm thick, while a barrier of 14 or 15 guard hairs flattens tightly over this underfur to provide some insulation (Frisch, Øritsland and Krog, 1974). The hair lengths of the coat decrease from the midback to the tarsus to the interdigital web (Tarasoff *et al.*, 1972).

Dimensions

Table 1 shows the minimum, maximum and average lengths of the different ages of harp seals in centimetres.

Using the formula:

$$\text{springtime fattening} = \frac{100 \times \text{maximal girth}}{\text{total length}}$$

the minimum, maximum and average values for girth apply. These are shown in Table 2.

Table 1. Lengths of harp seals (cm) (from Smirnov, 1924)

	Min.	Max.	Average
White coats	97	108	103
Moulting pups	90	123	110
Yearlings	126	148	131
2 year olds	138	155	144
3 year olds	158	170	160
Adult females	168	183	179
Adult males	171	190	183

Weights

The newborn harp seal pups weigh on the average about 11.8 kg at birth but increase their weight rapidly to about 22.8 kg within 4 to 5 days. Their weight continues to increase at the same rapid rate to a maximum of 33.3 kg at weaning, then declines to an average of 27.1 kg for the fully moulted pups. Adult male harp seals average 135 kg in weight and females about 119.7 kg (Sivertsen, 1941). There are circannial weight changes in all age groups, but approximately half their weight is in the hair, skin and blubber (Ronald and Steward, unpubl. MS).

Table 2. Girth of harp seals (cm) (from Smirnov, 1924)

	Min.	Max.	Average
White coats	67	81	75
Moulting pups	77	97	85
Yearlings	65	74	69
2 year olds	63	78	69
3 year olds	62	75	67
Adult females	63	71	67
Adult males	57	73	64

Distribution

P. groenlandicus inhabits the northern Atlantic and Arctic Oceans and ranges from northern Russia through Spitsbergen and Jan Mayen to Greenland then southwards to Newfoundland and north and east into Baffin Bay and Hudson Bay. It is found off the coasts of Europe and Asia from Severnaya Zemlya and Cape Chelyuskin to northern Norway, including the Kara Sea, Novaya Zemlya, Franz Josef Land, the White Sea, Spitsbergen and Jan Mayen , as well as on all the coasts of Greenland except the extreme north, and on Baffin Island, Southampton Island, Labrador, the east coast of Newfoundland and the Gulf of St. Lawrence (King, 1964). As a summer resident in the Arctic, it migrates as far north as Jones and Lancaster Sounds and Thule in northwest Greenland (Mansfield, 1967). The harp seal is not normally found far into Hudson Bay and rarely visits the northern coast of Iceland. Individuals are occasionally reported from Scotland and the Shetland Islands and even as far south as the Bristol Channel and the River Teign (King, 1964).

Migration

All 3 populations of harp seals migrate following the same general pattern of moving north in the summer and coming south for breeding in the winter to spring (King, 1964). During the summer the Jan Mayen or Greenland Sea population can be found in its most northerly feeding grounds between Spitsbergen and Greenland. These seals move south to Jan Mayen in the winter and pupping occurs on the ice in March. When the ice begins to drift south the adults mate, then move to the ice north of Jan Mayen where they moult during the month of April. By mid-May this herd has returned to the northern feeding grounds (King, 1964).

The White Sea population spends the summer period of intensive feeding and growth in the area close to the ice edge in the Barents and Kara Seas. At this time, groups are found at west Spitsbergen, at the north end of Novaya Zemlya, among the many islands of Franz Josef Land and in the Straits of Severnaya Zemlya. With the approach of the cold weather and the southward advancement of the ice border, the seals travel along the west and east coasts of Novaya Zemlya in search of food. In January and early February a rapid migration occurs to the funnel and basin of the White Sea where pupping takes place. The ice drift transports the new pups to the Barents Sea where they begin to feed independently (Popov, 1966). This passive migration northward occurs during lactation and for some time after weaning and brings the pups to the areas of rich food supply by April (Popov, 1970). The adults moult from mid-April to late May, then migrate north out of the White Sea (King, 1964).

During the summer, the northwest Atlantic population extends from Thule, Greenland and Jones Sound between Devon and Ellesmere Islands, south to northern Labrador waters and from Cape Farewell west to northwest and southeast Hudson Bay (Sergeant, 1965). The movement south out of the Canadian archipelago begins in late September and early October and by early November large numbers have passed Cape Chidley in northern Labrador (Mansfield, 1967), to reach the Strait of Belle Isle in late December (Sergeant, 1965). Only the adults and older immatures are involved in this migration. The remainder of the immatures move later, although some stay behind in west Greenland waters throughout the winter (Mansfield, 1967; Sergeant, 1965). In January, part of the population is thought to pass through the Strait of Belle Isle into the Gulf of St. Lawrence while the remainder moves down the east coast of Newfoundland. By late February the "Gulf" seals can be found on the ice to the north and west of the Magdalen Islands, while the "Front" seals are off the coast of Labrador

FIG. 1. – Front view of 10-20-year-old harp seal female moving up ice slope in the Gulf of St. Lawrence (photograph: D.M. Lavigne).

from Belle Isle to Hamilton Inlet (Mansfield, 1967). These 2 groups may or may not be separate although they are constant and distinct in location, numbers and breeding date (Sergeant, 1965, 1973). In early May, after breeding, the moulting adults begin to leave the Gulf and move north along the Labrador coast (Mansfield, 1967). The northward migration occurs by stages as a series of active northward movements followed by a drift southward on pack ice (Sergeant, 1970). This migration is deflected by ice towards the open water coast of west Greenland and most of the animals arrive in southwest Greenland around mid-June (Mansfield, 1967). After weaning, the young harp seal pups undergo 3 successive

FIG. 2. – Side view of female harp seal about to enter lead in ice of Gulf of St. Lawrence (photograph: D.M. Lavigne).

movements: an active move away from the ice where they were born to the ice edge where they can begin feeding, a passive drift with the current and an active migration northward. These young harp seals migrate alone, separately from and later than the adults and immatures (Sergeant, 1965).

The northward migration of the harp seals is extremely accurate, which is especially remarkable given the great distance that is covered. The Gulf of St. Lawrence herd migrates 4 000 km between 40°N, at its most southerly, and 70°N, at its most northerly (Sergeant, 1970). There is some understanding of how the harp seal achieves this migration. There is

evidence that the seal's eye is attuned to the blue green coloration of coastal waters (Lavigne and Ronald, 1975); it is also thought possible that the animal may orientate into the wind (Sergeant, 1970) or perhaps that its navigational capacity is innate since young animals find their way north in the absence of older animals who have travelled the route before, and since lone individuals may make crucial decisions involving orientation (Norris, 1966); or the animals may follow the temperature profile of the moving ice edge.

Tagging experiments have shown that young animals occasionally drift to other populations. The exchange eastward from Newfoundland is about 1 % while that eastward from Jan Mayen is about 10 %. No westward exchange has been observed (Sergeant, 1973).

Life history

Harp seals are born in late February and early March. At 2-4 weeks of age they lose their white coat and enter the water and are deserted by their mothers. After feeding for 4-6 weeks at the ice border they begin a northward migration and spend the summer feeding (Sergeant, 1965). Their southward migration begins in late fall when they return to the breeding grounds. Tagging results suggest that immatures return with great consistence to their place of birth (Sergeant, 1965). Immatures do not all appear from the north until early April, at which time they form moulting patches along with the adult males who have completed mating (Allen, 1975). Sexual maturity occurs at around 5½ years of age in females (Sergeant, 1966) and 8 years of age in males (King, 1964). In late February the females form whelping groups on the ice and give birth to their young a few days later. Breeding occurs in late March, following which the adult males move onto the ice to moult. The adult females join these moulting groups around April 20 to 27. Following the moult the harp seals begin their northward migration again. This cycle of migrating, whelping, mating, moulting and migrating occurs yearly for the adult seals until their death in their twenties or at the most thirties (Fisher, 1955).

Population dynamics

The numbers of seals at present in the 3 populations are thought to approximate: White Sea 600 000, Greenland Sea or West Ice 100 000, a drastic drop from 1 000 000 in 1956 (Dorofeev, 1956) — and Northwest Atlantic approximately 1 million. From 1924 to 1928 the White Sea population was composed of 20 % sexually mature males, 20 % sexually mature females, 40 % male and female immatures and 20 % pups less than 1 year old (Dorofeev, 1939a). During periods of heavy exploitation by man the harp seal populations show a compensatory increase in growth and maturation rates (Sergeant, 1973b). In order to ensure that the populations do not diminish, further catch quotas have been determined which the sealers must adhere to. The maximum sustainable yield (MSY) of white-coat pups is determined as a percentage of the annual production of pups within the herd. The 1974 production in the western North Atlantic was 267 000 pups. The MSY was believed to be 137 000 (Ronald, Capstick and Shortt, 1973). Unfortunately, accurate figures of censusing are only now being obtained by new techniques (Lavigne and Øritsland, 1974; Lavigne et al., 1974; Lavigne et al., 1976); this ultraviolet censusing technique will offer an absolute figure for management strategies.

Anatomical characteristics

SKULL, SKELETON AND TEETH

In the harp seal skull the nasals are long and narrow and taper gradually from the anterior to the posterior end. The posterior margin of the palate is round and the posterior palatine foramina lie in or anterior to the maxilla palatine suture (Doutt, 1942). The following are maximum, minimum and average measurements respectively in mm for different aspects of the skull: total length — 221, 190 and 204; width across the mastoids — 123.6, 107.5 and 114.6; interorbital width — 20.0, 8.3 and 11.7; length of the nasals — 52.6, 35.8 and 42.1; width of the nasals at the tip — 19.2, 14.6 and 16.6 (Doutt, 1942). The skulls of the adult

Greenland harp seal are described as being comparatively light, thin boned and smooth with the rostral part more shortened and the breadth at the auditory bullae on average being 54.7 % of the condylobasal length. The White Sea seal skulls are heavy, strong, and relatively thick boned with more conspicuous crests. The rostral part is more elongated with the breadth at the auditory bullae an average of 51.6 % of the condylobasal length (Smirnov, 1924).

The vertebral formula of *P. groenlandicus* is 7 cervical, 15 dorsal, 6 lumbar, 4 sacral and 13 caudal segments (Murie, 1870).

Harp seals are born with milk teeth which are separated from the jaw bones and are loose in the soft tissues of the gum, but never erupt. Sometimes the pups have molars at birth. The eruption of teeth begins immediately, in the order of molars, canines, premolars and incisors and the formation is very nearly complete by the time the seal begins to feed independently (Beloborodov, 1975). In the adult harp seal the teeth are comparatively small with the third molariform tooth the largest. There is 1 large central and 1 small posterior cusp. The anterior end of each ramus of the mandible is narrow and pointed and slopes backward to the lower margin of the ramus. The coronoid is long, slender and pointed. The mandibular teeth are small with 1 large central, 2 small posterior and 1 small anterior cusp (Doutt, 1942). The dental ormula of *P. groenlandicus* is i 3/2, c 1/1, pc 5/5 (King, 1964).

VISCERAL ANATOMY AND ORGAN WEIGHTS

The following is a description of the internal anatomy of a young male harp seal, 1.295 m long and weighing 18.6 kg. Its front flipper was 19 cm long, hind flipper 26.6 cm long. The viscera, including the tongue, weighed 2.325 kg, the brain 230.34 g. The heart had a well-defined bifid extremity with the cleft almost

1.2 cm deep. Its long diameter (root to apex) was 7.6 cm and its transverse diameter near the base was 9.5 cm. The right lung was without divisionary lobules while the left lung was partially divided into 2 lobes. Numerous and small dorsal papillae covered the terminally split tongue. The oesophagus was 40 cm long and the capacious stomach was cylindroid with a sharp pyloric bend, its long diameter being 23 cm. The small intestine from the pylorus to the caecum was 12.63 m long with an average diameter of 1.2 cm. The large intestine was 5.50 m long with a diameter of 1.9 cm at the caecal end and 1 of 3.1 cm at the rectum. The liver was deeply divided into 7 lobes; 5 large elongate taper-pointed hepatic divisions and 2 lobules. The kidneys were compound (Murie, 1870).

The lungs of the adult harp seal are oval in outline and correspond closely to the shape of the thoracic cage. Each compact lung has 3 lobes and they are topographically similar although the left lung is the larger and heavier (Tarasoff and Kooyman, 1973). The harp seal heart is dorso-ventrally flattened and has a blunt rounded apex. The midsagittal line lies midway between the axis of the 2 carotid arteries. The interior of the right ventricle follows the basic mammalian pattern. The configuration of the left ventricle, aorta and aortic valves is similar to that of terrestrial mammals. However, in the seal the valves are right, left and ventral in position rather than right, left and dorsal as in domestic animals (de Kleer, 1972). Macroscopically the harp seal kidney conforms to that of other pinnipeds, being composed of many renuli which are similar to unilobar kidneys. The respective length, width and depth of the pup kidneys (in centimetres) are, respectively: 7.6, 3.9 and 2.1, and the mean number of renuli is 136; in adults there are 12.2, 6.2 and 2.8, with the mean number of renuli being 136 (Dragert, Corey and Ronald, 1975).

The number of cartilaginous rings in the trachea is 42.7 ± 0.47 (Shustov and Iablokov, 1967). The length of the intestines exceeds the length of the body by as much as 10 (Murie,

1870) to 13.6 times (Shustov and Iablokov, 1967).

Weights of adult harp seal organs are: heart 0.33 ± 0.04 kg; liver 2.35 ± 0.22 kg; spleen 0.60 ± 0.16 kg (Shustov and Iablokov, 1967). The ratio of the total lung to body weight is 1.31 g/100 g (Tarasoff and Kooyman, 1973). Mean weights and volumes of kidneys for pups are 49.6 g and 47.3 ml and for adults 173.9 g and 163.1 ml. The difference in weight and volume between left and right adult kidneys is less than 11 % (Dragert, Corey and Ronald, 1975).

CENTRAL NERVOUS SYSTEM AND BRAIN WEIGHTS

Little work has been done on the central nervous system and brain of phocid seals (Dykes, 1973) and less still on harp seals. Some general descriptions of anatomy are available however. The bony tentorium between the cerebrum and the cerebellum is well developed and the brain is foreshortened and more spherical and convoluted than that of a land carnivore (Burne, 1909; Langworthy, Hesser and Kolb, 1938). The histological characteristics of the excito-motor cortex do not differ markedly from those of land animals. The auditory and trigeminal sensory areas are large and important (Alderson, Diamantopoulos and Downman, 1960). The entire trigeminal nuclear complex reaches its greatest size among carnivores in *Phoca*. The cerebellum and pons are large compared with other carnivores due to the well developed paraflocculus and the relatively enlarged flocculo nodular lobe. The lobus simplex and ansiform lobule are small (Harrison and King, 1965). The weight of the adult harp seal brain is about 442 g while that of a pup is around 243 g (Sacher and Staffeldt, 1974). The anatomy of the pituitary gland of *P. groenlandicus* indicates that this gland is similar in orientation to that of other types of mammals such as the ox (Leatherland and Ronald, pers. comm.).

Diving and swimming

Harp seals are noted for their ability to dive to great depths and stay submerged for long periods in their search for food. The mechanisms that allow them to do so are very complex. Harp seal skeletal muscle, in its adaptation for diving, is primarily geared for utilization of carbohydrates as the main fuel for muscular energy. The 2 most active locomotory muscles are the Ms *psoas* and *longissimus dorsi*, both equipped for sustained activity (George and Ronald, 1975). During a 10 to 18 min. dive the right ventricle of the heart becomes strikingly dilated with a large and systolic volume. This is an important compensatory mechanism in the maintenance of cardiac output and the external ventricular performance (Blix and Høl, 1973). When freely swimming the dive duration of the seal ranges from 0.2 to 10 min. and averages 2.5 min. (Øritsland and Ronald, 1975). During these spontaneous, short dives its heart rate drops to 41 % of its surface swimming rate of 147 beats per minute. There is a level of bradycardia associated with sinus arrythmia. Many short dives show an anticipatory bradycardia occurring 2.5 to 7.5 sec. before submergence. With trained dives there is a more profound bradycardia and less anticipation (Casson and Ronald, 1975). Along with the skeletal muscle and the heart, the circulatory system also undergoes changes during a dive. When a harp seal dives the blood flow in most of the veins, draining capillary beds, drops to virtually zero indicating a complete ischemia of many tissues (McCarter, 1973). This striking central distribution of the blood from the peripheral to the central capacitance vessels means that the blood flow in the posterior venae cavae is greatly reduced (Høl, Blix and Myhre, 1975).

The hepatic sinus expands in apparent response to an influx of blood from the splanchic reservoir. Blood is removed from the mesenteric veins by profound venoconstriction. At the initiation of the dive the caval sphincter appears to contract with the retained blood

277

engorging the hepatic sinus. The blood flow leaving the brain is maintained during the dive. Therefore, during the dive of a harp seal the blood is rerouted away from the heart-brain pattern to the posterior venae cavae (McCarter, 1973).

The principal means of propulsion when swimming is a sculling action of the flippers which provide alternate power strokes as they are moved from side to side with only 1 flipper extended at a time. The other main stroke is with the flippers pressed together beating rapidly in a horizontal plane. The forelimbs are used like paddles for slow forward propulsion. The seal uses its fore and/or hind limbs to maintain its position during inactive periods at the surface, when it adopts 2 main positions: head above water and body vertical, or prone, with the dorsal parts of the head and the mid-back exposed. The harp seal is capable of relatively high speeds for short periods of time in the water (Tarasoff *et al.*, 1972). Its highest speeds are attained when it is swimming ventro-dorsally.[1]

Behaviour

P. groenlandicus is gregarious, with only the very old males living alone or in small groups. It spends most of the year at sea and as well as being an agile and powerful swimmer, it can, when pressed, also move quickly over the ice. Its land movements are of 2 types: either a dragging motion using the claws of the front flippers or by a humping motion. Migrating harp seals are very active, leaping and cavorting in small groups and, sometimes, when near the surface, swimming on their backs. Southward migrant schools in January in open water are often observed swimming on their backs while close in to shore, where presumably they are able to see both the bottom

and their prey beneath them (Fisher, unpubl. MS). The harp seals use the large channels or leads in the ice to reach their breeding grounds, penetrating deep into the ice cover. These leads are also used for mounting the ice and so determine the haul-out sites, though these are also determined by the surface of the ice and its thickness. Seals prefer rough, hummocky ice at least 0.25 m thick. When pupping, females tend to stay close to a lead and near animals with pups of the same age (Dorofeev, 1939). The females appear to swim near their pups, visiting them at intervals to suckle. The greatest number of females are seen hauled out on the ice around 10:00 hrs and between 12:00 and 15:00 hrs (Terhune and Ronald, 1976, Terhune and Ronald, 1977). If the females are disturbed while in the water they do not defend their young but go out to sea. On land they will either "freeze" like the pups, defend their young vigorously or re-enter the water. When it is foggy or snowing the females tend to stay in the water but on clear, windless days they like to bask in the sun. Feeding occurs twice or 3 times a day after the female has found a comfortable place for herself and her pup (Popov, 1966).

Feeding habits

The harp seal feeds intensively in the winter and summer but eats less during the spring and autumn migrations and during spring whelping and moult (Mansfield, 1967; Sergeant, 1973a). Individual items are eaten by suction, with small fish taken in tail first. The pregnant females are partly segregated[2] in midwinter in the best feeding grounds, during and immediately following lactation. They tend to feed on decapods during these periods. In the spring all age classes are in the same

---

[1] Upside down.

---

[2] Segregated from non-lactating females and immature seals.

FIG. 3. – Harp seal pup approximately 3 hours old and still attached to placental membranes. Note the amniotic fluids are crystallizing on the white coated pup's hair (photograph: K. Ronald).

geographic area and feeding is stratified by size of organism and by depth (Sergeant, 1973a). The weaned young first feed in surface waters (Sergeant, 1973a) on small pelagic crustaceans such as the euphausid *Thysanoessa*, the amphipod *Anonyx*, and small fish such as polar cod *Boreogadus* (King, 1964). At the intermediate depth, immature harp seals eat capelin (*Mallotus villosus*) while the moulting adults are said to dive to depths of 150-200 m to feed on herring (*Clupea harengus*), cod (*Gadus morhua*) and other groundfish. Social beeding in pups, which may vary with the time of day (Lavigne *et al.*, 1975), begins at the age of 1 year as they shift from crustaceans to pelagic fish (Sergeant, 1973a).

The diet of the adult harp seal is varied, consisting of chiefly pelagic fish, especially capelin, and pelagic and benthic Crustacea (Euphausiacea, Mysidacea, Amphipoda, Decapoda) with smaller quantities of benthic fish (Sergeant, 1973a). The stomach of a seal was found to contain herring (Clupeidae), flatfish spp. including witch, *Glyptocephalus cynoglossus* and plaice, *Hippoglossoides platessoides*, redfish, *Sebastes marinus*, and the polychaete sea mouse, *Aphrodite linnaeus* (Myers, 1959).

A recent study showed that the annual weight of food items eaten by the Northwest Atlantic population of harp seals were: all organisms 2×10^6 t; capelin 0.5×10^6 t and herring 2×10^4 t. Predation on the capelin of eastern Canada occurs only in the winter when the pack ice is present (Sergeant, 1973a). The ecological efficiency of the harp seal, which is the weight of the annual increment of the population over the weight of the annual food eaten, has been said to be 0.005, a low figure (Sergeant, 1973a). Recently Lavigne *et al.*, (1976) have given further details on the metabolic activities of this species, and their figures can be used to indicate that the harp is a limited (240 000 t) feeder in waters that man fishes (Ronald, unpubl. MS). *

Social behaviour

Mating is believed to occur after the pups are weaned, which is about 2-3 weeks after their birth. It occurs on the ice and is often preceded by fights between males in which they use their teeth and flippers (Popov, 1966). It is also believed that copulation sometimes takes place in the water and that courtship involves fighting between male and female. The virgin females mate first followed by the whelped females (Popov, 1966). Each male is believed to mate with 1 (King, 1964) or more females (Merdsoy and Curtsinger, pers. comm.). Harp seals are at times very vocal, the many sounds they emit probably having a social and communicative function (Møhl, Ronald and Terhune, 1975; Terhune and Ronald, 1977).

When in the pack ice, seals keep natural openings in the ice free to be used as exit and breathing holes. These holes are 60 to 90 cm across at the top, widening towards the base of the ice. Harp seals, unlike Antarctic seals, use communal breathing holes, with as many as 40 seals in a pod around the hole.

Sound production, hearing and vision

A total of 15 underwater phonations have been recorded for the harp seal and grouped according to frequencies, harmonic structure and duration. They include sine waves, whistles, the morse call, trills, the gull's cry, chirps, warbles, dove cooing, the frequency shifting key, the distressed blackbird, the passerine call, the Tjok sound, grunts and squeaks (most common), knocking sounds and clicks (Møhl, Ronald and Terhune, 1975). It is only during whelping and breeding, with heavy concentrations of animals and the formation of breathing and access holes, that these calls are produced. No sounds are made during moult. 5 of the recorded sounds have been confirmed from captive harp seals. The only air call recorded from adult seals is produced by lactating females and sometimes by distressed captive females (Møhl, Ronald and Terhune, 1975), and captive males. It is similar to an "URRRH" sound. The pups cry or wail like a baby and this sound is probably used as a positive clue to allow the mother to find its young on the ice (Terhune and Ronald, 1970).

Hearing plays an important role in the harp seal's life for prey location, predator

---

* *Editor's note.* See "Pinniped bioenergetics", by Lavigne, Barchard, Innes and Øritsland.

avoidance and inter-animal communication (Terhune and Ronald, 1974), but is probably of little use in echolocation (Terhune and Ronald, 1976).

The anatomy of the harp seal ear is similar in some ways to that of cetaceans and also fulfills some of the requirements for bone conduction established in terrestrial mammals. The outer ear differs from that of land animals in the loss of pinna and the modifications of the auricular muscus to close the meatus. The loss of pinna is an adaptive modification to minimize hydrodynamic resistance and is also for effective directional hearing. Cavernous tissue and large, heavy ossicles are peculiarities of the seal's middle ear. These may be attributed to the seal's aquatic life or they may contribute to the general hearing mechanism in the animal. The harp seal inner ear is similar in anatomy to that of other mammals (Ramprashad, Corey and Ronald, 1973).

The underwater hearing abilities of *P. groenlandicus* are similar to those of humans in air (Terhune and Ronald, 1974). The harp seal freefield underwater audiogram, measured

from 0.76 to 100 kHz, has areas of increased sensitivity at 2 and 22.9 kHz. The lowest threshold is -37 db/μbar at 22.9 kHz. Above 64 kHz the threshold increases at a rate of 40 db/octave. The seal's ear is adapted to hearing underwater as is indicated by the decrease of sensitivity in air (Terhune and Ronald, 1972). The harp seal freefield air audiogram, measured from 1 to 32 kHz, has it lowest threshold at 4 kHz at a level of 29 db/0.0002 dynes/cm^2. Thus the harp seal's hearing in air is irregular and slightly insensitive with the air audiogram being generally flat. Critical ratios at 2 and 4 kHz are 10 % (Terhune and Ronald, 1971). The harp seal's audiogram is similar to that of other phocids (Terhune and Ronald, 1975).

Because seals utilize vision as a primary source of sensory information their eyes must be adapted for the two media in which they function, air and water. They must also be able to adjust to a variety of light conditions from the brightness of the sunlit snow to the underwater dimness (Lavigne *et al.*, 1976). The harp seal has large eyes with a sensitive retina and tapetum (Nagy and Ronald, 1970) and a widely dilated pupil. These characteristics are

FIG. 4. – Group of young and old mature harp seals in ice lead. Note the fifth seal from the right who is assuming a typical ventral dorsal swimming position (photograph: D.M. Lavigne).

281

typical of eyes adapted for nocturnal vision suggesting that the seal's eyes are adapted to dim light sensitivity (Lavigne and Ronald, 1972). The seal's rod-dominated retina is also adapted for increased sensitivity which allows for good underwater vision, especially at night. The presence of photoreceptors, which function optimally in bright light, permits effective vision during the day above ground (Lavigne, Bernholz and Ronald, 1977). Thus the harp seal possesses excellent visual sensitivity in both air and water (Lavigne and Ronald, 1972).

Not much is known about the other senses of seals. The small olfactory lobes of the brain and the reduced ethmoturbinals suggest that the sense of smell is not very acute. Although taste buds are definitely present this sense is probably not very subtle as these animals swallow their food whole. Seals vary in their awareness of touch and in their apparent liking of physical contact (Harrison and King, 1965). There is some evidence for the use of vibrissae as contact and receptor sensors (Dykes, 1973).

Captivity

When capturing harp seals the pups can be quietened by placing them in burlap bags. The adults can be captured in nylon nets by cutting off access to the breathing holes. They react either by fighting or "freezing" (Ronald et al., 1970).

Young seals should be kept in a small shallow tank with a dry resting area for the first few months. Adults should be kept in a tank that allows adequate swimming space – a minimum of 10 000 l per animal. The water, which may be fresh or sea water, should be temperature controlled to 10-12°C, and either flow through the tank once only or, if recirculated, pass through a gravel or sand and charcoal filter. When transferring seals it is advisable to put them in an empty tank which is then filled slowly. Routine maintenance of the tank consists of draining it once a week and scrubbing it with a detergent germicide. When it is refilled a benzalkonium chloride solution should be added in a concentration of 10 ppm. Ammonia-nitrogen tests should be conducted weekly to determine the efficiency of the charcoal-gravel filters. To prevent the seals' eyes from becoming opaque, sodium chloride can be added in a concentration of 3 %. The seals should be exposed to the salt solution for at least one hour before diluting the salt concentration by filling the tank with fresh water. As a preventative measure the seals can be vaccinated against erysipelas bacteria, 1 ml of vaccine, given intramuscularly, for pups and 2 ml for adults (Ronald et al., 1970).

To mark the seals for purposes of identification cryothermic branding with liquid nitrogen can be used. This requires a 4 to 5 second application to shaved skin (MacPherson and Penner, 1967). When it is necessary to restrain the seals a wheeled V-shaped trough lined with a sponge mattress with canvas straps or car safety belts can be used. Moult is characterized by the sloughing off of skin as well as hair and causes considerable stress in captivity. It is often accompanied by anorexia, opacity of the eye, lethargy and irritable behaviour. The complete moult varies with the individual from 10 to 90 days (Ronald et al., 1970). It has been found advisable not to stress the animal at these times as this can produce false chemical imbalance.*

Seal pups have difficulty learning to eat in captivity and often have to be force-fed. There are two methods. For the first few weeks, a food mixture can be administered by means of a stomach tube connected to a 2 l plexiglass syringe. The food mixture, which is given in doses of 0.5 l twice daily, should consist of homogenized herring flour, herring oil and tapwater plus cod liver oil, minerals and vitamins (Blix, Iversen and Pasche, 1973).

---

* *Editor's note.* Abnormal physiological condition of ionic imbalance.

FIG. 5. – Aerial view of early formation of harp seal herd on the ice in the Gulf of St. Lawrence. Picture taken from helicopter 100 m above the ice (photograph: K. Ronald).

The second method consists of force-feeding small pieces of herring 4 to 6 times a day. After the original period of 1 to 10 days the seals will be free feeding. The herring should be supplemented (Ronald *et al.*, 1970).

Harp seals respond to quiet handling and will soon learn to take larger and larger pieces of fish on their own. Throughout captivity the diet may remain mainly herring and later occasionally smelt (Ronald *et al.*, 1970). Only the best quality fish fit for human consumption should be used. Adult seals may consume 4 % to 7 % of their body weight daily (Geraci, 1975), while some captive seals have

283

been known to eat up to 10 % of their body weight per day (Ronald *et al.*, 1970). They can however be maintained on 1.5 %.

Hyponatremia occurs in captive harp seals and they need dietary salt supplementation. In freshwater, harp seals experience periods of electrolyte imbalance characterized by low plasma sodium concentrations. They can suffer mild to severe CNS disturbance and death. The cause of this condition is insufficient salt intake due to a low-salt diet in captivity with superimposed physiologic and pathologic stresses. Hyponatremia can be corrected with daily sodium chloride supplements of 3 gm/kg. This maintains the plasma electrolytes in normal or near normal condition (Geraci, 1972).

Captive harp seals which are maintained on herring and smelt, both high in thiaminase, develop thiamine deficiencies. If the diet is known to contain thiaminase, thiamine should be supplemented. The feeding of a wide variety of fish species will help to avoid or dilute high concentrations of thiaminase which might be present in any one of the species (Geraci, 1974).

It is often necessary to anaesthetise seals and this presents problems because of their adaptations for aquatic life. Intravenous or inhalation general anaesthesia sometimes re-

FIG. 6. – Adult female harp seal just prior to parturition (photograph: D.M. Lavigne).

sults in respiratory arrest. Thiopental sodium administration via the extra-dural vein is a rapid and dependable means of induction but rapid intubation and commencement of controlled ventilation are essential. Halothane/nitrous oxide induction is the safest and most controllable though slow. Halothane concentrations of 0.75 to 1.5 % are required (McDonnell, 1972). Valium may also be used prior to general anaesthetic (Gallivan and Ronald, unpubl. MS).

Reproduction

GESTATION

Gestation begins in June and lasts 7.5 months. The gap between this time and mating which occurs in March is accounted for by an 11 week delay in the implantation of the blastocyst (King, 1964). There is also evidence that the pregnant female can retain the foetus until suitable ice is available in February or even March (Ronald, unpubl. MS).

MATING

The seals mate about 2 weeks after parturition (King, 1964). It is only at this time, in a hunted herd, that males are seen in any number on the ice whereas males are commonly present both in the water and on the ice in a protected herd.

MATURITY

Sexual maturity in females or time of first ovulation occurs between 4 and 7 years of age with a mean age calculated as 4.0 years (Sergeant, 1973b) and 5.5 years (Sergeant, 1966). They bear their first young the following year and each successive year until they are at least 16 (King, 1964) and possibly until they are 30 years old. At Guelph 3 captive females have reached maturity in their fifth year. In the White Sea population the age of sexual maturity for females is 3 to 5 years, while in the Jan Mayen population it is 3 to 6 years with a mean age of 5 years. When a population approaches its maximum, sexual maturity is delayed and the fertility of older females is probably reduced. The 10 year old female seals dominate in whelping (Sergeant, 1966). Male harp seals are sexually mature by the age of 8 (King, 1964). They are however sexually active at 3 or younger. The maximum life span of *P. groenlandicus* is over 30 (Fisher, 1955; King, 1964). Both sexes are sexually active in their twenties (Fisher, 1955).

BREEDING SEASON

In the White Sea, pupping takes place from the end of January to the beginning of April but most of the young are born between February 20 and March 5. In Jan Mayen the breeding season is slightly later. After 2 weeks the adults mate, then move away to moult (King, 1964). In the Gulf, pups are born between February 25 and March 10; on the "Front" pupping is slightly later.

BIRTH

The pregnant females lie on the ice and the pups are born within 1.5 and 2.5 metres of one another. The breeding grounds are preferably some distance from the margins of the large ice fields in rough, hummocky ice which gives shelter to the pups (King, 1964). The pups are mostly born at night or early in the morning.

LACTATION

Suckling lasts 10 to 12 days during which time the female is said to feed very little (King, 1964), although there is considerable defeca-

Fig. 7. – Three day old whitecoat on the ice, Gulf of St. Lawrence, with female in the background (photograph: J.M. Terhune).

tion in the water (Merdsoy and Curtsinger, pers. comm.). Harp seal milk is greyish-white, with a strong fish-like odour and the consistency of thick cream. It is composed of 42.6 % fat, 10.4 % protein, 45.3 % water and 0.8 % ash (Sivertsen, 1941). The high fat content assists the rapid growth in pups during lactation. Lactose and ash contents are low compared to those of other mammals. About 27 % by volume of the fatty acid content of harp seal milk consists of fatty acids of chain lengths of 20 or more and about 69 % of the total fatty acids had one or more double bonds (Cook and Baker, 1969). Both the fat and protein contents decrease during suckling to a minimum on the

16th day postpartum, while the fatty acid composition of the fat follows no definite pattern of change during this period (Van Horn and Baker, 1971).

SIZE OF NEONATES

The whitecoat seals are between 97 and 108 cm long at birth (Smirnov, 1924) and weigh an average of 11.8 kg (Sivertsen, 1941). Little of this weight is blubber. At parturition, harp seal pups lack subcutaneous blubber, the wettable, infantile fur offers poor insulation and behavioural thermogenesis is not prominent. In order for them to survive a dramatic increase in heat production is necessary. Because these pups possess a layer of brown adipose tissue at birth it is thought that non-shivering thermogenesis through activated brown adipose tissue may help guard the animal from the cold (Grav, Blix and Pasche, 1974; Blix, Iversen and Pasche, 1973). The first feeding of milk is an important factor in the survival of the pup; any interference with normal life at this time could cause mortality.

Diseases

The most common symptoms of illness observed in captive harp seals are those of gastroenteritis. This consists of a general malaise with ocular opacity, anorexia and lethargy followed by emesis and diarrhoea (Ronald et al., 1970). In spite of a daily supplement of 100 mg thiamine/kg food, some captive seals still show signs of a vitamin B deficiency (Blix, Iversen and Pasche, 1973). The symptoms of this are shivering, anorexia and increasing lethargy (Ronald et al., 1970). This condition is invariably reversed within two days of an intramuscular injection of a vitamin B complex (12 mg thiamine chloride) (Blix, Iversen and Pasche, 1973). There are individual cases of captive seals developing a variety of illnesses. One had a gastric ulcer involving 60 % of the pyloric portion of the stomach. Another died from impaired thermoregulation caused by peritonitis and pleuritis from an infection of *Pasteurella multocida*. Polioencephalomalcia caused another death. Sometimes captive animals develop dry papules on their flippers which spread until the entire flipper is bare of hair, reddened and hot to touch (Ronald et al., 1970). *Staphyloccoccal granulomas* have been known to cause skin lesions in harp seals (Wilson and Long, 1970; Ronald et al., 1970). Infectious diseases caused by *Aeromonas* are found in pinnipeds. In one harp seal, aeromonads in the spleen, liver and intestines caused emaciation and inadequate feeding. Further examination showed very little content in the digestive tract, both sides of the heart dilated and the lungs oedematous and emphysematous (Dahle and Nordstoga, 1968). One captive *P. groenlandicus* suddenly developed severe and persistent tetanies and was given 1.2 g magnesium sulphate intramuscularly. After one more injection the next day the seal recovered fully. Convulsions never recurred after a daily supplement of 20 mg magnesium sulphate per kg body weight was added to its diet (Blix, Iversen and Pasche, 1973).

Blood values

Haemoglobin (Ronald, Foster and Johnson, 1969) and iron values (Vallyathan, George and Ronald, 1969) are, respectively, 21.80 ± 0.201 g/100 ml blood and 55.94 ± 0.48 mg/100 ml blood, considerably higher than those of other mammals, including man. Levels of glucose, 169.4 ± 2.27 mg/100 ml blood, total lipid, 854.4 ± 20.67 mg/100 ml blood, and total cholesterol, 242.2 ± 4.36 mg/100 ml blood, levels are also high. The levels of activity of the 3 enzymes involved in carbohydrate metabolism, amylase, aldolase and lactic dehydrogenase, are also higher than in other animals. LDH activity is particularly high. These blood properties reflect the pattern of metabolic adaptation to diving in the tissues of the harp seal, especially in its muscles. The low lipase (esterase) activity in seal blood indicates that fat is not the favoured metabolite for muscular energy (Vallyathan, George and Ronald, 1969).

A high erythrocyte number in March corresponds to the natural pupping and breeding periods. This count is depressed during moult. An initial increase in erythrocyte number occurs with development. A leucocyte count of over 12 000 cells/mm³ indicates an abnormal condition. The mean cell haemoglobin concentration of the harp seal is

287

unique, averaging 47.42 %. The high haemoglobin level enables the seal to carry greater quantities of oxygen than terrestrial species. A pH drop in January coincides with the southward migration to the breeding grounds while a maximum in March coincides with pupping and breeding. Individuals show a lower pH immediately preceding and during part of the moult. Decreases in erythrocytes, haemoglobin and haematocrit occur during moult (Ronald, Foster and Johnson, 1969). Erythrocyte, haematocrit and haemoglobin levels are maintained throughout life although cell volume and mean cell haemoglobin increase with age (Ronald, 1970; Geraci, 1971).

The following values for mercury, selenium and a number of biological parameters in blood were obtained (Geraci, 1971; Ronald, 1975).

Table 3. **Blood values of metals and biological parameters**

	Units	Pups	Adults
Total mercury	ppm.	0.16	0.19
Methyl mercury chloride CH_3HgCl	ppm.	0.20	0.13
Selenium	ppm.	1.21	1.45
Red cells	$mm^3 \times 10^6$	5.16	4.68
Mean cell volume (MCV)		109.02	125.96
Haematocrit vol %		56.7	59.5
Leucocyte differential counts % – neutrophils			
Plasma sodium levels	mEq/l	152.97	152.81
Plasma chloride levels	mEq/l	102.57	109.81
Plasma potassium levels	mEq/l	3.91	3.82
Blood urea nitrogen (BUN)	mg %	34.95	44.08
Lactic dehydrogenase	I.U.	151.29	118
Serum glutamic pyruvic transaminase (SGPT)	I.U.	7.81	38.82
Serum glutamic oxalacetic transaminase (SGOT)		71.86	39.3
Serum cholesterol	mg %	340.75	307.28
Serum protein	g %	6.49	7.53
Serum alkaline phosphatase	I.U.	34.5	10.0
Total bilirubin	mg %	0.34	0.38

Cytogenetics

The chromosome numbers of the harp seal are 2n = 32. Their karyotypic stability is attributed to a low level of reproduction (late sexual maturity and only one pup per year), good mobility and an environment without delimited niches. Because of the above characteristics, speciation caused by chromosal rearrangement is rare (Arnason, 1972).

Parasites

The commonest of the harp seal's parasites is the nematode *Contracaecum gadi* which is a normal part of the animal's parasitofauna (Ronald *et al.*, 1970). Specimens of *Contracaecum* sp. can be found in the oesophageal, gastric and small intestinal areas of the alimentary tract. This parasite may cause disease in the form of gastric lesions (Wilson and Stockdale, 1970). Another nematode is *Terranova decipiens* (= *Phocanema decipiens* = *Porrocaecum decipiens*). The gastro-intestinal tract is a site for the infection of nematodes where they become firmly attached to the intestinal mucosa (Montreuil and Ronald, 1957). *T. decipiens* also occurs in the stomach. Massive infestations of these nematodes do not seem to affect the harp seal's general health. After the seal's death some worms escape through its nostrils, mouth and rectum. Infection occurs after the consumption of fish containing the larvae which are thought to reach sexual maturity in the animal's digestive tract (Myers, 1960). Flatfish are the most common source of infection of *T. decipiens* (Myers, 1957a). *P. groenlandicus* plays some part in the dissemination of the nematode, *T. decipiens*, and has some importance as a definitive host (Ronald, Foster and Johnson, 1969). The harp seal is the host of preference as its internal temperature is ideal for the development of the parasite (Ronald, 1960). The harp seal is infective for the 4 months it spends in the Gulf. Its relative importance as a vector in the Gulf is 80.4 as compared to the harbour seal at 3.8 and the grey seal at 15.8 (Mansfield and Sergeant, 1965). The ascaroid parasites, *Contracaecum osculatum* (Rudolphi, 1802) and *Phocascaris* sp. are also found in the harp seal (Myers, 1957). The adult worms of these 3 are usually free in the lumen of the stomach and intestine but are sometimes attached to the mucosa (Myers, 1960). Other parasites of the harp seal are the Anasikinae, *Phocascaris phocae* (Ly-

ster, 1940), the cestodes, *Diphyllobothrium lanceolatum, D. cordatum, D. schistochilos* (King, 1964), *Anophryocephalus anophyrs* (Smith and Threlfall, 1973), the trematodes *Orthosplanchnus arcticus* (King, 1964) and *Pseudamphistomum truncatum* (Delyamure, 1955) and the Acanthocephala, *Corynosoma strumosum*. The anoplurans *Echinophthirus groenlandicus, E. phocae* (Kellogg and Ferris, 1915) and *E. horridus* are occasionally found on harp seals but in the case of the latter not on adults (Ronald *et al.*, 1970).

References

ALDERSON, A.M., E. DIAMANTOPOULOS and C.B.B.
1960   DOWNMAN, Auditory cortex of the seal (*Phoca vitulina*). *J. Anat.*, 94:506-11.

ALLEN, R.L., A life table for harp seals in the Northwest
1975   Atlantic. *Rapp. P.-V. Réun. CIEM*, 169:303-11.

ARNASON, U., The role of chromosomal rearrangement
1972   in mammalian speciation with special reference to Cetacea and Pinnipedia. *Hereditas*, 70:113-8.

BELOBORODOV, A.G., Postnatal dentition in the harp seal
1975   (*Pagophilus groenlandicus*). *Rapp. P.-V. Réun. CIEM*, 169:153-5.

BLIX, A.S. and R. HøL, Ventricular dilation in the diving
1973   seal. *Acta Physiol. Scand.*, 87:431-2.

BLIX, A.S., H.J. GRAV and K. RONALD, Brown adipose
1976   tissue and the significance of the venous plexuses in pinnipeds. *Acta Physiol. Scand.*, 94:133-5.

BLIX, A.S., J. IVERSEN and A. PASCHE, On the feeding and
1973   health of young hooded seals (*Cystophora cristata*) and harp seals (*Pagophilus groenlandicus*) in captivity. *Norw. J. Zool.*, 21:55-8.

BROWN, R., Notes on the history and geographical rela-
1868   tions of the Pinnipedia frequenting the Spitsbergen and Greenland Seas. *Proc. Zool. Soc. Lond. Commun. Sci. Corresp.*, 1868:405-40.

BURNE, R.H., Notes on the viscera of a walrus (*Odobenus rosmarus*). *Proc. Zool. Soc. Lond.*,
1909   1909:732-8.

BURNS, J.J. and F.H. FAY, Comparative morphology of
1970   the skull of the ribbon seal, *Histriophoca fasciata*, with remarks on systematics of Phocidae. *J. Zool.*, 161:363-94.

CASSON, D.M. and K. RONALD, The harp seal, *Pago-
1975   philus groenlandicus* (Erxleben, 1777). 14. Cardiac arrythmias. *Comp. Biochem. Physiol. (A Comp. Physiol.)*, 50:307-14.

COOK, H.W. and B.E. BAKER, Seal milk. 1. Harp seal
1969   (*Pagophilus groenlandicus*) milk: composition and pesticide residue content. *Can. J. Zool.*, 47:1129-32.

DAHLE, J.K. and K. NORDSTOGA, Identification of aero-
1968   monads in furred animals. *Acta Vet. Scand.*, 9:65-70.

DE KLEER, V.S., The anatomy of the heart and the
1972   electrocardiogram of *Pagophilus groenlandicus*. University of Guelph, M.Sc. Thesis.

DELYAMURE, S.L., Helminthofauna of marine mammals
1955   (ecology and phylogeny). Moscow, Akademii Nauk SSSR (in Russian). Translated by Israel Program for Scientific Translations, Jerusalem, IPST Cat. No. (18846):522 p. (1968).

DOROFEEV, S.V., The influence of ice conditions on the
1939   behaviour of harp seals. *Zool. Zh.*, 18:748-61 (in Russian).

—, The relationship of age groups in seals as indicative
1939a of the condition of the stock. *In* Volume in honour of scientific activity of N.M. Knipovich. Moscow, pp. 369-82 (in Russian).

—, Stocks of Greenland seals and their utilization.
1956 *Rybn. Khoz.*, 12:56-69. Issued also as *Transl. Ser. Fish. Res. Board Can.*, (113) (1957).

DOUTT, J.K., A review of the genus *Phoca. Ann. Carne-*
1942 *gie Mus.*, 29:61-125.

DRAGERT, J., S. COREY and K. RONALD, Anatomical as-
1975 pects of the kidney of the harp seal, *Pagophilus groenlandicus* (Erxleben, 1977). *Rapp. P.-V. Réun. CIEM*, 169:133-40.

DYKES, R.W., Characteristics of afferent fibers from the
1973 mystacial vibrissae of cats and seals. *Physiol. Can.*, 4:176.

FISHER, H.D., Utilization of Atlantic harp seal popula-
1955 tions. *Trans. N. Am. Wildl. Conf.*, 20:507-18.

FRISCH, J., N.A. ØRITSLAND and J. KROG, Insulation of
1974 furs in water. *Comp. Biochem. Physiol. (A Comp. Physiol.)*, 47:403-10.

GEORGE, J.C. and K. RONALD. Metabolic adaptation in
1975 pinniped skeletal muscle. *Rapp. P.-V. Réun. CIEM*, 169:432-6.

GERACI, J.R., Functional hematology of the harp seal
1971 *Pagophilus groenlandicus. Physiol. Zool.*, 44:162-70.

—, Hyponatremia and the need for dietary salt supple-
1972 ment in captive pinnipeds. *J. Am. Vet. Med. Assoc.*, 161:618-23.

—, Thiamine deficiency in seals and recommendations
1974 for its prevention. *J. Am. Vet. Med. Assoc.*, 165:801-3.

—, Pinniped nutrition. *Rapp. P.-V. Réun. CIEM*,
1975 169:312-23.

GRAV, H.J. and A.S. BLIX, Brown adipose tissue — a
1974 factor in the survival of harp seal pups *Vitam impendere vero. In* Depressed metabolism and cold thermogenesis, edited by L. Jansky. Prague, Academia Prague (in press).

GRAV, H.J., A.S. BLIX and A. PASCHE, How do seal pups
1974 survive birth in Arctic winter? *Acta Physiol. Scand.*, 92:427-9.

HARRISON, R.J. and J.E. KING, Marine mammals. Lon-
1965 don, Hutchinson.

HØL, R., A.S. BLIX and H.O. MYHRE, Selective redistri-
1975 bution of the blood volume in the diving seal (*Pagophilus groenlandicus*). *Rapp. P.-V. Réun. CIEM*, 169:423-31.

KELLOGG, V.L. and G.F. FERRIS, The Anoplura and
1915 Mallophaga of North American mammals. Stanford, Stanford University Publications, University Service in the Biological Sciences.

KING, J.E., Seals of the world. London, British Museum
1964 (Natural History) Trustees, 154 p.

LANGWORTHY, O.R., F.H. HESSER and E.C. KOLB, A
1938 physiological study of the cerebral cortex of the hair seal (*Phoca vitulina*). *J. Comp. Neurol.*, 68:351-69.

LAVIGNE, D.M. and N.A. ØRITSLAND, Ultraviolet pho-
1974 tography: a new application for remote sensing of mammals. *Can. J. Zool.*, 52:939-41.

LAVIGNE, D.M. and K. RONALD, The harp seal, *Pago-*
1972 *philus groenlandicus* (Erxleben, 1777). 23. Spectral sensitivity. *Can. J. Zool.*, 50: 1197-206.

—, Improved remote sensing technique for evaluating
1975 seal populations. ICES, C.M. 1975/N:12.

—, Pinniped visual pigments. *Comp. Biochem. Physiol.*
1975a *(B Comp. Biochem.)*, 52:325-9.

LAVIGNE, D.M., C.D. BERNHOLZ and K. RONALD, Func-
1977 tional aspects of the pinniped vision. *In* Functional anatomy of marine mammals, edited by R.J. Harrison. London, Academic Press, vol. 3:135-73.

LAVIGNE, D.M. *et al.*, Harp seal remote sensing. Uni-
1974 versity of Guelph (MS).

—, An aerial census of western Atlantic harp seals (*Pa-*
1976 *gophilus groenlandicus*) using ultraviolet photography. Paper presented to the Scientific Consultation on the Conservation and Management of Marine Mammals and their Environment, Bergen, Norway, 31 August-9 September 1976. Rome, FAO, ACMRR/MM/SC/33:9 p.

—, Pinniped bioenergetics. Paper presented to the
1976a Scientific Consultation on the Conservation and Management of Marine Mammals and

their Environment, Bergen, Norway, 31 August-9 September 1976. Rome, FAO, ACMRR/MM/SC/112:73 p.

LYSTER, L.L., Parasites of some Canadian sea mammals.
1940   Can. J. Res. (C Bot. Sci),, 18:395-409.

MacPHERSON, J.W. and P. PENNER, Animal identifica-
1967   tion. 2. Freeze branding of seals for laboratory identification. Can. J. Comp. Med., 31:275-6.

MANSFIELD, A.W., Seals of Arctic and eastern Canada.
1967   Bull. Fish. Res. Board Can., (137):35 p. Rev. of 1963 ed.

MANSFIELD, A.W. and D.E. SERGEANT, Relative impor-
1965   tance of seal species as vectors of codworm (Porrocaecum decipiens) in the Maritime Provinces. 10. Annu. Rep. Fish. Res. Board Can. Arct. Biol. Stn. Invest. Summ., (1964-65).

McCARTER, R.M., Venous circulation in Pagophilus
1973   groenlandicus. University of Guelph, M.Sc. Thesis.

McDONNELL, W., Anesthesia of the harp seal. J. Wildl.
1972   Dis., 2:287-95.

MØHL, B., K. RONALD and J. TERHUNE, Underwater calls
1975   of the harp seal, Pagophilus groenlandicus. Rapp. P.-V. Réun. CIEM, 169:533-43.

MONTREUIL, P.L.J. and K. RONALD, A preliminary note
1957   on the nematode parasites of seals in the Gulf of St. Lawrence. Can. J. Zool., 35:495.

MURIE, J., On Phoca groenlandica Muell., its modes of
1870   progression and its anatomy. Proc. Zool. Soc. Lond. Commun. Sci. Corresp., (1870):604-8.

MYERS, B.J., Ascaroid parasites of harp seals (Phoca
1957   groenlandica Erxleben) from the Magdalen Islands, Quebec. Can. J. Zool., 35:291-2.

−, Our present knowledge of Porrocaecum decipiens.
1957a   Quebec, MacDonald College, Institute of Parasitology, (MS).

−, The stomach contents of harp seals (Phoca groen-
1959   landica Erxleben) from Magdalen Islands, Quebec. Can. J. Zool., 37:378.

−, On the morphology and life history of Phocanema
1960   decipiens (Krabbe, 1878) Myers, 1959 (Nematoda: Anisakidae). Can. J. Zool., 38:331-44.

NAGY, A.R. and K. RONALD, The harp seal, Pagophilus

1970   groenlandicus (Erxleben, 1977). 6. Structure of retina. Can. J. Zool., 48:367-70.

NORRIS, K.S., Some observations on the migration and
1966   orientation of marine mammals. Proc. Annu. Biol. Colloq., 27:101-25.

ØRITSLAND, N.A. and K. RONALD, Energetics in the free
1975   diving seal. Rapp. P.-V. Réun. CIEM, 169:451-4.

POPOV, L.A., On an ice floe with the harp seals: ice drift
1966   of biologists in the White Sea. Priroda, 9:93-101. Issued also as Transl. Ser. Fish. Res. Board Can., (814) (1967).

−, Soviet tagging of harp and hooded seals in the North
1970   Atlantic. Fiskeridir. Skr. (Havunders.), (16):1-9.

RAMPRASHAD, F., S. COREY and K. RONALD, Anatomy of
1973   the seal's ear (Pagophilus groenlandicus) (Erxleben, 1977). In Functional anatomy of marine mammals, edited by R.J. Harrison. London, Academic Press, vol. 1:264-305.

RONALD, K., The effects of physical stimuli on the larva
1960   stage of Terranova decipiens (Krabbe, 1878) (Nematoda: Anisakidae). 1. Temperature. Can. J. Zool., 38:623-42.

−, Physical blood properties of neonatal and mature
1970   harp seals. ICES, C.M., Mar. Mamm. Comm., 1970/N: 5, 4 p.

−, The toxicity of methyl mercury to the harp seal.
1975   Report to Halifax Laboratory Fisheries and Marine Services, Environment Canada, Contrib. (717831).

RONALD, K. and C.K. CAPSTICK, Harp seal survival as
1975   predicted by a modification of Allen's model. ICNAF Res. Doc. 1975/12/141:35 p.

RONALD, K., C.K. CAPSTICK and J. SHORTT, Effect of
1973   alternative harp seal crops on populations 1974-1993. Report to Committee on Seals and Sealing, Ottawa.

RONALD, K., M.E. FOSTER and E. JOHNSON, The harp
1969   seal, Pagophilus groenlandicus (Erxleben, 1777). 2. Physical blood properties. Can. J. Zool., 47:461-8.

RONALD, K. et al., The harp seal, Pagophilus groenlan-
1970   dicus (Erxleben, 1777). 1. Methods of han-

291

dling, moult, and diseases in captivity. *Can. J. Zool.*, 48:1035-40.

RUDOLPHI, C.A., Fortsetzung der Beobachtungen über
1802   die Eingeweide Wuermer. *Arch. Zool. Zoot.*,
         2:1-67.

SACHER, G.A. and E.F. STAFFELDT, Relation of gestation
1974   time to brain weight for placental mammals:
         implications for the theory of vertebrate
         growth. *Am. Nat.*, 108(968):493-615.

SCHEFFER, V.B., Seals, sea lions and walruses: a review
1958   of the Pinnipedia. Stanford, Calif., Stanford
         University Press, 179 p.

SERGEANT, D.E., Migrations of harp seals *Pagophilus*
1965   *groenlandicus* (Erxleben) in the Northwest
         Atlantic. *J. Fish. Res. Board Can.*, 22(2):
         433-64.

–, Reproductive rates of harp seals, *Pagophilus groen-*
1966   *landicus* (Erxleben). *J. Fish. Res. Board Can.*,
         23(5):757-66.

–, Migration and orientation in harp seals. *In* Pro-
1970   ceedings of the 7th Annual Conference on
         Biological Sonar and Diving Mammals, 23-24
         Oct., 1970, Stanford Research Institute, Bio-
         logical Sonar Laboratory. Menlo Park, Calif.,
         pp. 123-31.

–, Transatlantic migration of a harp seal, *Pagophilus*
1973   *groenlandicus*. *J. Fish. Res. Board Can.*,
         30(1):124-5.

–, Feeding, growth and productivity of Northwest At-
1973a   lantic harp seals (*Pagophilus groenlandicus*). *J.
         Fish. Res. Board Can.*, 30(1):17-29.

–, Environment and reproduction in seals. *J. Reprod.*
1973b   *Fertil.*, (Suppl.), 19:555-61.

SHUSTOV, A.P. and A.V. IABLOKOV, Comparative mor-
1967   phological characteristics of the harp and rib-
         bon seals. *Tr. Poliarn. Nauchno-Issled.
         Proektn. Inst. Morsk. Rybn. Khoz. Okeanogr.*,
         21:51-9. Issued also as *Transl. Ser. Fish. Res.
         Board Can.*, (1084) (1968).

SIVERTSEN, E., On the biology of the harp seal, *Phoca*
1941   *groenlandica* Erxl., investigations carried out
         in the White Sea 1925-1937. *Hvalraad Skr.*,
         (26):166 p.

SMIRNOV, N.A., On the eastern harp seal *Phoca (Pago-*

1924   *phoca) groenlandica*. *Tromso Mus. Aarsh.*,
         47:3-11.

SMITH, F.R. and W. THRELFALL, Helminths of some
1973   mammals from Newfoundland. *Am. Midl.
         Nat.*, 90:215-8.

TARASOFF, F.J. and F.L. KOOYMAN, Observations on the
1973   anatomy of the respiratory system of the river
         otter, sea otter, and harp seal. 1. The topogra-
         phy, weight, and measurements of the lungs.
         Can. J. Zool., 51:163-70.

TARASOFF, F.J., *et al.*, Locomotory patterns and external
1972   morphology of the river otter, sea otter and
         harp seal (Mammalia). *Can. J. Zool.*,
         50:915-29.

TERHUNE, J.M. and K. RONALD, The audiogram and
1970   calls of the harp seal (*Pagophilus groenlandi-
         cus*) in air. *In* Proceedings of the 7th Annual
         Conference on Biological Sonar and Diving
         Mammals, 23-24 Oct., 1970, Stanford Re-
         search Institute, Biological Sona Laboratory.
         Menlo Park, Calif., pp. 133-43.

–, The harp seal, *Pagophilus groenlandicus* (Erxleben,
1971   1777). 10. The air audiogram. *Can. J. Zool.*,
         49:385-90.

–, The harp seal, *Pagophilus groenlandicus* (Erxleben,
1972   1777). 13. The underwater audiogram. *Can. J.
         Zool.*, 50:565-9.

–, Underwater hearing of phocid seals. ICES, C.M.,
1974   Mar. Mamm. Comm., 1974/N:5:9 p.

–, Underwater hearing sensitivity of ringed seals (*Pusa*
1975   *hispida*). *Can. J. Zool.*, 53:227-31.

–, Masked hearing thresholds of marine mammals. *J.*
1975a   *Acoust. Soc. Am.*, 58(2):515-6.

–, Examining harp seal behavioural patterns via their
1976   underwater vocalizations. *Appl. Ann. Ethol.*,
         2:261-4.

–, Influence of boat noise on the vocal activity of harp
1977   seals (*Pagophilus groenlandicus*). ICES, C.M.,
         Mar. Mamm. Comm., 1977/N:7:9 p.

VALLYATHAN, N.V., J.C. GEORGE and K. RONALD, The
1969   harp seal, *Pagophilus groenlandicus* (Erxleben,
         1777). 5. Levels of haemoglobin, iron, certain
         metabolites and enzymes in the blood. *Can. J.
         Zool.*, 47:1193-7.

VAN HORN, D.R. and B.E. BAKER, Seal milk. 2. Harp seal
1971   (*Pagophilus groenlandicus*) milk: effects of
        stage of lactation on the composition of the
        milk. *Can. J. Zool.*, 49:1085-8.

WILSON, T.M. and J.R. LONG, The harp seal, *Pagophilus*
1970   *groenlandicus* (Erxleben, 1777). 12. *Staphy-*

loccoccal granulomas (Botryomycosis) in harp
seals. *J. Wildl. Dis.*, 6:155-9.

WILSON, T.M. and P.H. STOCKDALE, The harp seal, *Pa-*
1970   *gophilus groenlandicus* (Erxleben, 1777). 11.
        Contracaecum sp. infestation in a harp seal. *J.*
        Wildl. Dis., 6:152-4.

AN AERIAL CENSUS OF WESTERN ATLANTIC HARP SEALS (*PAGOPHILUS GROENLANDICUS*) USING ULTRAVIOLET PHOTOGRAPHY

D.M. Lavigne, S. Innes, K. Kalpakis and K. Ronald

Abstract

Annual harp seal, *Pagophilus groenlandicus*, production in March 1975 in the western North Atlantic was estimated by an aerial census, using ultraviolet photography for low altitude sampling, at between 126 000 and 158 000 seals, with maximum estimates of 197 000 and 258 000, respectively. Of these, approximately one-third are thought to have been produced in the Gulf of St. Lawrence and two-thirds on the Front off the east coast of Newfoundland. Sampling problems associated with the uneven distribution of harp seals and their pups on the whelping grounds are discussed, and the census results are compared to the preliminary 1975 sealing statistics.

The above estimation suggests that western North Atlantic harp seals have continued to decline in abundance in recent years to between 630 000 and 790 000 animals in 1975. The present trend in annual production suggests that if current management policies are not changed, production will continue to decline and the population will be severely threatened before the end of this century.

Résumé

La production annuelle de phoques du Groenland, *Pagophilus groenlandicus*, dans l'Atlantique ouest a été estimée à 126 000-158 000 exemplaires en mars 1975 au cours d'un recensement aérien utilisant la photographie aux rayons ultraviolets pour un échantillonnage à basse altitude, avec des estimations maximales de 197 000 et 258 000, respectivement. Environ un tiers de la production se situait dans le golfe du Saint-Laurent et deux tiers sur la façade orientale de Terre-Neuve. Les auteurs décrivent les problèmes d'échantillonnage liés à la distribution inégale des phoques du Groenland et de leurs veaux sur les terrains de parturition. Les résultats du recensement sont comparés aux statistiques préliminaires de 1975 sur la chasse aux phoques.

L'estimation ci-dessus donne à penser que les stocks de *P. groenlandicus* du secteur ouest de l'Atlantique nord ont continué à fléchir ces dernières années, pour atteindre un niveau de 630 000 à 790 000 en 1970. La tendance actuelle de la production annuelle permet de dire que, si les politiques actuelles de gestion ne sont pas changées, la production continuera à fléchir et la population sera gravement menacée avant la fin du siècle.

Extracto

En un censo aéreo hecho en marzo de 1975, con fotografía con rayos ultravioleta para el muestreo a poca altura, se estimó la producción anual de foca de Groenlandia (*Pagophilus groenlandicus*) en el oeste del Atlántico entre 126 000 y 158 000 animales, con estimaciones máximas de 197 000 y 258 000, respectivamente. Se calcula que, de ese número, un tercio aproximadamente procede del Golfo de San Lorenzo, y dos tercios de la costa oriental de Terranova. Se examinan los problemas que plantea el muestreo debido a la desigual distribución de estas focas y sus cachorros en las zonas de cría, y se comparan los resultados de los censos con las estadísticas preliminares de caza de 1975.

Las estimaciones hechas sugieren que la población de *P. groenlandicus* del noroeste del Atlántico ha seguido disminuyendo en los últimos años, descendiendo en 1975 a cifras del orden de 630 000-790 000 animales. Extrapolando la trayectoria actual de la producción se llega a la conclusión de que, si no se modifican las políticas actuales de regulación, la producción seguirá disminuyendo y la población se encontrará gravemente amenazada antes de finales de este siglo.

D.M. Lavigne
College of Biological Science, University of Guelph, Guelph, Ontario N1G 2W1, Canada

S. Innes
Department of Zoology, University of Kansas, Lawrence, Kansas 66044, USA

K. Kalpakis
Department of Zoology, University of Guelph, Guelph, Ontario N1G 2W1, Canada

K. Ronald
College of Biological Science, University of Guelph, Guelph, Ontario N1G 2W1, Canada

Introduction

Ultraviolet photography has been introduced as a new technique for detecting certain white animals, including the whitecoated offspring of harp seals (*Pagophilus groenlandicus*) against a white background of ice or snow (Lavigne and Øritsland, 1974, 1974a). Extensive field experiments conducted in the Gulf of St. Lawrence in March 1974 suggested that aerial surveys of harp seals on their whelping grounds (Lavigne *et al.*, 1974) using this sensor might significantly improve population estimates, and specifically estimates of annual production.

In March 1975, further research was conducted on whelping harp seals, both in the Gulf of St. Lawrence and on the Front, off the coast of Labrador. The primary objective was to design a useful, feasible and precise sampling technique for routine use in aerial surveys of harp seals. A preliminary outline of this research has been prepared (Lavigne and Ronald, 1975) and a more detailed report has been produced (Lavigne *et al.*, 1975). This paper briefly summarizes only those results relevant to obtaining the best available estimate, from our aerial survey data, for production of western Atlantic harp seals in March 1975.

Methods

Four experimental remote sensing flights were conducted, 2 over the whelping herd in the Gulf of St. Lawrence west of the Magdalen Islands on 10 and 17 March 1975, and 2 over harp seals whelping on the Front off the east coast of Newfoundland on 11 and 15 March 1975. The latter group was divided into a northern patch and a smaller southern patch. Attempts were made to obtain total coverage of these areas by flying parallel grid lines over the herd at an altitude of 1 220 m

(4 000 ft) guided by an inertial navigation system on board the remote sensing aircraft. A 9 × 9 in (23 × 23 cm) aerial survey camera and black and white photography (Kodak 2402 aerial film) were used, since ultraviolet photography in this large format is not presently available. Subsequent sampling was conducted at random areas over the herd at an altitude of 305 m (1 000 ft) using ultraviolet photography in 70-mm format (Lavigne and Øritsland, 1974). The rationale was that the 1 220-m imagery should provide a second estimate of herd area, the first being made by observers in the field, as well as a direct count of the number of adult seals on the ice at the time of the flight. The sample obtained with ultraviolet photography at a lower altitude would give numbers of adults and pups which could then be extrapolated to the area of the herd. The estimate of adults would then be compared with the direct count of adults to evaluate the accuracy of the sampling technique. If satisfactory, the samples could then be used to estimate the numbers of white-coated pups on the ice (annual production) and, in turn, lead to a direct extrapolation of the number of breeding females in the population.

The data obtained from the 1975 imagery were analysed using a variety of sampling techniques (Lavigne and Ronald, 1975; Lavigne *et al.*, 1975). These included simple random sampling (Mendenhall, Ott and Schaeffer, 1971; Som, 1973) and ratio estimation (Snedecor and Cochran, 1967), the latter utilizing adult/pup ratios obtained from the 305-m imagery.

Results

Analysis of the imagery revealed that total coverage at 1 220 m was not obtained for the Front herd on either day. Herd area determinations made in the field (T. Curran, pers. comm.; Bergflødt, 1975) were thus used in calculations. Replicate coverage of Front and Gulf herds was not obtained, primarily because atmospheric conditions causing backscattering rendered some of the ultraviolet imagery at 305 m unusable. Somewhat fortuitously, however, satisfactory single coverage was obtained for each herd. Our calculations are thus based on aerial survey data from the Gulf of St. Lawrence on 10 March, approximately 3 days after pupping had been completed; from the north patch on the Front on 11 March when pupping was about 80 % completed (T. Curran, pers. comm.); and from the south patch on 15 March again when pupping was virtually complete (T. Curran, pers. comm.). These data were used in estimating annual production in 1975. The results of estimates obtained using ratio estimation techniques, and considered to be the best estimates available from our data (Lavigne et al.,

1975) are summarized in Table 1. The best estimate for annual production of harp seals in the western Atlantic in March 1975 was 125 958 with 37 % of these being born in the Gulf of St. Lawrence west of the Magdalen Islands. The upper confidence limit (p. < 0.05) on this estimate was 197 233. These calculations (Table 1) were based on the herd area estimates obtained from the aerial imagery from the Gulf on 10 March, from the mean herd area estimated by T. Curran (pers. comm.) and Bergflødt (1975) for the north patch on 11 March, and from the single estimate of herd area for the south patch on 15 March (T. Curran, pers. comm.).

The largest estimate of production provided by our data, using the area estimate of Bergflødt (1975) for the north patch on 11 March, was 157 900 (Table 1).

Table 1. Estimate of production of harp seals (*Pagophilus groenlandicus*) in the western Atlantic in March 1975

Location	Date	Herd area km²	Pup production f̂ ±95 % CI	Maximum estimate of production	
Gulf	10 March	519[1]	46 300 ± 5 158	51 458	
Front (N)	11 March	208[2]	53 583 ± 47 648	101 231	
Front (S)	15 March	52[3]	26 075 ± 18 469	44 544	145 775
			125 958	197 233	

[1] Herd area estimated from aerial imagery obtained at 1 220 m.
[2] Mean estimate of herd area based on the independent estimates of 2 observers.
[3] Herd area estimated by 1 observer.

Note:

If the larger of the 2 estimates of herd area for the north patch on the Front on 11 March (332 km²) is used in calculation, the mean estimate of total production becomes 157 900; the maximum estimate of production becomes 257 602 (see below).

Location	Date	Herd area	Pup production	Maximum estimate	
Gulf	10 March	519[1]	46 300 ± 5 158	51 458	
Front (N)	11 March	332	85 525 ± 76 075	161 600	
Front (S)	11 March	52[3]	26 075 ± 18 469	44 544	206 144
			157 900		

Discussion

Harp seals and their pups are distributed in a clumped or contiguous manner on their whelping grounds (Lavigne *et al.*, 1975). This causes certain difficulties when conducting an aerial census, since there are large areas of ice within the area of the herd which are devoid of seals, and other areas where the seals occur in dense concentrations. Such a non-random distribution is quite typical for gregarious species (Woolf, 1968), and the harp seal is gregarious (Mansfield, 1967) especially during the whelping and breeding seasons. In addition, habitat heterogeneity may also contribute to such distributions of animals (Poole, 1974) and this undoubtedly applies to the harp seal, which may actively seek out certain ice conditions for whelping, and which tends to congregate along the edge of open leads, and around breathing holes in the ice.

The problems associated with sampling a population distributed in this manner became readily apparent during initial calculations of production for the Gulf of St. Lawrence (Lavigne and Ronald, 1975). For example, in the Gulf of St. Lawrence on 10 March 1975, 35 418 adult harp seals were counted on the ice at the time of the flight on the 1 220-m imagery. This provided a reference for extrapolations from the samples obtained at 305 m using ultraviolet photography. On the basis of a simple random sample (Mendenhall, Ott and Scheaffer, 1971) the number of adults on the ice, predicted from 69 samples, was about 38 000 or within about 8 % of the direct count (Lavigne and Ronald, 1975). However, 95 % confidence limits on this estimate ranged from 12 727 to 63 934. These wide confidence limits are due to the large variances associated with sampling the contiguous distributions of seals on the ice and to the relatively small number of samples obtained. It has been shown that the means become normally distributed and the variances are greatly reduced simply by increasing the sample size (Lavigne and Ronald, 1975).

An alternative method which may prove to be more satisfactory is that of ratio estimation (Snedecor and Cochran, 1967). It has recently been observed that adult/pup ratios in our samples are rather normally distributed. This means that smaller sample sizes may be used to obtain precise estimates of production as long as an accurate estimate of the total number of adults on the ice, such as that provided by our 1 220 m imagery, is available. Ratio estimation was selected as the appropriate analysis to provide our best estimate of annual production of western Atlantic harp seals because it was the most powerful estimator. Estimates from the Front still have wide confidence limits (Table 1), primarily because of the small number of samples obtained at 305 m (Lavigne *et al.*, 1975). This emphasizes the need for larger samples in future aerial surveys. With more accurate estimates of herd area, a relatively minor problem to overcome, it would appear that aerial censusing, incorporating ultra-violet photography as the primary sensor for low altitude sampling, may provide very precise estimates of production for whelping harp seals, overcoming most of the difficulties encountered in the past (Sergeant, 1975).

The estimated number of harp seals produced in the western Atlantic in March 1975, between 126 000 and 158 000, is considerably lower than recent predictions of annual production made by other investigators. Using Sergeant's (1975) suggestion that the population other than young is between 4 to 5 times the number of young born, it follows that the number of harp seals in the western Atlantic may now total between about 630 000 and 790 000 animals. The distribution of 37 % of western Atlantic harp seals breeding in the Gulf and 63 % on the Front is in general agreement with the 1:2 ratio observed in the past (Sergeant, 1975).

It might be suggested that the photographic census did not cover all the whelping harp seals in the western Atlantic. However, this is not considered to be a large source of error in our estimates. The two concentrated patches

299

located on the Front by Canadian (T. Curran, pers. comm.) and Norwegian (Bergflødt, 1975) observers, and Canadian and Norwegian sealers, were surveyed. Harp seals in the Gulf of St. Lawrence near the Magdalen Islands were located in one concentrated area at the time of our surveys and were thoroughly covered in our census. To the best of our knowledge, only 2 small groups of seals were not included in our coverage or our estimates. The so-called Mecatina patch comprising some 3 000-4 000 seals, and a second group of old harps and bedlamers without pups were located by T. Curran (pers. comm.). Despite many searches by various experienced observers over wide areas, no other concentrations of whelping harp seals were reported to us.

Subsequent to the analysis of aerial census data and the preparation of a report (Lavigne et al., 1975) the preliminary sealing statistics from the 1975 hunt were obtained (Fisheries and Marine Service, Environment Canada, 1975 Sealing Statistics (Preliminary); Sergeant, pers. comm.). In total, some 140 629 harp seals born in the western Atlantic in March 1975, were taken by Canadian and Norwegian sealers, operating primarily on the Front. In addition, 33 435 harp seals aged 1 and older were also landed. The total kill for 1975, 174 064, is thus higher than the much publicized limit of 150 000 seals, because of the very successful hunt by landsmen (53 240).

The catch of pups thus provided a minimum estimate for production in the western Atlantic in 1975 (140 629). All Norwegian catches occurred on the Front (51 618). Although Canadian Sealing statistics are given in relation to the place of origin of the sealers, and do not provide detailed information on where the seals were killed, it would appear that some 7 550 pups were killed in the Gulf and the remainder (81 461) on the Front. This implies that 133 079 pups were taken on the Front. Although it is usually assumed that pups killed on the Front were born there, the possibility of catching Gulf animals as beaters on the Front or at least off the coast of Newfoundland cannot be ignored. Since this only involves some

38 750 animals, and lacking data to support or refute this hypothesis, we will also assume that all animals taken on the Front were, in fact, produced there.

Our best estimate of pup production on the Front (79 685) is obviously an underestimate of the actual production. However, if the upper confidence limits on the estimates of production for the north and south patches on the Front are taken as maximum estimates, production on the Front may have been as high as 145 775. This figure not only accounts for the number of pups killed, but allows for the escapement of 12 696 seals. If only Bergflødt's (1975) data are used to estimate the area of the north patch on 11 March 1975, the estimate of production on the Front becomes 111 600, again lower than the kill. However, maximum production may have been as high as 206 144 based on the upper confidence limits for each patch, and this allows for an escapement of as many as 73 065 seals from the Front. The survey results are thus reasonable, despite the admitted shortcomings, and still represent the best available direct estimate of production ever obtained from an aerial survey.

Taking the upper confidence intervals as maximum estimates of production for each of the 3 patches − the north and south patches on the Front, and the 1 patch in the Gulf − total production in the western Atlantic in March 1975 may have been as high as 197 233-257 602 animals. These figures, however, represent maximum estimates. In reality production probably did not exceed 200 000 and may have been considerably lower.

The results from the Gulf of St. Lawrence (46 300 ± 5 158) suggest that problems of sampling harp seal whelping patches can be overcome in the future, assuming continued support, and suitable weather and ice conditions.

Previous estimates of annual production are summarized in Fig 1. In the early fifties Fisher (1955) estimated that western Atlantic stocks of harp seals numbered about 3.3 mil-

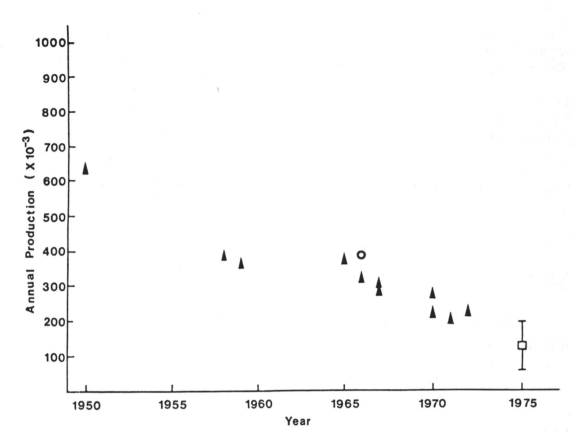

Fig. 1. – Annual production of western Atlantic harp seals, *Pagophilus groenlandicus*, estimated by aerial survey, capture-recapture experiments, greatest catch, and catch and survival estimates (Sergeant 1975a) ▲, by survival estimates (Benjaminsen and Øritsland 1975) O, and by aerial censusing using ultraviolet photography □, with error bars designating 95 % confidence intervals.

lion animals and estimated annual production to be in excess of 600 000 animals. Mansfield (1967) estimated that between 1951 and 1960 the stocks declined from more than 3 million to about 1.25 million seals. In 1970, it was suggested that western Atlantic harp seals numbered about 2.5 million (Mansfield, 1970) although no comment was made on the apparent increase in numbers during the sixties. Best estimates for annual production during the late sixties are between 270 000 (Sergeant, 1975) and 390 000 (Benjaminsen and Øritsland, 1975). Most recent estimates seem to suggest that harp seals now number some 1.10 to 1.35 million based on estimates of annual production of between 220 000 and 270 000 seals (Sergeant, 1975a). Our results indicate that production has continued to decline in recent years (Fig. 1), despite the reduced quota of 150 000 harp seals per year, and restricted sealing in the Gulf of St. Lawrence since 1972 (Anon., 1972). Extrapolation of the present trend in annual production (Fig. 1) suggests that if current management policies are continued, production will continue to decline, and the population will be severely threatened before the end of the twentieth century.

Acknowledgements

We thank Major E.J. McLaren, Head, Airborne Operations Section, Canada Centre for Remote Sensing, Energy, Mines and Resources Canada, and the officers and men of CF-ASU who, for the second consecutive year, participated in the field work and carried out the experimental aerial survey flights.

Mr. T. Curran continually supplied us with up-to-date information on the location of harp seals on the Front, and assisted our operations in the field. Mr. W. Hoek, Arctic Biological Station, Fisheries and Marine Service, Ste. Anne de Bellevue, provided us with information resulting from his survey flights, both in the Gulf of St. Lawrence and on the Front. Similarly, Mr. S. Dudka assisted with our field operations in the Gulf of St. Lawrence.

We also thank Mr. C. Levelton, Director General, Operations Directorate, Fisheries and Marine Service, Environment Canada; and Dr. G.A. Jarvis, Department of Mathematics and Statistics, University of Guelph, for his advice on the analysis of data.

Financial support was obtained through the Special Advisory Committee on Seals and Sealing to the Minister of State for Fisheries, and from grants to D.M. Lavigne and K. Ronald from the National Research council of Canada.

References

BENJAMINSEN, T. and T. ØRITSLAND, The survival of
1975   year-classes and estimates of production and sustainable yield of Northwest Atlantic harp seals. ICNAF Res. Doc. 75/121.

BERGFLØDT, B., Report on the sealing season and Norwegian seal investigations off Newfoundland-Labrador in 1975. ICNAF Res.
1975   Doc. 75/120.

FISHER, H.D., Utilization of Atlantic harp seal populations. *Trans. N. Am. Wildl. Nat. Resour. Conf.*,
1955   20:507-18.

LAVIGNE, D.M. and N.A. ØRITSLAND, Ultra-violet photography: a new method for remote sensing of mammals. *Can. J. Zool.*, 52:939-41.
1974

–, Black polar bears. *Nature, Lond.*, 251(5472):218-9.
1974a

LAVIGNE, D.M. and K. RONALD, Improved remote sensing techniques for evaluating seal populations. ICES C.M. 1975/N:12.
1975

LAVIGNE, D.M. *et al.*, Harp seal remote sensing. Report prepared for the Committee on Seals and Sealing, the Canada Centre for Remote Sensing, and the Arctic Biological Station, Fisheries and Marine Service, Environment Canada (MS).
1974

–, Harp seal aerial censusing. Report prepared for the Committee on Seals and Sealing, and Canada Centre for Remote Sensing (MS).
1975

MANSFIELD, A.W., Seals of arctic and eastern Canada.
1967   *Bull. Fish. Res. Board Can.*, (137) (2nd rev. ed.).

–, Population dynamics and exploitation of some arctic seals. *In* Antarctic ecology, edited by M.W. Holdgate. London, Academic Press, vol. 1:429-50.
1970

MENDENHALL, W., L. OTT and R.L. SCHEAFFER, Elementary survey sampling. Belmont, California, Wadsworth Publ. Co., Inc.
1971

POOLE, R.W., An introduction to quantitative ecology.
1974   New York, McGraw-Hill Book Co.

SERGEANT, D.E., Estimating numbers of harp seals.
1975   *Rapp. P.-V. Reun. CIEM*, 169:274-80.

–, Interrelations of the Gulf and Front herds of harp seals, *Pagophilus groenlandicus*. Paper presented to the Canadian Government-Industry Sealing Meeting, 25 February 1975, Doc. No. R/1.
1975a

SNEDECOR, G.W. and W.G. COCHRAN, Statistical methods. Ames, Iowa State University Press (6th ed.).
1967

SOM, R.K., A manual of sampling techniques. London, Heinemann Educational Books Ltd.
1973

WOOLF, C.M., Principles of biometry. New Jersey, Van Nostrand Co., Inc.
1968

Anon., Canadian-Norwegian agreement on sealing.
1972   *Polar Rec.*, 16:268-71.

HISTORY AND PRESENT STATUS OF THE CALIFORNIA SEA LION, *ZALOPHUS CALIFORNIANUS*

B.R. MATE

Abstract

Three sub-species of *Zalophus californianus* have been identified. *Z. c. californianus* is found along the eastern North Pacific coast of North America from British Columbia south to at least Manzanillo, Mexico; it breeds in late May and early June from the tip of Baja California north to San Miguel Island and throughout the Sea of Cortez. *Z. c. wollebaeki* breeds in the Galapagos Islands from October to December. *Z. c. japonicus* was in the past found in the Sea of Japan from 34 to 37°N. *Z. c. californianus* was heavily exploited in the 1800s; although estimates of population size are uncertain, there appear to be at least 75 000-100 000 animals present. Populations of this sub-species and of *Z. c. wollebaeki*, estimated to include 20 000 animals, are protected and are either growing in size or are stable, though some local populations in North America appear to fluctuate significantly and some animals there are killed in fishing gear or taken for public display. *Z. c. japonicus* is rare or extinct. Little is known about the reproductive biology of *Zalophus* and factors limiting population size and distribution have only been described qualitatively. Deliberate and unintentional interference by man through competition for food, pollution (especially the effects on reproduction of man-made toxicants) and disturbance of rookeries is present and can be expected to increase in some cases. The exchange of several diseases to and from man and *Zalophus* may also be important.

Résumé

Trois sous-espèces de *Zalophus californianus* ont été identifiées. On trouve *Z. c. californianus* le long de la côte pacifique septentrionale d'Amérique du Nord, de la Colombie britannique jusqu'à Manzanillo (Mexique) au moins. Il se reproduit fin mai-début juin de la pointe de la Basse-Californie jusqu'à l'île San Miguel et dans la mer de Cortez. *Z. c. wollebaeki* se reproduit dans les îles Galapagos d'octobre à décembre. On trouvait autrefois *Z. c. japonicus* dans la mer du Japon, entre 34 et 37°Nord. *Z. c. californianus* a été l'objet d'une exploitation intense vers les années 1800. Les estimations de la taille de la population sont incertaines mais il semble qu'il existe au moins 75 000-100 000 animaux. Les populations de cette sous-espèce et de *Z. c. wollebaeki* – celle-ci estimée à 20 000 sujets – sont protégées; leur taille augmente ou reste stable, bien que des oscillations appréciables semblent affecter certaines populations locales en Amérique du Nord; certains animaux sont tués dans les engins de pêche ou capturés pour être exhibés en public. *Z. c. japonicus* est rare ou sa population a disparu. On connaît très mal la biologie de la reproduction de *Zalophus* et les facteurs limitant la taille de la population et la distribution n'ont fait l'objet que de descriptions qualitatives. L'intervention délibérée et involontaire de l'homme due à la concurrence alimentaire, à la pollution (spécialement les effets des éléments toxiques artificiels sur la reproduction) et à la perturbation des rookeries, ne fera que s'accroître dans certains cas. Un élément peut-être important est l'échange de plusieurs maladies entre l'homme et *Zalophus.*

Extracto

Se han identificado tres subespecies de *Zalophus californianus. Z. c. californianus* se encuentra a lo largo de la costa oriental del norte del Pacífico, en América del Norte, desde Columbia británica hasta Manzanillo, en México. Se reproduce a finales de mayo y principios de junio, desde el extremo de Baja California hasta la isla de San Miguel y por el Mar de Cortez. *Z. c. wollebaeki* se reproduce en las islas Galápagos entre octubre y diciembre. *Z. c. japonicus* se encontraba antes en el Mar del Japón, entre 34 y 37°N. *Z. c. californianus* se explotó intensamente durante el siglo pasado; aunque no se dispone de estimaciones ciertas sobre el volumen de la población, parece que su número es del orden de 75 000-100 000 animales. Las poblaciones de esta subespecie y las de *Z. c. wollebaeki*, que se calcula representan unos 20 000 animales, están protegidas y van en aumento o se mantienen estables, aunque algunas poblaciones locales de América del Norte parecen experimentar notables fluctuaciones y algunos animales perecen en artes de pesca o se capturan para exposición. El león marino *Z. c. japonicus* es raro o está extinguido. Se sabe poco sobre la biología de la reproducción de *Zalophus* y los factores que limitan la población y la distribución sólo se han descrito cualitativamente. El hombre interfiere deliberada e inintencionalmente con estos animales, debido a la competencia alimentaria, la contaminación (especialmente los efectos de los productos tóxicos artificiales en la reproducción) y las alteraciones de las zonas de cría, interferencias que, en algunos casos, irán en aumento. El intercambio mutuo de varias enfermedades entre el hombre y *Zalophus* puede resultar también importante.

B.R. Mate
Marine Science Center, Oregon State University, Newport, Oregon 97365, USA

Stocks: identification and breeding distributions

Three sub-species of *Zalophus californianus* have been discerned by Scheffer (1958):

(i) *Zalophus californianus californianus*, which breeds from the tip of Baja California (23°N) north throughout the Sea of Cortez and north in the eastern Pacific to San Miguel Island, California (34°N). Although a single animal of this sub-species was reported from the Tres Marias (21-22°N) by Nelson (1899), its present status on those islands is unknown. The non-breeding season range of this sub-species extends from 19-51°N (Mate, unpublished data).

(ii) *Zalophus californianus wollebaeki*, which breeds on the Galapagos Islands (1°S).

(iii) *Zalophus californianus japonicus*, which has inhabited the Sea of Japan from at least 34-37°N but may now be extinct.

Few specimens of *Z. c. japonicus* are available, but it would appear that adult males are as large (if not somewhat larger) as *Z. c. californianus* and *wollebaeki*. Scheffer (1958) summarizes the morphological differences between the 2 latter sub-species, indicating that *Z. c. wollebaeki* is "smaller in both sexes" than *Z. c. californianus*. Orr, Schonewald and Kenyon (1970) found no morphological differences between *Z. c. californianus* from the Sea of Cortez and Pacific populations. Interbreeding between these 2 populations may be limited due to their distribution/density patterns (Mate, unpublished data).

The pupping and breeding season of *Zalophus* in the eastern North Pacific is from late May to early July, while Galapagos populations pup and breed from October to December. During the breeding season only a very few animals (usually sub-adult or bachelor males) are found outside of the breeding range. Although the exact age of sexual maturity is not well defined, males are likely to be capable of reproduction by age 5; however, because their physical (and perhaps social) development is insufficient to allow them to maintain territories, it is probable that few males are of breeding significance until they are between 7 and 9 years old. By age 5, males have started to develop a visible saggital crest (Orr, Schonewald and Kenyon, 1970), which becomes pronounced in full-grown adults and is frequently associated with a light coloured pelage over that area.

Seasonal distribution

Information on the non-breeding season distribution is limited to Pacific populations of *Z. c. californianus*, in which a northward post-breeding migration of males was first postulated by Fry (1939) and most recently reviewed and documented by Mate (1973, 1975). The northern extent of this migration appears to be Bull Harbor, Vancouver Island, British Columbia (51°N) during the winter months (Fisher and Benton, pers. comm.), a conservative 1 900 km from the northernmost rookery at San Miguel Island, California (34°N). A few males are found in British Columbia even during the breeding season. Female *Zalophus* have been documented as far north as Año Nuevo Island, California (37°N) by Morejohn (1968).

There is little data available for Sea of Cortez populations and the first collection of seasonal data has just been completed (Mate, unpublished data). As mentioned previously, morphological evidence shows little difference between Pacific and Gulf populations. Adult males, females and young of the year may be found throughout the entire breeding range of both populations all year round. In the Gulf, sexually distinct migrations are less conspicuous than in the Pacific. Some adult males and sub-adults in the Gulf population appear to move south following the breeding season along mainland Mexico to at least Manzanillo (19°N). Adult males have been found at Los Frailes (23°N) (the southeastern tip of Baja) in all seasons of the year. The Gulf population may be compressed during the breeding season by temperature constraints. Although many more areas of "apparently suitable" habitat exist than are occupied by *Zalophus*, some rookeries in the Gulf are semi- or fully aquatic. Those observed have always been close to the mainland or an island. Although the thermo-regulatory advantages of an aquatic territory are clear, the associated social and reproductive conditions may cause reduced recruitment. The use of such territories by *Zalophus* at San Nicolas Island (southern California) is described by Peterson and Bartholomew (1967) and Odell (1972).

Historic exploitation

References to sea lions during the 1800s have not always distinguished between *Zalophus* and its somewhat larger relative the northern (Steller) sea lion, *Eumetopias*. Although the breeding range of these 2 species only just overlaps at San Miguel Island (34°N), they are found together during their non-breeding season north of San Miguel and may in the past have cohabitated areas further to the south. Bailey (1936) identified bones of *Zalophus* among greater numbers of *Eumetopias* bones in Indian kitchen middens along the northern Oregon coast indicating that the species was used by native Americans for food and that it has been found this far north (probably as a migrant) for at least 150 years. The species was extensively exploited in the 1800s. Scammon (1874) described some of the products of sea lions, the associated economics, and hence some idea of the numbers exploited for harvest:

"The testes are taken out, and with the selected spires of the whiskers, find a market in China — the former being used medicinally, and the latter for personal ornaments. ... A few years ago great numbers of sea lions were taken along the coast of Upper and Lower California, and thousands of barrels of oil obtained. The number of seals slain exclusively for their oil would appear fabulous, when we realize the fact that it requires on an average, throughout the season, the blubber of three or four sea lions to produce a barrel of oil. Their thick, coarse-grained skins were not considered worth preparing for market in a country where manual labour was so highly valued. At the present time, however, they are valuable for glue-stock and the seal-hunter now realizes more comparative profit from the hides than from the oil."

During the early part of this century commercial harvest was primarily for dog food and some hides (Fry, 1939).

At present, *Zalophus* are protected throughout their breeding range (Mexico and the United States), although small numbers are killed annually by fishing gear. Small numbers are caught for display. *Zalophus* is considered the most readily trainable and economically feasible pinniped for zoos and aquaria. The United States Navy has used this species for deepwater object recovery operations. A harvest programme has been proposed in Mexico but none has been initiated.

"Natural" population regulators

There is little documentation of the reproductive biology of *Zalophus*. Pregnancy rates, ages of sexual maturity and longevity are poorly known. Similarly, mortality factors are still being defined in a qualitative manner. Sharks and killer whales are obvious predators, although the extent of their predation is unknown. A large factor governing early pup mortality may be sea state, either because of direct drowning, or because of injury to pups occurring when rookeries are crowded at times of storms or high tide.

Lungworm is a common parasite and may be responsible for significant mortality. An increase in the number of observed beach-cast animals and premature pups (presumably indicating a greater mortality rate) occurred during 1970-71 (Odell, 1970) and was attributed to leptospirosis (Vedros *et al.*, 1971). Subsequently, a virus known to produce abortions and premature births has been isolated from *Zalophus* (Smith *et al.*, 1974). It is unknown at present whether the *Lepospira* sp. bacterium or the virus are natural elements in *Zalophus* populations or if they have been introduced by man, as both are known to occur in domestic animals.

Zalophus appear to be shallow-water, opportunistic, day and night feeders, eating squid, including *Loligo*, and various small fishes including *Engraulis*, *Merluccius*, various rockfishes and *Clupea*. There is no evidence to indicate that food may be a factor limiting populations. However, they may be significant competition with *Eumetopias* and other nearshore pinnipeds for available food, habitat and other resources, which affects the distribution of each species. Mutual shifts in the historic breeding ranges of *Eumetopias* and *Zalophus*, short periods of cohabitation, use of similar hauling grounds and similar prey species indicate competition may be (or have been) a significant factor in the selective process of evolution.

Effects of man

Both man and sea lions compete for food, but human fisheries are selective, whereas sea lions are opportunists. The economic, social and biological effects of altering the balance of predation are unclear, though evidently human fisheries reduce the carrying capacity of the ecosystem for the sea lion, and may also have effects on other species. In some areas this competition goes beyond just hunting and capturing the prey. California sea lions are known to ascend some freshwater river systems during anadromous fish runs, have been "caught" in bottom trawling gear and have been observed to feed from gillnets. This has caused some aggressive retaliatory action by fishermen. The adversary relationship between fishermen and pinnipeds is both traditional and understandable.

Perhaps the greatest threat to pinnipeds as a group (and nearshore species such as *Zalophus* in particular) is the as yet unknown effect of increased levels of man-made toxicants in the marine environment. Numerous investigators have documented the high concentrations of heavy metals (mostly natural in occurrence), chlorinated hydrocarbons, and polychlorinated biphenyls found in marine mammal tissues (Buhler, Claeys and Mate, 1975). These may cause mortality by themselves or predispose an animal to natural or introduced diseases. The recent development of offshore oil production in the California Channel Islands and that proposed for the Guerrero Negro area of Baja may pose a potential threat to the two major areas of population for *Z. c. californianus*.

Both intentional and unintentional human disturbance of haulouts and rookeries occurs and will no doubt increase in the future. This may reduce the suitability of certain sites as rookeries and eliminate some entirely.

Population estimates

Population estimates and counts have been made sporadically over a century by various investigators and casual observers. Data have been collected by such a variety of methods at different times of the year for some areas that little can be done to project historic numbers of this species, except to say that it appeared common in the mid 1800s in a range

307

similar to its present breeding range.

In this century, population counts and estimates have been from direct observation or photographs taken from the ground, boats and aircraft. Counts from boats and aircraft have been highly variable, as have methods, photographic gear, emulsions and processing. While most counts have been made during the breeding season, some non-breeding seasonal data are available for some areas. Weather, tide, ocean state, time of day, and recent disturbance all influence the number of animals hauled out and make true population estimates from counts impossible at present. Tagging has been carried out on a few rookeries, primarily of pups, and few results have been reported to date.

The numbers and distribution of *Zalophus* in the California Channel Islands have changed markedly over the last 40 years according to Bartholomew (1967), who has estimated some 2 000 animals present in 1940 and 13 000 (excluding San Clemente) in 1958 (Bartholomew and Boolootian, 1960).

During the 1964 breeding season, Odell (1967) reported 34 382 *Zalophus* on the California Channel Islands, substantially higher than previous counts (18 363 in 1961 by Ripley, Cox and Baxter, 1962) or more recent estimates (17 169 in 1965 by Carlisle and Alpin, 1966; and 17 451 in 1969 by Frey and Alpin, 1970). Odell's figures are very nearly twice those found by Carlisle and Alpin (1966) just 1 year later for all California and may indicate the variability of controlled and "external" factors in producing "sampling error" problems during counting attempts. Alternatively, these gross differences may be interpreted as a comparison of "unusual regional-seasonal" distributions during those years. During the non-breeding season, as many as 14 000 *Zalophus* may be found in California north of the Channel Islands (Orr and Poulter, 1965), 2 500 in Oregon, 500 in Washington and perhaps as many as 1 000 in British Columbia (Mate, 1975).

An estimate of 16 566 *Zalophus* on San Benitos and Cedros Islands was made in 1965 (Rice, Kenyon and Lluch, 1965) and a conservative count of 35 000 has been made for all areas on the Pacific side of Baja (except Guadalupe) during 1975 (Mate, unpublished data). Gulf populations have been estimated by Orr, Schonewald and Kenyon (1970) at 5 411 in April 1966 (highest single-period count for 6 islands) and by Mate (unpublished data) at 8 500 for all areas during June of 1975. There is not enough data to judge stability of trends of Mexican populations. A conservative estimate of the *Zalophus californianus californianus* stocks would be 75 000-100 000. The Galapagos populations of *Z. c. wollebaeki* is estimated at 20 000 (King, 1964).

Summary

The present stocks of *Zalophus californianus wollebaeki* and *californianus* are protected and either growing or stable, while *Z. c. japonicus* is at best rare, and may be extinct. The eastern Pacific populations are not endangered at this time, although some local populations appear to fluctuate significantly. Man-made toxicants and several diseases may have a profound effect on reproductive success. The transmission of these diseases to and/or from man, domestic animals or wildlife may have significant consequences.

References

BAILEY, V., The mammals and life zones of Oregon. *N.*
1936   *Am. Fauna*, (55):416 p.

BARTHOLOMEW, G.A., Seal and sea lion populations of
1967   the California Islands. *In* Proceedings of the

Symposium on the Biology of the California Islands, held at Santa Barbara Botanic Gardens, 1965. pp. 229-44.

BARTHOLOMEW, G.A. and R.A. BOOLOOTIAN, Numbers
1960   and population structure of the pinnipeds on the California Channel Islands. *J. Mammal.*, 41:366-75.

BUHLER, D.R., R.R. CLAEYS and B.R. MATE, Heavy
1975   metal and chlorinated hydrocarbon residues in California sea lions. *J. Fish. Res. Board Can.*, 32(12):2391-7.

CARLISLE, J.G. and J.A. ALPIN, Sea lion census for 1965,
1966   including counts of other California pinnipeds. *Calif. Fish Game*, 52(2):119-20.

FREY, H.W. and J.A. ALPIN, Sea lion census for 1969,
1970   including counts of other California pinnipeds. *Calif. Fish Game*, 56(2):130-3.

FRY, D.H., A winter influx of sea lions from Lower
1939   California. *Calif. Fish Game*, 25:245-50.

KING, J.E., Seals of the world. London, British Museum
1964   (Natural History), 154 p.

MATE, B.R., Population kinetics and related ecology of
1973   the northern sea lion, *Eumetopias jubatus*, and the California sea lion, *Zalophus californianus*, along the Oregon coast. Ph.D. Thesis, University of Oregon, Eugene, 94 p.

—, Annual migrations of the sea lions *Eumetopias juba-*
1975   *tus* and *Zalophus californianus* along the Oregon coast. *Rapp. P.-V. Réun. CIEM*, 169:455-61.

MOREJOHN, G.V., A northern record of a female Cali-
1968   fornia sea lion. *J. Mammal.*, 49:156.

NELSON, E.W., Mammals of the Tres Marias Islands. *In*
1899   Natural history of the Tres Marias Islands, Mexico. *N. Am. Fauna*, (14):15-9.

ODELL, D.K., Premature pupping in the California sea

1970   lion. *Proc. Ann. Conf. Biol. Sonar Diving Mamm.*, 7:185-90.

—, Censuses of pinnipeds breeding on the California
1971   Channel Islands. *J. Mammal.*, 52(1):187-90.

—, Studies on the biology of the California sea lion and
1972   the northern elephant seal on San Nicholas Island, California. Ph. D. Thesis, University of California, Los Angeles. 168 p.

ORR, R.T. and T.C. POULTER, The pinniped population
1965   of Año Nuevo Island, California. *Proc. Calif. Acad. Sci.*, 32:377-404.

ORR, R.T., J. SCHONEWALD and K.W. KENYON, The Cal-
1970   ifornia sea lion: skull growth and a comparison of two populations. *Proc. Calif. Acad. Sci.*, 37:381-94.

PETERSON, R.S. and G.A. BARTHOLOMEW, The natural
1967   history and behavior of the California sea lion. *Spec. Publ. Am. Soc. Mammal.*, (1):79 p.

RICE, D.W., K.W. KENYON and D. LLUCH, B, Pinniped
1965   populations of Islas Guadalupe, San Benito, and Cedros, Baja California, in 1965. *Trans. San Diego Soc. Nat. Hist.*, 14(7):73-84.

RIPLEY, W.E., K.W. COX and J.K. BAXTER, California
1962   sea lion census for 1958, 1960 and 1961. *Calif. Fish Game*, 48:228-31.

SCAMMON, C.M., The marine mammals of the northwe-
1874   stern coast of North America. San Francisco, John H. Carmany Co., 319 p.

SCHEFFER, V.B., Seals, sea lions and walruses. Stanford,
1958   Stanford University Press, 179 p.

SMITH, A.W. *et al.*, A preliminary report on potentially
1974   pathogenic microbial agents recently isolated from pinnipeds. *J. Wildl. Dis.*, 48:228-31.

VEDROS, N.A. *et al.*, Leptospirosis epizootic among Cal-
1971   ifornia sea lions. *Science, Wash.*, 172:1250-1.

HISTORY AND PRESENT STATUS OF THE NORTHERN (STELLER) SEA LION, *EUMETOPIAS JUBATUS*

B.R. MATE

Abstract

The northern sea lion (*Eumetopias jubatus*) breeds from the Kurile Islands north and west through the Aleutian and Pribilof Islands and south along the North American coast to San Miguel Island. Populations in California, Oregon, Washington and British Columbia are estimated to number about 5 000-7 000, 2 000, 600 and 5 000 animals, respectively, though this varies seasonally. Combined estimates of the size of Soviet stocks exceed 20 000 animals. Nearly 200 000 northern sea lions are thought to inhabit Alaskan waters. Sea lions in the eastern Pacific migrate north following the breeding season (mid-May to mid-July) and seasonal movements have also been observed among those in the Bering Sea. The species moves south to inhabit waters around northern Hokkaido from late January to late May, reaching a maximum of 10 000-13 000 animals in March.

Northern sea lions have been taken for centuries by aboriginals, though the native harvest in Alaska has declined during this century. Commercial sealing from the late 1700s through the 1800s exterminated or reduced the abundance of the species in some areas. Aproximately 12 500 and 2 500 animals are killed each year in connexion with foreign and U.S. fishing operations, respectively.

Competition with other pinnipeds may be the most important factor affecting the abundance and distribution of northern sea lions — this may account in part for the decline of the species in the Channel Islands and for changes in its status in the Commander Islands. Competition with man for food may also be present though the trophic relations of the northern sea lion, other pinnipeds and man are poorly understood. Increased concentrations of man-made toxicants in the ocean is probably the greatest single threat to this species as well as to all marine mammals.

Résumé

L'aire de reproduction de l'otarie de Steller, *Eumetropias jubatus*, s'étend depuis les îles Kouriles, au nord et à l'ouest, en passant par les îles Aléoutiennes et Pribilof et, au sud, le long de la côte nord-américaine jusqu'à l'île San Miguel. Les populations de Californie, de l'Oregon, de l'Etat de Washington et de Colombie Britannique sont estimées à environ 5 000-7 000, 2 000, 600 et 5 000 animaux, respectivement, bien que ces chiffres soient sujets à des variations saisonnières. Les estimations combinées des stocks soviétiques dépassent 20 000 animaux. On pense que près de 200 000 otaries de Steller vivent dans les eaux de l'Alaska. Les otaries du Pacifique-est effectuent une migration vers le nord après l'époque de la reproduction (mi-mai à mi-juillet) et des déplacements saisonniers ont aussi été observés chez les animaux de la mer de Béring. L'espèce se déplace vers le sud pour vivre dans les eaux voisines du nord d'Hokkaido de la fin janvier à la fin mai, atteignant un maximum de 10 000-13 000 animaux en mars.

L'otarie de Steller est chassée depuis des siècles par les aborigènes bien que les chasses locales aient diminué en Alaska au cours du siècle. Depuis la fin du 18e siècle, et pendant tout le 19e siècle, la chasse commerciale a exterminé ou réduit les populations dans certaines régions. Environ 12 500 et 2 500 animaux sont tués chaque année, respectivement, dans les opérations de chasse étrangères et des Etats-Unis. La concurrence avec d'autres pinnipèdes pourrait être le facteur le plus important affectant l'abondance et la distribution des otaries de Steller, ce qui peut expliquer en partie le déclin de l'espèce dans les îles du Channel et la modification de son état dans les îles du Commandeur. La concurrence alimentaire avec l'homme peut aussi jouer un rôle, encore que les relations trophiques de l'otarie de Steller avec d'autres pinnipèdes et avec l'homme soient mal comprises. Les concentrations croissantes de produits toxiques mis en circulation par l'homme constituent probablement le plus grand danger menaçant cette espèce ainsi que tous les mammifères marins.

Extracto

El león marino septentrional (*Eumetopias jubatus*) se reproduce al norte y el oeste de las islas Kuriles a lo largo de las islas Aleutianas y Pribilof, y al sur de las Kuriles, a lo largo de la costa de América del Norte hasta la isla de San Miguel. El número de animales de las poblaciones de California, Oregón, Wáshington y Columbia Británica se ha calculado respectivamente en 5 000-7 000, 2 000, 600 y 5 000 animales, aunque las cifras varían según la estación. El total estimado de las poblaciones soviéticas arroja una cifra superior a 20 000 animales. Se estima que en aguas de Alaska viven aproximadamente 200 000 leones marinos de esta especie. Los leones marinos del este del Pacífico emigran hacia el norte después de la temporada de reproducción (mediados de mayo a mediados de julio) y también se han observado movimientos estacionales entre las poblaciones del mar de Bering. La especie se desplaza hacia el sur, a las aguas situadas en torno al norte de Hokkaido, desde finales de enero hasta finales de mayo, alcanzando puntas máximas de 10 000-13 000 en marzo.

El león marino septentrional ha sido cazado por los aborígenes durante siglos, aunque en Alaska las actividades de caza de los nativos han disminuido durante el presente siglo. La explotación comercial, desde finales del siglo XVIII hasta finales del XIX, acabó con esta especie o la redujo notablemente en algunas zonas. Durante las faenas de pesca de embarcaciones extranjeras y estadounidenses mueren todos los años 12 500 y 2 500 animales, respectivamente.

La competencia con otros pinnípedos puede ser el más importante de los factores que influyen en la abundancia y distribución del león marino septentrional, y a ella puede deberse en parte la disminución de esta especie en las islas del Canal y los cambios que su situación ha experimentado en las islas Commander. Es posible que compitan también con el hombre desde el punto de vista alimentario, aunque no se conocen bien las relaciones tróficas entre el león marino septentrional, otros pinnípedos y el hombre. Probablemente la amenaza más grave para esta especie, al igual que para todos los mamíferos marinos, es el aumento de las concentraciones de sustancias tóxicas artificiales en los océanos.

B.R. Mate
Marine Science Center, Oregon State University, Newport, Oregon 97365, USA

Identification and distribution of stocks

DISTRIBUTION

The northern sea lion, *Eumetopias juba-tus*, breeds from the Pribilof Islands (57°N) (Kenyon and Rice, 1961) south and west to the Kurile Islands (46°N) (Nishiwaki, personal communication 1975) and south and east to San Miguel Island, California (34°N). The wid-est gap in the species breeding range is the 650 km between the Aleutian and Commander Islands. No isolated or sub-specific populations have been identified over this large range.

The non-breeding distribution has been summarized by Scheffer (1958), elaborated by Kenyon and Rice (1961), and includes Hers-chel Island (69°N), Bering Straits, the Pribilofs, and extends south to northern Hokkaido, 43°N (Nishiwaki, personal communication 1975). Latitudinal seasonal movements have been noted throughout the range.

MIGRATION

In the eastern Pacific, adult and some sub-adult male *Eumetopias* migrate north after the pupping and breeding season (mid-May to mid-July). The migration appears to be unifi-ed, in that adult males are virtually absent from California waters (south of 42°N) by August and cannot be found south of British Columbia (48°N) by mid-October (Mate, 1975). It would appear that females also migrate north after breeding in the summer, for in mid-winter the number of females and young of the year drops in California, Oregon and Washington and in spring the number of fe-males with yearlings increases from north to south. It is probably necessary for females to delay their northward migration until their pups are capable swimmers. The primary fac-tors responsible for migration are as yet un-known, although some hypotheses have been proposed.

The bulk of the breeding population is found on the Aleutian Islands. In the Bering Sea some adult and sub-adult males appa-rently move north as the ice recedes. Fay (*in litt.*) (quoted by Kenyon and Rice, 1961) states that some of these animals arrive at St. Law-rence Island (63°N) in late June and accord-ing to local inhabitants the greatest numbers occur in September and depart in November when the ice returns. Further observation on the Pribilofs by Wilke and Kenyon (1952), re-ported by Kenyon and Rice (1961), indicated that the identifiable winter residents were males, suggesting a southward movement of females after the breeding season.

In the western Pacific, *Eumetopias* of unspecified sex appear from the north in north-ern Hokkaido (43°N) during late January, and depart by late May, presumably to breed in the Kurile Islands (Nishiwaki, personal communication 1965). No breeding occurs in Japanese waters.

Population estimates

Kenyon and Rice (1961) give detailed information on the occurrence of this species and estimated the total number to be 240 000-300 000 from their own work and that of others (Table 1). There have been certain rookeries which have maintained stable num-bers of animals over long periods, some of which have been deserted and others which apparently have developed, which makes comparison difficult. California populations appear to be fairly stable (5 000-7 000 indivi-duals) judging from aerial survey results from 1958-70 (Carlisle and Alpin, 1971). Oregon and Washington populations are approxima-tely 2 000 and 600 respectively (Mate, 1975). Fisher and Brenton (personal communication 1975) estimate the 1975 breeding population of British Columbia to be 5 000. The Alaska Department of Fish and Game now estimates that nearly 200 000 *Eumetopias* occur in Alas-kan waters. Estimates of Soviet stocks from the literature indicate a total in excess of 20 000 individuals, and the apparent occurrence of shifts in distribution over time. Nishiwaki (personal communication 1975) has estimated the numbers of non-breeding seals occurring seasonally in Japan to be approximately 10 000-13 000 during March.

History of exploitation and trends in abundance

Eumetopias has been harvested throughout its range for centuries for food, building material and wearing apparel as evidenced by kitchen middens, cultural artefacts and literature. This aboriginal harvest may have been significant in regulating some regional populations, but there is little documentation with which to establish this.

Sealing during the late 18th and entire 19th century certainly reduced or eradicated some "local" populations. The first indication of migration or immigration by *Eumetopias* may have been by a commercial sealer (Scammon, 1874):

"Doubts have been expressed as to the migratory habits of the sea lion; but we are fully convinced that there are individuals, at least, among all the northern herds, that change from the cold latitudes to the tropics, as we have killed several of the animals upon the southern coast of California, during the month of June, in which were found arrow or spear heads, such as are used by the northern sea-coast natives. Professor Davidson states that in June 1870, a spearhead, such as is used by the natives of Alaska, was found in a large male sea lion taken at Point Arenas, in latitude 39°, on the coast of California."

During the 1800s thousands of sea lions (including *Eumetopias*) were harvested for their oil, testes, whiskers, hides and gluestock value.

Table 1. Summary of population estimates of Steller sea lions (taken from Kenyon and Rice, 1961)

Area	Number	Authority
Southern California	50	Bartholomew and Boolootian (1960)
Northern California	6 002	California Department of Fish and Game (*in litt.*, 1960)[1]
Oregon	650-1 000	Rice, field notes, 1960
Washington	400-500	Kenyon and Scheffer (1959)
British Columbia	11 000-12 000	Pike and Maxwell (1958)
Southeastern Alaska to the Shumagin Islands	76 027	Mathisen (1959)
Aleutian Islands	100 205	Present report
Pribilof Islands:		
St. Paul Island and Sea Lion Rock	300	Kenyon, field notes, 1960
Otter Island	160	Kenyon, field notes, 1960
Walrus Island	4 000-5 000	Kenyon, field notes, 1960
St. George Island	1 200	Riley, field notes, 1960
Kamchatka (9 rookeries and hauling grounds)	No data	Rass *et al.* (1955)
Kurile Islands (23 rookeries and hauling grounds)	15 000-17 000	Klumov (1957)
Okhotsk Sea (Svyatov Iony)	5 000-6 000	Nikulin (1937)
Okhotsk Sea (9 other rookeries and hauling grounds)	No data	Rass *et al.* (1955)
Total	219 914-225 444	

[1] Ripley gives the following information: "We have made aerial estimates of sea lions on rookeries of California for the years 1958 and 1960. Although we do not have the species delineated in the aerial photos, it can be considered that the population north of Point Conception is nearly all Stellers. Therefore, based on this assumption, the counts for 1958 would be 7 116 and for 1960 would be 6 002. Our estimates this year did not include Southern California or the California islands.".

EASTERN PACIFIC

The pre-exploitation population in the southern extent of the eastern Pacific range is unknown, but the extensive harvest that took place there may have triggered off major changes in species distribution.

"When records of the pinniped population of the California Islands were first begun in the late twenties, the Steller sea lion was the most abundant pinniped in the Southern California group. Its population peaked at a little more than 2 000 in the late thirties and has been declining during the 30 subsequent years. In 1958 the total breeding population of this species in the Southern California Islands had fallen to less than 100 and was confined to a single rookery on the western tip of San Miguel." (Bartholomew, 1967.)

The population on San Miguel was even smaller in 1975 and 1976 than in 1958 (Mate, unpublished data). The population at Año Nuevo Island has remained fairly stable at 1 500-2 500 animals since 1921 (Evermann, 1921; Rowley, 1929; Ripley, Cox and Baxter, 1962; Carlisle and Alpin, 1971).

ALASKA

In Alaska, native take has reportedly been reduced during this century due to the influence of "white" culture and recent availability of alternative foods and manufactured goods. Recent records indicate that from 1963 to 1972 between 1 500 and 6 546 animals (average 4 518) were taken annually, primarily for the fur industry (Alaska Fish and Game, 1975). Alaska Fish and Game now feels that *Eumetopias* are "near or at carrying capacity for the habitat".

COMMANDER ISLANDS

Kenyon and Rice (1961) indicate that this species does not breed on the Commander Islands, but is found there from October to April. Although there may have been animals present during the breeding season, no population estimates were given. However, Chugunkov (1968) in his studies on the effect of sea lions on the fur seal rookeries of the Commander Islands, indicates the presence of up to 3 000 sea lions in several rookeries on the southeast tip of Medny Island between the end of May and early July. Considerable yearly fluctuation in these rookeries and a declining trend were attributed to increased fur seal populations and harassment of sea lions during fur seal harvest operations. This may indicate how easily changes in breeding status and stocks occur in this species, or it may merely reflect the lack of published citings for a long-established population.

JAPAN

Similarly, Wilke and Kenyon (in Kenyon and Rice, 1961) observed no sea lions during their fur seal studies near Hokkaido in the winter, spring and summer of 1949, 1950 and 1952, although Nishiwaki (personal communication 1975) believes the population to be as high as 10 000-13 000 during March in northern Hokkaido.

Natural population regulators

Competition may be the single most important factor both for population numbers and for distribution. In the Channel Islands the previously mentioned reduction of the breeding range of *Eumetopias* has been accompanied by a rapid increase in the numbers of *Zalophus* (Bartholomew, 1967), indicating there may be a niche competition (for some critical resource[s]) which *Zalophus* is winning. The observations of Chugunkov (1968) indicate that competition with fur seals for available rookery space may be a limiting factor for *Eumetopias* in the western Pacific. In addition,

315

it is likely that there may be considerable competition for prey species within pinniped species and between pinnipeds and others, including man. Commercial fisheries have increased dramatically over the last 15 years in the sea lions' range and may account for some reduced recruitment for Pribilof fur seals.

While there are several studies of the feeding habits of various marine mammal species, including *Eumetopias* (Imler and Sarber, 1947; Wilke and Kenyon, 1952; Pike and Maxwell, 1958; Mathisen, Baade and Lopp, 1962; Fiscus and Baines, 1966), it is not yet clear what effect these top carnivore populations have on each other by their consumption of mutually desirable prey species, nor how their populations interact with the rest of the marine food web. Such data may be essential to the definition of "carrying capacity", especially in view of man's intention to maintain and/or increase harvest from the same trophic level.

Direct predation of sea lions by sharks and killer whales is known to occur, but quantitative data are lacking. The species is known to have many parasites and some may cause considerable mortality, but very little data have been collected on which to base conclusions (Rausch, 1964; Dailey and Hill, 1970).

Effects of man

The most direct effect of man on *Eumetopias* populations is harvest:

— small numbers throughout the northern range are taken for human consumption;

— approximately 4 000 are captured in association with foreign and domestic fishing in gear conflicts, bait operations, or retaliations. Of this number most are alive when brought aboard and are allowed to escape (John Burns, pers. comm.);

— some dozen or so are captured each year for display and research purposes;

— some are taken by natives for use in traditional crafts and clothing;

— a proposal has been made to harvest sea lions as a protein source for animal breeding farms on the Commander Islands (Chugunkov, 1968). A feasibility analysis of commercial harvest in Alaska has also been made (Little Inc., 1964).

Probably the greatest single threat to the species is one shared by all marine mammals: increased concentrations of man-made toxicants. As a top carnivore, this species is the recipient of quantities of biologically persistent contaminants, which become more concentrated at each step up the food chain. The effects vary with different compounds, some of which may produce behavioural or physiological aberrations which would result in reduced reproductive success or even death.

Harassment, whether intentional or unintentional, may decrease breeding success by reducing the suitability of some habitats as rookeries.

This problem will, however, be restricted, since human density is low in most parts of this species' range.

References

Alaska Department of Fish and Game, Current takings 1975 of marine mammals in Alaska. Draft environmental impact statement. Juneau, Alaska, Department of Fish and Game (unpubl.).

BARTHOLOMEW, G.A., Seal and sea lion populations of
1967   the California Islands. *In* Proceedings of the
        Symposium on the Biology of the California
        Islands, held at Santa Barbara Botanic Gar-
        dens, 1965, pp. 229-44.

CARLISLE, J.G. and J.A. ALPIN, Sea lion census for 1970,
1971   including counts of other California pinni-
        peds. *Calif. Fish Game*, 57(2):124-6.

CHUGUNKOV, D.I., Sea lions and fur seal husbandry on
1968   the Commander Islands. *In* Pinnipeds of the
        North Pacific, edited by V.A. Arsen'ev and K.I.
        Panin. *Tr. Vses. Nauchno-Issled. Inst. Morsk.
        Rybn. Khoz. Okeanogr.*, 68:154-66.

DAILEY, M.D. and B.L. HILL, A survey of metazoan
1970   parasites infecting the California and Steller
        (*Eumetopias jubatus*) sea lion. *Bull. South.
        Calif. Acad. Sci.*, (69):126-32.

EVERMANN, B.W., The Año Nuevo Steller sea lion
1921   rookery. *J. Mammal.*, 2:16-9.

FISCUS, C.H. and G.A. BAINES, Food and feeding
1966   behaviour of the Steller and California sea
        lions. *J. Mammal.*, 47:195-200.

IMLER, R. and H.R. SARBER, Harbour seals and sea lions
1947   in Alaska. *Spec. Sci. Rep. USFWS*, (28):22 p.

KENYON, K.W. and D.W. RICE, Abundance and distri-
1961   bution of the Steller sea lion. *J. Mammal.*,
        42:223-34.

LITTLE, Inc., A.D., Feasibility of a commercial sea lion
1964   operation in Alaska. Report prepared for De-
        partment of Interior, Bureau of Indian Affairs,
        145 p.

MATE, B.R., Annual migrations of the sea lions *Eumeto-
1975   pias jubatus* and *Zalophus caliornianus* along
        the Oregon coast. *Rapp. P.-V. Réun. CIEM*,
        169:455-61.

MATE, B. and R.L. GENTRY, Northern (Steller) sea lion.
1979   *FAO Fish. Ser.*, (5) vol. 2:3-8 (in press).

MATHISEN, O.A., R.T. BAADE and R.J. LOPP, Breeding
162   habits, growth and stomach contents of the
        Steller sea lion in Alaska. *J. Mammal.*,
        43(4):469-77.

PIKE, G.C. and B.E. MAXWELL, The abundance and dis-
1958   tribution of the northern sea lions (*Eumetopias
        jubata*) on the coast of British Columbia. *J.
        Fish. Res. Board Can.*, 15(1):5-17.

RAUSCH, R.L., Studies on the helminth fauna of Alaska.
1964   41. Observations on cestodes of the genus *Di-
        plogonoporus* Lonnberg, 1892 (Diphylloboth-
        riidae). *Can. J. Zool.*, 42:1049-69.

RIPLEY, W.E., K.W. COX and J.K. BAXTER, California sea
1962   lion census for 1958, 1960 and 1961. *Calif. Fish
        Game*, 48:228-31.

ROWLEY, J., Life history of the sea lions on the California
1929   coast. *J. Mammal.*, 10:1-39.

SCAMMON, C.M., The marine mammals of the north-
1874   western coast of North America. San Francis-
        co, John H. Carmany Co., 319 p.

SCHEFFER, V.B., Seals, sea lions and walruses. Stanford,
1958   California, Stanford University Press, 179 p.

SPALDING, D.J., Comparative feeding habits of the fur
1964   seal, sea lion and harbour seal on the British
        Columbia coast. *Bull. Fish. Res. Board Can.*,
        (146):52 p.

WILKE, F. and K.W. KENYON, Notes on the food of fur
1952   seals, sea lions and harbour porpoises. *J. Wildl.
        Manage.*, 16(3):396.

STATUS OF NORTHERN FUR SEALS

R.H. LANDER and H. KAJIMURA

Abstract

This paper reviews the demographic and environmental biology of the northern fur seal, *Callorhinus ursinus* (Linnaeus, 1758), especially in relation to exploitation by man. Estimated current abundance (in parentheses), historical trends in abundance, and migration and subsequent intermixture of the 5 breeding populations recognized by the North Pacific Fur Seal Commission are reviewed: (1) Pribilof Islands (1 300 000). The likely size of the population before exploitation was between 2-2.5 million animals, falling to about 300 000 at its low point in 1911/12. Fluctuations in the annual kill occurred in the mid-1900s, leading to a major herd reduction programme (including harvesting), about 20 %. Latest computations indicate optimum annual production for maximum sustainable yield (MSY) at about 360 000 for both islands, a reduction from earlier estimates; (2) Commander Islands (265 000). This population included over 1 million animals before its rapid depletion around 1900 and its near-destruction by 1911. An annual yield of 40 000 is estimated when the population is restored; recent production trends indicate slow repopulation of decimated rookeries; (3) Robben Island (165 000). Seals of this population were also near depletion in 1911. MSY is projected for an annual pup production of 45 000-50 000; (4) Kuril Islands (33 000). This population was destroyed near the turn of the century; seals from the Commander Islands and Robben Island are contributing to the present repopulation of the central islands and (5) San Miguel Island (2 000). Breeding here was discovered in 1968, though the presence of fur seals has been known since early in the last century.

Pelagic sealing was banned by treaty in 1911; only the first 3 populations above are presently exploited commercially on land. Harvesting rate and data, birth and natural mortality rates and census methods and figures for these populations are presented. The northern fur seal is an opportunistic feeder, capable of long periods of fasting; its feeding habits and behaviour and principal food species (primarily fish on the continental shelf and squid in pelagic areas) are summarized, and additional ecological factors are reviewed. The northern fur seal's trophic relationships with other living resources and marine life of the North Pacific are poorly understood and represent a complex problem in resource allocation; its economic importance extends beyond its valuable skin and other oil and meal products to its impact on commercial fishery resources. While consumer demand for fur seal products is presently steady, increasing public interest in marine mammals suggest that aesthetic and educational values should also be considered in future management policies.

Résumé

Les auteurs étudient la biologie démographique et environnementale de l'otarie à fourrure des Pribilof, *Callorhinus ursinus* (Linnaeus, 1758), tout particulièrement du point de vue de son exploitation par l'homme. Ils donnent des indications (entre parenthèses) sur

319

l'abondance actuelle, l'évolution historique de l'abondance, les migrations et les mélanges subséquents des cinq populations de reproducteurs reconnues par la Commission du phoque à fourrure du Pacifique nord: (1) Iles Pribilof (1 300 000). Avant l'exploitation, la population se situait probablement entre 2 et 2,5 millions d'individus. Elle est tombée à son minimum, environ 300 000, en 1911/12. Vers le milieu du vingtième siècle, la mortalité par chasse a été variable si bien que de 1956 à 1963 les troupeaux ont été fortement réduits (on a tué même des femelles). L'île St Paul fournissait traditionnellement environ 80 pour cent des prises totales et l'île St George environ 20 pour cent. Cette île est aujourd'hui une zone réservée à la recherche, ce qui exclut l'exploitation. D'après les derniers calculs, la production annuelle optimale correspondant au MSY se situerait à environ 360 000 pour les deux îles, chiffre inférieur aux estimations antérieures. (2) Iles du Commandeur (265 000). Cette population dépassait le million avant son déclin rapide autour de 1900 et sa quasi-destruction en 1911. On pense que le rendement annuel sera de 40 000 quand la population se sera rétablie. Les tendances récentes de la production indiquent que les rookeries décimées se repeuplent lentement. (3) Ile Robben (165 000). Cette population était, elle aussi, pratiquement détruite en 1911. Le MSY correspondrait à une production annuelle de 45 000 à 50 000 jeunes. (4) Iles Kouriles (33 000). Cette population a été détruite au début du siècle. Les phoques des îles du Commandeur et de l'Ile Robben contribuent actuellement à repeupler les îles centrales. (5) Ile San Miguel (2 000). La reproduction y a été constatée en 1968, bien que la présence d'otaries à fourrure ait été connue depuis le début du siècle dernier.

La chasse pélagique a été interdite par le Traité de 1911; seules les trois premières populations énumérées ci-dessus font actuellement l'objet d'une chasse commerciale à terre. Les auteurs indiquent les taux et les données d'exploitation, les taux de natalité et de mortalité naturelle, les méthodes et les chiffres du recensement de ces populations. L'otarie à fourrure des Pribilof a une alimentation éclectique et peut demeurer longtemps sans manger. Les auteurs décrivent ses habitudes et son comportement alimentaires ainsi que les principales espèces qui composent sa nourriture (avant tout, des poissons sur le plateau continental et des calmars dans les régions pélagiques). Ils étudient aussi d'autres facteurs écologiques. Les relations trophiques de l'otarie à fourrure avec les autres ressources vivantes et les organismes marins du Pacifique nord sont peu connues et posent un problème complexe relatif à la distribution de la ressource. L'importance économique de cette espèce est liée non seulement à ses produits (peau, huile, farine) mais également à l'influence qu'elle exerce sur les ressources des pêches commerciales. Alors que la demande de produits se situe à un niveau stable, l'intérêt accru du public pour les mammifères marins laisse penser que les futures politiques de gestion devraient aussi tenir compte des valeurs esthétiques et didactiques.

Extracto

Se examina la biología demográfica y ambiental del oso marino o lobo de dos pelos, *Callorhinus ursinus* (Linnaeus, 1758), especialmente en relación con su explotación por parte del hombre. Se estudian la abundancia estimada actual (entre paréntesis), la trayectoria de la abundancia a lo largo de la historia, los movimientos migratorios y las mezclas consiguientes de las cinco poblaciones de reproductores reconocidas por la Comisión de Focas de Piel del Norte del Pácifico: (1) Islas Pribilof (1 300 000). El volumen probable de la población antes de comenzar la explotación era de 2-2,5 millones de animales, y disminuyó a unos 300 000 en el momento más bajo, en 1911-12. A mediados de este siglo se registraron fluctuaciones de las capturas anuales que dieron lugar a un programa importante de reducción del rebaño (incluidas capturas de hembras) entre 1956 y 1963. El 80 por ciento de las capturas totales han procedido siempre de la Isla St. Paul, y el 20 por ciento, aproximadamente, de la Isla St. George, reservada en la actualidad como zona de investigaciones (con prohibición de explotación). Los últimos cálculos indican una producción óptima anual para obtener el rendimiento máximo sostenible de unos 360 000 animales en ambas islas, lo que representa una reducción respecto de estimaciones anteriores. (2) Islas Commander (265 000). Esta población contaba con más de un millón de animales antes de su rápido depauperamiento en torno a 1900 y su destrucción casi total para 1911. Se calcula que, una vez restablecida la población, el rendimiento anual podría ser de unos 40 000 animales; la trayectoria de la producción en los últimos tiempos indica una lenta repoblación de las zonas de cría diezmadas. (3) Isla Robben (165 000). Esta población quedó también casi agotada en 1911. Se hacen proyecciones del rendimiento máximo sostenible sobre la base de una producción anual de cachorros de 45 000-50 000. (4) Islas Kuriles (33 000). Esta población se destruyó a comienzos de siglo; los osos marinos de las Islas Commander y Robben contribuyen a la actual repoblación de las islas centrales. (5) Isla de San Miguel (2 000). En 1968 se descubrió que *C. ursinus* acudía a esta isla para reproducirse aunque la presencia de estos animales se conocía ya desde principios del siglo pasado.

La caza pelágica se prohibió en 1911 por un tratado; sólo las tres primeras poblaciones mencionadas se explotan en la actualidad comercialmente, en tierra. Se dan índices y datos de explotación e índices de nacimiento y de mortalidad natural, y se indican las cifras obtenidas en los censos de esas poblaciones y los métodos utilizados. El otario *C. ursinus* es oportunista desde el punto de vista alimentario y puede soportar largos períodos de ayuno; se resumen sus hábitos alimentarios y su comportamiento en ese campo, así como las principales especies que le sirven de alimento (ante todo, peces que viven en la plataforma continental y calamares de zonas pelágicas). Se examinan también otros factores ecológicos. No se conocen bien las relaciones tróficas del oso marino con otros recursos vivos y con la vida marina en general del norte del Pacífico, y ello plantea un complejo problema por lo que se refiere a la asignación de los recursos. Para el hombre, la importancia económica no se limita a las pieles y otros productos, como aceite y harina, sino que hay que tener en cuenta también sus repercusiones en los recursos pesqueros comerciales. La demanda de consumo de productos derivados del oso marino está actualmente estabilizada, pero el creciente interés de la opinión pública por los mamíferos marinos sugiere que en las políticas futuras de ordenación habrán de tenerse también en cuenta los valores estéticos y educativos.

R.H. Lander
Marine Mammal Division, National Marine Fisheries Service, Building 32, 7600 Sand Point Way NE, Seattle, Washington 98115, USA

H. Kajimura
Marine Mammal Division, National Marine Fisheries Service, Building 32, 7600 Sand Point Way NE, Seattle, Washington 98115, USA

Description

IDENTIFICATION

Scheffer (1958) provides an account of pinniped systematics and a synoptic key to the genera. By contrast with the polytypic southern fur seal *Arctocephalus*, *Callorhinus* contains a single species, *ursinus*. No sub-species are recognized (Taylor, Fujinaga and Wilke, 1955; Repenning, Peterson and Hubbs, 1971).

DISTRIBUTION AND STOCK IDENTIFICATION

Table 1 summarizes by decreasing order of estimated current abundance (including newborn pups) the five breeding populations of northern fur seal recognized by the North Pacific Fur Seal Commission (NPFSC) through its member nations of Japan, USSR, Canada and USA. Breeding on San Miguel Island off southern California was discovered only in 1968 (Peterson, LeBoeuf and DeLong, 1968) but the island is known to have been at least a hauling ground early in the last century (Repenning, Peterson and Hubbs, 1971). Figure 1 shows the breeding islands and oceanic distribution.

The first three populations in Table 1 (Pribilofs, Commanders and Robben) are exploited commercially on land. The 1911 Treaty prohibited pelagic sealing but contained no provisions for research; the Treaty was abrogated by Japan in 1941 and pelagic sealing in the eastern and central North Pacific Ocean was prohibited by an interim US-Canadian agreement during 1942-57. The 1957 Convention then reiterated the ban on pelagic sealing and provided additionally for research on land and at sea. With effect from 1973 for an unspecified number of years, NPFSC set aside St. George Island in the Pribilof Islands as an area of intensive research (NPFSC, 1973; NOAA/NMFS, 1973) for the purpose of determining and quantifying, as a basic for im-

Table 1. Estimated abundance of northern fur seals (adapted from Johnson, 1975)

Population	Ownership and area	Estimated No. of seals (Thousands)
Pribilof Islands	US, eastern Bering Sea	1 300
Commander Islands	USSR, western Bering Sea	265
Robben Island	USSR, Sea of Okhotsk	165
Kuril Islands	USSR, Western North Pacific	33 [1]
San Miguel Island	US, eastern North Pacific	2 [2]
Total		1 765

[1] Exceeds by 18 000 seals the estimates in Johnson's Table 2 because of continuing repopulation on the Kuril Islands (NPFSC, 1975a).
[2] C.H. Fiscus and R.L. DeLong (personal communication) note that this small herd is growing rapidly, judging from pup production, and may number about 2 000.

proved management, the ecological and behavioural factors which control population size and structure. The presently unharvested population on St. George Island has traditionally contributed about 20 %, and the St. Paul Island population about 80 %, of the total kill from the Pribilof Islands; the only other rookery, which produces about 20 000 pups yearly, is on Sea Lion Rock and this group is not harvested.

Tag-recapture studies (Taylor, Fujinaga and Wilke, 1955; NPFSC, 1962, 1969, 1971 and 1975) demonstrate intermixture. For instance, an estimated 12-21 % of males (age 3-4 years) tagged as pups from the 1958-63 year-classes and killed on the Commander Islands (Bering and Medny) originated in the Pribilofs; 82-88 % were from home and only 0.1-0.5 % from Robben Island (NPFSC, 1969). On the Pribilof Islands with their much larger population (NPFSC, 1969), the kill contains a fraction of 1 % from all Asian rookeries; tags from Robben Island in particular are rare. Oddly, mixing is greater between Medny Island and the Pribilofs than between Medny

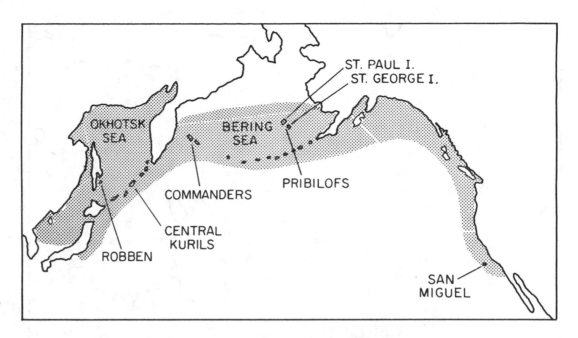

FIG. 1. – Breeding islands and general ocean distribution of the northern fur seal.

and nearby Bering Island. 93 % or more of the seals killed on Robben Island are from home, with only 0.3-1.9 % from the Commanders and 1.3-5.0 % from the Pribilofs. On San Miguel Island, most of the tagged animals observed are from the Pribilofs, but some are from the Commanders and 1 has appeared from Robben Island. Seals from the Commanders and Robben Island are contributing to repopulation of the central Kurils; a few tagged seals from the Pribilofs have been found there also (NPFSC, 1970, 1973).

The possibility exists of gene flow between populations.

Recovery rates on land from pup tagging are usually 5-10 %, or even higher when lost tags are accounted for by check marks made on flippers at the time of tagging. Recovery rates from research collections at sea, on the other hand, are often 0-1 % when broken down by area, time, age and sex. The few recoveries make oceanic intermingling estimates uncertain. Problems occur also in developing and reporting these estimates; for instance, the estimated annual total percentage contributions, by age and sex, of seals from the Pribilof Islands, Robben Island and the Commander Islands to pelagic catches off eastern Japan

during 1959-65 add up to values ranging from 0 to 286 % (NPFSC, 1969); the actual totals were clearly near 100 % because these are the main breeding populations (NPFSC, 1975).

Off eastern Japan during 1967-72, 63 % of 342 recoveries (i.e., 9 % of 3 756 seals collected of both sexes and all ages, year-classes and time periods combined) were from Robben Island, 30 % from the Commanders, 6 % from the Pribilofs and 3 % from the Kurils (NPFSC, 1975). Earlier, Taylor, Fujinaga and Wilke (1955) estimated tentatively that about 30 % (95 % confidence limits of 15-50 %) of the seals aged 3-5 years off eastern Japan were from the Pribilofs. Relative rates of pup tagging on the islands and recoveries at sea show more clearly that over 96 % of the animals off western North America south of the Bering Sea are from the Pribilofs.

MIGRATIONS

Seals from the Pribilofs and the Commanders migrate as far south as 30-32°N on both sides of the Pacific Ocean. Seals from Robben Island winter mainly in the Sea of

323

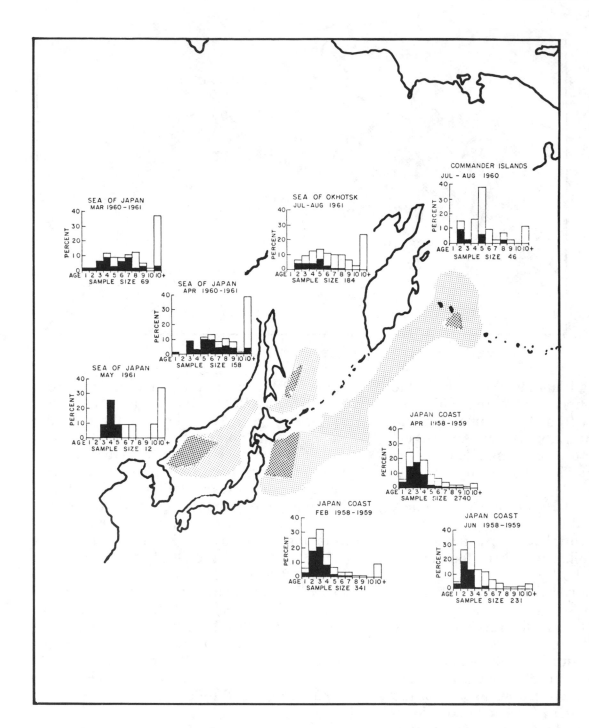

FIG. 2. – Distribution of northern fur seals in the western Pacific, 1958-61 (from NPFSC, 1962). Black bars are for males and white for females; dark and light shading indicates areas of intensive and limited sampling respectively.

324

Japan. Figs. 2 and 3 give typical distribution pictures illustrating that migrations are specific by age and sex. Males over 4 years old are not often taken on either side of the Pacific Ocean, but are taken commonly from the more self-contained Robben Island population in the Seas of Japan and Okhotsk. Harem bulls

(58 % 9-11 and 84 % 9-13 years old as shown in Table 1 of Johnson, 1968) are seldom taken at sea; they are the first arrivals on land and presumably winter closest to the breeding islands. One can only speculate as to why females predominate in the southernmost migrations; perhaps the energy requirements to

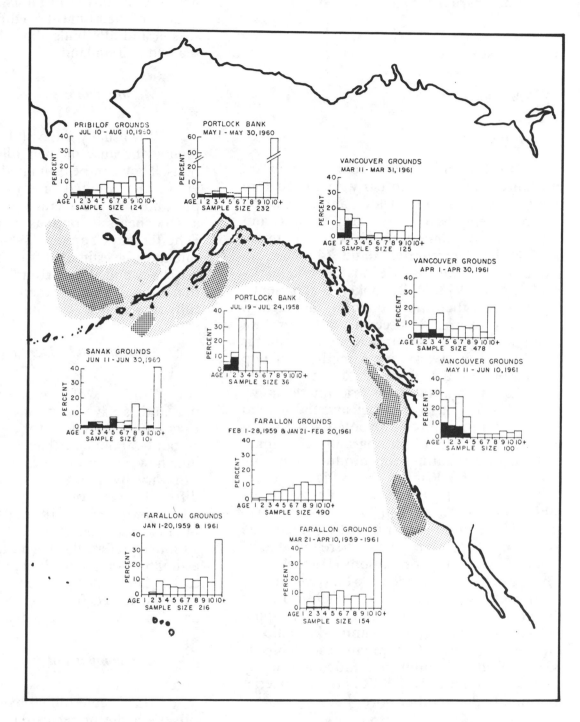

FIG. 3. – Distribution of northern fur seals in the eastern Pacific, 1958-61 (from NPFSC, 1962). Black bars are for males and white for females; dark and light shading indicates areas of intensive and limited sampling respectively.

sustain both mother and foetus cannot be met in colder waters to the north.

Pups migrate from the islands during October-November. They are the only age group for which total population counts or estimates may be obtained; the other age groups do not all come out on land at the same time, and they segregate on land and at sea by age, sex and maturity. Representative sampling is, therefore, difficult or impossible.

Vital parameters

CENSUS

Methods

Pups

On Robben Island (1 rookery) pups are normally rounded up in early August, before many have taken to the water, and counted by driving them past observers. Counts and tag-recapture estimates in the year of birth are used on the Commander Islands (4 rookeries). Direct counts were made on the Pribilof Islands during 1912-24 (21 rookeries at present); repopulation then made counting impractical on most rookeries. Pup census data were not taken during 1925-46 and Kenyon, Scheffer and Chapman (1954) give 6 methods of pup estimation on the Pribilofs during 1947-51 which are primarily of historic interest now; foggy weather, high pup density and limited image resolution have prevented a successful pup census by aerial photography. The main method of estimating pup production during 1947-60 on the Pribilofs was tagging pups, then recovering tags in the kill at ages 2-5 years (about 90 % were between 3 and 4 years old) to estimate the number of pups alive at the time of tagging. Tagging estimates were found to be higher than actual populations (Roppel *et al.*, 1966), however, and since 1961 have gradually been replaced by shearing a patch of fur off the head in early August and sampling about 1-2 weeks later for marked/unmarked ratios in the year of birth (Chapman and Johnson, 1968). Dead pup counts are added to live pup counts or estimates on USSR and US rookeries to estimate the number born.

Harem bulls and idle bulls

These are counted in June and/or July and August. Chapman (1964) suggests that harem bulls of the Pribilofs spend about one quarter of their time at sea during the breeding season and idle bulls about half their time at sea and half on land.

Mature females

It is usually impossible to count mature females because of their high density in harems. They can be estimated indirectly by dividing the counted or estimated number of pups born by the average pregnancy rate (i.e., a cow bears 1 pup as noted by Kenyon, Scheffer and Chapman, 1954). The pregnancy rate must be estimated from pelagic sampling, however, and this is complicated by the fact that animals younger than about 8 are seldom fully represented (Chapman, 1964).

Yearling and older animals

Estimates of numbers from tag-recapture studies have been made on the Pribilofs. Even after corrections for tag loss and for uncertainty about actual age at the time of tagging, however, estimated yearling abundance can vary by a factor of 2 or more between different ages of recovery from a given year-class (NPFSC, 1969, 1975). D.G. Chapman (various reports of U.S. fur seal investigations) prefers the tag returns at age 3 for estimating yearling abundance for kill forecasts. The latter are uncertain; errors for 1965-74 ranged from 25 to 48 % annually for ages 3 and 4 years combined.

Age composition

This is determined by counting annular ridges on the upper canine teeth from dead animals (Scheffer, 1950). The method is routinely applied to pelagic research collections, to the commercial kill, and less often to the relatively few animals older than pups that are found dead each year on land. On the Pribilofs, a daily 20 % sample is obtained to estimate the age composition of the kill (e.g., Marine Mammal Biological Laboratory, 1971); the accuracy of age readings from commercially killed animals (mainly 2-5 year males) exceeds 98 % (Anas, 1970).

Tags or check marks on flippers

These are detected on the killing grounds or during processing of carcasses after

pelts are stripped. Examination of flippers on slowly-moving, suspended carcasses at the processing plant on St. Paul Island (effective since 1965) may be the world's best system for detecting permanent tags and marks from marine mammals.

Results

Table 2 gives counted or estimated numbers of pups born in the exploited popu-

Table 2. Counted or estimated number of pups born on St. Paul Island (Pribilofs), Robben Island and the Commander Islands

Year	St. Paul Island [1]	Year	Robben Island [2]	Commander Islands [2]
1920	143	1958	32	38
1921	150	1959	35	41
1922	159	1960	38	45
1950	451	1961	41	48
1951	447	1962	45	52
1952	438	1963	49	56
1953	445	1964	51	58
1954	450	1965	48	59
1955	461	1966	45	61
1956	453	1967	56	55
1957	420	1968	46	61
1958	387	1969	44	59
1959	335	1970	32	62
1960	320	1971	41	66
1961	337	1972	44	61
1962	278	1973	35	54
1963	264	1974	33	69
1964	285			
1965	267			
1966	296			
1967	284			
1968	235			
1969	234			
1970	230			
1972	260			
1973	305			
1974	269			
1975	278			

[1] 1920-22 and 1950-65 from Chapman (1973);
1966 from Marine Mammal Biological Laboratory (1969);
1969 from Marine Mammal Biological Laboratory (1971);
1970 from Marine Mammal Biological Laboratory (1971a);
1967-68 and 1972-74 from NOAA Marine Mammal Division (1967);
counts or estimates for 1923-49 and 1971 are not available or are unrealistic.

[2] 1958-63 from NPFSC (1971);
1964-66 from Arseniev (1964, 1965, 1966);
1967-72 from NPFSC (1975);
1973 from NPFSC (1974);
1974 from NPFSC (1975a).

lations. St. Paul Island accounts for about 80 % of the Pribilofs' production, as noted earlier; values are not given for St. George Island because Chapman (1961, 1964, 1973) used only the St. Paul Island data to estimate maximum sustainable yield (MSY) for the Pribilofs' population (1912-24 values for both islands are in Table 5). Estimates for 1967-68 and 1972-74 are based on data collected only on sample rookeries in order to reduce disturbance of the seals, and no data were collected on any rookeries in 1971 (NOAA, Marine Mammal Division, 1976). The 1975 estimate indicates an increase of about 20 % above the low level of 1969-70.

Counts of harem and idle bulls are in Table 3 for the Pribilof Islands and in Table 4 for the Commander Islands and Robben Island. The 1975 counts on the Pribilof Islands indicate for both harem and idle bulls a reversal of the steady decline which followed the peak counts of 1961. Size limits on harvested animals have been adjusted to regulate the escapement of males into the breeding stock.

RATES

Birth rates — reproductive potential

Table 5 gives the numbers of pups born during periods of sustained increase from repopulation in the main breeding populations. Fig. 4 shows least squares regression lines. The expected number of pups born in the first and last years were equated by the average annual percentage increases in Fig. 4: 8.5 % per year for the Pribilofs, 6.5 % per year for the Commanders, and 6 % per year for Robben. The slight variability about regression is noteworthy: one can conclude with reasonable confidence that 6-10 % per year (average 8 % per year) is the maximum rate of increase when population density is low.

Natural mortality rates

Published estimates for the USSR rookeries emphasize the mortality of pups on land and the index, kill/newborn pup, which includes land and ocean mortality of males through the ages of harvest. One exception is Ichihara's (1972) work on the Robben Island population which gives the following: 20 % per year in males of 2-7 years, 32 % per year in bulls of 7 years and older, and 10 % per year in adult females of 3 years and older. The latter compares closely with 11 % per year by Chapman (1964) for adult Pribilof females.

Johnson (1968) estimated 38 % per year as the annual mortality of breeding males of 10 years and older. The rise in mortality rate of males with age is presumably due to fighting and fasting to hold breeding territories.

The mortality of pups on land is of special significance because it evidently can be density dependent. Table 11 of Kenyon, Scheffer and Chapman (1954) shows pup mortality was 7-8 % in pelagic sealing days before 1910, when pregnant and nursing females were killed. It then ranged from only 1.7 to 3.1 % during 1914-24 when the herd was small and growing rapidly. By 1949-51 when the population was very large, it increased to 12-17 %, and in the mid-fifties may have exceeded 20 % in a few year-classes (100 000 or more dead pups counted). Striking variations between rookeries are possible; e.g., 3-39 % on St. Paul Island in 1950 (Kenyon, Scheffer and Chapman, 1954). Recent pup mortality on US and USSR rookeries averages about 10 % per year, but can vary widely between years as well as rookeries. Hookworm disease, emaciation syndrome, and an infection caused by a spirochaete bacterium account for about 2/3 of all pup mortality of the Pribilofs (NOAA Marine Mammal Division, 1975). The proportion of deaths from hookworm disease can vary substantially between rookeries (Marine Mammal Biological Laboratory, 1971a); 2 % or less of the pups born on the Pribilof Islands in recent year-classes have died from hookworm disease although high proportions of the pups

Table 3. Counts or estimates of harem and idle bulls (mid-July) on the Pribilof Islands 1911-75 (A dash indicates no data)

Year	St. Paul Island		St. George Island		Both Islands	
	Harem	Idle	Harem	Idle	Harem	Idle
1911	1 090	258	266	71	1 356	329
1912	1 077	93	281	20	1 358	113
1913	1 142	77	261	28	1 403	105
1914	1 316	159	243	13	1 559	172
1915	1 789	546	362	127	2 151	673
1916	2 948	2 278	552	354	3 500	2 632
1917	4 116	2 341	684	365	4 850	2 706
1918	4 610	2 245	734	199	5 344	2 444
1919	4 573	2 158	585	81	5 158	2 239
1920	3 542	1 078	524	83	4 066	1 161
1921	3 443	711	466	36	3 909	747
1922	3 184	493	378	15	3 562	508
1923	3 051	303	361	9	3 412	312
1924	3 127	375	389	15	3 516	390
1925	3 103	283	423	28	3 526	311
1926	3 478	368	556	55	4 034	423
1927	3 916	846	727	126	4 643	972
1928	5 059	1 208	991	241	6 050	1 449
1929	5 998	1 339	1 189	294	7 187	1 633
1930	6 823	1 555	1 489	344	8 312	1 899
1931	7 557	1 519	1 676	369	9 223	1 888
1932	8 268	1 940	1 820	409	10 088	2 349
1933	8 334	1 933	1 879	408	10 213	2 341
1934	8 841	1 860	1 929	422	10 770	2 282
1935	9 444	2 082	2 103	453	11 547	2 535
1936	10 055	2 253	–	–	–	–
1937	10 689	2 516	2 411	515	13 100	3 031
1938	10 720	1 787	–	–	–	–
1939	9 122	2 616	1 858	357	10 980	2 973
1940	9 662	3 968	1 988	571	11 650	4 539
1941	10 089	5 059	1 942	396	12 031	5 455
1942	–	–	–	–	–	–
1943	10 948	3 523	2 107	330	13 055	3 853
1944	11 080	2 539	2 294	450	13 374	2 989
1945	10 750	4 055	2 434	750	13 184	4 805
1946	10 566	3 605	2 430	611	12 996	4 216
1947	10 160	3 331	1 808	479	11 968	3 810
1948	10 386	3 400	1 814	563	12 200	3 963
1949	9 554	2 976	1 746	552	11 300	3 528
1950	9 442	3 152	1 959	574	11 401	3 726
1951	9 434	3 581	1 825	549	11 259	4 130
1952	9 318	4 717	1 983	605	11 301	5 322
1953	9 848	5 912	2 285	826	12 133	6 738
1954	9 906	6 847	2 228	1 311	12 134	8 158
1955	9 034	8 650	2 130	1 902	11 164	10 552
1956	9 384	9 016	–	–	–	–
1957	9 562	10 060	2 423	2 693	11 985	12 753
1958	9 970	9 510	2 619	3 030	12 589	12 540
1959	10 003	11 485	2 527	2 699	12 530	14 184
1960	10 247	10 407	2 552	2 630	12 799	13 037
1961	11 163	11 791	2 843	2 489	14 006	14 280
1962	10 332	9 109	2 342	2 650	12 674	11 759
1963	9 212	7 650	2 071	1 890	11 283	9 540
1964	9 085	7 095	1 989	1 489	11 074	8 584
1965	8 553	5 616	1 917	1 113	10 470	6 729
1966	7 974	5 839	1 974	1 017	9 948	6 856

Table 3. **Counts or estimates of harem and idle bulls (mid-July) on the Pribilof Islands 1911-75 (A dash indicates no data)** *(concluded)*

Year	St. Paul Island		St. George Island		Both Islands	
	Harem	Idle	Harem	Idle	Harem	Idle
1967	7 230	4 439	1 646	1 268	9 876	5 707
1968	6 176	3 100	1 748	1 283	7 924	4 383
1969	5 928	2 535	1 457	677	7 385	3 212
1970	4 945	1 666	1 466	803	6 411	2 469
1971	4 200	1 900	1 235	534	5 435	2 434
1972	3 738	2 384	1 153	328	4 891	2 712
1973	4 906	2 550	875	375	5 781	2 925
1974	4 563	1 782	822	481	5 385	2 263
1975	5 018	3 535	877	1 427	5 895	4 962

contract it (M.C. Keyes, personal communication). Mortality on land lasts about 6 weeks and is mainly over by mid-August (Kenyon, Scheffer and Chapman, 1954).

Chapman (1964) noted for the Pribilofs population that a natural mortality of 50 % in the first year of life and 20 % per year from ages 1 to 3 years would be consistent with the observed return of males. He used 20 % per year for males of 3-7 years. There is some evidence (Chapman, 1964; Ichihara, 1972) that natural mortality of males exceeds that of females up to 3 years; in his latest work on MSY, Chapman (1973) uses 1.1 as the ratio of female to male recruitment at 3 years.

Harvesting rates, commercial and incidental kill

The USSR reports harvesting rates as the total kill of males divided by the number of male pups born (the sex ratio at birth and in foetuses from pelagic samples is very nearly 1:1). Values for the 1962-67 year-classes of 22-44 % for Robben Island and 32-42 % for the Commander Islands (NPFSC, 1975) include variations in land and ocean mortality up to the ages of harvest (mainly 2-5 years). The range of 20-31 % for the Pribilofs (1961-66 year-classes) suggests a lower average survival

in the eastern Bering Sea and North Pacific Ocean.

Age-specific exploitation rates are uncertain even for the Pribilofs population because of difficulty mentioned earlier with tag-recapture studies (i.e., where estimated yearling abundance varies widely with age at recovery). However, the tagging data do provide a good picture of relative rates and a fair guess at absolute rates: 5 % at age 2, 50 % at age 3, 70 % at age 4 and 30 % at age 5 (the latter figure is the most uncertain).

Table 6 gives the kill of males by age on the Pribilof Islands from the 1954-72 year-classes. Data from the Commander Islands and Robben Island for the 1956-72 year-classes are given in Table 7.

Annual kills during 1871-1975 for the Pribilofs are given in Table 8. To further speed repopulation after the 1911 ban on pelagic sealing, the US prohibited commercial sealing during 1912-17, when the only kill of males was for food. Kills of females were accidental or for research except during 1956-63, when the population was purposely reduced in the most important management action since the 1911 Treaty, and during 1964-68 when the calculated female contribution to MSY was harvested. Annual kills of males during 1871-90 and 1958-74 for the Commander Islands and during 1958-74 for Robben Island

Table 4. Number of harem and idle bulls counted on Robben Island and the Commander Islands, 1958-74[1]

Year	Robben Island		Commander Islands	
	Harem	Idle	Harem	Idle
1958	516	500	595	251
1959	666	700	691	399
1960	869	1 146	846	821
1961	935	1 490	933	1 032
1962	1 018	1 612	751	1 078
1963	1 056	1 409	1 215	927
1964	857	1 595	2 495	1 892
1965	741	1 472	1 573	4 670
1966	1 274	1 660	2 330	5 403
1967	1 008	930	1 789	3 853
1968	1 002	1 250	2 390	2 661
1969	754	1 250	2 170	1 661
1970	848	1 120	1 727	1 196
1971	910	954	1 541	813
1972	603	544	1 031	690
1973	356	208	750	858
1974	280	260	280	260

[1] 1958-61 from NPFSC, 1962; 1962-63 from NPFSC, 1971; 1964-66 and 1963 from Arseniev (1964, 1965, 1966, 1973); 1974 from Pacific Research Institute of Fisheries (TINRO) and All-Union Research Institute of Marine Fisheries and Oceanography (VNIRO), 1974.

are also in Table 8. Females have been killed only accidentally or experimentally on the USSR islands.

Fukuhara (1974) estimates that roughly 3 150-3 750 northern fur seals are killed incidentally each year by the Japanese mothership fishery for salmon west of 175°W. No estimates are available of the kill by origin, but these seals are undoubtedly from the Commander and Pribilof Islands. Nishiwaki (personal communication) believes the mothership fishery takes about 7 000 per year.

Table 5. Number of pups (thousands) born during 1912-24 on the Pribilof Islands (Kenyon, Scheffer and Chapman, 1954) and during 1958-64 on Robben Island and the Commander Islands (NPFSC, 1969)

Year	Pribilof Islands[1]	Year	Robben Island	Commander Islands
1912	82	1958	32	38
1913	92	1959	35	41
1914	93	1960	38	45
1915	104	1961	41	48
1916	117	1962	45	52
1917	128	1963	49	56
1918	143	1964	51	59
1919	157			
1920	168			
1921	177			
1922	186			
1924	208			

[1] No data available for 1923.

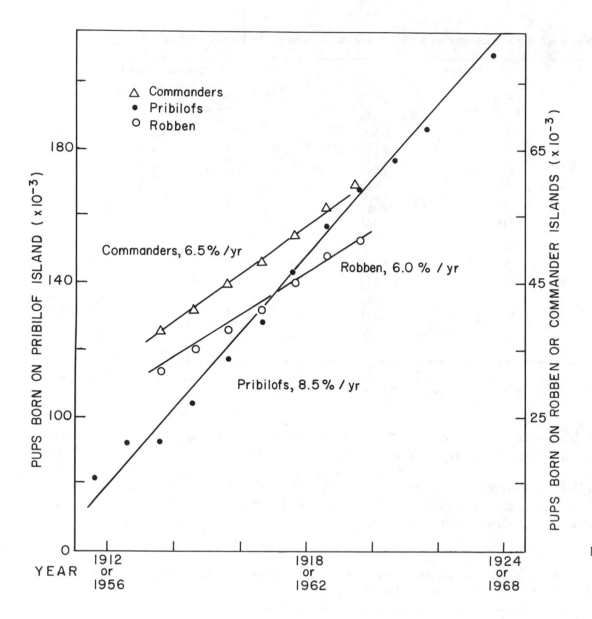

Fɪɢ. 4. – Numbers of pups born annually during periods of increase on the Pribilof Islands (1912-24) and on the Commander Islands and Robben Island (1958-64). Average annual percentage increases are from first and last years as expected from regression lines shown.

Trend in abundance (historical development)

The Commander Islands population was over 1 million before its rapid depletion at the turn of the century and near-destruction by 1911 (Nikulin, 1971). F.G. Chelnokov (personal communication) notes that there were 25 rookeries on the Commanders in the last century and the population may have numbered 1.5 to 2.0 million. It is interesting that the ratio of former to present rookeries (25/4 = 6.25), when multiplied by the current estimate of 265 000 (Table 1), by assuming no change in average number per rookery, suggests a population of 1.7 million.

The total kill of males is highly correlated in all exploited stocks with the kill at age 3 (r > 0.9). Fig. 5 shows the increasing trend of pup production during 1958-66 on the Commander Islands, along with an eye-fitted curve which indicates density-dependent mortality on land and MSY when 50 000-55 000 pups are born annually.

Nikulin (1971) projects an annual yield (of 2-5 year males) of at least 40 000 when the

Table 6. Kill of male seals by age on the Pribilof Islands, 1954-72 year-classes. (Dash indicates incomplete returns or no kill on St. George Island after 1972)

| Year-class | St. Paul Island | | | | | St. George Island | | | | | Total |
| | Age when killed | | | | Subtotal | Age when killed | | | | Subtotal | |
	2	3	4	5		2	3	4	5		
1954	2 918	23 473	5 599	554	32 544	535	6 651	2 779	162	10 127	42 671
1955	1 015	27 863	10 555	115	39 548	555	7 246	2 825	260	10 886	50 434
1956	885	10 671	2 762	532	14 850	171	2 251	1 387	218	4 027	18 877
1957	2 590	24 283	15 344	773	42 990	242	5 098	4 492	244	10 076	53 066
1958	1 977	48 458	14 149	1 587	66 171	431	9 413	3 707	540	14 091	80 262
1959	2 820	26 456	14 184	1 764	45 224	891	5 890	4 690	492	11 963	57 187
1960	1 619	14 310	10 533	1 240	27 702	636	4 332	2 579	178	7 725	35 427
1961	1 098	22 468	12 046	1 270	36 882	921	6 948	2 592	502	10 963	47 845
1962	2 539	19 009	12 156	1 287	34 991	1 139	3 736	3 881	392	9 148	44 139
1963	1 264	25 535	11 785	1 542	40 126	167	5 586	3 738	406	9 897	50 023
1964	3 143	26 991	13 279	1 469	44 882	391	7 622	3 680	680	12 373	57 255
1965	2 200	18 706	10 565	731	32 202	740	4 443	2 204	547	7 934	40 136
1966	1 673	17 826	11 548	1 338	32 385	443	2 645	2 274	467	5 829	38 214
1967	2 640	22 176	12 503	2 185	39 504	411	2 916	559	6 403	10 289	49 793
1968	1 725	12 888	14 932	721	30 266	98	1 456	2 125	—	—	—
1969	323	15 024	10 800	1 631	27 778	32	1 442	—	—	—	—
1970	916	16 337	15 533	—	—	57	—	—	—	—	—
1971	577	14 652	—	—	—	—	—	—	—	—	—
1972	1 025	—	—	—	—	—	—	—	—	—	—

population is restored. Declining pup production and numbers of bulls in recent years (Tables 2-4) have caused concern (NPFSC, 1973, 1974), however, and experience on the Kuril Islands population – destroyed near the turn of the century and presently with only about 33 000 animals despite the absence of a commercial kill (NPFSC, 1975a) – indicates slow repopulation on decimated rookeries. Considering the site-specific nature of harems, A.M. Johnson (personal communication) has postulated that density-dependent mortality may even occur at the harem level before a population rehabitates all other available sites on a rookery.

Seals on Robben Island were also near depletion in 1911 (Nikulin, 1971). Fig. 6 shows an increase in numbers of pups born during 1958-64. The curve is very poorly defined by comparison with the curve for the Commanders, but suggests MSY when about 50 000 pups are born. Ichihara's (1972) computations indicate MSY of 14 000 (6 000 males and 8 000 females) when 45 000 pups are born (Fig. 7).

Conflicting values have been reported for the primitive abundance of the Pribilofs population in 1786 when the islands were discovered and in 1911-12 when the population was at a minimum. Harry (1974) has reviewed the early reports and resolves them as follows in the light of present evidence that newborn pups are about 1/4 of the total population: when Alaska was purchased from Russia in 1867, the population was probably 2 to 2.5 million and this also seems likely to be the range for the pre-exploited population. The population was probably about 300 000 at the low point in 1911-12.

Fig. 8 (from Johnson, 1971) shows that the maximum rate of increase in the kill was during 1925-35. The "best estimate" of pups born was developed by assuming an increase of 8 % per year until 1930, when the rate of increase in the male kill began to decline.

Table 7. Kill of male seals by age on the Commander Islands (C) and Robben Island (R) 1956-72 year-classes. (Dash indicates no data available)

Year-class	Island	Age								
		2	3	4	5	6	7	8	9	10
1956	C	54	513	1 709	339	20	0	3	0	7
	R	89	1 976	1 670	460	214	226	166	3	46
1957	C	2	1 036	2 027	279	18	2	2	18	0
	R	88	2 116	1 584	496	205	73	3	113	74
1958	C	54	2 484	2 109	311	95	5	40	1	0
	R	124	3 221	1 711	684	52	13	157	121	45
1959	C	127	3 570	2 403	776	143	79	1	0	0
	R	340	3 070	1 734	379	77	110	141	83	7
1960	C	414	4 053	2 446	779	185	17	6	0	0
	R	480	3 387	1 852	450	130	255	105	18	4
1961	C	527	6 323	2 804	588	52	9	0	8	0
	R	459	4 320	1 869	557	594	175	28	9	87
1962	C	828	6 467	2 371	418	103	4	1	0	0
	R	1 032	4 678	1 598	1 119	420	34	42	69	1
1963	C	1 069	5 137	7 469	571	37	4	0	0	0
	R	1 336	4 199	1 839	673	93	96	53	1	0
1964	C	549	4 926	2 690	283	50	7	0	0	0
	R	2 238	3 582	811	242	127	70	2	2	0
1965	C	496	5 510	1 756	396	37	1	0	0	–
	R	1 014	1 341	575	275	200	13	0	0	–
1966	C	617	5 621	2 280	339	0	0	0	–	–
	R	1 486	3 360	1 026	517	107	3	0	–	–
1967	C	608	5 573	2 272	49	0	2	–	–	–
	R	1 833	4 580	1 662	362	10	0	–	–	–
1968	C	711	4 923	1 417	10	2	–	–	–	–
	R	874	3 525	786	30	0	–	–	–	–
1969	C	562	3 414	401	14	–	–	–	–	–
	R	613	2 975	544	5	–	–	–	–	–
1970	C	675	1 690	337	–	–	–	–	–	–
	R	1 657	2 609	174	–	–	–	–	–	–
1971	C	276	1 222	–	–	–	–	–	–	–
	R	935	1 747	–	–	–	–	–	–	–
1972	C	136	–	–	–	–	–	–	–	–
	R	556	–	–	–	–	–	–	–	–

From 1930 until 1947 (when pups were first tagged to estimate their abundance), the pup curve was fitted to reflect the shape of the male kill curve.

Fluctuations in the kill (3-year moving average) are evident during 1940-45 and (although not shown) occurred also in the next decade. Thus, the kill from the 1956 year-class was a record low of about 19 000 (Table 6)

despite the high population level. The dead pup count in 1956 exceeded 100 000: by this time it was evident that the rookeries were overcrowded and that the earlier increase in male kill had given way to erratic fluctuations.

The 4 nations recognized this in their discussions leading to the 1957 Interim Convention. Since Japan also advocated pelagic sealing on the grounds that excessive seal pop-

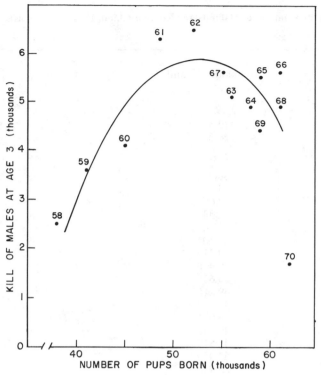

FIG. 5. – Harvest-pup relationship for Commander Islands fur seal populations.

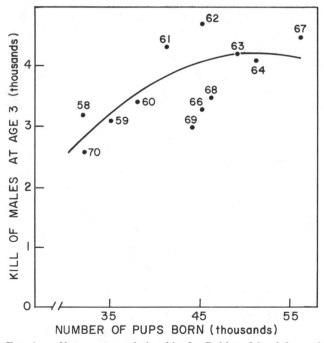

FIG. 6. – Harvest-pup relationship for Robben Island fur seal population.

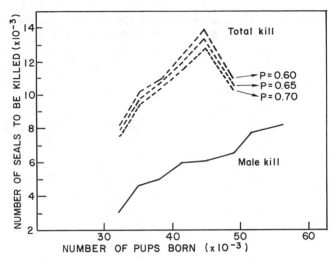

FIG. 7. – Sustainable yield from the Robben Island fur seal population; total kill includes both sexes, and P indicates average weighted pregnancy rate (from Ichihara, 1972).

ulations were damaging her fisheries (Japan abrogated the 1911 Treaty in 1941 on these grounds), the herd reduction programme with its female kills as mentioned earlier was begun in 1956, when 28 000 were taken (Table 8).

Nagasaki (1961) and Chapman (1961) published MSY estimates using the relation between the return or kill of males and the estimated pup production. These estimates, although tentative, agreed that optimum pup production on the Pribilofs was about 480 000. At this level the estimated annual MSY was

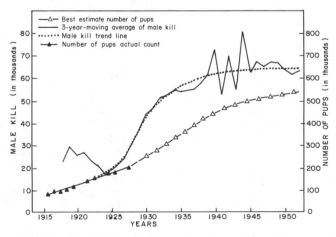

FIG. 8. – Trend of male kill and number of pups born on the Pribilof Islands, Alaska; values for pups born are translated 3.5 years to the right on the time scale (from Johnson, 1971).

335

Table 8. Kill of seals on the Pribilof Islands by sex and kill of males on the Commander Islands and Robben Island, 1871-1975. (Dash indicates no data available to present authors)

Year	Pribilof Islands [1]		Commander Islands [2]	Robben Island
	Male	Female		
1871	102 960	–	12 500	–
1872	108 819	–	26 898	–
1873	109 117	–	28 091	–
1874	110 585	–	28 584	–
1875	106 460	–	36 274	–
1876	94 657	–	24 326	–
1877	84 310	–	17 008	–
1878	109 323	–	31 340	–
1879	110 511	–	37 666	–
1880	105 718	–	48 504	–
1881	105 063	–	39 312	–
1882	99 812	–	40 468	–
1883	79 509	–	26 626	–
1884	105 434	–	49 216	–
1885	105 024	–	41 924	–
1886	104 521	–	54 021	–
1887	105 760	–	46 531	–
1888	103 304	–	43 518	–
1889	102 617	–	52 070	–
1890	28 859	–	55 432	–
1891	14 406	–	–	–
1892	7 509	–	–	–
1893	7 390	–	–	–
1894	15 033	–	–	–
1895	14 846	–	–	–
1896	30 654	–	–	–
1897	19 200	–	–	–
1898	18 047	–	–	–
1899	16 812	–	–	–
1900	22 470	–	–	–
1901	22 672	–	–	–
1902	22 386	–	–	–
1903	19 292	–	–	–
1904	13 128	–	–	–
1905	14 368	–	–	–
1906	14 476	–	–	–
1907	14 964	–	–	–
1908	14 996	–	–	–
1909	14 368	–	–	–
1910	13 586	–	–	–
1911	12 006	–	–	–
1912	3 191	–	–	–
1913	2 406	–	–	–
1914	2 735	–	–	–
1915	3 947	–	–	–
1916	6 468	–	–	–
1917	8 170	–	–	–
1918	34 890	–	–	–
1919	27 764	57	–	–
1920	26 568	80	–	–
1921	23 605	76	–	–
1922	31 063	93	–	–
1923	15 716	204	–	–
1924	17 053	166	–	–

Table 8. Kill of seals on the Pribilof Islands by sex and kill of males on the Commander Islands and Robben Island, 1871-1975. (Dash indicates no data available to present authors) *(concluded)*

Year	Pribilof Islands [1]		Commander Islands [2]	Robben Island
	Male	Female		
1925	19 750	110	–	–
1926	22 035	96	–	–
1927	24 912	30	–	–
1928	31 039	60	–	–
1929	40 023	45	–	–
1930	42 449	51	–	–
1931	49 462	62	–	–
1932	49 232	104	–	–
1933	54 471	79	–	–
1934	53 408	60	–	–
1935	57 061	235	–	–
1936	52 227	219	–	–
1937	55 010	170	–	–
1938	58 165	199	–	–
1939	60 312	161	–	–
1940	64 940	323	–	–
1941	92 802	2 211	–	–
1942	150	0	–	–
1943	116 407	757	–	–
1944	47 533	119	–	–
1945	76 391	573	–	–
1946	64 028	495	–	–
1947	61 153	294	–	–
1948	69 893	249	–	–
1949	70 553	337	–	–
1950	59 925	279	–	–
1951	60 503	186	–	–
1952	69 670	200	–	–
1953	65 824	845	–	–
1954	63 224	658	–	–
1955	64 727	743	–	–
1956	96 057	27 632	–	–
1957	46 219	47 426	–	–
1958	47 866	31 100	3 021	3 127
1959	30 191	28 060	2 261	4 860
1960	36 327	4 312	4 079	6 210
1961	82 798	43 849	5 023	6 947
1962	53 680	43 760	6 401	6 254
1963	42 386	43 952	7 312	6 469
1964	48 980	16 452	10 470	7 708
1965	42 123	10 434	11 287	8 423
1966	52 472	481	8 909	8 832
1967	55 720	10 096	8 381	8 758
1968	45 625	13 335	9 507	5 070
1969	38 678	230	8 309	6 221
1970	42 121	120	9 073	7 042
1971	31 795	103	8 140	7 003
1972	37 314	79	6 556	5 911
1973	28 457	25	2 395	4 187
1974	32 976	51	1 727	2 500
1975	29 093	55	–	–

[1] 1871-1911 data from Riley (1967), who also gives data back to 1876.
[2] 1871-1890 data from Table 1 of Nikulin (1971).

about 65 000 males and 35 000 females (NPFSC, 1962). Later, when it was known that estimates of pup production during the fifties, based on tagging, were too high, Chapman (1964) critically examined population estimates, recalculated MSY, and noted that the MSY level and the righthand limb of the return-pup relation were less well defined. The new MSY values (averaged from the same two models used earlier) were then about 55 000 males and at least 10 000 females. This would occur with about 761 000 females age 3 and older or, with a pregnancy rate of 60 %, when about 457 000 pups were born. His latest computation (Chapman, 1973) indicates that the annual pup production for MSY is about 360 000 on both islands or 283 000 on St. Paul Island alone.

The failure of the population to yield the annual expected kill of 55 000 males (versus 43 000 actually killed) after the herd reduction programme of female kills during 1956-63 cannot be explained by the high pup estimates from tagging in the fifties. Tables 3 and 8 show a decline in the kill starting in the sixties and a steady decline in bull counts during 1961-72. The number of pups born annually during 1929-33 and 1962-66 were probably very similar, yet the earlier year-classes yielded an average male kill of 53 600 vis-à-vis only 43 000 from the later year-classes (NOAA/NMFS, 1973). For reasons unknown, therefore, survival evidently has diminished by 20 % (53 600-43 000) (100/53, 600). Management policy since 1968 has been to increase escapement into the breeding stock.

Trophic relationships

FOOD AND FEEDING

Much biological information has been assembled for the northern fur seal including the type and quantity of food consumed throughout its range in the North Pacific Ocean, Bering Sea and the Seas of Okhotsk and Japan.

Fur seals are opportunistic feeders and appear to feed on available species. Seals generally swallow small prey whole below the surface, while larger prey are brought to the surface and shaken violently from side to side to break them into smaller pieces. Fresh, well preserved specimens found in stomachs of fur seals with no teeth puncture wounds indicate that teeth are used for seizing their prey but not for masticating their food. Fur seals collected on the Continental Shelf tend to feed on fishes, whereas seals taken beyond the shelf feed mostly on squids.

Squids are also one of the principal food prey species throughout the range of the fur seal. Many species have been described in the literature, but very little is known about their biology, distribution and abundance, except that they are assumed to be quite abundant in all oceans. All squids found in fur seal stomachs are considered to be pelagic, deep water species except for *Loligo opalescens*, a shallow-water species. Identification of squids in stomachs is made from remains of beaks, pens and whole specimens.

Feeding habits and food base

The food species consumed by fur seals vary by area, but the important food in the diet of fur seals in a given area (based on stomach content volume) generally does not change — only their ranking by volume (Table 9). Food volume information is from 1958-74 annual reports of the US on pelagic research.

The principal food of fur seals throughout their range (eastern Pacific) is as follows: (1) Pacific herring (*Clupea harengus pallasi*): (2) northern anchovy (*Engraulis mordax*); (3) Pacific salmon (*Oncorhynchus* spp.); (4) capelin (*Mallotus villosus*); (5) Pacific saury (*Cololabis saira*); (6) Pacific hake (*Merluccius productus*); (7) walleye pollock (*Theragra chalcogramma*); (8) rockfish (*Sebastes* spp.); (9) Atka mackerel (*Pleurogrammus monoptery-*

Table 9. Principal food of fur seals by area

Area	Year	Stomachs with food	Food species	Percent of total stomach volume	Area	Year	Stomachs with food	Food species	Percent of total stomach volume
California	1958	323	Squid	30.0		1964	22	Hake	47.7
			Saury	21.3				Eulachon smelt	17.2
			Hake	16.9				Rockfish	14.3
			Anchovy	14.3				Salmon	14.2
	1959	893	Anchovy	58.9		1965	98	Anchovy	47.6
			Hake	24.4				Smelt	17.7
			Squid	4.3				Salmon	11.3
			Saury	3.6				Herring	9.3
	1961	565	Squid	41.2		1967	89	Salmon	32.3
			Anchovy	29.7				Herring	24.3
			Saury	13.5				Rockfish	17.6
			Hake	7.1				Shad	11.5
	1964	228	Hake	73.8		1968	251	Salmon	31.7
			Squid	15.4				Anchovy	15.9
			Sablefish	7.5				Rockfish	14.3
			Anchovy	2.1				Eulachon	11.7
	1965	226	Hake	36.7		1969	190	Anchovy	32.7
			Squid	28.2				Rockfish	28.9
			Anchovy	15.0				Capelin	19.4
			Rockfish	11.6				Salmon	11.3
	1966	331	Anchovy	74.5		1970	299	Squid	48.4
			Hake	19.7				Anchovy	19.8
			Saury	2.7				Rockfish	6.4
			Squid	1.5				Salmon	5.9
						1971	204	Anchovy	31.7
Oregon	1958	36	Squid	60.0				Salmon	23.6
			Hake	18.1				Pacific hake	14.6
			Saury	12.4				Capelin	11.3
			Jack mackerel	7.1		1972	162	Squid	33.9
	1959	31	Hake	34.5				Anchovy	26.0
			Rockfish	28.6				Herring	17.5
			Squid	15.7				Rockfish	8.5
			American shad	4.2					
			Herring	2.1	Alaska	1958	372	Herring	45.7
	1961	26	Anchovy	60.3				Capelin	28.0
			Rockfish	32.2				Sand lance	9.7
			American shad	4.2				Walleye pollock	9.7
			Herring	2.1		1960	876	Sand lance	37.2
	1964	10	Hake	100.0				Capelin	28.2
								Herring	16.0
								Walleye pollock	10.5
Washington	1958	55	Herring	51.8		1962	795	Capelin	56.8
			Saury	13.6				Squid	19.0
			Squid	13.0				Walleye pollock	12.4
			Rockfish	12.9				Atka mackerel	4.8
	1959	120	Rockfish	40.2		1963	816	Squid	50.2
			Sablefish	21.8				Capelin	20.0
			Herring	14.0				Walleye pollock	7.7
			Salmon	10.9				Deepsea smelt	7.2
	1961	185	Anchovy	37.7		1964	369	Squid	35.6
			Rockfish	21.7				Herring	30.9
			Herring	17.3				Walleye pollock	14.0
			Salmon	9.5				Deepsea smelt	6.9

Table 9. Principal food of fur seals by area *(concluded)*

Area	Year	Stomachs with food	Food species	Percent of total stomach volume
	1968	324	Walleye pollock	37.8
			Squid	30.8
			Atka mackerel	16.3
			Capelin	7.4
	1973	519	Walleye pollock	67.2
			Gadidae	14.8
			Squid	10.3
			Deepsea smelt	4.0
	1974	201	Wammeye pollock	73.5
			Gadidae	12.3
			Atka mackerel	6.8
			Deepsea smelt	2.7

gius): (10) Pacific sand lance (*Ammodytes hexapterus*); (11) deepsea smelt (Bathylagidae); (12) and squids as follows: *Loligo opalescens, Onychoteuthis boralijaponicus, Moroteuthis robusta, Abraliopsis* spp., *Octopoteuthis* spp., *Gonatus* spp., *Berryteuthis magister, Gonatopsis borealis, Chiroteuthis* spp.

The principal foods of fur seals for the various areas in the eastern Pacific and Bering Sea are as follows:

California	— (2), (5), (6), (12)
Oregon	— (2), (6), (12)
Washington	— (2), (3), (4), (6), (8)
British Columbia	— (1), (12)
Alaska	— (1), (4), (7), (9), (10), (11), (12)

The principal foods of fur seals in the Sea of Japan, Sea of Okhotsk and the western Pacific (NPFSC, 1962, 1969, 1971, 1975) are similar to foods eaten in the eastern Pacific:

Sea of Japan - walleye pollock (*T. chalcogramma*) and squids *Ommastrephes sloani pacificus* and *Watasenia scintillans*

Sea of Okhotsk - walleye pollock

Western Pacific - cod-like fish (*Laemonema longipes*), lantern fish (*Notoscopelus elongatus*), chub mackerel (*Scomber japonicus*), walleye pollock and squids (*M. robusta, B. magister, G. borealis*).

Requirements and utilization

The energy requirements of fur seals are poorly known at present. From thousands of fur seal stomachs examined, it has been found that seals collected during the early morning have the fullest stomachs; food volume decreases during the day and increases toward dusk, indicating that some probably feed at least twice daily. Fur seals are also capable of fasting for long periods of time; e.g., breeding adult male fur seals may fast in the wild for more than 2 months (60 days) while nursing females may not feed for up to 4-5 days. Keyes (1968) reported that growing, pregnant and lactating seals require more food but that captive pinnipeds fed frozen fish and squids (with vitamin supplements) equal to 6-10 % of their body weight daily fared well in captivity.

Destruction of food supply

The northern fur seal is economically important for its valuable skin but is important also because of its impact on fishery resources. Some commercially important food species are consumed by fur seals throughout their range; the major foods of fur seals are not generally utilized as fresh seafood by the United States fishery but are fished extensively by foreign fisheries. Some of these species are: squids, hake, anchovy, herring, sand lance, capelin, walleye pollock, Atka mackerel and deepsea smelt.

The competition between man, the fur seal and other forms of marine life, for certain stocks of fish, is a problem in resource allocation. Sanger (1974) estimated the total annual consumption of fish by northern fur seals, from the Pribilof Islands, to be 965 000 metric tonnes (Table 10). Based on the fur seal food composition observed in the summer of 1973, he estimated that fur seal consumption is equivalent to about 15 % of the commercial walleye pollock catch (1.8 million metric tonnes in 1972) in the eastern Bering Sea. Walleye pollock was the principal food of fur seals in the eastern Bering Sea and contributed 2/3 of the total food volume of stomachs examined in 1973.

The relationship between fur seals and other living resources of the North Pacific Ocean is poorly understood and the problem is complex. We cannot conclude at this time that the reduction in stocks of a single species such as walleye pollock would affect the fur seal population because of a lowered food availability or, conversely, that the fur seal population would be greater if no commercial fishery existed for pollock. The availability of food is only one aspect of survival; a few others which

might affect survival and population changes of the herd are predators, diseases, pollution, density and storms.

ECOSYSTEM

The northern fur seal encounters many environmental changes annually, both at sea and on land. During the fur seal's annual migration to and from the breeding grounds, the animals are subjected to changing current systems, water masses and other oceanographic features (Figs. 1 and 9). Fur seal densities are often greatest near sea valleys, canyons, seamounts and along the Continental Shelf where there are abrupt changes in depth and upwelling of nutrient-rich bottom water. We will not attempt to relate here the characteristics of these oceanographic features in the path of the fur seal, but only mention that this information is available in Dodimead, Favorite and Hirano, 1963.

The role of the prey species consumed by fur seals is important in the ecosystem but equally important are the other animals that share the same ecosystem. Squids, for example, are a major item of food for fur seals; they are also food for many other kinds of marine animals including small and large cetaceans, fish, seabirds and are themselves active predators.

Predators on fur seals include sea lions and possibly sharks and killer whales. Sea lions were observed preying on fur seal pups during 1973-75 near St. George Island, Alaska (NOAA, Marine Mammal Division, 1975, 1976). There is no documentation of fur seals in killer whale stomachs, but Rice (1968) concluded that adult killer whales feed predominantly on mammals. During a pelagic sealing cruise off Washington State, a killer whale appeared on 16 May 1970, when fur seal hunting was in progress. Disturbance occurred at the surface near the fur seal being hunted; the fur seal was not seen again and may have been swallowed whole.

Table 10. Estimates of total annual or seasonal food consumption by northern fur seals from the Pribilof Islands [1]

Estimated herd size (thousands)	Area	Season	Food consumption (thousands of tons)
1 530	N. Pacific	Annual	689
1 300	Bering Sea	Annual	318-340
90	Aleut. Cent. SE Alaska	June-Nov.	49.4
236	Aleut. Cent. SE Alaska	Dec.-May	129.2
550	Eastern Bering Sea	June-Nov.	304.0
97	Eastern Bering Sea	Dec.-May	53.3
66 [2]	Gulf of Alaska	Annual	72.3
849 [3]	South of Alaska	Dec.-May	357.1
1 300	N. Pacific	Annual	956.3

[1] From Sanger (1974), who cites values in first two rows.
[2] Average of summer and winter.
[3] Assumes age and weight composition of 25 % yearlings at 10 kg, and 75 % "other" at 48 kg.

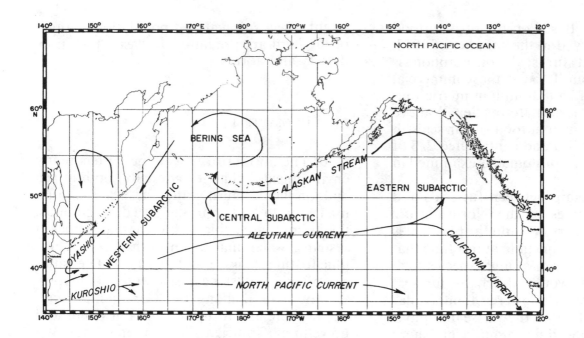

FIG. 9. – Major current
systems (Dodimead *et
al.*, 1963).

Man, sea lions and blue foxes are the principal predators of fur seals on the Pribilof Islands. Of special interest are the seabird rookeries on the Pribilofs which are among the largest in the world. These birds must also have a tremendous impact on the ecology of the area, but direct relations with the fur seal are at best speculative.

Other factors

AESTHETIC VALUES

Increasing public interest in marine mammals and concern for their welfare has been expressed in the United States, culminating in the Marine Mammal Protection Act of 1972. Section 2(6) of that legislation states as a policy declaration that "marine mammals have proven themselves to be resources of great international significance, aesthetic and recreational as well as economic, and it is the sense of the Congress that they should be pro-

tected and encouraged to develop to the greatest extent feasible commensurate with sound policies of resource management ...".

As a result of concern about whether harvesting procedures are humane, an expert panel of veterinarians examined in detail the traditional method of harvesting seals on the Pribilof Islands by stunning with a club followed by bleeding from the heart, and also investigated alternate methods. Stunning followed by bleeding was determined to be the most humane procedure (U.S. Congress, Sub-Committee on Commerce, 1972; Williams *et al.*, 1973). In this connexion, it should be noted that seals (except harem bulls) are extremely gregarious when on land. When a pod of young males (usually about 6-10) is isolated for killing from the large group driven inland from the beach, the individuals exhibit no panic when others in the pod are struck down. Seldom is it necessary, furthermore, for the expert stunners to administer more than one blow to the head.

St. Paul village on the island of that name has welcomed, in recent years, a sharply increasing number of tourists from the U.S. and distant lands. This trend undoubtedly will continue because of great interest in the pinniped with the longest oceanic migraiton of all.

FUTURE PRODUCT DEMANDS

W.G. Kirkness (personal communication) notes that the demand for seal skins for coats has been steady. Most of the processed skins are sold to buyers from West Germany and Italy. The US market has for some years been slow in its demand for skins, especially for heavy skins such as those of *C. ursinus*. A recent economic study by the National Marine Fisheries Service indicates no increasing or decreasing trend in demand.

OTHER USES OF MARINE MAMMALS

NPFSC (1975) states that "the fur seal resource has provided products other than fur (the principal product), such as mixed feeds for fish, poultry and fur-bearing animals, fertilizers, glycerin for munitions, oil for tanning, and oriental pharmaceuticals. In addition, a special type of peptide (callopeptide) can be extracted from the muscle protein of fur seals, but the study of its physiological and medical effects on the human body is incomplete.

"Increasing public concern over marine mammals, however, suggests that rational utilization of the fur seal resource should also consider these animals for their educational and aesthetic significance."

References

ANAS, R.E., Accuracy in assigning ages to fur seals. *J.*
1970   *Wildl. Manage.*, 34(4):844-52.

ARSENIEV, V.A., Report on USSR fur seal investigations
1964   in 1964. Moscow, VNIRO-TINRO, 101 p.
        (mimeo).

–, Report on USSR fur seal investigations in 1965.
1965   Moscow, VNIRO-TINRO, 95 p. (mimeo).

–, Report on USSR fur seal investigations in 1966.
1966   Moscow, VNIRO-TINRO, 92 p. (mimeo).

–, Report on USSR fur seal investigations in 1973.
1973   Moscow, VNIRO-TINRO, 78 p. (mimeo).

CHAPMAN, D.G., Population dynamics of the Alaska fur
1961   seal herd. *Trans. N. Am. Wildl. Nat. Resour.*
        Conf., (26):356-69.

–, A critical study of Pribilof fur seal population esti-
1964   mates. *Fish. Bull. U.S. Fish. Wildl. Serv.*,
        (63):657-69.

–, Spawner-recruit models and estimation of the level
1973   of maximum sustainable catch. *Rapp. P.-V.*
        Réun. CIEM, 164:325-32.

CHAPMAN, D.G. and A.M. JOHNSON, Estimation of fur
1968   seal pup populations by randomized sampl-
        ing. *Trans. Am. Fish. Soc.*, 97(3):264-70.

DODIMEAD, A.J., F. FAVORITE and T. HIRANO, Salmon of
1963   the North Pacific Ocean. Part 2. Review of
        oceanography of the subarctic Pacific region.
        Bull. INPEC, (13):195 p.

FUKUHARA, F.M., Estimated mortality of seabirds, fur
1974   seal, and porpoise in Japanese salmon drift
        net fisheries and sea lions in the eastern
        Bering Sea trawl fishery. Seattle, Wash.,
        NOAA/NMFS, 2 p. (unpubl. MS).

HARRY, G.Y., Fur seal population numbers. Memoran-
1974   dum, Seattle, Wash., NOAA/NMFS, July 3,
        1974, 2 p. (Unpubl.).

ICHIHARA, T., Maximum sustainable yield from the
1972   Robben Island fur seal herd. *Bull. Far Seas*
        Fish. Res. Lab., (6):77-94.

JOHNSON, A.M., Annual mortality of territorial male fur
1968   seals and its management significance. *J.*
        Wildl. Manage., 72(1):94-9.

–, Management of northern fur seals. Seattle, Wash.,
1971   NOAA/NMFS, Marine Mammals Biological
        Laboratory, 20 p. (Unpubl. MS).

–, The status of northern fur seal population. *Rapp.*
1975   *P.-V. Réun. CIEM*, 169:263-6.

KENYON, K.W., V.B. SCHEFFER and D.G. CHAPMAN, A

1954 population study of the Alaska fur seal herd. *Spec. Sci. Rep. U.S. Fish. Wildl. Serv. (Wildl.)*, (12):77 p.

KEYES, M.C., The nutrition of pinnipeds. *In* The
1968 behaviour and physiology of pinnipeds, edited by R.J. Harrison *et al.* New York, Appleton-Century-Crofts, pp. 359-95.

Marine Mammal Biological Laboratory, Fur seal
1969 investigations, 1966. *Spec. Sci. Rep. Fish, NOAA/NMFS*, (584):123 p.

–, Fur seal investigations, 1969. *Spec. Sci. Rep. Fish,*
1971 *NOAA/NMFS*, (628):99 p.

–, Fur seal investigations, 1970. Seattle, Wash.,
1971a NOAA/NMFS, 155 p. (mimeo).

NAGASAKI, F., Population study on the fur seal herd.
1961 *Spec. Publ. Tokai Fish. Lab.*, (7):60 p.

NIKULIN, P.G., Present condition and growth perspec-
1971 tives of the Commander Islands fur seal popu-lation. *In* Pinnipeds of the North Pacific, edit-ed by V.A. Arseniev and K.I. Panin. Moscow, Akademia Nauka, pp. 28-38 (1968). Translated by Israel Program for Scientific Translations, Jerusalem, IPST Cat. No. 5798.

NOAA, Marine Mammal Division, Fur seal investiga-
1975 tions, 1974. Seattle, Wash., NOAA/NMFS. 125 p. (mimeo).

–, Fur seal investigations, 1975. Seattle, Wash.,
1976 NOAA/NMFS.

NOAA/NMFS, Administration of the Marine Mammal
1973 Protection Act of 1972, December 21, 1972 to June 21, 1973. Report of the Secretary of Commerce. *Fed. Reg. U.S.*, 38(147):20601.

NPFSC, North Pacific Fur Seal Commission report on
1962 investigations from 1958-61. *NPFSC Rep. Invest.*, (1958-61):183 p.

–, North Pacific Fur Seal Commission report on inves-
1969 tigations from 1964 to 1966. *NPFSC Rep. Invest.*, (1964-66):161 p.

–, Proceedings of the twelfth annual meeting. *Proc.*
1970 *Annu. Meet. NPFSC*, (12):33 p.

–, North Pacific Fur Seal Commission report on inves-
1971 tigations in 1962-63. *NPFSC Rep. Invest.*, (1962-63):95 p.

–, Proceedings of the sixteenth annual meeting. *Proc.*
1973 *Annu. Meet. NPFSC*, (16):36 p.

–, Proceedings of the seventeenth annual meeting. *Proc.*
1974 *Annu. Meet. NPFSC*, (17):47 p.

–, North Pacific Fur Seal Commission report on inves-
1975 tigations from 1967 through 1972. *NPFSC Rep. Invest.*, (1967-72):212 p.

–, Proceedings of the eighteenth annual meeting. *Proc.*
1975a *Annu. Meet. NPFSC*, (18):41 p.

PETERSON, R.S., B.J. LeBOEUF and R.L. DeLONG, Fur
1968 seals from the Bering Sea breed in California. *Nature, Lond.*, 219(5157):899-901.

PINRO/VNIRO, Report on USSR fur seal investiga-
1974 tions in 1974. Moscow, PINRO-VNIRO, 66 p. (mimeo).

REPENNING, C.M., R.S. PETERSON and C.L. HUBBS, Con-
1971 tributions to the systematics of the southern fur seals, with particular reference to the Juan Fernandez and Guadeloupe species. *In* Ant-arctic Pinnipedia, edited by W.H. Burt. *Ant-arct. Res. Ser.*, (18):1-266.

RICE, D.W., Stomach contents and feeding behaviour of
1968 killer whales in the eastern North Pacific. *Norsk Hvalfangsttid.*, 57(2):35-8.

RILEY, F., Fur seal industry of the Pribilof Islands,
1967 1786-1965. *Circ. U.S. Fish. Wildl. Serv.*, (275):12 p.

ROPPEL, A.Y. *et al.*, Fur seal investigations, Pribilof Is-
1966 lands, Alaska, 1965. *Spec. Sci. Rep. Fish. U.S. Fish. Wildl. Serv. (Wildl.)*, (536):1-45.

SANGER, G.A., A preliminary look at marine mam-
1974 mal-food chain relationships in Alaskan wa-ters. Seattle, Wash., NOAA/NMFS, Marine Mammal Division, 29 p. (mimeo).

SCHEFFER, V.B., Growth layers on the teeth of Pinnipedia
1950 as an indication of age. *Science, Wash.*, 112(2907):309-11.

–, Seals, sea lions and walruses: a review of the Pinni-
1958 pedia. Stanford, Calif., Stanford University Press, 179 p.

TAYLOR, F.H.C., M. FUJINAGA and F. WILKE, Distribu-
1955 tion and food habits of the fur seals of the North Pacific Ocean. Report of Cooperative Investigations by Governments of Canada,

Japan and United States of America, February-July 1952. Washington, D.C., U.S. Govt. Printing Office, 86 p.

U.S. CONGRESS, Report of the veterinary panel evalua-
1972 ting humaneness of the harvest in the Pribilof Islands. *In* Ocean mammal protection; hearings before the sub-Committee on Commerce, United States 92nd Congress, 2nd session.

Washington, D.C., U.S. Govt. Printing Office. Part 1:456-71.

WILLIAMS, R.A. *et al.*, Final report on concept scrutiny,
1973 prototype development and field evaluations of improved fur seal slaughtering techniques to U.S. Department of Commerce, National Marine Fisheries Service. Batelle, Ohio, Columbus Laboratories.

HARBOUR SEALS IN THE NORTH PACIFIC - TAXONOMY AND SOME OTHER BIOLOGICAL ASPECTS

Y. Naito

Abstract

The taxonomic status of the harbour seal (*Phoca vitulina*) in the North Pacific Ocean remains unclear. Reviewing recent published discussions, two sub-species, partly overlapping in distribution, can at present be recognized - *P. v. largha* and *P. v. richardsi*. The former is a highly migratory form, breeding on pack ice in early spring, whose distribution is marked by association with the edge zone of the ice. It ranges from northern Bristol Bay to the coastal and pelagic areas of the Bering Sea, dispersing northward into the Chukchi Sea in summer as far as the northern coast of Alaska. To the southwest, it is found along the Asiatic coast to China and in the Sea of Okhotsk south to Hokkaido. Summer and autumn migrations in the latter area include southeastern Hokkaido and southern Japan. *P. v. richardsi* is a sedentary, coastal form breeding on land, widely distributed along the west and northwest coasts of North America from a southern limit near the latitude of Guadalupe through southern Alaska and the eastern Bering Sea, north to Herschel Island. It is also found in the Aleutian, Commander and Kurile Islands, reaching as far south as Point Erimo, Hokkaido. More information is needed on the identity of the harbour seal found in the coastal waters of the Gulf of Chili in China.

The pupping season of *P. v. largha* is from late winter to early spring, followed by a period of suckling lasting about 2-4 weeks. Pups are born to *P. v. richardsi* in the spring to early autumn, followed by a suckling period of 3-6 weeks. Little information is available on age at sexual maturity. Data on growth in body length in relation to age are given for several different areas, generally showing increasingly greater lengths at birth and physical maturity for *richardsi* seals in British Columbia and Alaska, *largha* seals in the southern Sea of Okhotsk and *richardsi* seals in Hokkaido, in that order. *Largha* seals in the Bering Sea and the Sea of Okhotsk live to about age 30-35; the longevity of *richardsi* seals is less certain, though animals in British Columbia reportedly live to about age 30. In both forms, females may perhaps live longer than males.

Taxonomic points deserving further study include the possible specific classification of *P. kurilensis*, denoting the land-breeding harbour seal in the Kurile and Commander Islands and in Hokkaido, and the raising of *P. v. largha* to specific status. (Recent comparative morphological studies in the Aleutian Islands and Alaskan Peninsula, where all forms appear to be found, do not support these suggestions, however.) Further studies, involving international cooperation, are needed to resolve taxonomic problems and provide information for accurate population estimates now mainly unavailable especially important in relation to fisheries and sealing.

Résumé

Du point de vue taxonomique, l'état du veau marin (*Phoca vitulina*) du Pacifique nord reste peu clair. Si l'on s'en tient aux débats récemment publiés, on peut actuellement reconnaître deux sous-espèces dont les distributions se recouvrent partiellement: *P. v. largha* et *P. v. richardsi*. La première fait de grandes migrations, se reproduit sur le pack au début du printemps et sa distribution est caractérisée par l'association avec la limite des glaces. Son domaine s'étend du nord de la baie de Bristol aux zones côtières et pélagiques de la mer de Béring; en été, les phoques se dispersent vers le nord dans la mer de Tchoukotsk jusqu'à la côte nord de l'Alaska. Au sud-ouest, on les trouve sur la côte asiatique jusqu'à la Chine et dans la mer d'Okhotsk, vers le sud, jusqu'à Hokkaido. Dans cette région, les migrations d'été et d'automne vont jusqu'au sud-est d'Hokkaido et jusqu'au sud du Japon. *P. v. richardsi* est une forme sédentaire, côtière, se reproduisant à terre, largement distribuée sur les côtes ouest et nord-ouest de l'Amérique du Nord, depuis une limite méridionale voisine de la latitude de la Guadeloupe jusqu'au sud de l'Alaska, à l'est de la mer de Béring et à l'île Herschel. On la trouve aussi dans les îles Aléoutiennes, l'île du Commandeur et l'archipel des Kouriles, jusqu'à une limite méridionale atteignant Point Erimo, à Hokkaido. Il est nécessaire d'acquérir plus d'informations sur l'identité des veaux marins qui se trouvent dans les eaux côtières du golfe de Chili, en Chine.

L'époque de la parturition de *P. v. largha* se situe à la fin de l'hiver et au début du printemps; elle est suivie d'une période d'allaitement de 2 à 4 semaines. La parturition de *P. v. richardsi* a lieu du printemps au début de l'automne; elle est suivie d'une période d'allaitement de 3 à 6 semaines; on connaît mal l'âge de la maturité sexuelle. Les données sur la croissance en longueur par rapport à l'âge sont fournies pour plusieurs zones différentes. On constate généralement une augmentation croissante de la taille à la naissance et à la maturité physique pour *P. v. richardsi* en Colombie Britannique et en Alaska, *P. v. largha* dans la mer d'Okhotsk méridionale et *P. v. richardsi* à Hokkaido, dans cet ordre. Les phoques *largha* de la mer de Béring et de la mer d'Okhotsk vivent jusqu'à 30-35 ans; la longévité de *P. v. richardsi* est moins certaine, encore qu'on ait rapporté que les animaux de la Colombie Britannique vivent jusqu'à 30 ans environ. Chez les deux sous-espèces, il est possible que les femelles vivent plus longtemps que les mâles.

Les aspects taxonomiques méritant une étude plus poussée comprennent l'éventuelle classification de *P. kurilensis* en tant qu'espèce de veau marin se reproduisant à terre dans l'archipel des Kouriles, l'île du Commandeur et à Hokkaido, et l'élévation de *P. v. largha* au rang d'espèce. (Cependant, de récentes études de morphologie comparée, effectuées dans les îles Aléoutiennes et dans la péninsule d'Alaska, où se retrouvent toutes les formes, n'étayent pas ces suggestions.) D'autres études, dans le cadre d'une coopération internationale, sont nécessaires pour résoudre les problèmes taxonomiques et donner des informations permettant l'estimation précise des populations – qui n'existent pratiquement pas à l'heure actuelle – dont l'importance est grande pour la pêche et la chasse au phoque.

Extracto

La posición taxonómica de la foca común (*Phoca vitulina*) del norte del Pacífico sigue siendo poco clara. Examinando los datos publicados recientemente es posible reconocer dos subespecies, que coinciden parcialmente en sus zonas de distribución: *P. v. largha* y *P. v. richardsi*. La primera es una especie muy migratoria, que se reproduce en los bancos de hielo a principios de la primavera y cuya distribución se caracteriza por la asociación con el límite de los bancos de hielo. Se encuentra desde el norte de la bahía de Bristol hasta las zonas costeras y pelágicas del mar de Bering, dispersándose en verano hacia el norte, hasta el mar de Chukchi, llegando hasta la costa septentrional de Alaska. Se extiende también hacia el sudoeste, a lo largo de la costa asiática, hasta China, y por el mar de Ojotsk hasta Hokkaido, con movimientos migratorios de verano y otoño en esta última zona que llegan hasta el sudeste de Hokkaido y el sur del Japón. *P. v. richardsi* es una especie sedentaria y costera, que se reproduce en tierra, con una amplia zona de distribución a lo largo de las costas occidentales y noroccidentales de América del Norte, desde latitudes próximas a Guadalupe, a través del sur de Alaska y el este del mar de Bering, hasta la isla Herschel como límite septentrional. Se encuentra también en las islas Aleutianas, Commander y Kuriles, llegando por el sur hasta Punta Erimo, en Hokkaido. Es necesario recoger más información para aclarar la identidad de la foca común que se encuentra en las aguas costeras del golfo de Chili, en China.

La estación de cría de *P. v. largha* va desde finales del invierno hasta principios de la primavera, con un período de lactación de unas 2-4 semanas. *P. v. richardsi* pare desde la primavera hasta principios del otoño, con un período de lactación de 3-6 semanas. Se dispone de poca información sobre la edad de madurez sexual. Se incluyen datos sobre la relación entre la longitud del cuerpo y la edad en diversas zonas, a partir de los cuales se observa que la talla de la foca *richardsi* de Hokkaido al nacer y al alcanzar la madurez física es mayor que la de la foca *largha* del sur del mar de Ojotsk, y la de ésta, mayor que la de la foca *richardsi* de Columbia Británica y Alaska. La foca *largha* del mar de Bering y del mar de Ojotsk, alcanza los 30-35 años de edad; los datos sobre la longevidad de la foca *richardsi* son menos seguros, aunque hay noticias de que focas de la Columbia Británica alcanzan los 30 años. En ambas subespecies es posible que la longevidad de las hembras sea mayor que la de los machos.

Entre las cuestiones taxonómicas que es necesario estudiar ulteriormente figuran la posibilidad de clasificar como especie a *P. kurilensis*, bajo cuyo nombre se agruparían las focas comunes que se reproducen en tierra en las islas Kuriles y Commander y en Hokkaido, y de elevar a la categoría de especie a *P. v. largha*. (Sin embargo, los estudios morfológicos comparativos hechos recientemente en las islas Aleutianas y en la península de Alaska, donde se encuentran todas estas formas, no son favorables a esta sugerencia.) Son necesarios, pues, nuevos estudios, que han de hacerse con colaboración internacional, para resolver los problemas taxonómicos y obtener información que permita hacer estimaciones exactas de la población, que hoy día faltan en general y que son especialmente importantes para la explotación pesquera y la caza de focas.

Y. Naito
National Institute of Polar Research, 9-10 Kaga 1-Chome, Itabashi-ken, Tokyo 173, Japan

Introduction

Biological studies on the harbour seal are needed in relation to human economic activities such as fishing and sealing. Furthermore, in recent years interest in the taxonomy and population study of the harbour seal in the North Pacific has increased. To solve taxonomical problems, both morphological and ecological studies on this seal are inevitably required. Population studies also require a lot of biological information. After the success in determining age in this seal (Mansfield and Fisher, 1960; Laws, 1962) such biological studies were successfully performed on some local populations. However, information on this seal is still scanty because of their widely-spread distribution in the North Pacific. To promote biological studies in all areas where this seal occurs, collaborative work and information exchange are very important and required.

It is quite difficult for me to review all the problems of the harbour seal; however, in the present paper I have tried to include information on the taxonomy, distribution and movements, on some aspects of growth, and on population size.

Taxonomy of the harbour seal

Many biologists are engaged in the taxonomy of the harbour seal in the North Pacific; however, its status is still confusing. In the past, according to Scheffer (1958), the harbour seal in the eastern North Pacific and the western North Pacific has been given 10 and 12 names, respectively, as shown below:

EASTERN NORTH PACIFIC

Halicyon richardii Gray, 1864; *Halichoerus antarcticus* Peale, 1848; *Phoca pealii* Gill, 1866; *Halicyon? californica* Gray, 1866; *Phoca vitulina* Trouessart, 1897; *Phoca richardii* Allen, 1902; *Phoca richardii pribilofensis* Allen, 1902; *Phoca richardii geronimensis* Allen, 1902; *Phoca vitulina richardsi* Trouessart, 1904; *Phoca vitulina richardii* Doutt, 1942.

WESTERN NORTH PACIFIC

Phoca largha Pallas, 1811; *Phoca tigrina* Lesson, 1827; *Phoca chorisi* Lesson, 1828; *Phoca nummularis* Tenminck, 1847; *Phoca vitulina* Trouessart, 1897; *Phoca ochotensis* Allen, 1902; *Phoca ochotensis macrodens* Allen, 1902; *Phoca stejnegeri* Allen, 1902; *Phoca vitulina largha* Smirnov, 1908; *Phoca vitulina largha* natig Pallasi Naumov and Smirnov, 1936; *Phoca petersi*, Mohr, 1941; *Phoca ochotensis kurilensis* Inukai, 1942.

In these names, many synonyms were included and Scheffer (1958) had reduced these names to two. One is *Phoca vitulina largha* for the seal in the area from the Bering Sea to Asia, northwestward into Chukchi Sea, and southwestward along the Asiatic coast to China. The other is *Phoca vitulina richardii* for the seal in the north and west coast of North America from Herschel Island to the eastern Bering Sea, the Aleutian Islands, and far south to northern Mexico. This reclassification of the North Pacific harbour seal was mainly based on some geographical separations and the breeding isolation (*P. v. largha* breeds on the packed ice and *P. v. richardii* breeds on the land). The reconstruction of the classification by Scheffer (1958) seemed to settle the arguments on the confusing taxonomy of the harbour seal in the North Pacific. However, since Belkin (1964) and Belkin, Kosygin and Panin (1969) claimed the new species *Phoca insularis* from the Kurile Islands from ecological and morphological studies on the land-breeding seal, *Phoca ochotensis kurilensis*, formerly reported by Inukai (1942), some argument began again. McLaren (1966) attempted to provide a new insight into the taxonomical problem of the harbour seal in the western

North Pacific and supported Belkin (1964) and Belkin, Kosygin and Panin (1969). He used the name *P. kurilensis* for this seal recognizing the priority by Inukai. Marakov (1968) studied the land-breeding harbour seal in the Commander Islands, recognizing that this seal is the same form described by Belkin (1964). He concluded that *P. kurilensis*, i.e., *P. insularis*, being almost identical with *P. v. largha* in many aspects, is nothing but a special form of the *P. v. largha* and used the name Commander *largha* for this seal. Rice and Scheffer (1968) followed McLaren (1966) and used the name *P. kurilensis* tentatively. Naito and Nishiwaki (1972; 1975) and Naito (1973) also used *P. kurilensis* following Belkin (1964) and McLaren (1966) in their papers on the comparative growth and the pelage pattern between *P. v. largha* and *P. kurilensis*. From all the above, *P. kurilensis* seemed to have specific status; unfortunately, however, any work on this seal has been inadequate and no comparisons were made with the same land-breeding seal *P. v. richardii*, and also no comparative work had been done in the area around the Alaska Peninsula and Aleutian Islands where 3 forms of the harbour seal exist – *P. v. largha*, *P. v. richardii* and *P. kurilensis*. The latest information is that Burns and Fay (1974) from their studies on the seals in the Aleutian Islands and Alaska stated that comparisons of pelage coloration, cranial characters, body form, number of tracheal rings, structure of the hyoid apparatus, and the proportional size and shape of internal organs show perfect correspondence between 2 forms (*P. kurilensis* and *P. v. richardii*) indicating that they are one and the same. They used the name for this seal *P. v. richardsi* (Gray, 1864). Therefore, being still more argument required, there exists only 1 species of the land-breeding form *Phoca vitulina richardsi* in the North Pacific.

On the other hand, concerning the taxonomical state of *P. v. largha*, there has been much argument since Scheffer's review (1958). Chapskii (1955, 1960, 1967) after much discussion of the osteology and breeding isolation, came to the conclusion that the ice-breeding harbour seal has specific status, *Phoca largha*. McLaren (1966) entered the discussion and reached the conclusion that the ice-breeding seal in the North Pacific deserved specific status, *P. largha*. Rice and Scheffer (1968) also followed them tentatively. However, Burns and Fay (1974) studied the seal in the Aleutian Islands and Alaska and, using *P. v. largha*, they stated "The geographic distribution of *P. v. richardsi* broadly overlaps that of *P. v. largha* in the southeastern sector of the Bering Sea. Specimens of the *richardsi* form from that area show signs of latent intergradation with *largha*". However, concerning *P. v. largha* or *P. largha* much more study seems to be required.

In addition to the above, we are very short of information on how to consider the taxonomy of the harbour seal which is resident in China. Only a few papers are known on this seal (Leroy, 1940; Shou-jen Huan, 1962) and further studies are expected.

From the above discussion, it is still difficult to reach taxonomic conclusions. However, to promote study of the above problem, we need international collaboration between America, Canada, China, U.S.S.R. and Japan. This collaboration is now steadily taking place in Alaska, where all the above-mentioned types of seals are found and which is the most important place for studies.

Distribution and movements

The distribution and movements should be considered from many biological aspects such as seasonal life cycle, life history, sexual segregation, feeding, relation to the environment, etc. However, at present, distribution and movements are still unknown in detail. Therefore, in this chapter only general geographical distribution ranges and some movements are described.

The harbour seal is widely known to be distributed in the temperate zone of the North-

351

ern Hemisphere. In the North Pacific they show a very wide distribution. They occur northward in the Chukchi Sea, southeastward in South California and North Mexico, and southwestward in Japan and China. They also appear in the chain of Aleutian and Kurile Islands. Furthermore, they are normally found both in the coastal and pelagic areas of the Bering Sea and the Sea of Okhotsk.

Phoca vitulina largha

The distribution of *largha* seal is marked by association with ice. This seal is noted for breeding on ice floes in early spring. Thus, the distribution ranges of this seal are generally believed to be limited to the Bering Sea, the Chukchi Sea and the Sea of Okhotsk, where the sea ice prevails. According to Burns (1970), Fay (1974) and Burns and Fay (1972), in the Bering Sea the seals are found in the 10-40 mile wide "front" zone at the southern edge of the packed ice, from the vicinity of northern Bristol Bay to the Koryak and Kamchatka coasts in winter and spring. Fay (1974) indicated that pups are usually born on heavy floes, 10-20 m in diameter, with a thick layer of snow and often with some remnant of pressure ridge, and the young seals utilize the ice blocks and caverns of the pressure ridge as shelter from the weather and as refuge from predators and scavengers. The breeding aggregations consist of isolated "family groups" of 3, comprising an adult male and female with a pup, and these groups are rarely closer together than 0.2 km (Burns *et al.*, 1972). Because of their wide spacing, males are presumed to be territorial and to defend the area around the natal floe. After the ice disappears, these seals become highly migratory, dispersing northward into the Chukchi Sea in summer, at least as far as the northern coast of Alaska, and returning again to the Bering Sea in late autumn to take up residence along the ice front (Fay, 1974). It is still uncertain how they share the habitats in this area. Though, as already mentioned in the former chapter, the geo-graphic distribution of *P. v. richardsi* broadly overlaps that of *P. v. largha* in the southern sector of the Bering Sea. Marakov (1968) stated that this seal (*P. v. largha*) rarely occurs in the Commander Islands. Therefore, habitat-sharing between 2 forms of the harbour seal may occur in the Commander Islands.

In the Sea of Okhotsk, sea ice appears from November in the north and prevails to the south in January with an ice-free area in the central parts of this sea (ice floes appear in the area about Hokkaido and on the Kamchatka side of the southern Okhotsk Sea). The sea ice retreats in March or April from the south and disappears in the north in June. The *largha* seal occurs very commonly in this sea and may stay for short periods (January to March or April) on the packed ice in the south and for longer periods (perhaps November to June) in the north. According to Naito and Nishiwaki (1972), in Hokkaido these seals appear on the lake ice of the inland sea (Lake Saroma, Odaito, Furen) or on the blocks of coastal ice that have drifted from the coast prior to the sea ice appearing from the north. When ice floes appear from the north the seals move to the offshore ice and breed, forming family groups. In the offshore ice floe region, they seemed to appear in waters less than 200 m in depth. This may be related to their feeding. Like the *largha* seal in the Bering Sea, these seals occurred more frequently in the edge zone of the packed ice, where the ice bay or ice tongue are developed, than in the area of densely packed ice. After the breeding season, young seals seemed to stay longer on the ice floe than the adult seals (Naito, unpublished). In summer and autumn these seals are highly migratory in Hokkaido, like the seals in the Bering Sea, and disperse and spread their distribution range and appear in the coast of southeastern Hokkaido where the *richardsi-kurilensis* seals commonly appear. Sometimes both forms of seals are found hauling out on the same rocks (Naito, 1973). Pups are much dispersed by the ice, or they are dependent on ice for the first 2-3 weeks after birth, and they sometimes appear far south, in the southern part of Japan. The same dispersion of pups is reported in the Bering Sea (Burns, 1970).

Phoca vitulina richardsi

The *richardsi* seal is known to occur along the western coast of North America, northern Alaska in the north, California and Mexico in the south and the Aleutian and Kurile Islands and Hokkaido in the east. The northern limit of the range is Herschel Island and Point Barrow and the southern limit of the range may be near the latitude of Cedros Island (28°12N) (Scheffer, 1958) or San Roque Island, Guadalupe (King, 1964). The eastern limit is Point Erimo in Hokkaido (Inukai, 1942). The distribution of local populations has been well examined in British Columbia (Fisher, 1952) and in Washington State by Scheffer and Slipp (1944). These seals are widely distributed along the coast in these areas and some of their main hauling grounds are Queen Charlotte Islands, Vancouver Island, Willappa Bay, Grays Harbour, Destruction Island, Neah Bay, Dungeness Spit, Minor Island, several of the small San Juan Islands, and the deltas of many rivers including Stikine, Skeena, Fraser, Samish, Skagit, Stillaguamish, Snohomish, Nisqually and Columbia. They are quite selective in choosing places to haul out on shore; their hauling sites are tidal sand bars, exposed rocks, mud flats, gravel bars where it is difficult or impossible for an enemy to approach unseen from the land side. It is noted that they are sedentary, and resident throughout the year in their habitat. They are not found more than 10-15 miles offshore from the coast in these areas. However, in the Skeena River definite seasonal upriver movements occur, coinciding in general with the salmon run; these are not mass migrations but gradual increases in numbers.

There is not much more information re-ported from other areas (in Alaska, Aleutian Islands and Kurile Islands). In Alaska, this coastal seal is divided into 2 groups with respect to their association with ice. One is that of the Bristol Bay area, where they have extensive contact with ice throughout the winter. The other is that of the Aleutian and Commander Islands, where sea ice is scarce or absent (Fay, 1972). It has been widely known that the *P. v. richardsi* is the land-breeding form and coastal seal, and they never make contact with ice, though in Hokkaido some *richardsi-kurilensis* seals (i.e., *P. kurilensis*) are said by fishermen to have contact with ice in early spring (before breeding season) as has been found in Bristol Bay. In Alaska, Alteutian Islands, Kurile Islands and all other areas of its distribution, this form of seal is sedentary to its coastal habitat and does not show any apparent migration throughout the year. *Richardsi* and *largha* are supposed to be distributed differently in winter excet for Bristol Bay, for *largha* moves to the pelagic ice and *richardsi* remains on the coast. However, in summer and autumn it is still uncertain how their ranges overlap in Alaska, Aleutian Islands and northern Kurile Islands.

POPULATION IN CHINA

According to Shou-jen Huang (1962), the population in China is observed all along the coastal waters of the Gulf of Chili. They are reported from the waters around Lüta, Chühüatao, Yingk'ou, Ch'anghsingtao, Laot'iehshanchiao and Chinhsien in Liaoning Province; the Miaotao Islands and off Yent'ai (Chefoo) in Shantung Province; and near Ch'inhuangtao and Peitaiho in Hopei Province. In late February many seals arrive from the southern Pohai Sea at the drift ice to the northeast for pupping. There appears to be no further information on the harbour seal in China.

353

Some information on growth

PUPPING SEASON

Table 1 is based on the report by Bigg (1969) and some additional information. Bigg tried to find some clines of the pupping season; however, in this paper, I have tried to separate the information into 2 groups; the ice-breeding *largha* seal and the land-breeding *richardsi* seal. From Table 1 it is indicated that the ice-breeding seal has an earlier pupping season than the land-breeding seal. The ice-breeding seal gives birth on the ice floe from late winter to early spring (from January to May, in most cases from March to early April) in the Bering Sea and the Sea of Okhotsk, including Tatar Strait. This also occurs in China. The harbour seal in China is supposed to be completely separated from the other harbour seals in Asia. According to Shou-jen Huang (1962), the seals bear the pups on the ice floes in spring, in the northeast of Pohai Bay. However, it is still uncertain that all of the seals in China are ice-breeding seals. On the other hand, the land-breeding seal shows a later pupping season. They give birth to their pups on land from spring to the beginning o autumn (from early March to the beginning of September). The pupping season of the land-breeding seal is supposed to show much more regional variation than the ice-breeding seal. This was often seen on the coast from British Columbia to southern California.

WEANING SEASON

Information on weaning is quite scarce; however, the variations appear to be small. In general as seen in Table 2, the ice-breeding *largha* seal showed shorter period of suckling; 2-4 weeks compared to 3-6 weeks in the land-breeding *richardsi* seal. In the former seal, Naito and Nishiwaki (1975) showed that the time of moulting of the white lanugo coat corresponds with the time of weaning.

The reason for the shorter period of suckling in the ice-breeding *largha* seal is unknown. However, long suckling may not be adaptive for this seal, which occupies the edge zone of packed ice. Pups in the white lanugo coat would not swim before moulting and are therefore quite dependent on ice and will sometimes be separated from their mother, and weaning may occur suddenly. On the other hand, the pups of the land-breeding *richardsi* seal can swim soon after birth and the mother and pup are always seen together (within 10-15 m diameter range) about 4 weeks after birth. Weaning takes place gradually (Naito, unpublished). The environmental difference mentioned above may relate to the difference of weaning time between these 2 types of seals.

SEXUAL MATURITY

The information on sexual maturity of the harbour seal is also quite scanty. According to Burns and Fay (1972), the ice-breeding *largha* seal becomes sexually mature at 4-5 years of age in males and 3-4 years of age in females; male maturity seems to occur 1 year later than the female. However, Tikhomirov (1966) showed different results on the same *largha* seal. According to him, 33 % males of 3 years of age (out of 12 seals) and 10 % females of the same age (out of 5 seals) attained maturity, 100 % males (out of 2) and 93 % females (out of 6) attained maturity at age 4, and 100 % males (out of 5) and 94 % females (out of 10) attained maturity at age 5. He noted that the male harbour seal in the North Pacific becomes sexually mature somewhat earlier than the female. Naito and Nishiwaki (1975) considered that males and females of the ice-breeding *largha* seal in the southern Sea of Okhotsk reach sexual maturity from 3 years of age and mostly mature at 5 to 6 years of age, noting the small sample sizes. From the above, it is quite difficult to know the ages of sexual maturity exactly.

In the land-breeding *richardsi* seal, Bigg

Table 1. **The regional variation of the pupping season of the ice-breeding and the land-breeding harbour seals in the North Pacific. (Information cited by Bigg, 1969 (no author))**

THE ICE-BREEDING HARBOUR SEAL

The Bering Sea

1. Late March to mid April (Burns, 1970; Fay, 1974)

The Sea of Okhotsk

2. Early February to mid March: with a peak from the end of February to the beginning of March in the Gulf of Peter the Great and in the Tatar Strait (Tikhomirov, 1966)
3. Mid March: in the Gulf of Terpenia and off the coast of Abashiri (Tikhomirov, 1966)
4. Late February to early May: with a peak in the middle of April in the northern part of the Sea of Okhotsk (Tikhomirov, 1966)
5. In April (including the ringed seal, the ribbon seal and the bearded seal): in the region of the Tauisk Lip and the adjacent waters (Tikhomirov, 1966)
6. Late January (the earliest) to mid April: off the coast of Abashiri (Wilke, 1954)
7. Mid March to late March: in the sea off the coast of Hokkaido and the southern Sea of Okhotsk (Naito and Nishiwaki, 1975)

China

8. Spring: northeast of Pohai Sea (Shou-jen Huang, 1962)

THE LAND-BREEDING HARBOUR SEAL

Western coast of North America

9. Early March to early April: in Nome
10. April to May: in the north of the Pribilof Islands
11. Early May to ?; 20 May to ?: in the Pribilof Islands
12. 5 May to 25 June: in Tugidak Island
13. Late May to late June: in the Copper, Stikine and Skeena Rivers
14. 24 June to 6 September: in the southeast of Vancouver Island
15. Mid August to early September: in McNeil Island
16. Late June to early August: in the Nisqually Flata
17. 12 May to ?: in Willapa Bay
18. Late April to early June: in Tillamouk Bay
19. 24 March to 7 May: in Humbolt Bay
20. Late March to late May: in Año Nuevo Island
21. Mid April to early May: in the Mugu Lagoon
22. 8 March: in San Martin Island
23. Mid March: in the Bahía San Quintin

Aleutian Islands, Kurile Islands and Hokkaido

24. Late April to early May: in the Commander Islands
25. Early April: in the Commander Islands (Marakov, 1968)
26. Mid May: in the Kurile Islands (Belkin, 1964)
27. Late March to mid April: in the southern Kurile Islands
28. Mid May to late May: in the southeast of Hokkaido (Naito and Nishiwaki, 1975)

Table 2. The suckling period of the harbour seal in the North Pacific

THE ICE-BREEDING *LARGHA* SEAL

1. about 4 weeks: in the Bering Sea (Burns *et al.*, 1972; Fay, 1974)
2. 3 to 4 weeks: in the Bering Sea and the Sea of Okhotsk (Tikhomirov, 1966)
3. 2 to 3 weeks: in the southern Sea of Okhotsk (Naito and Nishiwaki, 1975)
4. about 4 weeks: in the northeast of Pohai Sea (Shou-jen Huang, 1962)

THE LAND-BREEDING *RICHARDSI* SEAL

1. 3 to 4 weeks: in Alaska (Bishop; cited from Bigg, 1969a)
2. 4 to 6 weeks: in Washington State (Scheffer and Slipp, 1944)
3. 6 weeks: in the Skeena River (Fisher, 1952)
4. 6 weeks: in California (Finch; cited from Bigg, 1969a)
5. 5 to 6 weeks: in southern Vancouver Island (Bigg, 1969a)
6. 3 months: in the southern Kurile Islands (Belkin, Kosygin and Panin, 1969)
7. 4 to 6 weeks: on the southeast coast of Hokkaido (Naito and Nishiwaki, 1975)

(1969a) studied the sexual maturity in southern Vancouver Island. According to him 20 % of females attain sexual maturity at age 2, 58 % at 3, 82 % at 4 and 100 % at 5. Also 12 % of males attain sexual maturity by age 3, 72 % by age 5 and 100 % by age 6.

GROWTH IN BODY LENGTH

The growth in body length is little known in the ice-breeding *largha* seal and the land-breeding *richardsi* seal; data from several areas are shown below.

(1)   Bering Sea and the Sea of Okhotsk

According to Tikhomirov (1971), the birth length of the ice-breeding *largha* seal in the Bering Sea and the Sea of Okhotsk ranges from 76 to 81 cm (78 cm on average) and their weight from 6.9 to 7.3 kg (7.1 kg on average). On average, pups of common seals are almost half as long at birth as physically mature females (48 %) and sexually mature females (49 %). The weight of new-born pups is 10.4 % that of adult females. The length of 25-30 day-old pups (just after weaning) was 98-120

cm (average 108 cm), and 1.2-2 month-old pups were 98-122 cm (average 108 cm) in body length. The average body length of year-old seals is 124 cm. They grow 14 cm in 11 months. Body length increases until the seal attains physical maturity at 9 years of age: 168 cm in males and 162 cm in females. The size of sexually mature females ranges from 141 to 160 cm and the maximum length is 182 cm in females and 185 cm in males.

(2)   In the southern Sea of Okhotsk

Naito and Nishiwaki (1975) also reported the increase in body length of the ice-breeding *largha* seal in the southern Sea of Okhotsk. The birth length of this seal was 85 cm. The mean length at 1 year of age was 119 cm in males and 117 cm in females; growth in the first year is 34 cm for males and about 32 cm for females. About 35 % of the increase in body length during the first year seemed to occur in the first month after birth. From birth to 4 years of age both sexes increase their body length at almost the same rate. After 4 years of age, they showed different growth rates. Males continue to grow until 14-15 years of age and females grow until 10-11 years of age. The final body length was 169.9± 4.0 cm in males and 159.0 ± 3.1 cm in females.

The results in the above 2 areas seem to be difficult to compare because the measuring methods are different. Tikhomirov (1971) measured the body length from nose to tail along the curve of the back. Naito and Nishiwaki (1975) measured it by the straight length from nose to tail along the body axis. Therefore, the lengths measured by Tikhomirov will be a little longer for seals of the same size than those measured by Naito and Nishiwaki. The length given by Tikhomirov for mature female seals was longer by 3 cm than that given by Naito and Nishiwaki. However, the length of mature males measured by Tikhomirov was smaller by 2 cm than those measured by Naito and Nishiwaki. It is still difficult to conclude from the above results that the male seals in the southern Sea of Okhotsk are larger than those in other areas, for it may be that the results were influenced by the bias of the measuring method.

(3)   In British Columbia and Alaska

Bigg (1969a) showed the growth of the land-breeding *richardsi* seal in British Columbia and Alaska. According to him, the newborn length and weight in British Columbia were 81.6 ± 6.2 cm and 10.2 ± 1.5 kg. From after birth to 5 years of age both sexes grow at about the same rate. By 5 years of age most females are fully grown and attain physical maturity, averaging 147.7 ± 2.4 cm in length and 64.8 ± 4.4 kg in weight. Most males grow until 9-10 years of age averaging 161.1 ± 4.9 cm and 87.6 ± 6.6 kg. This length and weight are apparently smaller than those of ice-breeding *largha* seals shown above. However, no distinct differences seem to exist between the British Columbia and Alaska populations.

(4)   In Hokkaido

Naito and Nishiwaki (1975) showed the curve of growth in body length for the land-breeding *richardsi-kurilensis* seal in Hokkaido. According to them, birth length of this seal is 98.2 ± 3.2 cm. This birth length is the largest of all the 3 populations mentioned above. In this seal, males and females grow at about the same rate until 5 years of age. By 9-10 years of age most males are fully grown, averaging 186 cm. Most females are fully grown at 5-6 years of age, averaging 169 cm. The fully grown and mature length is apparently the largest of all 3 populations above. In this seal, the growth aspect is still uncertainly known; however, it is interesting to know that the land-breeding harbour seal shows wide variations in its growth. Furthermore, it is also important to know that they show some clines in their body size among the populations in the Aleutian Island chain and Alaska.

LONGEVITY

There is little information on longevity reported from the Bering Sea, the Sea of Okhotsk and British Columbia. With regard to the ice-breeding *largha* seal from the Bering Sea, Burns and Fay (1972) reported that maximal longevity is at least 35 years (both sexes included). Tikhomirov (1971) reported from the Sea of Okhotsk that the old males and females in his samples are 29 years of age and 35 years of age respectively, and indicated that the ice-breeding *largha* seal lives to an age of 30-35 years and possibly more. Naito and Nishiwaki (1975) also reported for the same seal that the oldest male and female seals of their 326 samples from the southern Sea of Okhotsk are 26 years of age and 32 years of age, respectively. From the above information, it may be concluded that the longevity of the *largha* seal in the Bering Sea and the Sea of Okhotsk is about 30-35 years of age. On the other hand, the longevity of the land-breeding *richardsi* seal is rather uncertain. Bigg (1969a) showed the life table of the seal in British Columbia, and according to this life table the oldest male of his 114 male samples is 20 years of age and the oldest female of 131 females is 29

357

years of age. This result seems not to suggest the longevity of this seal certainly; however, judging from the age composition in his life tables and also from the smaller body size of this seal (described in an earlier chapter), it may suggest that the land-breeding seal in British Columbia does not live longer than the ice-breeding seal, and its longevity may be about 30 years.

Differences in longevity of males and females are still uncertain; however, the results by Tikhomirov (1971), Naito and Nishiwaki (1975) and Bigg (1969a) may indicate that female seals live longer than males.

Population

The population studies on the North Pacific harbour seal are quite scarce. Some local populations of *richardsi* seal were estimated by observation counting or biological method. However, no such studies seem to have been performed in the Bering Sea and the Sea of Okhotsk.

Largha seal

Scheffer (1958) listed the estimated populations of all pinnipeds, and for the *largha* seal he estimated 20 000-50 000, though population studies seem to have been rare on the pelagic and migratory *largha* seal.

Richardsi seal

As to the coastal and sedentary *richardsi* seal, much information is reported. In British Columbia, Spalding (1964) indicated the population size as 17 000 seals. Bigg (1969a) also estimated the population of the same British Columbia population as 11 400 to 35 000 seals by the biological method. In Alaska, Imler and Sarber (1947) reported that at least 6 000 seals inhabit the mouth of the Copper River, and Bishop (MS 1968, cited in Bigg, 1969a) suggested that between 12 000 and 17 000 seals are found on Tugidak Island after the pupping season. In the Commander Islands, Marakov (1968) suggests that the population of these seals was reduced in the thirties and forties and has now recovered to exceed 1 500 seals. In the Kurile Islands, Belkin (1964) and Belkin, Kosygin and Panin (1969) reported that the island seal (*richardsi-kurilensis*) exists in all 28 southern Kurile Islands, and that 676 seals in Maloi Island, 286 in Shikotan Island, 238 in Iturup Island, 148 in Makanruski Island, 100 in Demina Island, 80 in Lisink Island, and 92 in Simushir Island were observed in August 1963. From these findings, he estimated that about 1 700 seals in total (except pups) exist in all 28 southern Kurile Islands and that the total population of the Kurile Islands is about 2 000 to 2 500 seals. The total population of *richardsi* seal from Alaska to California was estimated by Scheffer (1958) as 50 000 to 200 000.

References

BELKIN, A.N., A new species of seal, *Phoca insularis* n. sp.
1964   from the Kurile Islands. *Dokl. AN SSSR*, 158:1217-9.

BELKIN, A.N., G.M. KOSYGIN and K.I. PANIN, New ma-
1969   terials on Island seal (*Phoca insularis* sp. nova). *In* Morskie mlekopitayushchie (Third All-U-nion Conference on the Study of Marine Mammals, Vladivostock, 1966, edited by V.A. Arseniev, B.A. Zenkovich and K.K. Chapskii. Moscow, Nauka, pp. 157-75.

BIGG, Clines in the pupping season of the harbour seal
1969   *Phoca vitulina. J. Fish. Res. Board Can.*, 26(2):449-55.

–, The harbour seal in British Columbia. *Bull. Fish. Res.*
1969a   *Board Can.*, (172):1-33.

BURNS, J.J., Remarks on the distribution and natural
1970   history of pagohilic pinnipeds in the Bering and Chukchi Seas. *J. Mammal.*, 51 (3):445-54.

BURNS, J.J. and F.H. FAY, Comparative biology of Bering Sea harbour seal populations. *In* Proceedings of the 23rd Alaska Science Conference, August 1972, Fairbanks, Alaska (abstr.).
1972

–, New data on taxonomic relationships among North Pacific harbour seals genus *Phoca (sensu stricto)*. *In* Proceedings of the First International Theriological Congress, Moscow (abstr.).
1974

BURNS, J.J. *et al.*, Adoption of a strange pup by the ice-inhabiting harbour seal, *Phoca vitulina largha*. *J. Mammal.*, 53(3):594-8.
1972

CHAPSKII, K.K., An attempt at revision of the systematics and diagnostics of seals of the subfamily Phocinae. *Tr. Zool. Inst. AN SSSR.* 38:160-99. Issued also as *Transl. Ser. Fish. Mar. Serv. Can.*, (114).
1955

–, Morphologie systématique, différenciation intra-spécifique et polygenèse du sous-genre *Phoca (sensu stricto)*. *Mammalia, Paris*, 24:343-60.
1960

–, Morphological-taxonomical nature of the Pagetoda form of the Bering Sea largha. *Tr. Polyarn. Nauchno-Issled. Proektn. Inst. Morsk. Rybn. Khoz. Okeanogr.*, 21:147-76.
1967

FAY, F.H., The role of ice in the ecology of marine mammals of the Bering Sea. *Occas. Pap. Inst. Mar. Sci. Univ. Alaska*, (2):283-97.
1974

FISHER, H.D., The status of the harbour seal in British Columbia, with particular reference to the Skeena River. *Bull. Fish. Res. Board Can.*, (93):1-58.
1952

IMLER, R.H. and H.R. SARBER, Harbour seals and sea lions in Alaska. *Spec. Sci. Rep. U.S. Fish Wildl. Serv.*, (28):22 p.
1947

INUKAI, T., Hair seals in our northern waters. 1. *Shokubutsu Dobutsu (Bot. Zool.)*, 10(10):927-32 (in Japanese).
1942

KING, J.E., Seals of the world. London, British Museum, 154 p.
1964

LAWS, R.M., Age determination of pinnipeds with special reference to growth layers in the teeth. *Z. Säugetierkd.*, 27:129-46.
1962

LEROY, P., On the occurrence of a hair-seal *Phoca richardsi* (Gray) on the coast of North China. *Bull. Fan. Mem. Inst. Biol. (Zool.)*, 10:62-8.
1940

MANSFIELD, A.W. and H.D. FISHER, Age determination in the harbour seal, *Phoca vitulina. Nature, Lond.*, 186:192-3.
1960

MARAKOV, S.V., The ecology of the *largha* on the Commander Islands. *Tr. Polyarn. Nauchno-Issled. Proektn. Inst. Morsk. Rybn. Khoz. Okeanogr.*, 21:126-36. Issued also as *Transl. Ser. Fish. Mar. Serv. Can.*, (1079).
1968

McLAREN, I.A., Taxonomy of harbour seals of the western North Pacific and evolution of certain other hair seals. *J. Mammal.*, 47(3):466-73.
1966

NAITO, Y., Comparison in colour pattern of two species of harbour seal in adjacent waters of Hokkaido. *Sci. Rep. Whales Res. Inst., Tokyo*, (25):301-10.
1973

NAITO, Y. and M. NISHIWAKI, The growth of two species of the harbour seal in the adjacent waters of Hokkaido. *Sci. Rep. Whales Res. Inst.*, Tokyo, (24):127-244.
1972

–, Ecology and morphology of *Phoca vitulina largha* and *Phoca kurilensis* in the southern Sea of Okhotsk and northeast of Hokkaido. *Rapp. P.-V. Réun. CIEM*, 169:379-86.
1975

RICE, D.W. and V.B. SCHEFFER, A list of the marine mammals of the world. *Spec. Sci. Rep. Fish. U.S. Fish Wildl. Serv.*, (579):3-4.
1968

SCHEFFER, V.B., Seals, sea lions and walruses. Stanford, California, Stanford University Press, 179 p.
1958

SCHEFFER, V.B. and J.W. SLIPP, The harbour seal in Washington State. *Am. Midl. Nat.*, 32(2):373-416.
1944

SHOU-JEN HUANG, Economically important animals of China. Chungguo Jungji Dongwuzhi, pp. 414-7. Issued also as *Transl. Ser. Fish. Mar. Serv. Can.*, (2328):8 p.
1962

SPALDING, D.J., Comparative feeding habits of the fur seal, sea lion and harbour seal on the British Columbia coast. *Bull. Fish. Res. Board Can.*, (146):52 p.
1964

TIKHOMIROV, E.A., On the reproduction of the seals belonging to the family Phocidae in the North Pacific. *Zool. Zh.*, 14(2):275-81.
1966

–, Body growth and development of reproductive organs of the North Pacific phocids. *In* Pinnipeds
1971

359

of the North Pacific, edited by V.A. Arseniev and K.I. Panin. Jerusalem, Israel Program for Scientific Translations, pp. 213-41. *Transl. of Tr. Vses. Nauchno-Issled. Inst. Morsk. Rybn. Khoz. Okeanogr.*, 62:216-43 (1968).

WILKE, F., Seals of northern Hokkaido. *J. Mammal.*, 1954   35(2):218-24.

STATUS OF THE MAIN ICE-LIVING SEALS INHABITING INLAND WATERS AND COASTAL MARINE AREAS OF THE USSR

L.A. POPOV

Abstract

Information is given on the biology and exploitation of seals living on ice in waters within or near the Soviet Union, the forms being divided into three geographical areas: harp (*Pagophilus groenlandicus*) and hooded (*Cystophora cristata*) seals in seas of the eastern North Atlantic and adjacent southern Arctic Oceans; ribbon (*Histriophoca fasciata*) and largha (*Phoca largha*) seals in the western North Pacific; ringed (*Pusa hispida*) and bearded (*Erignathus barbatus*) seals in both these areas; and the Caspian seal (*Pusa caspica*) and Baikal seal (*P. sibirica*) in inland waters. Lengths, weights and pelage coloration of adults and pups are given for each species; other distinguishing characteristics are sometimes also included. There is some information on reproductive biology and natural mortality available for most kinds of seals: information given, though not always for all species, includes age at sexual maturity and at first mating, mean and maximum ages of breeding seals, pregnancy rate, timing of mating activities, length of gestation and nursing, causes and rates of natural mortality of pups and older animals. The trophic relations of these seals are poorly or only partly known for some species or for them in some areas of their distribution, though relatively more information is available for others, for example, for Caspian and largha seals; information given includes species eaten, seasonal pattern of eating and fasting, especially in relation to reproduction, and differences in diet by age.

Harp, Caspian and ringed seals are the most numerous species; the others are found in lesser numbers, especially hooded seals, which do not breed in Soviet waters. The distribution and movements of the seals are discussed, usually in relation to breeding, moulting, feeding and changing ice conditions and movements: most species undertake a migration to areas of heavy ice-cover to breed and moult in groups in the late winter or early spring, dispersing into a wider distribution when the ice melts, to feed throughout the summer.

A brief history of the exploitation and management of each species is given, this often including a period of decline due to over-hunting by landsmen, sealing vessels or both, followed by one of recovery after catch limits have been imposed. Caspian, harp and Baikal seals, ringed and bearded seals in the North Pacific and ribbon seals, have been studied more than the other forms, this depending largely on these seals' commercial value. Exploitation of bearded seals depends on the needs of the local coastal populations; for most of the other species, ready markets exist for their products, especially fur, but harvests are limited by the condition of the stocks and often the need to restore them.

Résumé

Des informations sont fournies sur la biologie et l'exploitation des pinnipèdes vivant sur la glace dans les eaux intérieures ou limitrophes de l'URSS, les formes se répartissant en trois

361

zones géographiques: les phoques du Groenland (*Pagophilus groenlandicus*) et les phoques à capuchon (*Cystophora cristata*) dans les eaux de l'Atlantique Nord-Est et les zones adjacentes du sud de l'océan Arctique; les phoques à bande (*Histriophoca fasciata*) et les phoques tachetés (*Phoca largha*) dans le Pacifique Nord-Ouest; les phoques annelés (*Pusa hispida*) et barbus *(Erignathus barbatus)* dans ces deux zones; les phoques de la Caspienne (*Pusa caspica*) et les phoques de Sibérie (*P. sibirica*) dans les eaux intérieures. La longueur, le poids et la coloration du pelage des adultes et des veaux sont indiqués pour chaque espèce; d'autres caractéristiques distinctives sont parfois aussi incluses. On trouve quelques informations sur la biologie de la reproduction et la mortalité naturelle de la plupart des espèces; les informations fournies, encore qu'elles ne couvrent pas toujours toutes les espèces, comprennent l'âge de la maturité sexuelle et au premier accouplement, les âges moyens et maximaux des reproducteurs, les taux de gestation, l'époque des accouplements, la durée de la gestation et de l'allaitement, les causes et les taux de mortalité naturelle des veaux et des animaux plus âgés. Les relations trophiques de ces phoques sont mal ou partiellement connues pour certaines espèces, ou pour certaines zones de distribution de ces espèces, bien qu'on possède relativement plus d'informations sur d'autres phoques, par exemple, les phoques de la Caspienne et les phoques tachetés; les informations fournies comprennent les espèces consommées, les modes saisonniers d'alimentation et de jeûne, spécialement pour ce qui est de la reproduction et des différences de régime alimentaire en fonction de l'âge.

Les phoques du Groenland, de la Caspienne et les phoques annelés sont les espèces les plus nombreuses; les autres se rencontrent en nombres moins importants, spécialement les phoques à capuchon, qui ne se reproduisent pas dans les eaux soviétiques. La distribution et les déplacements des phoques sont examinés, généralement en fonction de la reproduction, de la mue, de l'alimentation et des changements des états et du mouvement des glaces: presque toutes les espèces entreprennent une migration vers les régions où la glace est épaisse pour se reproduire et muer en groupes, à la fin de l'hiver ou au début du printemps; elles se dispersent ensuite, assumant une répartition plus large quand la glace fond, pour se nourrir pendant tout l'été.

Un bref historique de l'exploitation et de la gestion de chaque espèce est effectué; on y remarque une période de déclin due à une surexploitation par les chasseurs à terre, les bateaux — ou les deux — suivie d'une période de reprise après imposition de limites de capture. Les phoques de la Caspienne, du Groenland et de Sibérie, les phoques annelés et barbus dans le Pacifique Nord et les phoques à bande on été plus étudiés que les autres formes, ce qui dépend dans une grande mesure de leur valeur commerciale. L'exploitation des phoques barbus dépend des besoins des populations côtières locales; pour la majorité des autres espèces, il existe des marchés qui sont prêts à absorber les produits, spécialement la fourrure, mais l'exploitation est limitée par l'état des stocks et, souvent, la nécessité de les reconstituer.

Extracto

Se informa sobre la biología y la explotación de las focas de los hielos que se encuentran en aguas situadas dentro o cerca de la Unión Soviética, dividiéndolas por zonas geográficas: foca de Groenlandia (*Pagophilus groenlandicus*) y capuchina (*Cystophora cristata*) de los mares del nordeste del Atlántico y aguas meridionales adyacentes de los océanos árticos; foca fajada (*Histriophoca fasciata*) y larga (*Phoca largha*) del noroeste del Pacífico; foca marbreada (*Pusa hispida*) y barbuda (*Erignathus barbatus*) de ambas zonas; y foca del Caspio (*Pusa caspica*) y del Baikal (*P. sibirica*), que viven en aguas continentales. Se indica la longitud, peso y coloración del pelaje de los adultos y cachorros de cada una de las especies, indicando a veces otros elementos distintivos. Se dan algunos datos sobre la biología reproductiva y la mortalidad natural de la mayoría de estas especies de focas, en especial (aunque no siempre se dispone de datos sobre todas las especies): edad en el momento de la madurez sexual y de la primera cópula, edades media y máxima de los reproductores, índices de preñez, momento de la cópula, duración de la gestación y la lactación, causas e índices de mortalidad natural de los cachorros y de los adultos. Sobre las relaciones tróficas de estas focas en general o en determinadas partes de su área de distribución se sabe muy poco o se dispone sólo de datos parciales, aunque sobre algunas especies hay información relativamente más abundante, como, por ejemplo, sobre las focas del Caspio y larga. La información que se presenta incluye: especies que comen, distribución estacional de los períodos de alimentación y ayuno, especialmente en relación con la reproducción, y diferencias en la dieta según la edad.

La foca de Groenlandia, la del Caspio y la marbreada son las más numerosas, las demás se encuentran en menor número, especialmente la foca capuchina, que no se reproduce en aguas soviéticas. Se examinan la distribución y los movimientos migratorios de esas focas, que de ordinario están relacionados con la reproducción, la muda, la alimentación y las variaciones del estado de los hielos y sus desplazamientos: la mayoría de las especies se desplazan hacia zonas de hielos abundantes a finales del invierno o principios de la primavera, para reproducirse y mudar, dispersándose luego durante el verano cuando los hielos se funden, para buscar alimentos.

Se da una breve historia de la explotación y regulación de cada una de las especies, que muestra de ordinario un período en el que su número ha ido disminuyendo debido a la explotación excesiva (por los nativos o en cacerías industriales), seguido por otro de recuperación, una vez adoptados límites de captura. Las focas del Caspio, de Groenlandia y del Baikal, las focas marbreada y barbuda del norte del Pacífico y la foca fajada se han estudiado más a fondo que las demás especies, debido principalmente a su valor comercial. La explotación de la foca barbuda depende de las necesidades de los habitantes de las zonas costeras. Por lo que se refiere a las demás especies, los productos que de ellas se obtienen encuentran fácil mercado, sobre todo las pieles, pero la explotación se ve limitada por la situación de las poblaciones y, a menudo, por la necesidad de tomar medidas para que se recuperen.

L.A. Popov
VNIRO, 17 V. Karsnoselskaya, Moscow B-140, USSR

Introduction

This paper is concerned with the species of ice-inhabiting seals found in the inland waters and coastal marine areas of the USSR. The condition of the ice and the timing of annual, biological events in these seals are closely connected. Their distribution may be divided into 3 geographic areas:

(i)   seas of the northeastern Atlantic Ocean and adjacent waters of the Arctic Ocean (Barents Sea, White Sea and Kara Sea) – harp seal (*Pagophilus groenlandicus*), ringed seal (*Pusa hispida*), bearded seal (*Erignathus barbatus*) and hooded seal (*Cystophora cristata*);

(ii) seas of the North Pacific Ocean (Bering Sea and Sea of Okhotsk) – ringed seal (*Pusa hispida*), ribbon seal (*Histriophoca fasciata*), bearded seal (*Erignathus barbatus*) and largha seal (*Phoca largha*);

(iii) inland waters (Caspian Sea and Lake Baikal) – Caspian seal (*Pusa caspica*) and Baikal seal (*Pusa sibirica*).

The abundance of these seals varies over their distribution: the most numerous are the harp, Caspian and ringed seals; bearded, ribbon, largha and Baikal seals are found in lesser numbers; hooded seals, ranging over the North Atlantic seas, are found in very small numbers in the eastern Barents Sea.

Besides ice-living seals, very small numbers of other pinnipeds inhabit the inland waters and adjacent marine areas of the USSR: the Atlantic and Pacific walruses, northern fur seal, northern sea lion, grey and largha seals of the Barents and Baltic Seas, ringed seal of Lake Ladoga and the Baltic Sea, and the Kuril seal. Some of them are subject to strictly controlled small-scale sealing – the ringed seal of Lake Ladoga, northern fur seal and the Pacific walrus, the latter used only for the subsistence needs of the local population of Chukotsk –

while exploitation of species such as the Atlantic walrus of Arctic waters, island seal, Steller's sea lion, grey and common seals of the Baltic Sea and the grey seal of the southern Barents Sea is completely forbidden.

The amount of research devoted to the distribution, abundance, biology and ecology of the main ice-living seals varies by species and area of distribution. Thus, the Caspian harp and Baikal seals, the ringed and bearded seals of the North Pacific and the ribbon seal have received the most study in comparison with other forms.

Further, present knowledge and research programmes depend greatly on each species' commercial value in different parts of its range.

Seals of the northeastern Atlantic Ocean and adjacent waters of the Arctic Ocean

HARP SEAL

Adult harp seals have a maximum zoological length of 190 cm and a body weight of 160 kg. Newborn pups measure 80-90 cm in length and weigh 8-9 kg. Pups are born in the fluffy, white embryonic pelage which changes to a light grey background with small spots of brown and black after the pups' first moult. This basic coloration continues in immature seals 1 year and older. The background colour of adult animals is near-white, with 2 large, elongated spots on each side of the trunk, resembling joined wings; the head is black.

Distribution and Movements

The harp seal is found in the pelagic areas of the North Atlantic seas to the fringe of the drift ice in the Arctic Ocean. Waters to the east of Spitsbergen and to the west of the Novaya Zemlya archipelago serve as its western and eastern limits, respectively. The summer and winter limits of the ice fringe act as the species' northern and southern boundaries.

From summer to autumn, the seals inhabit the pre-fringe zone of ice in the Barents and Kara Seas, where they are usually observed in groups in the waters of western Spitsbergen, the gulf and straits of the Franz Josef Land archipelago, off northern Novaya Zemlya and in the straits of Severnaya Zemlya. In autumn, concurrent with the expansion of the ice fringe to the south, seals begin to migrate actively, mainly along the eastern and western shores of Novaya Zemlya; aggregations of seals appear near the coast of the Kapin Peninsula in late autumn and in the White Sea in January and February. During reproduction, the animals form dense concentrations on drifting ice in the White Sea and adjacent ice areas of the Barents Sea; passive migrations on ice from the middle part of the White Sea into the area of the ice fringe in the Barents Sea occur during reproduction and moulting. In the middle or end of May, the harp seals leave the ice and renew their active migrations to the southern areas of the Barents and Kara Seas, where they remain throughout the summer and early autumn.

Census and Status

The primary method of calculating the abundance of harp seals in Soviet waters is the use of aerial photography during the period of their greatest concentration on ice. In the past 25 years, censuses of this type have been regularly conducted every 3-4 years, making 2 different counts during each census: one of adult females during the breeding season following the mass pupping period, another of all animals on the moulting grounds, excluding pups of the year. In recent years, a mass collection of teeth has been made in order to determine the age composition of reproducing females. Both censuses are made using parallel air tracks, usually at a photographic scale of 1:1 500.

In calculating the number of adult fe-

Table 1. Census of reproducing female harp seals, before biological corrections

Year	Number of females
1963	65.0
1968	70.5
1970	82.1
1973	92.7

males, actual working counts are corrected in accordance with various biological factors, including, *inter alia*, seals remaining in the water, late parturition of some females and small aggregations not covered by the survey; males are excluded from the count by the former's characteristic distribution on the ice. The estimated number, before biological corrections, and mean age of reproducing harp seals determined in recent years are given in Tables 1 and 2.

Reproductive Capacity

Harp seal females reach sexual maturity at age 3, but most first take part in mating between 4 and 6; males become sexually mature at age 4. Females give birth annually; the

Table 2. Mean age of reproducing female harp seals

Year	Mean age (in years)
1963	8.1
1964	8.4
1969	12.2
1970	11.8
1971	13.0
1972	13.3
1973	13.6
1974	14.1

pregnancy rate appears to decrease from age 25 onward. Available data indicates that a high percentage of mature females do not become pregnant each year, perhaps as high as 20 % or more. Corrected photo-survey data show a total of 111 000 reproducing females present in 1973, presumably producing the same number of pups.

Natural Mortality

The causes of natural mortality and the associated vital rates have not been studied completely for all age and sex groups. Newborn and lactating pups have received the most attention in this area: pups may be still-born, may die from exhaustion when lost from females, or from serious injuries obtained from adult animals, or may be crushed or cut by the ice, especially during the first few days of life. Excluding the latter factor, the natural mortality rate for pups is 4-5 % during the lactation period.

Exploitation

Large-scale Soviet and Norwegian sealing operations have been based on the harp seal. The highest average combined annual catch of both countries was 353 000 for the period 1925-29; during the post-war period, 1947-51, the annual combined seal catch fluctuated between 146 000 and 192 000 animals.

As the number of seals decreased, annual Soviet harvest limits were established: from 1935, no more than 100 000 animals could be taken by sealing vessels, and from 1963 this limit was reduced to 60 000 and the taking of females during the breeding season was forbidden. As from 1965, sealing from vessels was stopped and the annual harvest by the local population was restricted to 20 000 pups. Sealing from vessels continues to be banned and the present annual catch limit for the local population is 30 000 pups; the killing of adult seals during the breeding season is forbidden.

Annual catches by Norwegian sealing vessels in the Barents Sea have fluctuated between 6 400 and 13 300 animals for the years 1963-74.

Regulation of sealing is provided for by the agreement between the USSR and Norway on the regulation of sealing and conservation of stocks in the northeastern Atlantic Ocean. As a result of regulations adopted during the past 10 years, there has been an increase in the numbers of harp seals in the White Sea stock, indicated by aerial photo censuses and changing factors in the age composition of reproductive females.

Trophic Relationships

Trophic relationships of the harp seal have not yet been studied thoroughly owing to the inaccessibility of the animals during the summer and autumn period of intensive feeding, when they are widely dispersed in small groups along the edge of the Arctic ice.

Some information can be gained during the breeding and moulting season, when seals form dense concentrations on ice in the White and Barents Seas; during that time (February-May) the seals almost never feed, living instead on the fat accumulated in the summer and autumn. In the summer, harp seals feed mainly on small crustaceans, including Euphausidae, and also on amphipods and small molluscs. In autumn, the seals' distribution is closely connected with that of the Arctic cod (*Arctogadus glacialis*) and capelin (*Mallotus villosus*) in the Barents and Kara Seas and in the White Sea in early winter.

Need for Seal Products

The products obtained from sealing (fur, fat and meat) are of great significance in the economy of the people living on the coast of the White Sea. Although the need for seal products increases annually, the present state of the harp seal population requires strict limits on exploitation to encourage the future restoration of the stock to its former abundance.

RINGED SEAL

Adults have a zoological length of 120-150 cm and a body weight reaching 80 kg. Newborn pups are 55-65 cm in length and weigh up to 5 kg. The pelage coloration of adult male and female ringed seals is the same: the main background colour of the back varies from brown, to grey with olive shading, to dark grey and almost black; the belly is light grey with silver shading.

Light-coloured veins are interlaced on the main background forming a net or lace design that produces oval rings; individuals are sometimes seen without the characteristic colouring of the species, but bearing a faint ring-like lace pattern instead. The embryonic coat of newborn pups is long and white, changing to a short pelage with the characteristic adult coloration, following the first moult.

Distribution and Movements

It is believed that only 1 sub-species of the ringed seal, i.e., *Pusa hispida hispida*, is found in the northeastern Atlantic (the White and Barents Seas) and Pacific (the Kara and Laptev Seas) Oceans. In the western part of its range, *P. h. hispida* inhabits the gulfs and bays of the Kola Peninsula, the White Sea coast and the southeastern Barents Sea; they are also usually found in the Cheshsky Gulf and Pechora Sea. To the east, numerous ringed seals occur in the southwestern Kara Sea, near the eastern coast of White (Bely) Island, and in Malygin Strait and Baydaratskaya Bay; seals are also observed in Tazovskaya and Obskaya Bays, off the coast of Yamal Peninsula and further east in gulfs and bays. In the Laptev Sea ringed seals are most abundant in its largest gulfs, including Hatangsky, Anabarsky, Ole-

neksky and Japsky. The distribution and abundance of the ringed seal in the East Siberian and Chuckchi Seas are poorly studied; it can be supposed that several stocks inhabit the entire Arctic coast. Seals can be observed not only in the coastal areas of Soviet Arctic waters, but also in the areas of drift ice of the central Arctic and on small islands and large archipelagos.

Ringed seals do not engage in long, mass migrations; their movements are mostly local and are connected with feeding and fluctuations in the condition of the ice. There are known cases, however, of animals swimming long distances to move up rivers, sometimes 10 km, when feeding on fish shoals.

Status

It is thought that ringed seals in the seas of the northeastern Atlantic Ocean and the seas of the Arctic Ocean are abundant enough to sustain commercial sealing. However, many areas have not been studied and censuses have not yet covered a large area; it is, therefore, impossible to estimate the number of ringed seals in Soviet waters.

Reproductive Capacity

Males and females become sexually mature at age 7-8 and age 5, respectively; however, females do not begin to reproduce until 2-3 years later. The number of mature females that do not become pregnant in any one year may reach 30 %. Females generally give birth to 1 pup and nursing occurs inside a snow den and lasts for about 1 month. The duration of the mating period is not known and gestation lasts about 11 months.

Exploitation

Organized exploitation of the ringed seal by local people only occurs in some areas along the entire Arctic coast and stocks are presently underexploited. Sealing is regular and intensive only in the White Sea, where an annual harvest limit of 3 500 has been established.

Trophic Relationships

The trophic relationships of the ringed seal have been poorly studied in the different areas of its distribution, especially in the Kara and Laptev Seas. In waters north of Europe, its main food items are crustaceans and fish. In winter and autumn ringed seals feed mainly on fish; polar cod (*Boreogadus sarda*) sometimes accounts for 90 % of all food taken, the remainder, including navaga (*Eleginus navaga*), capelin, smelt (*Osmerus eperlanus*), flounder (*Platichthys flesus flesus*) and sand eel (*Ammodytes* spp.). Crustaceans form the greater part of this species diet in the summer months. In the White and Barents Seas, the main food items include some commercial fish species such as herring (*Clupea harengus*) and navaga; ringed seals form dense concentrations while feeding on salmon (*Salmo salar*) during the latter's migration in the rivers of the Kola Peninsula. Because ringed seals feed on a wide range of prey, the future availability of their food supply is not endangered.

Need for Seal Products

The products obtained from ringed seals (pelts, fat and meat) are used by the local Arctic population for producing a variety of fur goods, as human and dog food and as bait in hunting (e.g., for polar fox). Future exploitation of the ringed seal in remote, as yet unexploited, Arctic areas will naturally provide additional seal products.

BEARDED SEAL

The bearded seal is a large animal, reaching a maximum zoological length of 270 cm and a maximum weight of 300 kg; newborns measure about 120 cm and weigh up to 25-30 kg. The species has somewhat unusual proportions, with a large body and a small head. Males and females have the same coloration: the back is of an olive-brown colour, while the belly has fairly numerous, small faded spots and touches unevenly distributed on a light grey background; the sides are often covered with brown spots. The mystacial vibrissae are sleek, muddy white in colour and hang over the lower lip like a beard. The embryonic pelage is shed before birth.

Distribution and Movements

In the White, Barents and Kara Seas, the bearded seal is found in practically all shallow coastal areas that are free of shorefast ice in the winter months. The distribution of this species is greatly affected by the ice conditions, as well as by the availability of currents and tidal flows, the presence of food items and other factors.

In March and April, the primary pupping grounds are Mezensky Bay and the entrance to the White Sea, southeastern Barents Sea and its adjacent gulf, the coast of Novaya Zemlya and waters near Spitsbergen; the lowest numbers of females are found in the southern White Sea, in western areas of the Kara Sea and near Medvezhy (Bear) Island in the Barents Sea. During the moulting season, from the end of April to the beginning of August, *E. barbatus* is most numerous in the shallow area between the Kolguev and Kanin Peninsulas, on the drift ice in the eastern Barents Sea and near Franz Josef Land. In the Kara Sea, concentrations of bearded seals are annually observed in the Kara Gate, Baydaratsky Bay, near the eastern shore of Novaya Zemlya, in the waters of the western Nordenshield Archipelago and off the southwestern coast of Severnaya Zemlya. With the formation of the shore ice and the onset of colder temperatures, bearded seals become more abundant in the coastal areas of the White and

Barents Seas and are found in concentrations on the drift ice when it arrives later in the season.

Bearded seals engage in long migrations, including passive movements with the ice. Adult seals have been recorded migrating on ice from the northern White Sea into the eastern Barents Sea. Young animals sometimes migrate into large shallow gulfs in the southern White Sea. Seals also migrate from the southeastern Barents Sea along the western shore of Novaya Zemlya and through the straits into the Kara Sea. Migrations on ice have been observed to southern areas of the Kara Sea. Seals sometimes enter river estuaries in summer and animals have even been recorded in the central Arctic not far from the North Pole.

Status

E. barbatus is not an abundant species. It is a solitary animal, though individuals found in the same area are sometimes observed in groups. Bearded seals do not congregate in large concentrations. It is difficult to provide an estimate of this species abundance because it has not been sufficiently studied.

Reproductive Capacity

The reproductive biology of the bearded seal in this area is poorly studied. Males reach sexual maturity at age 5 and females begin to take an active part in reproduction at 4. Fertilization occurs from the end of March through June and intensive development of the embryo begins in July and September; gestation normally last 10.5-11 months. Usually, 1 pup is born between the end of March to the end of May. Up to 25 % of mature females fail to get pregnant each year.

Natural mortality

The causes of natural mortality and associated vital rates have also received little study. The most dangerous predator of the bearded seal is the polar bear, especially in more northerly areas. The viscera have been found to be greatly infected with helminths.

Exploitation

Sealing vessels in the White and Barents Seas are prohibited from taking bearded seals because the species is not numerous. Coastal people do take this seal, but the number of animals killed annually is not known; the extent of the catch is mainly determined by the needs of the local population and this situation is expected to continue in the future.

Trophic Relationships

Trophic relationships of the bearded seal have received insufficient study. It is known, however, that its food consumption is diverse and includes about 70 different items: various species of molluscs, gephyreans and crustaceans are the main invertebrates consumed; polar cod is the most abundant fish in its diet, which also includes fair quantities of herring, navaga, flounder and sand eel.

HOODED SEAL

Cystophora cristata is a large animal: males reach a zoological length of 280 cm and weigh over 300 kg; females reach 230 cm and weigh 160 kg. Newborn pups measure 100-150 cm in length and weigh 22-25 kg.

Males have a characteristic hood on their head, which is absent in females. Adult pelage is generally of a dark grey colour, sometimes with a brown tint; different sizes spots varying in colour from dark brown to black are scattered on the back and sides. The belly is light grey, sometimes varying to either darker or lighter tints. The embryonic pelage is shed before birth; in newborns, the back, sides, dorsal sides of the back flippers and the tail are

369

dark grey with silver and blue tints while the chest and belly are white. Spots first appear at age 1 following the first postpartum moult.

Distribution and movements

The hooded seal is a pelagic animal, inhabiting areas of the open sea and drifting shore ice in the North Atlantic Ocean; only one stock is believed to exist, distributed from the Gulf of St. Lawrence, Newfoundland and Labrador in the west to an eastern limit near Novaya Zemlya and the Kanin Peninsula in the Barents Sea. The seals are concentrated in 2 areas of drift ice during their breeding and moulting periods: (i) Gulf of St. Lawrence and waters northeast of Newfoundland, and (ii) the area of Jan Mayen from 71°N-74°N. There are no aggregations of hooded seals in waters adjacent to the USSR during their moulting season, although some individuals are observed, including females with newborn pups.

The migrations of this species have been described in detail in other publications.

Status and Exploitation

The total population of *C. cristata* is approximately 500 000-600 000, of which 80-90 % are distributed in the Jan Mayen area and the remainder near Newfoundland. Up to 1955, hooded seals were exploited only by Norwegian sealing schooners in the Jan Mayen area; from 1955 to 1966, Soviet sealing vessels (8-10 ships) entered this area and harvested hooded and harp seals; during this period the annual Soviet catch of hooded seals was somewhat over 25 000 animals, mainly pups.

Concurrent research investigations were conducted by the USSR, primarily directed at general problems relating to morphology and reproduction biology, including distribution on ice during the breeding season, duration of whelping and lactation periods and age composition. The results of this research have been published in several articles; the investigations were terminated with the end of exploitation in 1966.

Indirect information on the status of the hooded seal in the Jan Mayen area from analysis of general biological data, catch statistics and age composition data indicate a decrease in the species' abundance in recent years due to intensive Norwegian sealing. Beginning in 1961, protection and management measures were begun as a result of the Agreement between the USSR and Norway: the taking of adult and immature animals was forbidden at the moulting grounds in the Denmark Strait and a spring harvest season was established in the Jan Mayen area. Soviet researchers further believe that a prohibition on taking females during the breeding season would be an effective conservation measure. At present the numbers of adult female hooded seals taken while breeding have been sharply reduced.

Trophic Relationships

Adult hooded seals do little, if any, feeding during the breeding season, although on rare occasions squid (*Gonatus fabricii*) are found in their stomachs. Pups feed initially near the ice edge, mainly on crustaceans and squid. The period of intensive feeding in the hooded seal has been poorly studied, although from information obtained in other areas of its distribution it can be supposed that the favoured food in the Barents Sea are bottom fishes like halibut (*Hippoglossus hippoglossus*), cod (*Gadus morhua*), redfish (*Sebastes marinus*) and flounders (*Pleuronecti formes*).

Seals of the North Pacific Ocean

RINGED SEAL

Two sub-species of *Phoca hispida* are found in the North Pacific region: *P. h. ocho-*

tensis in the Sea of Okhotsk and *P. h. krasheninn* in the Bering Sea. The sub-species are distinguished by morphological differences of the body and cranium and by their pelage coloration; *P. h. ochotensis* has grey, dark grey or almost black pelage on its back, while *P. h. krasheninn* is grey-brown, sometimes with a light greenish-yellow tint; both animals usually have a light grey belly, with light strips along the back and sides forming light irregular rings. Pups of both sub-species have a fluffy white birthcoat.

P. h. ochotensis is somewhat smaller than *P. h. krasheninn*: the zoological length of the former is between 85 and 140 cm and its body weight is from 14 to 55 kg; *P. h. krasheninn* is heavier by 8-11 kg. Newborns of *P. h. ochotensis* reach a length of 60 cm and a weight of 4 kg, while *P. h. krasheninn* pups are 62 cm in length and weigh about 5 kg.

Distribution and Migration

P. h. krasheninn is mainly found on fast shore ice in the gulfs and bays of the Bering Sea. With the disappearance of the ice, the seals remain sedentary along coastal inlets of Chulotsk and Kamchatka Peninsulas and the Commander Islands; the densest concentrations of *P. h. krasheninn* are found in Mechigmensky Gulf, Senyavina Strait, St. Lawrence Gulf and in Rudder Bay and Krest Gulf. Seals migrate to the Commander Islands in small numbers in spring and summer.

P. h. ochotensis inhabits moving sea ice for the greatest part of the year, avoiding fast shore ice. During the reproduction period (March-May), dense concentrations are mainly found near the western and northwestern coasts of the Sea of Okhotsk, and, in its southern part, near the Shantarske Islands, in Sakhalin Gulf and on the drift ice near the eastern shore of Sakhalin Island. *P. h. ochotensis* engages in both passive migrations on ice and in active migrations searching for ice flows within the Sea of Okhotsk. When the ice disappears, the species scatters widely to coastal inlets, spending much time in the water. With the coming of autumn and the reappearance of ice in the gulfs and bays, seals concentrate in coastal areas; during the winter pupping period, most animals are found on sea ice, although some inhabit the shore fast ice.

Census and Status

Biostatistical calculation of the population size of *P. hispida* in the Sea of Okhotsk gives an estimate of 800 000 animals, equal to the estimated level in 1966.

In 1968, an aerial census of this population was conducted; the flying altitude and the survey track width were both 100 m; by determining the area of sea ice and the number of seals per 1 km of sea ice, an estimation of the total number of seals in the survey area was obtained; census results show a total number of 818 000 and 865 000 ringed seals in the Sea of Okhotsk in 1968 and 1969, respectively, not including animals in the water. Data on the ringed seal in the Sea of Okhotsk indicated some decrease in population size in recent years.

The population of ringed seals in the Bering Sea is roughly estimated at 70 000 to 80 000 animals.

Reproductive Capacity

P. h. ochotensis females reach sexual maturity at age 5-6; at age 5, over 30 % and at 7 and over nearly 100 % of females give birth. The pregnancy rate begins to drop at about age 15.

The annual pregnancy rate is 80 %. Most males reach sexual maturity at age 6. *P. h. krasheninn* females become sexually mature at age 5-7; 25 %, 57 % and 73 % of females give birth at ages 6, 7 and 8, respectively. Annually, no more than 27 % of adult, mature females are not pregnant. Males reach sexual maturity at age 7-8.

371

Natural Mortality

The natural mortality rate by age of the ringed seal is given in Table 3.

From this data, the average natural mortality rate for the ringed seal is shown to be 10-11 % per year, excluding pups. For *P. h. krasheninn*, natural mortality in the first year of life is calculated to be 34 %, dropping to an average of 9 % for all other age groups.

Exploitation

From the end of the 1800s to the mid 1900s, the average annual take of ringed seals in the Sea of Okhotsk did not exceed 25 000-30 000 animals; such a harvest level did not reduce the abundance of the population. However, the average annual harvest of 72 000 seals taken from 1955 to 1965 led to a reduction in the population. From 1969, an annual limit of 32 000 animals was imposed on sealing conducted from ships, and this quota was subsequently reduced to 25 000 and 18 000 in 1972 and 1975, respectively. Catch restrictions were also introduced for sealing by the coastal people with a quota of 7 000 seals in 1975.

During the postwar years, the annual catch of ringed seals in the Bering Sea by the coastal population was between 30 000 and 35 000 animals; in latter years, however, the harvest decreased to 10 000-12 000 animals, mainly because there were fewer hunters. Vessel sealing was forbidden in the Bering Sea and, since 1970, the annual harvest by the coastal people has been restricted to low levels (2 000-3 000).

Trophic Relationships

In general, *P. h. ochotensis* feeds mainly on Euphausidae, though other food species seasonally assume major importance in some areas of its distribution: during breeding (March-April), the species feeds mainly on Euphausidae and to a lesser extent on Amphipoda and Decapoda; in May and June, when feeding is less intense, these latter 2 items make up the main part of the diet; and following June until the end of autumn, fish, including sand eel (*Ammodytes personatus*), herring (*Clupea haringus*), capelin, navaga and smelt (*Osmerus eperlanus*) assume primary importance.

In May and June, *P. h. krasheninn* feeds mainly on polar cod and sometimes on crustaceans. Because of the ringed seal's ability to shift seasonally between a number of varied food species, the availability (or lack) of specific food items should not be considered as the main factor limiting its abundance.

Need for Seal Products and Regulation of Exploitation

The primary objective of regulation measures is the restoration of the ringed seal stocks, especially in the Sea of Okhotsk. Demand for the products of sealing is unlimited, especially that for fur. The limits for ring seal catch are determined annually for vessel sealing, depending on the ring seal stocks. The sealing limits for local populations conducting their sealing operations near the shore are established annually as well.

Table 3. Natural mortality rates of *P. hispida* by age

Age	% Mortality
1 year old	35
2	15
3-5	11-13
6-7	10
8-9	5
10-11	10
12-13	14
14 and older	30-35

Ribbon seal

Adult ribbon seals reach maximum and mean zoological length of 190 and 165 cm, respectively, and weigh 70-80 kg, and up to 100 kg when in best condition. Newborns may be 80-90 cm in length and weigh about 9 kg.

The coloration of the ribbon seal is distinctive: the background of the adult male is brown to intensive black, that of the female generally somewhat lighter. Four white, sometimes yellow-tinted, ribbon-like strips, 10-12 cm in width are found, one covering the neck and occiput, another girding the body in the sacral area, and 2 covering the dorsal surface of the flippers and extending from the shoulder to the middle area of the trunk. Immature seals are dark pale yellow and lack the 4 strips. Newborn pups are in the fluffy, white embryonic pelage, which is replaced by a coat of dark grey on the back and lighter grey on the belly after the first moult.

Distribution and Movements

Ribbon seals are distributed in the Bering Sea and Sea of Okhotsk, and these populations may represent 2 separate local forms of the species; the species is also found in the southern Chukotsk Sea and northern Sea of Japan. *H. fasciata* always haul out on firm pack ice far from shore where cracks and leads are available; the primary hauling grounds in the Bering Sea are the Anadyr Gulf and adjacent southeastern St. Lawrence Gulf, the areas of ice massifs near St. Matthew Island and the Bering Strait. In the Sea of Okhotsk, the densest concentrations of seals are found in the ice area northeast of Sakhalin Island and northwest of the Babushkin Gulf.

The distribution of *H. fasciata* when not found on ice, and its migrations, especially during summer and autumn, have received very little study. Passive migrations on ice in the Sea of Okhotsk during the breeding season (April) and movements to ice areas preceding the moulting period have been observed.

Census and Status

The same aerial census method was used as for ringed seals. In the Bering Sea, the population was estimated at 80 000-90 000 animals in 1964, decreasing to 60 000 in 1969. More precise data was available for the Sea of Okhotsk, showing a total population of 133 000 animals in May 1969.

Reproductive Capacity

Most females first mate at age 4-5, with a very small number mating at age 3. Males reach sexual maturity 1-2 years later than females and first mate at age 5-6. Up to 15 % of mature females are not pregnant each year. The annual reproductive rate is 26 %. Females do not live beyond the age of 26.

Natural Mortality

Natural mortality during the first year of life has been calculated to be 44 %; the annual mortality for adults is 11.2 % before age 16-18. Predators include the killer whale, Greenland shark, polar bear and large marine birds.

Exploitation

During the past 18 to 20 years, ribbon sealing has been carried out primarily by sealing vessels in the Sea of Okhotsk and Bering Sea; from 1957 to 1961 the annual harvest ranged between 11 000 and 18 000 animals, and from 1961 an additional 8 000-9 000 animals were taken in the Bering Sea. From 1961 to 1968 the annual harvest increased to between 16 000 and 23 000 animals, and decreases in the seal stocks resulted. Sealing from vessels was thereafter restricted in order to restore stocks in both seas, and present annual quotas are 3 500 in the Sea of Okhotsk and 3 000 in the Bering Sea.

Trophic Relationships

The feeding of *H. fasciata* has received most study during the species' breeding and moulting seasons in the spring; during this time, crustaceans and, to a lesser extent, fish and cephalopods, form the seal's main diet. The composition of food species is more diverse in the Bering Sea than in the Sea of Okhotsk: in the former area, more than 14 species of crustaceans have been found in the stomach contents, primarily *Pandalus gonionus, Themisto* spp., *Pandalopsis* spp., *Enalus gaimardi* and Amphipodae, and more than 10 fish species, primarily polar cod (*Boreogadus saida*), lump fish (*Lumpenus medius*), navaga (*Elegenus navaga*), capelin (*Mallotus villosus*), and feed mainly on pollock (*Theragra chalcogramma*) and, to a lesser extent, on cod (*Gadus m. macrocephalus*) and crustaceans (*Pandalus borealis*).

Young seals feed mainly on crustaceans. In searching for food, *H. fasciata* can dive to a depth of 200 m. It is thought that the availability of food as well as favourable ice conditions determine the distribution of the species.

Need for Seal Products

Although a ready market exists for ribbon seal products, especially pelts, further exploitation is limited by the reduced condition of the stocks.

BEARDED SEAL

Adult bearded seals reach mean and maximum zoological lengths of 215 cm and perhaps 260 cm, respectively; the maximum weight of adult seals carrying maximum blubber is more than 300 kg. Newborns are 118-137 cm in length and weigh 27-35 kg; pups are ash grey, sometimes with a brown tint. Adult seals vary from light ash to dark grey, the belly lighter than the back.

Distribution and Movements

The largest concentrations of *E. barbatus* in the Bering Sea are found on inshore ice massifs on St. Lawrence, St. Matthew and Hall Islands; in the Sea of Okhotsk, large concentrations are found in the north and southwest and in Terpenye Gulf (Sakhalin Island). The species is sedentary, usually inhabiting shallow areas where the nearbottom organisms on which they feed are found.

Census

In 1969, a census of the bearded seals in the Sea of Okhotsk was conducted, using aerial surveys, indicating a total population as high as 180 000-200 000 animals, with 40 000-50 000 in the "southern" population (Sakhalin Island area) and 140 000-150 000 in the "northern" population. Aerial surveys were not used to count the Bering Sea population; the total number here is estimated to be approximately 250 000 animals.

Reproductive Capacity

Most females begin reproducing between 4 and 6 years of age; males become sexually mature between 5 and 6. The annual reproductive rate is estimated to be 19 %.

Natural Mortality

The natural mortality rate during the first year of life has been calculated to be 22 %; mortality rates in older animals are difficult to determine because of the worn condition of the teeth. It is supposed that the killer whale, Greenland shark and polar bear are predators, the latter attacking seals at their onshore rookeries.

Exploitation

Bearded seals have long been taken by the coastal peoples of the Bering Sea and Sea of Okhotsk; sealing vessels have also exploited the species, first in the Sea of Okhotsk and later also in the Bering Sea. In the former sea, annual vessel catches from 1947 to 1956 and from 1957 to 1964 ranged between 2 000-6 000 and 9 000-13 000 animals, respectively. Vessel sealing in the Bering Sea began in 1961; from 1964 to 1967 the annual harvest in both seas was 8 000-10 000 animals. The number of seals taken by the coastal population is generally unknown for these years.

A reduction in the bearded seal populations due to overexploitation led to the termination of vessel sealing in 1970 in both the Bering Sea and the Sea of Okhotsk, and the imposition of quotas (5 000 in the Sea of Okhotsk and 3 000 in the Bering Sea) on the harvest by the coastal population. Recently, the number of bearded seals has been increasing under this protection.

Trophic Relationships

Bearded seals feed on species found in less than 200 m of water. In the summer and autumn, crabs (Majdae), shrimp (Gragonidae), molluscs (Gastropoda) and worms (Echiurida and Polychaeta) are the primary foods. The seals also eat sand eels (*Ammodytes hexapterus*) and daubed shanny (*Leptoclinus maculatus*); of 11 species of crustaceans consumed, *Chinoecetes opilio* and *Grandon dalli* are most important; *Polynices* is the main mollusc eaten.

Need for Seal Products

Future demand for bearded seal products (skins, oil and meat) will be determined only by the needs of the coastal people of the Sea of Okhotsk and the Bering Sea.

LARGHA SEAL

The maximum and mean lengths and weights of adult largha seals is 214 cm and 167-169 cm, and 150 kg and 90-114 kg, respectively. Newborns aged 1 to 5 days are from 76 to 90 cm in length and weigh 7 to 10 kg.

The main background coloration of the largha seal varies from silver grey to dark grey, with the belly usually lighter than the back; black and brown spots of different sizes are scattered on the entire body. The embryonic pelage of newborn pups may be pure white to smoky grey.

Distribution and Migration

P. largha is found throughout the Sea of Okhotsk and the Bering Sea. Seals haul out on drift ice for breeding and moulting, mainly in the eastern Bering Sea and northern Sea of Okhotsk. The species performs passive migrations (on ice) during the breeding season and searches for firm ice flows before moulting. With the disappearance of the ice, seals move near coastal areas, and in autumn form rookeries on shore, which sometimes number 2 000 to 3 000 animals. The seals move out to sea again with the first appearance of ice.

Census

In 1969, a census of the largha seals in the Sea of Okhotsk was conducted using aerial surveys, indicating a population of 13 000. It is supposed that there are 135 000 largha seals in the Bering Sea.

Reproductive Capacity

Most females and males begin to take an active part in reproduction between 4 and 5 years of age and 5 and 6, respectively. During the reproduction period, families of 1 adult male, female and pup are formed. The annual reproduction rate is 20 %. Largha seals have a life expectancy of 35 years.

Natural Mortality

Data indicates that the natural mortality rate for seals in their first year is 45 % and about 8 % thereafter until the critical age (17-20). The main predator of this species is the brown bear; wolves and Arctic foxes are lesser predators. It is supposed that the natural mortality rate at land rookeries may be 10 %.

Exploitation

During the last 18 to 20 years, the combined annual catch of seals by vessels and by the coastal people in the Bering Sea and Sea of Okhotsk has not exceeded 10 000-15 000 animals. Although this level of exploitation did not affect the seal stock, catch limits allowing a harvest equal to 5 % of the total seal population were introduced in 1970, i.e., for vessel sealing, limits of 5 000 and 6 000 seals in the Sea of Okhotsk and Bering Sea, respectively; for exploitation by the coastal peoples, catch limits of 2 000 animals in each sea.

Trophic Relationships

P. largha feeds primarily on fish, cephalopods and crustaceans during the reproduction and moulting periods, with the most intensive feeding taking place in the morning and at night; bottom species and pelagic fish species predominate in the seals feeding during breeding and moulting, respectively. In the Bering Sea, food species consumed vary according to age: weaned pups eat mainly small Amphipodae, algae, shrimp and shoaling fish (sand eel); feeding on larger fish begins at 2 to 2.5 months of age. Immature animals (age 1-4 years) feed mainly on pelagic fish species (flounders, pollock (*Theragra chalcogramma*), cod (*Gadus m. macrocephalus*), halibut and gobies (Gobiidae)), Octopoda and crustaceans. In autumn, seals feed primarily on Salmonidae, including pink salmon, chum (*Oncorhynchus keta*) and coho salmon (*Oncorhynchus keta kisutch*).

Need for Seal Products

There is an unlimited market for the fur of this species; it is recommended, however, that stocks be held at the maximum sustainable level.

Seals of Inland Waters

CASPIAN SEAL

The length and weight of adult animals are 130-140 cm and 50-60 kg, respectively, and the latter may reach 90 kg. Newborns measure 65-79 cm in length and have a mean weight of 5 kg.

Coloration varies with age and sex; the back of adult seals is ash grey, changing to light grey on the sides and belly. Small black spots cover the body of males; in females, these spots are lighter in colour, fewer in number and found primarily on the back. The snout and head is of a reddish tint on some animals. The embryonic pelage of newborns is greenish yellow, moulting to silver grey, with a darker back and lighter belly and sometimes including small spots. Before autumn, the coloration again changes to olive yellow.

Distribution and Movements

Pusa caspica is distributed throughout the Caspian Sea. From September to midwinter, with the formation of shore ice, most animals migrate from the southern sections of the sea to the areas of pack ice and leads in the northern section, in preparation for the breeding season. This latter occurs from the end of January to the beginning of February. Young animals in poor condition, and sick adults do not leave the southern areas. Following reproduction and moulting, the majority of seals migrate back to the southern and middle areas of the sea; however, if the animals have not completed their moulting before the disappearance of the ice in May, they move to the northern islands where moulting is completed in late May or early June; some animals, mainly young, do not leave the northern area in the summer. Seals form rookeries for the entire summer in the groups of small islands.

Census and Status

Attempts to estimate numbers of reproductive females and total seal numbers were made, based on a considerable yield of pups in the 1965-66 season. The figure was estimated to be as high as approximately 520 000 seals. A counting method was used to estimate absolute numbers of seals in the water, during the summer in different areas of sea, and the data were then extrapolated to the whole area.

Aerial photographic surveys of females were made for the first time in 1973 during the breeding season. Treatment of the data gave an estimate of reproductive females as high as 90 000.

In recent years, the age composition of reproductive females – a factor determining the reproductive capacity of the population – has been established. Data are given in Table 4.

The increase in both the mean and maximum ages of reproducing females is perhaps a result of the management measures introduced during this period (see under Commercial Exploitation below).

Trophic Relationships

The Caspian seal feeds primarily on southern sprat (kilka) (*Clupeonella delicatula*),

Table 4. The mean and maximum ages (in years) of reproductive females for *Pusa caspica*

Date	Mean age	Age limit
1965	11.5	30.0
1972	12.5	32.0
1973	13.6	33.0
1974	13.7	34.0

which concentrates at depths of 10-40 m in the summer and autumn; crustaceans form only 1.0 % of their diet. Some data indicate that the mean and maximum weights of food found in the stomach at one time is 2.4 and 0.8 kg, respectively. As the Caspian seal is the only marine mammal now inhabiting the Caspian Sea, its food species are not affected by other mammalian predators. The composition of its diet depends on its distribution within the sea, e.g., in the Volga River delta seals prey on valuable fish species, principally small Caspian roach (vobla) (*Rutilus rutilus caspicus*), gobies, young sander (*Lucioperca lucioperca*), bream (*Abramis brama*) and silver bream.

During the breeding and moulting seasons, the species feeds only occasionally and loses a considerable amount of its blubber; storage of blubber begins again after the end of moulting when feeding becomes more intense; from mid-summer through autumn feeding and weight gain are at their highest rates. At this time only single animals or small groups are found, except in areas of greatest fish concentration, where up to several dozen animals may occur together.

Reproductive Capacity

Females and males become sexually mature at 4 to 5 and 6 to 7 years of age, respectively, although most females do not have their first pup until age 7. The majority of reproductive females (73.8 % in the 1974 sample) are aged between 8 and 17; females ages

26 to 34 were also recorded as giving birth. Available data indicate 2 different values for the percentage of annual missed pregnancies, i.e., 25 and 40 to 60 %.

Natural Mortality

The causes of natural mortality in pups have been thoroughly studied: (i) 5 to 15 % – exhaustion during the first days of nursing; (ii) over 3 to 4 % – crushing by moving ice; (iii) up to 2 % – stillborn, and (iv) 0.6 to 0.8 – freezing. Aborted premature births have also been recorded. Additionally, newborns are sometimes killed by large birds (eagles) and in recent years data has been obtained on mass killings of pups and females by wolf packs preying on the ice hauling grounds near islands. A possible epizootic disease, caused by the pathogene *Diplococus phocididae caspii* Badamschini, which affects the inner organs, muscles, skin and joints, has also been identified; the causes of other diseases in some seals have not been identified. The natural mortality rates for this species are not yet precisely known.

Commercial Exploitation

Average annual catches for this species from 1925 to 1955 are given in Table 5.

From 1956 to 1960, the maximum annual catch was 76 600 animals; in 1962, catch was 108 300 animals; and from 1963 to 1970, the catch ranged between 60 000 and 70 000.

Table 5. **Average annual catch of *Pusa caspica*, 1925-55**

Years	Average catch
1925-32	72 000
1933-40	169 000
1941-45	75 000
1946-50	65 000
1951-55	45 000

As the number of seals decreased, regulations were introduced. Since 1966, it has been illegal to take adult seals during the breeding season and since 1967, to take immature animals and pregnant females at the autumn rookeries. The harvest of pups has also been limited with a quota of 50 000. Observations now indicate that the population is being restored.

BAIKAL SEAL

Adults are 120-140 cm long and weigh 80-90 kg when in full blubber. Newborns are 70 cm long and weigh over 3 kg.

Baikal seals are brownish grey with an olive silver tint, changing to light grey on the sides and belly. Newborns are in the embryonic white coat and gain adult coloration after their first moult. Additional distinguishing characteristics of *Pusa sibirica* include thick, high claws with lateral ridge at the upper edge and a wrinkled snout.

Distribution and Movements

The species is distributed throughout all of Lake Baikal, with the greatest numbers found in the deep water areas of the north and the fewest found in the southern section. *P. sibirica* undertakes spring and autumn migrations: in the spring, the majority of the seals move from the middle part of Lake Baikal to its northern section where the ice remains longer; moulting seals may remain on the ice in this area until dispersing for the summer, when both groups and individuals are found scattered throughout all parts of the lake, with the largest concentrations in the north. Seals sometimes approach the shore, forming small rookeries. In autumn, with the first stages of the ice formation, the majority of seals move to shallow, easily-frozen areas in the pre-delta parts of rivers where rookeries, sometimes large, are formed on thin ice.

With the appearance of the drift ice, adult animals move to their breeding areas:

about 52 % of the females give birth in the northern part of Lake Baikal, 31 % in the middle section and 17 % in the south. After parturition, the main group of females and pups are found on the ice in an 8-15 km wide strip in the deepwater part of the lake; a small number of animals are found on both the 6-8 km strip extending along the eastern shore of the lake and along the 12-15 km strip along its western shore.

Census

In 1953 and 1960-61, censuses of seals remaining on ice using aerial photography were conducted; unfortunately, the method did not prove to be objective because of interference caused by aeroplane noise and other factors. The approximate numbers calculated from the 1953 and 1960-61 censuses were 20 000-25 000 and 30 000-40 000 animals, respectively.

Subsequently, the "snow holes" of female seals were counted, using motorcycles, in different areas of Lake Baikal; the number of "snow holes" counted was extrapolated to estimate the number of females and pups.

The present population is estimated to include 50 000-60 000 animals.

Reproductive Capacity

Females reach sexual maturity between 2 and 5, but do not immediately take part in reproduction; some females aged 4-6 give birth to pups and all do so at age 7. Almost 12 % of females age 7 and older are not pregnant each year. Males reach sexual maturity 2 years after females.

Females usually give birth to 1 pup, occasionally to twins. Pupping lasts 30-40 days, with the majority of females giving birth during a 10-15 day period with the peak in mid-March. Because pups are born in "snow holes", the mortality rate of pups is not high during the lactation period, which usually lasts

for 2-2.5 months. Mating takes place under the ice late in March until mid-April. It is thought that the species is polygamous.

Exploitation

The harvest of *P. sibirica* has historically been determined by the needs of the local people for skin, fur, oil and meat. In the early twenties, the annual harvest was 3 500-4 000 animals; subsequent annual catches have averaged 5 600 from 1931 to 1935, 1 500 from 1940 to 1950 and 800 from 1950 to 1960. The decrease in the number of seals taken was due both to a decrease in their abundance and a drop in the number of local sealers.

Beginning in 1966, management regulations were introduced in order to conserve the seal population; the killing of pups and of seals in the water was forbidden. In recent years, the seal population has been observed to be increasing; present regulations restrict the annual harvest to not more than 2 000-3 000 pups.

Trophic Relationships

P. sibirica feeds primarily on fish, which are also taken in very small amounts for human consumption. Its main food species are summarized in Table 6.

The greatest variety of species are consumed during the summer and autumn when

Table 6. **Main food items of *Pusa sibirica***

Species	Number %	Weight %
Golomanka (*Comephoris baicalensis*)	90.7	72.2
Sculpin (*Cottus* spp.)	9.2	25.8
Commercial species (Baikal omul (*Coregonus autumnalis migratorius*) and others)	1.1	2.0

379

feeding and growth are most intensive; during the moulting period, seals continue to feed but not so intensively. Feeding differences, mainly in the volume of food consumed rather than in species composition, are apparent for animals of different age groups.

Of the food species available to the Baikal seal, adult fish provide the best nutritional energy. Yearly variations in seal feeding are determined by annual fluctuations in the stock condition of pelagic fish species, such as golomanka and sculpin; these variations are appa-

rent in the age, size and weight structure of the fish, rather than in the species composition.

Need for Seal Products

Although there is no economic limit to the production of seal products, especially fur, exploitation will be determined by the abundance of seals and the need to restore the population to its earlier numbers.

Bibliography

BADAMSHIN, B.I., Resources of the Caspian seal and the
1961 means of its rational exploitation. *Tr. Soveshch. Ikhtiol. Kom.*, 12:170-9.

DOROFEEV S.V., Stocks of Greenland seals and their ex-
1956 ploitation. *Rybn. Khoz.*, 12:56-69.

FEDOSEEV, G.A., Biological characters and establishing
1973 of killing norms of bearded seal and sealing in the Sea of Okhotsk. *Izv. Tikhookean. Nauchno-Issled. Inst. Rybn. Khoz. Okeanogr.*, 86:148-57.

—, Morpho-ecological characteristics of ribbon seal po-
1973a pulations and the basis of preservation of its reserves. *Izv. Tikhookean. Nauchno-Issled. Inst. Rybn. Khoz. Okeanogr.*, 86:156-77. Issued also as *Transl. Ser. Fish. Res. Board Can.*, (3365) (1975).

—, Stock condition of the ice forms of the Far East
1975 pinnipeds. *In* Morskie mlekopitayuschchie. Sixth All-Union meeting on the study of marine mammals, Kiev. Moscow, Akademii Nauk, pp. 143-4.

FEDOSEEV, G.A. and Yu.A. BUKHTIYAROV, Feeding of
1972 seals in the Sea of Okhotsk. *In* Morskie mlekopitayuschchie. Fifth All-Union meeting on the study of marine mammals, 19-21 September, 1972. Makhachkala, Akademii Nauk, pp. 110-2.

FEDOSEEV, G.A. and V.N. GOLTSEV, New data on the
1975 distribution and the abundance of marine mammals in the Bering and Chuckchi Seas. *In* Morskie mlekopitayushchie. Part 2, Sixth

All-Union meeting on the study of marine mammals, Kiev. Moscow, Akademii Nauk, pp. 144-5.

FEDOSEEV, G.A. and Yu.I. NAZARENKO, On the intra-
1970 specific structure of the Arctic ringed seal. *Izv. Tikhookean. Nauchno-Issled. Inst. Rybn. Khoz. Okeonogr.*, 71:301-7.

GOLTSEV, V.N., Harbour seal (largha) feeding. *Ekologiia*,
1971 2:62-70.

IAKOVENKO, M.Ya., The White Sea population of the
1967 harp seal and prospects of their fishing. *Tr. Polyarn. Nauchno-Issled. Proektn. Inst. Morsk. Rybn. Khoz. Okeanogr.*, 21:6:18.

KRYLOV, V.I., Counting the numbers of Caspian seal.
n.d. *Rybn. Khoz.*, 5:18-21.

—, On the biology of Caspian seal, *Pusa caspica* Gmellin,
1976 1788. Bulletin MOIP, 81(1):15-28.

NAZARENKO, Yu.I., Feeding of the ringed seal in the
1976 north European part of the USSR. *Tr. Polyarn. Nauchno-Issled. Proektn. Inst. Morsk. Rybn. Khoz. Okeanogr.*, 21:81-5.

NAZARENKO, Yu.I. and Yu.K. TIMOSHENKO, Age struc-
1974 ture and sex ratio in the White Sea population of the Greenland seal *P. groenlandica* as an index of the efficiency of some protective measures. *Zool. Zh.*, 53(2):256-62.

PASTUKHOV, V.D., Economical value of the Baikal seal
1967 and rational exploitation of their stocks. *Tr.*

Polyarn. Nauchno-Issled. Proektn. Inst. Morsk. Rybn. Khoz. Okeanogr., 21:101-16.

–, Some indicators on the herd condition and fishery of
1967a the Baikal seal. *In* Morskie mlekopitayushchie. Third All-Union Conference on the Study of marine mammals, held in Vladivostok, 1966, edited by V.A. Arseniev, B.A. Zenkovich and K.K. Chapskii. Moscow, Nauka, pp. 117-26.

–, Number and distribution of pupping females of
1975 Baikal seal. *In* Morskie mlekopitayushchie. Part 2. Sixth All-Union meeting on the study of marine mammals, Kiev. Moscow, Akademii Nauk, pp. 39-41.

–, Terms of pupping and the duration of the pupping
1975a period of the Baikal seal. *In* Morskie mlekopitayushchie. Sixth All-Union meeting on the study of marine mammals, Kiev. Moscow, Akademii Nauk, pp. 41-3.

POPOV, L.A., Data on the general morphology of the
1961 Greenland hooded seal (*Cystophora cristata* Erxl.). *Tr. Soveshch. Ikhtiol. Kom.*, 12:180-91.

–, Juvenile period in the life of the hooded seal in the
1961a eastern Greenland area. *Tr. Vses. Nauchno-Issled. Inst. Morsk. Rybn. Khoz. Okeanogr.*, 7.

–, On an ice floe with the harp seals: ice drift of bio-
1966 logists in the White Sea. *Priroda*, 9:93-101. Issued also as *Transl. Ser. Fish. Res. Board Can.*, (814) (1967).

–, Modern marine animal hunting industry in the north
1968 Atlantic seas. *Probl. North*, 11:193-6.

–, On the estimation of the number of fertile female
1971 Greenland seals. *Tr. Vses. Nauchno-Issled. Inst. Morsk. Rybn. Khoz. Okeanogr.*, 79:102-8.

–, On the reasons and rates of natural mortality of harp
1971a seal pups during the nursing period. *Tr. Atl. Nauchno-Issled. Inst. Rybn. Khoz. Okeanogr.*,

39:102-8. Issued also as *Transl. Ser. Fish. Res. Board Can.*, (3185):159-76 (1976).

–, The influence of hydrometeorological conditions in
1975 the White Sea on the behaviour of harp seals in the breeding season. *Rapp. P.-V. Réun. CIEM*, 169:371-3.

POTELOV, V.A., On terms of the moulting of the bearded
1976 seal. *Sev. Odtel. Rab. Polyarn. Nauchno-Issled. Proektn. Inst. Morsk. Rybn. Khoz. Okeanogr.*, 9:52-6.

–, Distribution and migrations of the bearded seal in the
1969 White, Barents and Kara Seas. *In* Morskie mlekopitayushchie. Third All-Union conference on the study of marine mammals, Vladivostok, 1966, edited by V.A. Arseniev, B.A. Zenkovich and K.K. Chapskii. Moscow, Nauka, pp. 245-50.

–, Nutrition of the bearded seal. *Sev. Odtel. Rab. Po-
1971 lyarn. Nauchno-Issled. Proektn. Inst. Morsk. Rybn. Khoz. Okeanogr.*, 18:107-21.

RUMYANTSEV, V.D. *et al.*, State of Caspian seal stocks and
1975 prospects of their utilization. *Tr. Vses. Nauchno-Issled. Inst. Morsk. Rybn. Khoz. Okeanogr.*, 108:185-90.

SHUSTOV, A.P., Some biological features and reproduc-
1965 tive rates of the ribbon seal in the Bering Sea. *Izv. Tikhookean. Nauchno-Issled. Inst. Rybn. Khoz. Okeanogr.*, 39:183-92.

TIMOSHENKO, Yu.K., On the biology of reproduction in
1971 the Caspian seal. *Tr. Polyarn. Nauchno-Issled. Proektn. Inst. Morsk. Rybn. Khoz. Okeanogr.*, 17:224-5.

VOROZHTSOV, G.A. *et al.*, Food habits of seals from the
1972 north Caspian Sea. *Tr. Vses. Nauchno-Issled. Inst. Morsk. Rybn. Khoz. Okeanogr.*, 89:19-29.

–, Distribution of seals in the north Caspian Sea. *Tr.
1972a Vses. Nauchno-Issled. Inst. Morsk. Rybn. Khoz. Okeanogr.*, 89:30-7.

THE STATUS OF SEALS IN SOUTH AFRICA AND NAMIBIA

P.D. SHAUGHNESSY

Abstract

The Cape fur seal, *Arctocephalus pusillus pusillus*, is the only resident breeding pinniped found in Namibian and South African waters, being distributed in 23 breeding colonies from Cape Cross to Black Rocks in Algoa Bay, most colonies being found north of the Cape of Good Hope and on islands; 5 non-breeding colonies have also been recorded. Animals scatter freely about inshore waters; however, no definite migratory movements are known and colonies are believed to be fairly discrete. Distinguishing cranial and dental characteristics, and a comparison of serum protein transferrin in the 2 *A. pusillus* sub-species, are summarized. Adult males attain a length of 234 cm and an estimated weight (before breeding season) of 363 kg; the maximum reported length and weight of adult females are 176 cm and 122 kg, respectively. The pregnancy rate has been estimated to be 74 %; newborns are 60-70 cm long, most being born in November and December. No estimates of natural mortality rates are available. Possible causes of mortality are discussed.

Cape fur seals once inhabited most and perhaps all of the coastal islands of Namibia and South Africa, but by the early 1900s their numbers had been severely reduced by uncontrolled exploitation. The species first received legal protection in the early 1890s, and since the 1940s an increase in population size, including the formation of additional colonies, has been observed. Annual pup production before exploitation has been estimated at 290 700 and estimated production in 1940 and 1971 has been calculated as approximately 48 % (139 522) and 73 % (211 300-213 250) of this initial size, respectively; the latter figure indicates a total present population of 850 000 animals and this is thought to be about the optimum sustainable level.

Since 1947, the commercial harvest has gradually changed from almost entirely a Government operation to a private, but still Government controlled, concession system managed under the Sea Birds and Seals Protection Act, 1973, and the Sealing Regulations of 1976. In 1977, 14 colonies were under concession, with harvest quotas established for 8 of them, mostly set at 40 % sealing rate. The 9 unharvested breeding colonies contain about 21 % of the annual pup production; sealing at non-breeding colonies is prohibited. Exploitation has traditionally included 2 harvests: a winter harvest (June-October) of yearlings, averaging 72 586 animals for 1972-76 or 34.4 % of the number of pups born, and an early summer harvest (mainly November and December) of adult bulls, which ceased after 1975 when 786 bulls were taken at 4 colonies. The commercial value of the combined 1972 harvests has been estimated at Rand 982 038. Yearling seals are taken primarily for their pelts; bulls yield a less valuable skin that was used for leather or to produce a much inferior pelt. About 210 000 litres of oil from blubber was produced annually from 1974 to 1976. Although the skinned carcasses are now mostly discarded, they represent a potentially valuable source of protein and meal. The passage of the US Marine Mammal Protection Act (MMPA) in 1972 threatened, and at least temporarily halted the established export of most of the yearling skins to the United

States, through the imposition of import restrictions on seal products dependent, amongst other things, on minimum age at harvest and humaneness of kill. Steps have been taken to improve harvest standards, both to satisfy the MMPA and in response to increased interest of the South Africa public; meanwhile, there is a ready market for Cape fur seal pelts in Europe.

Some ecological relationships of this species are reviewed: pelagic shoaling fish and cephalopods are reported as the fur seal's most important food, though this has received little study in Namibian waters. Competition for commercial fish stocks is not considered significant. Of more importance is direct interference with purse-seine fisheries for pilchard, *Sardinops ocellata*, and anchovy, *Engraulis capensis*, especially in Namibian waters; preventive measures have had varying degrees of success and the number of fur seals killed by fishermen is unknown, but probably considerable. Seals also harass trawlers fishing for hake, *Merluccius capensis*, and line-fishing boats. Sea birds sharing islands with Cape fur seals have, in at least some cases, been adversely affected by the latter's population increase through habitat competition and loss.

The number of tourists regularly viewing 4 fur seal colonies may total 68 000 per year, with income exceeding Rand 70 000; although harvests are conducted at 3 of these sites, there is no conflict in the multiple use of the resource. Cape fur seals reportedly do well in captivity and, in recent years, most seals taken for foreign zoos (restricted to animals less than age 2) have come from Sea Island in False Bay, under Government licence (23 during 1971/77).

Résumé

L'otarie à fourrure du Cap, *Arctocephalus pusillus pusillus*, est le seul pinnipède indigène se reproduisant dans les eaux de l'Afrique du Sud et de la Namibie. Elle est répartie entre 23 colonies de reproducteurs, de Cape Cross à Black Rocks (baie d'Algoa); la plupart des colonies se trouvent au nord du cap de Bonne Espérance et dans les îles; on a également signalé cinq colonies de non-reproducteurs. Les animaux se dispersent librement dans les eaux côtières; on ne connaît cependant pas de mouvement migratoire défini et l'on croit que les colonies sont assez dispersées. L'auteur donne les caractères distinctifs du crâne et de la dentition, et indique une comparaison du transfert de protéines sériques dans les deux sous-espèces d'*A. pusillus*. Les mâles adultes atteignent une longueur de 234 cm et un poids (avant la saison de la reproduction) estimé à 363 kg; la longueur et le poids maximaux signalés pour les femelles adultes sont de 176 cm et 122 kg, respectivement. On a estimé le taux de gestation à 74 pour cent; les veaux nouveau-nés ont 60-70 cm de long et les naissances ont lieu en majeure partie en novembre et décembre. On ne possède pas d'estimations sur les taux de mortalité naturelle. L'auteur examine les causes possibles de la mortalité.

Les otaries à fourrure du Cap habitaient autrefois la plupart — et peut-être la totalité — des îles côtières de la Namibie et de l'Afrique du Sud, mais au début de ce siècle leur nombre avait été sérieusement réduit par une exploitation incontrôlée. L'espèce a bénéficié pour la première fois d'une protection juridique vers 1890; depuis les années 40, on a observé une augmentation de la population, avec la formation de colonies supplémentaires. La production annuelle de jeunes avant l'exploitation a été estimée à 290 700 sujets et l'on a calculé qu'en 1940 et 1971 la production avoisinait respectivement 48 pour cent (139 522) et 73 pour cent (211 300-213 250) de cette taille initiale. Le dernier chiffre indique un total de population actuelle de 850 000 animaux, que l'on considère être le niveau optimal soutenu.

Depuis 1947, l'exploitation commerciale, qui était autrefois une entreprise quasiment gouvernementale, est devenue un système de concessions privées mais toujours contrôlées par l'Etat dans le cadre de la Loi de protection des oiseaux de mer et des pinnipèdes de 1973 et de la Réglementation de la chasse aux pinnipèdes, de 1976. En 1977, 14 colonies étaient sous concession, des quotas de capture avaient été fixés pour 8 d'entre elles, pour la plupart à 40 pour cent du taux de chasse. Les colonies de reproduction non exploitées fournissent environ 21 pour cent de la production annuelle de jeunes. La chasse est interdite dans les colonies de non-reproducteurs. L'exploitation comprend traditionnellement deux campagnes: une campagne d'hiver, avec capture de jeunes de l'année, atteignant en moyenne 72 586 animaux pour 1972-76 ou 34,4 pour cent du nombre de jeunes nés, et une campagne au début de l'été (surtout en novembre et décembre) pour la capture des mâles adultes, qui a été interrompue après 1975, quand 786 mâles ont été tués dans quatre colonies. La valeur commerciale des captures combinées de 1972 a été estimée à 980 038 rands. Les jeunes de l'année sont surtout capturés pour leur peau; celle des mâles est bien moins bonne et sert à la fabrication du cuir ou de fourrures de qualité très inférieure. De 1974 à 1976, la production annuelle d'huile tirée du lard a été de 210 000 litres. Bien que les carcasses dépouillées soient à présent presque toutes jetées, elles représentent une source potentielle précieuse de protéines et de farine. L'adoption aux Etats-Unis de la loi sur la protection des mammifères marins (MMPA) en 1972 a menacé et a même temporairement interrompu l'exportation de la majeure partie des pelages des jeunes de l'année vers les Etats-Unis par l'imposition de restrictions à l'importation des produits de phoques, en se fondant — entre autres éléments — sur l'âge minimal à l'abattage et l'aspect humanitaire des méthodes de mise à mort. Des mesures on été prises pour améliorer les normes de capture, à la fois pour respecter la MMPA et pour répondre à l'intérêt croissant du public sud-africain; l'Europe constitue un débouché immédiat pour les fourrures d'otaries du Cap.

L'auteur examine certains rapports écologiques de cette espèce: on signale que les poissons pélagiques en bancs et les céphalopodes sont les aliments les plus importants de l'otarie à fourrure, bien que cet aspect ait été peu étudié dans les eaux de la Namibie. On considère que la concurrence pour les stocks de poissons commerciaux n'est pas importante. Ce qui, par contre, revêt plus d'importance, est l'interférence directe avec la pêche à la senne coulissante de *Sardinops ocellata* et *Engraulis capensis*, surtout dans les eaux de la Namibie. Les mesures préventives ont eu des succès divers et le nombre d'otaries à fourrure tuées par les pêcheurs est inconnu mais probablement considérable. Les otaries harcèlent aussi les chalutiers pêchant le merlu, *Merluccius capensis* et les bateaux pêchant à la ligne. Les oiseaux de mer partageant les îles avec les otaries à fourrure du Cap ont été — du moins dans certains cas — affectés par l'accroissement de la population de pinnipèdes par suite de la concurrence — et des pertes — pour l'habitat.

Le nombre de touristes se rendant régulièrement aux quatre colonies peut atteindre un total de 68 000 par an et le revenu qui en découle dépasse 70 000 rands. Bien que des captures soient effectuées sur trois de ces sites, il n'existe pas de conflits dans l'utilisation multiple de la ressource. D'après les rapports, les otaries à fourrure du Cap supportent bien la captivité; la plupart des animaux qui sont expédiés vers des zoos étrangers (il est interdit de capturer des animaux de plus de 2 ans) proviennent de Seal Island, dans False Bay, et ne sont pris qu'avec un permis gouvernemental (23 de 1971 à 1977).

Extracto

El lobo marino de dos pelos del Cabo (*Arctócephalus pusillus pusillus*) es el único pinnípedo que se reproduce en aguas de la Namibia y Sudáfrica, distribuido en 23 colonias de reproductores desde Cabo Cross hasta Black Rocks, en la bahía de Algoa; la mayor parte de las colonias se encuentran al norte del cabo de Buena Esperanza y en varias islas; se han registrado también cinco colonias de animales no reproductores. Los lobos marinos se dispersan libremente por las aguas costeras, pero no se sabe de movimientos migratorios definidos y se cree que las colonias están relativamente aisladas. Se resumen las características distintivas del cráneo y la dentición y se presenta una comparación de la transferencia de la proteína suérica en las dos subespecies de *A. pusillus*. Los machos adultos llegan a alcanzar una longitud de 234 cm y un peso estimado (antes de la temporada de reproducción) de 363 kg; la longitud y el peso máximos registrados en hembras adultas son 176 cm y 122 kg, respectivamente. El índice de gravidez se ha calculado en 74 por ciento; la longitud de los

385

cachorros al nacer es de 60-70 cm y la mayoría nacen en noviembre y diciembre. No se dispone de estimaciones sobre la mortalidad natural. Se examinan las posibles causas de mortalidad.

El lobo marino de dos pelos del Cabo vivía antaño en la mayoría de las islas costeras de la Namibia y de Sudáfrica, y quizás en todas ellas, pero a principios de este siglo su número se había reducido gravemente debido a la explotación incontrolada. La especie empezó a protegerse a principios del decenio de 1890 y desde los años cuarenta de este siglo se ha observado un aumento de la población, con formación de nuevas colonias. La producción anual de cachorros antes de la explotación se ha calculado en 290 700 y la producción de 1940 y 1971 se ha estimado aproximadamente en un 48 por ciento (139 522) y un 73 por ciento (211 300-213 500), respectivamente, de aquella cifra. La última de las cifras indicadas sugiere que la población total actual es del orden de 850 000 animales, cifra que se cree coincide aproximadamente con el nivel óptimo sostenible.

Desde 1947, la explotación comercial ha pasado gradualmente de ser una actividad totalmente estatal a un sistema de concesiones, en su mayoría a privados, controlado por el gobierno y administrado de acuerdo con la Ley de Protección de Aves Marinas y Focas de 1973 y el Reglamento para la Caza de Pinnípedos de 1976. En 1977, se habían cedido en concesión 14 colonias, estableciendo cupos de captura para ocho de ellas, de ordinario del orden del 40 por ciento de la producción. Las nueve colonias de reproductores no explotadas representan el 21 por ciento, aproximadamente, de la producción anual de cachorros; en las colonias de animales no reproductores está prohibida la caza. Tradicionalmente, las temporadas de explotación han sido dos: en invierno (junio-octubre), cuando se capturan animales de un año, con un promedio de 72 586 animales en 1972-76, o sea el 34,4 por ciento de los cachorros nacidos, y a principios del verano (sobre todo noviembre-diciembre), en que se cazan machos adultos. Esta última temporada de caza se interrumpió a partir de 1975, año en que se capturaron 786 machos adultos en cuatro colonias. El valor comercial de las capturas de 1972 se ha estimado en 982 038 Rand. Los lobos de un año se capturan ante todo por su piel; la piel de los machos es mucho menos valiosa y se utiliza para producir cuero o pieles de calidad inferior. Entre 1974 y 1976 se produjeron anualmente unos 210 000 litros de aceite. Aunque en la actualidad la mayor parte de los animales, una vez despojados de la piel, se descartan, representan una fuente potencialmente valiosa de proteínas y carne. La aprobación de la Ley de Protección de los Mamíferos Marinos de los Estados Unidos en 1972 puso en peligro la exportación de un importante porcentaje de pieles de animales de un año a los Estados Unidos, frenándola al menos temporalmente, debido a la imposición de restricciones de importación a los productos derivados de la foca, restricciones que dependen, entre otras cosas, de una edad mínima en el momento de la captura y de que se utilicen métodos humanos de caza. Se han tomado medidas para mejorar los procedimientos de explotación, tanto para ajustarse a la ley mencionada como para responder al creciente interés de la opinión pública sudafricana por esta cuestión; entre tanto, existe ya en Europa mercado para las pieles de lobos marinos de dos pelos del Cabo.

Se examinan algunas relaciones ecológicas de esta especie: los datos disponibles indican que los peces pelágicos que viven en cardúmenes y los cefalópodos constituyen los alimentos más importantes de este lobo marino, aunque esta cuestión se ha estudiado poco en aguas de la Namibia. La competencia por las poblaciones comerciales de peces no se considera importante. Más importante es la interferencia directa en las pesquerías de cerco de sardina (*Sardinops ocellata*) y anchoa (*Engraulis capensis*), especialmente en aguas de la Namibia; las medidas preventivas no han tenido siempre el mismo éxito, y no se conoce el número de lobos marinos que matan los pescadores, pero probablemente es considerable. Los lobos representan también una molestia para las actividades de pesca de merluza (*Merluccius capensis*) al arrastre y para la pesca con palangres. Las aves marinas que comparten algunas islas con este lobo marino han resultado, al menos en algunos casos, afectadas negativamente por el aumento de la población de éstos, debido a la mayor competencia por el hábitat.

El número de turistas que visitan regularmente cuatro de las colonias de lobos marinos puede llegar a unos 68 000 al año, con ingresos superiores a 70 000 Rand; aunque en tres de esas colonias se practica también la caza, el uso múltiple de ese recurso no plantea conflictos. Según los datos disponibles, los lobos marinos de dos pelos del Cabo viven bien en cautividad y en los últimos años la mayoría de los lobos capturados para parques zoológicos extranjeros (siempre animales de menos de dos años) han procedido de la isla Seal en la bahía False y se han capturado con licencia estatal (23 en 1971/77).

P.D. Shaughnessy
Director, Sea Fisheries Institute, Private Bag, Sea Point 8060, South Africa

Descriptive part

IDENTIFICATION

The only seal that breeds in South African and Namibian waters, the Cape fur seal (*Arctocephalus pusillus pusillus*), occupies the bulk of this report. Four other species visit the coasts of southern Africa: the Amsterdam Island fur seal, *A. tropicalis* (Nel, 1971); the southern elephant seal, *Mirounga leonina* (Ross, 1969; Best, 1971a); the crabeater seal, *Lobodon carcinophagus* (Courtenay-Latimer, 1961; Ross *et al.*, 1976; Ross *et al.*, 1978); and the leopard seal, *Hydrurga leptonyx* (Courtenay-Latimer, 1961; Best, 1971). With the exception of a single elephant seal that gave birth to a pup on the southern coast of South Africa in 1953 (Kettlewell and Rand, 1955), these four species are not known to breed in southern Africa.

Taxonomic classification of the Cape fur seal, *Arctocephalus pusillus* (Schreber, 1776), was considered by Rand (1956) and more recently by Repenning, Peterson and Hubbs (1971). The nominate sub-species (*A. p. pusillus*) breeds in South Africa and Namibia, and *A. p. doriferus* breeds on islands in Victoria, New South Wales and Tasmania (Warneke, 1976). The nomenclature used for *Arctocephalus* species in this report follows Repenning, Peterson and Hubbs (1971).

Data on the size of Cape fur seals are given by Rand (1956). Adult male Cape fur seals attain a zoological length[1] of 234 cm (7' 8"), and are estimated to reach 363 kg (800 lbs) prior to the breeding season, although the maximum weight recorded was 298 kg (657 lbs). The maximum reported length and weight of adult females were 176 cm (5' 9") and 122 kg (268 lbs), respectively. Most pups are born in November and December (Rand, 1956; Shaughnessy and Best, 1975): they are black, with a zoological length of between 60 and 70 cm (2' 0" and 2' 4"). Visible moult of black pups commences at the end of February, and is most obvious in March and April. After they lose their black coat, the seals are referred to as yearlings.

Skulls of the Cape fur seal were described by Repenning, Peterson and Hubbs (1971). With few exceptions they can be separated from those of other species of *Arctocephalus* by "the short maxillary shelf of the zygoma, by the prevalence of single-rooted first upper molars, by the very long rostrum and nasals, and by the very broad coronoid process of the mandible". They can be readily distinguished from other species of *Arctocephalus*, with the exception of *A. australis*, by the prominent posterior and anterior cusps on the postcanine teeth.

---

[1] Nose to tail measured over the back.

DISTRIBUTION AND STOCK IDENTIFICATION

Distribution

The Cape fur seal breeds in 23 colonies in Namibia and South Africa, from Cape Cross in the north to Black Rocks (Algoa Bay) in the east (Figs. 1 and 2). Most of these localities are described by Rand (1972). Six of the colonies are situated on the mainland (Cape Cross, Wolf Bay, Atlas Bay, Van Reenen Bay, Lion's Head, and Kleinzee); the others are on islands. In addition, at False Cape Fria, Pelican Point, Buchu Twins, Duikerklip, and on the rocks off Partridge Point on the western side of False Bay, aggregations of seals occur regularly with peak concentrations in the summer. Aerial photographs of False Cape Fria and Duikerklip taken in both the 1971-72 and 1974-75 breeding seasons failed to reveal any pups. The colonies at Pelican Point, Buchu Twins and Partridge Point were inspected in December, April and March 1974, respectively, but no pups or small yearlings were seen. Thus we conclude that these five areas are non-breeding colonies.

On the western coast of southern Africa, Cape fur seals are occasionally found as far north as Baia dos Tigres (latitude 16°30'S) in Angola, and isolated individuals have been reported in purse-seine nets in Baia Quicombo (latitude 11°19'S) by da Franca (1967). On the eastern coast, however, seals apparently do not move very far north: Rand (1967) reported that they do not extend beyond East London (latitude 33°S). In two recent breeding seasons (1974-75 and 1975-76) black pups have been washed ashore in the vicinity of East London (R. Horn, pers. comm.).

The distribution of Cape fur seals at sea was discussed by Rand (1959a), who reported that "they scatter freely about inshore waters and also extend out to sea for about 100 miles". Recently seals were sighted 120 nautical miles (220 km) off the south coast from a Sea Fisheries Branch trawler.

Stock Identification

A difference in the crania of *A. p. pusillus* and *A. p. doriferus* is described by Repenning, Peterson and Hubbs (1971): the crest that unites the mastoid process with the jugular process of the exoccipital is proportionately longer in *A. p. doriferus*.

In addition, Shaughnessy (unpubl. obs.) has made a preliminary comparison of the electrophoretic mobility of the serum protein

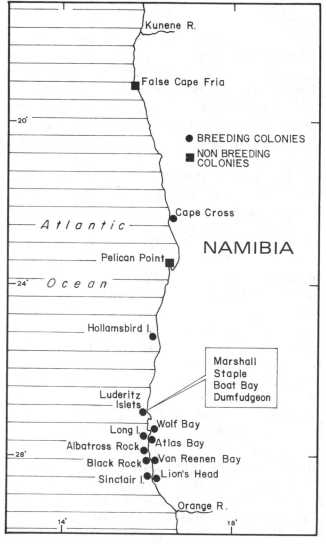

FIG. 1. — Seal colonies of Namibian waters. The Van Reenen Bay and Lion's Head colonies have been referred to in some previous reports as the beaches opposite Black Rock and Sinclair Island, respectively.

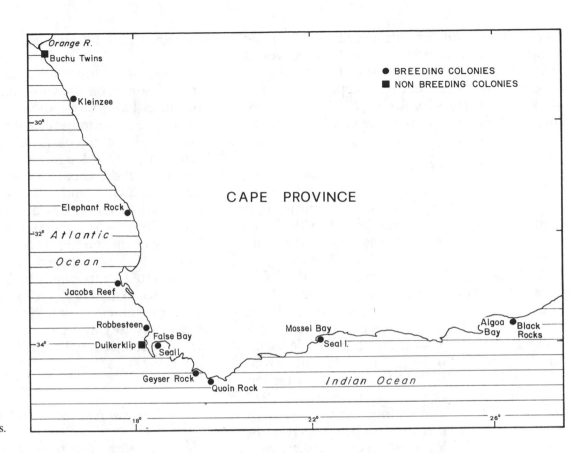

FIG. 2. – Seal colonies of South African waters.

transferrin in the two sub-species. A series of 11 blood samples from Cape fur seal yearlings taken in the winter harvest on Seal Island, False Bay in 1971 was compared with those from the Australia-New Zealand region that were reported by Shaughnessy (1970). Transferrin types of the False Bay series were Tf A, Tf AC and Tf AP. The Tf P zone has a faster anodal migration rate than Tf A. It was not observed in fur seals from the Australasian region, where the 53 *A. p. doriferus* examined where Tf A, Tf AC and Tf C. On the other hand, *A. forsteri* from Australian waters were all homozygous Tf D, a type not found at all in *A. pusillus*. In summary, transferrin of the 11 *A. p. pusillus* are much more similar to transferrin of *A. p. doriferus* than those of *A. forsteri*, but minor differences between the two subspecies of *A. pusillus* are apparent.

No attempt at stock identification within *A. p. pusillus* has yet been made, although

blood samples for this purpose were collected from seals at the following colonies: Wolf Bay (62 pups), Van Reenen Bay (48 pups), Seal Island, False Bay (93 pups), Geyser Rock (90 pups), Quoin Rock (36 yearlings), Black Rocks, Algoa Bay (11 pups and 3 subadults). Rand (1955) considered that "the herds are fairly discrete", since he believed that cows return to breed on the same rookery year after year. This statement is supported by evidence from the concentration of vitamin A in livers collected from adult bulls between 1943 and 1949 at seven colonies ranging from Cape Cross to Black Rocks, Algoa Bay (Black *et al.*, 1945; Shaughnessy, unpubl. rep).

MIGRATIONS

Although individual Cape fur seals may travel several hundred kilometers, there does not appear to be any definite migratory move-

389

ment. Two studies designed to provide information on movements are (a) recoveries of marked (tagged or branded) seals and (b) observations of seals at sea. Reports of earlier work in both areas by Rand (1959a), and work currently underway are reviewed briefly here.

Recoveries of Marked Seals

Rand (1959a) branded an unspecified number of seals at Sinclair Island in 1948 and 1949. Four animals were seen away from the colony; all had travelled at least 360 km.

Between 1954 and 1956, nearly 3 000 pups were tagged at Seal Island, False Bay. The 14 recoveries were of seals in their first or second year of life, and all had moved north along the west coast of southern Africa with the Benguela Current (Rand, 1959a). From January 1971 to 1977, 14 012 pups were tagged in 11 colonies (Table 1). Up to mid-July 1977 (the beginning of the sealing season) 10 825 of these were at risk during sealing operations, and 3 408 (31.5 %) were recovered at their natal colony as tagged yearlings. In the same period, 208 (1.5 % of those tagged) were recovered away from their natal colony, 59 as

yearlings and 149 as animals older than one year.

Most of the recoveries of tagged seals from colonies on the west coast and from Seal Island in False Bay indicate northward movements. Seals from other colonies on the south and on the east coasts seem to move more randomly. The longest movement recorded was a direct distance of 1 650 km. The seal was tagged at Seal Island in False Bay and drowned in a trawl net off Toscanini (100 km north of Cape Cross) 4.5 years later. On the south and east coasts the longest recorded movement was 780 km – a seal tagged at Geyser Rock and recovered 1 year 7 months later at the mouth of the Keiskamma River (33°18′S). Other notable movements were from Seal Island in False Bay to Cape Cross, a distance of 1 500 km (10 recorded by Rand (1959a) and six more since 1971).

Observations of Seals at Sea

Sighting records of seals from Sea Fisheries Branch ships operating on the west coast of Cape Province between 1950 and 1959 were discussed by Rand (1959a). Seals were

Table 1. Numbers of Cape fur seal pups tagged and recovered to mid-July 1977

Colony	Year	No. pups tagged	Recovered at natal colony yearlings	older than 1 year (− indicates no harvest)	Recovery away from natal colony	
Cape Cross	1972	1 365	510	2 [1]	8	(0.6 %)
Wolf Bay	1974	1 282	613	4	49	(3.8 %)
Atlas Bay	1974	2 203	539	25	93	(4.2 %)
Long Islands	1977	2 655	−	−	0	
Albatross Rock	1977	532	−	−	0	
Kleinzee	1973	2 012	584	28	19	(0.9 %)
Elephant Rock	1976	501	293	−	1	(0.2 %)
Seal Is., False Bay	1971	1 203	189	1	24	(2.0 %)
Geyser Rock	1976	1 000	−	−	3	(0.3 %)
Quoin Rock	1975	637	295	0	6	(0.9 %)
Seal Is., Mossel Bay	1975	622	385		5	(0.8 %)
Total		14 012	3 408	60	208	(1.5 %)

[1] Only one animal taken.

observed regularly up to 80 miles from shore (the most distant station) and were believed to go as far as 100 miles out to sea. Higher densities were noted in the vicinity of breeding colonies and deep-sea trawlers. Cows and bulls were relatively rare close inshore, bulls being more common further out. The number of yearlings sighted at sea (inshore only) increased during spring and summer.

Observations of seals at oceanographic stations of Sea Fisheries Branch ships were made between 1959 and 1971 at the instigation of Dr. R.W. Rand. Data from approximately 8 000 stations covering the waters of Namibia and South Africa south to latitude 40°S, and between longitudes 10°E and 36°E have now been transferred to computer punch cards. The number of seals per observation in half degree squares of latitude and longitude for each quarter of the year are to be compared. One quarter of the year will cover the breeding season (October to December). In this way it is hoped to determine the distribution of seals and whether there is a regular annual movement, either along or away from the coast.

Vital parameters

CENSUS

Estimates of the population size of the Cape fur seal were made by Rand (1959a, 1972), using harvest figures for bulls, and counts of bulls (and in some cases other classes) on aerial photographs of breeding colonies. These estimates were reassessed by Best (1973a).

The current research programme on Cape fur seals by the Sea Fisheries Branch includes estimates of the pup population of colonies by three methods: (1) counts of black pups on aerial photographs of colonies taken during the pupping season; (2) tag-recapture experiments made during January; and (3) collection of tags during the winter harvest (which is directed at yearlings). The number of pups born on Seal Island, False Bay, in the 1971-72 breeding season was estimated by a combination of these three methods (Best and Rand, 1975).

The relationship between the number of pups born and the total number of seals in a colony of the Cape fur seal has not yet been determined. For both the southern fur seal at South Georgia (*A. gazella*) and the northern fur seal (*Callorhinus ursinus*) at the Pribilof Islands the total population is considered to be four times the number of pups born (Bonner, 1968; Johnson, 1972). Until evidence to the contrary is available, this relationship will also be used for the Cape fur seal.

Methods

Aerial Photography

The South African Air Force made aerial surveys of most seal colonies in October 1955, November 1956 and November 1967. The methods used are described by Rand (1959a, 1972), who counted territorial bulls in each colony, and cows and pups or other animals in some colonies.

In recent years, black pups have been counted on aerial photographs of colonies, taken in December during the pupping season, preferably when the maximum numbers occur in the colonies. Near-vertical photographs are taken through the open window of an aircraft flying at a speed of 100 knots and an altitude of 110 m (360 feet). A variety of aircraft were used: good results were obtained from high-winged Cessnas. Photographs are taken with a hand-held Pentax Spotmatic camera with either a 55 mm f/1.4 or a 50 mm f/1.8 lens, using Ilford FP4 film rated at 200 ASA at a shutter speed of 1/1 000th of a second. Several transects of a colony are required to obtain sufficient overlap for counting. Black pups can be readily distinguished from other seals on 25 × 20 cm prints of high contrast.

391

Tagging

Black pups are tagged at one or two colonies per year as part of a continuing programme of population estimation by tag-recapture. Tagging has now been completed in 11 colonies (Table 1). Tags are applied to the rear edge of the fore flipper of pups in mid-January, when they average six weeks of age. At that time the harem structure has broken down, but the pups have not yet become too agile to escape. The monel metal tags (Hasco style 4-1005, size 49) bear a unique alphanumeric combination, and the inscription "GUANO ISLANDS CAPE TOWN". Recapture of samples of pups at the same colony takes place approximately a week later. An estimate of the number of pups in the colony is obtained from the proportion of pups examined that are tagged. Another estimate is made after tags have been collected at the winter harvest. Approximately half of the pups are double-tagged, and the proportion of yearlings killed that had been given two tags but lost one is used to make a correction for shedding of tags.

Results

Aerial Photography

From a combination of counts of bulls and other classes with harvest data from the years 1954 to 1956, Rand (1959a) estimated the population of seals in seven colonies in the Cape Province (Quoin Rock, Geyser Rock, Seal Island in False Bay, Duikerklip, Robbesteen, Jacob's Reef and Elephant Rock) to be 50 000. From aerial photographs taken in 1971 or 1972 (Table 2), a total of at least 29 176 pups was estimated to have been born, indicating that these colonies then numbered more than 100 000 seals.

Rand (1972) counted territorial bulls on photographs of all colonies (except Kleinzee)

taken in November 1956 and November 1967, and cows or other classes on some of the colonies. He considered that numbers of territorial bulls had changed little between the two series; however, Laws (1973) noted that the count for territorial bulls in the colonies included in both surveys decreased by 12 % (from 8 771 to 7 719). By combining the maximum catch of bulls at each colony with the highest counts from aerial photographs, Rand (1972), estimated the maximum number of bulls to be 19 500 (although summation of the appropriate column in his Table XXIII gives 20 219 bulls). The large colony at Kleinzee was omitted from this calculation, since no data were available for it. Using a harem size of 14 cows (the maximum in his Table XXIV), Rand estimated the population of mature females to be 273 000. These data were reassessed by Best (1973a) to obtain an estimate of 12 800 harem bulls, 91 000 to 858 000 mature females (mean 364 000), and 67 000 to 635 000 pups (mean 269 000), based on an estimate of 13 000 breeding bulls, harem size ranging from 7 to 66 (mean 28), and a pregnancy rate of 74 %.

Best (1973a) provided another estimate of pup production. He first estimated sealing rates at one island (Seal Island, False Bay) and one mainland (Cape Cross) colony, from tag recovery during sealing operations. He then applied the island rate (25 % of the pup population) and the mainland rate (50 % of the pup population) as appropriate to the average catch of yearlings, 1969-72, in all colonies. Populations on unexploited colonies were assumed to be the average size for exploited mainland or island colonies, as appropriate. He arrived at a figure of 276 300 pups. This estimate is now considered to be inflated for the following reasons. First, not all animals taken in winter harvests are yearlings (see "Commercial Harvest"). Second, the Duikerklip colony was included: this is not known to be a non-breeding colony, and so should not be included in an estimate of the size of the pup population. Last, and most important, counts of pups on a series of aerial photographs (mostly taken in December 1971) indi-

Table 2. Counts of Cape fur seal pups derived from aerial photographs

Colony	Count of pups on photos taken 4-6/12/71	Counts adjusted to 18/12/71	Counts of pups on photos taken on other occasions
False Cape Fria	0	0	
Cape Cross	11 840	17 826	
Hollamsbird Island	3 245	5 039	
Luderitz Islets:			
Marshall Reef	486	755	
Staple Rocks	1 873	2 908	
Boat Bay Rocks	1 088	1 689	
Dumfudgeon Rock	1 850	2 873	
Wolf Bay	–	–	8 805 (10/1/74)
Atlas Bay	–	–	23 295 (10/1/74)
Long Islands	7 869	12 219	
Albatross Rock	2 395	3 719	
Black Rock	–	–	
Van Reenen Bay	2 087	3 241	
Lion's Head	1 782	2 767	
Sinclair Island.	10 150	15 771	
Kleinzee	–	–	27 776 (19/12/72)
Elephant Rock	1 606	2 494	
Jacob's Reef	–	–	3 376 (19/12/72)
Robbesteen	1 562	2 425	
Duikerklip	0	0	
Seal Island, False Bay	–	–	14 449 (3/1/71)
Geyser Rock	1 725	2 679	
Quoin Rock	2 411	3 744	
Seal Island, Mossel Bay	2 083	3 234	
Black Rocks, Algoa Bay	1 096	1 702	
Total	54 788	85 085	77 701
		162 786	

cate that Best's extrapolation for the size of unexploited colonies was an overestimate.

Two new estimates of the pup population size (Shaughnessy and Best, 1976) are reviewed here. Both make use of a series of aerial photographs of the breeding colonies. Most of these photos were taken between 4 and 6 December 1971; others were taken more recently (Table 2). Since pupping had not finished when the aerial survey was carried out in early December, counts of pups on these photos underestimate the pup production. From counts of pups on aerial photos of Seal Island in False Bay taken during the 1974-75 pupping season, we deduced that the maximum number of pups on that colony occurs on about 18 December (Shaughnessy and Best, 1975). From the regression on time, of the number of pups present, we predicted that 64.4 % of pups are born by 5 December. Therefore counts in column 1 of Table 2 have been multiplied by 1/.644 to correct them to the maximum number that could be expected at each colony. Counts made after 18 December (column 3) have not been altered, since the number of pups decreases very slowly after the maximum is reached. From these counts of black pups on aerial photographs of the colonies, we estimate that at least 162 000 pups are born annually. This is still an underestimate because a small breeding colony was omitted from the aerial surveys (Black Rock, Namibia), and, more important, not all pups are seen on aerial photographs because of their clumping behaviour and the surface topography, the latter factor varying between colonies. In an attempt to determine to what extent counts of pups on aerial photographs underestimate the pup population size, aerial counts of four representative colonies are compared with final estimates of pup population size obtained from the combination of counts on aerial photographs, results of tag-recapture experiments, and estimates based on the recovery of tagged yearlings during sealing operations (Table 3). This comparison indicates that, for the colonies concerned (Cape Cross, Atlas Bay, Kleinzee and Seal Island in False Bay) an average of 76.3 % (83 346/109 255) of the pups are seen on aerial photographs. Consequently the total count of pups on aerial photographs (162 786) has been adjusted by multiplying it by 1/.763 (= 1.31) which gives an estimate of pup production of 213 250, for the 1971-72 pupping season.

The second estimate is derived from Best's (1973a) estimate of sealing rates and from the catch data for the winter harvest from 1969 to 1972. Unexploited colonies are esti- mated by making use of counts of pups on aerial photographs. In the 1969-72 seasons, the following colonies were exploited: Cape Cross, Wolf Bay, Atlas Bay, Long Islands, Albatross Rock, Sinclair Island, Kleinzee, Elephant Rock, Robbesteen, Seal Island (False Bay), Geyser Rock, Quoin Rock and Seal Island (Mossel Bay). For these colonies the average harvest figures have been reduced by a factor of 0.97 (or 0.94 at Wolf and Atlas Bay), since not all the animals taken are yearlings. The number of pups in each colony is estimated from these figures on the basis of an assumed sealing rate of 0.25 for island colonies and 0.50 for mainland colonies, as estimated previously. This gives an estimate of 178 011 pups produced in harvested colonies. From Table 2 it is apparent that these 13 colonies represent 85.0 % (138 436/162 786) of the total pup production, which can thus be estimated as 209 420 pups.

The average of these two estimates of the pup production of the Cape fur seal is 211 300 pups. Assuming that the number of pups born represents one quarter of the total population, the latter can be estimated as 850 000 animals.

Tagging

Estimates of pup population size have been made by the tag-recapture method at 11 colonies to date (Table 4). For the Kleinzee colony, an estimate of the pup population from the recovery of tags during sealing was made both on the basis of all animals (42 723), and of males only (37 719). The recovery rate of tagged male yearlings during that harvest was greater than that of tagged female yearlings, indicating a higher mortality of tagged females between tagging (at 1.5 months of age) and harvesting (at 6.5 to 10.5 months of age) (Best, 1974). Consequently, an estimate of pup population size based on recovery of males only will be more accurate in this case than one based on both sexes. This improvement has also been made to the estimates for other colonies where the proportion of tagged males

Table 3. Estimates of pup population size of Cape fur seal colonies by aerial photography and tag-recapture used to determine the proportion of pups visible on aerial photographs

Colony	Count of pups on aerial photos	Final estimate [2]	Season
Cape Cross	17 826 [1]	15 841	71-72
Atlas Bay	23 295	45 108	73-74
Kleinzee	27 776	33 900	72-73
Seal Is., False Bay	14 449 [1]	14 406	70-71
Totals	83 346 [1]	109 244	

[1] Photos taken 4/12/71, count of 11 480 adjusted to maximum expected on December 18.
[2] See Table 4.

Table 4. Estimates (with standard deviations) of pup population size of Cape fur seal colonies by aerial photography and tag-recapture

Colony	Aerial photographs		Estimate from tag-recapture	Estimate from recovery of tags at harvest	Final estimate [1]
	Date	Count of pups			
Cape Cross [2]	6/12/71	17 826 [5]	Incorrect method used	15 828 ± 1 221	15 828 ± 1 221 (3)
Wolf Bay	10/ 1/74	8 805	8 930 ± 1 968	21 655 ± 4 269 [6]	21 655 ± 4 269 (3)
Atlas Bay	10/ 1/74	23 295	37 931 ± 5 253	52 268 ± 3 936	45 108 ± 3 282 (2, 3)
Long Islands	17/12/76	10 119	15 155 ± 1 487	Harvest underway	
Albatross Rock	17/12/76	2 461	5 586 ± 927	Harvest underway	
Kleinzee [3]	19/12/72	27 776	30 006 ± 4 455	37 719 ± 5 042 [6]	33 900 (2, 3)
Elephant Rock	16/12/75	1 630 [5]	1 196 ± 153	1 532 ± 132	1 364 ± 110 (2, 3)
Seal Is., False Bay [4]	3/ 1/71	14 449	12 594 ± 3 671	16 176 ± 368	14 406 (1, 2, 3)
Geyser Rock	16/12/75	4 955 [5]	6 553 ± 850	No harvest	6 553 ± 850 (2)
Quoin Rock	20/12/74	1 730	2 292 ± 207	1 779 ± 166	2 036 ± 138 (2, 3)
Seal Is., Mossel Bay	18/12/74	1 262	2 095 ± 298	2 555 ± 189	2 325 ± 188 (2, 3)

[1] The figure in parentheses indicates the column no. on which the estimate was based.
[2] Best (1973).
[3] Best (1974).
[4] Best and Rand (1975).
[5] Count adjusted to maximum expected on December 18.
[6] Based on recoveries of tagged males only.

increased between the time of tagging and the harvest.

RATES

Birth Rates — Reproductive Potential

The pregnancy rate of the Cape fur seal was estimated by Best (1973a) as 74 %. This estimate was based on data from 144 females collected at sea between 1954 and 1956 by Rand (1959a). In March 1974 the Sea Fisheries Branch resumed pelagic collections of Cape fur seals aimed, *inter alia*, at refining this estimate of the pregnancy rate.

Cows produce their first pup at three years of age, according to Rand (1955), who determined the age of his specimens from an examination of skull sutures. However, in August and September 1975 seven females in their third year were killed at the Kleinzee colony. None was pregnant, indicating that first parturition in most females does not occur until age four or later.

The sex ratio of pups at birth has not been determined but pups are routinely sexed during tagging operations when their average age is 6 weeks. A total of 13 915 pups in 11 colonies has been examined (Table 5). The unweighted mean proportion of males in these samples is 0.561 with standard deviation ± 0.036.

Natural Mortality Rates

No estimates of natural mortality rates are available for the Cape fur seal. However, collections of known-age material are being made routinely and a reservoir of tagged animals of known age is being built up in the population. The causes of natural mortality were briefly discussed by Rand (1956). He indicated that both sharks, *Carcharodon* sp. and killer whales, *Orcinus orca* prey on the

Table 5. Sex ratio of Cape fur seal pups between one and two months of age

Colony	Date	Male	Female	Total	Proportion male
Cape Cross	4/1/72 & 10/1/72	824	540	1 364	.604
Wolf Bay	19/1/74	757	520	1 277	.593
Atlas Bay	21/1/74	1 169	1 023	2 192	.533
Long Islands	16/1/77	1 463	1 162	2 625	.557
Albatross Rock	13/1/77	284	246	530	.536
Kleinzee	11/1/73	1 211	793	2 004	.604
Elephant Rock	9/1/76	252	246	498	.506
Seal Is., False Bay	13/1/71 & 19/1/71	708	492	1 200	.590
Geyser Rock	15/1/76	512	482	994	.515
Quoin Rock	8/1/75	341	273	614	.555
Seal Is., Mossel Bay	10/1/75	360	257	617	.583

seals. We doubt that killer whales are a serious predator, judging by the disregard seals show for underwater playback of killer whale sounds (Anon., 1975). A number of second-hand reports suggest, however, that sharks may be a frequent predator.

Internal parasites in Cape fur seals have been discussed by Rand (1956, 1959a), but it is not known if any of them cause mortality in the host.

Rabies was identified in black-backed jackals (*Canis mesomelas*) at Cape Cross in August 1975. Since jackals scavenge in the mainland seal colonies and prey on pups, it is possible that they could transmit the disease to seals, though no cases of rabies in seals have yet been reported.

Morrell (1832) reported a large number of carcasses (estimated at not less than half a million), of Cape fur seals on Possession Island, and on Seal and Penguin Islands in Luderitz Bay in September 1828. He attributed the deaths to "the effects of a pestilence or plague" (p. 290) but later considered that they were "overwhelmed and suffocated by one of these sand-spouts ... accompanied by the sult-

ry, stifling sand-winds" (p. 312). No satisfactory explanation has been advanced for the cause of this mortality, nor has such a case been reported again.

It is thought that pups on small island colonies are subject to considerable risk of being washed away in the first few months of life, while they are still weak swimmers. This conclusion is based in part on events that occurred at the Black Rocks colony, Algoa Bay, during the 1974-75 breeding season. 904 black pups were counted on aerial photographs taken of this colony on 18 December 1974, but only a small number (less than 50) were observed when the colony was visited on 15 and 16 March 1975. Since hundreds of black pups were picked up on mainland beaches as far as 60 km from the colony within four days of a storm on 28 December 1974, we concluded that most of the pups had been washed off the island.

Reports of dead, prematurely born pups at the colonies on Elephant Rock, and on Seal Island, False Bay, were received during September and October, 1974. An examination of lungs of a sample of 35 pups indicated that more than half of them (20) had been born alive. 43 dead pups were picked up at Elephant Rock on 23 September, indicating that a not insignificant portion of the annual pup production of this colony (estimated as 2 500 pups, Table 2) must have been born prematurely in 1974. No indication of the cause of death was apparent from gross examination of the cadavers, nor from toxicological and bacteriological tests done by the State Veterinary Laboratory.

Harvesting Rates, Commercial and Incidental Kill

Commercial Harvest

Cape fur seals are currently managed under the Sea Birds and Seals Protection Act, 1973 and the Sealing Regulations of 1976. The harvest has traditionally been directed at seals of both sexes in their first year of life aged between 6.5 and 10.5 months (yearlings), and at adult bulls. The former harvest occurs during winter (June through October) after the first moult from the black pup stage is completed. The bull harvest occurs during early summer (primarily in November and December). In addition, a small proportion of sub-adult and adult seals are included in winter harvests. In recent years the winter harvest season has been limited to the months of August through October and bull sealing has ceased.

In the early 1890's when seals first received legal protection in the Cape Colony (which included islands off the coast of Namibia), all sealing there was done by the Government. The colony at Cape Cross in Namibia has been harvested by private enterprise since before 1903 (Schultze, 1907). The commercial harvest has gradually changed from being almost entirely a Government operation in 1947 to a privately operated one (though still under Government control) (Table 6). The last harvests by the Government occurred in 1975 at Kleinzee, Seal Island in False Bay and Geyser Rock.

Contracts issued since 1974 to private concessionaires for seal harvesting have included a limit to the number of seals that can be killed. Table 6 shows the status of the 14 colonies exploited in 1977. Aspects of these contracts and reasons for the absence of quotas prior to 1974 were discussed by Best (1973a). Quotas are generally introduced into contracts as they are renewed; an exception is the contract for Hollamsbird and the four Luderitz Islets which was renewed in 1975 without quotas. A quota was negotiated for the long-term concession for Wolf and Atlas Bays in 1974 and has been renegotiated since. However, there is still no quota for the other long-term concession at Cape Cross. Most of the quotas have been set at the 40 % sealing rate. The most recent one (that for Kleinzee in 1977) includes a quota at the 35 % rate. It is the only contract with a flexible quota that can be amended during the concession period as data on the size of the colony accrue. Concessions to harvest seals in specific colonies are granted for periods of 5, 10 or 25 years.

Seals are not harvested in all of the 23 breeding colonies. Table 7 shows those colonies exploited in 1973-1976. In 1977 private concessions were in effect for 14 of the colonies

Table 6. Colonies of the Cape fur seal harvested in 1977 — concessions and quotas

Colony	Concession first granted [1]	Current concession length (years)	Current concession expires	Quotas [3] yearlings	Quotas [3] adult bulls
Cape Cross	Before 1903	25	1985	No quotas yet	
Hollamsbird Island	1971	5	1980	No quotas yet	
Luderitz Islets [2]	1971	5	1980	No quotas yet	
Wolf Bay	1947	25	1985 }	30 000	0
Atlas Bay	1947	25	1985 }		0
Long Islands	1974	10	1983	5 000	500
Albatross Rock	1974	10	1983	1 500	400
Sinclair Island	1974	10	1983	4 000	700
Kleinzee	1977	10	1986	12 000	0
Robbesteen	1965	5	1978	300	0
Quoin Rock	1967	5	1978	1 800	0

[1] Some information from Best (1973a).
[2] Four colonies: Marshall, Staple, Boat Bay (or Eighty-four) and Dumfudgeon.
[3] At the beginning of the winter harvest.

(Table 6). Concessions for two colonies expired at the end of 1975 (Seal Island in Mossel Bay) and 1976 (Elephant Rock). They have not been renewed as the colonies showed signs of overharvesting. The other breeding colonies are either in Diamond Areas of restricted access (Van Reenen Bay and Lion's Head), within a military range (Jacob's Reef), too small and remote for consideration (Black Rock in Namibia and Black Rocks in Algoa Bay), or are still under consideration for harvesting by private enterprise following the cessation of Government sealing (Seal Island in False Bay and Geyser Rock). As pointed out by Best (1973a) seals in these nine unharvested colonies constitute "a substantial reservoir of unexploited animals" that is estimated (from Table 2) to contain 21 % of the annual pup production. Sealing is not permitted at the non-breeding colonies at False Cape Fria, Pelican Point, Buchu Twins, Duikerklip and Partridge Point, although a small experimental harvest of 148 seals took place at False Cape Fria in June 1976.

Catch figures for the commercial harvest up to 1972 (Best, 1973a) are brought up to date in Table 7. It has become apparent that not all seals taken in the winter harvest are yearlings. Some are adults, and have been declared as bulls by concessionaires (irrespective of their sex) and included in that category in Table 7. Others are sub-adults; animals in their second year (referred to as two-year-olds here) are particularly difficult to distinguish from yearlings using external characters. These sub-adults have all been included in the figures for the yearling harvest.

An idea of the proportion of seals older than one year that are taken in winter harvests has been obtained from inspection of teeth in the lower jaw. In yearlings the canines are lower than, or at the same level as, the post-canines, while in animals older than one year the canines are considerably higher. Another guide (although less accurate) is obtained from an inspection of the belly blubber for cestode

Table 7. **Winter and summer harvests of Cape fur seals in South Africa and Namibia 1973 to 1976** [1]

Colony	1973	1974	1975	1976
Black Rocks, Algoa Bay	–	–	–	–
Seal Island, Mossel Bay	2 150	2 054	1 638	–
Quoin Rock	1 421	1 207	970	806
Geyser Rock	2 310	1 493	138	–
Seal Island, False Bay	2 839	1 635	139	–
Robbesteen	458	292	350	365
Jacob's Reef	–	–	–	–
Elephant Rock	449	1 550	872	1 097
Kleinzee	15 582	17 000	13 615	5 318
Sinclair Island	454	–	4 222	4 294
Albatross Rock	224	–	1 668	1 125
Long Islands	1 543	3 740	5 282	3 831
Atlas Bay	} 45 891	31 506	23 236	19 420
Wolf Bay			12 380	11 548
Luderitz Islets	–	–	744	1 689
Hollamsbird Island	–	–	–	1 879
Cape Cross	7 353	6 339	9 543	11 095
Total Yearling Catch	80 674	66 816	74 945 [3]	62 467
Total Bull Catch [2]	2 246	1 167	786	0

[1] See Best (1973a) for earlier figures.
[2] This class includes some adults taken during the winter (yearling) harvest.
[3] Including an experimental harvest of 148 at False Cape Fria.

cysts (absent from yearlings). In winter harvests at five colonies, the proportion of seals older than one year has been estimated as: 3 % at Cape Cross in 1972; 6 % at Wolf and Atlas Bays in 1974; 0.8 % at Kleinzee in 1974; 11.3 % at Elephant Rock in 1976. The age composition of these older animals is not yet determinable; information from tag returns may eventually provide an indication.

Sealing rates (see Results) were estimated by Best (1973a) to be 50 % for Cape Cross when pup population size was estimated in the 1971-72 season and 25 % at Seal Island when pup population size was estimated in the 1970-71 season (see Table 3).

A mathematical population model designed to predict the effects of various harvesting rates of yearling females in a stable population of females has been developed by Shaughnessy and Best (1975a, 1976a) in collaboration with Dr. T.D. Smith, of the University of Hawaii. At present the model utilises estimates of some population parameters (mortality and pregnancy rates) obtained from studies of the northern fur seal (*Callorhinus ursinus*). As the corresponding parameters for the Cape fur seal become available they will be incorporated into the model. The current model indicates that a harvesting rate of 33 % of the number of female pups surviving to the beginning of the sealing season is the rate that will maximise the catch of pups on a sustainable basis. Because of the polygynous nature of the Cape fur seal, it may be possible to exploit male pups on a sustainable basis at a higher rate. Further, there are several observations that suggest that the seal population has been increasing (discussed under Historical Development). Consequently, the maximum sealing rate for each colony has been set at a slightly higher rate (35 %, and in some colonies, 40 %), though this may be revised in the future in the light of management experience. A harvesting rate greater than 40 % based on the estimate of the population in 1972 has probably been maintained at the Cape Cross colony since 1961, and according to Zur Strassen (1971), the population has

increased.

The winter harvest for the whole population peaked in 1973 at 80 674. The following decrease was caused by the introduction of quotas, not by a scarcity of seals. The winter harvest for the last five years (1972-76) averaged 72 586 animals representing 34.4 % of the pup population estimate.

Calculations indicate that the Cape fur seal is currently at about the optimum sustainable population level (Shaughnessy and Best, 1975a). The number of mature females in the population in 1971 was estimated to be 63 % of the number in the population before commercial exploitation commenced. This is somewhat higher than the proportion that would be present if the population were at the maximum sustainable yield level (52 %).

Quotas have also been set for summer sealing (Table 6). This form of sealing has been decreasing in recent years, and ceased after 1975 when bulls were only taken at four colonies (Wolf Bay, Atlas Bay, Elephant Rock and Seal Island in Mossel Bay).

Incidental Harvest

Cape fur seals are taken incidentally in the pelagic purse-seine fisheries for pilchard (*Sardinops ocellata*) and anchovy (*Engraulis capensis*), especially in Namibian waters. In those fisheries, seals are attracted to the seine boats and readily jump over the cork line into (and out of) the net. They create problems by eating fish, frightening fish from the net before it is pursed and by damaging nets after they are pursed and are being hauled aboard. Weighted firecrackers that explode underwater were developed and marketed from 1974 to 1976 under the name "Seal Deterrents". They were partially effective in frightening seals from the nets, but only if set off at frequent intervals. Their use was banned in 1976 at the request of the fishing industry on the grounds that they interfered with the fish shoals. Firearms are also effective. The number of seals killed by pelagic fishermen is not known, but the number of cadavers on beaches north of Walvis Bay indicates that it is considerable.

A project designed to frighten seals from purse-seine nets with underwater sounds is currently being undertaken by the Central Acoustics Laboratory and the Department of Zoology of the University of Cape Town, in conjunction with the Sea Fisheries Branch, and funded by the South African Society for the Prevention of Cruelty to Animals and the fishing industry (Anon., 1975). Two tape recordings of killer whales have been used: one obtained from Dr W.C. Cummings of the U.S. Naval Undersea Center at San Diego, the other made in McMurdo Sound by Dr G.A. Kooyman of the Scripps Institute at San Diego. The tests were performed on Sea Fisheries Branch research ships near Cape Town and on a purse-seiner near Cape Cross. The seals were obviously aware of the sounds on the first mentioned tape: they responded by diving rapidly, and on resurfacing "spied out" the vessel before resuming their previous activities. However, neither tape elicited an apparent escape response from the seals. On the other hand, jackass penguins (*Spheniscus demersus*) rapidly fled on hearing the killer whale sounds underwater (Frost *et al.*, 1975). Further trials have indicated that .303 bullets fired into the water next to seals at 15 second intervals (or shorter) are an effective deterrent. Efforts are being made to build and test an electronic shock wave generator with similar sound pressure level to that of a .303 bullet hitting the surface.

Fur seals are also attracted to trawlers fishing for hake (*Merluccius capensis*). The mortality of seals incidental to this fishery has been recorded on Sea Fisheries Branch research vessels and on a small number of South African commercial trawlers. For the 12 months beginning August 1976, the mortality rate in 356 drags was 0.045 seals per drag.

Individual seals also harass line-fishing boats, particularly those catching snoek (*Thyrsites atun*). Fishermen take retaliatory action.

Historical Development

"Historically fur-seals have lived on most (if not all) islands round the coast of South Africa and South West Africa. However, foreign sealers (who hunted by clubbing over 300 years ago) and guano-workers effectively destroyed all herds associated with the guano-islands off the West Coast" (Rand, 1972). Brief comments on some islands that no longer harbour fur seals (Mercury, Ichaboe, Seal and Penguin Islands in Luderitz Bay, Possession, the Saldanha Bay Islands, Dassen and Robben) were provided by Rand (1972). The location of former colonies of the Cape fur seal in Namibia and South Africa is shown in Figures 3 and 4, including 8 not shown by Rand (1972) which are briefly described here.

A colony was reported on Robbe Islet near Port Nolloth in 1779 by the traveller William Patterson (Forbes, 1965). Seals were harvested there as recently as 1835 (Alexander, 1838). A colony on the mainland, in or near St. Helena Bay, was briefly referred to in the journal of Jan van Riebeeck (first governor of the settlement at the Cape of Good Hope) for 11 October 1953 (Thom, 1952). Three extinct colonies were mentioned by Ross (1971): St. Croix Island in Algoa Bay, and Robberg Peninsula and Beacon Island in Plettenberg Bay. Seals on St. Croix and its small neighbours Jahleel and Brenton were reported by Moresby in his survey of the coast in 1820 (Moresby, 1972). The colony at Robberg was also referred to by Klein (1972), who found bones of the Cape fur seal in deposits in Nelson Bay Cave. The Report of the Guano Islands Commission (Cape of Good Hope, 1907) recommended that the Robberg colony and a colony near Walker Point be opened to harvesting by private enterprise. Since 1893, when conservation measures for the Cape fur seal were included in the Fish Protection Act, only the last two colonies have been eliminated. There are strong indications that the population of the Cape fur seal was severely reduced by the early part of the twentieth century (Gilchrist, in Cape of Good Hope, 1907; Schultze, 1907;

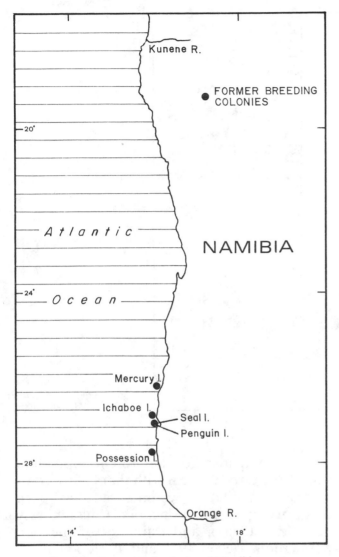

FIG. 3. – Former seal colonies of Namibian waters.

Thompson, 1913). Observations suggesting that the population of the Cape fur seal has increased since the 1940's were presented by Best (1973a). These observations concerned the five breeding colonies at Wolf Bay, Atlas Bay, Van Reenen Bay (the beach opposite Black Rock, Namibia), Lion's Head (the beach opposite Sinclair Island) and Seal Island in False Bay, which were all very small or non-existent during the 1940's and now produce substantial numbers of pups annually (Tables 2 and 4). The formation of mainland colonies has been attributed by Rand (1972) to

"the destruction of large desert carnivores, known predators of the seals", together with the "stringent diamond regulations which have curtailed human traffic on this coast for many years".

Another newly-formed colony and three non-breeding colonies can be added to these. Firstly, Albatross Rock was not listed with the breeding colonies by Rand (1949), who thought that seals present on the island in 1947 may have been the harbingers of a new breeding herd. At least 3 700 pups are estimated to have been produced there in the 1971-72 breeding season (Table 2). Secondly, a non-breeding colony has formed at False Cape Fria in recent years (Zur Strassen, 1971). The Sea Fisheries Branch learnt of this colony in 1970 and photographed it from the air in December 1971 and January 1975. Finally, we first heard of, and visited, two other non-breeding colonies at Pelican Point and Buchu Twins in December and April, 1974, respectively. The existence of these new non-breeding colonies is indicative of an increase in numbers of the Cape fur seal. The increase in the number of hauling-out areas is probably encouraged by the disturbance caused by sealing activities in long-established colonies. In addition to this evidence for an increase in seal numbers, there is an unsubstantiated statement by Zur Strassen (1971) that the seal population at Cape Cross has increased, despite the effect of intense winter and summer harvests.

The recent establishment of several colonies indicates that legislation controlling harvesting of the Cape fur seal has been effective in allowing the numbers to increase. Efforts have been made to compare the present population size with that immediately before commercial exploitation commenced. Harvest figures for some of the now-extinct colonies have been obtained from the journals Jan van Riebeeck (Thom, 1952). Much valuable information on sealing in the early days of the Cape Colony is also contained in Muller (1942) and Rand (1973). The largest of the extinct colonies must have been Possession Island where

401

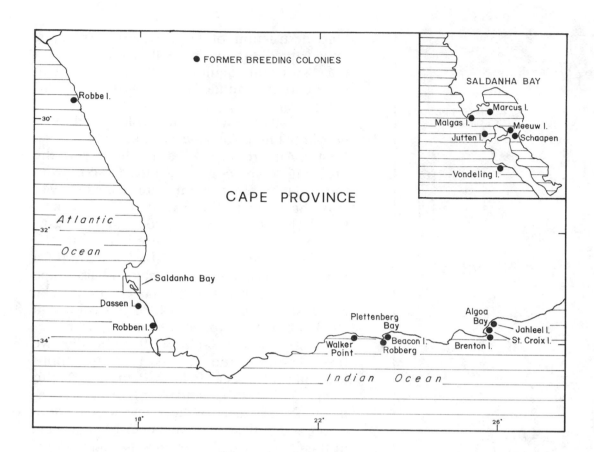

FIG. 4. – Former seal colonies of South African waters.

Morrell (1832) estimated that not less than half a million seals had been dead about five years. Because Morrell is reputed to be an unreliable source (e.g. Eden, 1846), and because estimates of population sizes of other extinct colonies are insignificant when compared with Morrell's for Possession, the veracity of the latter should be examined. The traveller S.V. van Reenen visited Thomson's (i.e., Possession) Island in January 1793 in the *Meermin* and noted that over 21 000 seal skins had been taken during three successive years and shipped from Possession in the schooner *Betsy*. Some of these skins were possibly taken from nearby Long Island where the sealers were working (Franken, 1938). Rand (1972) noted that as many as 30 sealing ships were operating out of Possession in 1796, though it is quite likely that these vessels were also taking seals at nearby colonies (Long, Albatross, Sinclair), since Possession provides the best anchorage in that area.

A comparison of the present population size of the Cape fur seal with that before commercial exploitation commenced has been made, using a population model (Shaughnessy and Best, 1975a), and estimates of the pup population sizes in 1940 and 1971. The comparison has been included in an appendix to that report. It is briefly described here.

Since the population is believed to have increased since the 1940's, observations of the rate of increase should provide an indication of where the 1940 population was on the growth curve, and thus, indirectly, of the size of the initial population. To do this, the size of the 1940 population was roughly estimated by assuming that the six newly-formed breeding colonies referred to above did not produce any pups in 1940. From counts of pups on aerial photographs taken in 1971 or later, a total of $52\,276 \times 1.31$ pups is estimated to have been produced in these six colonies (Table 2). Thus the pup population size in 1940 is estimated as

213 250-72 722, i.e., 139 528 pups, approximately two-thirds of the estimate for 1971. The 1940 population was then assigned the biological parameters (pregnancy rate and mortality rate of pups) pertaining to a population considered to be at various proportions of an initial population size, and its progress simulated by the population model for 31 cycles with actual catches (Best, 1973a) substituted for a constant sealing rate. Predictions of the pup population size in 1971 (Table 8) compared with the estimated pup population size for 1971 (taken as 213 250) indicate that the 1940 pup population was 48 % of the initial size. Thus the initial pup population size can be estimated as 290 700 pups, and the 1971 pup population estimated as 73 % of its initial value.

Trophic relationships

FOOD AND FEEDING

The food of Cape fur seals collected off the south-western coast of Cape Province between 1954 and 1956 was studied by Rand

Table 8. Predictions of the pup population size in 1971 when the pup population of 1940 was various proportions (I) of the unexploited population size

Proportion of the initial pup population present in 1940 (I)	Pup population size in 1971 ($P_{0,1971}$) predicted by the model
0.1	496 065
0.2	372 973
0.3	301 164
0.4	247 032
0.48	213 079
0.5	205 628
0.6	173 313
0.7	147 559

(1959a). The frequency of occurrence of food items in 245 stomachs was: 50 % fish, 37 % cephalopods, and 13 % crustaceans. By volume the composition was 70 % fish, 20 % cephalopods and 2 % crustaceans, with another 8 % of miscellaneous matter. The most numerous prey were squid (mainly *Loligo* spp.), maasbankers (*Trachurus trachurus*), and pilchards. Competition between Cape fur seals and the commercial fishery in Cape Province was discussed by Rand (1959a). Although the seals (other than yearlings) consume considerable amounts of fish (estimated at 600 lbs annually) as well as other marine animals, Rand concluded that their effect was much less than that of the commercial fishery.

The population of the Cape fur seal is now estimated at 211 300 pups (see Aerial Photography) and 634 000 seals older than one year (assuming that the number of pups born represents approximately one quarter of the total population). The annual consumption of fish by these seals is approximately 173 000 m tons, considerably less than the 2.4 million m tons of fish removed by the commercial fishery in Namibia and the Cape Province (Best, 1973a).

More important than the amount of fish eaten by seals is their tendency to approach fishing boats, especially pelagic purse-seine boats fishing for pilchards and anchovies, and trawlers fishing for hake. Seals frequently jump into purse-seines, eat fish, damage nets and sometimes chase the fish from the net before it is pursed.

Stomachs of 520 seals in their first year of life were examined at the winter harvests at Cape Cross, Wolf Bay and Atlas Bay (Best and Shaughnessy, 1975): 31 % contained milk and 8 % contained solids. The most common items of solid food in stomachs of these seals at Cape Cross were crustaceans (in 22 stomachs), cephalopods (in 3) and fish (in 2). This is the only study of the food of the Cape fur seal in Namibian waters.

Since Rand's study of food of the Cape fur seal, the composition of pelagic fish populations in the waters of Cape Province has

403

changed as a result, primarily, of the decrease of the maasbanker and pilchard populations, and an increase of the anchovy (Geldenhuys, 1973; Stander and Le Roux, 1968). A similar change has occurred in Namibian waters where the pilchard stocks declined (Cram, 1974) and the anchovy increased (Newman, 1970). Presumably therefore, the availability of food to the seals has also changed.

In March 1974, the Sea Fisheries Branch resumed collections of Cape fur seals. Examination of their stomach contents will provide a better understanding of their current food habits.

ECOSYSTEM

The inshore range of the Cape fur seal was divided into three distinct zoo-geographic zones by Rand (1967): the West Coast; the area between Cape Point and Cape Agulhas on the south coast; and a third zone between Mossel Bay and Algoa Bay on the southeast coast. Waters in these three zones have been described by Rand (1967) and Shannon (1970). The West Coast zone is dominated by the cold (10°C to 15°C) upwelled waters of the northward-flowing Benguela Current, which is found within 160 km off shore. The second zone includes the area of nearshore mixing between cold Atlantic water and warmer water flowing south in the Agulhas Current. The third zone includes the Agulhas Current, but the two seal rookeries (Seal Island in Mossel Bay and Black Rocks in Algoa Bay) are in areas where moderately strong upwellings and countercurrents periodically occur inshore.

Other aspects of the seals' environment (wind, fog, rain and air-temperature) have been considered by Rand (1967).

Other organisms that form part of the Cape fur seal's ecosystem are mentioned briefly. Its most important prey are pelagic shoaling fish and cephalopods (see Food and Feeding). Species that share the same prey are the Cape gannet (*Morus capensis*), jackass penguin and various cormorants (*Phalacroco-*

rax spp.) (Rand, 1959, 1960, 1960a) and dolphins (Delphinidae) (P.B. Best and G.J.B. Ross, pers. comm.). Its predators include sharks, possibly the killer whale (see Natural Mortality Rates), and man, both as a commercial harvester (sealer) and as a commercial fisherman taking seals incidentally to fishing operations (see Harvesting Rates). Avian scavengers of the Cape fur seal have been discussed by Rand (1967). The black-backed jackal is both a predator of pups and a scavenger of carcasses on the desert coast. The strandwolf, or hyaena, (*Hyaena brunnea*) is another scavenger of seals on the desert coast.

Most of the islands on the coasts of South Africa and Namibia are inhabited either by sea birds or by Cape fur seals, while some islands contain populations of both, e.g. Hollamsbird, Sinclair, Elephant Rock, Seal Island in False Bay, Duikerklip, Geyser Rock and Quoin Rock (Rand, 1963, 1970). The increase in the population size of the Cape fur seal may have been disadvantageous to sea birds on islands shared by both groups (Rand, 1970); for example, seals displaced the sea bird colony on Albatross Rock where guano was once collected (D.B. Price, pers. comm.). Similarly, expansion of the seal population was responsible for the white pelican (*Pelecanus onocrotalus*) vacating nesting sites on Quoin Rock in the early 1900's and on Seal Island, False Bay in recent years (Rand, 1963).

Other factors

AESTHETIC VALUES

In the winter harvest, Cape fur seals are killed by clubbing followed by severing of the heart or great vessels with a knife ("sticking"); in summer harvests bulls are shot. Provision is made in the Sealing Regulations for the harvests to be inspected by officials of the Sea Fisheries Branch.

The aesthetic aspects of clubbing have

been discussed by Best (1973a), who pointed out that (1) if a better method was available, it would be used, and (2) most scientists who investigated killing methods of the northern fur seal at the Pribilof Islands were satisfied that clubbing is humane (U.S. Senate, 1972; Williams *et al.*, 1973). The winter harvest of Cape fur seals at two colonies was inspected in August 1974 by two independent U.S. veterinarians in connection with the application of the Fouke Company to import seal skins from South Africa. The veterinarians judged that the harvest did not attain the standard of humaneness required by the U.S. Department of Commerce. However, they stressed that sealing was done by the recognised method of clubbing and sticking. In the following season, the same veterinarians visited these colonies again and decided that the harvest satisfied their standards of humaneness. In 1976 and 1977 Sea Fisheries Inspectors were stationed at the colonies where the majority of the harvesting took place.

PRODUCTS OF THE SEALING INDUSTRY

Yearling seals are taken primarily for their pelts, oil from their blubber being a by-product. In the past, a large proportion of yearling skins was sent to the USA for processing by the Fouke Company, where the outer guard hairs are removed, leaving the soft underfur. Alternatively skins are sent to Europe, where they are processed "in the hair" by shaving off the guard hairs to the level of the fur. Skins of bulls are less valuable than those of yearlings; they were used for leather or treated in the hair to produce a much inferior pelt.

Blubber from most of the animals harvested is used for the production of seal oil. Production in the 3 years 1974-76 was 203 000 litres, 233 000 litres and 198 000 litres, respectively.

Although seal meat was frequently used as human food in the early years of the Cape settlement (Thompson, 1913), during the pres-

ent century skinned carcasses have usually been dumped into the sea or buried. Small amounts of fresh seal meat are eaten by the sealers (Rand, 1973), and seal meat has also been canned for human and pet food, but marketing was not successful. Carcasses are utilised at one rookery (Cape Cross), where about half of the catch (yearlings and adult bulls) is rendered into meat-meal and bone-meal (32 550 kg and 9 850 kg, respectively, in 1974). In 1974 the Department of Industries actively encouraged sealing concessionaires to increase their utilisation of seal carcasses, and a total of 2 507 carcasses of yearling seals from the harvests at Wolf and Atlas Bays and Seal Island (False Bay) was frozen and sold for pet food. This form of utilisation has not been repeated.

The quantity of raw material available annually from sealing operations was calculated by Black *et al.* (1945), using the weights of pups (five of each sex) and five bulls that were weighed whole and in pieces. The weight distribution of these components, together with their gross weights for the 1974 harvest are presented in Table 9. By discarding the carcasses after the skin and blubber have been

Table 9. **Weight distribution of components of yearlings and bull seals: averages and totals for the 1974 harvest [1]**

Component	Yearlings		Adult Bulls	
	Average of 10 animals	Totals for 1974 harvest (tonnes)	Average of 5 animals	Totals for 1974 harvest (tonnes)
Total weight	23.2 kg	1551.9	285.5 kg	310.9
Skin	11.5 %	178.5	9.0 %	28.0
Blubber	26.0 %	403.5	16.1 %	50.1
Liver	2.5 %		3.8 %	
Intestines	3.5 %	183.1	2.1 %	37.9
Flippers	5.8 %		6.3 %	
Residual carcass	50.7 %	786.8	62.7 %	194.9

[1] Based on Black *et al.* (1945).

removed, 63 % of the weight of pups, and 75 % of the weight of bulls, are wasted. This loss would have amounted to about 1 203 tonnes in 1974 if some of the carcasses at Cape Cross and some other sealing stations had not been utilised.

The potential value of the carcass can be realised from a breakdown of individual organ weights for a juvenile female Cape fur seal (Table 10). The dressed carcass (i.e. body without skin, most blubber, head, flippers and viscera) comprised half the weight of the seal, and of this, about 54 % could be readily filleted off as meat (as might be practicable in a commercial fishery) with a further 24.6 % available as "bonings" (or meat obtained by more careful cleaning of individual bones). More than three-quarters of the dressed carcass is therefore a potential source of red-meat protein, and this would have amounted to a total of 609 tonnes (= 1551.9 × .499 × .786) of meat from the 1974 yearling harvest.

The calorific value of the muscle of 3 yearling seals averaged 5.700 Kcals per gm dry weight (J. Field, University of Cape Town, pers. comm.). The chemical composition of muscle and bone of an immature female was:

Table 10. Weight (kg) of the components of a juvenile female Cape fur seal

	Weight (kg)	Percentage of total
Skin (deblubbered)	2.62	9.7
Blubber	1.91	7.1
Stomach (and contents)	2.07	7.7
Liver	0.88	3.3
Kidneys	0.23	0.9
Heart	0.18	0.7
Tongue, trachea and lungs	1.17	4.3
Intestines	1.39	5.1
Head	1.26	4.7
Flippers	1.84	6.8
Dressed carcass	13.49	49.9
Total (of parts)	27.04	100.2
Total (weighed whole)	29.09	
Filleted meat	7.27	26.9
All meat, including bonings	10.60	39.2
Cleaned bones	2.89	10.7

22.9 % protein, 0.80 % fibre, 6.60 % fat, 68.4 % moisture, 1.53 % ash, 0.08 % calcium and 0.23 % phosphorus.

In 1974 some yearling carcasses were sold for pet food at 30 cents per kg. Maximum utilisation of the 786.8 tonnes of residual carcasses (Table 9) is probably an impossibility due to the remoteness of some concessions, but if it were, a further R236 000 might have been added to the value of the industry from the yearling harvest. For comparison, the commercial value of the 1972 seal harvest was estimated by Best (1973a) as R982 038.

FUTURE PRODUCT DEMANDS

The influence of the US Marine Mammal Protection Act, 1972 (MMPA) on the South African seal harvest has been reviewed by Shaughnessy (1976). Since 1925 most of the skins from Cape fur seals have been exported to the Fouke Company in the USA for processing. After the passage of the MMPA this export trade ceased, with the exceptions of skins sent to the Fouke Company in 1973 under an economic hardship exemption, and in 1976 under a waiver to the moratorium.

According to Section 102 (b) of the MMPA, marine mammals or their products may not be imported into the US if the animals concerned were, inter alia, (1) pregnant at the time of taking; (2) nursing at the time of taking; or less than 8 months old, whichever occurs later; (3) taken in a manner deemed inhumane. The first of these conditions does not apply to the South African harvest since it is directed at yearlings, and the skins of any adult cows accidently taken in the harvest are not currently sought by the Fouke Company.

The nursing part of the second condition was the subject of a report by Best and Shaughnessy (1975) who considered evidence from published data on the time of moult, shedding of milk teeth, stomach contents and intestinal parasites in pups, movements of pups and yearlings, and survival rates of animals caught for display purposes. They tentatively concluded that nursing is no longer obligate (defined as necessary for the health and survival of the pup) from July onwards, that is, from the age of between 7 and 8 months.

The "8 months old" limit in the second condition required an accurate determination of the pupping season. This was achieved at Seal Island, False Bay by counting black pups on aerial photographs taken at weekly intervals between 15 October 1974 and 13 January 1975 (Shaughnessy and Best, 1975). The maximum number of pups was present at the colony on 18 December. From the regression analysis of number of pups on time, it was calculated that the median pupping date was 1 December, and that 90 % of the pups were born in a time span of 34 days between mid-November and mid-December. The beginning of the harvest was then postponed to 1 August to ensure that more than half of the seals were older than 8 months.

The third condition, concerning humane killing has been discussed above (Aesthetic Values). Steps have been taken to improve the standard of the sealing operations, not only to satisfy the requirements of the MMPA, but also in response to the increasing interest being shown in sealing operations by the public in South Africa.

The Fouke Company's application for a waiver of the importation moratorium for the 1974 harvest was unsuccessful because the South African harvest was judged inhumane. A waiver to the MMPA was granted for the 1975 and 1976 harvests, with the added proviso that the annual harvest be limited to 70 000 animals. The 1975 harvest was completed before the waiver was granted and exceeded 70 000 skins, hence none of those skins were imported into the US. Some skins were imported from the 1976 harvest. The waiver was invalidated in July 1977 by an appeal court on the basis of infraction of those parts of the MMPA concerning nursing and the age of harvested animals.

A ready market for Cape fur seal skins currently exists in Europe. One of the sealing concessionaires is now interested in obtaining pelts from sub-adults. Such skins are larger than those of yearlings, and are considered to be suitable for treatment in the hair. A harvest of sub-adults in lieu of yearlings would require a re-evaluation of harvest quotas.

OTHER USES OF CAPE FUR SEALS

Live Cape fur seals are also utilised for display purposes at their colonies and in captivity. 4 colonies are visited by tourists. The island colonies of Duikerklip, Seal Island (False Bay) and Seal Island (Mossel Bay) were visited regularly by a total of 6 boats in 1975. The Duikerklip and False Bay boats operated year-round, with the emphasis on the 3-month-long summer season, while the 4 smaller boats at Mossel Bay operated only during summer. No landings are allowed at these, or any other colonies, without permission of the Director of Sea Fisheries. In addition, the colony at Cape Cross is also visited by tourists under the supervision of the Division of Nature Conservation and Tourism of the South West Africa Administration. The other mainland colonies are either of limited access (False Cape Fria) or within restricted Diamond Areas and so are rarely visited. Information on the number of visitors in 1972 to Seal Island, False Bay (9-10 000) and to Cape Cross (6 308) was provided by Best (1973a). During the tourist season at Mossel Bay at the beginning of 1975, 17 000 people viewed Seal Island from boats in a 5 week period. For the 12 months ending February 1975, 35 000 visitors viewed the Duikerklip colony. Overall, therefore, as many as 68 000 people per year may view Cape fur seals at their colonies, with monetary takings exceeding R70 000.

As Best (1973a) noted, harvesting of the seals regularly takes place at 3 of these 4 colonies (the exception being Duikerklip) without conflict of interest in the multiple use of the resource.

Cape fur seals are reported to thrive in captivity (Rand, 1956). Most Cape fur seals

407

caught for shipment to overseas zoos in recent years have come from Seal Island in False Bay under licence from the Sea Fisheries Branch. Only animals in their first and second years are taken, and Sea Fisheries Branch scientists have suggested that catching be limited to the months between July and October to avoid the breeding and pupping seasons, and because it is considered that "obligate nursing" of yearlings ceases during July (Best and Shaughnessy, 1975). According to that report, 23 seals were taken from Seal Island during 1971 and 1972.

In South Africa, captive Cape fur seals are displayed at the Port Elizabeth Oceanarium, East London Aquarium, Johannesburg Zoological Gardens, National Zoological Gardens (Pretoria), Tygerberg Zoopark (Cape Town) and Hartebeestpoort Dam. The 8 yearlings now at the East London Aquarium were among the hundreds that were stranded as black pups on nearby beaches during late

December 1974, after a storm washed most of the pups away from the colony at Black Rocks, Algoa Bay (Shaughnessy, unpubl. rep.).

In addition to Cape fur seals, other species that have come ashore near Port Elizabeth (crabeater, southern elephant, and Amsterdam Island fur seals) have been displayed in the Port Elizabeth Oceanarium (Ross et al., 1976; G.J.B. Ross, pers. comm.).

Acknowledgements

For support in the preparation of this report I am grateful to my colleague Dr P.B. Best, with whom much of the previously unreported work was carried out. I also thank C.S. Bosman, D.B. Price, R.W. Rand and G.J.B. Ross for information, and Ms G.L. Shaughnessy for criticising the manuscript.

References

ALEXANDER, J.E., An expedition of discovery into the
1838   interior of Africa. London, Coulson, 2 vols. (facsimile reprint by Struik, Cape Town, 1967).

BEST, P.B., A leopard seal from Hout Bay, South Africa.
1971   Zool. Afr., 6:177-9.

—, Stalked barnacles Conchoderma auritum on an ele-
1971a   phant seal: occurrence of elephant seals on South African coast. Zool. Afr., 6:181-5.

—, Estimates of pup population size and sealing at Cape
1973   Cross, S.W.A. Cape Town, Sea Fisheries Branch, 19 p. (unpubl. rep.).

—, Seals and sealing in South and South West Africa. S.
1973a   Afr. Shipp. News Fish. Ind. Rev., 28(12):49-57.

—, Seal tagging at Kleinzee, 1973 — final report. Cape
1974   Town, Sea Fisheries Branch, 11 p. (unpubl. rep.).

BEST, P.B. and R.W. RAND, Results of a pup-tagging
1975   experiment on the Arctocephalus pusillus rookery at Seal Island, False Bay, South Africa. Rapp. P.-V. Réun. CIEM, 169:267-73.

BEST, P.B. and P.D. SHAUGHNESSY, Nursing in the Cape
1975   fur seal Arctocephalus pusillus pusillus. Cape Town, Sea Fisheries Branch, 19 p. (unpubl. rep.).

BLACK, M.M. et al., South African fish products. Part 19.
1945   The South African seal fishery. J. Soc. Chem. Ind., Lond., 64:326-31.

BONNER, W.N., The fur seal of South Georgia. Sci. Rep.
1968   Br. Antarct. Surv., 56:1-81.

Cape of Good Hope, Department of Agriculture, Guano
1907   Islands Commission's Report. In Annexures to the votes and proceedings of the House of Assembly. Cape Town, Cape of Good Hope, No. 114 of 1907, 272 p.

COURTENAY-LATIMER, M., Two rare seal records for
1961   South Africa. Ann. Cape Prov. Mus., 1:102.

CRAM, D.L., South West African pilchard stock conti-
1974   nues to recover. S. Afr. Shipp. News Fish. Ind. Rev., 29(9):74-5.

EDEN, T., The search for nitre and the true nature of

1846   guano: being an account of a voyage to the S.W. coast of Africa. London, R. Groombridge and Sons, 133 p.

FORBES, V.S., Pioneer travellers of South Africa. Cape
1965   Town, Balkema, 177 p.

FRANCA, P. da, Sur la présence d'*Arctocephalus pusillus*
1967   (Schreber) (Otariidae) et de *Mirounga leonina* (Linné) (Phocidae) au sud de l'Angola. *Mammalia*, 31:50-4.

FRANKEN, J.L.M., Duminy-dagboeke; Duminy diaries.
1938   Cape Town, Van Riebeeck-Vereniging, 355 p.

FROST, P.G.H. *et al.*, The response of jackass penguins to
1975   killer whale vocalisation. *S. Afr. J. Sci.*, 71:157-8.

GELDENHUYS, N.D., Growth of the South African maas-
1973   banker *Trachurus trachurus* Linnaeus and age composition of the catches, 1950-1971. *Invest. Rep. Sea Fish. Branch S. Apr.*, (101):1-24.

JOHNSON, A., Affidavit. *In* Ocean mammal protection:
1972   hearings before the Sub-Committee on Oceans and Atmosphere of the Committee on Commerce, United States Senate 92nd Congress, 2nd session, Part I. Washington, US Government Printing Office, pp. 783-7.

KETTLEWELL, H.D.B. and B. RAND, Elephant seal cow
1955   and pup on South African coast. *Nature, Lond.*, 175:1000-1.

KLEIN, R.G., The late quaternary mammalian fauna of
1972   Nelson Bay Cave (Cape Province, South Africa): its implications for mega-faunal extinctions and environmental and cultural change. *Quatern. Res.*, 2:135-42.

LAWS, R.M., The current status of seals in the Southern
1973   Hemisphere. *IUCN (New Ser.) Suppl. Pap.*, 39:144-61.

MORESBY, F., Remarks on the rivers and coast between
1972   Cape Recife and the mouth of the Keiskahama, with particular description of Port Elizabeth, Algoa Bay, southern Africa. *Looking Back*, 12:98-102.

MORRELL, B., A narrative of four voyages, to the South
1832   Sea, North and South Pacific Ocean, Chinese Sea, Ethiopic and southern Atlantic Ocean, Indian and Antarctic Ocean – from the year 1822 to 1831. New York, J. and J. Harper, 492 p.

MULLER, C.J.F., Die geskiedenis van die visserye aan die
1942   Kaap tot aan die middel van die agtiende eeu. *Argief-Jaarb. Suid Afr. Gesk.*, 5(1):1-100.

NEL, J.A.J., Order Pinnipedia. Part 9. *In* The mammals
1971   of Africa – an identification manual, edited by J. Meester and H.W. Setzer. Washington, D.C., Smithsonian Institution Press.

NEWMAN, G.G., Stock assessment of the pilchard *Sardi-*
1970   *nops ocellata* at Walvis Bay, South West Africa. *Invest. Rep. Div. Sea Fish.*, S. Afr., (85):1-13.

RAND, R.W., Studies on the Cape fur seal. 2. Attendance
1949   at the rookery. Department of Agriculture, South Africa, Guano Islands Administration, 19 p. (unpubl. progress rep.).

–, Reproduction in the Cape fur seal, *Arctocephalus*
1955   *pusillus* (Schreber). *Proc. Zool. Soc. Lond.*, 124:717-40.

–, The Cape fur seal *Arctocephalus pusillus* (Schreber):
1956   its general characteristics and moult. *Invest. Rep. Div. Sea Fish.*, S. Afr., (21):1-52.

–, The biology of guano-producing seabirds. The dis-
1959   tribution, abundance and feeding habits of the Cape gannet, *Morus capensis*, off the south western coast of the Cape Province. *Invest. Rep. Div. Sea Fish.*, S. Afr., (39):1-36.

–, The Cape fur seal (*Arctocephalus pusillus*). Distribu-
1959a   tion, abundance and feeding habits off the south western coast of the Cape Province. *Invest. Rep. Div. Sea Fish.*, S. Afr., (34):1-75.

–, The biology of guano-producing seabirds. The dis-
1960   tribution, abundance and feeding habits of the Cape penguin, *Spheniscus demersus*, off the south western coast of the Cape Province. *Invest. Rep. Div. Sea Fish.*, S. Afr., (41):1-28.

–, The biology of guano-producing seabirds. 3. The
1960a   distribution, abundance and feeding habits of the cormorants *Phalacrocoridae* off the south west coast of the Cape Province. *Invest. Rep. Div. Sea Fish.*, S. Afr., (42):1-32.

–, The biology of guano-producing seabirds. 4. Com-
1963   position of colonies on the Cape Islands. *Invest. Rep. Div. Sea Fish.*, S. Afr., (43):1-32.

–, The Cape fur seal (*Arctocephalus pusillus*). 3. Gener-
1967   al behaviour on land and at sea. *Invest. Rep. Div. Sea Fish.*, S. Afr., (60):1-39.

409

—, Some hazards to sea-birds. *Ostrich Suppl.*, 8:515-20.
1970

—, The Cape fur seal (*Arctocephalus pusillus*). 4. Esti-
1972   mates of population size. *Invest. Rep. Div. Sea
Fish., S. Afr.*, (89):1-28.

—, Management of the South African fur-seals. *J. S. Afr.
1973   Wildl. Manage. Assoc.*, 3:85-7.

REPENNING, C.A., R.S. PETERSON and C.L. HUBBS, Con-
1971   tributions to the systematics of the southern fur
seals, with particular reference to the Juan
Fernández and Guadalupe species. *In* Antarctic Pinnipedia, edited by H.W. Burt. *Antarct. Res. Ser.*, 18:1-34.

ROSS, G.J.B., The southern elephant seal, *Mirounga leo-
1969   nina*, on South African coasts. *Ann. Cape Prov.
Mus.*, 6:137-9.

—, Notes on seals and sealing in the Eastern Cape. *East
1971   Cape Nat.*, 44:6-8.

ROSS, G.J.B. *et al.*, Observations on two captive crab-
1976   eater seals (*Lobodon carcinophagus*) at the Port
Elizabeth Oceanarium. *Int. Zoo Yearb.*,
16:160-4.

—, New records of crabeater seals (*Lobodon carcino-
1978   phagus*) from South Africa. *Ann. S. Afr. Mus.*,
75(6):153-8.

SCHULTZE, L., Die Fischerei an der Westküste Süd-Af-
1907   rikas. Bericht über Untersuchungen an der
Deutsch S-W-Afrikanischen Küste und am
Kap der guten Hoffnung. *Abh. Dtsch. Seefis-
chereiver.*, 9:1-57.

SHANNON, L.V., Oceanic circulation off South Africa.
1970   *Fish. Bull. Div. Sea Fish. S. Afr.*, (6):27-33.

SHAUGHNESSY, P.D., Serum protein variation in south-
1970   ern fur seals, *Arctocephalus* spp., in relation to
their taxonomy. *Aust. J. Zool.*, 18:331-43.

—, Controversial harvest. *Afr. Wildl.*, 30:26-31.
1976

SHAUGHNESSY, P.D. and P.B. BEST, The pupping season
1975   of the Cape fur seal *Arctocephalus pusillus pusillus*. Cape Town, Sea Fisheries Branch, 8 p.
(unpubl. rep.).

—, A simple population model for the South African fur
1975a   seal, *Arctocephalus pusillus pusillus*. Cape
Town, Sea Fisheries Branch, 8 p. (unpubl.
rep.).

—, Population estimates of the Cape fur seal, *Arctoce-
1976   phalus pusillus pusillus*. Paper presented to the
First Interdisciplinary Conference on Marine
and Freshwater Research in Southern Africa.

—, A discrete population model for the South African
1976a   fur seal, *Arctocephalus pusillus pusillus*. Paper
presented to the Scientific Consultation on the
Conservation and Management of Marine
Mammals and Their Environment, Bergen,
Norway, 31 August-9 September, 1976. Rome,
FAO, ACMRR/MM/SC/127:8 p.

STANDER, G.A. and P.J. LE ROUX, Notes on fluctuations
1968   of the commercial catch of the South African
pilchard (*Sardinops ocellata*) 1950-1965. *Invest.
Rep. Div. Sea Fish., S. Afr.*, (65):1-14.

THOM, H.B. (ed.), Journal of Jan van Riebeeck. Vol. 1.
1952   1651-1655. Cape Town, A.A. Balkema, 395 p.

THOMPSON, W.W., The sea fisheries of the Cape Colony.
1913   Cape Town, Maskew Miller, 163 p.

U.S. SENATE, Report of the Veterinary panel evaluating
1962   humaneness of the northern fur seal harvest in
the Pribilof Islands. *In* Ocean mammal protection: hearings before the Sub-Committee
on Oceans and Atmosphere of the Committee
on Commerce, United States Senate, 92nd
Congress, 2nd session, Part I. Washington, US
Government Printing Office, pp. 456-71.

WARNEKE, R.M., Preliminary report on the distribution
1976   and abundance of seals in the Australian
region. Paper presented to the Scientific
Consultation on the Conservation and
Management of Marine Mammals and their
Environment, Bergen, Norway, 31 August-9
September, 1976. Rome, FAO,
ACMRR/MM/SC/42:46 p.

WILLIAMS, R.A. *et al.*, Final report on concept scrutiny,
1973   phototype development and field evaluation of
improved fur seal slaughtering techniques to
U.S. Department of Commerce, National
Oceanic and Atmospheric Administration,
National Marine Fisheries Service. Columbus,
Ohio, Batelle Memorial Institute, Columbus
Laboratories.

ZUR STRASSEN, W.H., The fur seal of southern Africa.
1971   Cape Town, Howard Timmins, 71 p.

Anon., Phantom killer whales — SPCA backs project to
1975   overcome seal problem in purse-seine fishery.
S. Afr. Shipp. News Fish. Ind. Rev., 30(7):50-3.

THE STATUS OF THE AMSTERDAM ISLAND FUR SEAL

P.D. Shaughnessy

Abstract

The Amsterdam Island fur seal, *Arctocephalus tropicalis*, is found in 3 main populations, all north of the Antarctic Convergence: Tristan da Cunha and Gough Island; the Prince Edward Islands; and New Amsterdam and St. Paul Islands. This fur seal is not reported to be migratory. Dentition and the distinctive cream-coloured chest, throat and face are distinguishing features of the species. Adult males and females reach standard lengths and weights of about 180 cm and 165 kg, and 145 cm and 55 kg, respectively; length and weight at birth average 63 cm and 4.9 kg. Information on reproductive biology and on mortality rates in young animals is reviewed.

Uncontrolled sealing in the late 18th through the 19th centuries brought this species near extinction; estimates made between 1951 and 1973 show a thriving population of more than 23 400 animals, which is continuing to increase, with breeding on all major inhabited islands. Legal and illegal harvesting of up to several hundred animals per year has been conducted on Gough Island, where a sustained yield could perhaps be taken; small numbers have been taken on New Amsterdam and Marion Islands in recent years. Trophic relationships are briefly reviewed, revealing no evidence of direct competition between *A. tropicalis* and commercial fishing operations. Competition for space between *A. tropicalis* and the southern elephant seal, *Mirounga leonina*, presently occupying different parts of the same islands, may become acute as numbers of the former species continue to increase.

Résumé

L'otarie à fourrure de l'île Amsterdam, *Arctocephalus tropicalis*, constitue trois populations principales, toutes au nord de la convergence antarctique: île Tristan da Cunha et île Gough; îles du Prince Edouard; et îles de la Nouvelle-Amsterdam et St Paul. On n'a pas signalé de migrations pour cette espèce. La dentition, ainsi que le poitrail, la gorge et la face couleur crème sont les signes distinctifs de cette espèce. Les mâles et les femelles adultes ont des tailles et des poids normaux d'environ 180 cm et 165 kg et de 145 cm et 55 kg, respectivement – la longueur et le poids à la naissance sont en moyenne de 63 cm et 4,9 kg. L'auteur passe en revue les informations sur la biologie de la reproduction et sur les taux de mortalité.

Une exploitation incontrôlée, qui s'est étendue de la fin du 18e à la fin du 19e siècle a pratiquement provoqué l'extinction de l'espèce; d'après les estimations effectuées entre 1951 et 1973, il existe une population vigoureuse de plus de 23 400 animaux qui continue à s'accroître et se reproduit sur toutes les grandes îles désertes. Des captures légales et illégales, atteignant jusqu'à plusieurs centaines d'animaux par an, ont été réalisées sur l'île de Gough, où un rendement soutenu a peut-être été obtenu. De petits nombres d'exemplaires ont été capturés ces dernières années sur l'île de la Nouvelle-Amsterdam et sur l'île Marion. Les relations trophiques sont brièvement passées en revue, ne faisant apparaître aucune preuve de concurrence entre *A. tropicalis* et les opérations de pêche commerciale. La concurrence pour l'habitat entre *A. tropicalis* et *Mirounga leonina*, qui occupe à présent diverses parties des mêmes îles, pourrait devenir grave à mesure que les effectifs des otaries à fourrure continuent à augmenter.

Extracto

El lobo marino de dos pelos de la isla de Nueva Amsterdam (*Arctocephalus tropicalis*) se agrupa en tres poblaciones principales, todas al norte de la convergencia antártica: Tristan da Cunha e isla Gough; islas del Príncipe Eduardo; e islas de Nueva Amsterdam y San Pablo. No se sabe que este lobo marino sea migratorio. Características distintivas de esta especie son la dentición y el color crema en el pecho, la garganta y la cara. La longitud y peso medio de los machos y hembras adultos es del orden de 180 cm y 165 kg y 145 cm y 55 kg, respectivamente; la talla y el peso en el momento del nacimiento son por término medio de 63 cm y 4,9 kg. Se examina la información disponible sobre biología de la reproducción y mortalidad de animales jóvenes.

La caza incontrolada a finales del siglo XVIII y en el siglo XIX ha llevado a esta especie a un punto próximo a la extinción; las estimaciones hechas entre 1951 y 1973 muestran una población en aumento de más de 23 400 animales, que sigue aumentando y se reproduce en todas las principales islas habitadas. Anualmente se han capturado legal e ilegalmente varios centenares de animales en la isla Gough, donde quizás podría obtenerse un rendimiento sostenido; en los últimos años se ha capturado también un pequeño número de estos animales en las islas de Nueva Amsterdam y Marion. Se examinan brevemente las relaciones tróficas, que no indican ninguna competencia directa entre *A. tropicalis* y las pesquerías comerciales. La competencia por el espacio entre *A. tropicalis* y el elefante marino del sur, *Mirounga leonina*, que actualmente ocupa partes diversas de las mismas islas, podría agudizarse si sigue aumentando el número de lobos marinos.

P.D. Shaughnessy
Director, Sea Fisheries Institute, Private Bag, Sea Point 8060, South Africa

Descriptive part

IDENTIFICATION

The Amsterdam Island fur seal (*Arctocephalus tropicalis*) was for many years regarded as conspecific with the Kerguelen fur seal (*A. gazella*). They were first separated on the basis of cranial and dental characteristics, at the sub-specific level by King (1959), following a similar suggestion by Paulian (1957). King (1959a) recognised *A. tropicalis gazella* from Kerguelen, Bouvet, and South Georgia, and *A. tropicalis tropicalis* from Marion, Gough and New Amsterdam Islands. She noted that the line of the Antarctic Convergence runs in between the two groups of islands. Bonner (1968) concurred with King's differentiation. Although he considered that the differences between the two taxa rated recognition at the specific level, he did not revise the nomenclature. In a taxonomic review of the genus *Arctocephalus*, Repenning, Peterson and Hubbs (1971) distinguished between these two taxa at the specific level as *A. gazella* (Kerguelen fur seal) from islands south of the Antarctic Convergence and *A. tropicalis* (Amsterdam Island fur seal) from islands north of the Convergence. No important changes in nomenclature have been made since then, although Erickson and Hofman (1974) wondered if the differences between the two taxa warranted specific recognition. The epithet *pusillus* was applied incorrectly to fur seals at Gough by some earlier authors (e.g., Elliott, 1953).

Repenning, Peterson and Hubbs (1971) noted that no vernacular name had been regularly applied to *A. tropicalis*. They proposed the name "Amsterdam Island fur seal" for it because, firstly, the type specimen was believed to have been collected on or near that island, and secondly, it was there that the most detailed study of the species had been made (Paulian, 1964). The vernacular names "Subantarctic fur seal" and "Kerguelen fur seal" have also been used by Rice and Scheffer (1968). The former is only partly justified because, although this seal breeds on sub-Antarctic islands in the Atlantic and Indian Oceans rather than those south of the Antarctic Convergence, it does not occur on sub-Antarctic islands in the Pacific Ocean, where it is replaced by the New Zealand fur seal, *A. forsteri*. The vernacular name Kerguelen fur seal should only be used for *A. gazella*, which occurs on islands south of the Antarctic Convergence, and Kerguelen which lies on the Convergence. Because taxonomical usage for the genus *Arctocephalus* in this report follows that of Repenning, Peterson and Hubbs (1971), their vernacular name for *A. tropicalis* is also used.

One of the most distinguishing external features of the Amsterdam Island fur seal is the conspicuous cream-coloured chest, throat, and face of the bulls contrasting with their black head, which is topped with a crest that can be raised when the animal is excited. The colour of the females and immatures is less striking, although a yellowish colour occurs on the chest, throat and face of these animals.

Adult males attain a standard length of about 180 cm and weigh about 165 kg; females reach 145 cm and 55 kg (Paulian, 1964). At birth, the average length and weight of male pups is 63 cm and 4.9 kg, respectively. Pups are born with a black coat which is shed by four months of age.

Cranial and dental characteristics of *A. tropicalis* have been considered by Rand (1956), King (1959), Paulian (1964) and Repenning, Peterson and Hubbs (1971). The last authors considered that *A. tropicalis* was closely related to *A. australis* from South America, and differed from it primarily in its simplified dentition and distinctive pelage. Differences between *A. tropicalis* and *A. gazella* have been discussed by King (1959) and Bonner (1968). On the basis of these differences, King (1959) was able to recognise a specimen of *A. gazella* from Marion Island. Condy (1975) also recognised a second species of *Arctocephalus* on Marion. Consequently it is possible that both species were included in Rand's (1959) report on fur seals at Marion.

413

DISTRIBUTION AND STOCK IDENTIFICATION

A. tropicalis is known to breed on Gough (Swales, 1956), New Amsterdam (Paulian, 1964), Saint Paul (Segonzac, 1972), Prince Edward (de Villiers and Ross, 1976), and Marion (Rand, 1956) Islands.

It has been recorded as breeding on Nightingale (Wace and Holdgate, 1976) and Inaccessible (Elliott, 1953) Islands. At Tristan da Cunha five fur seal pups were recorded in the colony at Cave Point on the southwest coast in 1962 when the islanders were in England, but no pups were seen there in 1967/68 (Wace and Holdgate, 1976). No pups were seen among 30 fur seals at Cave Point on 16 December 1973 (M.E. Richardson, *in litt.*). One pup was sighted in December 1975 (van Ryssen, 1976).

The Crozet Archipelago has been included in its breeding range by, for example, Rand (1956) and Scheffer (1958), but a recent report by Despin, Mougin and Segonzac (1972) indicates that although fur seals bred there last century, only stragglers identified as *A. tropicalis* have been reported since 1962. Despin, Mougin and Segonzac attribute the error made by Rand and Scheffer to misinterpretation of a complicated sentence in French, concerning both fur seals and elephant seals at the Crozet Archipelago written by Aubert de la Rüe (1950).

A single *A. tropicalis* was reported from Macquarie Island by Csordas (1962) who suggested that this species may have been the original fur seal there. Eight stragglers have been reported from the South African coast since 1966 (Nel, 1971; G.J.B. Ross, P.B. Best and P.D. Shaughnessy, unpubl. obs.).

The Amsterdam Island fur seal can be considered as consisting of three main populations which occur at the Tristan da Cunha — Gough group, at the Prince Edward Islands, and at New Amsterdam and St. Paul Islands. No attempts have been made to differentiate between these populations.

Series of blood samples from these seals have been collected at Marion Island (by Dr P.R. Condy) and at Gough Island (by the author). I plan to compare by electrophoresis the transferrins, haptoglobins and other proteins of these seals with those of Australasian fur seals (Shaughnessy, 1970) and a large series of *A. p. pusillus.*

MIGRATIONS

A. tropicalis is not reported to be migratory. Some long movements have been reported, namely the single male sighted at Macquarie Island in 1959 (Csordas, 1962) and a single animal recorded by Nel (1971) from the South African coast near Port Elizabeth (a juvenile female that came ashore in 1966). Another seven Amsterdam Island fur seals have been recorded on the South African coast since 1966, four adult and one juvenile male and two adult females.

More information on movements of *A. tropicalis* may come from tagging studies. At Marion Island, by April 1975, 67 fur seals had been tagged on the fore-flipper with monel metal tags bearing the inscription RSA, MARION and a unique number. At Gough Island, by November 1975, 30 fur seals had been given similar tags bearing the inscription RSA, GOUGH and a unique number. In November 1973, 74 fur seals were given tags marked GUANO ISLANDS CAPE TOWN (Condy and Bester, 1975; Shaughnessy, 1975). At Amsterdam Island seals were tagged on the external ear with "Identix-Hauptner" marks (Tollu, 1974). In 1972, 755 animals were tagged and in January 1973, 482 pups were tagged.

Vital parameters

CENSUS

Attempts to census Amsterdam Island fur seals have been made on several islands by direct counting.

For Gough Island, Swales (1956) making allowance for animals absent from beaches during counting, estimated that the population in the 1955/56 breeding season consisted of 1 645 adult bulls, 5 210 immature males and females, 3 295 mature females and 2 754 pups, a total of almost 13 000 animals. He estimated that the population at Gough had been increasing at the rate of 8 % annually from a nucleus of 300 animals in 1892. Swales counted 394 seals on some east coast beaches of Gough Island in 1955/56. On the same beaches, Shaughnessy (1975) counted 787 seals in October and November 1973. Although the two counts are not strictly comparable, the large difference between them suggests that an increase in population size on Gough may have occurred since 1955.

Swales (1956) believed that there were another 600 seals on nearby Nightingale and Inaccessible Islands, most of them on the latter island. A small number of seals has also been recorded from Tristan da Cunha, referred to above, under Distribution.

On Marion Island, Rand (1956) counted fur seals during the 1951/52 breeding season and estimated the population at not more than 500 animals. In 1972 and 1973, de Villiers and Ross (1976) estimated from counts that at least 1 600 fur seals were on Marion Island, an increase of at least threefold in 20 years. Another 1 100 fur seals were estimated to be on Prince Edward Island. A more recent estimate for Marion Island is 3 500 animals, made by P.R. Condy (Anon., 1974).

On New Amsterdam Island, Paulian (1964) observed 500 pups and 1 818 older animals in March 1956, while in March 1970, Segonzac (1972) observed 1 498 pups and another 3 370 animals. Segonzac believed that methods used for counting pups were identical in both studies, indicating that a threefold increase in the population had occurred in 14 years. In January 1973, Tollu (1974) used the mark-recapture method to estimate the pup population size (at 2 months of age) at the largest colony (Plateau de la Recherche) at 950. He then estimated that another 700 pups

occurred on the island, and estimated the total population at 4 600 animals. As Tollu pointed out, this is an underestimate as it does not allow for mortality of pups in their first 2 months nor for non-reproductive females. Neither does it allow for sub-adult males.

On neighbouring St. Paul Island, Segonzac (1972) counted 350 adults in February 1970 and the first pups (3) known to have been born there. Another 7 pups were seen in 1971.

Despite the scarcity of recent data on population sizes, we must agree with Laws (1973) that *A. tropicalis* "appears to be thriving after near extinction last century", since the population figures given above total more than 23 400 animals.

RATES

Birth Rates, Reproduction Potential

Data on sex ratio at birth are provided by Paulian (1964) for New Amsterdam Island: of 129 pups examined (newborn or less than 8 days old) only 54 (41.9 %) were male.

Paulian (1964) estimated the harem size in 1955 to be between 6 and 8 females with a maximum of 14, while Tollu (1974) stated that the harem size there in 1971 and 1972 was 7 to 9 with a maximum of 20. Tollu attributed the change in harem size to the increase in the population and referred to Captain Péron's observation at St. Paul Island of harem sizes of between 20 and 30 females in 1792-5 before harvesting.

The pupping season extends from 25 November to 1 January according to Paulian (1964) and between mid-November and mid-December according to Tollu (1974). Pups are born between several hours and several days after the females arrive ashore (Tollu, 1974). The gestation period is 360 days. The period of delayed implantation was estimated as 5 months by Tollu (1974) and can be estimated as 3-4 months from Rand's (1956) data. Nursing continues until mid-October (Tollu, 1974) when the pups would average 10 months of age. Paulian (1964) stated that weaning occurs at 7 months.

Natural Mortality Rates

Paulian (1964) recorded the mortality rate at birth as 0.9 % among more than 300 births at New Amsterdam Island. The mortality rate of pups aged between 1 and 3 weeks at the colony at Plateau de la Recherche was 63 %. Most deaths were attributed to storms washing pups away. At two other colonies (Goodyear and d'Entrecasteaux) pups were able to move further inland and the mortality rate during this period was much lower, being 32 %. From 3 weeks to 5 months of age, the mortality rate was estimated to be very small (1 to 2 %). For all three colonies, Paulian estimated that mortality to age 5 months averaged 47 %. However, he considered that the pup mortality rates for the 1955/56 season were higher than normal because good weather at the beginning of the breeding season had induced bulls to take up territories closer to the water's edge than usual.

Between weaning (at 7 months) and 2 years, Paulian (1964) estimated that the mortality rate was of the order of 40-50 %. No estimates of mortality rates are available for older animals.

Parasites of *A. tropicalis* were briefly described by Paulian (1964). Of 13 animals that were dissected, 10 contained nematodes in their stomachs and 11 had cestode larvae in their blubber. Neither cestodes nor acanthocephalans were found in their intestines. Paulian did not consider parasites to be an important factor in the mortality of these seals.

Harvesting Rates

The most recent harvest of fur seals at Marion Island was in 1921 when 785 were taken (Rand, 1956). Since Rand estimated the population on Marion in 1951/52 at not more than 500 animals, it seems that the sealers took a large proportion of the population in 1921. Rand (1956) discussed the prospects for sealing at Marion Island, but concluded that protection would be more pertinent than exploitation. Seals at Marion and Prince Edward Islands are now protected, by the Minister of Transport, under the Sea Birds and Seals Protection Act, 1973 of the Republic of South Africa. No concessions to harvest seals there have been granted under the Act, although seals have been collected at Marion Island since 1972 for scientific purposes.

Gough and Tristan da Cunha Islands form part of the British Protectorate of St. Helena. Marine mammals at Gough and the Tristan Islands are protected under the Tristan da Cunha Conservation Ordinance, 1976, which is included as an appendix in Wace and Holdgate (1976). The fishing company that has the concession to take seals in the Tristan – Gough group has taken a few hundred animals under permit from the Tristan administration (Wace and Holdgate, 1976). About 400 immature seals per year were taken on average illegally from Gough in the early 1950's, according to Swales (1956). That harvest, from a population of 2 750 pups, represented a sealing rate of 15 % of the number of pups born. Swales considered that fur seals at Gough Island could be harvested on a sustainable yield basis. He estimated that 500 2- and 3-year-old seals could be taken in the 1956/57 summer between October and February, followed by 440 in 1957/58. The harvest could then be increased by 8 % annually, this being the rate at which he estimated the population had been increasing since harvesting ceased in the 1890's. Holdgate (1957) and Wace and Holdgate (1976) also considered that fur seals at Gough could be harvested on a sustainable yield basis.

No harvesting in recent years on New Amsterdam or St. Paul was reported by Paulian (1964) or Segonzac (1972). Seals on these islands (together with those on the Crozet Archipelago and parts of Kerguelen) were protected in 1924 by the French Chamber of Deputies (King, 1959). However, Paulian (1964) reported that small numbers of seals were taken annually from New Amsterdam by expedition members and others.

Trend in Abundance (Historical Development)

Indiscriminate and uncontrolled sealing on sub-Antarctic islands during the 18th and 19th centuries soon reduced the size of the seal populations. The reduction of the several populations of *A. tropicalis* will be discussed briefly. Statements by various authors that fur seals did not occur on the island they visited should not be accepted uncritically, for the fur seals have a propensity for hauling out on the rugged western coasts of sub-Antarctic islands (discussed by Paulian (1964) and by Segonzac (1972)), while human visitors tend to land on the protected eastern side. Further, a small number of fur seals must be very difficult to find on boulder-strewn beaches.

The earliest known catch of fur seals at Gough Island was of 1 100 seals taken in 1811 (Swales, 1956). Morrell (1832) visited the island in November 1829 and saw very few seals. A total of only 396 fur seals was taken from Gough in a period of about 18 months between 1887 and 1889 by men from the *Francis Allyn* (Verrill, 1895). The seals were virtually undisturbed from 1892 (when few were reported) until the early 1950's when a small number of immature animals (up to 400 annually) was taken illegally from the north and east coasts (Swales, 1956). Rand (1956) also referred to recent sealing on Gough.

Fur seals were once very common on Tristan da Cunha, but were exterminated there late last century (Swales, 1956). The Tristan Islands were first visited for sealing purposes in 1790 when 5 600 skins were taken (Allen, 1899). Swales (1956) reported that

fur seals were occasionally seen on Tristan, but considered that the presence of humans on the island prevented the population from increasing (the presence of a colony at Cave Point has been referred to above, under Distribution and Stock Identification). In 1955/56 he estimated that the population on Nightingale and Inaccessible Islands was 600 animals, with most on the latter island.

Early sealing at the Prince Edward Islands commenced at about the end of the 18th century (Rand, 1956) and several vessels were taking fur seals there by 1806 (Allen, 1899). No fur seals were seen on Marion Island by members of the Challenger Expedition in 1872. The last harvest of fur seals at the Prince Edward Islands occurred in 1921 (Rand, 1956). Unfortunately, the Cape Town-based sealing company (Irvin and Johnson) that was most active in sealing on the Prince Edward (and Crozet) Islands during the early years of this century recently informed the Government Archives in Cape Town that they had long since destroyed their sealing records.

Sealing at New Amsterdam began in the last years of the 18th century (Paulian, 1964). Perhaps the earliest catch was of 1 200 animals within a period of 10 days by the *Mercury* in 1789. Fur seals were still abundant on these islands in the 1820's, but Paulian (1964) considered that only about 100 individuals remained on the two islands at the beginning of this century, while none was seen by Aubert de la Rüe or by Jeannel in the 1930's. However, the population on New Amsterdam had recovered by 1955/56 when Paulian (1964) counted a total of 2 318 animals, and estimated the population there to be between 2 550 and 2 800. Later, in 1970, the population had increased even further, when Segonzac (1972) counted 4 868 animals. Recovery on St. Paul has been much slower: only 350 animals were counted in 1970 (Segonzac, 1972).

The fur seal still existed on all islands of the Crozet Archipelago up to about 1825, but had disappeared completely by about 1850 (Despin, Mougin and Segonzac, 1972; Derenne *et al.*, 1976). The former authors argue from

417

the catch figures that the fur seal was not abundant on the Crozets before commercial exploitation commenced. When Fanning rediscovered the Crozets in 1805, he estimated that an abundance of fur seals occurred on the islands, but Despin, Mougin and Segonzac, 1972 considered this to be imprecise and contrary to estimates made by sealers who followed only a few years later.

Fur seals were not recorded from the Crozets again until 1962, and had not begun to recolonise the archipelago by 1971 (Despin, Mougin and Segonzac, 1972).

Trophic relationships

FOOD

Rand (1956) examined an undisclosed number of stomachs of fur seals collected at the colony on Marion Island and reported that fish (Nototheniidae), cephalopods and euphausiids formed the bulk of the food. 50 % of the females had eaten cephalopods.

At New Amsterdam Paulian (1964) found that squid was present in 11 of the 12 stomachs he examined and penguin remains were present in 2 stomachs. No stomachs contained fish remains or euphausiids. Paulian was puzzled by the absence of fish in the stomachs, as fish were numerous at New Amsterdam and had been reported as important food items of *A. tropicalis* at Marion.

According to Tollu (1974), the main food of fur seals at New Amsterdam between August and April is rockhopper penguins, *Eudyptes chrysocome*. For the remainder of the year they consume mainly squid, fish (especially tazards, *Thyristes atun*) and octopus. Although lobster (*Jasus paulensis*) are common at the island, they are not an important food item. Beurois (1975) noted that the seals concentrate on squid although fish are abundant

at the island.

Stones were found in stomachs of a small number of specimens from New Amsterdam and Marion (Paulian, 1964; Rand, 1956).

Fish and lobster are caught commercially at New Amsterdam (Paulian, 1964; Beurois, 1975) and crawfish at the Tristan – Gough group. Food habits of the fur seal at Gough have not been reported. Since fish and lobster do not seem to be an important food item of the fur seals at New Amsterdam, direct competition between fur seals and commercial fishing operations would seem to be unimportant, unless the fur seals at Gough feed on crawfish (*Jasus tristani*).

SPECIES AND ITS ECOSYSTEM

Both Paulian (1964) and Segonzac (1972) have noted that *A. tropicalis* (and *A. gazella*) prefer boulder strewn beaches on the west coasts of islands. Paulian first suggested that it might be necessary for fur seals to haul out on the exposed side of islands in order to thermoregulate satisfactorily. His second suggestion was favoured by Segonzac, namely that the present populations have grown from remnants left on the most inaccessible regions of the islands after sealing activity had ceased. However, Marsallon (1969) disagreed with these authors and considered that fur seals at New Amsterdam preferred shores exposed to maximum sunshine.

Suspected predators of *A. tropicalis* include sharks and the killer whale (*Orcinus orca*). Although Paulian (1964) noted that the shark *Isurus glaucus* occurred at New Amsterdam, he found no evidence that it preyed on seals. Killer whales at New Amsterdam were assumed to prey on the fur seals (Paulian, 1964), but no direct observations supporting that assumption were made. However, he did note that fur seals were more common ashore and in the breakers when killer whales were present.

Killer whales were also recorded at the

Prince Edward Islands by van Zinderen Bakker (1967). He noted that their activity increased during the seals's pupping season, but did not specify whether he was referring to elephant seals or fur seals.

Since there are no vertebrate scavengers at New Amsterdam (Paulian, 1964), foetal membranes remain in the colony. On the other islands in the range of *A. tropicalis* there are skuas (*Stercorarius skua*), and sheathbills (*Chionis minor*) occur on the Prince Edward Islands (Winterbottom, 1971). Presumably, these birds scavenge in the seal colonies, and probably also harass young pups.

Although rockhopper penguins constitute part of the diet of fur seals at New Amsterdam Island, they exhibit little fear of the fur seals on land (Paulian, 1964). Similarly, at Gough Island, I observed the apparent disregard of rockhopper penguins for fur seals on land.

Southern elephant seals (*Mirounga leonina*) occur on the same islands as *A. tropicalis*. On New Amsterdam Island, elephant seals tend to frequent sandy beaches or beaches on the more protected north coast. Consequently, the two species have little contact with each other there (Paulian, 1964). On the few occasions that I saw elephant seals on the same beach as fur seals at Gough Island, the two groups kept well apart. However, as the population size of southern fur seals increases, competition with elephant seals for space for breeding and hauling-out may become problematical.

Other factors

ANIMALS TAKEN FOR DISPLAY

No live Amsterdam Island fur seals have been taken from the Prince Edward Islands or from Gough Island (where South Africa maintains a weather station) for display purposes since the early 1960's. Requests for the collection of fur seals (and other animals) for display or research from the Prince Edward Islands are considered by a specialist panel on the fauna of Antarctica and the sub-Antarctic islands appointed by the South African Scientific Committee for Antarctic Research. Paulian (1964) noted that a small number of young animals was sent to zoos each year from New Amsterdam Island. Three *A. tropicalis* that came ashore on the South African coast near Port Elizabeth were displayed at the Port Elizabeth Oceanarium along with *A. p. pusillus* (G.J.B. Ross, pers. comm.). A fourth is currently on display.

CURRENT STUDIES

The biology of *A. tropicalis* at Marion and Gough Islands is currently being studied by P.R. Condy and M.N. Bester from the Mammal Research Institute, University of Pretoria, South Africa. Brief notes on Condy's work were published recently (Anon., 1974). B. Tollu of the Muséum National d'Histoire Naturelle, Paris, recently studied fur seals at French sub-Antarctic islands (Tollu, 1974).

References

ALLEN, J.A., Fur-seal hunting in the Southern Hemisphere. *In* The fur-seals and fur-seal islands of the North Pacific Ocean, edited by D.S. Jordan, Washington, D.C., Government Printing Office, Part 3:307-19. 1899

AUBERT DE LA RÜE, E., Notes sur les îles Crozet. *Bull. Mus. Natl Hist. Nat.*, 22(2):197-203. 1950

BONNER, W.N., The fur seal of South Georgia. *Sci. Rep. Br. Antarct. Surv.*, (56):1-81. 1968

BEUROIS, J., Etude écologique et halieutique des fonds de pêche et des espèces d'intérêt commercial (langoustes et poissons) des îles Saint-Paul et Amsterdam (océan Indien). *CNFRA (Com. Natl Fr. Rech. Antarct.)*, 37:1-91. 1975

CONDY, P.R., Mammal research on the Prince Edward
1975   Islands. *In* Die Soogdiernavorsings-instituut
        1966-1975. *Publ. Univ. Pretoria (Nuwe Reeks)*,
        97:56-9.

CONDY, P.R. and M.N. BESTER, Notes on the tagging of
1975   seals on Marion and Gough Islands. *S. Afr. J.*
        Antarct. Res., 5:45-7.

CSORDAS, S.E., The Kerguelen fur seal on Macquarie
1962   Island. *Vict. Nat.*, 79:226-9.

DERENNE, P. *et al.*, Les oiseaux de l'île aux Cochons,
1976   archipel Crozet. *CNFRA (Com. Natl Fr. Rech.*
        Antarct.), 40:107-48.

DESPIN, B., J.L. MOUGIN and M. SEGONZAC, Oiseaux et
1972   mammifères de l'île de l'Est, archipel Crozet
        (47°25'S, 52°12'E). *CNFRA (Com. Natl Fr.*
        Rech. Antarct.), 31:1-106.

DE VILLIERS, A.F. and G.J.B. ROSS, Notes on numbers
1976   and distribution of fur seals, *Arctocephalus*
        tropicalis (Gray), on Marion and Prince Ed-
        ward Islands, Southern Ocean. *J. Mammal.*,
        57:595-600.

ELLIOTT, H.F.I., The fauna of Tristan da Cunha. *Oryx*,
1953   2:41-53.

ERICKSON, A.W. and R.J. HOFMAN, Antarctic seals. *In*
1974   Antarctic mammals, edited by V.C. Bushnell.
        Antarct. Map Folio Ser., 18:4-13.

HOLDGATE, M.W., Gough Island – a possible sanctua-
1957   ry. *Oryx*, 4:168-76.

KING, J.E., The northern and southern populations of
1959   Arctocephalus gazella. *Mammalia*, 23:19-40.

–, A note on the specific name of the Kerguelen fur
1959a   seal. *Mammalia*, 23:381.

LAWS, R.M., The current status of seals in the Southern
1973   Hemisphere. *IUCN Publ. (New Ser.) Suppl.*
        Pap., (39):144-61.

MARSALLON, A., Note sur l'otarie de l'île Amsterdam.
1969   *Sci. Nat., Paris*, 96:2-7.

MORRELL, B., A narrative of four voyages, to the South
1832   Sea, North and South Pacific Ocean, Chinese
        Sea, Ethiopic and southern Atlantic Ocean,
        Indian and Antarctic Ocean; from the year
        1822 to 1831. New York, J. and J. Harper.

NEL, J.A.J., Order Pinnipedia – Part 9. *In* The mam-
1971   mals of Africa – an identification manual,
        edited by J. Meester and H.W. Setzer. Wash-
        ington, Smithsonian Institution Press.

PAULIAN, P., Note préliminaire sur la systématique de
1957   l'otarie de l'île Amsterdam. *Mammalia*,
        21:9-14.

–, Contribution à l'étude de l'otarie de l'île Amsterdam.
1964   *Mammalia*, 28 (Suppl. 1): 3-146.

RAND, R.W., Notes on the Marion Island fur seal. *Proc.*
1956   *Zool. Soc. Lond.*, 126:65-82.

REPENNING, C.A., R.S. PETERSON and C.L. HUBBS, Con-
1971   tributions to the systematics of the southern
        fur seals, with particular reference to the Juan
        Fernández and Guadalupe species. *In* Ant-
        arctic Pinnipedia, edited by W.H. Burt. *An-
        tarct. Res. Ser.*, 18:1-34.

RICE, D.W. and V.B. SCHEFFER, A list of the marine
1968   mammals of the world. *Spec. Sci. Rep.*
        USFWS (Fish.), (579):1-6.

SCHEFFER, V.B., Seals, sea lions and walruses. Stanford,
1958   Stanford University Press, 149 p.

SEGONZAC, M., Données récentes sur la faune des îles
1972   Saint-Paul et Nouvelle-Amsterdam. *Oiseaux,*
        Rev. Fr. Orn., 42 (No. Spec.): 3-68.

SHAUGHNESSY, P.D., Serum protein variation in south-
1970   ern fur seals, *Arctocephalus* spp., in relation
        to their taxonomy. *Aust. J. Zool.*, 18:331-43.

–, Observations on the seals of Gough Island. *S. Afr. J.*
1975   *Antarct. Res.*, 5:42-4.

SWALES, M.K., The fur seals of Gough Island. London,
1956   Colonial Office, 13 p. (unpubl. rep.).

TOLLU, B., L'otarie de l'île Amsterdam *Arctocephalus*
1974   *tropicalis tropicalis* (Gray 1872). Thèse de
        doctorat de troisième cycle, Université Paris-
        VII.

VAN RYSSEN, W.J., The birds of the Tristan da Cunha
1976   group and Gough Island. Cape Town, Uni-
        versity of Cape Town, 31 p.

VAN ZINDEREN BAKKER, E.M., Jr., Observations on ani-
1967   mal life on Marion and Prince Edward Is-
        lands. *S. Afr. J. Sci.*, 63:242-6.

VERRILL, G.E., On some birds and eggs collected by Mr.
1895   Geo Comer at Gough Island, Kerguelen Island, and the island of South Georgia, with extracts from his notes, including a meteorological record for about six months at Gough Island. *Trans. Conn. Acad. Arts Sci.*, 9:430-78.

WACE, N.M. and M.W. HOLDGATE, Man and nature in
1976   the Tristan da Cunha Islands. *IUCN Monogr.*, (6):1-114.

WINTERBOTTOM, J.M., The position of Marion Island in
1971   the sub-Antarctic fauna. *In* Marion and Prince Edward Islands, edited by E.M. van Zinderen Bakker *et al.*, Cape Town, A.A. Balkema, pp. 241-8.

Anon., Seals of the Antarctic. *Afr. Wildl.*, 28:12-6.
1974

THE STATUS OF THE ANTARCTIC FUR SEAL, *ARCTOCEPHALUS GAZELLA*

W.N. Bonner

Abstract

The Antarctic fur seal, *Arctocephalus gazella*, is found on islands south of the Antarctic Convergence and north of about 60°S latitude: South Georgia, with a major breeding population of about 369 000, and smaller groups, whose state is not well known, at the South Shetland, South Orkney and South Sandwich Islands, Bouvet Island, the Kerguelen Islands, Heard Island and McDonald Island. The species can be identified by the arrangement and form of the postcanine teeth. Adult males and females average lengths and weights of 184.3 cm and 140.4 kg, and 127.9 cm and 38.2 kg, respectively. The movements and vital parameters of the species are mostly unknown, though there is data from which to calculate the population dynamics of the breeding females at South Georgia.

The Antarctic fur seal is now recovering from earlier uncontrolled hunting and shows promise of attaining its former abundance: the rapidly expanding stock centred on South Georgia may increase to perhaps 1-2 million animals, and Kerguelen may show similar growth; a substantial population (perhaps 500 000) might develop at the South Shetland, but elsewhere in the Atlantic sector, only small colonies of some tens of thousands will develop. Although this fur seal yields a high quality pelt competitively equal with that of the northern fur seal, *Callorhinus ursinus*, there is currently no commercial harvest of the species; controlled exploitation based on scientific studies now in preparation would not endanger stocks, though lack of segregation of age-classes would increase harvest costs. The Antarctic fur seal is protected by law over most of its range. Krill, *Euphausia superba*, forms the staple diet of the species at South Georgia; increased availability of this food due to large reductions of southern baleen whale stocks may be connected with the rapid increase of fur seals. Conversely, major expansion of present small-scale commercial krill fishing is a potentially serious threat to Antarctic pinnipeds and emphaizes the necessity for international control beforehand. `

Résumé

L'otarie à fourrure de l'Antarctique, *Arctocephalus gazella*, vit dans les îles au sud de la convergence de l'Antarctique et, au nord, jusqu'à environ 60°S. On a en Géorgie du sud une grosse population de reproducteurs d'environ 369 000 animaux, et des groupes plus petits dont on connaît mal l'état dans les îles Shetland du sud, les Orcades du sud, les îles Sandwich du sud, l'île Bouvet, les Kerguelen, l'île de Heard et l'île McDonald. L'espèce peut être identifiée par l'implantation et la forme des dents post-canines. Les mâles et les femelles

423

adultes ont une longueur et un poids moyens de 184,3 cm et 140,4 kg et 127,9 cm et 38,2 kg, respectivement.

On ne connaît pratiquement rien des déplacements et des paramètres biologiques de cette espèce encore qu'il existe des données permettant de calculer la dynamique de la population de femelles reproductrices en Géorgie du sud.

On constate une reprise de la population de l'otarie à fourrure après une période d'exploitation incontrôlée. L'espèce semble devoir redevenir aussi nombreuse que dans le passé; le stock en expansion rapide vivant autour de la Géorgie du sud pourrait atteindre un ou deux millions d'animaux et l'augmentation aux Kerguelen pourrait être du même ordre. Une population importante (peut-être 500 000 individus) pourrait se développer aux Shetland du sud mais dans le reste du secteur atlantique, seules se développeront de petites colonies de quelques dizaines de milliers d'animaux. Bien que cette otarie à fourrure fournisse une très belle peau qui peut concurrencer, sur le plan de la qualité, celle de *Callorhinus ursinus*, l'espèce ne fait actuellement l'objet d'aucune exploitation commerciale. Une exploitation contrôlée, fondée sur les études scientifiques en cours ne mettrait pas les stocks en danger; cependant, l'absence de ségrégation des classes d'âge accroîtrait les coûts d'exploitation. L'otarie à fourrure de l'Antarctique est protégée par la législation sur presque toute son aire géographique. Le krill (*Euphasia superba*) constitue le principal aliment de l'espèce en Géorgie du sud. Les disponibilités de krill, accrues par suite de la réduction considérable des stocks méridionaux de mysticètes, pourraient être en rapport avec l'augmentation rapide des otaries à fourrure. Par contre, une expansion considérable de la pêche commerciale du krill, actuellement pratiquée à petite échelle, constitue une grave menace potentielle pour les pinnipèdes de l'Antarctique et souligne la nécessité d'un contrôle international préalable.

Extracto

El lobo marino del Antártico, *Arctocephalus gazella*, se encuentra en islas situadas al sur de la Convergencia Antártica y al norte de los 60° de latitud sur: hay una importante población de reproductores, de unos 369 000 animales en Georgia del Sur, y grupos menores, cuyo estado no se conoce bien, en la Shetland del Sur, las Orcadas del Sur y las Sandwich del Sur, la Isla Bouvet, las Islas Kerguelen, la Isla Heard y la Isla McDonald. Es posible identificar esta especie por la disposición y forma de los dientes postcaninos. La longitud y peso medios de los machos y hembras adultos son respectivamente 184,3 cm y 140,4 kg y 127,9 cm y 38,2 kg. Los movimientos y los parámetros vitales de esta especie son en su mayor parte desconocidos aunque se dispone de datos para calcular la dinámica de población de las hembras reproductoras de Georgia del Sur.

A. gazella se está recuperando después de una explotación incontrolada y parece que podrá retornar a su abundancia anterior: la población de Georgia del Sur, que está aumentando rápidamente, podría llegar quizás a 1-2 millones de animales, y la de las Kerguelen podría aumentar en forma similar; en las Islas Shetland del Sur podría surgir una población importante (quizás de 500 000 animales), pero en el resto del sector del Atlántico sólo se formarán pequeñas colonias de algunas decenas de millares. Aunque *A. gazella* produce pieles de gran calidad, que pueden competir con las del oso marino septentrional *Callorhinus ursinus*, en la actualidad no se explota comercialmente esta especie: una explotación controlada basada en los estudios científicos actualmente en preparación no representaría una amenaza para las poblaciones, aunque la ausencia de segregación entre las diversas clases de edad aumentaría los costos de explotación. *A. gazella* está protegido por la ley en la mayor parte de su zona de distribución. El alimento principal de *A. gazella* en Georgia del Sur es el krill, *Euphausia superba*; el aumento de las disponibilidades de esta especie, debido a la notable disminución de las poblaciones de ballenas de barbas del sur, podría ser una de las causas del rápido aumento del número de lobos marinos. Por otro lado, la posibilidad de que aumente en grado importante la explotación comercial del krill, que actualmente se hace a pequeña escala, representa una grave amenaza para los pinnípedos del Antártico y pone de relieve la necesidad de un control preventivo internacional.

W.N. Bonner
Life Sciences Division, British Antarctic Survey, Madingley Road, Cambridge CB3OET, England

Nomenclature

All the fur seals that normally breed on islands south of the Antarctic Convergence can be referred to a single species *Arctocephalus gazella* (Peters, 1875). Bonner (1968) discussed the confusion surrounding the taxonomic status of this species but unfortunately opted to accept King's (1959 and 1959a) decision to regard *A. gazella* as conspecific with *A. tropicalis*, and to adopt the latter name on grounds of priority, the two populations being *A. tropicalis tropicalis*, north of the Antarctic Convergence, and *A. t. gazella* south of it. It was left to Repenning, Peterson and Hubbs (1971) to demonstrate conclusively that the Antarctic fur seals constitute a single valid species, *A. gazella*.

Identification

Adult males:
  Nose to tail length:
  172-197 cm ($\bar{x}$ 184.3, SD 8.46, n 15)
  Weight: 126-160 kg
    ($\bar{x}$ 140.4, SD 14.2, n 4)

Adult females:
  Nose to tail length:
  113-139 cm ($\bar{x}$ 127.9, SD 7.87, n 21)
  Weight: 30-51 kg
    ($\bar{x}$ 38.2, SD 5.9, n 17)

The coat coloration has been fully described by Bonner (1968). In the cow the back and sides are grey to slightly brownish, almost russet; the throat and breast are creamy. The bull is similar but the great development of the mane showing many white hairs gives it a very grizzled appearance. There is no variation in colour between the chest and the back of the neck.

A. gazella is a medium-sized fur seal. It may be readily distinguished from the only other member of the genus to share the same hauling grounds, *A. tropicalis*, by the conspicuous nicotine-yellow chest of the latter. It is more difficult to separate it from *A. australis*, which approaches the range of *A. gazella* in South America and the Falkland Islands, though *A. australis* has been described as more timid than *A. gazella*.

The species is instantly recognisable from a skull if post-canine teeth are present. The maxillary tooth rows diverge posteriorly on either side of a wide palate; there are diastemata between the 4th and 5th, and 5th and 6th upper post-canines and the very small unicuspid teeth show conspicuous abrasion surfaces (usually black) on the medial side.

DISTRIBUTION AND STATUS OF STOCKS

The Antarctic fur seal is found on islands south of the Antarctic Convergence and north of about 60°S latitude. Major breeding populations are found at South Georgia, the South Sandwich Islands and Bouvetøya; smaller

425

groups are found at the South Shetland Islands, the South Orkney Islands, Îles Kerguelen and Heard Island.

Payne (1977) has recently reviewed the population increase at South Georgia. The seals mostly occur at the north-west extremity of the main island and on some of the smaller islands to the west, notably Bird Island. In the 1930's the total population was probably of the order of 100 animals. In 1957 Bonner (1968) calculated that it had increased to about 15 000 and recent research indicates a population of about 369 000 (based on an annual pup production of 90 000 in 1975).

In the South Sandwich Islands about 400 fur seals including some pups were found on a beach at Visokoi Island in 1960 (O'Gorman, 1961) and two years later 800-900 were seen at the same place and ten pups at Saunders Island (Holdgate, 1963). Sivertsen (1954) estimated that at Bouvetøya there was a breeding stock of 1 000-1 200 in 1927-29. Holdgate, Tilbrook and Vaughan (1968) recorded about 500 seals with an estimated pup production of 150-180 in 1964.

Recent reports of fur seals in the South Shetland Islands date from 1958 when O'Gorman (1961) reported 42 seals at Livingstone Island; the following year two pups were born at Cape Shireff. Aguayo and Torres (1968) recorded 200 fur seals on Livingstone Island, and 300 on Elephant, Cornwallis and Clarence Islands in 1966. Breeding occurred on Elephant and Livingstone Islands. Erickson *et al.* (1971) counted 204 on the northwest coast of King George Island in 1970. A count in 1971 at Cape Shireff gave a total of 201 fur seals, including 27 pups (Laws, 1973a).

The first 20th century sighting of a fur seal in the South Orkney Islands was at Signy Island in 1947 (Laws, 1973). Breeding was first recorded at Meier Point, Coronation Island in 1955 and Michelson Island in 1956 (Øritsland, 1960) and at Signy Island in 1976/77 (British Antarctic Survey, unpublished records). At least 61 pups were born in the South Orkneys in 1971. The summer population however is mainly composed of male seals, and probably consists of non-breeders or spent breeders from South Georgia. It is now likely to be well over 3 000, as more than 2 000 were recorded at Signy Island alone in 1976/77 (British Antarctic Survey, unpublished records).

Îles Kerguelen were at one time an important breeding station but the status of the species there today is doubtful. The first record there this century appears to be that of a single adult male in 1951 (Paulian, 1952). Budd and Downes (1969), reviewing the situation, could find no evidence of breeding, and suggest that the increase in sightings (up to 143 in 1967) might reflect wider searching by observers in recent years.

The same authors record increased sightings of fur seals at Heard Island. In 1963 there were up to 500, including two suckling pups and by 1969 numbers had increased to 3 000 (Budd, 1970). Two years later he confirmed the existence of breeding fur seals at McDonald Island, some 38 km west of Heard Island (Budd, 1972).

It is possible that *A. gazella* was once the fur seal inhabiting Macquarie Island (Csordas and Ingham, 1965; Falla, 1962), though the position of the island north of the Antarctic Convergence makes *A. tropicalis* a more likely candidate for this role. *A. forsteri* has colonised the island in this century following the extermination of the indigenous seals by hunters in the nineteenth century.

Antarctic fur seals leave their breeding grounds in the autumn, but we do not know where they go to feed in the winter, nor whether there is a directional migration or simply a dispersion. The great majority of sightings away from known breeding grounds are of young males, and these do appear to be more mobile. However, the establishment of new colonies away from traditional breeding grounds is certain evidence that females occasionally disperse to new localities. A colony of about 200 *A. gazella* breed sympatrically with a much larger group of *A. tropicalis* at Marion Island.

Reliable figures for the status of the species are available only from South Georgia, where the vast majority of the seals occur. At

THE ANTARCTIC FUR SEAL

South Georgia, the South Shetlands and the South Orkneys, the evidence is that the seals are increasing in numbers and extending their range (Bonner, 1964, 1968; Laws, 1973; Payne, 1977). There is no firm evidence available from the South Sandwich Islands, and sightings from Bouvetøya indicate a decline, but neither these localities nor the South Orkney Islands appear to have supported a large stock of fur seals before exploitation by nineteenth century sealers began. This may be because conditions are not suitable for breeding, either because of pack ice (Bonner, 1968) or lack of protected beaches.

At Kerguelen the status is also unknown. Substantial numbers of breeding seals may exist, possibly on the west coast, and these may be the source of the non-breeding seals seen at Heard Island. The existence of breeding fur seals at McDonald Island may also account for some of the animals at Heard. Whether the McDonald stock was a relict group which has recently expanded, or whether it represents new colonisation from elsewhere (perhaps Kerguelen?), cannot be established. The presence of a pale-coated morph at Heard (Budd, 1972), similar to those recorded at South Georgia (Bonner, 1958), may suggest a common origin. Heard Island and McDonald Island do not appear to have been important breeding stations prior to the activities of the sealers.

The general picture is of a rapidly expanding stock centred on South Georgia. If conditions remain unchanged this may be expected to continue to increase, perhaps to between one and two million animals (based on early sealers' records of abundance). The South Georgia stock has probably supplied recruits to other islands of the Scotia Arc (Bonner, 1964) and a substantial population (perhaps around half a million) might develop at the South Shetlands; elsewhere in the Atlantic sector only small colonies (some tens of thousands) will develop. In the Indian Ocean sector Kerguelen may eventually show a similar development to South Georgia, though the situation may be complicated if the stock of *A. tropicalis* at Îles Crozet and Île Amsterdam increases concurrently. The original status of fur seals at Kerguelen is less well known than at South Georgia.

Table 1 summarises the numerical data.

VITAL PARAMETERS

There is currently (August 1977) no available life table for *A. gazella*. From inadequate samples Bonner (1968) concluded that males entered the breeding stock at age 6 or 7 though much younger ones were potent. Two-year old females were found to be virgin, but two three-year old females were pregnant. Maximum determined ages are 23 for cows and 14 for bulls (Payne, pers. commun.). However, Payne (1977) has provided many statistics from which the population dynamics of the breeding cow herd at South Georgia can be worked out. He determined an age-structure from a sample of 195 breeding cows and calculated pregnancy rates as 55 % at age 3, 75 % at age 4, 85 % at age 5 (by which time the cows were fully recruited to the breeding stock) and 90 % thereafter up to the age of 11. He assumed that the pregnancy rate would fall in older ageclasses as in *Callorhinus* (North Pacific Fur Seal Commission, 1965). An annual mortality rate of 7.9 % could be applied to all age groups from 1 year upward, though this would tend to underestimate mortality at each end of the age range. If allowance is made for falling pregnancy rates for older animals, a value of 4.6 % for annual mortality of adult cows is obtained. This gives an estimate for first-year mortality of 23.9 %.

FOOD HABITS AND RELATION TO FISHERIES

Bonner (1968) concluded that the staple diet of the fur seal at South Georgia was krill, *Euphausia superba*. Fish were occasionally eaten, most often by juvenile and non-breeding animals. Occasional squid-beaks were recovered from stomachs. There are a few records of seals feeding on birds but these are unlikely to form a significant part of the diet.

The great reduction of baleen whales in

427

Table 1. Review of stocks of *Arctocephalus gazella*

Locality	Estimated Stock size	Annual Pup Production	Reliability	Source
South Georgia	369 000 (increasing)	90,000	Good	Payne 1977
South Orkney Is.	1 000 ? (increasing)	100 ?	Poor	Laws 1973a
South Sandwich Is.	1 000 ?	200 ?	Poor	Holdgate 1963
Bouvetøya	1 000 ?	200 ?	Poor	Holdgate. Tilbrook and Vaughan 1968
South Shetland Is.	1 000	200 ?	Poor	O'Gorman 1961 Aguayo and Torres 1968 Erickson *et al.* 1970 Laws 1973a
Îles Kerguelen	?	?		
Heard Island	3 000	?		Budd and Downes 1969

Note: The estimated stock sizes have in some cases been modified from the counts or estimates given in the sources cited.

southern waters may have resulted in increased availability of food for other krill-eating species (Sladen, 1964), and Laws (1973a) connected the rapid increase of fur seals with this. Although factory fishing for stocks of sub-adult and adult *Notothenia rossii* is carried on by Russian trawlers at both Îles Kerguelen and South Georgia (where 240 000 tons were taken in one season) no complaints of the effects of fur seals on this fishing have been recorded. It may be noted here that *A. pusillus* is regarded as a serious threat by fishermen off South Africa.

A major expansion of commercial krill-fishing could have disastrous effects on fur seals (and on much other Antarctic marine life) but at the present krill-fishing is a small-scale operation only.

ECONOMIC VALUE

There is currently no commercial exploitation of *A. gazella* (though Prévost, quoted in Laws, 1973, suggests that some poaching may go on at Kerguelen). The Antarctic fur seal yields a high-quality pelt, significantly better than that from *A. pusillus* or *A. australis*, which could compete on equal terms with that of the northern fur seal, *Callorhinus ursinus*. The polygynous nature of the seals would allow the cropping of a large proportion of the young males without detriment to the reproductive potential of the stock. However, the age classes are not segregated, as they are in the northern fur seal, and the labour required to collect the skins would therefore be very much greater than in the Pribilofs. For the same reason the profit from the carcasses would be small and it would probably never be economic to collect them for processing.

CONSERVATION LEGISLATION

Fur seals are protected in South Georgia and the South Sandwich Islands by the Falkland Islands Dependencies Conservation Ordinance which prohibits the taking of native mammals except under permit. Permits can be issued for, *inter alia*, regulating the management and use of living resources, but none have so far been issued for this purpose (nor were any licences granted under the earlier Seal Fishery Ordinance to take fur seals commercially).

The taking of fur seals is banned by

Norway at Bouvetøya and by France at Kerguelen, but it would seem that enforcement is not practicable at either place. Bouvetøya however is so remote and the stock of seals there so small that organised poaching is not likely.

South of 60°S the Antarctic Treaty and the Convention for the Conservation of Antarctic Seals prohibit the taking of fur seals on land or at sea (or on pack ice), by signatory nations, which include those likely to develop the technology of sealing.

CONCLUSIONS

The Antarctic fur seal affords a happy example of a mammal, once numerous then almost exterminated by uncontrolled hunting, which is now recovering rapidly and shows every promise of regaining its former status. Existing conservation legislation is adequate and does not need to be tightened up, except perhaps at Kerguelen. Controlled exploitation would not endanger the stocks and current work on population dynamics (Payne, 1977, 1978) will provide the proper scientific basis for rational harvesting, should this ever be contemplated. A serious potential threat would be human competition for krill and, as with the Antarctic phocids, penguins, etc., this emphasises the necessity for international agreement and control before any proposed major exploitation of this key species occurs.

References

AGUAYO, A.L. and D. TORRES, A first census of Pinnipedia in the South Shetland Islands, and other observations on marine mammals. *In* Symposium on Antarctic oceanography, Santiago, Chile, organised by SCAR/SCOR/IAPO/IUBS. Cambridge, Scott Polar Research Institute, pp. 166-8.
1968

BONNER, W.N., Notes on the southern fur seal in South Georgia. *Proc. Zool. Soc. Lond.*, 130:241-52.
1958

–, Population increase in the fur seal *Arctocephalus tropicalis gazella*, at South Georgia. *In* Biologie antarctique, Premier symposium organisé par le SCAR, edited by R. Carrick *et al.* Paris, Herman, pp. 433-43.
1964

–, The fur seal of South Georgia. *Sci. Rep. Brit. Antarct. Surv.*, (56):1-81.
1968

BUDD, G.M., Rapid population increase in the Kerguelen fur seal, *Arctocephalus tropicalis gazella*, at Heard Island. *Mammalia, Paris*, 34:410-4.
1970

–, Breeding of the fur seal at McDonald Islands, and further population growth at Heard Island. *Mammalia, Paris*, 36:123-7.
1972

BUDD, G.M. and M.C. DOWNES, Population increase and breeding in the Kerguelen fur seal, *Arc-*
1969

tocephalus tropicalis gazella, at Heard Island. *Mammalia, Paris*, 33:58-67.

CSORDAS, S.E. and S.E. INGHAM, The New Zealand fur seal, *Arctocephalus forsteri* (Lesson) at Macquarie Island, 1949-64. *CSIRO Wildl. Res.*, 10:83-99.
1965

ERICKSON, A.W. *et al.*, Distributional ecology of Antarctic seals. *In* Symposium of Antarctic ice and water masses, Tokyo, 19 September, 1970, edited by G. Deacon. Cambridge, Scientific Committee on Antarctic Research, pp. 55-76.
1971

FALLA, R.A., Exploitation of seals, whales and penguins in New Zealand. *Proc. N.Z. Ecol. Soc.*, 9:34-8.
1962

HOLDGATE, M.W., Fur seals in the South Sandwich Islands. *Polar Rec.*, 11(73):474.
1963

HOLDGATE, M.W., P.J. TILBROOK and R.W. VAUGHAN, The biology of Bouvetøya. *Brit. Antarct. Surv. Bull.*, (15):1-7.
1968

KING, J.E., The northern and southern populations of *Arctocephalus gazella. Mammalia, Paris*, 23:19-40.
1959

–, A note on the specific name of the Kerguelen fur seal. *Mammalia, Paris*, 23:381.
1959a

LAWS, R.M., The current status of seals in the Southern
1973   Hemisphere. *IUCN Publ. (New Ser.) Suppl.*
        Pap., (39):144-61.

—, Population increase of fur seals at South Georgia.
1973a   *Polar Rec.*, 16(105):856-8.

North Pacific Fur Seal Commission, Standing Scientific
1962   Committee, Report on investigations from
        1958 to 1961. Washington, D.C., NPFSC, 183
        p.

O'GORMAN, F.A., Fur seals breeding in the Falkland
1961   Islands Dependencies. *Nature, Lond.*, 192:
        914-6.

ØRITSLAND, T., Fur seals breeding in the South Orkney
1960   Islands. *Norsk Hvalfangsttid.*, 49(5):220-5.

PAULIAN, P., Sur la présence aux îles Kerguelen d'*Hy-*
1952   *drurga leptonyx* (BI) et d'*Arctocephalus gazella*
        (Pet.) et notes biologiques sur deux phocidés.
        Mammalia, Paris, 16:223-7.

PAYNE, M.R., Growth of a fur seal population. *Philos.*
1977   *Trans. R. Soc. Lond. (B)*, 279:67-79.

—, Population size and age determination in the Ant-
1978   arctic fur seal *Arctocephalus gazella*. *Mamm.*
        Rev., 8:67-73.

REPENNING, C.A., R.S. PETERSON, and C.L. HUBBS, Con-
1971   tribution to the systematics of the southern fur
        seal, with particular references to the Januan
        Fernandez and Guadeloupe species. *Antarct.*
        Res. Ser., (18):1-34.

SIVERTSEN, E., A survey of the eared seals (family Ota-
1954   riidae) with remarks on the Antarctic seals
        collected by M/K NORWEGIA in 1928-9.
        Sci. Results Nor. Antarct. Exped., (23):1-76.

SLADEN, W.J.L., The distribution of the Adelie and
1964   chinstrap penguins. *In* Biologie antarctique,
        Premier symposium organisé par SCAR,
        edited by R. Carrick *et al.* Paris, Hermann, pp.
        359-65.

THE DISTRIBUTION AND ABUNDANCE OF SEALS
IN THE AUSTRALASIAN REGION,
WITH SUMMARIES OF BIOLOGY AND CURRENT RESEARCH

R.M. Warneke

Abstract

This paper is a broad summary of pinnipeds resident in the waters of Australia and New Zealand: Australian fur seal, *Arctocephalus pusillus doriferus*; New Zealand fur seal, *A. forsteri*; Australian sea lion, *Neophoca cinerea*; New Zealand sea lion, *Phocarctos hookeri*; and southern elephant seal, *Mirounga leonina*. All 5 species were subjected to a long period of unregulated, geographically expanding exploitation, both colonial and foreign, resulting in disastrous reductions of breeding stocks and extremely slow recovery. Total protection was given to seals in New Zealand, Western Australia and Victoria in the early 1890s, although a few seasonal harvests were allowed up to 1925 and harvests were conducted in New Zealand and Victoria in the mid forties in response to complaints by fishermen. As far as is known, seals have not been taken elsewhere in Australia for commercial purposes or control for at least 50 years.

Data on the recent and historical distribution of each species, with reference to breeding state and past exploitation, is appended to the report. Information on reproductive biology and behaviour, movements and mortality is given when available. *A. p. doriferus* is found from Seal Rocks, New South Wales (32°28'S, 152°33'E), to southern Tasmania (43°51'S) and throughout Bass Strait to a western limit of Lady Julia Percy Island (142°00'E). More than 2/3 of the present population of about 20 000 animals is concentrated at 3 sites in Bass Strait and, in general, the species does not appear to be increasing in numbers. *A. forsteri* is found in separate Australian and New Zealand populations; the species is widely distributed, but not common along southern Australia from about 117°E to 136°E with occasional stragglers to about 145°E in Bass Strait. Before exploitation, its range extended to the Furneaux Group; however, the present Australian population is not increasing significantly and recolonization of this and adjacent vacant areas in the foreseeable future seems unlikely. In New Zealand, *A. forsteri* is increasing throughout its range: breeding colonies are found along the south and southwest coasts of South Island with non-breeding colonies distributed north to Three Kings Islands; substantial populations (1 000 or more) are found on Chatham, Solander and Stewart Islands and on adjacent sub-Antarctic islands. The present estimated population of about 40 000 animals should be able to expand substantially, especially on remote islands. The biology of these 2 fur seals is generally similar; however, their breeding seasons do not coincide and marked behavioural differences are evident.

Although *N. cinerea* is the most widely distributed of Australian pinnipeds — breeding from Houtmann's Abrolhos (28°S) to Kangaroo Island (138°E) — it is nowhere abundant and the present total population is probably between 3 000 and 5 000 animals. The species has a relatively mild fixation to inhabited sites, often isolated islands, and it may naturally congregate in only small numbers as well; it is the only Australasian pinniped with no fixed breeding season. The main population of *P. hookeri*, estimated to be between 3 000 and 3 500 animals, is centred on several of the small islands of the Auckland Group; these, together with small groups on Campbell Island and the Snares and some wide-ranging males, form a total population of perhaps 4 000. Only the general outline of these sea lions' biology is known.

In the Australasian region, *M. leonina* is centred on Macquarie Island, where the colony is now stable at its maximum sustainable level of about 95 000 animals before whelping; a small but thriving breeding colony, including at least 300 females, is present on Campbell Island. The species ranges widely and regularly visits Antipodes and Auckland Islands and the Snares; eventual recolonization of more northern sites, especially in western Bass Strait, is a possibility. Long-term life history studies of this species have yielded a good understanding of its biology. Of all the Australasian seals, only *M. leonina* could presently support commercial exploitation on a sustained-yield basis, offering 2 population surpluses at Macquarie Island: harvesting of weaned pups appears safe from both numerical and behavioural standpoints while the taking of surplus males at maximum weight presents difficulties, with possible disruption of reproduction activities.

Data on food, feeding and effects on fisheries are presented, though information is not complete for all species. In general, cephalopods and fish (especially barracouta, *Thyrsites* for the fur seals) are reported as the important food items. Crustaceans are also reported as main food items of *P. hookeri* and *M. leonina*, and penguins and sea birds are eaten by seals in some cases. Charges by fishermen of drastic reductions of commercially valuable fish stocks by pinnipeds are unsubstantiated. However, individual Australian fur seals do cause sporadic direct interference to sedentary mesh fisheries in Port Phillip and Westernport Bays, Victoria, and prompt destruction of the offending seal is the only effective remedy; immature seals of the same species also drown in nets and traps and are shot by fishermen. In general, other species do not occur in sufficient numbers near fishing grounds to be considered pests.

The colonies of *A. p. doriferus* at Seal Rocks, Phillip Island, and of *N. cinerea* in South Australia, are important tourist attractions; the general inaccessibility or remoteness or both of the other resident species has prevented their use as a tourist resource. *A. p. doriferus*, *N. cinerea* and lately *M. leonina* are successfully exhibited in Australia. Recent and ongoing research is summarized.

Résumé

La présente communication donne une récapitulation générale des pinnipèdes vivant dans les eaux territoriales d'Australie et de Nouvelle-Zélande: l'otarie à fourrure australe, *Arctocephalus pusillus doriferus*; l'otarie à fourrure de Nouvelle-Zélande, *A. forsteri*; l'otarie d'Australie, *Neophoca cinerea*; l'otarie de Nouvelle-Zélande, *Phocarctos hookeri* et l'éléphant de mer austral, *Mirounga leonina*. Ces cinq espèces ont fait l'objet, pendant longtemps, d'une exploitation effrénée, coloniale et étrangère, s'étendant sur une aire géographique en expansion, qui a entraîné une réduction catastrophique des stocks de reproducteurs ainsi qu'une grande lenteur de la reprise. Les pinnipèdes de Nouvelle-Zélande, d'Australie-Occidentale et de Victoria ont fait l'objet d'une protection totale au début des années 1890. Cependant, quelques campagnes ont été autorisées jusqu'en 1925 et des animaux ont été abattus en Nouvelle-Zélande et dans l'Etat de Victoria au milieu des années 40 à la suite de revendications des pêcheurs; pour autant que l'on sache, aucun phoque n'a été capturé dans une autre région d'Australie à des fins commerciales ou de contrôle depuis au moins 50 ans.

Les données sur la distribution récente et historique de chaque espèce, notamment pour ce qui concerne l'état de la reproduction et l'exploitation passée, sont jointes au rapport. Des informations sont données sur la biologie de la reproduction et sur le comportement correspondant, les déplacements et la mortalité chaque fois qu'on en a disposé. On trouve *A. p. doriferus* depuis Seals Rocks (Nouvelle-Galles du Sud) (32°28'S-152°33'E) jusqu'à la Tasmanie méridionale (43°51'S) et dans tout le détroit de Bass jusqu'à une limite occidentale représentée par l'île de Lady Julia Percy (142°E). Plus des deux tiers de la population actuelle d'environ 20 000 animaux sont localisés dans trois sites du détroit de Bass et, dans l'ensemble, il ne semble pas que cette espèce augmente en nombre. *A. forsteri* existe sous forme de populations distinctes, australienne et néo-zélandaise: cette espèce occupe une aire géographique vaste mais n'est pas très commune; on la trouve depuis le sud de l'Australie (environ 117°E) jusqu'à 136°E, avec des spécimens isolés jusqu'à 145°E dans le détroit de Bass. Avant l'exploitation, l'espèce arrivait jusqu'au groupe de Furneaux. Toutefois, la population australienne actuelle n'augmente pas sensiblement et une recolonisation de cette région et des autres aires vacantes adjacentes semble peu probable dans un avenir proche. En Nouvelle-Zélande, *A. forsteri* est en augmentation dans toute son aire géographique; des colonies de reproducteurs existent le long des côtes sud-est et sud-ouest de l'île du Sud; la distribution des colonies de non-reproducteurs atteint les îles Three Kings au nord; des populations importantes (1 000 individus ou davantage) existent sur les îles Chatham, Solander et Stewart et sur les îles subantarctiques voisines. La population actuelle, évaluée à environ 40 000 animaux, devrait être en mesure de croître sensiblement, surtout sur les îles éloignées. Dans l'ensemble, la biologie de ces deux otaries est comparable mais leurs saisons de reproduction ne coïncident pas et des différences de comportement marquées sont évidentes.

Bien que *N. cinerea* soit le pinnipède australien dont la distribution est la plus vaste (son aire de reproduction s'étend depuis Houtman's Abrolhos (28°S) jusqu'à l'île Kangaroo (138°E) — on ne le trouve nulle part en abondance et la population totale actuelle est probablement de 3 000-5 000 animaux. L'espèce se fixe relativement peu dans les lieux habités, souvent dans des îles isolées, et peut aussi bien ne se rassembler naturellement qu'en petit nombre. C'est le seul pinnipède australien ne possédant pas de saison de reproduction fixe. La principale population de *P. hookeri*, que l'on estime à 3 000-3 500 animaux, a son centre sur plusieurs petites îles du groupe d'Auckland; avec des petits groupes de l'île Campbell et des Snares et quelques mâles se déplaçant au loin, le chiffre total de la population atteint peut-être 4 000 sujets. On ne connaît que les généralités de la biologie de ces otaries.

En Australasie, *M. leonina* a son centre de peuplement sur l'île de Macquarie, où la colonie a atteint son niveau eumétrique d'environ 95 000 animaux avant parturition et s'y maintient; une petite colonie en plein essor, comportant au moins 300 femelles, existe à l'île Campbell. L'espèce a une aire très vaste et visite régulièrement les îles Antipodes et Auckland ainsi que les Snares. Une recolonisation éventuelle des sites les plus septentrionaux, notamment à l'ouest du détroit de Bass, n'est pas improbable. Des études prolongées sur le cycle biologique de cette espèce ont permis d'avoir une bonne connaissance de sa biologie. De tous les pinnipèdes d'Australasie, seul *M. leonina* pourrait actuellement supporter une exploitation commerciale sur une base eumétrique, du fait qu'il existe deux excédents de population sur l'île Macquarie; la capture de nouveau-nés sevrés semble pouvoir se faire sans difficulté, tant du point de vue numérique que du comportement. Par contre, la capture des mâles excédentaires ayant atteint leur poids maximal présente des difficultés, avec la possible interruption des activités de reproduction.

Des données sur l'alimentation, la nourriture et les incidences sur les pêches sont présentées, bien que les informations ne soient pas complètes pour toutes les espèces. On signale qu'en général, la principale nourriture est constituée de céphalopodes et de poissons (notamment, *Thyrsites* pour les otaries à fourrure). On signale aussi que les crustacés constituent les principaux aliments de *P. hookeri* et *M. leonina* et que les pinnipèdes mangent à l'occasion des manchots et des oiseaux de mer. Les assertions des pêcheurs, selon lesquelles les pinnipèdes provoqueraient une réduction considérable des stocks de poissons ayant une importance commerciale, sont sans fondement. Cependant, il est exact que des otaries à fourrure australiennes isolées interfèrent directement et sporadiquement avec les pêcheries au filet fixe des baies de Port Phillip et de Westernport (Etat de Victoria) et qu'une destruction immédiate du pinnipède en cause semble le seul remède efficace. Des sujets immatures de la même espèce se noient aussi dans les filets et les pièges ou sont tués au fusil par les pêcheurs.

Dans l'ensemble, les autres espèces ne sont pas assez nombreuses à proximité des fonds de pêche pour être considérées comme une nuisance.

Les colonies de *A. p. doriferus* de Seals Rocks, de l'île Phillip et de *N. cinerea* en Australie-Méridionale constituent des attractions touristiques importantes. Le fait que les autres espèces résidentes soient en général trop inaccessibles ou trop éloignées a fait obstacle à leur utilisation en tant qu'attraction touristique. *A. p. doriferus, N. cinerea* et, récemment, *M. leonina* ont été exhibés avec succès en Australie. Les recherches récentes et en cours sont récapitulées.

Extracto

En este documento se trata en general de los pinnípedos que viven en las aguas territoriales de Australia y Nueva Zelandia: lobo marino de dos pelos de Australia, *Arctocephalus pusillus doriferus*; lobo marino de dos pelos de Nueva Zelandia, *A. forsteri*; león marino de Australia, *Neophoca cinerea*; león marino de Nueva Zelandia, *Phocarctos hookeri*, y elefante marino del sur, *Mirounga leonina*. Las cinco especies han sido objeto de explotación por parte de los colonizadores y de cazadores extranjeros durante largo tiempo, sin regulaciones y en un ámbito geográfico cada vez más vasto, lo que ha determinado una desastrosa disminución de las poblaciones de reproductores, que están recuperándose con gran lentitud. En Nueva Zelandia, Australia occidental y Victoria los pinnípedos están totalmente protegidos desde principios del decenio de 1890, aunque hasta 1925 se permitió a veces su explotación estacional y a mediados de los años cuarenta se hicieron algunas expediciones de caza en Nueva Zelandia y Victoria para atender a las quejas de los pescadores. A juzgar por los datos disponibles, en otras zonas de Australia no se capturan pinnípedos con fines comerciales o para limitar las poblaciones desde hace al menos 50 años.

En apéndice a este informe se dan datos sobre la distribución de cada una de las especies en los últimos tiempos y en el pasado teniendo en cuenta su situación desde el punto de vista de la reproducción y la explotación de que han sido objeto en el pasado. Cuando se dispone de datos, se da también información sobre la biología reproductiva, el comportamiento, los desplazamientos y la mortalidad. *A. p. doriferus* se encuentra desde Seal Rocks, en Nueva Gales del Sur (32°28'S, 152°33'E), hasta el sur de Tasmania (43°51'S), y a través del Estrecho de Bass hasta el extremo occidental de la Isla de Lady Julia Percy (142°00'E). Más de dos tercios de la población actual, cuyo total asciende a unos 20 000 animales, se concentran en tres zonas del Estrecho de Bass, y, en general, no parece que el número de animales de esta especie vaya en aumento. De *A. forsteri* existen poblaciones separadas en Australia y Nueva Zelandia: esta especie está muy extendida, aunque no es común, a lo largo del sur de Australia, desde los 117°E hasta los 136°E, encontrándose en ocasiones animales dispersos hasta cerca de los 145°E, en el Estrecho de Bass. Antes de que comenzara la explotación, su zona de distribución se extendía hasta el Archipiélago Furneaux, pero la población actual de Australia no está aumentando en forma significativa y no parece probable que recolonice en un próximo futuro esta y otras zonas adyacentes, actualmente vacías. En Nueva Zelandia, en cambio, *A. forsteri* va en aumento en toda su zona de distribución: se encuentran colonias de reproductores a lo largo de las costas meridionales y sudoccidentales de la Isla Meridional, con colonias de animales no reproductores al norte de las Islas Tres Reyes; se encuentran también poblaciones importantes (1 000 o más) en las Islas Chatham, Solander y Stewart, y en algunas islas subantárticas adyacentes. La población actual se estima en unos 40 000 animales, y probablemente podrá aumentar sustancialmente, especialmente en las islas remotas. La biología de estos dos lobos marinos es en general similar, aunque las temporadas de cría no coinciden y existen claras diferencias de comportamiento.

N. cinerea es el pinnípedo con ámbito más vasto de distribución en Australia — desde el Archipiélago Pelsart, en Houtman's Abrolhos (28°S), hasta la Isla Kangaroo (138°E) — pero en ninguna zona es abundante y la población total debe ser en la actualidad del orden de 3 000 a

5 000 animales. La especie manifiesta un apego relativamente moderado a las zonas que habita, con frecuencia islas aisladas, y puede encontrarse también en grupos naturales formados por un pequeño número de animales; es el único pinnípedo australiano que no tiene una temporada fija de reproducción. La población principal de *P. hookeri*, calculada en unos 3 000-3 500 animales, se encuentra en torno a varias de las pequeñas islas del Archipiélago de las Auckland; este grupo, junto con otros pequeños grupos de la Isla Campbell y de las Snares y algunos machos que recorren grandes distancias, forman una población total del orden quizás de 4 000 animales. Sólo se conocen algunos elementos generales de la biología de estos leones marinos.

En la región de Australasia, *M. leonina* se encuentra en torno a la Isla Macquarie, cuya colonia es en la actualidad estable, en torno a cifras equivalentes al nivel máximo sostenible (unos 95 000 animales antes de la reproducción); en la Isla Campbell se encuentra una colonia de reproductores, pequeña pero floreciente, que cuenta al menos con 300 hembras. La zona de distribución de esta especie es muy vasta: visitan regularmente las Islas Antípodas y Auckland y las Snares y es posible que lleguen a recolonizar algunas zonas situadas más al norte, especialmente al oeste del Estrecho de Bass. Los estudios a largo plazo que se han hecho sobre el ciclo vital de esta especie han permitido conocer bien su biología. De todos los pinnípedos de Australasia, sólo *M. leonina* podría sostener en la actualidad una explotación comercial con rendimiento sostenido, aprovechando los dos tipos de animales excedentarios en la Isla Macquarie; la captura de cachorros destetados no parece entrañar ningún peligro, a juzgar por su número y por el comportamiento de la especie, pero la captura de los machos excedentarios en el momento en que alcanzan su peso máximo plantea algunas dificultades, y pudiera determinar alteraciones de las actividades reproductivas.

Se presentan datos sobre los alimentos de esos pinnípedos y los efectos que su alimentación tiene en las pesquerías, aunque no se dispone de información completa para todas las especies. En general, los alimentos más importantes son cefalópodos y peces (especialmente barracuda, *Thyrsites*, en el caso de los lobos marinos de dos pelos). También los crustáceos son alimentos importantes de *P. hookeri* y *M. leonina* y en algunos casos los pinnípedos comen pingüinos y aves marinas. Las acusaciones de los pescadores de que las especies de pinnípedos que se encuentran en las zonas de pesca reducen radicalmente algunas poblaciones de peces comercialmente valiosos no se han probado. Sin embargo, algunos lobos marinos de Australia interfieren a veces con las pesquerías de redes de enmalle en las Bahías de Port Phillip y Westernport (Victoria), y el único remedio eficaz es acabar inmediatamente con los animales que causan daños; algunos lobos inmaduros de la misma especie perecen ahogados en redes y trampas o son muertos a tiros por los pescadores. Las demás especies, en general, no se encuentran cerca de los caladeros en número suficiente para considerarlas perjudiciales.

Las colonias de *A. p. doriferus* de Seal Rocks, en la Isla Phillip, y las de *N. cinerea* de Australia Meridional, ofrecen un importante atractivo para el turismo. La dificultad general de acceso y/o la lejanía de las demás especies ha impedido su aprovechamiento para el turismo. *A. p. doriferus*, *N. cinerea* y últimamente *M. leonina* se exhiben con éxito en Australia. Se resumen las investigaciones recientes y en curso.

R.M. Warneke
Arthur Rylah Institute for Environmental Research, 123 Brown Street, Heidelberg, Victoria 3084, Australia

Scope of the report

This report summarizes both historical and recent data on the distribution and status of seals in the territorial waters of Australia and New Zealand. Its geographical scope is therefore limited to the coastline of Australia, Tasmania and adjacent islands; New Zealand, Antipodes I., Auckland Is., Bounty Is., Campbell I., Chatham Is., Snares Is., Solander I. and Stewart I. Although Macquarie I. is an Australian territory under the direct jurisdiction of Tasmania, it is geographically and biologically part of New Zealand's sub-Antarctic group, and I have treated it as such.

A brief summary of European exploitation of seals in the region is also included; data on the biology and population dynamics of each species, where these are available; food, feeding and effects on fisheries; references to recent and on-going research, and a comment on aesthetics.

Sources of information include published material, museum records, unpublished data from research workers, the files of various government agencies concerned with wildlife and fisheries, professional fishermen, and my own field observations. My review of the literature is by no means complete, and is especially meagre as far as precise historical records are concerned. This is due largely to the uncertainty of interpreting early accounts of fur seals in south eastern Australian waters according to current species concepts. However where sites are currently occupied I have assumed conspecificity of historical and recent (post 1945) records, unless there is evidence to the contrary. I have for the most part accepted authors' identification of species.

Data on distribution (see appendices) have been grouped by locality, in alphabetic listing for each territorial entity, i.e. the two main islands comprising New Zealand and the associated islands to the south and southeast, including Macquarie I., and separately for each Australian State.

The status of each existing colony has been defined in terms of the most recent estimate of numbers, if one is available, and whether breeding is known to occur, does not occur, or the matter is uncertain. The source of these data is cited in each instance. For some of the more important and better known sealing grounds I have been able to include data on the initial haul of skins, which give some idea of the original abundance of the resource.

Species

Five species are resident within the region: two fur seals, two sea lions and the southern elephant seal. The nomenclature followed here is basically that of King (1964), modified according to the review of Australian fur seals by King (1969) and of the genus *Arctocephalus* by Repenning, Peterson and Hubbs (1971).

Family OTARIIDAE

Arctocephalus pusillus doriferus (Wood Jones) 1925.
    Type locality unknown.
    Nominate race *Arctocephalus pusillus pusillus* (Schreber) 1776, type locality, Cape of Good Hope, South Africa.
Arctocephalus forsteri (Lesson) 1828.
    Type locality, Dusky Sound, New Zealand.
Neophoca cinerea (Peron) 1816.
    Type locality, Kangaroo I., South Australia.
Phocarctos hookeri (Gray) 1844.
    Type locality, Auckland Is., New Zealand.

Family PHOCIDAE

Mirounga leonina (Linnaeus) 1758.
    Type locality, Masa Afuera I.

The Antarctic species *Hydrurga lepto-nyx, Lobodon carcinophagus* and *Leptonychotes weddelli* have been recorded as stragglers to New Zealand and southern Australia. Records of *Hydrurga* are typically of winter incidence and are sufficiently frequent and regular to suggest that an extensive northward movement at this season is normal for this species.

Historical background

All five species were subjected to a long period of exploitation by Europeans for skins and oil. The pelt of *A. forsteri* was considered to be the most valuable of the two fur seals and often both species were killed merely for the skin (Dunderdale, 1898). The pelts of sea lions were much less valuable and their bodies were often rendered down for oil. Elephant seals were important only as a source of oil.

Historically this exploitation occurred in three phases:

Phase I (1798 to about 1820) consisted of an intense and unregulated industry, which was associated with the colonization and early economic development of Australia (Hainsworth, 1972). The initial effort was concentrated in Bass Strait and along the southern Australian coast, but the industry soon spread to New Zealand (Murray, 1929; Dunbabin, 1931; McNab, 1909), where seals had been known since the time of Cook's visit in 1773. Initially seal products found ready markets in China and then in Europe, and the trade which developed was the first export industry of the colony at Sydney (Hainsworth, 1972; Abbott and Nairn, 1969).

In addition to colonial enterprise the sealing grounds were also worked by English, French and American gangs. The intense competition which developed and the rapid dwindling of the seal colonies forced wider ranging by the sealing captains and eventually led to the discovery of the rich grounds beyond New Zealand and in the sub-Antarctic. By 1825 all the significant and accessible colonies had been reduced to very low levels or eliminated entirely. Sealing as a primary activity then virtually ceased.

Phase II was generally associated with expanding settlement and involved only local enterprise. Residual colonies were persistently exploited along with other species of wildlife, or in association with agricultural activities near to seal colonies. This phase continued into the latter half of last century, both in Australia and New Zealand, and was eventually brought to a close or under some form of regulation by government action. Such regulation characterises the third, or current, phase.

In 1875 the New Zealand Government moved to prohibit sealing during the months October to May. This restriction remained in force until 1894, when sealing was totally prohibited. In 1913 a three month season was reintroduced, in which it was legal to take seals under regulation. Licences were not required and no check was made on the numbers taken each year to 1916, when the season was again closed. An exception was made in the case of the Campbell Island Co., an agricultural concern, which was permitted to take up to 400 fur seal skins in 1922 and 1924; however, this quota was not reached in either year and no further permits were granted.

In 1946, an open season of four months was declared by the New Zealand Government, in response to pressures by local fishing interests. It was restricted to parts of the south coast of the South I. of New Zealand, Solander I. and parts of Stewart I. The conditions of the licences were such that they were effectively only available to commercial fishermen. The total yield was 6 187 skins, mostly of females and pups (Sorensen, 1969a).

The corresponding period in Australia, where each State is quite independent in the administration of its wildlife, has not yet been fully researched. In Western Australia seals have been legally protected since 1892, but at least one open season has been permitted since then, in 1920. In that year a sealing party took

494 *A. forsteri* and 327 *N. cinerea* in the Recherche Archipelago (Serventy, 1953). In South Australia seals were first protected in 1919, but only within St. Vincent and Spencer Gulfs and adjacent waters to the north of Kangaroo I. They are now fully protected in all South Australian waters under the Fauna Conservation Act of 1964.

In Victorian waters (to 39°12′S) seals were given legal protection in 1890, and only once since then has a season been declared, in 1948-1949. As in New Zealand in 1946, this was in response to complaints from the local fishing industry. Permits were available only to licensed fishermen, who were required to forward all carcasses to Melbourne for commercial processing. Despite vociferous complaint against the seals prior to the season, only 619 were accounted for (McNally and Lynch, 1954). As far as I am aware seals have not been legally culled elsewhere in Australia for commercial purposes or control for at least 50 years.

It is clear, from even the most cursory examination of historical accounts and recent data, that the initial reduction of the breeding stocks of all five species was disastrous and that recovery has been extremely slow. In the case of the fur seals this may have been due, in part at least, to sporadic harvesting despite low economic return (Phase II, and to some extent in Phase III) and, more recently, to illegal "control" shooting by fishermen (Sorensen, 1969a; Victorian Fisheries and Wildlife Division, unpubl. data) which is impossible to prevent in open waters distant from mainland coasts.

Current distribution and status

Arctocephalus pusillus doriferus (see Appendix C)

The present range extends from Seal Rocks, New South Wales, to southern Tasma-nia and throughout Bass Strait to as far west as Lady Julia Percy I., i.e. from 32°28′ to 43°51′S and from 152°33′ to 142°00′E. On present evidence the breeding range does not include the east and south coasts of Tasmania but it is likely that breeding does occur at some of the known sites there. More detailed and appropriately timed field surveys are required to improve estimates of colony size and status.

On the basis of the most recent estimates the total for the whole region is about 20 000, of which more than two thirds are concentrated at three sites in Bass Strait: Judgement Rocks, Seal Rocks off Phillip I., and Lady Julia Percy I.

Historical records do not reveal a wider distribution in the past, and the uncertainty of much of these data does not permit any estimate of original abundance. The lack of colonization or recolonization of the many vacant sites within the present range of this species suggests that most of these may have originally been occupied by *A. forsteri* or *N. cinerea*. Conversely, it is possible that the existing breeding colonies represent the major foci of the species prior to European exploitation.

There is some suggestion that a slight redistribution in relation to other species may have occurred, e.g. *A. p. doriferus* now occurs in the Anser Group, said to have once been occupied by hair seals (Doome, 1874), but no indisputable evidence now exists.

Arctocephalus forsteri (see Appendix D)

The Australian and New Zealand populations are apparently geographically isolated, and may have been so long before European activity began in the region (Shaughnessy, 1970). The species is by no means common although it is widely distributed from about 117° to 136°E, with occasional stragglers penetrating Bass Strait to about 148°E. Information on individual colonies (post 1945) is so meagre that no satisfactory estimate of total numbers can be made. It may be as low as several thousand.

Historical evidence indicates that its range formerly extended to the Furneaux Group in eastern Bass Strait, and that it was quite abundant there (Flinders, 1814; Roe, 1967). However, as there is no evidence at all that the species is increasing significantly in numbers anywhere in Australian waters, it seems unlikely that these vacant sites will be recolonized in the foreseeable future.

The situation in New Zealand is very different. According to various authors (Crawley, 1972) *A. forsteri* is increasing throughout its range there. There is reasonable evidence of an upward trend in numbers at many breeding sites in the past two decades and there has also been a marked increase in numbers hauling out at non-breeding sites to the north (Kaikoura, Wellington, Three Kings Is.) and south (Macquarie I.) of the present range. Breeding has actually commenced at Macquarie I. but as yet the number of pups born is still very small (Johnstone, 1972). Viewed against historical records of this species' former abundance to the east of the Tasman Sea, the current population estimate of about 40 000 (Wilson, 1974a) indicates that there is great scope for further expansion of present colonies, and especially those on the remote islands.

Neophoca cinerea (see Appendix E)

This sea lion is the most widely distributed of Australian seals. In recent times individuals have been seen as far east as Portland, Victoria (142°E) and north to Shark Bay, Western Australia (25°S) (Burbidge, pers. comm.). The breeding range extends from Kangaroo I., South Australia (138°E) to Houtmans Abrolhos off the Western Australiancoast at 28°S, but the species is nowhere abundant. The lack of estimates of colony size probably reflects the isolation of many of the islands it inhabits, a less tenacious fixation to site compared with *Arctocephalus* and lack of a fixed breeding season. I have the impression that it has a natural tendency to congregate only in relatively small numbers at any one site, for there are few records of colonies in excess of 200. This is certainly true of most recent records and appears to have been the case prior to exploitation by Europeans (Flinders, 1814, (1), p. 91; Peron and Freycinet, 1816, p. 118).

Recent censuses in South Australian waters (Ling and Walker, 1976) grossed a total of nearly 2 000, including pups. This survey covered less than half of the total range of the species, but even allowing the most generous interpretation of the estimates of all known colonies the total population would appear to be within the range 3 000-5 000, which is near the lowest estimate of Scheffer (1958, p. 3).

Phocarctos hookeri (see Appendix F)

The main population is centred on several of the small islands of the Auckland Group, rather than on the main island itself, but it is by no means abundant. Best (1974) estimates that there are about 1 000 on Enderby I., 2 000 on Dundas I. and 68 were counted on Figure of Eight I. A few haul-out at various points throughout the Group, so that the total for the Group as a whole would be of the order 3 000-3 500 (Wilson, pers. comm.).

Some breeding occurs at Campbell I. and at the Snares, but those islands are predominantly male hauling grounds. A small group of males has been noted at Stewart I., but most other records are of lone individuals, all males. The northern limits of this ranging by males is about 46°S, to the Otago Peninsula in the South I., and south to 53°S at Macquarie I., which has been visited regularly over a period of years by several known individuals until they were fully mature.

It would appear then, that the entire population is of the order of 4 000.

Historical records do not indicate a wider breeding range or any clear indication of its former abundance. There is some evidence (e.g. Musgrave, 1865) that *Phocarctos* will vacate a breeding site if subjected to undue dis-

439

turbance by man (cf. *Neophoca*, Marlow, 1968) so that counts at selected sites over a period of years may give an erroneous idea of population trends.

Mirounga leonina (see Appendix G)

The main focus of this species in the Australasian Region is Macquarie I., and there is a small but thriving colony at Campbell I. There is clear evidence (Johnstone, 1972) that the former colony is now at its maximum sustainable level – about 95 000 not including pups of the year. The most recent counts for Campbell I. indicate a breeding population of at least 300 females and a larger number of males, mostly immature.

Early last century a commercially important breeding colony of unknown size existed on the north and east coasts of King I. in Bass Strait and on the nearby New Years Is., but it was quickly eliminated as a breeding species (Micco, 1971).

The species ranges widely and regularly visits Antipodes Is., Auckland Is., and the Snares. In recent times stragglers have been recorded at the Chathams and the South I. of New Zealand and in Australian waters at Tasmania, several islands in Bass Strait, and on the Victorian and South Australian coasts. Both heavily pregnant females and fully mature males are involved. This suggests the possibility of eventual recolonization of more northern sites, if not in New Zealand waters, where opportunities are limited, then in western Bass Strait at the ancestral grounds.

Biology and population dynamics

Arctocephalus pusillus doriferus

Breeding habitat varies from basalt reef and shore platforms of low elevation, to caves, boulder stacks and, marginally, cobblestone beach, smooth granite ledges and slopes.

The colony at Seal Rocks, Victoria, which has been studied extensively for some years, breeds during November and December. Males are rigidly territorial and polygamous but harems are not formed. The ratio of males to females is 1:8-10.

Parous females copulate 6 days after parturition, but implantation is delayed until the following March-April. Pups are normally suckled for 11-12 months, but a few are carried through a second year, and in rare instances through a third. This may happen if the subsequent pup dies soon after birth. A significant proportion of immature of both sexes up to the age of 3 or 4 are to be found among the breeding females throughout the breeding season.

Females reach puberty at 4 years or later, occasionally at 3. Males probably reach puberty at 4 or 5 years, but attainment of breeding status is deferred until a competitive size is reached, which may be as early as the ninth year but more generally occurs about the twelfth year or later.

As yet there are little quantitative data on mortality in relation to age or sex. Counts of dead pups in the breeding areas reveal a minimum loss of the order of 15 % in the first two months, when they are sedentary and do not readily enter the sea. During the later period of immaturity many more die at sea, and an analysis of tag returns (Warneke, 1975) indicates that a significant proportion of these losses is due to fishermen, through accidental drowning in nets and traps and by shooting. Large sharks, and the white pointer (*Carcharodon carcharias*) in particular, prey heavily on seals of all ages, but the extent of this mortality is unknown.

Young seals (ages 3-5) tagged at Seal Rocks have been found to be rather sedentary, few moving beyond 150 km of the natal colony. Males range more widely than females, to distances of at least 750 km (Warneke, 1975). As yet there is no evidence of interchange of breeding animals between colonies.

The two largest breeding colonies, at Seal Rocks and Lady Julia Percy I., appear to have been stable for at least 30 years and it is likely that most of the very small seal islands are also at saturation e.g. Tenth I. and Moriarty Rocks (Fowler, unpubl. data). There is little convincing evidence of increase in numbers in recent years except at Judgement Rocks.

Arctocephalus forsteri

The favoured breeding habitat of this species appears to be boulder stacks, fronting cliffs or slopes of high relief. Wilson (1974) has coined the term "tumbledown beach" to describe such localities, and has stressed that they provide shelter for females and pups. The species climbs well and retreats to higher situations to avoid breaking seas (e.g. at the Aucklands, Wilson, 1974; and at the South Neptunes, Warneke, pers. obs.).

In broad outline the biology of this species is essentially the same as *A. p. doriferus*, but there are marked behavioural differences and the breeding seasons do not precisely coincide (Stirling and Warneke, 1971). Wilson (1974) has defined three main types of colony: breeding, bachelor bull and immature. These aggregations may be quite isolated geographically (e.g. wintering colonies of males around the North I. of New Zealand) but, even if all three types are present at the one site, they are still clearly segregated.

Bachelor males are automatically excluded from breeding areas by the territorial behaviour of the dominant males. In contrast to *A. p. doriferus*, no juveniles occur in the breeding areas during the breeding season.

Although no precise data are available on birth and mortality rates, age at first breeding etc., one attempt has been made to calculate the size of the colony at Taumaka from pup counts, using the known population parameters of *Callorhinus* (Crawley and Brown, 1971). Although several sources of bias could not be allowed for, the result was not inconsistent with field estimates.

Neophoca cinerea

The biology of this species has not been closely studied and only a general outline can be given.

In contrast to the fur seals *Neophoca* prefers sandy beaches and smooth rock for breeding purposes, although individual sea lions often haul out among resting fur seals. *Neophoca* has a well marked tendency to penetrate inland and individuals have been found several kilometres from shore (King, 1964).

This species is unique among Australasian otariids in that the timing and duration of the breeding season is variable and unpredictable. Adult males usually become territorial in September and pupping commences in October, but the timing of these events can vary by as much as two months in some years (Marlow, pers. comm.). In 1975 the pupping season at Seal Bay, Kangaroo I., began in February and extended over the following eight months (Ling and Walker, 1976).

The areas defended by breeding males may alter or be abandoned depending on environmental factors (Stirling, 1972) and the presence of females about to give birth (Marlow, 1968, 1975). Social, territorial and reproductive behaviour have recently been described in detail by Marlow (1975) and compared with that of *Phocarctos hookeri*. The normal ratio of males to females at breeding sites appears to be 1:4-6 (Flinders, 1814; Marlow, 1868; Stirling, 1972).

Copulation occurs 6.5 days after parturition (Marlow, 1968). Pups may suckle for two years or longer and individual females have been observed nursing both a newborn pup and a yearling concurrently (Marlow, 1968; Stirling, 1972).

441

Limited data on the age structure of populations in South Australia (Stirling, 1972a) reveal that adults commonly reach nine years, but the limitations of the ageing technique prevented reliable estimation beyond 12 years. On the basis of these data and comparable species of otariids Stirling (1972) suggested that *Neophoca* females commence breeding at three years in compensation for their limited life expectancy.

No quantitative data are yet available on mortality. As appears to be common in many otariids, a proportion of late-term foetuses are lost through abortion (Marlow, 1968) and the presence of wounds and scars on some animals indicates that the species is subject to predation by large sharks (Marlow, 1968). The white pointer (*Carcharodon carcharias*) abounds in southern Australian waters and has frequently been taken by sport fishermen in the vicinity of seal rookeries.

Phocarctos hookeri

Only the broad outline of the biology of this species is known from general accounts (e.g. Musgrave, 1865) and a mass of incidental observations. Breeding occurs on beaches from late October to January; males are territorial and polygamous, the ratio at breeding sites being 1:12 (Gaskin, 1972). Pups are born from November to January, and females are mated only a few days after parturition. The period of lactation appears to be 6-8 months, but pups may remain with their mothers for some months after weaning. The activities of the young pups are closely supervised by their mothers.

In some respects the behaviour of *Phocarctos* seems rather similar to that of *Neophoca*, but there are striking contrasts which are due in part to differences in habitat and also to innate behaviour patterns. Marlow (1975) considers *Phocarctos* to be advanced behaviourly in that it is much more tolerant of its own kind and excessive aggression is avoided by highly ritualized behaviour.

Mirounga leonina

This species returns annually to ancestral breeding sites on sandy beaches, which are usually characterized by their ease of access from the sea. Mature males are found on shore from early August to early December. The first mature and pregnant females arrive in September and congregate in small groups. As each group forms it is taken over by the larger males (beachmasters) and later arrivals join these established harems. These aggregations may eventually contain 600 or more females, which is far more than a single beachmaster can control. Assistant beachmasters are admitted and take over individual sections. Harems of 50 or less never contain more than one breeding bull.

On average a female is present at a breeding site for 28 days (5 days pre-partum and 23 days of lactation) and fasts the whole time. Oestrus occurs in the third week of lactation, or earlier if the pup is lost. During the short period of dependence pups gain weight at a rate of about 5 kg per day.

Carrick and Ingham (1962b) have shown that the breeding population at Macquarie I. is stable at 36 000 females and 3 500-4 000 breeding males, with an annual maximum of the order of 110 000 including pups. Survival of branded, weaned pups to the fourth year of life is over 40 % in both sexes; 20 % of females survive to the eighth year of life, but few may live longer than 12 years. 15 % of males survive to the eighth year of life, but the small number of breeding males may include individuals 20 years old. In this unexploited population females do not reach puberty until the third year at the earliest and for many it does not occur until the fourth or fifth year. Males are thought to reach puberty at 5 years or older, but attainment of reproductive status is deferred until the twelfth to fourteenth year of life.

Growth and development is strikingly different in the exploited population at South Georgia (54°30S, 36°40W). South Georgia females generally reach puberty and mate at 2 years and males are mature and present at the breeding sites at 4 years of age and may hold harems at 7. The rate of growth of South Georgia elephant seals is significantly greater and both males and females achieve larger size than do Macquarie I. seals, suggesting that nutritional factors, i.e. competition for food, are limiting in the latter population (see review in Johnstone, 1972).

Of all the Australasian seals *Mirounga* is the only species which could be commercially exploited at the present time on a sustained yield basis.

Carrick and Ingham (1962b) have considered the feasibility of harvesting the two surpluses that are available as a result of the dynamics of the Macquarie I. population: adult males and weaned pups. Surplus males would have to be taken when they first haul out for breeding or moulting i.e. those times at which they are carrying maximum blubber reserves. Killing of breeding males would probably cause serious disturbance to pregnant and parturient females and the taking of the most economically desirable males, the largest and most experienced harem bulls, would reduce reproductive efficiency. The alternative of selecting younger males at the time of moult did not appear feasible, owing to their less synchronized haul-out habits, and to intermixing with other ages and mature females.

Harvesting of fat weaned pups as they leave the harems appears to be safe, from both the numerical and behavioural view-points. Carrick and Ingham argue that, pending experimental evidence, it might be possible to take up to 80 % of males and 50 % of females without affecting future breeding stocks and success. One likely advantage of such action would be to increase the food resource available to developing females, enabling them to breed at puberty or even increase their survival rate. Carrick and Ingham stressed that these figures are tentative and may be excessive if the causes of juvenile mortality were not approximately density dependent, and further cautioned that large scale trials would be

necessary to determine the most appropriate levels and methods of harvesting.

Food, Feeding and Fisheries

Arctocephalus pusillus doriferus

This fur seal feeds predominantly on squid (*Notodarus* and *Sepioteuthis*), cuttlefish (*Sepia*) and octopus (*Octopus*), but a wide range of fish are also eaten depending on seasonal availability and local opportunity (McNally and Lynch, 1954). Of these barracouta (*Thyrsites*), which often occurs in large shoals in Bass Strait in summer, is undoubtedly the most important. Some of the other species that are taken, though not regularly, nor apparently in large numbers except under favourable circumstances, are salmon (*Arripis*), gurnards (Trigilidae) whiting (*Sillaginodes*) flathead (*Platycephalus*) red mullet (*Upeneichthys*), parrot fish (*Pseudolabrus*), leather-jackets (Aluteridae) and small fishes such as pilchards (Clupeidae). Crayfish (*Jasus*) are taken from time to time, but possibly only when in the "soft shell" stage. Crabs have been found in the stomachs of starveling juveniles, but not in any from healthy, active seals.

Very few seals are seen feeding in bays, estuaries or along the coast, which suggests that the principal feeding grounds are out in open waters over the Continental Shelf. This may also be inferred from the many observations of discrete groups of seals swimming purposefully out to sea from Seal Rocks, Victoria, on a fixed bearing to the southeast.

Although several seals may be seen herding and feeding on a shoal of fish it is not known whether co-operative hunting actually occurs; it is more usual to see seals feeding individually (Lewis, 1929, 1930).

Recoveries of drowned seals from traps and trawl nets indicate that this species is quite able to hunt at depths of at least 118 m. This suggests that the whole of the Continental

443

Shelf is available as a feeding area and there is some evidence that adults work the deeper water off the shelf edge as well.

It is widely maintained by fishermen that seals drastically reduce the stocks of commercially valuable fish, but this claim is not substantiated by evidence from fisheries statistics or the contents of stomachs and ejecta. This fur seal does however, pose a problem to sedentary mesh-net fisheries in Port Phillip and Westernport Bays in Victoria, which are near the large colony at Seal Rocks. Even though these two bays are not significant feeding areas for seals, lone individuals can do extensive damage to a fleet of nets, and losses are compounded by the escape and/or mauling of enmeshed fish. The problem arises sporadically and the only effective remedy is prompt destruction of the offending seal. Seals can also disrupt line fishing for barracouta, but this only appears to be a problem in seasons of short supply.

Arctocephalus forsteri

Data from stomach-contents (Rapson in Sorensen, 1969a; Street, 1964) indicate that *A. forsteri*, in the vicinity of the South I. of New Zealand, feeds mainly on squid (*Notodarus* and *Sepioteuthis*), octopus (*Octopus*) and barracouta, and not on prime commercial fish as claimed by fishermen working those waters. Street's analysis showed that barracouta comprised 38 % by weight of the diet, with octopus, squid and other fish in the percentages 29, 24 and 9 respectively. Of the variety of other fish identified none were of commercial significance, and it was clear that any commercial fish taken by seals would be incidental to their main diet. Further south, off Campbell I., the main diet is penguins and squid (Bailey and Sorensen, 1962).

According to Street, *A. forsteri* feeds principally in near-surface waters (on barracouta and squid) and at night, but takes octopus on the bottom at any time.

There are no data on the species' food

preferences in Australian waters, but squid, octopus and barracouta are all abundantly available. Mutton birds and presumably other small sea birds are occasionally taken (Warneke, pers. obs.). As far as I am aware *A. forsteri* does not occur in sufficient numbers near fishing grounds in South or Western Australia to be considered a problem.

Neophoca cinerea

Very little has been recorded of the diet and feeding behaviour of this sea lion. Wood Jones (1925) records that Little penguins (*Eudyptula*) are commonly taken by adult males when both are ashore for the breeding season. Penguins breed on many of the islands inhabited by *Neophoca* and would be easy prey when moving to and from their burrows. They may also be caught at sea. Wood Jones also observed a sea lion tearing up a large fiddler ray (*Trygonorhina*) at the surface by gripping it firmly in its teeth and shaking vigorously. This fish is common in the shallow coastal waters of South Australia.

Apart from the general antipathy of fishermen towards seals there appears to be no widespread complaint against sea lions by the industry, probably because they do not occur in large numbers in any one place. Storr (1961) records that sea lions are "disliked" by fishermen netting salmon (*Arripis*) at Cheynes Beach, Western Australia, because they attack the nets to reach the enclosed fish.

Phocarctos hookeri

According to Gaskin (1972) this sea lion feeds mainly on small fish, crustaceans, sea birds and penguins. Waite (1909) found the remains of octopus and fish in one stomach and quoted information to the effect that octopus remains were frequently found in their stomachs. A red crab (*Nectocarcinus antarcticus*) is eaten and the indigestible remains regurgitated (King, 1964).

Visiting sea lions at Macquarie I. have been observed preying on Gentoo penguins (*Pygoscelis*) and the technique has been described in detail by Gwynn (1953).

Mirounga leonina

The feeding habits of this seal in the New Zealand region have not been studied in detail, but fish, cephalopods and small crustaceans appear to be the major items of the diet (Gaskin, 1972).

Research and Aesthetics

Arctocephalus pusillus doriferus

As a direct result of long controversy over the effects of this species on local fisheries in Victoria, field studies of behaviour, diet, reproductive physiology, population structure and status were conducted during the period 1965-1977. This project involved an extensive marking programme and monthly sampling during two successive years (Warneke, 1966, 1975; Stirling and Warneke, 1971). The results of these studies will provide the basis for future conservation and management policies.

Apart from its importance to field research, the Seal Rocks colony is a rather unique tourist attraction. For many years it has been one of the important wildlife assets of Phillip Is., which is a major tourist outlet for Melbourne, a city with a population of approximately 3 million. Seal Rocks harbours the only large breeding colony of seals in Australia that may be easily and safely viewed by the public, either from Pt. Grant, an adjacent headland of Phillip I., or from a ferry which runs out to the colony in good weather during the tourist season. A tourist facility at Pt. Grant provides high-power binoculars for viewing and a free information brochure. The feasibility of using closed circuit television to view the colony at close range and improve the scope and detail of the visual experience is currently beeing considered.

The only other colony of this species which at present offers scope for tourism is at Lady Julia Percy I., Victoria. Boat parties are occasionally taken out to view the seals from the nearest ports (a distance of about 20 km) but there is as yet no regular service.

Australian fur seals are exhibited in both the Melbourne Zoological Gardens, Victoria, and at Taronga Zoo in Sydney, New South Wales.

Arctocephalus forsteri

The totally inadequate biological basis for the 1946 open season in New Zealand led to field surveys by Falla (Sorensen, 1969a; Falla, 1953) and recommendations for future studies. An encouraging series of publications have since appeared, covering a modest breadth of topics: feeding habits (Rapson in Sorensen, 1969a; Street, 1964), the increase in non-breeding colonies to the north (Tunbridge in Sorensen, 1969; Stonehouse, 1965; Stirling, 1970; Singleton, 1972; Wilson, 1974a), isolated strandings in tropical waters at New Caledonia (King, 1976), recolonization of Macquarie I. (Gwynn, 1953; Csordas, 1958; Csordas and Ingham, 1965), diurnal rhythms of activity (Stirling, 1968; Crawley, 1972), social and reproductive behaviour (Stirling, 1970; Miller, 1971, 1974, 1974a, 1975a; Crawley, 1972; Crawley and Wilson, 1976), vocal communication (Brown, 1974), body and organ weights (Miller, 1975), a population estimate from pup counts (Crawley and Brown, 1971), and the distribution and summer abundance throughout New Zealand (Wilson, 1974, 1974a).

Current investigations are aimed at determining the magnitude and rate of the increase in numbers of this species throughout its range (Crawley, pers. comm.).

Research in Australia has been limited to social and reproductive behaviour (Stirling, 1971, 1971a; Stirling and Warneke, 1971).

445

I am unable to give any worthwhile assessment of the aesthetics of this species. In Australia it is by no means an accessible animal, and the only colony that can be viewed with comparative ease is hardly known to the public. This is a small, mainly non-breeding colony near Cape du Couedic, Kangaroo I., a locality that is visited by tourists because of its picturesque lighthouse and rugged rock formations.

Neophoca cinerea

Despite its wide range this species has received little attention from biologists until recent years. Apart from general accounts of its natural history and morphology (e.g. Wood Jones, 1925) there have been only brief contributions on reproductive and maternal behaviour (Marlow, 1968; Stirling, 1972), population structure (Stirling 1972) and pup abduction (Marlow, 1972).

More recently Marlow (1975), in the context of comparing the two Australasian sea lions, presented a detailed description of non-interactive, social, territorial, reproductive and maternal behaviour, and development of the pup. Ling and Walker (1976) are currently studying the population dynamics of *Neophoca* at several colonies and are attempting to assess accurately the current status and distribution of the entire population.

It is a species of great importance to tourism in South Australia, and its economic value to that state can only increase as tourism expands. This has been clearly shown by conservative estimates of tourist expenditure in relation to the seals at Seal Bay, Kangaroo I. (Stirling, 1972a). A non-breeding colony at this locality has become so accustomed to humans that tourists are able to mingle with the seals on the beach. Conducted tours to Seal Bay began in 1955 and the service has expanded in recent years. Stirling has stressed that management authorities must anticipate future pressures if this important natural resource is not to be lost.

Neophoca is held in captivity at a number of zoos and aquaria in Australia and appears to be a hardy and tractable species in confinement.

Phocarctos hookeri

This is the least known of all the seals in the Australasian Region, because of its restricted distribution and the remoteness of its breeding grounds.

However, as activity in seal research has increased in recent years, some preliminary work has been done on distribution, abundance and social and reproductive behaviour at the Auckland Is. and the Snares (Crawley and Cameron, 1972; Best, 1974).

Mirounga leonina

This species has been the subject of long-term life history studies by Australian biologists at Macquarie I. since 1951 (Carrick and Ingham, 1960). The main findings, based on marked individuals of known age, were published by Carrick, Csordas and Ingham (1962); Carrick et al., (1962); Carrick and Ingham (1962, 1962a and 1962b), and Nicholls (1970).

Subsequent studies have been on more specialized physiological topics: growth and development (Bryden, 1967, 1968, 1968a, 1968b, 1968c, 1969, 1969a, 1969b, 1971, 1971a, 1972, 1973; Bryden and Lim, 1969), and the integument (Ling, 1965, 1966, 1968; Ling and Thomas, 1967).

The remoteness and general inaccessibility of the major breeding and hauling out grounds of this species prevents their exploitation as a tourist resource. Captive display is the only alternative and the first attempt, using 2 juveniles, at the Mount Mauganui Marineland at Hauranga, New Zealand, is proving successful (Gaskin, 1972).

Acknowledgements

I am most grateful to the various government agencies, institutions, colleagues and other individuals who, by their interest in the object of my enquiries and their prompt response, assisted very materially in the compilation of this report. I am especially indebted to Judith King of the Department of Zoology, University of New South Wales; John Ling, Director, and Peter Aitken, Senior Curator of the South Australian Museum; and to Peter Shaughnessy, formerly of the Mawson Institute, Adelaide.

Reviewing the Australian situation was difficult enough from within, but the New Zealand region would have been impossible from the opposite side of the Tasman Sea without the generous assistance of Dr. Malcolm Crawley and Mr. Graham Wilson of the University of Canterbury.

Appendix A

ABBREVIATIONS USED IN TEXT

CSIRO	Commonwealth Scientific and Industrial Research Organization: Division of Fisheries and Oceanography.
HRA	Historical Records of Australia. (1913-1925). Series I, Vols. 1-26 III, Vols. 1-6; IV, Vol. 1, Sydney.
HRNSW	Historical Records of New South Wales (1893-1901). 7 vols. Sydney.
HRNZ	Historical Records of New Zealand (1908, 1914). 2 vols. Wellington.
HTG	Hobart Town Gazette and Southern Reporter (1816-1819). Facs. Ed. Hobart, Platypus Publications, 1965, 1967.
NSW:FISH	Fisheries Branch, Chief Secretary's Department, New South Wales.
NSW:NPWS	National Parks and Wildlife Service, New South Wales.
SAM	South Australian Museum, Adelaide.
SG	Sydney Gazette and New South Wales Advertizer (1803-1810). Facs. Ed. Sydney, Pub. Lib. NSW and Angus and Robertson, 1963-1970.
TAS:CC	W.E.L.H. Crowther Collection, State Library of Tasmania.
TAS:FISH	Fisheries Division, Department of Agriculture, Tasmania.
TAS:NPWS	National Parks and Wildlife Service, Tasmania.
VIC:FWD	Fisheries and Wildlife Division, Ministry for Conservation, Victoria.
VIC:NPS	National Parks Service, Ministry for Conservation, Victoria.
WA:DFW	Department of Fisheries and Wildlife, Western Australia.

Appendix B

NON-SPECIFIC RECORDS OF SEALS IN AUSTRALIAN WATERS

Key to status. A breeding colony.
B non-breeding colony.
C status unknown.

BABEL I. (39°57′S, 148°20′E).
1801, sealers camp (Murray). Lee, 1915:85.
1817, Dec. many seals seen. (C) King, 1827(1):7.

BRUNY I. (43°15′S, 147°20′E).
1802, Jan. seals observed in Adventure Bay. Peron and Freycinet, 1816:36.

BUFFALO REEF (34°43′S, 136°27′E).
1945, Apr. c. 12 (Fowler). (B) CSIRO.

447

CAPE BLANCHE (33°01′S, 134°09′E).
1945,   May. c. 6 on rocks of cape (Fowler). (C) CSIRO.

CAP I. (33°57′S, 135°08′E).
1945,   May. c. 6 (Fowler). (C) CSIRO.

CAT. I. (39°58′S, 148°22′E).
1798,   Jan. a boat-load of seals and gannets obtained by Bass. Flinders, 1814(1):cxcii.
1798,   Jan. seals encountered by Bass, males territorial. (A) Collins, 1802:191.

CLARKE I. (41°33′S, 148°11′E).
1802,   Mar. a great number of seals (Bailly). Peron, 1807:357.

COMBE I. (34°05′S, 122°57′E).
1945,   May. c. 6 (Fowler). (C) CSIRO.

COUNCILLOR I. (39°49′S, 144°11′E), once known as

ELEPHANT ROCK and ELEPHANT I.
1802,   Jan. fur seals killed on Elephant Rock, 6-7 000 ashore (Murray). Lee, 1915:122.
1802,   Jun. 600 obtained by gang from the *Margaret*, mainly from Elephant I. HRNSW, 5:8; Cumpston, 1973:52.
1802,   Dec. covered with seals (Grimes). Shillinglaw, 1879:16.
1813,   Jan. 2 skins obtained. Kelly Log, TAS:CC.

CRAGGY I. (39°41′S, 147°41′E).
1830's,   sealers camp (Robinson). Plomley, 1966:612.
(1871),   sealing ground known as "The Stacks". Gould, 1872:66.
1890,   breeding colony. (A) Le Souef, 1891:123.

CURTIS GROUP (39°28′S, 146°39′E).
1820's,   sealers camp for 5 years (Robinson). Plomley, 1966:326.
1820's,   seals taken at THE SLIPPER. Plomley, 1966:337.

DOUBTFUL IS. (34°22′S, 119°35′E).
1802,   seals seen on small islet nearby. Flinders, 1814(1):76.

EASTERN GROUP (33°50′S, 124°06′E).
1945,   Jun. 20-30 on NW Island; 100-150 for group, not including S island (Fowler). (C) CSIRO.

FENELON I. (32°35′S, 133°17′E).
1945,   Apr. c. 12 (Fowler). (C) CSIRO.

GODFREY IS. (37°05′S, 139°44′E), once known as BAUDIN'S ROCKS.
1831,   Dec. 30 seals killed by men from the *Elizabeth*. (C) Bride, 1898:52.

HELBY I. (34°08′S, 123°04′E).
1945,   Jun. 3 (Fowler). (C) CSIRO.

HUGO I. (34°09′S, 122°18′E).
1945,   Jun. 8 (Fowler). (C) CSIRO.

HUNTER GROUP (40°30′S, 144°50′E).
1802,   Dec. Islet off Three Hummock I. covered with seals (Freycinet). Peron and Freycinet, 1816:31; Cumpston, 1973:57
1832,   Jun. sealers camp (Robinson). Plomley, 1966:612.
1834,   Feb. sealing occurring (Robinson). (C) Plomley, 1966:845.
1830's,   seals killed on islet off S. coast of Three Hummock, I. (Robinson). (C) Plomley, 1966:670.

KENT GROUP (39°30′S, 147°20′E).
1791,   some seals seen. Flinders, 1814(1):cxliv.
1801,   Nov. seals seldom ashore, evidence of sealers found (Murray). Lee, 1915:98.
1801,   Dec. 2 seals killed (Murray). Lee, 1915:98.
1802,   Dec. many seals and sealions (Grimes). Shillinglaw, 1879:15.
1803,   500 skins obtained by the JOHN. SG, 11 Sept. 1803.
1830's,   home of the black fur seals. *Gippsland Mercury*, 2 Feb. 1875.

KING I. (39°50′S, 144°00′E).
1802,   Jan. fur seals killed at Seal Bay, vast number on shore (Murray). (A) Lee, 1915:85.
1802,   Mar-May. 4 300 skins taken by gangs from the *Harrington*. HRA, I, 3:524, 637, 641.

1804, Feb. none of any consequence. Delano, 1817:462.

Note: localities named for seals: Phoques Bay, Seal Bay, Sea Elephant Bay, Seal Point.

LAWRENCE ROCKS (38°25'S, 141°11'E).
1830-31, 400 skins obtained (Hart). Bride, 1898:51.

LOW FLAT IS. (34°01'S, 123°32'E).
1945, May. 6 on main island (Fowler). (C) CSIRO.

MARTS IS. (34°01'S, 122°39'E).
1945, May. 6-8 on W islands, E islands not inspected (Fowler). (C) CSIRO.

NEW YEARS IS. (39°41'S, 143°49'E), classified as a Conservation Area, TAS:NPWS.
1802, covered with innumerable legions of various species (Faure). Peron and Freychinet, 1816:22.

NINTH I. (30°50'S, 147°15'E), once known as TWENTY-DAY I.
1817, abounds with seal. (C) HTG, 21 June, 1817.

NUYTS REEFS (32°06'S, 132°10'E).
1945, Apr. 30-40 on E rock (Fowler). (C) CSIRO.
1945, May. 15-20 on E rock (Fowler). (C) CSIRO.

POINT BELL (32°12'S, 133°06'E).
1945, May. 4 on rocks off point (Fowler). (C) CSIRO.

PRIME SEAL I. (40°04'S, 147°46'E), also known as HUMMOCK I.
1832, formerly the resort of vast herds ... a few seen on an adjacent rock. Backhouse, 1843:172.

RED I. (33°51'S, 121°20'E).
1945, Jul. c. 20 (Fowler). (C) CSIRO.

ROCKY I. (34°16'S, 135°17'E).
1945, May. c. 80 (Fowler). (C) CSIRO.

SINCLAIR I. (32°08'S, 133°00'E).
1945, May. c. 20 (Fowler). (C) CSIRO.

SISTERS, THE (EAST: 39°30'S, 148°00'E; WEST: 39°42'S, 147°55'E), classified as Conservation Areas, TAS:NPWS.
1802, Oct. sealing by French gang. Peron and Freychinet, 1816:4, 33; Cumpston, 1973:15-16.

SLIPPER I. (34°03'S, 122°44'E).
1945, May. 1 (Fowler). CSIRO.

SWAN I. (40°44'S, 148°06'E).
1802, Mar. seals abounded on this island (Bailly). Peron, 1807:358.

THISTLE I. (islet at 35°04'S, 136°10'E).
1945, Apr. c. 60 (Fowler). (C) CSIRO.

WARD I. (33°44'S, 134°17'E).
1945, Apr. 6 (Fowler). (C) CSIRO.

WATERHOUSE I. (40°48'S, 147°38'E).
1898, covered with hair seals. * Flinders, 1814(1):cli.
1802, Mar. frequented by a great number of seals (Bailly). Peron, 1807:359.

WEST I. (34°06'S, 120°18'E).
1802, Jan. frequented by seals. Flinders, 1814(1):78.

Appendix C

DATA ON THE DISTRIBUTION AND STATUS OF THE AUSTRALIAN FUR SEAL, *ARCTOCEPHALUS PUSILLUS DORIFERUS*

Known to the early sealers as sea bear, brown fur seal, grey fur seal; aboriginal names "wayanna" and "cartela" but specific identify uncertain.

Key to status: A breeding colony.
B non-breeding colony.
C status unknown.

---

* A doubtful record of this species as Flinders passed at a distance of about 1.5 km and none of his party landed.

NEW SOUTH WALES

MONTAGUE I. (36°15'S, 150°13'E), lighthouse site under the control of the Federal Government.

1798,	Feb. many seals in water. Flinders, 1814(1):cxxi: Rawson, 1946:72.
1925,	Aug.-Nov. estimate of 200. Le Souef, 1925:114.
1963,	Summer peak. NSW:NPWS.
1970,	Nov. estimate of 150. NSW:NPWS.
1971,	300 maximum, pups born (report from fishermen). NSW:NPWS.
1974,	200, numbers increasing. (C) NSW:NPWS.

SEAL ROCKS (32°28'S, 152°33'E), dedicated as a Nature Reserve.

1925,	estimate of 500. (A) Le Souef, 1925:115.
1970,	22, including 1 large male. (A) NSW:NPWS.
1972,	minimum of 1 pup born. (A) NSW:NPWS.
1974,	count of 12. (C) NSW:NPWS.

TASMANIA AND BASS STRAIT, north to 39°12'S.

ALBATROSS I. (40°23'S, 144°39'E), classified as a Conservation Area, TAS:NPWS.

1798,	Dec. seals taken by Bass. (A) Flinders, 1801, 1814(1):clxxii.
prior 1813,	minimum of 12 000 (Kelly). (A) Plomley, 1966:697.
1813,	Feb.-Mar. 5 783 skins taken from "seal rock" near Hunter I. (= Albatros I.?). Kelly Log, TAS:CC.
1832,	Oct. 1 seal seen (Robinson). Plomley, 1966:665.
1895,	Skeletal remains of seals found in large cave. Ashworth and Le Souef, 1895:138.
1973,	Jan.-Feb. 5 seen, including a sub-adult male tagged at Seal Rocks, Victoria. (B) Warneke, pers. obs.; skeletal remains of *A.p.d.* found in large cave. Warneke, field catalog.

BETSY I. (43°03'S, 147°29'E), classified as a Conservation Area, TAS:NPWS.

| 1974, | estimate of 10-20. (C) TAS:FISH. |

BLACK PYRAMID (40°29'S, 144°19'E), also known SEAL (Sailing Directions for Victorian and Bass Strait, 1970), Classified as a Conservation Area, TAS:NPWS.

1842,	colony said to exist. (C) Stokes, 1846(1):299.
1972,	small colony (Olsen). (C) VIC:FWD.
1973,	Feb. no seals seen from boat (Warneke). VIC:FWD.

CAPE PILLAR, TASMANIA (43°13'S, 148°00'E).

1910,	colony known. (C) Barrett, 1918:146.
1945,	estimate of 2 000 (Challenger). VIC:FWD.
1972,	60-80 (Dinger). (C) VIC:FWD.
1974,	30-50. TAS:FISH.
1974,	25-50. TAS:NPWS.

FRIAR ROCKS (43°32'S, 147°18'E).

| 1972, | small colony (Olsen). (C) VIC:FWD. |

GEORGE ROCKS (40°55'S, 148°20'E).

1816,	Jan. 172 skins taken in 9 days, pups present (Kelly). (A). Kelly, 1920:174-80.
1827,	worked by sealers. O'May (n.d.):29.
1840's,	sealing ground. Stokes, 1846(2): 450.
1972,	small colony (Olsen). (C) VIC:FWD.

HIPPOLYTE ROCKS (43°07'S, 148°03'E).

1945,	Mar. c. 120 (Fowler). (C) CSIRO.
1945,	Apr. 70-80 (Fowler). (C) CSIRO.
1972,	May-Jul. 50 (Dinger). (C) VIC:FWD.
1974,	12-20. (C) TAS:NPWS.

HOGAN GROUP (39°13'S, 147°00'E).

1840's,	sealing in large cave. (C) Doome, 1874.
1840's,	home of brown fur seal. *Gippsland Mercury*, 2 Feb. 1875.
1842,	fur seals in cave on largest island. Stokes, 1846(2):426.
1871,	seals in large cave. Gould, 1872:66.
1905,	colony known (Vietheer). CSIRO.
1925,	300 (fisherman). (C) Le Souef, 1925:114.
1973,	Dec.-Jan. 1974. 20-40 on East Islet (Murray-Smith). VIC:FWD.
1975,	Apr. 30-40 on East Islet (Warneke). VIC:FWD.

JUDGEMENT ROCKS (39°30'S, 147°08'E).

| 1890, | seals breeding on centre islet, sealing |

still occurring. (A) Le Souef, 1891:123.

1921, 350 skins taken by Cape Barren Islanders (Vietheer). CSIRO.

1945, Mar. 800-1 000 (Fowler). CSIRO.

1945, Apr. 1 000 (Fowler). CSIRO.

1965, Jan. 300-400 (Dorward). VIC:FWD.

1973, Jan. 4 000 (Murray-Smith). (A) VIC:FWD.

1975, Apr. 1 500-2 000 (Warneke). VIC:FWD.

KENT GROUP (39°30′S, 147°20′E).

1820's and 30's, small sealing settlement on Deal I. Whinray, 1971:2.

1925, 200 (fishermen). (C) Le Souef, 1925:114.

MAATSUYKER IS. (43°39′S, 146°17′E).

1971, 60 on Needle Rocks. (C) TAS:NPWS.

1974, 10-20 on north side. (C) TAS:FISH.

1975, 800-1 000 on rocks SW of lighthouse. (A) TAS:NPWS.

MARIA I. (42°40′S, 148°05′E), once known as OYSTER I., now Maria Island National Park, TAS:NPWS.

1802, innumerable seals. (A) Peron, 1807:301.

1802, Mar. object of sealing vessel *Endeavour*. Peron, 1807:309.

1804-05, c. 2 000 skins lost by gang from *Sophia* sealing at Oyster Bay (Knopwood). Nicholls, 1977:78.

1805, sealing gang on island. HRNSW, 5:697.

1972, small colony on Ilot Du Nord (Olsen). (C) VIC:FWD.

1972, 2 or 3 groups = 200 (Dinger) (C) VIC:FWD.

1974, a few, seen regularly. (C) TAS:NPWS.

MONCOEUR IS. (39°14′S, 146°31′E).

1921, 400 skins taken by Cape Barren Islanders (Vietheer). CSIRO.

1925, 300 on Western Island (fishermen). (C) Le Souef, 1925:114.

1945, Apr. 300-400 on W island (Fowler). (C) CSIRO.

1945, colony reported on E island (in error for W?), said to be larger than Seal Rocks, Vic. VIC:FWD.

1967, Jan. minimum of 200 at E end of W island (Mirrabella). VIC:FWD.

1975, Apr. c. 420 (Warneke). (C) VIC:FWD.

MORIARTY ROCKS (40°36′S, 148°16′E), once known as COUNCIL ROCKS.

1925, 150 (fishermen). Le Souef, 1925:114.

1925, 1 800-2 000 (Mansfield). Le Souef, 1925:114.

1945, Apr. 800-1 000 (Fowler). (C) CSIRO.

1971, Jul. c. 620 (Warneke). (C) VIC:FWD.

PEDRA BLANCA (43°52′S, 146°58′E), also known as PEDRA BRANCA or PEDRO BLANCO.

1939, Feb. c. 300 (Fowler). (C) CSIRO.

1945, 5 000 (Challenger). VIC:FWD.

1945, minimum of 1 000 (Fowler). (C) VIC:FWD.

1947, Apr. estimate of 400-500 (Palfreyman). (C) Fowler, 1947:22-6.

1972, small colony (Olsen). (C) VIC:FWD.

1974, 12-20. TAS:NPWS.

1975, Apr. c. 90 (Warneke). (C) VIC:FWD.

"PINEAPPLE" (= PARTRIDGE I.) (43°24′S, 147°06′E).

1974, 5-10. (C) TAS:FISH.

PORT DAVEY, TASMANIA (43°20′S, 145°55′E), within the SW Fauna District, a conservation area, TAS:NPWS.

1972, seals seen at Window Pane Bay, (Olsen). (C) VIC:FWD.

1974, maximum of 20. (C) TAS:NPWS.

PYRAMID, THE (39°49′S, 147°14′E).

1830, Dec. 400 skins taken (Robinson). (C) Plomley, 1966:177, 302-3, 337, 443.

1974, 300-400, increasing. (C) TAS:NPWS.

1975, Apr. c. 150 (Warneke). (C) VIC:FWD.

REID'S ROCKS (40°15′S, 144°10′E).

1854, Nov. large herd. (C) Nixon, 1857:96.

1910, colony known. (C) Barrett, 1918:146.

1925, 1 500-2 000 (fishermen). Le Souef, 1925:114.

1945, Apr. 2 000 (Fowler). (C) CSIRO.

1974, Jun. 300-500. TAS:NPWS.

1975, Apr. c. 1 300 (Warneke). (A) VIC:FWD.

SCHOUTEN I. (42°20′S, 148°20′E).

1972, small colony (Olsen). (C) VIC:FWD.

SISTERS, THE (43°39′S, 146°23′E). The eastern island also known as SEAL ROCK or FLAT TOP I.

1871,   colony known. (C) Gould, 1872:66.
1944,   seals numerous. *Aust. Pilot*, 1944(2): 219-20.
1945,   4 000 (Challenger). (C) VIC:FWD.
1972,   small colony (Olsen). VIC:FWD.
1974,   50-150 on "Flat-top Sister". (C) TAS:FISH.

TENTH I. (39°57′S, 146°59′E), commonly known as BARRENJOEY.
1798,   Nov. covered with hair (?) seals, Flinders, 1814(1):cli.
1910,   colony known. (C) Barrett, 1918:137.
1925,   200 (fishermen). (C) Le Souef, 1925:114.
1925,   1 000 (Mansfield). (C) Le Souef, 1925:114.
1945,   Apr. 300-400 (Fowler). (C) CSIRO.
1971,   Jul. minimum of 400 (Warneke). (A) VIC:FWD.
1974,   200. TAS:NPWS.
1975,   Apr. minimum of 500 (Warneke). (A) VIC:FWD.

WHITE ROCK (42°25′S, 148°10′E), once known as ISLE DES PHOQUES.
1802,   Feb. covered with a prodigious number of seals (Bailly). (C) Peron, 1807:294; Cumpston, 1973:48.
1802,   Feb. covered with seals (Baudin). (B) Cornell, 1974:349.
1816,   Jan. 6 skins collected. Kelly, 1920:181.
1832,   fur seals taken occasionally. Backhouse, 1843:73.
1910,   Jan. 50 seals in cave. Barrett, 1918:114.
1925,   estimate of 100. Le Souef, 1925:114.
1945,   500 (Challenger). (C) VIC:FWD.
1974,   10-20. (C) TAS:FISH.

WRIGHT'S ROCK (39°36′S, 147°32′E).
1803,   May. seals heard at night. (C). Flinders, 1814(2):271.
1945,   Apr. none seen (Fowler). (C) CSIRO.
1971,   Jan. 40 ashore, including males, females and young. (C). Marginson and Murray-Smith, 1972:213.
1975,   Apr. c. 190 (Warneke). (B) VIC:FWD.

VICTORIA, south to 39°12′S.

CAPE BRIDGEWATER (38°23′S, 141°25′E).
1948,   60 in caves at E point; "young" seen

(Patterson). (C) VIC:FWD.
1948,   80-100 (Sealey). (C) VIC:FWD.
1971,   seals seen· in cave (Beinssen). VIC:FWD.
1971,   young seen (abalone fishermen). VIC:FWD.
1975,   July. c. 40 in cave at E point (Beinssen). VIC:FWD.
1976,   Jan. 25-30 in cave (Warneke). (B) VIC:FWD.

CAPE NELSON (38°25′S, 141°34′E).
1948,   60 in caves at E point (Sealey). (C) VIC:FWD.
1948,   50; bulls seen Nov.-Dec., young seals in Jan.-Feb. (Patterson). (A) VIC:FWD.
1971,   seals in cave, to be seen at any time of year (Beinssen). VIC:FWD.

KANOWNA (39°10′S, 146°18′E), part of Wilsons Promontory National Park, VIC:NPS.
1874,   seals on adjacent islets. (C) Doome, 1874.
1925,   600 (fishermen). Le Souef, 1925:114.
1945,   1 500-2 000; 250 on adjacent islets (Fowler). (A) VIC:FWD.
1964,   Jun. maximum of 300, on N slope and adjacent rocks (Dorward and Pizzey, mimeogr. report). VIC:FWD.
1966,   Oct. 500-650 on N slope (Baum.). VIC:FWD.
1974,   July. 1 800 on Island and adjacent islets (Warneke). (A) VIC:FWD.
1975,   Apr. 2 000-2 500 on island and adjacent islets (Warneke). (A) VIC:FWD.

LADY JULIA PERCY I. (38°25′S, 142°00′E), a State Faunal Reserve, VIC:FWD.
1822-28,   sealers at island. Mahoney, 1937:332.
1866,   seals in great numbers (Griffiths). (C) Mahoney, 1937:332.
1925,   3 000-4 000 (fishermen). (C). Le Souef, 1925:114.
1936,   Dec. 3 000-4 000; more than 1 000 pups. (A) Tubb and Brazenor, 1937:435.
1945,   5 000 (Lewis). (A) VIC:FWD.
1945,   Apr. minimum of 1 000 (Fowler). CSIRO.
1948,   Nov.-Dec. 2 000 (Tarr). Coleman, 1951:177.

1963,   Dec. colony larger than Seal Rocks (c. 5 000). (A) Pescott, 1965:294.

1967,   Dec. slight increase (from 1963); some bachelor sites now maternal sites. (A) Pescott, 1968:127.

1974,   Feb. 962 pups tagged, of estimated 1 800 (Warneke). VI:FWD.

1975,   Jan. 1 380 pups tagged (Warneke). VIC:FWD.

1976,   Jan. 1 786 pups tagged (Warneke). VIC:FWD.

1977,   Jan. 1 342 pups tagged (Warneke). VIC:FWD.

LAWRENCE ROCKS (38°25'S, 141°41'E), a State Faunal Reserve, VIC:FWD.

1948,   25, in water only (Patterson). (B) VIC:FWD.

1948,   estimate of 30 (Sealey). VIC:FWD.

SEAL IS. (38°56'S, 146°40'E), also known as DIRECTION IS.

1798,   Jan. the number of seals was by no means equal to what we had been led to expect. It is certain, however, that great numbers had been destroyed ... pups seem now to be nearly full grown ... a speculation on a small scale might be carried on with advantage (Bass). (A) Flinders, 1814(1):cxvii; Rawson, 1946:36.

1966,   Dec. 60-70 yearlings, 3 adult females at SW end of Rag I. (Baum). Normally only up to 6 old seals at E end (Truscott). (C) VIC:FWD.

SEAL ROCKS, off Phillip I. (38°32'S, 145°06'E), a State Faunal Reserve, VIC:FWD.

1801,   Mar. covered with seals ... of a large size ... I judged them to be of that species ... called by the fishermen Sea Elephants ... they may be found in great numbers. (C) Grant, 1803:123.

1801,   Dec. several thousand pups lying on shore ... evidence of sealers found (Murray). (A) Lee, 1915:104.

1850's,   estimate of 20-40. Lewis, 1942:24.

1860,   100 (fishermen). VIC:FWD.

1869,   estimate of 20 (Kennon). (C) Coleman, 1951:176.

1879,   seals taken for oil (Kennon). Gliddon, 1963:229.

1907,   1 000-2 000. (C) *Vict. Nat.*, 24:54.

1913,   Mar. 400-600. (C) Gabriel, 1913:31.

1925,   3 000-4 000 (fishermen). Le Souef, 1925:114.

1945,   Apr. c. 3 000 (Fowler). CSIRO.

1945,   5,000 (Lewis). VIC:FWD.

1966-74,   colony stable at about 5 500 (shore counts); producing an annual crop of about 2 000 pups. Warneke, 1975.

SKERRIES, THE (37°45'S, 149°31'E), part of Wingan National Park, VIC:NPS.

1910,   colony known. (C) Barrett, 1918:146.

1945,   Apr. 400-500 (Fowler). CSIRO.

1946,   300-400, maximum of 800 (Fowler). (A) VIC:FWD.

1974,   Feb. about 50 pups (Warneke). (A) VIC:FWD.

WHITE ROCK (38°55'S, 146°39'E).

1966,   Dec. 180 in two groups; mainly yearlings but including 4 bulls and 6 adult females (Baum). (C) VIC:FWD.

1975,   Apr. 190-200 (Baum). (C) VIC:FWD.

1977,   Apr. c. 135 (Cherry). (C) VIC:FWD.

Appendix D

DATA ON THE DISTRIBUTION AND STATUS OF THE NEW ZEALAND FUR SEAL, *ARCTOCEPHALUS FORSTERI*

Known to the early sealers as sea bear or black fur seal; maori name "Kekeno".

Key to status: A breeding colony.
                 B non-breeding colony.
                 C status unknown.

SOUTH AUSTRALIA

ALTHORPE I. (35°22'S, 136°51'E), Althorpe Island Conservation Park, SA:NPWS.

1969,   breeding colony. (A) King, 1969:850.

CASUARINA IS. (36°06'S, 136°42'E), also known as THE BROTHERS; part Flinders Chase National Park, SA:NPWS.

453

1912, 20 fur seals killed. Wood Jones, 1925:377.

1925, presence practically certain. Wood Jones, 1925:377.

1945, Apr. c. 60 on N island (Fowler). (C) CSIRO.

1969, fur seals on N island. (C) King, 1969:851.

1974, Feb. minimum of 40 on N island, mostly males (Warneke). VIC:FWD.

1975, Mar. 240, (a few newborn pups in previous Jan.). (A) Ling and Walker, 1976:65.

FENELON I. (32°35′S, 133°17′E).
1975, Jun. 40 (Delroy). (C) Ling and Walker, 1976:65.

FLINDERS I. (33°43′S, 133°17′E).
1802, Feb. 3 seals, of blackish colour, seen on the rocks (Brown). Cooper, 1955:69.

FOUR HUMMOCKS (34°46′S, 135°01′E).
1968, colony known. King, 1968:632.
1969, 50-100. (C) King, 1969:850.

FREELING I. (32°39′S, 133°21′E).
1975, Jun. 5 (Delroy). Ling and Walker, 1976:65.

GAMBIER IS. (35°10′S, 136°27′E).
1969, mapped as seal locality. (C) King, 1969:850.
1975, Nov. 26 on South-West Rocks. Ling and Walker, 1976:65.

GREENLY I. (34°49′S, 134°47′E).
1947, Nov. present, no estimate. (C) Finlayson, 1948:38; (less than 100, see Mitchell and Behrndt, 1949:172).

KANGAROO I. (35°50′S, 137°20′E), part Flinders Chase National Park, SA:NPWS.
1803, Jan. great number of seals at Anse des Phoques (= Western Cove). (C) Peron and Freycinet, 1816:70.
1803, 1 400 hair and fur seal skins taken (Pendleton). Fanning, 1833:319.
1969, colony at Cape du Couedic. (C) King, 1969:850.
1974, Feb. non-breeding group, mostly of

sub-adult males (Warneke). (B) VIC:FWD.

1975, Jan. 3 pups at Cape du Couedic. (A) Ling and Walker, 1976:65.

1975, Mar. peak of 240 seals. Ling and Walker, 1976:65.

SOUTH NEPTUNE IS. (35°19′S, 136°06′E), Neptune Islands Conservation Park, SA:NPWS.
1970, several breeding colonies on N island, including a minimum of 920 females. (A) Stirling, 1971:247.
1975, Sep. 1 100 on N island, 200 on Middle Rock (Needham). Ling and Walker, 1976:65.

THISTLE I. (35°00′S, 136°08′E).
1969, maximum of 20. (C) King, 1969:850.
1975, Jun. count of 8. Ling and Walker, 1976:65.

TASMANIA AND BASS STRAIT

CAPE BARREN I.[1] (40°25′S, 148°15′E).
1798, main concentration at Cone Pt. (A) Flinders, 1814(1): cxxix, cxxxiii.
1798, 9 000 skins taken by pioneer gang (Bishop). Roe, 1967:317.

CLARKE I.[1] (40°33′S, 148°11′E).
1798, fur seals abundant at S end. (C) Flinders, 1814(1):cxxxiii.

KENT GROUP (39°30′S, 147°20′E).
1840's, home of the black fur seal. (C) *Gippsland Mercury*, 2 Feb. 1875.

---

[1] My identification of these seals as *A. forsteri* is based on Flinders' description, which on points of size and especially of colour is indicative of this species rather than *A.p. doriferus*. Admittedly Flinders was comparing these seals with sea lions nearby, but in later references he described other fur seals with reddish fur of poorer quality, e.g. at Albatross I. which was then occupied by *A.p. doriferus*, (see Flinders, 1814(1):clxxii). Skeletal material from Albatross I., which I have reason to believe pre-dates 1832, is of *A.p. doriferus* (VIC:FWD Collection). Other writers have stated without reservation that both black (*A. forsteri*) and brown (*A. p. doriferus*) fur seals originally occurred in Bass Strait, e.g. Dunderdale (1898:305) and Gould (1872:62).

LOW IS.[1] (40°08′S, 147°44′E).
1798,   Oct. a few seals killed. Flinders, 1814(1):cxlv.

PASSAGE IS.[1] (40°31′S, 148°19′E).
1798,   seals abundant. Flinders, 1814(1):cxxxiii.
1830,   24 skins taken in 1 yr by sealer at W island (known as Forsyth or Penguin I.) (Robinson). (C) Plomley, 1966:295.

SALTPETRE ROCKS, reported off W coast of KING I. (39°50′S, 144°00′E), but not on modern charts.
1925,   c. 100, colony known locally as black seals (Knight). (C) Le Souef, 1925:114.

WESTERN AUSTRALIA

BALD I. (34°55′S, 118°27′E), Reserve A25869, Conservation of Flora and Fauna, WA:DFW.
1971,   Oct. c. 30 on main island and adjacent islets (Smith and Burbidge). (C) WA:DFW.

BOXER I. (34°00′S, 121°40′E), part Reserve A22796, Conservation of Flora and Fauna, WA:DFW.
1968,   mapped as fur seal locality. (D) King, 1969:851.

CAPPS I. (33°59′S, 121°41′E), part Reserve A22796.
1945,   May. none seen (Fowler). CSIRO.
1969,   mapped as fur seal locality. (C) King, 1969:851.

DAW I. (33°51′S, 124°07′E), also known as CHRISTMAS I., part Reserve A 22796.
1948,   Jun. 100 counted from FRV *Wareen*. (C) Serventy, 1953:46.
(n.d.),   most abundant on off-lying Coopers Reef. Serventy, 1953:46.
1969,   mapped as fur seal locality. (C) King, 1969:851.

ECLIPSE I. (35°11′S, 117°23′E), lighthouse site under control of Federal Government.
1967,   breeding colony, minimum of 12 pups born. (A) King, 1969:849.

FIGURE OF EIGHT I. (34°01′S, 131°36′E), part Reserve A22796.

1969,   mapped as fur seal locality. (C) King, 1969:851.

FUR ROCK (34°01′S, 121°38′E).
1945,   Jul. 30-40 (Fowler). (C) CSIRO.

HOOD I. (34°09′S, 122°02′E), part Reserve A22796.
1969,   mapped as fur seal locality. (C) King, 1969:851.

KERMADEC I. (34°06′S, 122°50′E), also known as WEDGE I.
1969,   mapped as a fur seal locality. (C) King, 1969:851.

MIDDLE I. (34°06′S, 123°11′E), part Reserve A22796.
(n.d.),   once occupied by sealers. Serventy, 1953:46.
1833-34, salt obtained by sealer (Hart). Bride, 1898:53.

MONDRAIN I. (34°08′S, 122°14′E), part Reserve A22796.
1802,   Jan. seals of reddish fur taken. (C) Flinders, 1814(1):83.
1969,   mapped as a fur seal locality. (C) King, 1969:851.

ROUND I. (34°12′S, 122°06′E), part Reserve A22796.
1969,   mapped as a fur seal locality. (C) King, 1969:851.

SALISBURY I. (34°21′S, 123°32′E), part Reserve A22796.
1950,   Nov. 50 adults. Serventy, 1953:46.
1969,   mapped as a fur seal locality. (C) King, 1969:851.

SEAL ROCK (34°01′S, 121°39′E), part Reserve A22796.
1945,   May. 60-70 (Fowler). (C) CSIRO.
1945,   Jul. 100-150 (Fowler). (C) CSIRO.
1969,   mapped as a fur seal locality. (C) King, 1969:851.

TERMINATION I. (34°28′S, 122°02′E), part Reserve A22796.
1969,   mapped as a fur seal locality. (C) King, 1969:851.

All these localities except Eclipse I. are part of the Recherche Archipelago, of which Flinders (1814(1):91) said, "All the islands seem to be more or less frequented by seals; but I think not in numbers sufficient to make a speculation from Europe advisable on their account ... the seals being mostly of the hair kind, and the fur of such others as were seen was red and coarse".

NEW ZEALAND

The following listing of seal localities in New Zealand was compiled from my own reading and with the help of a very detailed gazetteer presented as an appendix to Wilson (1974a). I have grouped the localities alphabetically under three broad geographical divisions: North Island; South Island; and the major island groups distant to the south and southeast, including Macquarie I.

NORTH ISLAND

CAPE PALLISER (41°37'S, 175°16'E).
1972,   1972, wintering colony. (B) Singleton. 1972:649.
1972,   May. c. 200. Wilson, 1974a:193.

CAPE TERAWHITI (41°17'S, 174°37'E).
1962,   Aug. 300, including "pups" (Tunbridge). (C) Sorensen, 1969:10.
1972,   wintering colony. (B) Singleton, 1972:649.

GANNET I. (37°58'S, 174°34'E).
1958,   3-400 counted (Fish. Mgt. Files). Wilson, 1974a:194.
1971,   2 seals seen. Young, 1971:15.
1972,   May 70-100. Wilson, 1974a:194.

MOTUPIA I. (34°36'S, 172°48'E).
1969,   wintering colony of c. 130 (Jose). (B) Singleton, 1972:649.
(1974),   Jan.-Feb. estimate of 5-25. Wilson, 1974a:195.

SINCLAIR HEAD (41°22'S, 174°42'E).
1972,   wintering colony. (B) Singleton, 1972:649.
1972,   May. c. 30 counted. Wilson, 1974a:193.

SUGARLOAF IS. (34°03'S, 174°02'E).
1927,   May. 4 seen, first for many years (Fish. Mgt. Files). Wilson, 1974a:194.

1951,   Sep. 12 seen on Lion Rock. Wilson, 1974a:194.
1960,   Sep. 30 on Lion Rock, minimum of 200 on Saddleback I. (Merton). Wilson, 1974a:194.
1972,   May. c. 30 counted. Wilson, 1974a:193-4.

THREE KINGS IS. (34°10'S, 172°08'E).
1967,   Dec. seals first seen (Jose). (B) Singleton, 1972:649.
1968,   Oct. 20 on western-most of Princes Is. Singleton, 1972:649.
1969,   70-80. Singleton, 1972:649.
(1974),   Jan.-Feb. estimate of 0-15. Wilson, 1974a:195.

TURAKIRAE HEAD (41°26'S, 174°55'E).
1972,   wintering colony. (B) Singleton, 1972:649.
1972,   May. c. 140 counted. Wilson, 1974a:193.

SOUTH ISLAND

ABUT HEAD (43°07'S, 170°16'E).
(1974),   Jan.-Feb. estimate of 40-200. Wilson, 1974a:180.

ARCHWAY IS. (40°30'S, 172°40'E).
1968,   Aug. 35 (Taylor). Wilson, 1974a:189.
1972,   Jul. 47-55. (B) Wilson, 1974a:189.

BANKS PENINSULA (43°50'S, 173°00'E).
1973,   Jul-Sep. 32 Horseshoe Bay; 55-65 at Pompeys Pillar; 13 on mainland opposite Crown I.; 55-70 at Ducksfoot Bay; c. 50 at Pa Bay. Wilson, 1974a:185-8.

BIG RIVER (46°12'S, 166°56'E).
1947-48, colony known (Falla). Wilson, 1974a:169.
(1974),   possibly several hundred, pups present (Dorizac). (A) Wilson, 1974a:169.

BLIGH SOUND (44°45'S, 167°34'E) to **CASWELL SOUND** (45°00'S, 167°08'E). See also LOOKING GLASS BAY and HOUSEROOF ROCK.
(1974),   Jan-Feb. estimate of 500-1 500. Wilson, 1974a:176.

BREAKSEA I. (45°34′S, 166°38′E).

1792, Nov. great number of seals (Murry). HRNZ, 2:512.

1795, Oct. 15 killed on "seal islands" (Murry). HRNZ, 2:523.

1947, Dec. less than 100 (Falla). (C) Sorensen, 1969a:52.

(1974), Jan.-Feb. estimate of 110-160. Wilson, 1974a:174.

CAPE PROVIDENCE (46°00′S, 166°28′E).

1969, Dec. c. 150 counted (Begg and Begg). (A) Wilson, 1974a:171.

(1974), Jan.-Feb. estimate of 100-400. Wilson, 1974a:171.

CASCADE POINT (44°01′S, 168°22′E).

1909, a few occur. Waite, 1909:548.

1934, Nov. 200 on offshore reef (Falla). (B) Sorensen, 1969a:52.

1946, 300 killed (Roderique). Wilson, 1974a:178.

1947, Dec. 25 on offshore reef, maximum of 500 on point (Falla). Sorensen, 1969a:52-3.

1964, May. 132 on point (Gaskin). Sorensen, 1969:11.

(1974), Jan.-Feb. estimate of 1 500-3 000. Wilson, 1974a:178.

CASWELL SOUND (45°00′S, 167°08′E) to CHARLES SOUND (45°02′S, 167°05′E).

(1974), Jan.-Feb. estimate of 50-300. Wilson, 1974a:175.

CHALKY I. (46°03′S, 166°32′E).

1947, Dec. 1 000 (Falla). Sorensen, 1969a:68.

1963, Feb. 1 200 (Murrell). Wilson, 1974a:171.

(1974), Jan.-Feb. estimate of 1 100-1 800. (B) Wilson, 1974a:171.

CHETWODE IS. (40°54′S, 174°05′E).

1955, 36 (Street). Wilson, 1974a:192.

1974, Oct. 33 on Outer Island. (B) Wilson, 1974a:192.

DOUBTFUL SOUND (45°17′S, 166°52′E).

1964, May. 109 on Seal Rock (Gaskin). Sorensen, 1969:11.

(1974), Jan.-Feb. estimate of 100-750. Wilson, 1974a:175.

D'URVILLE I. (40°50′S, 173°52′E).

1964, colony reported. (C) Street, 1964:1.

(1974), Jan.-Feb. estimate of 15-40. (B) Wilson, 1974a:191.

DUSKY SOUND (at 45°50′S, 166°25′E), see also SEAL IS.

1773, Apr. seals hunted on small rock islands (Pickersgill). HRNZ, 2:187; Beaglehole, 1961:111 et seq.

1792, Dec.-Sep. 1793. c. 4 500 skins taken by gang of the *Brittania*. HRNZ, 1:178,182.

1974, colony reported, estimated at 25-100. (C) Wilson, 1974a:172.

FIVE FINGERS PENINSULA (45°44′S, 166°28′E).

Colonies undoubtedly worked by sealers based at Dusky Sound during first half of the 19th Century, see HRNZ, HRA.

1946, Jul. 1 047 skins taken. (A) Sorensen, 1969a:40.

1947, Nov. estimate of 2 000 (Falla). Sorensen, 1969a:68.

(1974), Jan.-Feb. estimate of 2 500-5 000. (A) Wilson, 174a:173.

GEORGE SOUND (at 44°50′S, 167°21′E).

1958, Jul. colony of 200, photo in Sorensen, 1969:35.

(1974), see Wilson 1974a:176 for details of other colonies in this region.

GILLESPIES BEACH (43°24′S, 169°50′E).

1972, Aug.-Sep. maximum of c. 500 Wilson, 1974a:179.

(1974), Jan.-Feb. estimate of 15-25. (B) Wilson, 1974a:179.

GREEN IS. (46°14′S, 166°47′E) and WINSOR POINT (46°12′S. 166°39′E).

(1974), Jan.-Feb. estimate of 250-800. Wilson, 1974a:170.

GULCHES HEAD (46°06′S, 166°34′E).

1946, Jun. 39 skins taken, including pups. (A) Sorensen, 1969a:40-1.

(1974), Jan.-Feb. doubtful estimate of 50-175. Wilson, 1974a:170.

HAMURI BLUFF (42°33′S, 173°31′E).

1972, Jul. 108 counted (Hay and Challies).

Wilson, 1974a:188.

(1974),   Jan.-Feb. estimate of 10-40. (B) Wilson, 1974a:188.

HOUSEROOF ROCK (44°52′S, 167°16′E).
(1974),   several hundred. Wilson, 1974a:176.

KAIKOURA PENINSULA (42°26′S, 173°43′E).
1950-51,   seals first observed in quantity. (Gorman). Sorensen, 1969:27.
1956,   May. 46 (Bell). Stonehouse, 1965.
1957,   Dec. count of 7. Stonehouse, 1965.
1958,   maximum of 270 (Gorman). Sorensen, 1969:27.
1960-64,   estimate of 60-150. Stonehouse, 1965.
(1964),   estimate of 150-270. Street, 1964:1.
1964,   May-Jun. 520 (Gaskin). Sorensen, 1969:11.
1967-69,   May-Jul. maximum of 800. Stirling, 1970:767.
1973,   Jan. 233 (Hay). Wilson, 1974a:188.
(1974),   Jan.-Feb. estimated 235-250. (B) Wilson, 1974a:188.

LONG REEF (44°20′S, 167°59′E).
(1974),   Jan.-Feb. estimate of 100-300. (A) Wilson, 1974a:177.

LOOKING GLASS BAY (44°45′S, 167°15′E).
1964,   May 63 counted (Gaskin). Sorensen, 1969:11.

MOTUNAU I. (43°04′S, 173°05′E).
(1974),   regular haul-out; numbers peak at c. 10 in Sep. Wilson 1974a:177.

NANCY SOUND (45°06′S, 167°05′E).
(1974),   Jan.-Feb. estimate of 100-400, on islands off Anxiety Point. (?A) Wilson, 1974a:175.

NUGGET POINT (46°27′S, 169°49′E).
1934,   seals first reported (Fish. Mgt. Files). Wilson, 1974a:183.
1964,   up to 30 seen. Street, 1964:1.
1971,   Nov. 62 counted (lighthouse keeper). Wilson, 1974a:184.
(1974),   Jan.-Feb. estimate of 5-8. Wilson, 1974a:183.

OPEN BAY IS. (43°52′S, 168°53′E).
1964,   May. 1 300 (Gaskin). Sorensen, 1969:11.

1968,   Sep. 1 000. Stirling, 1970:768.
1970,   Jan. 545 pups on Taumaka I.; population estimated at 2 750. (A) Crawley and Brown, 1971:394.
1973,   Feb. 156 pups on Popotai I.; population estimated at 825. (A) Wilson, 1974a:178.
(1974),   Jan.-Feb. estimate of 2 700-3 900 for island group. Wilson, 1974a:179.

OTAGO PENINSULA (45°51′S, 170°44′E).
1913,   seals first sighted at Taiaroa Head. Wilson, 1974a:185.
1964,   650 counted. (C) Street, 1964:1.
(1974),   Jan.-Feb. estimate of 270-290 for Cape Saunders only; estimate for rest of peninsula 550-700. Wilson, 1974a:184-5.

POISON BAY (44°39′S, 167°38′E).
(1974),   Jan.-Feb. estimate of 100-300. Wilson, 1974a:177.

PRESERVATION INLET (46°06′S, 166°46′E).
1930's,   important centre for whaling and sealing, see McNab, 1913:85 et seq. for details of skins taken.

RUAPUKE IS. (46°45′S, 168°30′E).
1946,   small rookeries on many of the outliers (Falla). (A) Sorensen, 1969a:67.
(1974),   Jan.-Feb. doubtful estimate of 50-200. Wilson, 1974a:165.

SEAL I. (BREAKSEA SOUND at 45°35′S, 166°37′E).
1773,   seals ... here in plenty (Cook). Beaglehole, 1961:135.
1947,   Dec. c. 100 (Falla). Sorensen, 1969a:52.
1971,   Dec. 68 (A) Wilson, 1974a:174.
(1974),   Jan.-Feb. estimate of 125-160. Wilson, 1974a:174.

STEPHENS I. (40°40′S, 174°00′E).
1972,   Jul. estimate of 110-135. Wilson, 1974a:191.
(1974),   Jan.-Feb. estimate of 20-30. Wilson, 1974a:191.

TAURANGA BAY (41°46′S, 171°27′E).
1972,   Oct. c. 30 on headland; 60-75 on island. Wilson 1974a:182.

THREE STEEPLES (41°44′S, 171°28′E).
1874,   Jan. 11 seals collected (Hector). (A)
         Clark, 1875:659.
1909,   a few. Waite, 1909:548.
1940's, seals breeding (Falla). Wilson,
         1974a:182.
1964,   May a dozen or so (Gaskin). Wilson,
         1974a:182.
1969,   7 counted (Gaskin). Sorensen, 1969:11.
1972,   Oct. 168 counted. Wilson, 1974a:182.
(1974), Jan.-Feb. estimate of 250-450. Wilson,
         1974a:182.

WANGANUI RIVER (43°02′S, 170°26′E).
1972,   Aug. c. 400 seen, mainly at Greens
         Beach. Wilson, 1974a:181.
(1974), Jan.-Feb. estimate of 20-30. Wilson,
         1974a:181.

WEKAKURA POINT (40°55′S, 172°02′E).
1974,   Jun. c. 250 counted (Meredyth-Young).
         (A) Wilson, 1974a:183.
(1974), Jan.-Feb. estimate of 200-300 (A) Wil-
         son, 1974a:183.

YATES POINT (44°30′S, 167°49′E).
1972,   Sep. 250-300 pups (Cragg). (A) Wilson,
         1974a:177.
(1974), Jan.-Feb. estimated total of 300-650.
         Wilson, 1974a:177.

MAJOR ISLANDS, including Macquarie I.

ANTIPODES IS. (49°41′S, 178°43′E), discovered 1800.
1804-06, 60 000 skins taken by pioneer gang. (A)
         Redwood, 1950:30.
(1927), seals rarely seen (Bollons). Sorensen,
         1969a:64.
1946,   no re-establishment (Falla). Sorensen,
         1969a:23.
1969,   Feb. 1 100 counted, between North
         Cape and Albatross Point (Taylor). (C)
         Sorensen, 1969a:79.

AUCKLAND IS. (50°50′S, 166°00′E), discovered 1806.
Flora and Fauna Reserve.
1807,   sealing begun. Redwood, 1950:44.
1823,   13 000 fur seal skins taken by gang from
         the *Henry*. (A) Morrell, 1832:363.
prior   main period of sealing. McNab,
1826   1909:344.

1830,   Jan. no fur seals found. Morrell,
         1832:360.
1864,   black seals in W arm of Carnley Har-
         bour. (C) Musgrave, 1865:19.
1939-45, few seen. Sorensen, 1951:33.
1945,   many of best rookery sites still deserted
         (Falla). Sorensen, 1969a:23.
(1948), possibly several thousand, but no real
         data available (Falla). Sorensen,
         1969a:65.
1972,   Dec.-Jan. 1973. estimate of 1 000. (A)
         Wilson, 1974.

BOUNTY IS. (47°41′S, 179°03′E), discovered 1788.
Flora and Fauna Reserve.
1804,   Feb. a few seals round them. Delano,
         1817:475.
1807,   8 000 skins taken in 6 months. Red-
         wood, 1950:26.
1831,   5 only seen at breeding time (Biscoe).
         Falla, 1948:154.
1904,   winter. more than 60 (Cockayne).
         Darby, 1970:174.
1907,   one or two seen. Waite, 1909:548.
1909,   quite a small colony (Bollons). (B)
         Waite, 1909:548.
1927,   3 000, estimated from photos (Falla).
         (A) Sorensen, 1969a:64.
1948,   Jan. several thousand, many of them
         new pups. *The Press*, Christchurch.
1950,   Nov. estimate of 5 000-6 000 (Falla).
         Wilson, 1974a:203.
1968,   Jan. estimate of 10 000. Darby,
         1970:177.
1974,   5 500. Wilson, 1974a.

CAMPBELL I. (52°33′S, 169°08′E), discovered 1810.
Flora and Fauna Reserve.
1810,   15 000 skins taken by pioneer gang.
         Falla, 1948:148.
1831,   170 skins obtained by *Venus*, prospects
         encouraging (Harvey). McNab,
         1913:88.
1834-38, 165 skins obtained by gang of 4.
         McNab, 1913:243, 470, 479.
1922,   284 skins declared for royalty. Soren-
         sen, 1969a:16.
1924,   66 skins declared for royalty. Sorensen,
         1969a:16.
1927,   maximum of 1 000 (Bollons). (A) So-
         rensen, 1969a:65.

459

1948,   minimum of 2 000 (Falla). (A) Sorensen, 1969a:65.

1958,   Jan.-Feb. count of 771, including 71 pups, considered well below actual number (Street). (A) Bailey and Sorensen, 1962.

CHATHAM IS. (44°50′S, 176°30′E), discovered 1791.

1809,   visited by sealing vessel *Pegasus*. McNab, 1909:161.

1818,   visited by sealing vessel *Sophia*. McNab, 1909:230.

1830,   Feb. seals skin bought off by the *Samuel*. McNab, 1913:84.

1831,   Nov. 7 skins obtained by the *Tula*. at the Forty-Fours (Biscoe). McNab, 1913:87, 419; HRNZ, 2:558.

1831,   Dec. 16 skins obtained at Sisters Rocks (Biscoe). McNab, 1913:87, 421.

1831,   Dec. no seals on likely grounds at Cornwallis Is. (Biscoe). McNab, 1913:420.

1937,   breeding colonies on outlying Star Keys and Forty Fours, the latter densely populated (Falla). (A) Sorensen, 1969a:64.

1946,   steady increase (Falla). (A) Sorensen, 1969a:23.

1948,   non-breeding groups on main island; c. 10 seen at South-East I. (Abernathy). (C) Sorensen, 1969a:64.

1948   maximum of 2 000 (Falla). (A) Sorensen, 1969a:64.

1974   2 100. Wilson, 1974; see 1974a: 196-201 for detailed counts.

MACQUARIE I. (54°40′S, 158°50′E), discovered 1810.

1810-11,   57 000 skins taken by pioneer gang. Cumpston, 1968:17.

1815,   fur seal colonies exhausted. Cumpston, 1968:35.

1831,   no success by the *Venus*. McNab, 1913:88.

1852,   gang taking elephant seals found no fur seals. Gwynn, 1953:2.

1919-48,   a few fur seals in summer. Gwynn, 1953:2.

1929-30,   none seen by research expedition. Gwynn, 1953:2.

1946,   no re-establishment (Falla). Sorensen, 1969a:23.

1948,   small group found by A.N.A.R.E. team. Csordas, 1962:226.

1950,   174 at North Head. Csordas, 1963a:256.

1955,   first record of breeding. (A) Csordas, 1963a:257.

1950-64,   summer counts at North Head, rising to maximum of 474. (A) Csordas and Ingham, 1965:88.

1959,   540 counted on E. coast. (A) Csordas, 1962:256.

1965,   Feb. 2 fur seals on Clerk Islet. MacKenzie, 1968:245.

1965,   Mar. 637 at North Head, new groups in excess of 100 at NW and SE ends of island. Johnstone, 1972:522.

1971,   total population estimated at 900-1 000. (A) Johnstone, 1972:522.

SNARES IS. (48°00′S, 166°35′E), discovered 1791. Flora and Fauna Reserve.

1791,   Nov. vast number of oceanic birds, seals and penguins (Menzies). HRNZ, 2:495.

1803,   visited by sealing vessel *Endeavour*. McNab, 1909:136.

1804,   Feb. a number seen swimming offshore. Delano, 1817:474.

1810-17,   marooned gang took only 1 300 skins. McNab, 1909:224.

1830,   Jan. no fur seals found. Morrell, 1832:363.

1880,   only 2 seen (Fairchild). Chapman, 1891.

1909,   colony known. Waite, 1909:548.

1915,   300 skins taken by one gang (Falla). (B) Sorensen, 1969a:24.

1944,   maximum of 20 young bulls at Boat Harbour (Falla). Sorensen, 1969a:66.

1947,   Nov.-Dec. 2 000 on main island, less than 1 000 on Broughton I. and Western Reef (Falla). (A) Sorensen, 1969a:66.

1948,   Jan.-Feb. maximum of 200 on main island. Richdale, (n.d.):113.

1970,   Nov.-Dec. 1 150 on main island; 115 on Broughton I. Crawley, 1972:120.

SOLANDER I. (46°35′S, 166°54′E), discovered 1770.

1803,   May. few seals found by sealers. McNab, 1909:135.

1808-13,   5 sealers on the island. McNab, 1909:207-212.

1946,   Jun. 95 skins taken, mainly females and
          pups (Rapson). (A) Sorensen, 1969a:40.
1947,   Dec. maximum of 1 000, including not
          more than 300 females (Falla). Sorens-
          en, 1969a:51.
1948,   Aug. Herd augmented by non-breeders,
          total about 2 000 (Falla). Sorensen,
          1969a:68.
1974,   5 000. Wilson, 1974a, see pp. 167-9 for
          detailed counts.

STEWART I. (47°00'S, 168°00'E) and associated is-
     lands. Charted in part 1770, found to be an island
     1809, or earlier. McNab, 1909:158.
1808-09, several vessels from Sydney sealing in
          the area. McNab, 1909:156.
1948,   Jul. 300 on Bench I., total population of
          Stewart I., Big South Cape I., and Pou-
          tama I. about 2 000. Seals seen but not
          counted on Breaksea I., Mogi I. and
          Codfish I. (Falla). Sorensen, 1969a:67.
1961,   Jan. 150 on Bench I. Street, 1964:1.
1974,   summer population c. 3 150. Wilson,
          1974a, see pp. 150-65 for detailed
          counts.

Appendix E

DATA ON THE DISTRIBUTION AND STATUS OF THE AUSTRALIAN SEA LION, *NEOPHOCA CINEREA*.

Also known as Councillor seal and White capped sea
lion; known to the early sealers as hair seal.

Key to status: A breeding colony.
                    B non-breeding colony.
                    C status unknown.

TASMANIA AND BASS STRAIT

ANSER I. (39°08'S, 146°19'E).
1840's,   said to occur (locality possibly in error,
          most probably Kanowna I. nearby).
          Doome, 1874.

BATTERY I. (40°28'S, 148°11'E).
1798,   Feb. large hair seals seen. (C) Flinders,
          1814(1):cxxviii.

CLARKE I. (40°35'S, 148°11'E).
1798,   Feb. large hair seals at Seal Point. (C)
          Flinders, 1814(1):cxxviii.

KENT GROUP (39°30'S, 147°20'E).
1802,   Dec. seals and hair seals seen (Grimes).
          (C) Shillinglaw, 1879:15.

PASSAGE I. (40°31'S, 148°20'E), once known as SEA
     LION I. Plomley, 1966:442; Delano, 1817:433.
1788,   Feb. possibly on this island at that time.
          (C) see Flinders, 1814(1):cxxxiii.

LITTLE ANDERSON I. (40°17'S, 148°07'E), once
     known as HAIR SEAL I.
1830's.   evidence of name only. See Plomley,
          1966:273.

TASMANIAN COAST.
     Remains found in aborigines' kitchen middens.
     Wood Jones, 1925:363.

WATERHOUSE I. (40°48'S, 147°37'E).
1798,   covered with sea birds and hair seals.
          (C) [1] Flinders, 1814(1):cli.

SOUTH AUSTRALIA

CASUARINA I. (36°06'S, 136°42'E), also known as
     THE BROTHERS, part Flinders Chase National
     Park, A:NPWS.
1973,   Feb. about 10 in view, among fur seals
          (Warneke). (C) VIC:FWD.

DANGEROUS REEF (34°49'S, 136°12'E).
1925,   colony known. (C) Le Souef, 1925:113.
1966,   Oct. large number of very young pups.
          (A) Marlow, 1968:39.
1967,   Jul. count of 160. Marlow, 1968:42.
1967,   Oct. 30 (decline thought due to disturb-
          ance). Marlow, 1968:42.
1974,   possibly the major breeding colony in
          South Australian waters. (A) Marlow
          and King, 1974:126.
1974,   maximum of 400 during the breeding
          season. (A) King, pers. comm.
1975,   Sep. 580-670, including 200-500 live

---

[1] A doubtful record for this species as Flinders passed at
a distance of about 1.5 km and none of his party landed.

pups; 64 dead pups (Needham). (A) Ling and Walker, 1976:64.

1975, Nov. 410-460, including 180-220 pups (Needham). (A) Ling and Walker, 1976:64.

DOG I. (32°29'S, 133°20'E), part Isles of St. Francis Conservation Park, SA:NPWS.

1802, Feb. seals killed (Flinders Rough Log). Cooper, 1953:69.

1975, Jun. 22, including 6 pups. (A) Ling and Walker, 1976:64.

ENGLISH I. (34°38'S, 136°12'E), part Sir Joseph Banks Groups Conservation Park, SA:NPWS.

1965, Nov. 42, including males, females and juveniles. (C) (Aitken), SAM.

1972, population, with that of Lewis I., about 50 (Fairbank). Stirling, 1972a:8.

1975, Jun. count of 53. Ling and Walker, 1976:64.

1975, Nov. 115, including 36-40 pups (Needham). (A) Ling and Walker, 1976:64.

EVANS I. (32°22'S, 113°28'E).

1925, colony known. (C) Le Souef, 1925:116.

FENELON I. (32°35'S, 133°17'E), part Isles of St. Francis Conservation Park, SA:NPWS.

1972, small colony. (C) Wace, pers. comm.

1975, Jun. 28, no pups. (C) Ling and Walker, 1976:64.

FLINDERS I. (33°43'S, 134°30'E).

1802, Feb. seals numerous (Brown). Cooper, 1955:69.

1802, Feb. harems of 4 to 5 females, every 200 to 300 yards of beach. (A) Flinders, 1814(1):125.

1802, Feb. several hair seals killed (Flinders Fair Log). Cooper, 1953:39.

1968, Jun. 2 males. (Aitken), SAM.

FOUR HUMMOCKS (34°46'S, 135°01'E), part Whidbey Isles Conservation Park, SA:NPWS.

1966, Oct. non-breeding colony. (C) Marlow, 1968:39.

FRANKLIN I. (32°29'S, 133°21'E).

1969, Feb. 11, including females and juveniles. (Aitken), SAM.

1971, Apr. count of 8. (Aitken), SAM.

1974, Jun. 63, including 12 pups. (A) Ling and Walker, 1976:65.

FREELING I. (32°29'S, 133°21'E).

1975, Jun. count of 20. (C) Ling and Walker, 1976:65.

GAMBIER IS. (35°10'S, 136°27'E).

1945, Apr. 2 on South-West Rock (Fowler). (C) CSIRO.

1975, Nov. 72, including 8 pups on North I.; 74 on E Peaked Rock; 18 on W Peaked Rock; 32 on South-West Rock. (A) Ling and Walker, 1976:64.

GOAT I. (32°18'S, 133°30'E), part Nuyt's Archipelago Conservation Park, SA:NPWS.

1802, Feb. 4 hair seals taken. Flinders, 1814(1):113.

1802, Feb. the seals killed were of the hair kind and not numerous (Flinders Rough Log). Cooper, 1953:70.

1925, colony known. (C) Le Souef, 1925:116.

GREENLY I. (34°39'S, 134°47'E).

1947, Nov. more numerous than fur seals. Finlayson, 1948:38.

1947, Dec. minimum of 100, including pups. (A) Mitchell and Behrndt, 1949:172.

1974, Mar. c. 10 (Field Naturalists group). S. Aust. Nat. 49:43.

HOPKINS I. (34°58'S, 136°04'E).

1974, Mar. 17, including males, females and juveniles. (Aitken), SAM.

1975, Jun. 40-50. Ling and Walker, 1976:64.

1975, Nov. count of 79. Ling and Walker, 1976:64.

KANGAROO I. (35°50'S, 137°15'E).

1802, Apr. hair seals at Kangaroo Head. Flinders, 1814(1):169.

1803, Jan. great number of otaries on the beach (Baudin). Cornell, 1974:467.

1803, 14 000 fur and hair seal skins taken (Pendleton). Fanning, 1833:319.

1969-70, minimum of 200 at Seal Bay, Stirling 1972a:4.

1972, abundant skeletal remains on small islet at West Bay. Stirling 1971a:276; 1972a:10.

1972, colonies at Capes Bouger and Borda. (C) Stirling, 1972a:1.

1974, 383 counted at Seal Bay; breeding occurs at adjacent bay, of prohibited entry. (A) SA:NPWS.

1975, Feb. 5 at West Bay; 16 at Cape du Couedic. Ling and Walker, 1976:64.

1975, Oct. 370 at Seal Bay; 16 at Cape Gantheaume; 29 at Cape Bouger. Ling and Walker, 1976:64.

KIRKBY I. (34°33′S, 136°13′E).

1802, Mar. a few hair seals ashore. Flinders, 1814(1):153.

1802, Mar. a few killed (Flinders Fair Log). Cooper, 1953:50.

LEWIS I. (34°58′S, 136°01′E), part Lincoln National Park, SA:NPWS.

1972, population, including that of English I., about 50 (Fairbank). (C) Stirling, 1972a:8.

1975, Jun. 56, count minimal. Ling and Walker, 1976:64.

1975, Sep. 45-65, including pups. (A) Ling and Walker, 1976:64.

1975, Nov. count of 26. Ling and Walker, 1976:64.

LITTLE I. (34°57′S, 136°02′E).

1975, Jun. count of 20. (C) Ling and Walker, 1976:64.

1975, Nov. count of 10. Ling and Walker, 1976:64.

LOUND I. (32°16′S, 133°22′E).

1945, Apr. 4 (Fowler). (C) CSIRO.

NEPTUNE IS. (N GROUP: 35°14′S, 136°04′E; S GROUP: 35°19′S, 136°06′E), Neptune Islands Conservation Park, SA:NPWS.

1945, Apr. c. 12 on N island of S group; none on N group (Fowler). (C) CSIRO.

1966, Oct. no evidence of breeding at S Neptunes. Marlow, 1968:39.

1969-70, summer. 80-100, including adult males and females with pups, mainly at N end. (A) Stirling, 1972:272.

1972, breeding colony at N group. (A) Stirling, 1972a:10.

1975, Sep. 55 at N island (of S group). Ling and Walker, 1976:64.

PAGES, THE (34°47′S, 138°17′E), The Pages Conservation Park, SA:NPWS.

1837, some seals of a yellowish colour, with black muzzles. Backhouse, 1843:508.

1945, Apr. 20-25 (Fowler). (C) CSIRO.

1972, colony known. (C) Stirling, 1972a:8.

PERSON I. (33°27′S, 134°17′E), part Investigator Group Conservation Park, SA:NPWS.

prior rookery visited during breeding season.

1925, (A) Wood Jones, 1925:372.

1945, Apr. 30-40 on E side (Fowler). (C) CSIRO.

1966, Oct. non-breeding colony. (B) Marlow, 1968:39.

POINT LABATT (33°09′S, 134°16′E), a prohibited area, SA:NPWS.

1966, over 50 at haul-out site. (B) Stirling, 1972a:7.

1969, Mar. 32, including males, females and juveniles. (Aitken), SAM.

1970, less than 30. Stirling, 1972a:7.

1975, May. count of 35. Ling and Walker, 1976:65.

PRICE I. (34°42′S, 135°17′E), part Whidbey Isles Conservation Park, SA:NPWS.

1925, colony known. (C) Le Souef, 1925:116.

PURDIE I. (32°16′S, 133°14′E).

1945, Apr. 30-40 (Fowler). (C) CSIRO.

1945, May. 80 (Fowler). (C) CSIRO.

SINCLAIR I. (32°08′S, 133°00′E).

1945, May. count of 20 (Fowler) (C) (CSIRO).

SMOOTH I. (33°29′S, 133°20′E), part Isles of St. Francis Conservation Park, SA:NPWS.

1802, Feb. seals killed (Flinders Rough Log). (C) Cooper, 1953:69.

ST. FRANCIS I. (32°30′S, 133°17′E), part Isles of St. Francis Conservation Park, SA:NPWS.

1802, Feb. seals seen, 2 shot (Brown) (C) Cooper, 1955:64.

1802, Feb. a few hair seals seen (Flinders Rough Log). Cooper, 1953:33.

1975, Jun. 3, including 1 pup. (a) Ling and Walker, 1976:65.

ST. PETER I. (32°17′S, 133°35′E).
1802, Feb. a few individuals. Peron and
  Freycinet, 1816:118.

THISTLE I. (35°00′S, 136°08′E).
1802, Feb. seals on the beach. (C) Flinders,
  1814(1):133.
1975, Nov. 1 only seen. Ling and Walker,
  1976:64.

WALDEGRAVE I. (33°36′S, 134°49′E), Waldegrave
Islands Conservation Park, SA:NPWS.
1802, Feb. abundance of seals ... several families (Brown). (A) Cooper, 1955:68.
1802, Feb. a few hair seals killed. Flinders,
  1814(1):123.

WARDANG I. (34°30′S, 137°21′E).
1972, small colony on nearby island (C)
  Stirling, 1972a:7.

WILLIAMS I. (35°02′S, 135°58′E).
1974, Mar. 3 females observed. (Aitken),
  SAM.

WESTERN AUSTRALIA

BALD I. (34°55′S, 118°27′E), Reserve A25869. Conservation of Flora and Fauna, WA:DFW.
1959, May. one seen ashore. Storr, 1961:196.
1971, Oct. 15 on main island and adjacent
  islets (Smith and Burbidge). (C)
  WA:DFW.

BEAGLE I. (29°48′S, 114°53′E), Reserve 26411, Conservation of Flora and Fauna, WA:DFW.
1963, count of 100. (C) Ford, 1963:139.

BOXER I. (34°00′S, 121°10′E), part Reserve A22796,
Conservation of Flora and Fauna, WA:DFW.
1950, Nov. one seen resting ashore. (C) Serventy, 1953:48.

CARNAC I. (32°08′S, 115°39′E).
1975, 1-18 commonly seen over past 6 years
  (Burbidge). (C) WA:DFW.

CERVANTES IS. (30°31′S, 115°03′E), Reserve 29253.
Conservation of Flora and Fauna, WA:DFW.
1945, Jun. 2 on N island (Fowler). (C)
  CSIRO.

1963, N and S islands frequented. (C) Ford,
  1963:139.

CHEYNE'S BEACH (34°53′S, 118°23′E).
1959, common. (C) Storr, 1965:196.

DAW I. (38°41′S, 124°07′E), also known as CHRIST-
MAS I., part Reserve A22796.
1950, Nov. 65 on beach, and number of harems. (A) Serventy, 1953:48.

DEPUCH I. (20°38′S, 117°43′E).
1801, seals recorded. (C) Peron and Freycinet, 1816:33, but see report of Ronsard,
  in Peron, 1807:131.

DOUGLAS I. (34°10′S, 123°08′E), part Reserve
A22796.
1945, May. c. 6 (Fowler). (C) CSIRO.
1950, Nov. c. 10, including 1 harem. (A) Serventy, 1953:48.

DYERS I. (Off Rottnest I.: 32°01′S, 115°31′E).
1975, estimate of 110 (Burbidge). (C)
  WA:DFW.

EASTER GROUP (28°41′S, 113°47′E), part Reserve
A20253, Conservation of Flora and Fauna, tourism and purposes associated with the Fishing
Industry, WA:DFW.
1840, Jan. many hair seals seen (Moore).
  Grey 1841(2):125.
1840, Apr. a few seals on Rat. I. (C) Stokes,
  1846(2):145.

ECLIPSE I. (35°11′S, 117°52′E), lighthouse site under
the control of the Federal Government.
1974, small numbers. (C) Marlow and King,
  1974:126.

ESSEX ROCKS (30°24′S, 115°01′E), Reserve 29257,
Conservation of Flora and Fauna, WA:DFW.
1963, N rock regularly inhabited. (C) Ford,
  1963:139.

FIGURE OF EIGHT I. (34°01′S, 121°36′E), part Reserve A22796.
1950, Nov. 2, and about 20 on off-lying rock.
  (C) Serventy, 1953:48.

FISHERMAN IS. (30°08′S, 114°57′E), Reserve 29256,
Conservation of Fauna, WA:DFW.

1945,   Jun. c. 20 on N island (Fowler). (C) CSIRO.

1945,   Jul. 22 on N island (Fowler). (C) CSIRO.

1963,   60 on N island. (C) Ford, 1963:139.

GARDEN I. (32°12′S, 115°41′E), named L'ILE BUA-CHE by the French, see below.

1801,   covered with seals. (C) Peron and Freycinet, 1816:33.

1801,   Jun. a great number killed. Peron, 1807:184.

GEORGE I. (34°04′S, 123°15′E).

1945,   Jun. 30 (Fowler). (C) CSIRO.

GLENNIE I. (34°06′S, 123°06′E).

1945,   May c. 40 including young (Fowler). (A) CSIRO.

1945,   Jun. 1 adult and juvenile (Fowler). CSIRO.

GOOSE I. (34°05′S, 123°11′E), part Reserve A22796.

1802,   Jan. a few hair seals. (C) Flinders, 1814(1):89.

1803,   May. party sent to kill seals. Flinders, 1814(1):265-6.

1950,   Nov. dead seal in cave. Serventy, 1953:48.

GREEN ISLETS (30°41′S, 115°06′E).

1945,   Jun. 1 on S islet (Fowler). CSIRO.

HAUL-OFF ROCK (34°42′S, 118°39′E).

1945,   Jun. c. 40 (Fowler). (C) CSIRO.

1945,   Jul. 20-40 (Fowler). (C) CSIRO.

HOUTMAN'S ABROLHOS: see EASTER and WAL-LABI GROUPS.

ISRAELITE BAY (at 33°36′S, 123°55′E).

1945,   May. c. 6 on rocks (Fowler). (C) CSIRO.

KERMADEC I. (34°06′S, 122°50′E), part Reserve A22796.

1950,   Nov. c. 40 seals and a number of ha-rems. (A) Serventy, 1953:48.

LION I. (33°53′S, 122°01′E), part Reserve A22796.

1956,   Jan. 1 bull, 3 females and 1 pup. (A) Lindgren, 1956:101.

MIDDLE I. (34°07′S, 123°11′E), part Reserve A22796.

1803,   Jan. a few hair seals. (C) Flinders, 1814(1):89.

MONDRAIN I. (34°08′S, 122°14′E), part Reserve A20253.

1950,   Nov. 5 ashore. (C) Serventy, 1953:48.

POINT MALCOLM (33°48′S, 123°44′E).

1945,   May. 12 on rocks to SW (Fowler). (C) CSIRO.

RED ISLET (34°02′S, 119°47′E).

1945,   Jun. c. 20 (Fowler). (C) CSIRO.

ROCKY IS. (34°03′S, 120°57′E).

1945,   May. 1 (Fowler). CSIRO.

ROTTNEST I. (32°01′S, 115°31′E), Reserve A16713, Recreation.

1801,   Jun. a great number ... some were black ... The furs of these animals were mostly fine and thick (Freycinet). (C) Peron, 1807:189.

1803,   Mar. a few seals (Baudin). Cornell, 1974:512.

1822,   Jan. a great many in bay at NE end; 3 killed, not of the fur species. (C) King, 1827(2):163.

ROUND I. (34°12′S, 122°06′E), part Reserve A22796.

1950,   Nov. about 20, and at least 3 harems. (A) Serventy, 1953:48.

SALISBURY I. (34°21′S, 123°32′E), part Reserve A22796.

1950,   Nov. 20 ashore. (C) Serventy, 1953:48.

SANDLAND I. (30°12′S, 114°59′E), Reserve 29255, Conservation of Fauna, WA:FWD.

1963,   10; a breeding colony. (A) Ford, 1963:139-40.

SEAL I. (32°04′S, 117°58′E), Reserve A25645, Conservation of Fauna, WA:FWD.

1791,   20 seen at one time. (C) Vancouver, 1798:73-4.

1801,   Dec. seals encountered. (C) Flinders, 1814(1):54.

1803,   only 30 found (Pendleton). Fanning, 1833:316.

1803,   Feb. no seals (Baudin). Cornell, 1974:485.

1818,   Jan. several seals of the "hairy" species; 3 killed. King, 1828(1):11,19.

1821,   Dec. seal killed in Oyster Harbour. King, 1828(2):126.

1822,   Jan. 5 seals killed. King, 1828(2):152.

SEAL I. (32°18′S, 115°42′E), part Reserve A24204, Conservation of Flora and Fauna, WA:DFW. No evidence other than name.

SMOOTH ROCKS (34°30′S, 119°07′E).

1945,   May. 5 on largest rock (Fowler). (C) CSIRO.

1945,   Jun. c. 20 on S rock (Fowler). (C) CSIRO.

SOUTHERN GROUP (28°28′S, 13°49′E), once known as the PELSART GROUP, part Reserve A20253.

1727,   survivors of the *Zeewyk* ate 147 seals in 10 months at Gun I. (van der Graeff). O'Loughlin, 1967:415.

1840,   a quantity of seals bones found in Gun I. Stokes, 1846(2):150.

1840,   Apr. a few seals on "Pylsart I". (C) Stokes, 1846(2):138.

1966,   Aug. 1 male, 1 female and 2 juveniles on Jubilee I. O'Loughlin, 1967:415.

TERMINATION I. (34°28′S, 122°02′E), part Reserve A22796.

1950,   Nov. c. 20, including 1 harem. (A) Serventy, 1953:48.

THOMAS I. (33°58′S, 121°58′E), part Reserve A22796.

1950,   Nov. 1 seal ashore. (C) Serventy, 1953:48.

THUNDALDA (32°76′S, 126°00′E), below coastal cliffs near head of Great Australian Bight.

1973,   Oct. 22 in cave, including bulls, females, pups and sub-adults. (A) Reilly and Johnstone, pers. comm.

WALLABI GROUP (28°25′S, 113°43′E), part Reserve A20253.

1729,   survivors of the *Batavia* named one of the Group "Seal I.", presumably because of the presence of seals (Pelsaert). (C) Drake-Brockman, 1963:111 et seq; Edwards, 1966.

WEST I. (34°04′S, 120°28′E).

1945,   May. 70-80 (Fowler). (C) CSIRO.

WESTALL I. (34°05′S, 122°57′E), part Reserve A22796.

1950,   Nov. c. 10 resting ashore. (C) Serventy, 1953:48.

Appendix F

DATA ON THE DISTRIBUTION AND STATUS OF THE NEW ZEALAND SEA LION, *PHOCARCTOS HOOKERI*.

Known also as Hooker's sea lion, and to the early sealers as hair seal or tiger seal (see Musgrave, 1865).

Key to status: A breeding colony.
                 B non-breeding colony.
                 C status unknown.

AUCKLAND IS. (50°50′S, 166°00′E), discovered 1806.

prior   main period of sealing. McNab, 1826, 1909:344.

1830,   Jan. survey of coastline revealed not more than 20 hair seals. (C) Morrell, 1832:360.

1840,   specimens collected, voyage of *Astralabe* and *Zelee* (Doumoutier, Hombron, and Jacquinot). Clark, 1873:750,759.

1840,   specimens collected, voyage of *Erebus* and *Terror*. Clark, 1873:756.

1864,   Jan. great numbers seen in Carnley's Harbour ... appears to be more numerous at Figure of Eight I., and at head of W arm of Carnley's Harbour. (A) Musgrave, 1865:16,33.

1907,   quite numerous at Enderby I., Carnley Harbour, and Masked I. (A) Waite, 1909:543-8.

1971,   more than 1 000 at Sandy Bay, Enderby I. during the breeding season. (A) Taylor, 1971.

1972-73, about 1 000 at Enderby I., minimum of 2 000 at Dundas I. and 68 on Figure of Eight I., including at least 24 pups. (A) Best, 1974:2-3.

1972,   Dec.-Jan. 1973 total population at the islands estimated at 3 000-3 500. (A) Wilson, pers. comm.

CAMPBELL I. (52°32′S, 169°08′E).
1815-16, 300 hair skins obtained by gang from the *Governor Bligh* which apparently worked Foveaux Strait and Campbell I. Cumpston, 1963:102: HRNZ, 1:559-60.
prior sea lions taken for oil and skins. (C)
1864, Musgrave, 1865:18.
1909, quite numerous at certain seasons. (C) Waite, 1909:542.
1942-47, a female with pup seen near Camp Cove in most years; up to 150 males, mostly immature, at Northwest Bay; maximum of 20 females, minimum of 200 males on the island. (A) Bailey and Sorensen, 1962:52-4.
1948, minimum of 50 at Northwest Bay. Sorensen, 1951:17.
1948, a considerable population, mainly non-breeding. (A) Falla, 1948:147.
1958, Feb. main concentration at Northwest Bay, of 84 males, and 5 females (Street). (A) Bailey and Sorensen, 1962:55.

MACQUARIE I. (54°40′S, 158°50′E), discovered 1810.
1810-11, no evidence of occurrence. Csordas, 1963:32.
1949-52, lone male, named "Blackie", recorded in all seasons. Csordas, 1963:32.
1954, one or two seen chasing penguins. Csordas, 1963:33.
1955-60, lone male, "Mr. Brown", recorded each winter-spring, until mature. Csordas, 1963:33-35.
1957-59, a few other individuals seen, for only a day at a time. Csordas, 1963:33.
1966, winter. medium-sized male on isthmus near Buckles Bay. Shaughnessy, pers. comm.
1966, Nov. a large male at Lusitania Bay. Shaughnessy, pers. comm.
1971, Nov. one near-mature male near North Head (Warneke). VIC:FWD.

SNARES IS. (48°00′S, 166°35′E), discovered 1791.
1810-17, 4 marooned sealers lived on sea birds and seals; collected 1 300 skins (most probably of fur seals, but possibly some sea lions as well). (C) McNab, 1909:223. (Note: fur seal flesh is quite unpalatable compared with that of sea lion. See Musgrave, 1865:22,57.)
1830, Jan. no fur seals (or sea lions?) found.

Morrell, 1832:365.
1907, Feb. quite numerous at certain seasons; female with pup found. (A) Waite, 1909:544.
1948, Jan.-Feb. less than 100, mostly males, at Boat Harbour. (B) Richdale, (n.d.): 112.
1961, 67, small number of females in a predominantly male population (Knox). (C) Crawley and Cameron, 1972:129.
1968-69, mother and pup seen on Main I., later near Boat Harbour with male. (A) Crawley and Cameron, 1972:130.
1970-71, mother and pup seen; summer population to maximum of 50. (A) Crawley and Cameron, 1972:128-32.

SOUTH I., NEW ZEALAND (north to 46°S).
1964, included within species range. King, 1964:36.
1972, lone males haul out in winter, S of Dunedin (Street). Gaskin, 1972:155.
1974, lone males haul out on S coast, to as far N as Otago Peninsula. Wilson, pers. comm.

STEWART I. (47°00′S, 168°00′E).
1972, a few males ashore in winter (Street). (C) Gaskin, 1972:155.
1974, Feb. group of 9 males at Small Crafts Retreat; lone males seen elsewhere. (C) Wilson, pers. comm.

Appendix G

DATA ON THE DISTRIBUTION AND STATUS OF THE SOUTHERN ELEPHANT SEAL, *MIROUNGA LEONINA*, IN THE AUSTRALASIAN REGION.

Key to status: A breeding colony.
B non-breeding colony.
C status unknown.

TASMANIA AND BASS STRAIT

HUNTER I. (40°30′S, 144°45′E), originally known as BARREN I.
1802, Dec. in large numbers. (C) Peron and

467

Freycinet, 1816:37; (see translation in Micco, 1971:23).

KING I. (29°50′S, 144°00′E), discovered 1799.

1801,   taking of elephant seals possibly begun by gang from the *Harrington*. Footnote in Micco, 1971:12; Cumpston, 1968:36.

1802,   Jan. Elephant Bay named because of large numbers encountered (Murray). (A) Lee, 1915:117.

1802,   Jan. specimen of oil taken for Government (Murray). Lee, 1915:118.

1802,   Mar.-May. 600 killed for oil by gangs from the *Harrington*. HRA, I. 3:524, 637, 641.

1802,   Apr. 1 killed at NE point. Flinders, 1814(1):206.

1802,   Jun.-Jul. c. 50 killed by gang from the *Margaret*. Cumpston, 1973:52.

1802,   Dec. the elephant seal oil industry described in detail in Peron and Freycinet, 1816: chap. XXII, XXIII. (see translation in Micco, 1971).

1802,   Dec. they are becoming scarce already (Baudin). HRNSW, 5:832.

1802,   Dec. many elephant seals on NW coast; in greatest plenty at mouths of fresh freshwater streams (Grimes). Shillinglaw, 1879:17.

1803,   Jun. large quantity of oil obtained by the *Margaret*. SG, 26 June, 1803.

1803,   Feb. sealing party relieved by the *Surprise*. SG, 12 Mar. 1803.

NEW YEARS IS. (39°41′S, 143°51′E).

1801,   Oct.-Nov. pioneer gang landed from the *Harrington*. Footnote in Micco, 1971:12.

1802,   Apr. *Harrington* at New Years Islands. Footnote in Flinders, 1814(1):209.

1802,   Dec. in large numbers on ... New Years Islands. (A) Peron and Freycinet, 1816:37; Micco, 1971:23; Cumpston, 1973:58.

SISTERS IS. (39°42′S, 147°57′E).

1802,   Dec. a few stragglers. (C) Peron and Freycinet, 1816:23; Micco, 1971:23; Cumpston, 1973:58.

TASMANIA, WEST COAST.

9 000BP * common in archeological site. Ride, 1970:189.

TASMANIA, WEST POINT (40°56′S, 144°37′E).

1 850-1 300 ± 80 BP. thousands of bones of young individuals in middens of aborigines. Jones, 1967:363.

Stragglers occasionally haul-out on the Tasmanian and Victorian coast and some of the islands, e.g. Flinders I. (VIC:FWD), Lady Julia Percy I. (Simpson, 1961:227, 307) and Seal Rocks (VIC:FWD). These include several records of adult males and of females coming ashore to give birth (Davies, 1961, Tyson, 1977, VIC:FWD).

NEW ZEALAND AND MAJOR ISLANDS, including Macquarie I.

ANTIPODES I. (49°41′S, 178°43′E).

1969,   Feb. 35 counted, from North Cape to Leeward I. (Taylor). Sorensen, 1969a:79.

AUCKLAND IS. (50°50′S, 166°00′E).

1948,   a regular visitor. Falla, 1948:142.

CAMPBELL I. (52°33′S, 169°08′E).

1870-1930, not recorded as breeding. (B) Falla, 1948:148.

1880-1929, no breeding seals ashore. (B) Sorensen, 1951:10.

1941,   small breeding population of about 1 000. (A) Sorensen, 1950.

1944,   Nov. 1 100, including 26 bulls and 105 pups. (A) Bailey and Sorensen, 1962:74.

1947,   15 harems, including 32 bulls, 194 cows and 191 pups (Sorensen). (A) Bailey and Sorensen, 1962:68.

1957,   Oct. 16 bulls, 211 females and 190 pups (Thompson). Bailey and Sorensen, 1962.

1958,   post-breeding haul-out of 84 large bulls, 129 medium bulls, 281 females and 42 pups (Street). Bailey and Sorensen, 1962:74.

_____

* Before present.

CHATHAM I. (44°50'S, 176°30'W).

1972, Nov. stragglers only. Wilson, pers. comm.

MACQUARIE I. (54°40'S, 158°50'E).

c.1814- elephant seals taken for oil, initially by
1919, gangs from Sydney, later by gangs from New Zealand. (A) Cumpston, 1968:36 et seq.

1831, no sign of seals found by gang of *Venus*. McNab, 1913:88.

1834, Mar.-Feb. no oil obtained. McNab, 1913:94.

1920, Feb. sealing licence held by J. Hatch of NZ cancelled by Tasmanian Government. Cumpston, 1968:316.

1949, population stable in numbers. (A) Nicholls, 1970:599.

1952-58, counts made which indicate population stabilized at natural level: 33 000 breeding cows, 28 500 weaned pups, 3 000 beachmasters and challengers. (A) Carrick and Ingham, 1960:336.

1960, provisional estimate of total population of 110 000, including pups; breeding population of 36 000-37 000 females and 3 500-4 000 males. (A) Carrick and Ingham, 1962b:200-1.

1972, review of population dynamics, and of research on growth and development. Johnstone, 1972:519-32.

SNARES IS. (48°00'S, 166°35'E).

1948, suitable beaches available only at Boat Harbour, with space for 5. (C) Falla, 1948:137.

1948, Jan.-Feb. fighting among large males; no estimate of numbers. Richdale, (n.d.):111-12.

SOUTH I., NEW ZEALAND (north to 41°30'S).

1969, isolated records of females pupping on shore. Sorensen, 1969:6.

1974, a few stragglers haul-out; records to as far N as Wellington. Wilson, pers. comm.

References

ABBOTT, G.A. and N.B. NAIRN, (eds.), Economic growth
1969 of Australia 1788-1821. Melbourne, Melbourne University Press.

ASHWORTH, H.P.C. and D. LE SOUEF, Albatross Island
1895 and the Hunter Group. *Vict. Nat.*, 11:134-44.

BACKHOUSE, J., A narrative of a visit to the Australian
1843 colonies. London, Hamilton, Adams and Co.

BAILEY, A.M. and J.H. SORENSEN, Subantarctic Campbell
1962 bell Island. *Proc. Denver Mus. Nat. Hist.*, 10:1-305.

BARRETT, J.W., The twin ideals. London, Lewis and Co.,
1918 2 vols.

BEAGLEHOLE, J.C., (ed.), The journals of Captain James
1961 Cook on his voyages of discovery. The voyage of the *Resolution* and *Adventure*, 1772-75. Cambridge, Hakluyt Society.

BEST, H.A., A preliminary report on the natural history
1974 and behaviour of Hooker's sea-lion at Enderby Island, Auckland Islands, New Zealand, December 1972 to March 1973. *Fish. Tech. Rep. Minist. Agric. Fish. N.Z.*, (132):12 p.

BRIDE, T.F., Letters from Victorian pioneers, edited by
1898 C.E. Sayers. Melbourne, Heinemann, reprint. 1969.

BROWN, D.L., Vocal communication of the New Zealand
1974 land fur seal on Open Bay Islands, Westland. *Fish. Tech. Rep. Minist. Agric. Fish. N.Z.*, (130):15 p.

BRYDEN, M.M., Testicular temperature in the southern
1967 elephant seal, *Mirounga leonina* (Linn.). *J. Reprod. Fert.*, 13:583-94.

—, Control of growth in two populations of elephant
1968 seals. *Nature, Lond.*, 217:1106-8.

—, Development and growth of the southern elephant
1968a seal (*Mirounga leonina*) (Linn.). *Pap. Proc. R. Soc. Tasm.*, 102:25-30.

—, Growth and function of the subcutaneous fat of the
1968b elephant seal. *Nature, Lond.*, 220:597-9.

469

−, Lactation and suckling in relation to early growth
1968c   of the southern elephant seal, *Mirounga leonina* (L.). *Aust. J. Zool.*, 16:739-48.

−, Growth of the southern elephant seal, *Mirounga*
1969   *leonina* (L.). *Growth*, 33:69-82.

−, Regulation of relative growth by functional demand:
1969a   its importance in animal production. *Growth*, 33:143-56.

−, Relative growth of the major body components of
1969b   the southern elephant seal, *Mirounga leonina* (L.). *Aust. J. Zool.*, 17:153-77.

−, Size and growth of viscera in the southern elephant
1971   seal, *Mirounga leonina* (L.). *Aust. J. Zool.*, 19:103-20.

−, Myology of the southern elephant seal *Mirounga*
1971a   *leonina* (L.). *Antarct. Res. Ser.*, 18:109-40.

−, Body size and composition of elephant seals (*Mi-*
1972   *rounga leonina*): absolute measurements and estimates from bone dimensions. *J. Zool.*, *Lond.*, 167:265-76.

−, Growth patterns of individual muscles of the ele-
1973   phant seal, *Mirounga leonina* (L.). *J. Anat.*, 116:121-33.

BRYDEN, M.M. and G.H.K. LIM, Blood parameters of
1969   the southern elephant seal (*Mirounga leonina*, Linn.) in relation to diving. *Comp. Biochem. Physiol.*, 28:139-48.

CARRICK, R. and S.E. INGHAM, Ecological studies of the
1960   southern elephant seal, *Mirounga leonina* (L.), at Macquarie Island and Heard Island. *Mammalia, Paris*, 24:325-42.

−, Studies on the southern elephant seal, *Mirounga*
1962   *leonina* (L.). 1. Introduction to the series. *CSIRO Wildl. Res.*, 7:89-101.

−, Studies on the southern elephant seal, *Mirounga*
1962a   *leonina* (L.). 2. Canine tooth structure in relation to function and age determination. *CSIRO Wildl. Res.*, 7:102-18.

−, Studies on the southern elephant seal, *Mirounga*
1962b   *leonina* (L.). 5. Population dynamics and utilization. *CSIRO Wildl. Res.*, 7:198-206.

CARRICK, R., S.E. CSORDAS and S.E. INGHAM, Studies on
1962   the southern elephant seal, *Mirounga leonina* (L.). 4. Breeding and development. *CSIRO Wildl. Res.*, 7:161-97.

CARRICK, R. *et al.*, Studies on the southern elephant seal,
1962   *Mirounga leonina* (L.). 3. The annual cycle in relation to age and sex. *CSIRO Wildl. Res.*, 7:119-60.

CHAPMAN, F.R., The outlying islands south of New
1891   Zealand. *Trans. N.Z. Inst.*, 23:491-522.

CLARK, J.W., On the eared seals of the Auckland Is-
1873   lands. *Proc. Zool. Soc. Lond.*, 1873:750-60.

−, On the eared seals of the islands of St. Paul and
1875   Amsterdam, with a description of the fur seal of New Zealand, and an attempt to distinguish and re-arrange the New Zealand Otariidae. *Proc. Zool. Soc. Lond.*, 1875:650-77.

COLEMAN, E., Save the seals. Part 2. *Vict. Nat.*, 67:171-7.
1951

COLLINS, D., An account of the English Colony in New
1802   South Wales. London, Cadell and Davis, vol. 2.

COOPER, H.M., The unknown coast. Adelaide, the au-
1953   thor.

−, The unknown coast: a supplement. Adelaide, the
1955   author.

CORNELL, C., The journal of Post Captain Nicholas
1974   Baudin. Adelaide, Libraries Board of South Australia.

CRAWLEY, M.C., Distribution and abundance of fur
1972   seals on the Snares Islands, New Zealand. *N.Z.J. Mar. Freshwat. Res.*, 6:115-26.

CRAWLEY, M.C. and D.L. BROWN, Measurements of
1971   tagged pups and a population estimate of New Zealand fur seals on Taumaka, Open Bay Islands, Westland. *N.Z.J. Mar. Freshwat. Res.*, 5:389-95.

CRAWLEY, M.C. and D.B. CAMERON, New Zealand sea
1972   lions, *Phocarctos hookeri* on the Snares Islands. *N.Z.J. Mar. Freshwat. Res.*, 6:127-32.

CRAWLEY, M.C. and G.J. WILSON, The natural history
1976   and behaviour of the New Zealand fur seal. *Tuatara*, 22(1):1-29.

CSORDAS, S.E., Breeding of the fur seal, *Arctocephalus*
1958   *forsteri* Lesson, at Macquarie Island. *Aust. J. Sci.*, 21:87-8.

–, The Kerguelen fur seal on Macquarie Island. *Vict.*
1962   *Nat.*, 79:226-9.

–, Sea lions on Macquarie Island. *Vict. Nat.*, 80:32-5.
1963

–, The history of fur seals on Macquarie Island. *Vict.*
1963a   *Nat.*, 80:255-8.

CSORDAS, S.E. and S.E. INGHAM, The New Zealand fur
1965   seal *Arctocephalus forsteri* (Lesson) at Mac-
        quarie Island, 1949-64. *CSIRO Wildl. Res.*,
        10:83-99.

CUMPSTON, J.S., Shipping arrivals and departures Syd-
1963   ney, 1788-1825. Canberra, the author.

–, Macquarie Island. *ANARE Sci. Rep. (A Narr.)*, (93).
1968

–, First visitors to Bass Strait. *Roebuck Soc. Publ.*
1973   *Canberra*, (7).

DARBY, M., Natural history of the Bounty Islands. *Ani-*
1970   *mals*, 13:170-7.

DAVIES, J.L., Birth of an elephant seal on the Tasmanian
1961   Coast. *J. Mammal.*, 42:113-4.

DELANO, A., Narrative of voyages and travels in the
1817   Northern and Southern Hemispheres: com-
        prising three voyages round the world;
        together with a voyage of survey and discovery,
        in the Pacific Ocean and Oriental Islands.
        Boston, House.

DOOME, U., A cruise in Bass's Straits. *Illus. Sydney News*,
1874   28 Feb. 1874.

DRAKE-BROCKMAN, H., Voyage to disaster: the life of
1963   Francisco Pelsaert. Sydney, Angus and Ro-
        bertson.

DUNBABIN, T., Sailing the World's edge. London,
1931   Newnes.

DUNDERDALE, G., The book of the bush. London, Ward,
1898   Lock and Co.

EDWARDS, H., Islands of angry ghosts. London, Hodder
1966   and Stoughton.

FALLA, R.A., The outlying islands of New Zealand. *N.Z.*
1948   *Geogr.*, 4:127-54.

–, Southern seals: population studies and conservation
1953   problems. *Proc. Pac. Sci. Congr.*, 7(4):706.

FANNING, E., Voyages round the world; with selected
1833   sketches of voyages to the South Seas, North
        and South Pacific Oceans, China, etc. New
        York, Collins and Hannay.

FINLAYSON, H.H., Greenly Island (South Australia).
1948   *Walkabout*, 1 (May Issue): 35-40.

FLINDERS, M., Observations on the coasts of Van Die-
1801   men's Land on Bass's Strait and its islands,
        and on part of the coasts of New South Wales.
        London, John Nichols.

–, A voyage to Terra Australis. London, Nicol, 2 vols.
1814

FORD, J., The reptilian fauna of the islands between
1963   Dongara and Lancelin, Western Australia.
        West. Aust. Nat., 8:135-42.

FOWLER, S., A landing on Pedra Branca. *Proc. R. Zool.*
1947   *Soc. N.S.W.*, 1947:22-6.

GABRIEL, J., Excursion to Phillip Island. *Vict. Nat.*,
1913   30:29-34.

GASKIN, D.E., Whales, dolphins and seals with special
1972   reference to the New Zealand region. London,
        Heinemann.

GIPPSLAND MERCURY, The, 2 Feb. issue.
1875

GLIDDON, J.W., (ed.), Phillip Island in picture and story.
1963   Phillip Island, Committee of Trust, Cowes
        Bush Nursing Hospital.

GOULD, C., The islands in Bass's Strait. *Pap. Proc. R.*
1872   *Soc. Tasm.*, 1871:57-67.

GOULD, J., The mammals of Australia. Part 12. London,
1860   the author.

GRANT, J., The narrative of a voyage of discovery, per-
1803   formed in His Majesty's vessel *The Lady Nel-*
        son in the years 1800, 1801, and 1802, to New
        South Wales. London, Egerton.

GREY, G., Journals of two expeditions of discovery in
1841   north-west and Western Australia, during the
        years 1837, 38 and 39. London, Boone, 2 vols.

GWYNN, A.M., Notes on the fur seals at Macquarie
1953   Island and Heard Island. *ANARE Interim*
        Rep., (4).

HAINSWORTH, D.R., The Sydney traders. Melbourne,
1972   Cassell.

HOPE, J.H., Mammals of the Bass Strait islands. *Proc. R.*
1973   *Soc. Vict.*, 85:163-95.

JOHNSTONE, G.W., A review of biological research by
1972   Australian National Antarctic Research Expedition, 1947-71. *Polar Res.*, 16:519-32.

JONES, R., Middens and man in Tasmania. *Aust. Nat.*
1967   *Hist.*, 15:359-64.

KELLY, J., First discovery of Port Davey and Macquarie
1920   Harbour, by James Kelly. *Pap. Proc. R. Soc.
Tasm.*, 1920:160-81.

KING, J., Seals of the world. London, British Museum
1964   (Natural History).

–, On the identity of the fur seals of Australia. *Nature,*
1968   *Lond.*, 219:632-3.

–, The identity of the fur seals of Australia. *Aust. J.*
1969   *Zool.*, 17:841-53.

–, On the identity of three young fur seals (genus *Arc-*
1976   *tocephalus*) stranded in New Caledonia
(Mammalia, Pinnipedia). *Beaufortia*, 25:
97-105.

KING, P.P., Narrative of a survey of the inter-tropical
1827   and western coasts of Australia performed
between the years Australia performed
between the years 1818 and 1822. London,
Murray, 2 vols.

LEE, I., The logbooks of the *Lady Nelson*. London,
1915   Grafton and Co.

LE SOUEF, A.S., Notes on the seals found in Australian
1925   seas. *Aust. Zool.*, 4:112-6.

LE SOUEF, D., Expedition of Field Naturalists' Club to
1891   Kent Group, Bass Straits. *Vict. Nat.*, 7:121-31.

LEWIS, F., Report of the Chief Inspector of fisheries and
1929   game on an investigation into the feeding
habits, etc., of seals in Victorian waters.
Melbourne, Government Printer.

–, Seals on the Victorian coast and their feeding habits.
1930   *Aust. Mus. Mag.*, 4:39-44.

–, Notes on Australian seals. *Vict. Nat.*, 59:24-6.
1942

LINDGREN, E., Bird notes on Lion Island, Esperance.
1956   *West. Aust. Nat.*, 5:97-101.

LING, J.K., Hair growth and moulting in the southern
1965   elephant seal, *Mirounga leonina* (Linn.). *In*
Biology of the skin and hair growth, edited by
A.G. Lyne and B.F. Short. Sydney, Angus and
Robertson, pp. 525-44.

–, The skin and hair of the southern elephant seal,
1966   *Mirounga leonina* (Linn.). The facial vibrissae.
Aust. J. Zool., 14:855-66.

LING, J.K., The skin and hair of the southern elephant
1968   seal, *Mirounga leonina* (L.). 3. Morphology of
the adult integument. *Aust. J. Zool.*,
16:629-45.

LING, J.K. and C.D.B. THOMAS, The skin and hair of the
1967   southern elephant seal, *Mirounga leonina* (L.).
2. Pre-natal and early post-natal development
and moulting. *Aust. J. Zool.*, 15:349-65.

LING, J.K. and G.E. WALKER, Seal studies in South
1976   Australia: progress report for the year 1975. *S.
Aust. Nat.*, 50:59-68, 72.

MACKENZIE, D., The birds and seals of the Bishop and
1968   Clerk Islets, Macquarie Island. *Emu*, 67:241-5.

MAHONEY, D.J., Reports of the Expedition of the
1937   McCoy Society for Field Investigation and
Research. 2. Historical introduction. *Proc. R.
Soc. Vict.*, 49:331-2.

MARGINSON, M.A. and S. MURRAY-SMITH, Craggy Is-
1972   land, Bass Strait. *Vict. Nat.*, 89:212-22.

MARLOW, B.J., The sea-lions of Dangerous Reef. *Aust.
1968   Nat. Hist.*, June Issue: 39-44.

–, Pup abduction by the Australian sea lion *Neophoca
1972   cinerea. Mammalia, Paris*, 36:161-5.

–, The comparative behaviour of the Australasian sea
1975   lions *Neophoca cinerea* and *Phocarctos hookeri* (Pinnipedia: Otariidae). *Mammalia,
Paris*, 39:159-230.

MARLOW, B.J. and J.E. KING, Sea lions and fur seals of
1974   Australia and New Zealand – the growth of
knowledge. *Aust. Mammal.*, 1:117-35.

MCNAB, R., Murihiku. Wellington, Whitcombe and
1909   Tombs.

–, The old whaling days: a history of Southern New

1913   Zealand from 1830-1840. Auckland, Golden Press. Reprinted 1975.

McNALLY, J. and D.D. LYNCH, Notes on the food of
1954   Victorian seals. *Fauna Rep. Vict.*, (1).

MICCO, H.M., King Island and the sealing trade 1802.
1971   *Roebuck Soc. Publ. Canberra*, (3).

MILLER, E.H., Social and thermoregulatory behaviour
1971   of the New Zealand fur seal *Arctocephalus forsteri* (Lesson 1828). M.Sc. Thesis, Department of Zoology, University of Canterbury, Christchurch, New Zealand.

–, Social behaviour of the New Zealand fur seal on
1974   Open Bay Islands, Westland. *Fish. Tech. Rep. Minist. Agric. Fish. N.Z.*, (131):33 p.

–, Social behaviour between adult male and female
1947a   New Zealand fur seals, *Arctocephalus forsteri* (Lesson) during the breeding season. *Aust. J. Zool.*, 22:155-73.

–, Body and organ measurements of fur seals, *Arcto-*
1975   *cephalus forsteri* (Lesson), from New Zealand. *J. Mammal.*, 56:511-3.

–, Social and evolutionary implications of territoriality
1975a   in adult male New Zealand fur seals, *Arctocephalus forsteri* (Lesson, 1828), during the breeding season. *Rapp. P.-V. Réun. CIEM*, 169:170-87.

MITCHELL, F.J. and A.C. BEHRNDT, Fauna and flora of
1949   the Greenly Islands. Part 1. Introductory narrative and vertebrate fauna. *Rec. S. Aust. Mus.*, 9:167-79.

MORRELL, B., Jr., A narrative of four voyages to the
1832   South Sea, North and South Pacific Ocean, Chinese Sea, Ethiopic and Southern Atlantic Ocean, Indian and Antarctic Oceans from the years 1822 to 1831. New York, J. and J. Harper.

MURRAY, L.C., Notes on the sealing industry of Van
1929   Diemen's Land. *Rep. Aust. Assoc. Adv. Sci.*, 19:274-81.

MUSGRAVE, T., Castaway on Auckland Isles: A narrative
1865   of the wreck of the *Grafton*. Melbourne, Dwight.

NICHOLLS, D.G., Dispersal and dispersion in relation to
1970   the birthsite of the southern elephant seal, *Mirounga leonina* (L.), of Macquarie Island.

Mammalia, Paris, 34:598-616.

NICHOLLS, M., (ed.), The diary of the Reverend Robert
1977   Knopwood 1803-1838. Hobart, Tasmanian Historical Research Association.

NIXON, F.R., The cruise of the *Beacon*. London, Bell and
1857   Daldy.

O'LOUGHLIN, P.M., Houtmans Abrolhos. *Aust. Nat.*
1967   *Hist.*, 15:413-7.

O'MAY, H., Sealers of Bass Strait. Hobart, Government
n.d.   printer.

PERON, F., Voyage de découvertes aux Terres Australes.
1807   1. Historique. Paris, L'Imprimerie Impériale.

PERON, F. and M.L. FREYCINET, Voyage de découvertes
1816   aux Terres Australes. 2. Historique. Paris, L'Imprimerie Royale.

PESCOTT, T., A visit to Lady Julia Percy Island. *Vict.*
1965   *Nat.*, 81:290-301.

–, Lady Julia Percy Island revisited. *Vic. Nat.*, 85:125-8.
1968

PLOMLEY, N.J.B., Friendly mission: the Tasmanian
1966   journal and papers of George Augustus Robinson 1829-1834. Hobart, Tasmanian Historical Research Association.

Press, The, 27 January, 1968 issue. Christchurch, N.Z.
1968

RAWSON, G., Matthew Flinders' narrative of his voyage
1946   in the schooner *Francis*: 1798. London, Golden, Cockerel Press.

REDWOOD, R., Forgotten islands of the South Pacific.
1950   Wellington, Reed.

REPENNING, C.A., R.S. PETERSON and C.L. HUBBS, Con-
1971   tributions to the systematics of the southern fur seals, with special reference to the Juan Fernandez and Guadalupe species. *Antarct. Res. Ser.*, 18:1-34.

RICHDALE, L.E., Wild life on an island outpost. Dune-
n.d.   din, the author.

RIDE, W.D.L., A guide to the native mammals of Aus-
1970   tralia. Melbourne, Oxford University Press.

ROE, M., (ed.), The journal and letters of Captain
1967   Charles Bishop on the northwest coast of

473

America, in the Pacific and in New South Wales. Cambridge, Cambridge University Press for Hakluyt Society, Second Series No. 131.

SCHEFFER, V.B., Seals, sea lions and walruses: a review
1958   of Pinnipedia. Stanford, California, Stanford University Press, 179 p.

SERVENTY, V.N., The archipelago of the Recherche. Part
1953   4. Mammals. *Rep. Aust. Geogr. Soc.*, (1).

SHAUGHNESSY, P.D., Serum protein variation in south-
1970   ern fur seals, *Arctocephalus* spp. in relation to their taxonomy. *Aust. J. Zool.*, 18:331-43.

SHILLINGLAW, J.J., (ed.), Historical records of Port Phil-
1879   lip: the first annals of the Colony of Victoria. Melbourne, Government Printer.

SIMPSON, K., Fauna Survey Group reports for 1 Dec.
1961   1960, 12 Jan. 1961. *Vict. Nat.*, 77:277, 307.

SINGLETON, R.J., New Zealand fur seals at Three Kings
1972   Islands. *N.Z.J. Mar. Freshwat. Res.*, 6:649-50.

SORENSEN, J.H., Elephant seals of Campbell Island.
1950   *Cape Exped. Ser. Bull.*, (6).

–, Wildlife in the sub-Antarctic. Christchurch, N.Z.,
1951   Whitcombe and Tombs.

–, New Zealand seals with special reference to the fur
1969   seal. *Fish. Tech. Rep. Mar. Dep. N.Z.*, (39).

–, New Zealand fur seals with special reference to the
1969a   1946 open season. *Fish. Tech. Rep. Mar. Dep. N.Z.*, (42).

STIRLING, I., Diurnal movements of the New Zealand
1968   fur seal at Kaikoura. *N.Z.J. Mar. Freshwat. Res.*, 2:375-7.

–, Observations on the behaviour of the New Zealand
1970   fur seal (*Arctocephalus forsteri*). *J. Mammal.*, 51:766-78.

–, Studies on the behaviour of the New Zealand fur
1971   seal, *Arctocephalus forsteri* (Lesson). 1. Annual cycle, postures and calls, and adult males during the breeding season. *Aust. J. Zool.*, 19:243-66.

–, Studies on the behaviour of the New Zealand fur
1971a   seal, *Arctocephalus forsteri*. 2. Adult females and pups. *Aust. J. Zool.*, 19:267-73.

–, Observations on the Australian sea lion *Neophoca*
1972   *cinerea* (Peron). *Aust. J. Zool.*, 20:271-9.

–, The economic value and management of seals in
1972a   South Australia. *Publ. S. Aust. Dep. Fish.*, (2).

STIRLING, I. and R.M. WARNEKE, Implications of a
1971   comparison of the airborne vocalizations and some aspects of behaviour of the two Australian fur seal species. *Arctocephalus* spp., on the evolution and current taxonomy of the genus. *Aust. J. Zool.*, 19:227-41.

STOKES, J.L., Discoveries in Australia, with an account
1846   of the coasts and rivers explored and surveyed during the voyage of H.M.S. *Beagle* in the years 1837-43. London, Boone, 2 vols.

STONEHOUSE, B., Marine birds and mammals at Kai-
1965   koura. *Proc. N.Z. Ecol. Soc.*, 12:13-20.

STORR, G.M., Notes on Bald Island and the adjacent
1965   mainland. *West. Aust. Nat.*, 9:187-96.

STREET, R.J., Feeding habits of the New Zealand fur seal
1964   *Arctocephalus forsteri*. *Fish. Tech. Rep. Mar. Dep. N.Z.*, (9).

TAYLOR, R.H., Influence of man on vegetation and wild-
1971   life of Enderby and Rose Islands, Auckland Islands. *N.Z.J. Bot.*, 9:225-68.

TROUGHTON, E. LeG., Furred animals of Australia.
1941   Sydney, Angus and Robertson.

TUBB, J.A. and C.W. BRAZENOR, Reports of the expedi-
1937   tion of the McCoy Society for Field Investigation and Research. 2. Historical introduction. *Proc. R. Soc. Vict.*, 49:331-2.

TYSON, R.M., Birth of an elephant seal on Tasmania's
1977   east coast. *Vict. Nat.*, 94:212-3.

VANCOUVER, G., A voyage of discovery to the north
1798   Pacific Ocean, and around the world ... performed in the years 1790-1795. London, Robinson and Edwards, 3 vols.

WAITE, E.R., Vertebrata of the sub-Antarctic islands of
1909   New Zealand. Art. 25. *In* The sub-Antarctic islands of New Zealand. Canterbury, N.Z., Philosophical Institute, vol. 2, 542-600.

WARNEKE, R.M., Seals of Westernport. *Vict. Resour.*,
1966   5:24-5.

—, Dispersal and mortality of juvenile fur seals *Arcto-*
1975   *cephalus pusillus doriferus* in Bass Strait, southeastern Australia. *Rapp. P.-V. Réun. CIEM*, 169:296-302.

WHINRAY, J.S., A list of the birds of the major Kent's
1971   Group islands. *Tasm. Nat.*, (24):2-3.

WILSON, G.J., A preliminary report on the distribution
1974   and abundance of the New Zealand fur seal (*Arctocephalus forsteri*) at the Auckland Islands, December 8, 1972 to January 15, 1973. *Fish. Tech. Rep. Minist. Agric. Fish. N.Z.*, (133).

WILSON, G.J., The distribution, abundance and popu-
1974a   lation characteristics of the New Zealand fur seal. M.Sc. Thesis, Department of Zoology, University of Canterbury, Christchurch, Christchurch, Zew Zealand.

WOOD JONES, F., The mammals of South Australia. Part
1925   3. The Monodelphia. Adelaide Government Printer.

YOUNG, J., Gannet Rock — west coast dive. *South Pac. Underwat. Mag.*, 10(6):15.

Anon., *Aust. Pilot*, 1944(2):219-20.
1944

OTARIA FLAVESCENS (SHAW), SOUTH AMERICAN SEA LION

R. VAZ-FERREIRA

Abstract

The South American sea lion (*Otaria flavescens*) is distributed along the Atlantic and Pacific shores of South America. Despite the lack and limited significance of recent estimates of abundance, the total number on land can be estimated at 275 000, excluding the Chilean coast south of Punta Maiquillahue. A reduction in numbers is generally found over most of the species' range and sea lions are no longer found in many areas where they once lived. In Brazil, the species reaches north to Rio de Janeiro, though probably does not breed north of Recife da Torres. In Uruguay, the population has maintained a size of about 30 000 animals with rookeries distributed on several islands, mainly Isla de Lobos. In the early fifties, 168 270 animals were estimated to inhabit Argentine waters; sea lions there are presently distributed from Bahía Blanca to Tierra del Fuego and Isla de los Estados. The species is found mostly on offshore islets in the Falkland Islands — the drop in the population there from an estimated 371 500 or 389 500 animals in the thirties to no more than 30 000 animals in 1964-65 may be due to population movements or a reduction in the food supply. On the Pacific coast, *O. flavescens* is distributed from the Diego Ramirez Islands to Zorritos, Peru, and to the Galapagos Islands; it probably does not breed north of Isla Lobos de Tierra. The size of the population in Peru was estimated to be 20 000 in 1975. Although South American sea lions apparently do not migrate, movements at certain times of the year, along land and out at sea, can be significant, and important seasonal and daily changes in the size of populations on land do occur.

Identifying skull characters and important aspects of external form and pelage, including coloration, are reviewed. Common and scientific names are given. Males and females, between which there is a marked difference in size, colour and form, may reach lengths and weights of 256 cm and more than 300 kg, and 200 cm and 144 kg, respectively. Sexual maturity may be reached at age 4 in females and age 5 in males. Natural mortality rates in young pups are variable, reported from 2 to nearly 50 %, the latter in more crowded rookeries; mortality again increases at age 1 following weaning.

Sea lions were taken by South American Indians; exploitation by Europeans for oil, hides and meat, the latter now used for animal feed, began as early as 1520. The Uruguayan harvest, conducted by the Government, now consists mainly of young males, 3 240 animals being killed in 1976. Argentine sea lions are under provincial administration; there is no exploitation, though it is legal under licence, except for poaching. Sea lions in the Falkland Islands and Chile are protected by law, but significant poaching and some killing in response to complaints by fishermen occur in Chile. Limited, experimental exploitation under government supervision has been permitted in Peru since 1967. South American sea lions adapt well to captivity and young animals are taken for exhibition from the Uruguayan Islands; sea lion colonies on Isla de Lobos and Peninsula Valdes are visited by tourists.

Sea lions feed mostly in shallow waters; limited reports indicate that fish, crustaceans and molluscs are their most common foods. Penguins and other birds are eaten in some areas.

477

The species competes with shore fisheries for food resources and also causes direct interference with fisheries, though the degree of interference and competition is difficult to quantify. No competition is apparent between sea lions and South American fur seals (*Arctocephalus australis*). Research should include study of possible morphological differences between populations, population dynamics, vital parameters and relation to fisheries.

Résumé

L'otarie à crinière (*Otaria flavescens*) est distribuée le long des côtes atlantiques et pacifiques de l'Amérique du Sud. Bien que les estimations récentes de l'abondance soient très rares et que leur signification soit limitée, on peut estimer le nombre total à terre à 275 000 animaux, compte non tenu de la côte chilienne au sud de Punta Maiquillahue. On a constaté en général une réduction des effectifs sur la majeure partie de l'aire géographique de l'espèce et il existe de nombreuses zones, autrefois peuplées, d'où les otaries à crinière sont absentes. Au Brésil, l'espèce atteint Rio de Janeiro vers le nord, encore qu'elle ne se reproduise probablement pas au nord de Recife das Torres. En Uruguay, la taille de la population s'est maintenue à 30 000 animaux, avec des rookeries sur plusieurs îles, notamment Isla de Lobos. On estimait au début des années 50 que 168 270 animaux habitaient les eaux argentines; les otaries à crinière y sont actuellement distribuées de Bahia Blanca à la Terre de Feu et à Isla de los Estados. L'espèce se trouve surtout sur les petites îles du large dans le groupe des Falkland. Le fléchissement qu'on y a constaté, d'une population estimée à 371 500 ou 389 500 au cours des années 30, à 30 000 animaux au maximum en 1964-65 peut être dû à un déplacement de la population ou à une réduction des disponibilités alimentaires. Sur la côte pacifique, *O. flavescens* est distribuée des îles Diego Ramirez à Zorritos (Pérou), et aux îles Galapagos; elle ne se reproduit probablement pas au nord d'Isla Lobos de Tierra. On a estimé la taille de la population péruvienne à 20 000 animaux en 1975. Bien que les otaries à crinière n'effectuent apparemment pas de migrations, les déplacements qui se produisent à certaines époques de l'année, le long des côtes et vers la mer, peuvent être importants, et l'on a observé de sensibles changements saisonniers et quotidiens de la taille des populations à terre.

L'auteur passe en revue les caractéristiques craniennes distinctives ainsi que les aspects importants de la forme extérieure et du pelage, y compris la couleur. Il indique les noms communs et scientifiques. Les mâles et les femelles, entre lesquels il existe une différence marquée de taille, de forme et de couleur, peuvent atteindre respectivement une longueur de 256 cm et un poids supérieur à 300 kg et une longueur de 200 cm pour un poids de 144 kg. L'âge de la maturité sexuelle peut être de 4 ans chez les femelles et 5 ans chez les mâles. Les taux de mortalité naturelle des nouveau-nés peuvent être variables; on rapporte qu'ils vont de 2 pour cent à près de 50 pour cent, ce dernier chiffre s'appliquant aux rookeries surpeuplées; la mortalité augmente de nouveau à un an, après le sevrage.

Les otaries à crinière étaient capturées par les Indiens sud-américains; dès 1520, les européens ont commencé à les exploiter pour l'huile, les peaux et la viande, qui est à présent utilisée pour l'alimentation animale. Les captures uruguayennes, dirigées par le gouvernement, comprennent maintenant une majorité de jeunes mâles; 3 240 animaux ont été tués en 1976. Les otaries à crinière d'Argentine dépendent de l'administration provinciale; elles ne sont pas exploitées, sauf avec des permis, mais il y a des braconniers. Les otaries des îles Falkland et du Chili sont protégées par la législation mais le braconnage est important et certains animaux sont tués au Chili à la suite des plaintes des pêcheurs. Une exploitation expérimentale limitée a été autorisée sous le contrôle du gouvernement péruvien depuis 1967. Les otaries à crinière s'adaptent bien à la captivité et de jeunes animaux sont capturés dans les îles uruguayennes aux fins d'exhibition; les touristes visitent les colonies d'Isla de Lobos et de la péninsule Valdez.

Les otaries à crinière s'alimentent surtout sur les hauts fonds; des rapports limités indiquent que les poissons, les crustacés et les mollusques sont les aliments les plus communs.

Les manchots et d'autres oiseaux sont mangés dans certaines zones. L'espèce concurrence les pêches côtières pour les ressources alimentaires et interfère aussi directement avec les activités de pêche, encore que ces actions soient difficiles à quantifier. Aucune concurrence n'apparaît entre l'otarie à crinière et l'otarie à fourrure d'Amérique du Sud (*Arctocephalus australis*). Les recherches devraient porter sur l'étude d'éventuelles différences morphologiques entre les populations, de la dynamique des populations, des paramètres biologiques et des rapports avec les pêches.

Extracto

El león marino de América del Sur (*Otaria flavescens*) se encuentra en las costas del Atlántico y el Pacífico de América del Sur y, a pesar de la falta de estimaciones recientes de la población y de las limitaciones de las estimaciones existentes, el número total de animales en tierra puede calcularse en 275 000, excluyendo la costa de Chile al sur de Punta Maiquillahue. En general, su número ha disminuido en la mayor parte de su zona de distribución, y en muchas áreas que antiguamente poblaba ya no se encuentran animales de esta especie. En Brasil, la especie llega por el norte hasta Río de Janeiro, aunque probablemente no se reproduce más arriba de Recife das Torres. En Uruguay, la población se ha mantenido en torno a unos 30 000 animales, con criaderos distribuidos en varias islas, principalmente la isla de Lobos. A principios de los años cincuenta se calculó que vivían en aguas argentinas 168 270 animales; en la actualidad se encuentran leones marinos desde Bahía Blanca hasta la Tierra del Fuego y la isla de los Estados. Esta especie se encuentra sobre todo en varios islotes de las islas Malvinas (Falkland), donde ha disminuido radicalmente, pasando de una cifra estimada en 371 500-389 500 animales en los años treinta a no más de 30 000 en 1964-65, debido quizá a algunos desplazamientos de la población o a la disminución de sus alimentos. En la costa del Pacífico, *O. flavescens* se encuentra desde las islas Diego Ramírez hasta Zorritos, en Perú, y las islas Galápagos, y probablemente el límite septentrional de su zona de cría se encuentra en la isla de Lobos de Tierra. La población del Perú se calculó en 1975 en 20 000 animales. Aunque el león marino de América del Sur no realiza aparentemente movimientos migratorios, sus desplazamientos a lo largo de la costa y mar adentro en determinadas épocas del año pueden ser importantes y se registran notables variaciones estacionales y diarias en el número de animales en tierra.

Se examinan las características del cráneo y de la dentición y algunos aspectos importantes de su forma exterior y de su pelaje, incluido el color. Se dan los nombres común y científico. Los machos y hembras, que se diferencian evidentemente en talla, color y forma, pueden alcanzar tallas y pesos de 256 cm y más de 300 kg, y 200 cm y 144 kg, respectivamente. Las hembras pueden alcanzar la madurez sexual a los cuatro años y los machos a los cinco. La mortalidad natural de los cachorros es variable, y los datos disponibles oscilan entre el 2 por ciento y cerca del 50 por ciento, este último porcentaje en zonas de cría donde hay gran apiñamiento; la mortalidad aumenta de nuevo a partir de un año de edad, después del destete.

Los indios de América del Sur capturaban ya leones marinos; los europeos empezaron a explotar esa especie para aprovechar el aceite, el cuero y la carne (esta última utilizada hoy para piensos) hacia 1520. En Uruguay, la explotación, controlada por el Gobierno, se limita casi exclusivamente a los machos jóvenes, de los que en 1976 se mataron 3 240. Las poblaciones de Argentina dependen de las administraciones provinciales; con excepción de algunos cazadores furtivos, no se explota el león marino, aunque pueden obtenerse licencias para ello. Los leones marinos de las islas Malvinas (Falkland) y de Chile están protegidos por la ley, pero en Chile abundan los cazadores furtivos y se matan algunos animales debido a quejas de los pescadores. En Perú se ha permitido desde 1967 la explotación limitada de esta especie, con carácter experimental, bajo supervisión estatal. El león marino de América del Sur se adapta bien a la cautividad y se capturan animales jóvenes para tal fin en las islas del Uruguay; las colonias de leones marinos de isla de Lobos y península Valdés son meta de turistas.

El león marino se alimenta sobre todo en aguas poco profundas; los limitados datos disponibles indican que come sobre todo peces, crustáceos y moluscos. En algunas zonas come también pingüinos y otras aves. Esta especie compite con las pesquerías costeras por los recursos alimenticios e interfiere directamente con algunas de ellas, aunque es difícil cuantificar esas interferencias y la competencia que esos animales representan. No hay pruebas de que exista competencia entre el león marino y el lobo marino de dos pelos de América del Sur (*Arctocephalus australis*). Es preciso hacer investigaciones, en especial sobre posibles diferencias morfológicas entre poblaciones, dinámica de población, parámetros vitales y relación de estos animales con las pesquerías.

R. Vaz-Ferreira
Universidad de la República, Departamento de Zoología Vertebrados, Juan L. Cuestas 1525, Montevideo, Uruguay

Identification of the species

CHARACTERISTICS

General

Otaria flavescens (Shaw), the South American sea lion, is yellow-brown with a wide, slightly upturned, flattened muzzle. It is markedly dimorphic, the males having a mane and reaching weights of 300-340 kg and body lengths of 256 cm; the females, which have no mane, reach 144 kg and 200 cm. Its main skull characteristics are: palate very long, almost reaching the hamular processes of the pterygoids, with the hind border almost straight and transverse to the sagittal plane of the skull.

The following measurements are greater than in any other otarid: from the palatal hind border to the incisors (palatilar length) which is about 57-65 % of skull length (Sivertsen, 1954); from the gnathion to the posterior palatal end of the maxilla, which is 49-56.5 % of the skull length, and from the gnathion to the palatal notch, which is 52-65 % of skull length. The lateral margins of the palate of adults are raised, the surface being deeply concave on its posterior area.

The skull in normal males reaches a maximum of 382 mm, and in females 286 mm, expressed as condylo basal length.

The snout is upturned and very broad (breadth of skull at canines about 20-35 % of skull length). The pterygoid processes are very long, surpassing the plane defined by the tips of canine teeth and mastoid processes. There are temporal processes and a process on or near the intersection of the fronto-parietal suture with a transverse plane passing through the hammuli.

The tooth formula is: I:3/2, C:1/1, PM:4/4, M:2/1, the last upper cheek teeth very often lacking. The fifth upper cheek teeth are bent markedly backward, and there is no widened space between the bases of the 4th and 5th upper cheek teeth.

External form

The common name "sea lion" refers to the thickened neck and the presence of a "mane", which emphasizes the massive head and foreparts of the male *Otaria*, and contrasts markedly with the small hind quarters.

The front of the body, as pointed out by Murie (1872) carries an important mass of subcutaneous fat and fibrous tissues, muscular layers of considerable thickness, and massively developed shoulder regions.

480

The so-called "mane" consists of an area of longer, coarser, erectile hair, which extends backwards from a line going throughout the forehead, the posterior border of the eyes, and the mentoneal surface, to the nape and anterior chest.

The hair of the "mane" is longer on the back, where sometimes it divides mesially in two lateral lobes. The comparatively small ears are sometimes difficult to see even when the coarse hair is not very long in this area.

The muzzle is blunt, comparatively short, slightly upturned and erectile; as Beddard (1890) has pointed out, the nose pad of the southern sea lion is markedly large, and the mystacial vibrissae are stiff and curvilineous; the eyes are surmounted by two vibrissae and by a medium-sized area without specially elongated hairs. The lower jaw is massive, vertically extended, and wide. The female, about half as heavy, and 15-22 % shorter than the male, has no mane at all, and the head is much smaller and lighter, and not massive at the back.

In general shape young males resemble the cows, but even before the mane begins to develop they have the massive head and lower jaw characteristic of their sex; the females are slighter in build and have a more pup-like head.

The pups, apart from their hair, colour and size, resemble females in shape, but their heads are larger in relation to their body size.

Hair

The coarse hairs on the neck of the males may grow as long as 80 mm; they are flattened in shape.

The little underhair that sea lions possess consists of a very few, individually spaced, flexible hairs of very small diameter, 1-2 mm long, found among several guard hairs.

In cows, the hair is shortest on the belly and longest on dorsal and neck areas.

From birth to about 1 month old, the pups have black, curly hair, which contains a mixture of hair of different diameters, 4-7 mm long on the belly, 9-13 mm long on the back, and 15-18 mm long on the future mane area in males. The vibrissae, 33-42 mystacials and 2 supraoculars on each side, reach 250 mm on adult males, 170 mm on adult females and 60 mm on neonates: they have a rich supply of nerves and vessels which come forward in a large sheaf straight from the infraorbital foramen, under the dilatator naris (Murie, 1872).

Colour

The colour of adults and sub-adults varies from dark brown to orange, sometimes to very pale gold; chocolate brown is common in pups after their first moult, and shiny black is the natal colour for about the first month of life.

The common colours of adult males in the Lobos Islands are: dark orange-brown body, with some scarlet tinge, mane either of the same colour or with areas of yellowish orange; or light yellowish orange or straw coloured body with the back area of the mane of a lighter yellow; or dark orange body and lighter and yellower mane.

Hamilton (1934) found, in order of frequency, the following colours for bulls (Falkland Islands): (i) dark brown all over, mane sometimes paler; (ii) very dark brown almost black, mane dull yellow; (iii) grey often with a slight greenish cast, mane pale; (iv) very pale gold all over.

No grey individuals have been observed in Uruguay. On the Lobos Islands, sub-adult males are often yellowish brown to orange on the face and body with a straw-coloured mane; they are also often very dark brown.

The coloration pattern of adult females, which are brown-orange, tends to vary within the population; at Lobos Islands their masks are sometimes of different colours. Common patterns on these islands are: muzzle, nape and fore-part of the back to halfway down the sides, light orange; body and hinder part of the back and sides of the head, dark orange. In some specimens the mask is dark, as is the body, but parts of the neck and head are lighter; often

481

the muzzle is a greyish orange, which may or may not extend to the preocular area. The superolateral and posterior part of the body are the same colour, and one area around the neck, sometimes extended to the base of the foreflippers, is lighter orange.

Hamilton (1934) gives the following predominant patterns for adult cows: (i) dark brown, with the back of the head and neck yellow, face dark; (ii) dark brown with the whole head and neck yellow, muzzle dark; (iii) very dark brown, usually with a paler colour at the muzzle; (iv) dull yellow all over, face dark; (v) pale cream all over, face dark.

The yearlings and some other very young individuals are commonly light orange with whitish parts on the face and around the mouth.

The pups are mostly black: the hair is curled and of a very shiny black on the back; on the belly, the hair has no curls and is dark greyish orange; upper parts of the flippers have very dark orange hair. After the first moult, when they are a month old, the colour is dark or chocolate brown, becoming much paler later on.

Hair moult in adults occurs mostly after breeding in early autumn, though moulting specimens may be found throughout the year. The moult takes place in patches, sometimes denuding extensive areas of skin which show a matt black colour. Such areas take on a yellow tint as the new, yellow-tipped hair grows through.

COMMON NAMES

In Brazil, *Otaria flavescens* is called "leão marino" or "lobo". In Uruguay the names commonly employed are: "lobo de un pelo" and "lobo ordinario", occasionally "lobo grueso" and "leon marino" are also used; the adult male is called "peluca" and the sub-adult "pelucon"; "bayon" is a young male and "baya" is the female, the pup is a "cachorro". In Argentina, the names employed are about the same, though Carrara (1964) gives, in addition, "lobo de aceite" and "lobo marino del sur".

According to Hamilton (1934) the sea lion is known in the Falkland Islands (Islas Malvinas) to most of the inhabitants as "seal" or "hair seal" to distinguish it from the fur seal. The adult male *Otaria* is generally termed a "lion" and the female a "clapmatch" (a name derived from the Scandinavian name for *Cistophora cristata*).

In Chile (Aguayo and Maturana, 1973), the most frequent common names are, besides the Spanish names used on the Atlantic side, "lobo chusco", "urine", "lame", "ama", "leon marino austral"; the pups are called "popitos"; Carrara (1964) gives for Chile also "toruno". In Peru, Piazza (1959) gives "lobo marino de un pelo" and "lobo chuzco".

SCIENTIFIC NAMES

Otaria flavescens (Shaw, 1800), should be accepted as valid name for the South American sea lion.

Allen (1905) has given an extensive list of synonyms under *Otaria byronia* (Blainville, 1820).

Some of the many scientific names for the South America sea lion have had conflicting history and use. The specific epithet *flavescens* (Shaw, 1800) from the "eared seal" of Pennant, which was based on a young otarid in the Leverian Museum about 2 feet in length taken from the Straits of Magellan, was considered by Allen as quite indeterminable from the description given and "resting on a basis too unsatisfactory to warrant its use for any species". Notwithstanding this, Cabrera (1940) and in personal communication to Scheffer (Scheffer, 1958), concluded that "the yellow seal" *Phoca flavescens* (Shaw) could only have been a "southern sea lion pup after its first moult"; this name was adopted also by Osgood, (1943) and Hershkovitz pointed out (in letters to Scheffer, 1957, see Rice and Scheffer, 1968) that "the type of *flavescens* was a tangible specimen preserved in the old Leverian Museum. It was adequately described and figured, is perfectly identifiable and has a valid type locality, its name has priority, usage and currency".

Other names which have been used many times by different authors for the South American sea lion are:

The specific epithet *jubata* (from *Phoca jubata* Schreber, 1775, in part) was used by most authors until about 1830, and, as recombined by Desmarest (1820) as *Otaria jubata* by many writers until 1905 and still for a few until some years ago. The use of this name for the South American sea lion is not suitable, since Peron (1816) who noticed that southern and northern sea lions were different, restricted *jubata* to the northern species.

The specific epithet *byronia* Blainville (1820) has been widely used by many modern authors until *flavescens* was adopted. Allen (1905) accepted *byronia* as the only available name for this species, considering that the skull on which the name *Phoca byronia* was based was beyond doubt a skull of the sea lion found on the islands and coasts of southern South America and also considering that name to be the first exclusively based on a clearly identified animal, and not preoccupied. The skull mentioned (Scheffer, 1958) was that of an adult male "brought to England by Commodore John Byron in 1769, placed in the British Museum, purchased in 1809 by the Museum of the Royal College of Surgeons of England; listed in Flower's catalogue under *O. jubata* as osteological collection No. 3966".

The skull, destroyed during the Second World War, belonged to a specimen of *Otaria flavescens*, even though it was mistakenly labelled "Tinian Island", one of the Caroline Islands (not populated by pinnipeds); its correct provenance, according to Scheffer, was probably either the Straits of Magellan or the Islas Juan Fernandez. Among the users of *byronia*, besides Allen, were Hamilton (1934, 1939), Scheffer (1958), King (1964), Vaz-Ferreira (1950, 1952) and others, who based their choice on the fact that this name was derived from a tangible specimen.

Some of the other names proposed to nominate specimens of this species (for full references, see Allen, 1905 and Osgood, 1943) have been: *Otaria guerin* Quoy and Gaimard, 1824 (Falkland Islands – Islas Malvinas); *Otaria molossina* Lesson and Garnot, 1826 (Falkland Islands – Islas Malvinas); *Platyrhynchus uraniae* Lesson, 1827 (Falkland Islands – Islas Malvinas); *Otaria pernettyi* Lesson, 1828 (Falkland Islands – Islas Malvinas); *Otaria chilensis* Muller, 1841 (Chile); *Otaria ulloae* Tschudi, 1845 (coast of Peru); *Otaria godeffroyi* Peters, 1866 (Chincha Islands) Peru; type specimen lost (Scheffer, 1958); *Otaria minor* Gray, 1874 (locality unknown); *Otaria pygmaea* Gray, 1874 (locality unknown); *Otaria velutina* Philippi, 1892 (coast of Atacama Prov., Chile); *Otaria fulva* Philippi, 1892 (coasts of Algarrobo, Talcahuano and Ancud, Chile); *Otaria rufa* Philippi, 1892 (locality not given).

All these names must be considered synonyms, as long as population differences within the extensive geographic area of distribution of the species have not been demonstrated.

As Hamilton (1934) has pointed out, this large number of species, proposed during the nineteenth century each time a skull not previously seen turned up, had, as a source of error, the lack of knowledge of the species. Even among the adults there is a considerable individual variation, the animals take several years to become adult, the specimens of various ages differ in form, colour, size and skull characteristics, and there is a very marked difference in size and form between the sexes.

Distribution and movements

DISTRIBUTION

Areas inhabited or reached by the South American sea lion include the Atlantic and Pacific shores of South America, from Rio de Janeiro, Brazil, about 23°S, to the southern tip of South America, and from there, on the Pacific side, to Zorritos, Peru, 4°S latitude and to the Galapagos Islands.

483

In Brazil, some specimens have been found as far as Rio de Janeiro (Vieira, 1955) but the northernmost place in which some breeding may occur is Recife das Torres, between Estado Santa Catharina and Rio Grande (29°19′S; 49°41′W).

In Uruguay (Vaz-Ferreira, 1950, 1952) they live and breed on the Island group of Coronilla (33°56′S; 53°29′W) which contains 2 islands; on the Isla del Marco (34°21′S; 53°45′W) of the Castillos group; on the islands of the Torres group (34°24′S), and mainly on the Isla de Lobos (35°01′S) and on its islet. They also haul out but do not breed on other islands off the Atlantic shore of Uruguay. A few non-breeding sea lions come ashore on the islands of Las Pipas, in the mouth of Rio de la Plata. No continental shore colonies exist today in Brazil or Uruguay.

In Argentina, Holmberg and Aubone (1948, 1949) and Carrara (1952, 1954) studied sea lion populations. Carrara (1952) described 71 places in Argentina inhabited by sea lions of which 41 were on continental shores and 30 were on islands. Of the first group, 17 were between Bahía Blanca (38°43′S; 62°17′W) and Cabo Virgenes (52°19′S; 68°21′W) and 24 are between Cape Espiritu Santo (52°40′S; 62°36′W) and Ushuaia (54°49′S; 68°16′W). Of the 30 island sea lion colonies, 26 are between Bahía Blanca and Cabo Virgenes and the others near the shore of Tierra del Fuego, between Cape Espiritu Santo and Ushuaia. The most northerly Argentinian populations are the ones situated on Isla Trinidad (39°14′S; 61°52′W) (non-breeding) and a breeding area on Isla de los Riachos (40°24′S; 61°58′W); the southernmost group mentioned by Carrara are on Cabo Hall (54°58′S; 65°42′W), on the Gobernacion of Tierra del Fuego and the one on Islote San Martin de Tours (55°00′S; 66°20′W); there are also islands and rocks of the Beagle Channel which are accidentally populated by sea lions. Three areas of the Isla de los Estados situated on 54°43′ to 54°47′S; 64°32′ to 64°43′W have breeding groups. Lopez (1950) has described colonies living near Bahía Thetis.

On the Falkland Islands (Islas Malvinas) (51°30′S; 59°30′W) Hamilton (1939) recorded 64 rookeries, very few of which are on the shore of the main islands and most of which are on small islets or rocks of very difficult access.

According to Aguayo (in litt.), creditable information exists that a population of *Otaria* lives on the Pacific side on the Diego Ramirez Islands (56°30′S; 68°44′W) in the Magallanes Province.

Aguayo (in press) has observed specimens on the Fallo and Chacabuco Channels, and Inchnemo Island in the Province of Chacabuco, and Aguayo and Torres (1967) have recorded sea lion groups on Cockburn, Ocasion and Brecknoe Channels (54°20′ to 40′S; 71°30′ to 72°00′W), in the Province of Magallanes. Markham (1971) mentions the existence of several hundred sea lions along the Toro Fjord, and a cave used as a resting place by this species. The area studied is at 53°23′S; 72°35′W.

Aguayo and Maturana (1973) searched carefully both from the sea and from the shores of Chile, between Punta Maiquillahue and Arica, and found rookeries and groups of sea lions in islands or on the shore of the mainland, distributed as follows: from Punta Maiquillahue (39°27′S; 73°15′W) to Roca Pan de Azucar (35°38′S; 73°08′W) several groups, situated specially on Isla Mocha; northwards to Punta Toro (33°47′S; 71°49′W), 9 inhabited points and capes; to Punta Virgen (31°22′S; 71°38′W), 22 populated points; to Punta Guanilla (22°41′S; 70°17′W), groups on 2 islands and 13 points; to Arica (18°20′S; 70°20′W) 23 capes and bays populated by sea lions.

According to Aguayo, Maturana and Torres (1971) there is no reliable evidence that the species either exists or existed on Juan Fernandez Islands.

Piazza (1959) and Grimwood (1968, 1969) published the distribution of *Otaria* along the Peruvian coast. The latter author establishes that "the coast from 13°45′S to 15°30′S was always a favoured region, and it still holds the greatest number of animals during the breeding season ...".

Principal rookeries in this area are, according to Grimwood, on the cliffs of the

Paracas Peninsula and islands such as the Chinchas and Ballestas groups, islands of San Gallan and Las Viejas groups. Breeding areas also utilized are Morro Sama (18°00'S; 70°53'W), Punta Coles (17°45'S; 71°23'W), Punta Corio (17°20'S; 71°27'W), Punta Isla (17°00'S; 72°05'W), Isla el Saltadero and Cueva del Ladron (16°35'S), Isla Oscuyo (16°30'S; 73°02'W), Punta Vilcayo (16°05'S; 73°55'W), Isla San Lorenzo (12°05'S; 77°13'W), Islas Guanapo (8°33'S; 78°57'W), Isla Macabi (7°48'S; 79°27'W) and Isla Lobos de Tierra (6°30'S; 80°51'W).

The northernmost breeding area is probably Isla Lobos de Tierra, but specimens as aforementioned have been obtained in Zorritos (4°S) and the species has been recorded nearly as far as 3°S, but has not been known to breed there (Grimwood, 1969).

Some authors (Osgood, 1943) have included Galapagos Islands in the distribution of *Otaria*; this inclusion was based on mis-identified specimens from the Hassler Expedition (Scheffer, 1958) and according to Sivertsen (1954) the species does not live at all on the Galapagos. But it is now known that it arrives there at least as a straggler: Wellington and de Vries (1976) have described 1 specimen, an adult male, 356 mm in condylo-basal length, found on 10 October 1973 on Pinta (Abingdon Island) west of Cape Ibbetson, Galapagos Island.

MOVEMENTS

The South American sea lion is not migratory on the whole: even when the adult males retire to water after breeding for variable periods, all the colonies which have been observed maintain, at least in part, their land connexion throughout the year; notwithstanding this, movements of groups and spreading at sea, sometimes directional, are significant. Hamilton (1934) has recorded, late in December, the existence of groups playing and feeding about 120 miles north of the Falkland Islands (Islas Malvinas), and, early in November, he observed parties of sea lions apparently heading south. Hamilton (1939) noticed that the herd at Cape Dolphin gradually becomes smaller after the breeding season and continues to diminish as the winter progresses. He interpreted this as the result of a genuine partial migration, distinct from the daily changes caused by the coming and going of individuals between land and sea. The same author saw on 13 December a herd of perhaps 500 sea lions some distance offshore to the north, gradually drawing into land and coming ashore. According to that author, the unusual features of this phenomenon were that the whole herd was moving steadily in the same direction and there was no reason to believe that they were feeding; for this reason, Hamilton adopted the view that this was a party returning from migration, and considered it possible that a large part of the *Otaria* herd of the Falklands (Islas Malvinas) may put to sea in winter.

In our studies of the changes of land populations on Lobos Islands (Vaz-Ferreira and Palerm, 1961; Vaz-Ferreira 1975a) we concluded that they are caused by behavioural responses to accidental causes, to changes of weather and to reproducltive cycles. These changes of population on land, which are important even in breeding periods and in breeding areas, may even account for population changes of the order of nearly 50 % in the case of *Otaria*.

Important increases in land populations are observed with marked drops in atmospheric pressure, preceding hurricanes and high storms; in these instances, the increase in land populations is observed before the storm starts. Daily, sun-caused temperature increase on sandy areas can drastically reduce land populations.

In the Falkland Islands (Islas Malvinas) (Hamilton, 1934) and in the Isla de Lobos (Vaz-Ferreira, 1975) some sandy beaches used for breeding during the summer are deserted in winter.

Some of the breeding areas on which a section of the population remains all year

485

round may be occupied by increased numbers during the summer; for example, important changes in population on Cape Dolphin have been recorded by Hamilton (1939), who noticed a change from 2 545 individuals, including 183 bulls, in August, to 5 854, including 723 bulls in January.

Certain breeding areas on flat rocky zones of Lobos Island have an increased population in winter, probably as a result of being occupied by populations leaving sandy localities.

Purely accidental landing of *Otaria* occurs on some rocks situated far away from the normal breeding grounds; these resting places show even more important changes of population than the regular areas.

Sea lions often enter the Rio de la Plata estuary, sometimes reaching areas of fresh water, such as the Uruguay River and the freshwater lagoons of Uruguay and Rio Grande do Sul (Vaz-Ferreira, 1965a). In Chile they enter the Valdivia Fluvial system about 49 km along the river (Schlatter, *in litt.*).

Specimens of *Otaria* tagged as pups on Uruguayan islands have been recovered 835 km to the southwest of their birthplace, near Puerto Quequen.

Many specimens of sea lions travel along the coast of Brazil and often arrive at Rio de Janeiro, at least 1 930 km away from their regular breeding areas.

Stocks

COUNTS AND ESTIMATIONS

Census of estimates of *Otaria* have been made from time to time in different areas during the last 45 years, but no recent or simultaneous counts exist for all the zones.

In April 1953, in Brazil, I estimated the population of adult sea lions on Recife das Torres to be around 200-300 individuals (quoted by Scheffer, 1958).

In Uruguay in February-March 1953 and again in 1956, I counted the live pups on all the islands, and in 1953, also counted adult *Otaria* on Isla de Lobos; the results were a total of 7 159 pups for 1953 on all the Uruguayan islands, and 9 116 pups in 1956 for the same islands excluding the Coronilla group. Estimated totals for 1954 (adults plus pups) were about 30 000. Ximenez (1964) gives figures for a total of 8 020 *Otaria* pups counted in summer 1959 over all the islands of Uruguay. In recent visits to the islands (January and February 1973, 1974, 1975), I have verified that the areas occupied by breeding groups and their population are roughly the same, with the exception of Isla Verde de Coronilla, where the number of pups born in 1975 diminished to about 100 as against 516 in 1953. The number of pups born in Uruguay in the last few years has been estimated by I. Ximinez, Manager of Sealing, Industrias Loberas y Pesqueras del Estado (personal communication) to be about 11 000 annually.

In Argentina, Carrara (1952, 1954) made several censuses of sea lions; his counts from 1946 to 1949 resulted in a figure of 143 905 sea lions including 19 467 pups (Carrara, 1952) and later on, as a result of his studies of 1952, 1953 and 1954, he gave a figure of 168 270. No information has been published since the Carrara counts of 1952-54. According to J.C. Godoy, Office of Nature Conservancy (personal communication) several unpublished aerial censuses were made in following years, which showed important changes in the location of some of the herds. An aerial census of the population of *Otaria* living in the Province of Buenos Aires between Bahía Blanca and the mouth of the Rio Negro in December 1973, showed the existence there of 3 populations, one of 900 animals at Punta Lobos, a second of 1 000 animals at Banco Culebra and a third group, further south, numbering 60 to 80 animals (R.H. Aramburu, University of La Plata – personal communication).

On the Falkland Islands (Islas Malvinas) an extensive aerial survey of all known sea lion colonies was carried out in 1965, followed by a check survey in 1966 (Strange, 1972). The total number counted and estimated in the 1965 survey was 18 876, of which approximately 5 500 were pups; the 1966 check confirmed the count. The same author shows that with all counts erring on the optimistic side, the grand total of sea lions of all age groups in 1964-65 was a maximum of 30 000 animals. This figure shows a drastic reduction if compared with the figures given by Hamilton (1939) who counted the pups of the 64 rookeries on the Falklands (Islas Malvinas) from December 1930 to February 1936. He found a total of 80 555 pups and estimated the total herd related to these islands to be 371 500 or 389 500 individuals. This dramatic reduction of the herds occurred without any important exploitation on the islands and may have been caused, among other factors, by the movement of populations to other areas or by the reduction of available sources of food. According to Strange (1973), checks made in 1970 on specific colonies showed little change in the state of the species since 1966.

In Chile, Aguayo (in press) has taken a census, still unpublished, of the sea lions of the southern part of the country, and Aguayo and Maturana (1973) have taken censuses from 1965 to 1971, which cover from Punta Maiquillahue to Arica, counting and/or estimating a total for the 7 areas included, of 21 887 to 25 342 comprising a very small number of pups.

For Peru, the Servicio de Pesquerias took censuses and estimates of 13 000 for 1964; of 16 800 for 1968 (data from an anonymous unpublished report of the Department) and Grimwood (1969) gives an estimate of about 20 000 for 1966. A census made in February 1975 showed that the Peruvian herd lives now from Isla Foca (05°12′S, 81°13′W) to the Chilean frontier, the total number being about 20 000 (H. Tovar-Serpa, *in litt.*).

In spite of the limited significance of the figures available, adding partial counts and estimates of different years, some of them recent, others very old, the number of individuals on land for the whole range can be estimated at 275 000, with the exception of the sea lions of the Chilean coast from Maiquillahue to the south, for which no counts or estimates have yet been published.

ACTUAL AND PAST STATE OF THE STOCKS

Sea lions are decimated by human agency, including regular exploitation, clandestine exploitation, and killing by fishermen on account of damage to nets; and a reduction in population is the rule over most of its area of distribution.

Over the whole area of its distribution there are islands or shore areas which historically have been populated by sea lions and which are not now inhabited by them (Vaz-Ferreira, 1956; Holmberg and Aubone, 1948, 1949; Grimwood, 1969).

Sea lion populations, according to the very scanty comparative information on former and later population sizes, have maintained numbers in some areas (Uruguay), increased in some others and diminished in areas such as the Falkland Islands (Islas Malvinas).

MORTALITY RATES AND CAUSES OF MORTALITY

The death rate of pups from natural causes, especially in the first month, may be very high, as is shown by the great numbers of dead pups of this age found in the rookeries. When the pups are 1 year old, they again appear to suffer an increase in mortality; at this stage they are frequently found emaciated or dead on shore, probably as a consequence of the starting of completely independent living because of the definitive weaning imposed by the new maternity of their mother. Mortality on land diminishes considerably afterwards, since dead animals of older ages are seldom seen.

The mortality of young pups is very variable: it is sometimes very high, nearing 50 % on crowded rookeries, especially those situated

487

near hauling grounds containing young males who perform aggressive activities and kill pups (Vaz-Ferreira, 1965); it is much smaller, sometimes 2 %, in uncrowded rookeries.

Hamilton (1934) found a pup mortality of 5 to 6 % before the break-up of the harems on the Falkland Islands (Islas Malvinas).

Among the causes of mortality, other than disease, in young pups, are: parasites, smashing by bulls and cows, drowning on the shore area, bites by females other than the mother, and the aforementioned aggressive activities of sub-adult males, which occur not only because of direct biting and killing of pups and displacement of them, but also because the increase of conflicts on the rookeries favours mortality from some of the causes quoted above.

Increased activity in males in areas that are not particularly suitable for breeding, or too early in the season, can prevent flight by females (Vaz-Ferreira, 1973) and this can also increase pup mortality (Hamilton, 1934, 1939; Vaz-Ferreira, 1973).

Non-human causes of mortality of more aged individuals include attacks by sharks of unidentified species. This is evidenced by the author's findings of wounded females and young males on the beaches of Rio Grande do Sul, Brazil, and on the islands of Uruguay.

Killer whales, *Orcinus orca*, are sometimes seen around the rookeries and probably constitute, as stated by Cabrera and Yepes (1940) an effective predator of even adult sea lions. A leopard seal, *Hydrurga leptonyx*, killed on Falkland Islands (Islas Malvinas) in October (Hamilton, 1934) contained lumps of pups from the previous season; the same author reports having heard of 2 leopard seals attacking and killing a large specimen of sea lion. Brandenburg (1938) reports on remains of young sea lions found in a cave where a puma was later trapped, mentioning that pumas' tracks were in evidence at the colony on the beach. The colony of sea lions studied by Brandenburg is situated on the eastern coast'of Patagonia, near the town of Santa Cruz.

Vital parameters

SIZES AND WEIGHTS

The maximum size from muzzle to tip of tail recorded on Isla de Lobos for males is 245 cm and for females 200 cm (Vaz-Ferreira, unpubl.). Hamilton (1934) in the Falkland Islands (Islas Malvinas) found that the largest males measured 211 to 256 cm and the largest females 160 to 190 cm.

The greatest weight we recorded in Isla de Lobos for males is 305 kg; bulls in January commonly weigh from 200 to 300 kg (for animals between 216 cm and a maximum length of 245 cm), and they lose some 50 kg in February; it is possible that some adult males in November or December may weigh as much as 350 kg. A male of 340 kg was reported by Fava de Moraes *et al.* (1967).

The maximum weight for adult females verified by us was 144 kg.

The medium size of adults from the Falkland Islands (Islas Malvinas) (Hamilton, 1934) is 234 cm for males and 179 cm for females.

The medium length of newborn pups in 81.7 cm (males) and 75.0 cm (females) and medium weight is 14.157 kg (males) and 11.436 (females) at Isla de Lobos (Vaz-Ferreira, unpubl.). Carrara (1952) has recorded medium lengths of 84.5 cm for males, 75.0 cm for females and medium weights of 15 kg for males and 12.5 kg for females.

AGES AT SEXUAL MATURITY

Of 72 cows and 11 sexually-active bulls, the range of lengths was 142.2-195.6 cm for females and 210.7-256.4 cm for males (Hamilton, 1939). For 19 pregnant cows, the range was 146.1-190.4 cm.

Hamilton (1934, 1939) established a series of development groups for males and for females, to which he assigned definite ages. To delimit these groups he took as the basis of criterion the following variables: length of the animal; coat colour; length of skull (condylobasal); skull length to body length ratio; ratio between various skull measurements and skull length; osteological development; dental development and condition of the reproductive glands, characters which are not now considered adequate for age determination (Bryden, 1972). As a result of these values, he found the following groups, to which he assigned the ages shown in the second column. These ages have not been confirmed, as no teeth of southern sea lions have been studied for that purpose and the result of marking operations have not been published until now in any area of the distribution of *Otaria* (Table 1).

These age groups at any rate may be useful to study the population of *Otaria* if, in the future, they can be adequately aged by means of tagging.

If the ages attributed to the sizes are correct, then the beginning of active sexual life occurs at 4 years of age for the females and at 5 years for the males.

LONGEVITY

Some specimens have lived 14 years at the Montevideo Zoo; Flower (1931) mentions 2 females which lived 15.5 and 17.5 years at the London Zoo; as the last one was about 2 years old when she arrived there she must have been 19 or 29 years old when she died.

No studies of longevity in natural environments have ben published.

The economic value and state of regulations and management of exploitation

ECONOMIC VALUE

Magellan (Kellogg, 1942) recorded having seen sea lions in the straits, and Europeans started making use of them in 1520.

Table 1. Stages of development of *Otaria flavescens* according to Hamilton (1934, 1939)

Group	Presumed months of age	Total length cm	Skull length mm
MALES			
0 (newborn)	0	83.8	148.0
I	6	120.3 (106.6-137.1)	195.6 (186-203)
II	18	135.7 (126.9-139.6)	227.4 (215-238)
III	30	152.4 (144.7-162.6)	239.0 (233-247)
IV	42	172.7 (152.3-195.5)	270.6 (261-288)
V	54	210.7 (205.7-215.8)	308.5 (301-321)
VI (and over)	66 (and over)	234.3 (210.7-256.4)	344.9 (388-382)
FEMALES			
(newborn)	0		
I	6	112.7 (96.5-119.7)	186.4 (166-189)
II	18	118.5 (114.3-124.4)	201.0 (199-205)
III	30	125.0 (121.9-129.5)	212.5 (212-213)
IV	42	147.4 (137.1-158.8)	228.4 (220.0-233.5)
V	54	161.2 (153.6-170.2)	237.8 (228.0-247.5)
VI	66	170.5 (160.0-177.8)	248.5 (242.5-255.0)
VII	78	180.1 (170.2-190.5)	255.7 (247.0-263.5)
VIII	90	184.6 (177.8-193.0)	261.7 (254.5-264.0)
IX	102	188.0 (172.7-195.6)	261.9 (257.0-269.0)
X (and over)		186.2 (175.3-195.6)	266.7 (255.0-276.0)

It soon became the custom to provision ships with sea lion meat and the blubber of this large seal provided them with oil.

According to the same author, as early as 1535 Alcazaba took sea lions from Chubut, Patagonia, and Sir Francis Drake in 1577 provisioned his vessels with some 200 sea lions killed at Port Desire, Patagonia. In the same paper, Kellogg quotes from Balch that 52 000 sea lion skins were taken in 1821-22 by the shore crews of the American brigs *Alabama* and *Frederick* on the islands of Mocha and St. Marys, off the coast of Chile.

Numbers of sea lions killed and accounts of killings in some areas of its distribution and during several periods have been given by: Devincenzi (1895), who gives numbers killed in Uruguay from 1873 to 1894, apparently of both *Arctocephalus australis* and *Otaria flavescens* together; and by Perez Fontana (1943) who mentions 108 116 sea lions killed in Uruguay from 1910 to 1942. The Uruguayan kill from 1943 to 1952 (Vaz-Ferreira, unpublished) was 25 192. Holmberg and Aubone (1948, 1949) Carrara (1964), Lopez Arregui and Gonzales Regalado (1940) and Urraga (1937) give some data on exploitation in Argentina. Strange (1972) quotes 39 696 sea lions harvested on the Falkland Islands (Islas Malvinas) from 1928 to 1940, and 3 045 from 1949 to 1952. Kellogg (1942) gives an account of human exploitation for several places including the Pacific coast.

Acosta y Lara (1884, 1900), Arechavaleta (1882), Peso Blanco (1911), and Devincenzi (1925), Smith (1927) and De Buen (1947) have given accounts of exploitation in Uruguay.

Sea lions are difficult to kill; sealers beat the seal on the nose with large and stout wooden clubs which have to be very strong as adult males are difficult to knock out. The animal is normally then stabbed in the heart with a knife and killed. On Cape Polonio in the past the killing was done with long lances.

According to Carrara (1964), the natives of the southern tip of South America used to kill sea lions during 2 seasons each year: in July-August they killed particularly old males and in December-January they killed adult females and pups. From the sea lions they obtained oil, which they stored in sea lion stomachs, and hides, with which they made small inflated boats or rafts. To make these they sewed 2 skins together and inflated air between them.

The meat was also used to a large extent for human consumption, the preferred parts being the heart, brain, liver and tongue.

The same author after quoting Lizarraga tells of the drinking by primitive Peruvian natives of the sea lions' blood, and says that haematophagy with sea lion blood is still practised by some sealers who believe that it is good to strengthen themselves.

Sea lion meat, which was eaten by man in the days of sailing vessels, is no longer consumed by Europeans.

The hides of adults, used in the past for making harnesses and trunks, are employed now for suede, carpets, boots, belts, industrial gloves and other leather goods where the many scars which appear on the skin of males, and, to a lesser degree, of females, do not affect production. The hides of 3-5 week old pups, which are used for ladies' coats, fetch much better prices.

Oil obtained mostly from the subcutaneous blubber and, at Isla de Lobos, from the boiled meat, is employed for tannery and other uses. Meat, when produced, is used as animal feed. According to Perez-Fontana (1943) a sea lion of 260 kg produces (no season given) 34.125 kg of oil and 39.750 kg of meat.

Regulation and management of exploitation

The Uruguayan herd is exploited by ILPE (Industrias Loberas y Pesqueras del Estado, formerly SOYP), a government agency which has the exclusive right to exploit and manage the resource. The annual harvest of young individuals is conducted on the several islands populated by the species.

The majority of animals taken in the harvests are now males; to accomplish this, the sea lions, when possible, are driven to the interior of the islands where the sexes are separated. According to I. Ximenez (personal communication), 500 females were among the 3 260 and 3 150 individuals killed in 1974 and 1975, respectively.

The Argentinian sea lion colonies come under the provincial administrations, which have especially in Chubut been developing research and management programmes. Even though the granting of licences to private persons to harvest sea lions is allowed by law, no exploitation now occurs in Argentina, except for poaching.

On the Falkland Islands (Islas Malvinas), a moderate kill took place in 1962 and 1963 but afterwards, when it was known that a drastic reduction of the population, for unknown reasons, had occurred, the killing was stopped.

In Chile, according to Laws (1973), sea lions are protected by law but, according to Aguayo and Maturana (1973), some private sealers kill them indiscriminately. According to A. Aquayo, Naturhistoriska Riksmuseet (*in litt.*, 24/5/76), G.A. Atalah, Instituto de la Patagonia (*in litt.*, 18/3/76) and to R.P. Schlatter, Universidad Austral, Chile (*in litt.*, 30/4/76),

Table 2. **Numbers killed from 1963 to 1976**

Year	Lobos Islands and Islote	Cabo Polonio Islands	Total
1963	2 300	700	3 000
1964	2 063	332	2 395
1965	1 718	598	2 316
1966	–	2 061	2 061
1967	–	2 800	2 800
1968	1 208	1 859	3 067
1969	944	1 987	2 931
1970	988	1 900	2 888
1971	985	1 840	2 825
1972	1 075	2 010	3 085
1973	1 042	2 022	3 064
1974	1 050	2 210	3 260
1975			3 150
1976	1 020	2 220	3 240

important poaching, especially of pups, takes place in Chile, but no regular or legal exploitation has occurred in recent years; the killing of seals has been stopped since 1970, except under special permits. However, according to Schlatter, some killing to control populations of *Otaria* is done by the authorities in areas in which there are many complaints from fishermen.

In Peru, the exploitation of sea lions has been permitted since July 1967 (Information Fishery Service of Peru, 1971) but in a limited and experimental way; the government holds the right of and responsibility for, determining the areas of exploitation and the ages and sexes of the animals which may be killed.

Recreational and aesthetic values

Specimens of sea lions are kept in zoological gardens in many parts of the world, as they adapt themselves easily to life in captivity. For this reason, a certain number of sea lions from 6 to 18 months old are captured on the Uruguayan islands, and taught to accept hand-feeding with small pieces of filleted fish. Once adapted to feeding in captivity, they are exported to other zoos and aquaria.

Some sea lion colonies are exploited to attract tourism. On Isla de Lobos there is a rookery with a hauling ground on the beach, which is visited daily in the summer by guided tours going by boat from the nearby Punta del Este. The breeding areas of Peninsula Valdes in Argentina together with the rookeries of sea elephants are visited annually by many tourists.

Food and relation to other resources

FOOD HABITS

The South American sea lion feeds mostly in shallow waters, often less than 5 miles from shore or near its hauling or breeding areas. They often swim inside fish banks with sea birds or cetaceans. This happens near Lobos Islands, where schools of anchovies, *Engraulic anchoita*, and some of its predators form compact schools during the late summer; the same fact has been mentioned by Hamilton (1934), for an area of water about 120 miles north of the Falkland Islands (Islas Malvinas) in which many *Otaria* gather during November and December.

From the scanty information on the food content of stomachs, it can be inferred that the more common items are fish, crustaceans and molluscs. On Isla de Lobos (Vaz-Ferreira, 1950), I studied the gastric content of 200 adult males taken in late February from a hauling ground, and always found in these land-stationed specimens, either empty stomachs (28 %) or much digested food, which was 40 % fish and 31 % a yellow, unidentifiable liquid; some of the stomachs contained squid or *Octopus* beaks, or egg shells of elasmobranch fishes. One adult male caught in the Islote near Cabo Polonio in February 1974, contained egg shells and vertebrae of an elasmobranch.

In the Falklands (Islas Malvinas), Hamilton (1934) found that the diet of *Otaria* is varied, the commonest food being squid (*Loligo*), then the crustacean *Munida* and finally fish; he based this conclusion on the assumption that by the action of the gastric juice of the sea lion the ink of *Loligo* becomes a bright yellow and that colour is maintained even in the faeces; similarly, with *Munida*, the faeces are brick red and the skeletal parts of the crustaceans are found on them; the faeces derived from fish are grey and contain bones. The same author states that occasionally, the species eats large Medusae.

Aguayo and Maturana (1973) upon examination of food from 32 stomachs of *Otaria* obtained in Valparaiso (February and March) conclude that, excluding 12 empty stomachs, and 4 corresponding to pups containing milk, the 16 remaining individuals contained a high percentage (75 %) of fish, including "cabrilla" *Sebastodes oculatus*, "merluza" *Merluccius*

gayi, "sardina" *Clupea bentinckii* and, in a lesser amount, 35 %, remains of molluscs — "jibia" *Dosidicus gigas*, "caracol" *Tegula* sp., "loco" *Concholepas concholepas* — and crustaceans "camaron" *Heterocarpus reedi*.

Murphy (1920) (quoted by Piazza, 1959) studied one stomach from the Peruvian coast, finding in it remains of at least 5 species of fish. In some areas *Otaria* eat penguins and other birds. Hamilton (1934) describes how large parties of sea lions pursue the groups of penguins coming ashore on Bird Island, West Falkland (where there is a very large rookery of rockhopper penguins), surround them and catch some of the birds.

The same author also has reports of sea lions eating logger or steamer ducks (*Tachyeres*). Boswall (1972) gives a summary of existing information dealing with predation on penguins by *Otaria* which shows that Magellanic penguins *Spheniscus magellanicus*, rockhopper penguins *Eudyptes crestatus* and gentoo penguins *Pigoscellis papua*, are caught at sea or land and eaten by sea lions. Quoted observations are from point Tombo, Chubut, Argentina, where Conway has seen predation on *Spheniscus magellanicus*; and Falkland Islands (Islas Malvinas) where Hamilton, Rumboll, Strange and earlier travellers, have reported the capture by sea lions of the 3 species of penguins mentioned above. Apparently, particular adult individuals have learned to do this.

Other observations refer to Staten Island, where about 20 rockhoppers were caught in about 4 hours by one male *Otaria*. According to O.S. Petingill (quoted by Boswall) "a common sight on the beaches in the Falkland Islands are skins of gentoo and rockhopper penguins turned inside out with head, flippers and feet still attached". This manoeuvre, well-known in the leopard seal *Hydrurga leptonyx*, is attributed in this case by the author to sea lions.

At the harbour of Punta del Este, Uruguay, it is common to see 5 to 30 sea lions which have learned local and specialized feeding ways, eating fish residues which have been thrown by fishermen or by people who want to watch the very tame seals.

Stones are a very common non-food item in the sea lion stomach content; the stomachs of most of the 200 males referred to above, killed on Isla de Lobos, Uruguay (Vaz-Ferreira, 1950) contained from 1 to 7 stones, with diameters from 1 to 22 cm; the total weight for the stones found in each stomach varied from 180 to 1 525 g; Hamilton (1934) found in 1 adult male from the Falkland Islands (Islas Malvinas) 6 stones with a total weight of 1 460 g and, in three females with body lengths of 96-157 cm, from 3 to 22 stones weighing 57-709 g; the stones are often beachworn, but sometimes have sharp angles.

RELATION TO OTHER RESOURCES

Competition of sea lions with man for food resources is evident, as a part of the sea lion feeding grounds coincides with shore fisheries, but no estimation of the total competition can be worked out with the scanty data available.

In contrast with *Arctocephalus australis*, the South American sea lion is well-known for its habit of following fishing boats for several days, taking fish from the nets and causing severe damage to fishing tackle.

Direct interference with fisheries occurs particularly with fishing gear and with fish already hooked or caught in the nets.

The damage is more pronounced in shore trammel nets or fishing lines which are thoroughly examined by the sea lions, which eat and destroy many of the fish, consuming particularly the visceral parts.

Apart from this, there is sometimes very serious damage to the mesh of the nets. No estimates of the damage are available.

There is no apparent competition between *Otaria flavescens* and *Arctocephalus australis*, as the second species feed on areas which are deeper and farther offshore than the ones exploited by the sea lions.

Other interferences of sea lions are with penguins, which are themselves a human resource and are consumed by sea lions, and with vegetation, which may be destroyed by the passage of sea lions; this happens specially with the "tussac grass" *Poa flabellata* on the Falkland Islands (Islas Malvinas).

Recommendations

Research should be encouraged into different zones of its area of distribution, dealing especially with the following subjects:
- possible morphological differences between populations;
- population dynamics;
- vital parameters;
- relation with fisheries.

References

ACOSTA Y LARA, F., La pesca de lobos. *Rev. Soc. Univ.,*
1884   *Montevideo,* 1:337-52.

—, La pesca de lobos. *In* Diccionario geográfico del
1900   Uruguay por Orestes Araujo. Montevideo, Imp. de Dornaleche y Reyes, pp. 420-9.

AGUAYO, A., Marine mammals observation on board R/V *Calypso* during the cruise Punta Are-

na-Puerto Montt, Chile, early autumn 1973. *Bull. Inst. Oceanogr., Monaco,* (in press).

AGUAYO, A. and R. MATURANA, Presencia del lobo ma-
1973   rino común (*Otaria flavescens*) en el litoral chileno. *Biol. Pesq. Santiago,* 6:45-75.

AGUAYO, A. and D. TORRES, Observaciones sobre
1967   mamíferos marinos durante la Vigésima Co-

misión Antártica Chilena. *Rev. Biol. Mar.*, 13(1):1-57.

AGUAYO, A., R. MATURANA and D. TORRES, El lobo fino
1971   de Juan Fernández. *Rev. Biol. Mar.*, 14(3):135-49.

ALLEN, J.A., The Mammalia of southern Patagonia.
1905   *Rep. Princeton Exped. Patagonia 1896-1899 (Zool.)*, 3(1):210 p.

ARECHAVALETA, J., Reino animal. Orden de los pinní-
1882   pedios. *In* Album R.O. del Uruguay. Monte-video, Imp. Rius and Becchi.

BEDDARD, P.E., On the structure of Hooker sea lion
1890   (*Arctocephalus hookeri*). *Trans. Zool. Soc. Lond.*, 12(10):369-80.

BOSWALL, J., The South American sea lion *Otaria byro-
1972   nia* as a predator on penguins. *Bull. Br. Orni-thol. Club*, 92(5):129-32.

BRANDENBURG, F.G., Notes on the Patagonian sea lion.
1938   *J. Mammal.*, 19(1):44-7.

BRYDEN, M.M., Growth and development of marine
1972   mammals. *In* Functional anatomy of marine mammals, edited by R.J. Harrison. London, Academic Press, vol. 1:2-79.

BUEN, F. DE, Algunas observaciones sobre los lobos
1947   marinos de la costa uruguaya. *Rev. Soc. Mex. Hist. Nat.*, 8(1-4):221-7.

CABRERA, A., Notas sobre carnívoros sudamericanos.
1940   *Notas Mus. La Plata (Zool.)*, (29):1-22.

CABRERA, A. and J. YEPES, Mamíferos sudamericanos
1940   (Vida, costumbres y descripción). Buenos Aires, Compañía Argentina de Editores, 370 p.

CARRARA, S.I., Lobos marinos, pingüinos y guaneras de
1952   las costas del litoral marítimo e islas adyacen-tes de la República Argentina. *Publ. Espec. Univ. Nac. Fac. Cienc. Vet., La Plata*, (15) 189 p.

—, Observaciones sobre el estado actual de las pobla-
1954   ciones de pinnipedios de la Argentina. Uni-versidad Nacional Eva Perón, 17 p.

—, Zoorrecursos naturales de la Antártida. La Plata,
1964   Universidad Nacional de La Plata, Facultad de Ciencia Veterinaria. 89 p.

DEVINCENZI, E.J., Importancia de las islas de Lobos.
1895   Necesidad de su administración en forma por medio de licitación pública. Montevideo, Dornaleche y Reyes, 16 p.

DEVINCENZI, G.J., Le foche dell'Uruguay. *Vie Ital. Am.*
1925   *Latina*, 31:11 p.

FAVA DE MORAES, F. *et al.*, Morphological and chemical
1967   studies on the salivary glands and pancreas of two species of Pinnipedia. *Ann. Histochem.*, 2:199-212.

FLOWER, S.S., Contributions to our knowledge of
1931   the duration of life in vertebrate animals. 5. Mammals. *Proc. Zool. Soc. Lond.*, 1931(1):145-234.

GRIMWOOD, I.R., Endangered mammals in Peru. *Oryx*,
1968   9:411-21.

—, Notes on the distribution and status of some Peru-
1969   vian mammals. *Publ. Am. Comm. Int. Wild Life Prot. N.Y. Soc.*, (21):1-86.

HAMILTON, J.E., The southern sea lion *Otaria byronia*
1934   (De Blainville). *Discovery Rep.*, (8):269-318.

—, A second report on the southern sea lion, *Otaria
1939   byronia* (De Blainville). *Discovery Rep.*, (19):121-64.

HOLMBERG, A.D. and G. AUBONE, Documentación que
1948   ha servido de base para reconstruir el mapa de las foquerías del Virreinato del Río de la Plata en 1776-1810. Part 1. 80 p. (mimeo).

—, Documentación que ha servido de base para re-
1949   construir el mapa de las foquerías del Virrei-nato del Río de la Plata en 1776-1810. Part 2. 79 p. (mimeo).

KELLOGG, R., Tertiary, quaternary and recent marine
1942   mammals of South America and the West Indies. *Proc. Am. Sci. Congr.*, 8(1940) vol. 3:445-73.

KING, J.E., Seals of the world. London, British Museum
1964   (Natural History) 154 p.

LAWS, R.M., The current status of seals in the Southern
1973   Hemisphere. *IUCN Publ. (New Ser.) Suppl. Pap.*, (39):144-61.

LÓPEZ, R.B., Lobos marinos en las inmediaciones de
1950   Bahia Thetis. *In* Primer Congreso Nacional de Pesquerías Marítimas e Industrias Derivadas,

Mar del Plata, 24-29 Oct., 1949. Buenos Aires, Coni, vol. 2:43-54.

López Arregui, E. and T. Gónzalez Regalado, Lobos
1940   marinos en la Argentina. *Bol. Fom. Ganad. B. Aires*, 5(18):3-19.

Markham, B.J., Reconocimiento faunístico del área de
1971   los fiordos Toro y Cóndor, Islas Riesco, Magallanes. *An. Inst. Patagonia*, 1(1):41-56.

Murie, J., Researches upon the anatomy of the Pinni-
1872   pedia. Part 2. Descriptive anatomy of the sea lion (*Otaria jubata*). *Trans. Zool. Soc. Lond.*, 7(8):527-96.

Osgood, W.H., The mammals of Chile. *Publ. Field Mus.*
1943   *Nat. Hist. (Zool.)*, 30:268 p.

Pérez Fontana, H., Informe sobre la industria lobera
1943   (ciento diez años de explotación de la industria lobera en nuestro país). Montevideo, Servicio Oceanográfico y de Pesca, 70 p.

Peso Blanco, J. del, Focas de la República O. del
1911   Uruguay. Granada, Spain, P.V. Travesset, 27 p.

Piazza, L.A., Los lobos marinos en el Perú. *Pesca Caza,*
1959   *Lima*, (9):1-29.

Rice, D.W. and V.B. Scheffer, A list of the marine mammals of the world. *Spec. Sci. Rep. U.S. Fish. Wildl. Serv.*, (579):16 p.

Scheffer, V.B., Seals, sea lions and walruses: a review
1958   of Pinnipedia. Stanford, Stanford University Press, 180 p.

Shaw, G., Seals – *Phoca flavescens. In* General zoology
1800   or systematic natural history, edited by G. Kearsley. London, vol. 1. Pt.2:260-1.

Sivertsen, E., A survey of the eared seals (family Ota-
1954   riidae) with remarks on the Antarctic seals. Collected by M/K *Norvegia* in 1928-1929. *Sci. Results Norw. Antarct. Exped. 1927-1928*, (36):76 p.

Smith, H.M., The Uruguayan fur-seal islands. *Zoologi-*
1927   *ca, N.Y.*, 9:271-94.

Strange, I., Sealing industries of the Falkland Islands.
1972   *Falkland Isl. J.*, 1972:9 p.

–, The silent ordeal of a south Atlantic archipelago.
1973   *Nat. Hist.*, 82:30-9.

Urraga, E. de, La explotación del lobo marino en el
1937   sur. *Mem. Jard. Zool. La Plata*, (7):184-8.

Vaz-Ferreira, R., Observaciones sobre la Isla de Lobos.
1950   *Rev. Fac. Hum. Cienc. Univ. Urug.*, 5:145-76.

–, Observaciones sobre las Islas de Torres y de Castillo
1952   Grande. *Rev. Fac. Hum. Cienc. Univ. Urug.*, 9:237-58.

–, Características generales de las islas uruguayas ha-
1956   bitadas por lobos marinos. *Trab. Islas Lobos*, (1):24 p.

–, Comportamiento antisocial en machos subadultos
1965   de *Otaria byronia* (de Blainville), ("lobo de un pelo"). *Rev. Fac. Hum. Cienc. Univ. Urug.*, 22:203-7.

–, Ecología terrestre y marina de los pinnipedios del
1956a   Atlántico sudoccidental. *An. Acad. Bras. Cienc. Suppl.*, (37):179-91.

–, Ocupación de espacios y reproducción de *Otaria*
1973   *flavescens* (Shaw) "lobo de un pelo", en áreas periféricas o apartadas del criadero. *Bol. Soc. Zool. Uruguay*, (2):8-12.

–, Behaviour of southern sea lion, *Otaria flavescens*
1975   (Shaw) in Uruguayan islands. *Rapp. P.-V. Réun. CIEM*, 169:219-27.

–, Factors affecting numbers of sea lions and fur seals
1975a   on the Uruguayan islands. *Rapp. P.-V. Réun. CIEM*, 169:257-62.

Vaz-Ferreira, R. and E. Palerm, Efectos de los cam-
1961   bios meteorológicos sobre agrupaciones terrestres de pinnipedios. *Rev. Fac. Hum. Cienc. Univ. Urug.*, 19:281-93.

Vieira, C. da Cunha, Lista remissiva dos mamíferos do
1955   Brasil. *Arq. Zool. Estado S. Paulo*, 8(1): 341-477.

Wellington, G.M. and Tj. de Vries, The South Ameri-
1976   can sea lion, *Otaria byronia*, in the Galapagos Islands. *J. Mammal.*, 57(1):166-7.

Ximénez, I., Estudio preliminar de la distribución
1964   geográfica actual de los pinnipedios en América Latina. *Bol. Inst. Biol. Mar., Mar del Plata*, (7):65-72.

ARCTOCEPHALUS AUSTRALIS ZIMMERMANN, SOUTH AMERICAN FUR SEAL

R. VAZ-FERREIRA

Abstract

The South American fur seal (*Arctocephalus australis*) is distributed along the Atlantic and Pacific coasts of South America, reaching north to at least São Paulo, Brazil, and to Paracas Peninsula in southern Peru, with rookeries on about 6 islands along the coast of Uruguay, several populations along the coast of the province of Chubut and on Isla de los Estados in Argentina, and colonies in the Falkland Islands, Chile and Peru. Although the Uruguayan population is not migratory, fur seals there may spread widely at sea during winter, travelling several hundred miles north or south along the coast. Distinguishing skull characteristics and general aspects of the pelage are reviewed. Common and scientific names are given. Adult males and females reach maximum lengths and weights of 188.5 cm and 159 kg, and 142.5 cm and 48.5 kg, respectively. Limited data on reproductive parameters are available. Fur seals feed over a wide area of the continental shelf and beyond, causing little or no disturbance to commercial fishing operations. Different breeding seasons and other mechanisms allow convivence of this species with the South American sea lion (*Otaria flavescens*) without major interference.

Fur seals have been harvested in South America for several centuries. Review of exploitation records of Uruguayan fur seals shows a drastic reduction in the population following the beginning of this century with a drop in the average annual harvest from 16 175 animals (1873-1900) to 3 400 animals (1943-47), after which a government programme of management and exploitation was begun. The population has been increasing since 1949, with total estimated numbers in 1953 at 26 444 animals, more than two-thirds of them on Isla de Lobos, and in 1972 at 252 000 animals. Present numbers are probably similar to those around 1900 and the species now constitutes a very important Uruguayan resource, earning revenues of the same order as the fisheries. Harvests for the past 5 years have averaged near 12 000 animals, mostly males; the oil and meat are used in some cases.

There is apparently no present exploitation of fur seals, except perhaps poaching, in other areas of its distribution. Estimates published in 1954 give a total of 2 700 fur seals in Argentina, mostly on Isla de Los Estados; 40 000 animals were found to be living in Magallanes Province, Chile, in 1976; and in Peru, 1968 figures show 11 806 fur seals distributed mostly in 3 areas. It appears that populations in these countries are either stable or diminishing. The Falkland Islands' population was stable between 1951 and 1966 and may be so today; it was estimated to include 15 000-16 000 fur seals in 1965-66. The difficult access of most rookeries discourages the recreational use of this species and it has only rarely been maintained successfully in captivity. Recommendations for further research include investigation of possible morphological differences between populations and studies of the state of southern stocks.

Résumé

L'otarie à fourrure d'Amérique du Sud (*Arctocephalus australis*) est distribuée le long de la côte atlantique et pacifique d'Amérique du Sud, allant au moins vers le nord jusqu'à São Paulo (Brésil) et jusqu'à la péninsule de Paracas, au sud du Pérou, avec des rookeries sur au moins 6 îles de la côte uruguayenne, plusieurs populations le long de la côte de la province de Chubut et sur Isla de los Estados, en Argentine, et des colonies aux îles Falkland, au Chili et au Pérou. Bien que la population uruguayenne ne pratique pas de migrations, les otaries à fourrure de cette région s'éloignent sensiblement en mer pendant l'hiver et parcourent plusieurs centaines de milles le long des côtes, vers le nord ou le sud. L'auteur passe en revue les caractéristiques craniennes distinctives ainsi que les aspects généraux du pelage. Il indique les noms communs et scientifiques. Les mâles et les femelles adultes atteignent, respectivement, des longueurs et des poids maximaux de 188,5 cm et 159 kg, 142,5 cm et 48,5 kg. On possède des données limitées sur les paramètres de la reproduction. Les otaries à fourrure s'alimentent sur une vaste surface du talus continental et au-delà de celui-ci et perturbent peu, ou pas du tout, les opérations de pêche commerciale. Les différences de saisons de reproduction et d'autres mécanismes permettent à cette espèce de coexister avec l'otarie à crinière (*Otaria flavescens*) sans interférences majeures. Les otaries à fourrure ont été exploitées en Amérique du Sud pendant des siècles. Une étude des archives d'exploitation des otaries à fourrure d'Uruguay montre un fléchissement colossal de la population au début du siècle accompagné d'une chute des captures, de 16 175 animaux (1873-1900) à 3 400 (1943-47); un programme gouvernemental de gestion et d'exploitation a été ensuite appliqué.

La population a augmenté depuis 1949; on a estimé que la population totale était de 26 444 sujets en 1953, plus des deux tiers se trouvant sur Isla de Lobos, et de 252 000 animaux en 1972. Les effectifs actuels sont probablement comparables à ceux qu'on relevait vers 1900 et l'espèce constitue maintenant une très importante source de revenus pour l'Uruguay, dont les montants sont comparables à ceux des pêches. Au cours des cinq dernières années, le chiffre moyen des captures a été de 12 000 animaux environ, surtout des mâles; l'huile et la chair sont utilisées occasionnellement.

A l'heure actuelle, les otaries à fourrure ne sont apparemment pas exploitées, à l'exception peut-être du braconnage, dans d'autres régions de leur distribution. Les estimations publiées en 1954 indiquent un total de 2 700 animaux en Argentine, surtout sur Isla de los Estados; on a constaté que 40 000 animaux vivaient en 1976 dans la province de Magallanes (Chili); au Pérou, les chiffres relatifs à 1968 indiquent 11 806 otaries à fourrure, qui sont distribuées en majeure partie dans trois zones. Il apparaît que les populations de ces pays sont stables ou diminuent.

La population des îles Falkland était stable entre 1951 et 1966; elle l'est encore peut-être aujourd'hui. En 1965-66, on estimait qu'elle comprenait 15 000-16 000 otaries. La difficulté d'accès de la plupart des rookeries décourage l'utilisation récréative de cette espèce, qu'on a rarement pu tenir avec succès en captivité. Les recommandations relatives à la recherche future comprennent la détermination d'éventuelles différences morphologiques entre les populations et l'étude de l'état des stocks du sud.

Extracto

El lobo marino de dos pelos de América del Sur (*Arctocephalus australis*) se encuentra a lo largo de las costas del Atlántico y el Pacífico de América del Sur, llegando por el norte al menos hasta São Paulo, en Brasil, y la península de Paracas, en el Perú; se encuentran criaderos en seis islas de la costa del Uruguay, varias poblaciones a lo largo de la provincia de Chubut y en la isla de los Estados (Argentina), y algunas colonias en las islas Malvinas (Falkland), Chile y Perú. Aunque la población de Uruguay no es migratoria, los lobos pueden dispersarse mucho por el mar durante el invierno, recorriendo varios centenares de millas hacia el norte o hacia el sur a lo largo de la costa. Se examinan las características cránicas distintivas y los aspectos generales del pelaje. Se dan los nombres vulgar y científico. La talla y peso máximos de los machos y hembra adultos son, respectivamente, 188,5 cm y 159 kg y 142,5 cm y 48,5 kg. Los datos disponibles sobre los parámetros de reproducción son limitados. Estos lobos se alimentan en una vasta zona de la plataforma continental y fuera de ella, sin interferir, o apenas, con las actividades de pesca comercial. La diferencia de las temporadas de cría y otros mecanismos permiten la convivencia de esta especie con el león marino de América del Sur (*Otaria flavescens*) sin interferencias importantes.

El lobo marino de dos pelos se ha cazado en América del Sur desde hace varios siglos. Los datos sobre la explotación de este lobo en Uruguay reflejan una reducción radical de la población a partir de principios de este siglo, con una disminución de la producción media anual de 16 175 animales (1873-1900) a 3 400 (1943-47), como consecuencia de lo cual el Gobierno inició un programa de regulación y de explotación. La población ha ido en aumento desde 1949, y su número total se estimaba en 1953 en 26 444 animales, más de la mitad de ellos en la isla de Lobos, y en 1972 en 252 000 animales. En la actualidad su número es probablemente similar al de 1900 y hoy día la especie constituye un recurso muy importante para el Uruguay, con ingresos del mismo orden que los de las pesquerías. Durante los últimos cinco años la captura media ha sido de 12 000 animales, en su mayoría machos; en algunos casos se aprovecha también el aceite y la carne.

Este lobo marino no se explota, según parece, en el resto de su zona de distribución, excepto, quizás, clandestinamente. Las estimaciones publicadas en 1954 dan un total de 2 700 lobos en Argentina, principalmente en la isla de los Estados; en la provincia de Magallanes, en Chile, se encontraron 40 000 animales en 1976; en Perú, las cifras correspondientes a 1968 arrojan 11 806 lobos, distribuidos principalmente en tres zonas. Parece que las poblaciones de esos países son estables o están en disminución. La población de las islas Malvinas (Falkland) se mantuvo estable entre 1951 y 1966 y es posible que lo sea aún hoy; el número de lobos en esa zona se estimó en 15 000-16 000 en 1965-66. Las dificultades de acceso a la mayoría de los criaderos no permiten aprovechar con fines recreativos esta especie, y sólo en raros casos se ha logrado mantener a estos animales en cautividad. Entre las recomendaciones para investigaciones futuras hay que citar la necesidad de estudiar las posibles diferencias morfológicas entre las diversas poblaciones y la situación de las poblaciones meridionales.

R. Vaz-Ferreira
Universidad de la República, Departamento de Zoología Vertebrados, Juan. L. Cuestas 1525, Montevideo, Uruguay

Identification of the species

CHARACTERISTICS

General

Arctocephalus australis (Zimmermann), the South American fur seal, is grey with a silver, orange or red tinge on the back, and orange-grey on the belly. Like other members of the genus *Arctocephalus, A. australis* has a pointed nose and is markedly dimorphic; the neck area of the males has hair which is stiffer and longer than that of females, which have very little specialised hair on the neck. Large males reach lengths of 188.5 cm (Isla de Lobos – Vaz-Ferreira, unpublished) and weights of 159 kg (recorded by Repenning, Peterson and Hubbs, 1971, from the Falkland Islands, (Islas Malvinas)). The females reach 142.5 cm and 48.5 kg (specimens on Isla de Lobos). The maximum recorded skull length for males is 258.5 mm and 209 mm for females (specimens from Isla de Lobos, Uruguay – Vaz-Ferreira, unpublished).

As established in the revision of the genus *Arctocephalus* by Repenning, Peterson and Hubbs (1971), the skull of *A. australis* is characteristic in that the palate is moderately broad and slightly arched anteriorly, wider than in *A. tropicalis* and narrower than in *A. forsteri*. The nasals widen markedly anteriorly; the rostrum is moderately long and the occipital crest just covers the braincase, the forehead being almost flat above the orbits. The depth of the jugal bone in the region of its postorbital process is, in old males, according to Repenning, Peterson and Hubbs (1971), probably extreme for the genus; the maxillary shelf is long.

The dental formula, as in other *Arctocephalus* is I 3/2, C 1/1, PC 6/5; the accessory cusps of the postcanines are more pronounced than in the other species of the genus, except *A. pusillus*, which has even more pronounced accessory cusps.

External aspect, colour and hair

No distinctive characteristics of the external form of *Arctocephalus australis* have been worked out at a specific level.

The colour of adult males may vary in different specimens between black or silvery grey or grey-orange and grey-yellowish orange on the back, with a lighter neck area of grey or of a greyish orange, and belly sometimes more reddish.

The pattern of colours in females is more or less constant, even if the colours themselves vary considerably. The pattern is composed of about four areas: (i) chin and back of the neck – dark grey-orange; (ii) front of the neck to anterior border of foreflippers – light orange or light orange-yellow or yellowish; (iii) the breast areas, delimited by the lines of the anterior and posterior borders of the foreflippers, have 2 more or less circular dark areas, which are continued on the middle by a lighter area, and (iv) the belly area, from a line joining the posterior border of the foreflippers backward, is bright orange or brick red.

The young males have similar colours to the females, but less vivid.

The pups from birth to the first moult are uniformly black and they acquire a lighter greyish colour later on. Many adults of both sexes, especially females, are of a silver-grey colour or sometimes completely red (apparently erythrine specimens).

The hair is longer on the neck, especially in males; the guard hair is bicoloured whitish or reddish with grey, and the fur brownish, with a dark base and lighter tips.

For each guard hair, there are bundles of underfur fibres, each of 29 to 47 underfur elements.

Common names

In Brazil, *Arctocephalus australis* is called "lobo marinho", "leão marinho" or "lobo de dois pelos"; in Uruguay and Argentina "lobo fino" or "lobo de dos pelos"; in the Falkland Islands (Islas Malvinas) the name in use is "fur seal" and in Chile and Peru, either "lobo fino" or "lobo de dos pelos".

Scientific names

Arctocephalus australis (Zimmermann, 1783) is the valid specific name for the South American fur seal.

Allen (1905) and Osgood (1943), have given extensive lists of synonyms; among the specific epithets which have been used are: *falklandicus* (as *Phoca falklandica* Shaw, 1800, employed in different combinations by many authors), *nigrescens* (*Arctocephalus nigrescens* Gray, 1859), *gracilis* (*Arctocephalus "Arctophoca" gracilis* Nehring 1887 or *Arctocephalus falklandicus* var. *gracilis* Nehring, 1887a) and several names proposed by Molina (1782) and by Philippi (1892).

King (1954), admitting that the populations of the Falkland Islands (Islas Malvinas) could differ at a sub-specific level from those of the mainland of South America, adopted *A. a. australis* (Zimmermann) for the fur seals of the Falkland Islands and *A. a. gracilis* (Nehring) for those of the mainland. The basis for the recognition of these 2 sub-species is a number of skulls which appear to be too small to constitute a good sample representative of the populations of the mainland of S. America. Until further and stronger evidence of the contrary is published, different sub-species among *Arctocephalus australis* do not seem justified at present.

Distribution and movements

DISTRIBUTION

Areas inhabited or reached by the South American fur seal are the Atlantic and Pacific shores of South America, from São Paulo, Brazil, to the southern tip of South America and Falkland Islands (Islas Malvinas) and northward on the west coast to southern Peru.

In Brazil, the species, according to Vieira (1955) reaches São Paulo, and Nehring (1887b) reported the capture of specimens at Ponta Negra (22°56′S); we have recorded a few fur seals on Recife das Torres, in Santa Catalina (29°19′S; 49°41′W).

In Uruguay the species breeds on the Isla del Marco (34°21′S; 53°5′W) (Castillos group); on the Islote, Isla Encantada and Isla Rasa (Torres group 34°24′S); and, mainly on the main Isla de Lobos (35°01′S) and on its Islote. They also haul out on other islands of the Atlantic shore of Uruguay, on which they do not breed; some adult males of this species also haul out during the breeding season on the shore of the mainland of Cabo Polonio. The islands of the Coronilla group, where the southern sea lion breeds, are not used for breeding by the fur seals.

In Argentina, Holmberg and Aubone (1948, 1949) and Carrara (1952, 1954) studied the populations of southern fur seals; Carrara (1952, 1954) mentions the existence of colonies of southern fur seals in 3 places: Isla Escondida (43°43′S; 65°17′W), Bahía de San Antonio, on the Isla de los Estados (43°43′ to 47′S; 64°32′W) and Bahía Flinders on the same island. Daciuk (1974) mentions the existence of populations of the species at Cabo Dos Bahías (44°54′S; 65°32′W) and on some islands of the province of Chubut, the occasional hauling out of specimens at Península Valdés and also the finding of a dead pup on Puerto Madryn on 21 September 1973.

On the Falkland Islands (Islas Malvinas), Laws (1953) surveyed the fur seals, finding colonies on Volunteer Rocks, the Bird Islands, on rocky islets south of Elephant Jason, in a cove between Precipice Hill and Landsend Bluff of New Island and on rocky islets of the same islands; he also had references to colonies on North Island and on Beauchene Island. Strange (1972) and Laws (1973) have later pointed out that the Beauchene Island colony does not exist any more.

As far as it is known, no other islands of the Atlantic are populated by this species. South Georgia, South Orkney, South Shetland and other islands in or south of the Antarctic Convergence, formerly supposed to be populated by *A. australis*, are inhabited only by *Arctocephalus gazella* (Peters, 1875).

Some colonies exist in Chile, but they have not been recorded during recent research on populations of *Otaria flavescens*. L.A. Aguayo, Naturhistoriska Riksmuseet (*in litt.* 24/5/76 and in press) has confirmed that this species still lives in Chile: "This animal was observed in the Magallanes Strait, in the Castro Channel, in Puerto Caracciolo, in the Paso del Abismo (Chasm Reach), on the Pierre Islets, in the Fallos Channel, in the Messier Channel and in Abra Kelly". According to Aguayo and Maturana (1970), the only population of fur seals on the Islands of Juan Fernández is *Arctocephalus philippi* (Peters).

The distribution of the South American fur seal on Peruvian shores is given by Piazza (1959) and Grimwood (1968, 1969); according to the latter it has a northern breeding limit at approximately 13°45′S, the only breeding site known to have been used during 1965 and 1966 being located at the foot of the cliffs of Paracas Peninsula even though in previous years fur seals were breeding at Punta Corio (17°20′S) and Punta Coles (17°45′S). A typewritten report prepared by the fisheries Service of Peru shows a much better situation for 1968 (see under COUNTS AND ESTIMATIONS).

MOVEMENTS

The Uruguayan populations are not migratory, part of the herd maintaining its attachment to land all the year round.

Very important changes in land populations may occur (Vaz-Ferreira and Palerm, 1961; Vaz-Ferreira, 1975), with increases or decreases of the order of 50 % of the population sometimes occurring in certain areas in a few hours.

Increases and decreases in ground temperature are the main causes of changes produced during the breeding season.

During the winter, the fur seals, mostly 6-month old individuals and larger young males, come as far as several hundred metres from inshore (Vaz-Ferreira, 1956). The places occupied in summer by the breeding structures which have a complex integration (Vaz-Ferreira and Sierra, 1961) are inhabited by varied populations during the rest of the year.

The fur seals spread widely at sea; groups of 15 to 20 have been seen travelling between 60 and 105 miles to the east of the island during the winter. To the southwest, the Uruguayan specimens spread at least to Mar del Plata, as Uruguayan tags have been recovered there; northeastward they travel very often to Rio Grande and Santa Catalina, and probably as far as São Paulo and Rio de Janeiro.

No studies have been published of the land attendance of fur seal populations on the Falkland Islands (Islas Malvinas) and other southerly areas; it is possible, but not proven, that, as suggested by King (1964) part of the populations of these areas migrate to more northerly areas during the winter.

Stocks

COUNTS AND ESTIMATIONS

In Uruguay in February-March 1953 and again in 1956 (Vaz-Ferreira, unpublished), we counted the live pups of *Arctocephalus australis* on all the islands and, in January 1953, counted also the adults of this species; the results were as shown in Table 1.

The total number counted and estimated for 1953 was 26 444 individuals, including 9 149 pups and 17 295 adults.

In subsequent years, the number of pups born has grown steadily, extending the areas formerly occupied by the breeding grounds of

Table 1. Counts of pups and adults of S. American fur seal in Uruguay

Group	Islands	Pups 1953 [1]	Pups 1956	Adults 1953 [2]
Lobos	Lobos	4 435	7 460	10 578
	Islote	500		500
Torres	Rasa	15	178	1 599
	Encantada	2 128	2 383	1 400
	Islote	280	337	667
Castillos	Marco	1 791	2 332	2 541
Total		9 149	12 690	17 295

[1] February-March.
[2] January.

fur seals. During the last 3 years, I have been able to find at Isla de Lobos extensive areas formerly not occupied by breeding groups of this species which are now occupied by them. According to Ximenez (1973), the number of pups born increased in 1970 to 7 625 for the Encantada Island, to 11 211 for Isla del Marco and in Isla Rasa the number of pups born in 1970 would be 23 118. According to I. Ximenez, Manager of Sealing, Industrias Loberas y Pesqueras del Estado (U.S. Federal Register, 38(147):20572, 1973), the total estimated population was 129 000 in 1960, 174 000 in 1965 and 252 000 for 1972. Ximenez (personal communication) obtained the following counts for the pups born in the 1972-73 breeding season: Isla de Lobos, 58 930; Islote de Lobos, 341; Isla del Marco, 11 087; Isla Rasa, 23 408; Islas Encantada, 7 704, for a total of 101 470 animals.

In Argentina, Carrara gives counts in 1954 of a total of 2 700 *Arctocephalus australis* (400 at Isla Escondida, 100 at Bahia San Antonio on Isla de los Estados and 2 200 in Bahia Flinders, of the same Island). No additional information on population sizes has been published since this census but, according to Ximenez (personal communication) about 600 adult males, presumed to belong to this spe-

cies, are currently seen at Cabo dos Bahias in Chubut Province.

For the Falkland Islands (Islas Malvinas) according to Strange 1973, the counts made in 1965-66 showed 15 000-16 000 fur seals inhabiting the Archipelago.

In Chile according to Lieutenant I. Petrowitsch F., Director of the Division of Fisheries Protection of Chile (*in litt.*, 4/6/76), a census of fur seals was made in Magallanes Province in 1976 and 7 rookeries with about 40 000 animals were found; of these, about two-thirds were pups.

The aforementioned breeding populations belong probably to *A. australis*, which is the species formerly living in the area, even though M.R. Payne has reported that a fur seal tagged at South Georgia (presumably *A. gazella*) was recovered at Isla Hoste, located near the southern tip of Chile, south of Tierra del Fuego (Schlatter, *in litt.*, 30/4/76).

For Peru, the Department of Fisheries has given the following figures for 1968.

ACTUAL AND PAST STATE OF THE STOCKS

Over the whole area of distribution of the South American fur seal, there are islands which were populated historically which they do not inhabit today.

The population of fur seals has been

Table 2. Numbers of S. American fur seals in Peru, 1968

Place	Males	Females	Pups	Total
North of Lagunillas	724	2 042	1 119	3 885
Infiernillo	99	542	261	902
San Fernando	648	2 994	3 078	6 720
Tres Hermanas	5	30	8	43
Sombrerillo	21	22	10	53
Cachuco	4	1		5
Island 4 km from San Juan	23	106	69	198
Total	1 524	5 737	4 545	11 806

increasing in Uruguay since 1949 to the present, having now probably reached levels of population similar to the ones which were present at the end of the last century and at the beginning of the present, and which had been drastically diminished in following years.

On the Falkland Islands (Islas Malvinas) the population appears to be stable, or at least it was more or less so between 1951 and 1966 (Strange, 1972; Laws, 1973).

No comparative figures of the last years are available from other areas, where it appears that populations are either stable or diminishing.

Vital parameters

SIZES AND WEIGHTS

Maximum sizes recorded by us in Uruguay were 188.5 cm for males and 142.5 cm for females.

Maximum weights recorded were 159 kg for males and 48.5 kg for females.

Four neonates weighed between 3 350 and 5 450 g.

AGES AT SEXUAL MATURITY

Tagged female fur seals recovered during the fourth year of life were found to be pregnant; it is evident from this that the females may be impregnated when they are 3 years old. It may be possible, but it is not proven, that some females may be impregnated when they are 2 years old.

No knowledge of the age of breeding males is available.

The minimum size of pregnant females recorded was 1.06 m.

PREGNANCY RATES

An experimental kill of 40 females, ranging from 1.06 to 1.36 m in total length, was made on 15 July 1953, and I found the relationship between pregnant females and size shown in Table 3. The sex ratio of the herd was taken to be more or less the undisturbed ration, since there had been selective killing for only a short time.

PROPORTION OF SEXES

Of 572 live pups sexed on 4-6 February 1953, when they were about 1 ½ months old, we found (Vaz-Ferreira, unpublished) 321 males and 251 females (56.11 % males).

In breeding groups (December), the proportions of males to females may vary from 1:1 to 1:13. Numbers counted on Lobos Island were: 33 males with 213 females; 7 males with 33 females; 10 males with 63 females. Another group recorded had 6 males and 45 females (Vaz-Ferreira,1956).

The economic value and state of regulation and management of exploitation

According to Kellogg (1942), the first cargo of seal skins exported from the Falkland Islands (Islas Malvinas) was carried by Bougainville's ship.

Several authors, including Kellogg (1942) and Strange (1972) have given historic accounts of the exploitation of the Falkland Island (Islas Malvinas) herds. According to Strange (1973), in 1784 about 13 000 fur seal

Table 3. **Pregnancy data for S. American fur seals**

Size class	Pregnant	Non-pregnant	Total
1.18 or less	4	7	11
1.19 - 1:31	25	0	25
1.32 - 1.36	4	0	4
Total	33	7	40

skins were taken on these islands by an American vessel out of Boston; in 1919, the 2 sealers holding licences for that region, after spending 2 months on Beauchene Island, which had formerly been "the home of thousands of fur seals", returned with only 11 skins. Recovery has been slow, even allowing for unreported exploitation since 1919.

The past status and exploitation of the herds of Argentina was reviewed by Holmberg and Aubone (1948, 1949) and by Carrara (1964). No exploitation of this species is allowed by law and no record of clandestine killing has been found.

In Uruguay, the exploitation of fur seals began shortly after the discovery of the country by Juan Diaz de Solis in 1515, whose mates, after his death, made up a cargo of fur seal skins for sale in the market of Sevilla. Sealing has been conducted in all the islands populated by the species: Isla de Lobos and Islote de Lobos, off Punta del Este and on Marco, Encantada, Rasa and Islote, near Cabo Polonio. Killing is and has been mainly done during the winter, out of the breeding season, thereby taking advantage of some of the ecological and behavioural characteristics of this species; during the winter, populations of *A. australis* remain on the islands, occupying the space utilized in spring and summer by the rookeries, and others also move to the higher parts of the islands.

According to several authors, such as Devincenzi (1895) and the Bering Sea Tribunal of Arbitration (1895), the number of fur seals killed on Uruguayan islands from 1873 to 1900 was as shown in Table 4.

The data in Table 4 gives a total of 454 491 animals killed and a medium annual catch, apparently sustained at least during 28 years, of 16 175.

No records from 1901 to 1909 are available. The catch for 1910-42 (either no killing was done or no records are available for 1913, 1915, 1917, 1918, 1930, 1931, 1932, 1933, 1938, 1939) was, according to Perez-Fontana (1943) 71 955 fur seals, a medium annual catch for the 23 years in which killing was done or recorded

Table 4. Kills of S. American fur seals on Uruguayan islands, 1873-1900

Year	Number
1873	8 190
1874	9 449
1875	9 204
1876	11 353
1877	13 066
1878	14 493
1879	14 093
1880	16 382
1881	14 473
1882	13 595
1883	12 843
1884	14 872
1885	12 247
1886	17 072
1887	17 788
1888	21 150
1889	15 700
1890	20 150
1891	13 871
1892	15 870
1893	17 779
1894	20 763
1895	17 421
1896	23 639
1897	19 234
1898	17 685
1899	17 235
1900	18 828

of 3 128. From 1943 to 1947 a total of 17 000 or a yearly yield of 3 400 was obtained.

In 1948 and 1949 no killing was done and a management project began under which the killing, which was started again in 1950 at Isla de Lobos, was restricted exclusively to males.

To achieve this, groups of 200 to more than 2 000 fur seals were driven from shore, or mostly from a special area called the "explanada", where many young seals congregate in winter, to an inland corral in which they were enclosed. Once in the corral, small groups were driven to a much smaller corral, caught and individually sexed; the young males were killed, and undersized seals of both sexes, females and overlarge males, were released.

Later, this manoeuvre was considered unnecessary as it was established from expe-

505

rience that most of the individuals, sometimes as many as 80 % of the total of the population of the higher areas of the island during winter, are young males 6 months old and older. So the use of these populations reduces to a minimum the killing of females; this being improved by the fact that many of the adult females may be recognized and released. Adult females tend to overwinter on the breeding areas on the shore (Ximenez, 1962).

On other parts of Isla de Lobos and the other Uruguayan Islands, the selective killing of young males is much more difficult.

Starting a selective kill of males only in 1950, 1 692 pelts were obtained. This number has been increasing and the annual harvest has been, during the last 5 years, around 12 000 specimens, mostly males.

The management and exploitation of the Uruguayan herds has been done by the SOYP (Servicio Oceanografico y de Pesca), which has now been restructured into the ILPE (Industrias Loberas y Pesqueras del Estado), both of them government offices. The pelts are processed by a plant belonging to the same institution which is now one of the few in the world doing this kind of processing.

Oil from fur seals is obtained on Isla de Lobos and also on Cabo Polonio from the seals killed on the islands nearby; the meat is processed into meal only on Isla de Lobos; there are now plans to sell the carcasses whole or cut in the middle for animal food. Apparently, no exploitation of fur seals, other than poaching, is done at present on other areas of South America populated by *Arctocephalus australis*.

Recreational and aesthetic values

Most of the rookeries of the South American fur seal are in places of difficult access; the one situated on the southern shore of the Isla de Lobos, Uruguay, is an exception to this since it offers a possibility to observe a great many fur seals; however, it is at present forbidden to visit this areas because of possible disturbance to the herd.

The South American fur seal has been only rarely maintained successfully in captivity.

Food and relation to other resources

FOOD HABITS

In specimens caught on land we found (Vaz-Ferreira, 1950, and unpublished) either empty stomachs or very much digested materials, including remains of fish, beaks of cephalopods, crustaceans, lamelli-branchs and sea snails.

Brownell (personal communication) was able to study the stomach contents of 13 specimens of *Arctocephalus australis* drowned in trammel nets, and found the following fish: *Engraulis anchoita, Trachurus lathami, Cynoscion striatus, Pneumatophorus japonicus, Peprilus*, sp.

RELATION TO OTHER RESOURCES

Arctocephalus australis feeds over a wide area of the continental shelf and beyond.

In contrast to *Otaria flavescens*, which has about the same geographical distribution, and to the South African fur seal, *Arctocephalus pusillus*, *Arctocephalus australis* is not a boat follower, does not enter the nets during the fishing operations and causes no important damage to fishing gear, except perhaps some interference with fishing gear placed too close to the rookeries.

As described elsewhere (Vaz-Ferreira and Sierra, 1963), the different breeding seasons and other mechanisms allow *Arctocephalus australis* and *Otaria flavescens* to co-exist without major interference.

The fur seal population constitutes a very important resource for the Government of Uruguay, which obtains from it revenues of the same order as from the fisheries.

Recommendations

To encourage research dealing especially with:

1. Possible morphological differences of populations.

2. Studies of southern populations such as those in southern Chile and on the Falkland Islands (Islas Malvinas).

References

AGUAYO, A. and R. MATURANA, Primer censo de lobos
1970 finos en el archipiélago de Juan Fernández. *Biol. Pesq., Barc.*, (4):3-15.

ALLEN, J.A., The Mammalia of southern Patagonia.
1905 *Rep. Princeton Exped. Patagonia 1896-1899, (Zool.)*, 3(1):210 p.

Bering Sea Tribunal of Arbitration, Fur seal arbitra-
1895 tion: Proceedings of the Tribunal of Arbitration, convened at Paris under the Treaty between the United States and Great Britain, concluded at Washington, 29 February 1892, for determination of questions between the two governments concerning jurisdictional rights of the United States to the waters of Bering Sea. Washington, D.C., Government Printing Office, vol. 6:213-5.

CARRARA, S.I., Lobos marinos, pingüinos y guaneras de
1952 las costas del litoral marítimo e islas adyacentes de la República Argentina *Publ. Espec. Univ. Nac. Cienc. Vet., La Plata*, (15):189 p.

−, Observaciones sobre el estado actual de las pobla-
1954 ciones de pinnípedos de la Argentina. Universidad Nacional Eva Perón, Argentina, 17 p.

−, Zoorrecursos naturales de la Antártida. La Plata,
1964 Universidad Nacional de La Plata, Facultad de Ciencia Veterinaria, 89 p.

CUNHA VIEIRA, C. DA, Lista remissiva dos mamíferos do
1955 Brasil. *Arq. Zool. Estado, Sao Paulo*, 8(11):341-74.

DACIUK, J., Notas faunísticas y biológicas de Península
1974 Valdés y Patagonia. 12. Mamíferos colectados y observados en la Península Valdés y zona litoral de los golfos San José y Nuevo (Provincia de Chubut, República Argentina). *Physis (C), B. Aires*, 33(86):23-39.

DEVINCENZI, E.J., Importancia de las Islas de Lobos.
1895 Necesidad de su administración en forma por medio de licitación pública. Montevideo, Dornaleche y Reyes, 15 p.

GRIMWOOD, I.R., Endangered mammals in Peru. *Oryx*,
1968 9:411-21.

−, Notes on the distribution and status of some Peru-
1969 vian mammals. *Publ. Am. Comm. Int. Wild Life Prot. N.Y. Zool. Soc.*, (21):1-86.

HOLMBERG, A.D. and G. AUBONE, Documentación que
1948 ha servido de base para reconstruir el mapa de las foquerías del Virreinato del Río de la Plata en 1776-1810. Part 1. 80 p. (mimeo).

−, Documentación que ha servido de base para re-
1949 construir el mapa de las foquerías del Virreinato del Río de la Plata en 1776-1810. Part 2. 79 p. (mimeo).

KELLOGG, R., Tertiary, quaternary and recent marine
1942 mammals of South America and the West Indies. *Proc. Am. Sci. Congr.*, 8(1940) vol. 3: 445-73.

KING, J.E., The otariid seals of the Pacific coast of
1954 America. *Bull Br. Mus. Nat. Hist. (Zool)*, 2(10):311-37.

−, Seals of the world. London, British Museum (Natu-
1964 ral History), 154 p.

LAWS, R.M., The seals of the Falkland Island and de-
1953 pendencies. *Oryx*, 2:87-97.

−, The current status of seals in the Southern Hemi-
1973 sphere. *IUCN Publ. (New Ser.) Suppl. Pap.*, (39):144-61.

MOLINA, G.I., Saggio sulla storia naturale del Cile. Bo-
1782   logna, S. Tomaso d'Aquino, 368 p.

NEHRING, A., Uber eine Pelzrobben-Art von der Kuste
1887   Sud-Brasiliens. *Arch. Naturgesch.*, 1:75-94.

—, Uber die sudbrasilienische Pelzrobbe. *Sitzungsber.*
1887a   *Ges. Naturforsch. Freunde Berl.*, 1887:142-3.

NEHRING, A., Uber eine Pelzrobbe von Rio de Janeiro.
1887b   *Sitzungsber. Ges. Naturforsch. Freunde Berl.*,
        1887:207-8.

OSGOOD, W.H., The mammals of Chile. *Publ. Field Mus.*
1943   *Nat. Hist. (Zool.)*, 30:1-268.

PÉREZ FONTANA, H., Informe sobre la industria lobera
1943   (ciento diez años de explotación de la indus-
        tria lobera en nuestro país). Montevideo, Ser-
        vicio Oceanográfico y de Pesca, 70 p.

PHILIPPI, R.A., Las focas chilenas del Museo Nacional.
1892   *Ann. Mus. Nac. Chile (Zool.)*, 1892:52 p.

PIAZZA, L.A., Los lobos marinos en el Perú. *Pesca Caza*,
1959   *Lima*, (9):1-29.

REPENNING, C.A., R.S. PETERSON, and C.L. HUBBS, Con-
1971   tributions to the systematics of the southern
        fur seals, with particular reference to the Juan
        Fernandez and Guadalupe species. *Antarct.
        Res. Ser.*, (18):1-34.

STRANGE, I., Sealing industries of the Falkland Islands.
1972   *Falkland Isl. J.*, 1972:9 p.

—, The silent ordeal of a South Atlantic archipelago.
1973   *Nat. Hist.*, 82(2):30-9.

U.S. Federal Register, 38(147):20572.
1973

VAZ-FERREIRA, R., Observaciones sobre la Isla de Lobos.
1950   *Rev. Fac. Hum. Cienc. Univ. Urug.*, 5:145-76.

—, Etología terrestre de *Arctocephalus australis* (Zim-
1956   mermann) ("lobo fino") en las islas uru-
        guayas. *Trab. Islas Lobos* (2):22 p.

—, Ecología terrestre y marina de los pinnipedios del
1965   Atlántico sudoccidental. *An. Acad. Bras.
        Cienc.*, Suppl. (37):179-91.

—, Factors affecting numbers of sea lions and fur seals
1975   on the Uruguayan islands. *Rapp. P.-V. Réun.
        Ciem*, 169:257-62.

VAZ-FERREIRA, R. and E. PALERM, Efectos de los cam-
1961   bios meteorológicos sobre agrupaciones te-
        rrestres de pinnipedios. *Rev. Fac. Hum. Cienc.
        Univ. Urug.*, 19:281-93.

VAZ-FERREIRA, R. and B. SIERRA, División funcional del
1961   habitat terrestre y estructura de las agregacio-
        nes sociales de *Arctocephalus australis* (Zim-
        mermann), estudio gráfico. *Acta Congr.
        Sudam. Zool*, 1:175-83.

—, Tolerancia en grupos biespecíficos de pinnipedios.
1963   *Proc. Int. Congr. Zool.*, 16:250 (abstr.).

XIMÉNEZ, I., Frecuencia y fluctuaciones estacionales en
1962   la población de *Arctocephalus australis* en al-
        gunas zonas de la Isla de Lobos. *Rev. Inst.
        Invest. Pesq. Univ. Urug.*, 1(2):141-58.

—, Nota preliminar sobre la repoblación de *Arctoce-
1973   phalus australis* en la Isla Rasa. *Trab. Congr.
        Latino-am. Zool.*, (5) vol. 1:281-8.

ZIMMERMANN, E.A.W. von, Geographische Geschichte
1783   des Menschen, und der allgemein verbreiteten
        vierfussigen Thiere — *Phoca australis*. Leip-
        zig, vol. 3: p. 276 *Phoca australis*.

SIRENIANS AND OTTERS

AERIAL SURVEY OF THE DUGONG, *DUGONG DUGON*, IN KENYA

S.H. Ligon

Abstract

From 29 October to 1 November 1975, an aerial survey of dugongs (*Dugong dugon*) was made along the entire coast of Kenya, following a grid pattern covering 25 percent of the area between the shore and the end of the continental shelf and totalling 12.17 hours of observation. Even with favourable conditions, only 8 animals were seen, 4 of them alone and 2 cows with calves; the smaller calf was seen riding on its mother's back. The discrepancy between these results and earlier reports of large numbers of dugongs off Kenya, may be due to their absence because of migration or to the deliberate or incidental capture of dugongs by native fishermen, which has probably greatly reduced the population in this region.

Résumé

Du 29 octobre au ler novembre 1975, une étude aérienne des dugongs (*Dugong dugon*) a été effectuée le long de toute la côte du Kenya, en suivant un carroyage couvrant 25 pour cent de la zone entre le rivage et la limite du talus continental et atteignant un total de 12h17 d'observation. Même avec des conditions favorables, on n'a pu apercevoir que 8 animaux, dont 4 étaient isolés, et 2 étaient des femelles avec leur petit. Le plus petit des veaux était porté sur le dos de sa mère. La discordance entre ces résultats et les rapports antérieurs signalant la présence de grands nombres de dugongs au large du Kenya peut être due à leur absence par suite de migrations ou à la capture délibérée ou accidentelle de dugongs par les pêcheurs indigènes, qui a sans doute grandement réduit la population de cette région.

Extracto

Del 29 de octubre al 1 de noviembre de 1975, se realizó un reconocimiento aéreo de la presencia de dugones (*Dugong dugon*) a lo largo de la costa de Kenya, en una cuadrícula que cubría el 25 por ciento de la superficie comprendida entre la costa y el borde de la plataforma continental, durante un total de 12,17 horas de observación. A pesar de que las condiciones eran favorables, sólo se avistaron ocho animales, cuatro de ellos solos y dos hembras con cría, la más pequeña de las cuales cabalgaba sobre los lomos de su madre. La discrepancia entre estos resultados y los datos comunicados anteriormente sobre la presencia de gran número de dugones frente a las costas de Kenya puede deberse a movimientos migratorios o a la captura deliberada o accidental de dugones por parte de los pescadores nativos, que probablemente ha reducido en forma notable la población de esta región.

S.H. Ligon
Department of Biology, University of New Mexico, Albuquerque, NM 87131, USA

Philip and Fisher (1970) report that dugongs, *Dugong dugon*, are more common off the coasts of Kenya and the Somali Republic than elsewhere in Africa. Major populations have been located in both the Kiunga Archipelago and the Lamu inland sea of Kenya (Kingdon, 1971; Jarman, 1966), and large herds of dugongs have been sighted at both Mombasa and Malindi (Jarman, 1966). This information is based largely on incidental sightings and reports of local fishermen. This paper reports results of the first aerial survey of dugongs in Kenya.

Methods

A Cessna 182 was flown at a constant altitude of 900 feet, at an average ground speed of 70-80 knots. The flight path followed was not the single-strip census used by Husar (1976) for dugong surveys in Queensland; rather, a grid pattern was followed which resulted in 25 % coverage of the water surface. This grid covered the entire Kenya coast (300 miles long), from the shore line out to the drop off of the continental shelf (roughly 50 fathoms). Greater depths are thought to be unsuitable dugong habitat.

Two observers, seated in the rear of the plane, one on each side, monitored transects (600 m wide) defined by two rigid poles fixed to the wing struts. The pilot and a third passenger were responsible for navigation and reporting water conditions. Sightings of dugongs were tape recorded, as were observations of sea turtles, dolphins, whale sharks and native fishing vessels.

Results

Surveys were flown in 1975 on 29 October (03.00 h), 30 October (04.33 h), 31 October (02.17 h) and 1 November (02.67 h), totalling 12.17 h of survey. Only 8 dugongs were sighted during the entire survey. Water and light conditions were favourable. The fact that 21 whale sharks, 142 sea turtles and 447 dolphins were recorded as well as millions of jellyfish (each approximately 1 foot in diameter) confirms that viewing conditions were satisfactory. Four dugongs were alone and two were cows with calves. One calf (ca. 1.5-2 m in length) was about 2/3 the size of its mother and swam close beside her. The other calf was very small (ca. 1 m in length). We observed it for several minutes as it rode upon its mother's back while she swam near the surface. Each time the cow submerged deeper into the water, the calf moved to her side and swam beside the cow until she again approached the surface. The calf then repositioned itself above the cow.

Discussion

The discrepancy between fishermen's reports and sightings of "herds" of dugongs, and these results may be explained in either of two ways:

(1) Dugongs are no longer present in any numbers in Kenyan waters, owing to illegal hunting. Within the transects alone, 173 native fishing vessels were counted, indicating that about 700 native boats were active along the coast during the survey. Nylon fishing nets are frequently used, and dugongs are captured, either deliberately or accidentally. Thus, it is likely that human predation has drastically reduced the dugong population in this region.

(2) The dugong population of the East African coast may be migratory (no data on migration of dugongs exist) and the animals were merely absent during the sur-

vey period. Another survey may resolve the question of migratory movement.

The World Wildlife Fund provided financial support for this initial survey, conducted in conjunction with Michael D.

Gwynne and Harvey Croze of the United Nations Development Programme (UNDP).

Although a similar follow-up survey supported by UNDP was planned for April 1976, funds to support this second effort were not obtained.

References

HUSAR, S.L., A survey of dugongs (*Dugong dugon*) in Queensland. *J. Mammal.*, (in press).

JARMAN, P.J., The status of the dugong (*Dugong dugon* 1966   Muller); Kenya, 1961. *E. Afr. Wildl. J.*, 4:82-8.

KINGDON, J., East African mammals, an atlas of evolu-
1971   tion in Africa. Vol. 1. London and New York, Academic Press, 446 p.

PHILIP, Prince (Duke of Edinburgh) and J. FISHER, 1970   Wildlife crisis. New York, Cowles Book Co., 256 p.

DUGONG HUNTING AND CONSERVATION IN QUEENSLAND, AUSTRALIA, WITH UNDERWATER OBSERVATIONS OF ONE INDIVIDUAL IN THE WILD

C. BARNETT and D. JOHNS

Abstract

A description of the traditional methods used to hunt dugongs (*Dugong dugon*) in north-eastern Australia is given. Although legislation only permits hunting by indigenous people, the length and ruggedness of the coast make this restriction impossible to enforce – it is doubtful, in any case, that hunting now significantly affects the dugong population in northern Australia, already much reduced in size. Dugongs are taken in shark nets and may also be affected, directly or indirectly, by pollution and other disturbances associated with coastal development. Action to conserve dugongs should include measures to reduce these forms of interference, the continuance of the ban on commercial hunting and assessments of their abundance. Observations of a female dugong, 2.1 m long, at Green Island on the Great Barrier Reef, are summarized in an appendix. The animal was observed for 5 hours, 2 of them underwater, over 3 months; tide and weather conditions associated with inshore movements, observations of swimming, foraging and breathing, and the presence of other animals, are summarized. Much more complete studies of dugongs in their natural habitat are needed.

Résumé

Une description des méthodes traditionnelles de chasse du dugong (*Dugong dugon*) en Australie du nord-est est fournie. Bien que la législation n'autorise que la chasse par les indigènes, la longueur et le caractère accidenté de la côte rendent impossible la stricte application de cette disposition. On peut douter, quoi qu'il en soit, que la chasse affecte maintenant de façon significative les populations de dugongs de l'Australie du nord, dont la taille est déjà très réduite. Les dugongs sont capturés dans des filets à requins et peuvent aussi être affectés, directement ou indirectement, par la pollution et les autres perturbations liées au développement côtier. La conservation du dugong devrait comprendre des mesures pour réduire ces formes d'interférence, le maintien de l'interdiction de la chasse commerciale et l'évaluation de leur abondance. Les observations portant sur une femelle longue de 2,10 m, à Green Island, sur la Grande Barrière, sont résumées en annexe. L'animal a été observé pendant cinq heures, dont deux sous l'eau, sur une période de 3 mois; les conditions de marée et les conditions météorologiques liées aux déplacements côtiers, ainsi que l'observation de la nage, de la recherche de la nourriture, de la respiration et la présence d'autres animaux sont résumées. Il est nécessaire d'effectuer des études beaucoup plus complètes des dugongs dans leur habitat naturel.

Extracto

Se describen los métodos utilizados tradicionalmente en el nordeste de Australia para cazar el dugón (*Dugong dugon*). Aunque la legislación sólo permite la caza de estos animales a los indígenas, la longitud y aspereza de la costa hace imposible velar por la aplicación de esas disposiciones. De todas formas, es muy poco probable que hoy día la caza afecte en modo importante a la población de dugones del norte de Australia, ya muy reducida. Los dugones resultan apresados en las redes tiburoneras, y pueden sufrir los efectos, directos o indirectos, de la contaminación y de otras alteraciones del hábitat motivadas por el desarrollo de las zonas costeras. Para conservar los dugones es necesario tomar disposiciones para reducir esas formas de interferencia, mantener la prohibición de explotación comercial de esos animales y proceder a evaluar su abundancia. En un apéndice se resumen las observaciones hechas de un dugón hembra de 2,1 m de longitud en la Isla Green, en la Gran Barrera Coralina. Se observó a ese animal durante cinco horas, dos de ellas debajo del agua, a lo largo de tres meses. Se indican brevemente las condiciones de las mareas y del tiempo durante los desplazamientos medios cerca de la costa por el animal estudiado y los resultados de las observaciones de sus movimientos natatorios, su alimentación y su respiración, y se señala la presencia de otros animales. Son necesarios estudios mucho más completos sobre los dugones en su hábitat natural.

C. Barnett
Museum of Vertebrate Zoology, 2593 Life Sciences Building, University of California, Berkeley, California 94720, USA

D. Johns
Department of Zoology, University of Kansas, Lawrence, Kansas 66044, USA

Introduction

This paper outlines the hunting methods for dugongs in parts of Australia, the threats to their survival and recommends measures to be taken for their conservation. Underwater observations of a free-living dugong are given in an appendix.

Most of our scant knowledge of the dugong (*Dugong dugon*) comes from anatomical descriptions (Dexler and Freund, 1906; Gohar, 1957; Hill, 1945; Nair *et al.*, 1975; Petit, 1955 cited in Spain and Heinsohn, 1974), analyses of stomach contents (Heinsohn and Birch, 1972; Heinsohn and Spain, 1973), censusing efforts (Bertram and Bertram, 1973; Heinsohn, 1972, 1975; Heinsohn *et al.*, 1976; Hughes and Oxley-Oxland, 1971), allometric studies (Spain and Heinsohn, 1974, 1975), interviews with native dugong hunters (Jarman, 1966), anecdotal observations by divers and sailors, and accounts of early naturalists (Troughton, 1928). In addition, behavioural observations have been made on captive animals (Jones, 1967; Johnklass, 1961; Kenny, 1967; Oke, pers. comm.). However, no underwater studies of dugongs in their natural habitat, studies comparable to Hartman's (1971) on manatees, have yet been made. This gap represents a major obstacle to successful conservation efforts.

Dugong hunting

HUNTING METHODS [1]

Torres Strait Islanders hunt dugongs with a 4-m spear made of heavy, dense wood from the indigenous wongai tree. The upper 60

---

[1] All descriptions of hunting procedures are derived from interviews and demonstrations; the authors never observed a successful hunt.

cm are made from bamboo. The other end is thicker than the shaft, and blunt. Designs are often carved on this end. This spear, called a "wap", receives a detachable spearhead, which can either have 3 prongs or a single point. The prongs may be cut from 5-gallon fuel drum handles, filed to a point, splayed slightly, and bound together at one end; the single point is usually a 3-sided file with barbs notched along its edges. The spearhead is packed into the wap using palm leaves. A line runs from the head to the dinghy, where it is coiled into buckets. Dugongs are hunted from both wooden and aluminium boats. Islanders prefer wooden dinghies because they are not so noisy as the more durable aluminium; the wood absorbs the impact of slapping waves and dropped objects more quietly. We saw or knew of no hunting platforms mounted over the water.

Dugongs are located by drifting quietly for hours in likely spots. If a dugong surfaces nearby to breathe, its noisy exhalation gives it away. Sometimes the hunter can spot a trail of discoloured water resulting from mud stirred up by a feeding dugong. In Papua New Guinea, hunters may walk out over beds of sea grasses exposed at low tide. They locate a pathway of cropped vegetation which cuts through the dark grasses. At one end of the path they plant a stick tall enough to be seen at high tide. They assume the dugong will return there at flood tide, to resume feeding at the end of the trail, and wait for it there in their boats.

An old hunter, who claimed he had killed hundreds of dugongs (and called himself "King of the Dugongs"), explained how he approaches the animal. He notes the spot the dugong surfaces and starts a steady count beginning when the dugong submerges. When the dugong surfaces again, the hunter stops his count at, say, 160, and mentally draws a line between the two places where the dugong has surfaced. He now predicts that the dugong will continue to forage along this line, surfacing again after another count to 160. He rows the boat upcurrent of the predicted location and

517

drifts down on it, timing his approach to place the boat right next to the dugong when it comes up for air. Silence is essential. The scrape of an oar in its lock can frighten the animal.

The spearer braces himself in the bow of the dinghy. As the dugong's back arcs over the surface, the spearer jumps, using his full weight to push the spear into the blubber just anterior to the caudal peduncle. The spear-head penetrates only a few centimetres but splays and holds fast. The wap falls into the water; its bamboo end keeps it floating upright. The dugong swims away, uncoiling the line from the boat. The spearer clambers back in the dinghy and grabs the wap from the water. As the line becomes taught, the dinghy starts to move. Some hunters have been caught in the tightening line and drowned (Haddon, 1914; pers. comm. from hunters). The dugong then tows the boat until it is tired, which for a full-size dugong can be up to 4 h, although we could not obtain a reliable figure.

As the animal tires, the 2 or 3 men in the dinghy gradually take in the line until eventually the spent and exhausted dugong is lying alongside the boat. The men tie it and drown it by holding its tail out of the water and keeping its head under. New Guineans flip the tied animal on its back in the water; one man then sits on its, feet hooked under the tail flukes, thus preventing the animal from breathing. The dugong, having towed the men, is now towed home. This procedure has not changed greatly from the fascinating account given by Haddon (1912) during his expedition to the Torres Strait at the end of the nineteenth century.

Dugongs are also hunted from luggers in the same basic fashion. Luggers, 17.4-m gaff-rigged, engine-driven ketches, are the ubiquitous work horses of the Torres Strait. The spearer jumps from the bowsprit onto the dugong. When the animal is pulled in, it may be lifted onto the deck and its nostrils plugged until it suffocates.

One reliable report explained that a dugong could be chased onto a shallow coral reef with an outboard, forcing it to bump into the coral and exhaust itself in an effort to flee. When the dugong tires, a man could get in the water, ride it and presumably kill it. This is not, however, a traditional hunting method.

Use of products

Dugongs are caught for feasts, weddings or sale. While we were in the Torres Strait, no regular supply of dugong meat could be obtained, although it is in demand by both native and European Islanders. Once, the meat from 2 adult dugongs was quickly sold on the beach at Thursday Island for A$0.75 per longitudinal strip.

Aboriginals, particularly those who hunt dugongs in the Gulf of Carpentaria, have prescribed rules for dividing up the animal after the hunt. The chief of the village, the man who speared the dugong, the one who guided the boat, and other participants receive specific portions of the dugong depending on their role (pers. comm.).

Conservation problems

LEGISLATION

Australian legislation, in force since 1973, permits dugong hunting only by "Torres Strait Islanders and aboriginal people living on reserves, missions and other settlements established specifically for them" (Heinsohn, 1972) and then only for food. Thus only traditional hunting by indigenous peoples is permitted. Europeans may not hunt dugongs at all.

As far as we could observe, these laws are impossible to enforce. In Queensland, dugongs can potentially be hunted over a coastline of about 4 000 km. 2 200 km of this coastline is the Cape York Peninsula, where the greatest dugong concentrations are found. The Peninsula contains numerous small, isolated habitations. The terrain is rugged, difficult to patrol, and, in places, impenetrable. We were told by people living there that anybody, white or black, could take dugongs in small numbers regardless of the law.

IMPACT OF HUNTING

Successful dugong hunts are comparatively few. Green turtles (*Chelonia mydas*) for example, are far easier to catch because they are more abundant. While there is no doubt that hunting has caused the reduction of the dugong from vast herds at the turn of the century to its present endangered status, we doubt if current hunting pressure has an appreciable impact on the population, at least in northern Australia. Dugongs are simply too scarce to permit their capture in large numbers.

We could better assess the effects of hunting if we knew the fecundity of killed animals. Aboriginal hunters will sometimes capture a calf from its mother; the mother persists in trying to remain near the calf, facilitating her own capture (pers. comm.). Cropping of calves and mothers has a greater impact on the population size than cropping males or post-reproductive animals.

OTHER THREATS

Shark netting takes its toll of dugongs (Heinsohn, 1972). We cannot determine how severely netting reduces Australian stocks until we know to what extent dugong herds follow foraging paths which bring them repeatedly into netted beaches. Perhaps, if netting were confined to discrete, permanent, well-populated beaches, dugongs could learn, by cultural transmission, to avoid those areas. The noise of swimmers could, in fact, scare them off.

Non-human predation on dugongs is rare (pers. comm.). We heard unconfirmed anecdotes of sharks occasionally taking young dugongs.

Coastal towns bring with them dredging of harbours, erosion of hillsides with a subsequent increase in silt and fresh water carried to sea, commercial vessels and small pleasurecraft, bathers, and water pollution in the form of heat, sewage and oil. As these effects encroach on previously uninhabited coastlines, they may, singly or synergistically, further depress dugong populations. For example, the dugong's food supply, extensive as it is, may be reduced or contaminated. Subtle physiological effects may plague the animals. Courtship and mating behaviours may be disrupted.

Proposed conservation action

We offer 3 general recommendations to conserve natural populations of dugongs. First, we need an accurate census to determine not only how many dugongs there are, but also whether stocks are increasing, decreasing or stable. Secondly, commercial hunting, if it should again become feasible, should be prohibited, unless perhaps dugongs were raised like cattle on sea ranches. Thirdly, large-scale dredging operations, sewage and waste outfalls, land erosion from mining and agricultural efforts, thermal pollution and heavy boat traffic should be prohibited in areas where dugongs are known to forage. These factors are harmful to either the dugongs directly, or to their food supply (Thayer, Wolfe and Williams, 1975). This last recommendation is admittedly unrealistic, for such activities accompany economic "progress". Australia, despite her leadership in enacting conservation legislation for the dugong, cannot be expected to curtail coastal development everywhere dugongs might exist or potentially increase. But workable compromises, such as the location of marine reserves, cannot be

519

proposed until the migratory, feeding and breeding habits of dugong are known.

Acknowledgements

We thank Drs Colin Bertram of Cambridge University, Harry Messel of the University of Sydney and Glen McBride of the University of Queensland, three senior scientists who took the time to advise and help us at the outset of our study. Additionally, Dr McBride provided lodgings in Brisbane and made possible our visits to some restricted island reservations.

Dr George Heinsohn provided lodging, advice and first-hand experience at dissecting dugongs. We are grateful to him, to Dr Alister Spain, to the staff of James Cook University, and to the Queensland Department of Harbours and Marine for their outstanding help.

We could not have stayed in the Torres Strait had it not been for the courtesy and hospitality of Laddy Doricich, Bruce and Beverly Gillison, Jerry Holmes, Reg Scott and Gene Cox. They extended themselves more than they should have. The Reverend and Mrs Fox were kind to us as well. We also thank Roland Cantley. This generous man not only provided us with inter-island transportation but helped us meet the most important source of our information, the Islanders themselves. Tanu Nona graciously allowed us passage on his luggers. Mawie Gibuma and Mota Charley taught us how to hunt dugongs. Lenny Foxcroft and the crew of the *Wallach* kindly gave us a dugong skull.

Our survey of the Cape York coastline was made possible by Eddie Kurvers, skipper of the *Matthew Flinders*, by the owners and crew of the freighter *Maluka*, and by the skilful aeronautics and boatmanship of Mat McDonald.

Mr George Craig and his family gave unselfishly of their facilities at Marineland, Green Island, and provided complete support for our work there. They were patient, encouraging and helpful for the many months we imposed on them. Alex and Paddy Azzopardi provided additional assistance at Green Island. Dr William Birch, of James Cook University, identified the sea grasses we collected there, often from less than complete material.

This report was prepared by the senior author, who thanks Sandra Peterson, William Rogers and Terrance Lim for their critical comments on the manuscript. The research it describes was made possible by a Fellowship to C. Barnett from the Thomas J. Watson Foundation. Through the warmth, energy and interest of the Director, Dr Dan Arnaud, and the Executive Secretary, Mrs Dorothy Campbell, the Foundation provided an intangible support surpassing their financial generosity.

APPENDIX

Underwater observations of a dugong

These observations are merely notes. For generalizable results a study would need to be made of a stable herd living in clear water.

Our observations were made at Green Island (lat. 16°46S, long. 145°158E), 36 km from the mainland on the Great Barrier Reef. The island is a tourist resort, and has a long pier extending about 180 m over the coral. At low tide, the exposed reef stretches about 275 m from the shoreline in places. Where coral is absent, patches of sea grasses grow amidst large areas of empty sand. It was reported from Green Island and from Cairns, the closest mainland town, that a dugong had been seen off the island for 5 to 10 years prior to our arrival. Observers believe that there used to be a mated pair but that when one was shot the spouse continued to frequent the island.

For 3 months, from January to March, we established a watch from the pier. We saw the dugong infrequently; sometimes its husky exhalation gave its location away. While one of us continued to observe from the pier, the other would try to swim to the animal (usually 50-100 m away). This dugong was a female 2.1 m long, greyish-brown dorsally and creamy-white ventrally. She could be identified by 3 distinctive notches on her tail resembling fish bites. She fled when approached the first few times. Later she would tolerate us if we were quiet, deliberate and calm. By the eighth sighting, 1 month after we started, we were close enough to touch her. Our presence no doubt modified her normal behaviour.

All underwater observations were made with mask and snorkel; notes were taken on plastic slates. Our study coincided with the beginning of the wet season, which, along with some local dredging, may have been responsible for the steadily decreasing water visibility: 20 m on our first visit, less than half a metre when we left.

Throughout the 3 months, we stood watch on the pier for 32 days, from sunrise to sunset. In addition, everybody who worked at the resort was ready to tell us of any sightings. Our total observation time over the 3 months amounted to 5 h from the pier and 2 h under water. Because of this extremely short contact time and because we observed only 1 animal, the data presented below should not be treated as a generalization for the species. Moreover, it is likely that if the dugong did indeed regularly frequent this tourist resort, some aspects of her behaviour could be considered adaptations to boats and swimmers. Finally, coral reefs are considered atypical habitats for dugongs (Bertram and Bertram, 1973; Husar, 1975). Despite these qualifications, our observations represent perhaps the only detailed behavioural record of a free-living dugong.

They are summarized under 6 headings:

Tide and weather conditions associated with inshore movements

The dugong was always seen to come inshore on a flood tide and, with one exception, within 3 h after low water (Table 1).

She may have come inshore even earlier; some of our sightings could have occurred after she had been present for a while. We do not know how long the dugong foraged in the grass beds around Green Island, but on one occasion she stayed at least 3.5 h.

Dugongs probably avoid foraging when the depth of water drops below a minimal figure, to avoid both the risk of stranding and to keep away from boats and hunters. Indigenous people hypothesize that the increased depth at flood tide allows dugongs to come closer inshore without getting into waters below this critical depth. Our sightings provide some evidence for this. We found a significant inverse correlation between the water level at low water and the time elapsed between the start of the flood tide and our sightings (correlation coefficient,

$$r = -.712, t_r = 2.87 > t_{df} = 8, \alpha = .05 = 2.306).$$

Thus, when low tide level was very low, we would wait longer after low water before seeing the dugong. If the low water mark was high, then the dugong could come inshore virtually coincident with the start of flood tide.

The dugong always appeared at dawn or dusk; we never saw her at midday. She may have been kept away

Table 1. Sightings of the same dugong from the pier at Green Island, Queensland, Australia (1973). Watches mounted: 20 December; 5-24 January; 7-12 February; 14-15 February; 14-16 March; 19 March.

Sighting number	Date	Time	Hours after start of flood tide	Sea temperature (°C)	Underwater visibility (m)
1	20 Dec.	16.30	less than 3 h	—	—
2	8 Jan.	18.15	0 h 45 min	—	12.2
3	11 Jan.	06.34	0 h 7 min	27.8	12.2
4	18 Jan.	18.45	3 h 43 min	29.4	4.6
5	19 Jan.	18.35	2 h 53 min	30.0	4.6-6.1
6	20 Jan.	06.05	2 h 38 min	27.8	4.6
7	7 Feb.	18.25	0 h 58 min	—	6.1-7.6
8	8 Feb.	06.30	1 h 16 min	27.8	7.6
9	9 Feb.	07.27	1 h 11 min	28.8	6.1-7.6
10	16 Mar.	16.05	2 h 20 min	26.1	0.9-1.2
11	19 Mar.	17.05	1 h 54 min	30.0	4.0

at that time by boats and swimmers, but we could never unambiguously assess her reaction to them. Weather conditions for the sightings ranged from sunny to overcast with drizzle. Seas were more often moderate than calm; wind ranged from gentle to moderate (Beaufort scale: 3-4).

Swimming

The dugong swam with smooth, slow strokes of her tail, keeping the pectorals pressed to her side. Sometimes she used them as hydroplanes to alter direction, rolling 20° as she did so. Occasionally, she would roll over completely. She usually swam closer to the bottom than the surface, and never shallower than 3 m. She travelled in straight lines, periodically veering sharply. Her cruising speed was as fast as a diver could swim using fins at full force, a speed chosen probably to keep her distance from us. She could easily accelerate beyond this by arching her body and increasing tail speed, as she did when she left our sight. Several times we saw the dugong lying belly down on a sandy bottom, motionless for up to 7 minutes.

Foraging

We cannot estimate the extent of the dugong's daily foraging, either in terms of duration or area covered, since we made all our observations from one spot. Of the 4 grasses available to her, *Halophile ovalis, Thalassia hemprichii, Halodule (= Diplanthera) uninervis* and *Cymodocea rotundata*, she ate the last 2, which we collected by literally pulling the grasses which the dugong had uprooted out of her grasp. Surprisingly, she did not flee. These species correspond in part with Heinsohn and Birch's (1972) findings from gut analysis. We never saw her eat anything else. The patches she fed on ranged from sparse to luxuriant.

She fed with her body either 45° to the bottom or resting completely on it, pectorals touching the sand. As she ate, she shook her head from side to side, uprooting grasses with her bristled lip pads, which caused sandy clouds to obscure her head, and left a trail of muddy water. In contrast to Husar's (1975) report, we did not see her use her pectorals to shovel plants into her mouth. When she moved along the substrate, her pectorals sometimes dragged in the sand, but whether they provided some force for her forward movement is hard to say. Such friction could account for the callouses on the anterior tips of her pectorals.

Bright green trails through the dark beds of sea grasses appeared to represent new vegetation. We did not see the dugong making or following these trails. The dugong foraged at a depth of about 3-6 m. On the one occasion that we saw her dive in deep water she was out of sight at about 12 m.

Breathing

The dugong surfaced for air every 3-5 minutes on the average. On about a third of her ascents, she would start to exhale about 15 cm before surfacing. She broke the surface for 3-5 seconds, making a husky exhalation. She would submerge by lowering her head and sinking to the bottom or, more commonly, by arching her back out of the water in a smooth roll, the tail flukes being the last part of the body to re-enter.

Inverted swimming

The dugong would swim upside down, back rubbing against sea grasses. Examination of the area over which the dugong swam revealed no hard objects, though it may be that the sand in which the grasses grew provided a scratching or grooming effect. We did not see the dugong rub against dead coral although she had about a dozen 20-25 cm long scars above her left pectoral and a few superficial ones on her tail. We saw no behaviour which could explain the presence of the scars.

Actions to other animals

The dugong had from 1 to 3 remoras (*Remora remora*) on her every time we saw her. They clung posteriorly and ventrally, although they would at times move off the animal briefly. Remoras may have been more concentrated around Green Island than elsewhere because sharks were frequently fished out of the water and the attendant remoras would fall off. Remoras are carnivores (Strasburg, 1959) and those attached to sharks scavenge scraps of meat from the shark's meal. Since the herbivorous dugong could clearly not provide them with such benefits, their presence may be due to non-feeding factors such as transportation or predator avoidance.

Small banded fish (perhaps juvenile pilot fish, *Naucrates ductor*) sometimes preceded the dugong. A

1.5 m grouper (*Promicrops lanceolatus*) – a Green Island "regular" – could approach the dugong to within 60 cm with no immediate effect.

The dugong tolerated our presence to within about 1.2 m. We were able to scratch its back once but it swam away afterwards. Our powerful camera flash had no obvious effect. An approaching rowboat apparently caused it to swim away in a straight line.

References

BERTRAM, G.C.L. and C.K.R. BERTRAM, The modern
1973   Sirenia: their distribution and status. *J. Linn. Soc.*, 5:297-338.

DEXLER, H. and L. FREUND, External morphology of the
1906   dugong. *Am. Nat.*, 40:567-81.

GOHAR, H.A.F., The Red Sea dugong. *Publ. Mar. Biol.*
1957   *Stn. Al Ghardaqa*, (9):3-49.

HADDON, A.C., Reports of the Cambridge anthropolog-
1912   ical expedition to Torres Straits. Cambridge, Cambridge University Press, vol. 4:166-71.

–, Reports of the Cambridge anthropological expedi-
1914   tion to Torres Straits. Cambridge, Cambridge University Press, vol. 5:339.

HARTMAN, D.S., Behavior and ecology of the Florida
1971   manatee. Ph.D. Thesis, Cornell Univ.

HEINSOHN, G.E., A study of dugongs (*Dugong dugon*) in
1972   Northern Queensland, Australia. *Biol. Conserv.*, 4:205-313.

–, Report on aerial surveys of dugongs in northern
1975   Australian waters. Report to Department of Environment, Canberra, 10 p.

HEINSOHN, G.E. and W.R. BIRCH, Feeding habits of the
1972   dugong, *Dugong dugon* (Erxleben) in Northern Queensland, Australia. *Mammalia, Paris*, 36:414-22.

HEINSOHN, G.E. and A.V. SPAIN, Cyclone associated
1973   feeding changes in the dugong (Mammalia: Serenia). *Mammalia, Paris*, 4:679-80.

HEINSOHN, G.E., A.V. SPAIN and P.K. ANDERSON, Popu-
1976   lations of dugongs (Mammalian: Sirenia): aerial survey over the inshore waters of tropical Australia. *Biol. Conserv.*, 9(1):21-3.

HILL, W.C.O., Notes on the dissection of two dugongs.
1945   *J. Mammal.*, 26:153-75.

HUGHES, G.R. and R. OXLEY-OXLAND, A survey of du-
1971   gong (*Dugong dugon*) in and around Antonio Enes, northern Mozambique. *Biol. Conserv.*, 3(4):299-301.

HUSAR, S.L., A review of the literature of the Dugong
1975   (*Dugong dugon*). *Wild. Res. Rep. U.S. Fish Wildl. Serv.*, (4).

JARMAN, P.J., The status of the dugong (*Dugong dugon*
1966   Müller): Kenya, 1961. *E. Afr. Wildl. J.*, 4:82-8.

JONES, S., The dugong, *Dugong dugon* Müller: its pres-
1967   ent status in the areas around India, with observations on its behaviour in captivity. *Int. Zoo Yearb.*, 7:215-20.

JONKLASS, R., Some observations on dugongs. *Loris*,
1961   9:1-8.

KENNY, R., The breathing pattern of the dugong. *Aust.*
1967   *J. Sci.*, 29:372-3.

NAIR, R.V., R.S. LAL MOHAN and K.S. RAO, The dugong,
1975   *Dugong dugon. Bull. Centr. Mar. Fish. Res. Inst., Cochin*, (26).

PETIT, G., Ordre des siréniens. *In* Traité de zoologie,
1955   edited by P.P. Grasse, Paris, Masson et Cie vol. 17:918-1001.

SPAIN, A.V. and G.E. HEINSOHN, A biometric analysis of
1974   measurement data from a collection of North Queensland dugong skulls, *Dugong dugon* (Müller). *Aust. J. Zool.*, 22:249-57.

–, Size and weight allometry in a North Queensland
1975   population of *Dugong dugon* (Müller). (Mammalia: Sirenia). *Aust. J. Zool.*, 23:159-68.

STRASBURG, D.W., Notes on the diet and correlating

1959   structures of some central Pacific echeneid fishes. *Copeia*, 1959 (3):244-8.

THAYER, G.W., D.A. WOLFE and R.B. WILLIAMS, The
1975   impact of man on seagrass systems. *Am. Sci.*, 63:288-96.

TROUGHTON, F., Sea-cows: The story of the dugong.
1928   *Aust. Mus. Mag.*, 3:220-8.

THE SEA OTTER, *ENHYDRA LUTRIS*

A.M. Johnson

Abstract

The sea otter, *Enhydra lutris*, is the only marine member of the order Carnivora, generally inhabiting near-shore waters of less than 20 fathoms and distinguished from the other Lutrinae by its larger body size and weight and other substantial anatomical and behavioural differences. Non-migratory, resident populations of 2 sub-species are distributed as follows: *E. l. lutris* from the Commander Islands east along the Aleutian Islands and from Prince William Sound south to southern California, and *E. l. gracilis* from the southeastern coast of Sakhalin, the Kuril Islands and southern Kamchatka. Quantitative data needed for estimates of population parameters and dynamics of the species are generally lacking. A 2-year reproduction cycle with year-round whelping and breeding including annual peak periods has been documented. Females reach sexual maturity at age 3 or 4 years; age at sexual maturity in males is unknown. Data on mortality are not well known.

Commercial exploitation of *E. lutris* for its valuable pelt began in 1741, eventually eliminating it from most areas by the late 19th century. With nearly complete protection since 1911, *E. lutris* is increasing in abundance and extending its range; recent estimates indicate a total population of 132 000 or less, with 1 600-1 800 others off California, near 50 off Oregon, Washington and British Columbia, 101 000-121 000 off Alaska and 9 000 in the U.S.S.R. Although it has yet to become re-established in about 75 percent of its historic range, once extending to Honshu and to near 28°N in the eastern Pacific, populations in some areas have reached maximum levels of abundance.

At the same time, the sea otter's aesthetic value has been recognized. The present and potential indirect economic benefits of recreational use of the species are unknown, but probably substantial. *E. lutris* is also especially interesting scientifically due to its distinctive environmental adaptations. Conversely, the presence of sea otters substantially reduces the abundance of some commercially valuable invertebrate species (including abalone, crab, urchins and clams, all major food species of *E. lutris*), creating conflicts between the restoration of the species and the harvest of invertebrates (notably, the California sea otter/abalone conflict). The total effect of *E. lutris* on the near-shore marine community, however, is unknown.

Résumé

La loutre marine, *Enhydra lutris*, est le seul animal marin de l'ordre des carnivores; vivant généralement dans les eaux côtières à moins de 36 mètres de fond, elle se distingue des autres lutrinés par ses dimensions et son poids corporels plus considérables, ainsi que par d'autres différences substantielles relevant tant de l'anatomie que du comportement. Les populations résidentes et non migratoires de deux sous-espèces sont réparties comme suit: *E. l. lutris*, des îles du Commandeur vers l'est en suivant les îles Aléoutiennes et du Prince William Sound vers le sud jusqu'à la Californie méridionale, et *E. l. gracilis*, de la côte sud-est de

Sakhaline en passant par les îles Kouriles jusqu'au Kamchatka méridional. Les données quantitatives nécessaires aux estimations des paramètres et de la dynamique des populations de cette espèce font généralement défaut. On a recueilli des documents sur le cycle de reproduction qui s'étend sur deux ans, la parturition et la reproduction survenant pendant toute l'année avec des sommets annuels. Les femelles atteignent la maturité sexuelle à l'âge de trois ou quatre ans; on ignore à quel âge les mâles atteignent la leur. Les données sont imprécises sur la mortalité.

On a commencé à chasser *E. lutris* pour sa fourrure en 1741; l'exploitation de cette espèce a finalement provoqué son élimination dans la plupart des régions à la fin du 19e siècle. Bénéficiant d'une protection quasi totale depuis 1911, *E. lutris* redevient plus abondante et élargit son habitat; d'après des estimations récentes, la population totale de loutres marines atteindrait 132 000 unités au maximum, dont 1 600 à 1 800 au large de la Californie, une cinquantaine au large de l'Oregon, du Washington et de la Colombie Britannique, de 101 000 à 121 000 au large de l'Alaska et 9 000 en U.R.S.S. Bien que la loutre marine ne se soit encore rétablie que sur 75 pour cent de son habitat historique, qui s'étendait jadis jusqu'à Honshu à l'ouest et jusqu'à près de 28° de latitude Nord dans le Pacifique oriental, ses populations ont dans certains secteurs retrouvé des niveaux maximaux d'abondance.

Par ailleurs, la valeur esthétique de la loutre marine a été reconnue. On ignore quels avantages économiques indirects, tant actuels que potentiels, on pourrait tirer de son utilisation à des fins récréatives, mais ils sont sans doute substantiels. *E. lutris* est en outre particulièrement intéressante au point de vue scientifique par suite de son adaptation à un environnement bien distinct. Par contre, la présence de ce lutriné réduit notablement l'abondance de certaines espèces d'invertébrés qui ont une valeur commerciale (y compris les ormeaux, les crabes, les oursins et les clams, les principales espèces dont se nourrit *E. lutris*); il en résulte une incompatibilité entre le rétablissement de cette loutre et la récolte des invertébrés (notamment entre la loutre marine de Californie et l'ormeau). Toutefois, on ignore quel est au total l'influence de *E. lutris* sur les communautés marines côtières.

Extracto

La nutria marina, *Enhydra lutris*, es el único miembro marino del orden de los carnívoros. Vive, en general, en zonas costeras de menos de 20 brazas de profundidad y se distingue de las demás Lutrinae por su mayor talla corporal y peso y por otras importantes diferencias anatómicas y de comportamiento. Existen dos subespecies, cuyas poblaciones residentes, no migratorias, están distribuidas como sigue: *E. l. lutris* desde las Islas Commander hacia el este a lo largo de las Islas Aleutianas, y desde la Bahía de Príncipe William hacia el sur, hasta California meridional, y *E. l. gracilis* desde la costa sudeste de Sakhalin hacia las Islas Kuriles y el sur de Kamchatka. Faltan en general datos cuantitativos para estimar los parámetros de población y la dinámica de la especie. Los datos disponibles revelan un ciclo reproductivo de dos años, con alumbramientos y cópulas a lo largo de todo el año, con períodos máximos en determinados momentos. Las hembras llegan a la madurez sexual a los tres o cuatro años de edad, mientras no se conoce la edad de madurez sexual de los machos. No se dispone de buenos datos sobre mortalidad.

La explotación comercial de *E. lutris* por su piel, considerada valiosa desde hace mucho tiempo, comenzó en 1741, y para finales del siglo XIX la especie había desaparecido de la mayor parte de las zonas en que se encontraba. Desde 1911, en que empezó a gozar de protección casi completa, el número de *E. lutris* va en aumento y la especie está extendiendo su zona de distribución: algunas estimaciones recientes indican una población total de 132 000 o menos animales, con 1 600-1 800 frente a California, cerca de 50 frente a Oregón, Wáshington y Columbia Británica, 101 000-121 000 frente a Alaska y 9 000 en la U.R.S.S. Aunque queda aún por repoblar el 75 por ciento, aproximadamente, de su zona tradicional de distribución, que antaño llegaba hasta Honshu y hasta cerca de los 28°N en el este del Pacífico, las poblaciones de algunas zonas han alcanzado ya niveles máximos.

Simultáneamente se ha ido reconociendo el valor estético de la nutria marina. Los beneficios indirectos actuales y potenciales derivados del aprovechamiento para fines recreativos de esta especie son desconocidos, pero probablemente importantes. *E. lutris* es también especialmente interesante desde el punto de vista científico, debido a su adaptación al medio ambiente. Por otro lado, la presencia de nutrias marinas reduce sustancialmente la abundancia de algunas especies de invertebrados valiosos desde el punto de vista comercial (entre ellos, orejas de mar, cangrejos, erizos de mar y almejas, especies todas que figuran entre los principales alimentos de *E. lutris*), lo que plantea conflictos entre la restauración de esta especie y la explotación de los invertebrados (es de notar especialmente el conflicto entre la nutria marina de California y la oreja de mar). Sin embargo, no se conocen los efectos totales de *E. lutris* en las comunidades marinas costeras.

A.M. Johnson
Sea Otter/Walrus Project, Fish and Wildlife Service, National Fish and Wildlife Laboratory, Anchorage Field Station, 4455 Business Park Boulevard, Anchorage, Alaska 99503, USA

Classification and identification

Sea otters are the largest member of the family Mustelidae, the only marine member of the order Carnivora, and the smallest marine mammals. 2 sub-species are recognized: *Enhydra lutris gracilis*, found in southern Kamchatka and the Kuril Islands; and *Enhydra lutris lutris*, which ranges from the Commander Islands east and south to Alaska and southern California (Roest, 1973). Although the California population of *E. l. lutris* has features distinct from the northern population, Roest (1973) considers the California population as a southern extreme of a cline.

In general structure or form the sea otter resembles other otters; the head appears flattened dorso-ventrally and the body elongated and cylindrical. However, there are also substantial distinguishing features; the sparse guard hairs are about 1-1/2 inches long, underfur dense and about 1 inch long; the rear paws are flattened, the phalanges connected by webs with individual pads near the tips, the outer (fifth) digit longest thus, like flippers; pelage colour is variable from nearly black to light brown with the head, neck, and occasionally anterior body tending to be lighter, in some animals becoming silver or white with age; the tail is horizontally flattened, about one-third body length and bluntly tapered; the forepaws are short and blunt with retractile claws and the external pinnae rolled, appearing pointed. A skin fold on each side of the chest between the forelegs is used with the foreleg for holding food or other items. The dental formula is 3/2, 1/1, 3/3, 1/2 with molars flattened and rounded.

The body size of sea otters changes with age and varies somewhat among populations (Kenyon, 1969). Generally adult males are from 135 to 140 cm long and weigh nearly 30 kg. Adult females are slightly smaller, with body length ranging from 125 to 130 cm and weigh 20 to 25 kg. Newborn pups are 50 to 60 cm long and weigh nearly 2 kg.

Probably the most distinctive characteristic of the sea otter is the tendency to rest and swim on its back. The typical resting position in water is on its back with head and both front and rear paws out of the water. When swimming on its back the head, chest, and front paws are out of the water, and the hind paws and tail are used for propulsion and steering.

527

Distribution and movements

Resident populations are found from central California north to Prince William Sound, westward along the Aleutian, Commander, and Kuril Islands; on the southern tip of Kamchatka Peninsula and the southeastern coast of Sakhalin Island (Kenyon, 1969; Nikolaev, 1961). The sea otters found from central California to Prince William Sound are small groups recently translocated to the coasts of Oregon, Washington, Vancouver Island, and southeast Alaska. Historically, sea otters ranged to near 28°N lat. (Scammon, 1870) in the eastern Pacific and to northern Honshu Island (Nikolaev, 1961) in the western Pacific. Although sea otters are widely distributed, most are found relatively near shore in water less than 20 fathoms with few found in water deeper than 30 fathoms.

There appear to be seasonal changes in local distribution but little evidence to indicate that sea otters migrate.

State of stocks

Commercial exploitation of the sea otter began in 1741 with the return to Kamchatka of the survivors of the crew of Bering's last voyage. By the late 19th century the number of sea otters had been greatly reduced throughout its range and eliminated from most areas. With nearly complete protection since 1911, the remnant populations have gradually increased in numbers and in some areas the population is believed to be near the maximum level, but in most areas range extension and increase continue (Lensink, 1960; Kenyon, 1969; Klumov, 1968; Wild and Ames, 1974).

Recent estimates of the sea otter population indicate a total population of 132 000 or less, with 1 600 to 1 800 off California (Wild and Ames, 1974); near 50 off Oregon, Washington, and British Columbia; 101 000 to 121 000 off Alaska (Alaska, Department of Fish and Game, 1973); and 9 000 in the USSR (Klumov, 1968).

Population characteristics (vital parameters)

The characteristics describing the dynamics of sea otter populations have not been studied in depth. Studies by Barabash-Nikiforov (1947), Kenyon (1969), and Schneider (1972) provide descriptive information but generally quantitative data for a basis of estimates of population parameters are lacking.

Reproduction in the sea otter has received a considerable amount of attention. Investigators generally agree on the timing of peaks in activity and the total length of the reproductive cycle, but disagree on other aspects (Barabash-Nikiforov, 1947; Kenyon, 1969; Sandegren, Chu and Vandevere, 1973; Schneider, 1972). By examining both a tooth, for age estimation, and the reproductive tract, in over 1 300 females, Schneider (1972) concluded females are reproductively mature at age 3 or 4 years; the reproductive cycle requires 2 years; peak of breeding occurs in October and November; implantation occurs approximately 2 months after fertilization; the gestation period is 5 months; the peak of pupping occurs in late May or early June; and although there is a peak pupping and breeding period, these activities occur throughout the year. From field observations and the examination of reproductive tracts from 278 females from Amchitka Island, Kenyon (1969) reported 4 years as the age of reproductive maturity for females; a 2-year cycle; an unimplanted period of 7-8 months; a total gestation period of 12-13 months; and an annual reproductive rate of near 15 %. Age at maturity of males is not known.

Partial segregation by age and sex limit the value of counts and collections as a basis for determining the sex ratio but generally these data show a preponderance of females.

The sex ratio of foetus collections, which have no obvious source of bias, also show more females (55 %) than males (Kenyon, 1969; Schneider, 1972).

Mortality is a characteristic of the population for which it is difficult to obtain data. Kenyon (1969) reported that the greatest mortality occurs from February through May, and estimated the annual death rate was 8 to 11 % of the Amchitka Island population. Although this estimate of the death rate seems reasonable, it is based on limited data. From counts of annuli in the cement of teeth, Schneider (pers. comm.) has estimated the age of nearly 2 000 female sea otters and has found the oldest to be 23 years, but only 5 or 6 were 20 years or older, indicating sea otters are relatively long lived but that mortality essentially eliminates a year class prior to reaching age 20.

Factors causing death among sea otters are not well known. Predation generally appears insignificant, but recent observations of eagle nests of Amchitka Island indicate that substantial predation on pups may occur there (Sherrod, Estes and White, 1975). Malnutrition, parasites, physical injuries, and diseases have also been identified as causes of death.

Relation to humans

The economic value of sea otter skins is well known. However, since 1911 when sea otters were first protected the only harvest has been the experimental take of about 2 500 from 1962 to 1971 by the State of Alaska. Sea otters continue to be protected by the Marine Mammals Protection Act of December 1972 and no animals have been taken since. The tremendous demand and resulting high price paid for sea otter skins in the 18th and 19th centuries shows the appeal of this skin. There is no way of predicting what the present or future value might be, but it was certainly one of the most sought after skins historically.

A crude estimate of the sustainable yield of sea otter skins from a maximum population can be developed in the following way. Kenyon (1969) assumed that there were 30 000 sea otters occupying about one-fifth of the historic range in the mid-1960's and postulated that the original population of sea otters was probably between 100 000 and 150 000. Estimates of the sea otter population by other investigators (Lensink, 1960; Alaska, Department of Fish and Game, 1973; Estes and Smith, 1973) are generally greater than Kenyon's estimates. If it is assumed that Kenyon's estimate was too low and there were nearer 60 000 sea otters occupying one-fifth of the historic range, the original population should have been near 300 000; this is probably a more realistic estimate based on recent data. Kenyon (1969) estimated the population was increasing at a rate of 4 to 5 % in the late 1950's and early 1960's. Assuming 5 % is the highest possible utilization rate for sustainable yield, a population of 300 000 could provide 15 000 skins annually. Obviously, this is a very crude estimate of the potential sustained yield.

Recent studies of sea otters in the USSR have shown the sea otter has reached maximum abundance in some areas (Belkin, 1966; Klumov, 1968) and harvesting is being considered (Marakov, 1966; Voronov, 1965).

More and more important is the aesthetic or recreational use of sea otters — a use or value which has increased dramatically as the otters' range has expanded, particularly in areas of human population. The otters' appearance and behaviour, particularly the maternal care of the young, appeals strongly to humans. The present and potential indirect economic effect of recreational use of sea otters is not known, but is probably substantial.

Sea otters have several features of interest to science and education. They are the only marine members of the order Carnivora, they are "tool users", they have no blubber for insulation or as an energy source, and their metabolic rate is high.

Some interactions between sea otters and humans are considered detrimental, at least by some segments of the human population. The so-called sea otter-abalone conflict (California Senate, 1963), which has plagued resource managers in California for more than 10 years, is the most obvious interaction of this type. Actually, several commercially valuable marine invertebrates, such as abalone, crab, urchins, and clams, are major food species of sea otters. In the absence of sea otters in the near-shore marine environment these invertebrates, which are predominantly grazers, reach high levels of abundance and are a commercially valuable resource. Studies of sea otters and their environment have shown quite conclusively that the abundance of these invertebrate species is substantially reduced when sea otters occur, creating a conflict between those people wanting the sea otter restored throughout its historic range and the people competing with the sea otter for the invertebrates. Additional discussion can be found in reports of hearings and conferences on this conflict (California Seanate, 1963, 1965; Anon, 1969; Ebert, 1968; McLean, 1962; Miller, 1974; Vandevere, 1973; Wild and Ames, 1974). Unfortunately, we cannot describe all the changes in a marine community resulting from the presence of sea otters. It is quite reasonable to speculate that the presence of sea otters in a marine community would result in a potentially beneficial increase in the total biomass of the community (McLean, 1962).

Conclusion

The following are believed to be the most important conclusions that can be made regarding sea otters:

1. Sea otters as a species are increasing in abundance and extending their range.

2. Populations in some areas have reached maximum level but they have not yet become re-established in about 65 % of their historic range.

3. The presence of sea otters, through feeding, substantially reduces the abundance of some commercially valuable invertebrate species, but the total effect sea otters have on the near-shore marine community is not known.

References

ALASKA, Department of Fish and Game, Alaska's wil-
1973   dlife and habitat. Anchorage, Alaska, Van Cleve Printing, 144 p.

BARABASH, I.I., The sea otter (Kalan). Moscow, Soviet
1947   Ministrov RSFSR. Issued also by Israel Program for Scientific Translations, Jerusalem, IPST Cat. No. (621):232 p. (1962).

BELKIN, A.N., On the present numbers and status of the
1966   sea otter population of the Kuril Islands. *Izv. Tikhookean. Nauchno-Issled. Inst. Rybn. Khoz. Okeanogr.*, 58:3-13. Issued in English, translated by Nancy McRoy, Seattle, 1966.

California Senate, Affect [sic] of the sea otter on the
1963   abalone resource Subcommittee on Sea Ot-ters. Hearing, San Luis Obispo, Nov. 19, 1963, 148 p. (mimeo).

California Senate, The sea otter and its effect on the
1965   abalone resources. *In* Third progress report to the legislature by the Senate Permanent Fact-finding Committee on Natural Resources. Sacramento, California Office of State Printing, pp. 129-44.

EBERT, E.E., A food habits study of the southern sea
1968   otter, *Enhydra lutris nereis. Calif. Fish Game*, 54(1):33-42.

ESTES, J.A. and N.S. SMITH, Research on the sea otter,
1973   Amchitka Island, Alaska. *Fin. Rep. Amchitka Bioenviron. Program AEC Contract Natl.*

Tech. Inf. Serv. U.S. Dep. Commer. Springfield, AT(26-1)-520.

KENYON, K.W., The sea otter in the eastern Pacific
1969   Ocean. *North Am. Fauna*, (68):352 p.

KLUMOV, S.K., The transplantation of sea otters as a
1968   fundamental method for the re-establishment of their former area and increase of the abundance of population. *Okeanologiya*, 8(5):900-3.

LENSINK, C.J., Status and distribution of sea otters in
1960   Alaska. *J. Mammal.*, 41(3):172-82.

MARAKOV, S.V., Sea otters (Kalany) (Krai nepuganykh
1966   ptits). Zhivotnyi mir Komandorskikh ostrovov. Moskva, Izd-vo Nauka, pp. 20-30. Translated by the Indian National Scientific Documentation Centre, New Delhi, (1969).

MCLEAN, J.H., Sublittoral ecology of kelp beds of the
1962   open coast area near Carmel, California. *Biol. Bull. Mar. Biol. Lab. Woods Hole*, 122(1):95-114.

MILLER, D.J., A summary of taxonomic status, life his-
1974   tory, and some ecological interactions of the sea otter, *Enhydra lutris*. Monterey, California Department of Fish and Game, Marine Resources Region, 18 p. (mimeo).

NIKOLAEV, A.M., O rasprostranenii, chislennosti i bio-
1961   logii kalanov (The distribution, quantity and biology of the sea otter). *Tr. Soveshch. Ikhtiol. Kom.*, 12:214-7. Issued also as *Transl. U.S. Naval Oceanogr. Off.*, (520) (1970).

ROEST, A.I., Subspecies of the sea otter, *Enhydra lutris*.

1973   *Contrib. Los Ang. County Nat. Hist. Mus.*, (252):17 p.

SANDEGREN, F.E., E.W. CHU and J.E. VANDEVERE, Ma-
1973   ternal behaviour in the California sea otter. *J. Mammal.*, 54(3):668-79.

SCAMMON, C.M., The sea otters. *Am. Nat.*, 4(2):65-74.
1870

SCHNEIDER, K.B., Sea otter report. *Progr. Rep. Alaska
1972   Dep. Fish Game*, (1) (mimeo).

SHERROD, S.K., J.A. ESTES and C.M. WHITE, Depreda-
1975   tion of sea otter pups by bald eagles at Amchitka Island, Alaska. *J. Mammal.*, 56(3):701-3.

VANDEVERE, J.E., Testimony relating to the status of
1973   marine mammals under the Protection Act. Paper presented to the House Subcommittee on Fisheries and Wildlife Conservation and the Environment in La Jolla, California, August 21, 1973, 5 p. (mimeo).

VORONOV, V., Present problems in the study and indus-
1965   trial use of the Kuril sea otter. *In* Marine mammals, edited by E.N. Pavlovskii *et al.* Moscow, Izd-vo Nauka. Translated by Nancy McRoy, Seattle (1966).

WILD, P.W. and J.A. AMES, A report on the sea otter,
1974   *Enhydra lutris* L. in California. *Tech. Rep. Calif. Fish Game*, (20):94 p.

ANON, Sea otter-abalone controversy. Paper presented
1969   at a Conference held at Moss Landing Marine Laboratory, November 24, 89 p. (mimeo).

FAO SALES AGENTS AND BOOKSELLERS

Algeria	Société nationale d'édition et de diffusion, 92, rue Didouche Mourad, Algiers.
Argentina	Librería Agropecuaria S.A., Pasteur 743, 1028 Buenos Aires.
Australia	Hunter Publications, 58A Gipps Street, Collingwood, Vic. 3066; Australian Government Publishing Service, P.O. Box 84, Canberra, A.C.T. 2600; and Australian Government Service Bookshops at 12 Pirie Street, Adelaide, S.A.; 70 Alinga Street, Canberra, A.C.T.; 162 Macquarie Street, Hobart, Tas.; 347 Swanson Street, Melbourne, Vic.; 200 St. Georges Terrace, Perth, W.A.; 309 Pitt Street, Sydney, N.S.W.; 294 Adelaide Street, Brisbane, Qld.
Austria	Gerold & Co., Buchhandlung und Verlag, Graben 31, 1011 Vienna.
Bangladesh	ADAB, 79 Road 11A, P.O. Box 5045, Dhanmondi, Dacca.
Belgium	Service des publications de la FAO, M.J. de Lannoy, 202, avenue du Roi, 1060 Brussels. CCP 000-0808993-13.
Bolivia	Los Amigos del Libro, Perú 3712, Casilla 450, Cochabamba; Mercado 1315, La Paz; René Moreno 26, Santa Cruz; Junín esq. 6 de Octubre, Oruro.
Brazil	Livraria Mestre Jou, Rua Guaipá 518, São Paulo 05089; Rua Senador Dantas 19-S205/206, 20.031 Rio de Janeiro; PRODIL, Promoção e Dist. de Livros Ltda., Av. Venáncio Aires 196, Caixa Postal 4005, 90.000 Porto Alegre; A NOSSA LIVRARIA, CLS 104, Bloco C, Lojas 18/19, 70.000 Brasilia, D.F.
Brunei	SST Trading Sdn. Bhd., Bangunan Tekno No. 385, Jln 5/59, P.O. Box 227, Petaling Jaya, Selangor.
Canada	Renouf Publishing Co. Ltd, 2182 St Catherine West, Montreal, Que. H3H 1M7.
Chile	Tecnolibro S.A., Merced 753, entrepiso 15, Santiago.
China	China National Publications Import Corporation, P.O. Box 88, Beijing.
Colombia	Editorial Blume de Colombia Ltda., Calle 65 N° 16-65, Apartado Aéreo 51340, Bogotá D.E.
Congo	Office national des librairies populaires, B.P. 577, Brazzaville.
Costa Rica	Librería, Imprenta y Litografía Lehmann S.A., Apartado 10011, San José.
Cuba	Empresa de Comercio Exterior de Publicaciones, O'Reilly 407 Bajos entre Aguacate y Compostela, Havana.
Cyprus	MAM, P.O. Box 1722, Nicosia.
Czechoslovakia	ARTIA, Ve Smeckach 30, P.O. Box 790, 111 27 Prague 1.
Denmark	Munksgaard Export and Subscription Service, 35 Nørre Søgade, DK 1370 Copenhagen K; telephone: (01)128570.
Dominican Rep.	Fundación Dominicana de Desarrollo, Casa de las Gárgolas, Mercedes 4, Apartado 857, Zona Postal 1, Santo Domingo.
Ecuador	Su Librería Cía. Ltda., García Moreno 1172 y Mejía, Apartado 2556, Quito; Chimborazo 416, Apartado 3565, Guayaquil.
El Salvador	Librería Cultural Salvadoreña S.A. de C.V., Calle Arce 423, Apartado Postal 2296, San Salvador.
Finland	Akateeminen Kirjakauppa, 1 Keskuskatu, P.O. Box 128, 00101 Helsinki 10.
France	Editions A. Pedone, 13, rue Soufflot, 75005 Paris.
Germany, Fed. Rep. of	Alexander Horn Internationale Buchhandlung, Spiegelgasse 9, Postfach 3340, 6200 Wiesbaden.
Ghana	Fides Enterprises, P.O. Box 14129, Accra; Ghana Publishing Corporation, P.O. Box 3632, Accra.
Greece	G.C. Eleftheroudakis S.A., International Bookstore, 4 Nikis Street, Athens (T-126); John Mihalopoulos & Son S.A., International Booksellers, 75 Hermou Street, P.O. Box 73, Thessaloniki.
Guatemala	Distribuciones Culturales y Técnicas "Artemis", 5a. Avenida 12-11, Zona 1, Apartado Postal 2923, Guatemala.
Guinea-Bissau	Conselho Nacional da Cultura, Avenida da Unidade Africana, C.P. 294, Bissau.
Guyana	Guyana National Trading Corporation Ltd, 45-47 Water Street, P.O. Box 308, Georgetown.
Haiti	Librairie "A la Caravelle", 26, rue Bonne Foi, B.P. 111, Port-au-Prince.
Hong Kong	Swindon Book Co., 13-15 Lock Road, Kowloon.
Hungary	Kultura, P.O. Box 149, 1389 Budapest 62.
Iceland	Snaebjörn Jónsson and Co. h.f., Hafnarstraeti 9, P.O. Box 1131, 101 Reykjavik.
India	Oxford Book and Stationery Co., Scindia House, New Delhi 110001; 17 Park Street, Calcutta 700016.
Indonesia	Inti Buku Agung Ltd, 13 Kwitang, Jakarta.
Iraq	National House for Publishing, Distributing and Advertising, Jamhuria Street, Baghdad.
Ireland	The Controller, Stationery Office, Dublin 4.
Italy	Distribution and Sales Section, Food and Agriculture Organization of the United Nations, Via delle Terme di Caracalla, 00100 Rome; Libreria Scientifica Dott. Lucio de Biasio "Aeiou", Via Meravigli 16, 20123 Milan; Libreria Commissionaria Sansoni S.p.A. "Licosa", Via Lamarmora 45, C.P. 552, 50121 Florence.
Japan	Maruzen Company Ltd, P.O. Box 5050, Tokyo International 100-31.
Kenya	Text Book Centre Ltd, Kijabe Street, P.O. Box 47540, Nairobi.
Kuwait	Saeed & Samir Bookstore Co. Ltd, P.O. Box 5445, Kuwait.

FAO SALES AGENTS AND BOOKSELLERS

Luxembourg	Service des publications de la FAO, M.J. de Lannoy, 202, avenue du Roi, 1060 Brussels (Belgium).
Malaysia	SST Trading Sdn. Bhd., Bangunan Tekno No. 385, Jln 5/59, P.O. Box 227, Petaling Jaya, Selangor.
Mauritius	Nalanda Company Limited, 30 Bourbon Street, Port Louis.
Mexico	Dilitsa S.A., Puebla 182-D, Apartado 24-448, Mexico 7, D.F.
Morocco	Librairie "Aux Belles Images", 281, avenue Mohammed V, Rabat.
Netherlands	Keesing Boeken V.B., Joan Muyskenweg 22, 1096 CJ Amsterdam.
New Zealand	Government Printing Office. Government Printing Office Bookshops: Retail Bookshop, 25 Rutland Street, Mail Orders, 85 Beach Road, Private Bag C.P.O., Auckland; Retail, Ward Street, Mail Orders, P.O. Box 857, Hamilton; Retail, Mulgrave Street (Head Office), Mail Orders, Cubacade World Trade Centre, Private Bag, Wellington; Retail, 159 Hereford Street, Mail Orders, Private Bag, Christchurch; Retail, Princes Street, Mail Orders, P.O. Box 1104, Dunedin.
Nigeria	University Bookshop (Nigeria) Limited, University of Ibadan, Ibadan.
Norway	Johan Grundt Tanum Bokhandel, Karl Johansgate 41-43, P.O. Box 1177 Sentrum, Oslo 1.
Pakistan	Mirza Book Agency, 65 Shahrah-e-Quaid-e-Azam, P.O. Box 729, Lahore 3; Sasi Book Store, Zaibunnisa Street, Karachi.
Panama	Distribuidora Lewis S.A., Edificio Dorasol, Calle 25 y Avenida Balboa, Apartado 1634, Panama 1.
Paraguay	Agencia de Librerías Nizza S.A., Tacuarí 144, Asunción.
Peru	Librería Distribuidora "Santa Rosa", Jirón Apurímac 375, Casilla 4937, Lima 1.
Philippines	The Modern Book Company Inc., 922 Rizal Avenue, P.O. Box 632, Manila.
Poland	Ars Polona, Krakowskie Przedmiescie 7, 00-068 Warsaw.
Portugal	Livraria Bertrand, S.A.R.L., Rua João de Deus, Venda Nova, Apartado 37, 2701 Amadora Codex; Livraria Portugal, Dias y Andrade Ltda., Rua do Carmo 70-74, Apartado 2681, 1117 Lisbon Codex; Edições ITAU, Avda. da República 46/A-r/c Esqdo., Lisbon 1.
Republic of Korea	Eul-Yoo Publishing Co. Ltd, 46-1 Susong-Dong, Jongro-Gu, P.O. Box Kwang-Wha-Moon 362, Seoul 110.
Romania	Ilexim, Calea Grivitei N° 64-66, B.P. 2001, Bucharest.
Saudi Arabia	The Modern Commercial University Bookshop, P.O. Box 394, Riyadh.
Sierra Leone	Provincial Enterprises, 26 Garrison Street, P.O. Box 1228, Freetown.
Singapore	MPH Distributors (S) Pte. Ltd, 71/77 Stamford Road, Singapore 6; Select Books Pte. Ltd, 215 Tanglin Shopping Centre, 19 Tanglin Road, Singapore 1024; SST Trading Sdn. Bhd., Bangunan Tekno No. 385, Jln 5/59, P.O. Box 227, Petaling Jaya, Selangor.
Somalia	"Samater's", P.O. Box 936, Mogadishu.
Spain	Mundi Prensa Libros S.A., Castelló 37, Madrid 1; Librería Agrícola, Fernando VI 2, Madrid 4.
Sri Lanka	M.D. Gunasena & Co. Ltd, 217 Olcott Mawatha, P.O. Box 246, Colombo 11.
Sudan	University Bookshop, University of Khartoum, P.O. Box 321, Khartoum.
Suriname	VACO n.v. in Suriname, Dominee Straat 26, P.O. Box 1841, Paramaribo.
Sweden	C.E. Fritzes Kungl. Hovbokhandel, Regeringsgatan 12, P.O. Box 16356, 103 27 Stockholm.
Switzerland	Librairie Payot S.A., Lausanne and Geneva; Buchhandlung und Antiquariat Heinimann & Co., Kirchgasse 17, 8001 Zurich.
Thailand	Suksapan Panit, Mansion 9, Rajadamnern Avenue, Bangkok.
Togo	Librairie du Bon Pasteur, B.P. 1164, Lomé.
Tunisia	Société tunisienne de diffusion, 5, avenue de Carthage, Tunis.
United Kingdom	Her Majesty's Stationery Office, 49 High Holborn, London WC1V 6HB (callers only); P.O. Box 569, London SE1 9NH (trade and London area mail orders); 13a Castle Street, Edinburgh EH2 3AR; 41 The Hayes, Cardiff CF1 1JW; 80 Chichester Street, Belfast BT1 4JY; Brazennose Street, Manchester M60 8AS; 258 Broad Street, Birmingham B1 2HE; Southey House, Wine Street, Bristol BS1 2BQ.
United Rep. of Tanzania	Dar-es-Salaam Bookshop, P.O. Box 9030, Dar-es-Salaam; Bookshop, University of Dar-es-Salaam, P.O. Box 893, Morogoro.
United States of America	UNIPUB, 1180 Avenue of the Americas, New York, N.Y. 10036.
Uruguay	Librería Agropecuaria S.R.L., Alzaibar 1328, Casilla de Correos 1755, Montevideo.
Venezuela	Blume Distribuidora S.A., Gran Avenida de Sabana Grande, Residencias Caroni, Local 5, Apartado 50.339, 1050-A Caracas.
Yugoslavia	Jugoslovenska Knjiga, Trg. Republike 5/8, P.O. Box 36, 11001 Belgrade; Cankarjeva Zalozba, P.O. Box 201-IV, 61001 Ljubljana; Prosveta, Terazije 16, P.O. Box 555, 11001 Belgrade.
Zambia	Kingstons (Zambia) Ltd, Kingstons Building, President Avenue, P.O. Box 139, Ndola.
Other countries	Requests from countries where sales agents have not yet been appointed may be sent to: Distribution and Sales Section, Food and Agriculture Organization of the United Nations, Via delle Terme di Caracalla, 00100 Rome, Italy.

The volume was designed by Ferruccio Martellacci

Finito di stampare con i tipi della fotocomposizione della lito-lito SAGRAF - Napoli

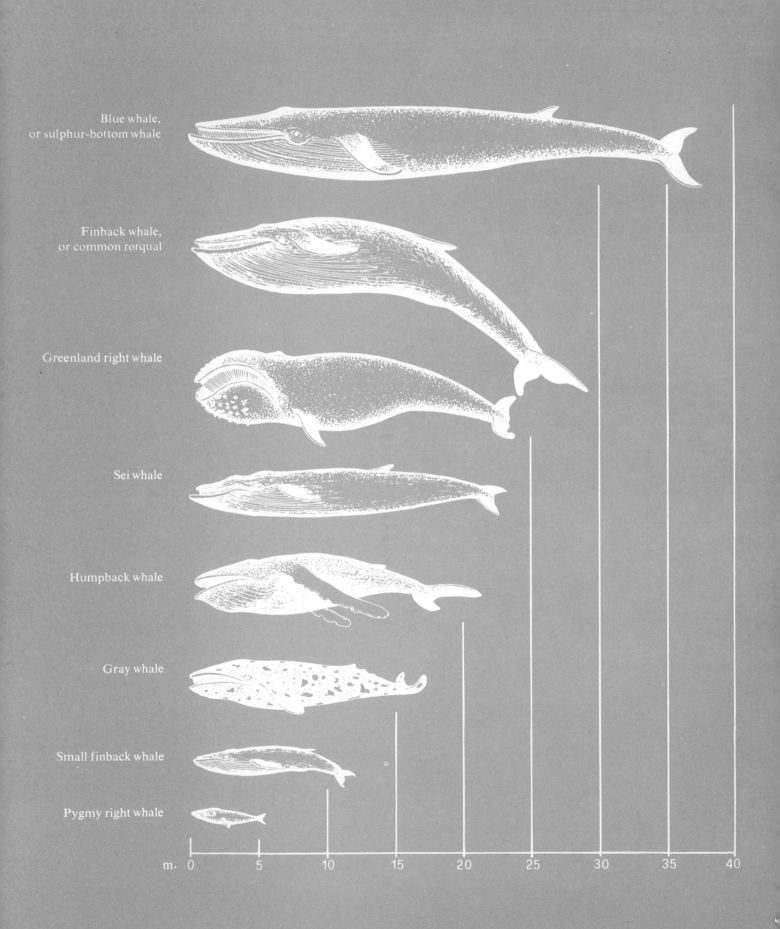

Blue whale,
or sulphur-bottom whale

Finback whale,
or common rorqual

Greenland right whale

Sei whale

Humpback whale

Gray whale

Small finback whale

Pygmy right whale

m. 0   5   10   15   20   25   30   35   40